RELIGION and the CLINICAL PRACTICE of PSYCHOLOGY

RELIGION and the CLINICAL PRACTICE of PSYCHOLOGY

EDITED BY Edward P. Shafranske

American Psychological Association
Washington, DC

First printing May 1996
Second printing June 1997

Published by
American Psychological Association
750 First Street, NE
Washington, DC 20002

Copies may be ordered from
APA Order Department
P. O. Box 92984
Washington, DC 20090-2984

In the UK and Europe, copies may be ordered from
American Psychological Association
3 Henrietta Street
Covent Garden, London
WC2E 8LU England

Typeset in Goudy by PRO-IMAGE Corporation, Techna-Type Div., York, PA

Printer: Braun-Brumfield, Inc., Ann Arbor, MI
Jacket Designer: Kachergis Book Design, Pittsboro, NC
Technical/Production Editor: Edward B. Meidenbauer

Library of Congress Cataloging-in-Publication Data
Religion and the clinical practice of psychology / Edward P.
    Shafranske, editor.
        p.   cm.
    Includes bibliographical references and index.
    ISBN 1-55798-321-6 (acid-free paper)
    1. Psychology and religion.   2. Psychiatry and religion.
3. Experience (Religion)—Psychological aspects.   I. Shafranske,
Edward P.
BF51.R45   1996
291.1'75—dc20   95-51499
                                                                                CIP

British Library Cataloguing-in-Publication Data
A CIP record is available from the British Library.

Printed in the United States of America

CONTENTS

PART II: RELIGION, MENTAL HEALTH, AND CLINICAL PRACTICE

PART III: PSYCHOTHERAPY WITH RELIGIOUSLY COMMITTED PERSONS

CONTRIBUTORS

Allen E. Bergin, PhD, is Professor and former Director of Clinical Psychology at Brigham Young University, Past President of the Society for Psychotherapy Research, and coeditor (with Sol Garfield) of the *Handbook of Psychotherapy Research and Behavior Change.* He is a recipient of the APA Distinguished Professional Contributions to Knowledge Award and of the APA Division 36 William James Award for Research in the Psychology of Religion.

James W. Fowler, PhD, is Charles Howard Candler Professor and Director of the Center for Ethics in Public Policy and the Professions at Emory University. Dr. Fowler is the author of a number of books and articles, including *Stages of Faith: The Psychology of Human Development and the Quest for Meaning, Faith Development and Pastoral Care,* and *Weaving the New Creation.* Dr. Fowler is the recipient of the Oskar Pfister Award of the American Psychiatric Association and the William James Award of APA Division 36: Psychology of Religion.

Marc Galanter, MD, is Professor of Psychiatry at New York University School of Medicine. He is the author of numerous works on religious sects, including *Cults: Faith, Healing and Coercion* and *Cults and New Religious Movements: A Report of the American Psychiatric Association.*

John Gartner, PhD, is Clinical Assistant Professor of Psychiatry at Johns Hopkins University Medical School and is in private practice in Baltimore, Maryland.

Paul Giblin received the PhD from Purdue University and MDiv from Westin School of Theology. He is Assistant Professor of Pastoral Studies and coordinates the MA Program in Pastoral Counseling at Loyola University's Institute of Pastoral Studies in Chicago.

Dean R. Hoge, PhD, is Professor of Sociology, the Catholic University of America, Washington, DC. He is a graduate of Harvard Divinity School (BD) and Harvard Graduate School (PhD). His recent books include *Patterns of Parish Leadership: Cost and Effectiveness in Four Denominations* (coauthored, 1988); *American Catholic Laity in a Changing Church* (coauthored, 1989); *Research on Factors Influencing Giving to Religious Bodies* (coauthored, 1992); *Vanishing Boundaries: The Religion of Mainline Protestant Baby Boomers* (coauthored, 1994).

Ronald E. Hopson, PhD, is Associate Professor of Psychology and Adjunct Professor of Religious Studies at the University of Tennessee, Knoxville. His work is in the area of the interface between therapeutic psychology and religion. He is also engaged in work on the social psychology of Christian fundamentalism, and the psychological dynamics of substance abuse and addiction. He has published in the *Journal of Religion and Health*, the *Alcoholism Treatment Quarterly*, and *Psychotherapy: Theory, Research, Practice*. Dr. Hopson is a licensed clinical psychologist and an ordained minister.

Stanton L. Jones, PhD, is Provost and Professor of Psychology, Wheaton College, Wheaton, Illinois. Until recently, he maintained a private practice as a licensed clinical psychologist. He has been a Postdoctoral Scholar in the Divinity School of the University of Chicago, a Research Fellow of the Evangelical Scholars Program of the Pew Foundation, and a Visiting Scholar on the Faculty of Divinity of the University of Cambridge. He wrote, with Richard E. Butman, *Modern Psychotherapies: A Comprehensive Christian Appraisal* and edited *Psychology and the Christian Faith: An Introductory Reader*. He has published articles in such periodicals as *Journal of Abnormal Psychology*, *Behavior Therapy*, *Journal of Studies on Alcohol*, *Journal of Psychology and Theology*, and *Behavior Modification*.

Robert J. Lovinger, PhD, is Professor of Psychology at Central Michigan University where he has taught in the Clinical Psychology Program since 1970. He was Director of the Psychological Training and Consultation Center from 1979 to 1995. Lovinger received his PhD in Clinical Psychology from New York University in 1969 and is a member of the Board of Directors of the Michigan Psychoanalytic Council, serving as its Treasurer since its founding in 1989. He is the author of *Working With Religious Issues in Therapy* and *Religion and Counseling*.

Alvin R. Mahrer, PhD, is Professor, School of Psychology, University of Ottawa, Ottawa, Canada. He is author of 11 books and approximately 200 other publications, mainly on his experiential psychotherapy and also on theory, practice, training, and research in the field of psychotherapy. Recipient of the University of Ottawa Award for Excellence in Research, perhaps his most timely books include *Experiencing: A Humanistic Theory of Psychology and Psychiatry, Dream Work in Psychotherapy and Self-Change,* and *The Complete Guide to Experiential Psychotherapy.*

H. Newton Malony, PhD, is Senior Professor of Psychology in the School of Psychology, Fuller Theological Seminary. He is a past president of APA Division 36: Psychology of Religion, and has more than 30 books to his credit including *Current Perspectives in the Psychology of Religion, Psychology and Faith, Psychology of Religion: Personalities, Problems, Possibilities,* and *The Psychology of Religion for Ministry.*

W. W. Meissner, SJ, MD, is University Professor of Psychoanalysis at Boston College and is a training and supervising psychoanalyst at the Boston Psychoanalytic Institute. He was formerly Clinical Professor of Psychiatry at Harvard Medical School. He is the author of 20 books, among which are *Psychotherapy and the Paranoid Process, Treatment of Patients in the Borderline Spectrum, Psychoanalysis and Religious Experience,* and *Ignatius of Loyola: The Psychology of a Saint,* plus 223 articles and chapters in books. In 1989, he received the Oskar Pfister Award of the American Psychiatric Association for his work in psychiatry and religion.

Kenneth I. Pargament, PhD, is Professor of Psychology, Department of Psychology, Bowling Green State University, Bowling Green, Ohio. Dr. Pargament consults with churches and synagogues and conducts psychotherapy with clergy and religious groups. He has published extensively in the psychology of religion. He is coeditor of *Religion and Prevention in Mental Health: Research, Vision and Action* and author of the forthcoming book *The Psychology of Religion and Coping.*

I. Reed Payne, PhD, is Professor Emeritus of Psychology at Brigham Young University, and a frequent contributor to the psychology of religion literature. He has been active in forensic psychology, rural mental health, and Native American psychology. He has also contributed to business consultation methods and the psychology of music.

L. Rebecca Propst, PhD, is associate professor of counseling psychology in the Graduate School of Professional Studies at Lewis and Clark College. She is author of *Psychotherapy With a Religious Framework:*

Spirituality in the Emotional Healing Process published by Human Sciences Press (1988), as well as numerous articles dealing with theology and psychology. She has also published outcome studies examining the role of religious values in cognitive therapy in the *Journal of Consulting and Clinical Psychology* as well as other journals. She also maintains a private practice.

P. Scott Richards, PhD, is Associate Professor and Director of Counseling Psychology at Brigham Young University. He previously taught at Central Washington University and University of Minnesota, Duluth. His research interests are in religious and spiritual issues in mental health and psychotherapy. He is also a part-time psychologist at the Center for Change.

Ana-Maria Rizzuto, MD, is training and supervising psychoanalyst at the Psychoanalytic Institute of New England, East. She is author of *The Birth of the Living God: A Psychoanalytic Study* and several papers on the psychodynamic aspects of religious beliefs.

Edward P. Shafranske, PhD, is Professor of Psychology, Graduate School of Education and Psychology, Pepperdine University, and is a member of the faculty of the Southern California Psychoanalytic Institute. He is a past president of APA Division 36: Psychology of Religion and has written extensively on the psychoanalytic study of religion. In addition to academic and research activities, Dr. Shafranske maintains a private practice in clinical psychology and psychoanalysis in Irvine, California.

Len Sperry, MD, PhD, is Professor of Psychiatry and Preventive Medicine at the Medical College of Wisconsin. He is Director of the Division of Organizational Psychiatry and Corporate Health, and Co-Director of the Center for Aging and Development. He completed Psychiatric and Preventive Medicine training at the Medical College of Wisconsin and his fellowship at the University of Wisconsin Medical School. He is on the editorial board of nine journals including the *Journal of Pastoral Counseling* and *Journal of Christian Healing*. He is board certified in both Psychiatry and Clinical Psychology, is a fellow of the Division of Psychology and Religion of APA, and has lectured and published widely on health and impairment in executives and professionals. He was the Cochair of the Psychiatry and Religion Committee of the Wisconsin Psychiatric Association and is a member of the American Family Therapy Academy.

Siang-Yang Tan, PhD, is Director of the Doctor of Psychology Program and Associate Professor of Psychology at the Graduate School of Psychology, Fuller Theological Seminary, in Pasadena, California. Dr. Tan is a licensed psychologist with a part-time private practice.

He has authored or coauthored five books, including *Lay Counseling*. He is Associate Editor of the *Journal of Psychology and Christianity*, and Consulting or Contributing Editor of three other journals, including *Professional Psychology: Research and Practice*. He is also a Fellow of APA.

John R. Van Eenwyk, MDiv, PhD, is an Episcopal priest, clinical psychologist, training analyst with the Pacific Northwest Society of Jungian Analysts, and clinical supervisor at the University of Washington School of Medicine. Dr. Van Eenwyk is a nonstipendiary Associate at Saint John's Episcopal Church and maintains a private practice in Olympia, Washington. He also lectures internationally on the treatment of torture survivors.

Hendrika Vande Kemp, PhD, is Professor of Psychology, Graduate School of Psychology, Fuller Theological Seminary. Dr. Vande Kemp is a Past President of APA's Division 36, the author of *Psychology and Theology in Western Thought, 1672–1965: A Historical and Annotated Bibliography*, and the editor of *Family Therapy: Christian Perspectives*. Her primary scholarly commitment is to document the historical relationship between psychology and religion.

Frances Vaughan, PhD, is a psychologist in private practice in Mill Valley, California. She was formerly president of the Association for Transpersonal Psychology and clinical faculty at the University of California Medical School at Irvine. She is the author of several books on psychology and spirituality, including *Awakening Intuition*, *The Inward Arc*, and *Shadows of the Sacred*.

Roger Walsh, MD, PhD, is professor of psychiatry, philosophy, and anthropology at the University of California, Irvine. His publications include *Meditation: Classic and Contemporary Perspectives*, *Paths Beyond Ego*, and *The Spirit of Shamanism*.

Bryan Wittine, PhD, is a psychotherapist in private practice in Oakland and San Rafael, California and was the founding director of the Department of Transpersonal Psychology at John F. Kennedy University, Orinda, California. He has authored several papers bridging spirituality and depth psychotherapy, and is a psychoanalytic candidate at the C. G. Jung Institute of San Francisco.

David M. Wulff is Professor of Psychology at Wheaton College, Norton, Massachusetts. He has a PhD in personality psychology from the University of Michigan and in 1993 received an honorary Doctor of Theology from the University of Lund, Sweden. He is the author of *Psychology of Religion: Classic and Contemporary Views* (Wiley, 1991; Swedish translation, 1993), which was awarded the 1990

Quinquennial Prize by the International Commission for Scientific Psychology of Religion. He was the 1991 recipient of the William C. Bier Award given by Division 36: Psychology of Religion, of the American Psychological Association. He is a Fellow both of Division 36 and of the Society for the Scientific Study of Religion.

PREFACE

The genesis of this book is located in many sources, both personal and professional. Indeed, it is a major premise of this volume that personal values inevitably participate in the practice of psychology, whether the practice is as a clinician, scientist, or, in this instance, as editor and author. The values that inform this book emanate from a personal sensitivity to the ontological discourse to which religion contributes and to continuing observations of the salience that religion and spirituality hold for many clients.

The sensitivity to which I first allude finds its origins in my own personal history as well as in ongoing clinical work and consultation. In both contexts I am struck with the organizing capacity of religious faith to shape the construction of personal identity and to maintain and transform meaning in times of comfort and in moments of adversity. Religion, at its heart, provides a language to begin to capture the fact of human existence and to provide a context for locating personal history within the universe of eternity. The surround that religion articulates provides the ground upon which the tasks of human existence are worked through. As a psychologist and psychoanalyst I have had the opportunity to understand in an immediate and often direct way the impact that religious experience, belief, and commitment has on a person's life. And yet, this observation is in marked contrast to the conspicuous lack of attention placed on the religious dimension within the training of most psychologists, psychiatrists, and other mental health professionals.

This book is an attempt to address the chasm between the observations of the salience attributed to religion by so many people and the seeming lack of focused attention given to religion within most graduate education and clinical training programs. Further, it intends to contribute to the necessary and ongoing dialogue concerning the nature of the therapeutic relationship and process. The understanding that values are inherent in the therapeutic measures we employ, in the observations we make, and in the recommendations we offer, render past claims of therapeutic neutrality obsolete. If as clinicians we function, in Perry London's words, as *secular priests*, or if we hold that psychotherapy offers *hope* as an anecdote to demoralization, as suggested by Jerome Frank, then it becomes self-evident that psychological treatment enters into the noetic realm—a realm once solely occupied by religion. As a clinician, I have been mindful that a great deal of psychotherapeutic work occurs within that realm or at least contiguous to it, to employ a spatial term. Although I was fortunate to be directly exposed to the contributions of Victor Frankl and Rollo May and others who conceived of psychology as being concerned with *meaning*, there was a significant void in the discussion concerning institutional expressions of meaning. I found in discussions with other clinicians and through surveys I conducted and texts that I reviewed that the religious dimension in the clinical practice of psychology was rarely addressed in a systematic manner. Ongoing dialogue within APA Division 36 (The Psychology of Religion) and with colleagues from other disciplines corroborated these observations and led to the development of this volume.

The book brings together a number of scholars and clinicians who share in an appreciation of religion as a clinical variable and, for some, a personal value as well. Each author provides a window of perception and a guiding opinion to address a particular issue in the interface of religion and psychology. I wish to acknowledge and thank these scholars and clinicians for their contributions. Their work has not only provided salient commentaries, but has laid a foundation for ongoing dialogue in the spirit of forthright exchange. A project such as this could not be undertaken without the encouragement of colleagues. I wish to express my appreciation for the institutional and personal support of Pepperdine University.

A book would remain a manuscript without the encouragement and support of a publisher. I wish to express my appreciation to APA Books, in particular to Julia Frank-McNeil for her early and steadfast support of the project, to Theodore J. Baroody for his shepherding the manuscript through its development, and to Ed Meidenbauer for his careful attention to detail throughout its production. I am honored that my primary professional affiliation, the American Psychological Association, is the publisher of this volume. This fact signifies the growing appreciation of religion as an important force in human psychology. It is my hope that this volume will contribute to our appreciation of the religious dimension in clinical practice and therefore further our understanding of the persons with whom we assist in their difficulties in living.

EDWARD P. SHAFRANSKE, PhD

INTRODUCTION: FOUNDATION FOR THE CONSIDERATION OF RELIGION IN THE CLINICAL PRACTICE OF PSYCHOLOGY

EDWARD P. SHAFRANSKE

This book holds that religious sentiment appears within human experience in a multitude of forms, moods, and intensities.[1] As a force in the culture of and as an expression of the surround within the individual, religion plays an essential role in human psychology. The form that religion takes varies for each person. For some, religious experience is housed within the credos and traditions of a given religion and expressed within a faith community; for others, it is a private semblance of spiritual ideas and practices. The vast majority of individuals in western society are raised within some religious tradition, and indeed recent surveys have found that 93 percent of Americans identified with a religious group (Kosmin & Lachman, 1993) and over 80 percent reported that religion is "fairly" or "very" important in their lives (Gallup, Jr., 1995, p. 72; see also Hoge, Chapter 1, this volume). Even for the unchurched or irreligious, the atheist or agnostic, the influence of religion cannot be dismissed. Culture through its

---

[1] In this introduction I draw on a number of sources from the functional analysis of religion. Among the approaches to the study of religion, the functional analysis is most useful for this present discussion because we are concerned with the functions religion serves in individual psychology and psychosocial adjustment. I am indebted in particular to the following authors and their works: Clifford Geertz (1966), Religion as a cultural system; Peter Berger (1967), *The Sacred Canopy: Elements of a Sociological Theory of Religion*; Peter Berger and Thomas Luckman (1966), *The Social Construction of Reality: A Treatise in the Sociology of Knowledge*; Talcott Parsons (1977), *Social Systems and the Evolution of Action Theory*; and Max Weber (1963), *The Sociology of Religion*.

popular rituals and traditions underscores the threads of religious sentiment that are woven within its cohesive fabric of meaning and social affiliation.

Religion appears in one's conscious and veiled representations of awe, majesty, and fear toward a sacred object, in the beliefs that one holds, in the attributions that one constructs, and in the affiliations that locate the individual with the human community. It is one of the "webs of significance" that culture provides and that the human community constructs. It informs the creation of a sense of personal identity and provides a "sacred canopy" under which spheres of relevancy are created that orient human values and ultimately determine behavior.

With each form of belief and communal practice, moods are elicited that motivate the individual to action. These moods are prompted and encoded through institutional and private religious involvement throughout the life of the person. Beliefs, practices, and affiliations conjoin to establish moods that propel the individual into behavior. Religious beliefs, unlike scientific and commonsense understanding, allow the inexplicable to be comprehended and the challenges and tragic discontinuities of life to be accepted through faith. Through its function of going beyond explanation to acceptance, faith instills a sense of meaning, coherence, and at times, courage in the face of confusion, disappointment, loss, suffering, and anomie. Through symbols and rituals—together with beliefs—religious practices inspire and encourage behaviors in accordance with religion's prescribed values. Affects that are induced through religious involvement serve as important elements in motivation and influence behavior.

A variance of religious commitment and expression exists between individuals and within individuals. In nexus points, religion may be a silent, almost imperceptible thread of influence and coherence in a person's life. At other points, religion may appear as a clear and potent source of influence, support, or conflict. Religion, in its intrinsic and extrinsic dimensions, shapes the commitments and affiliations through which an individual lives. Religion's influence may wax and wane both within the individual and within the culture. The intensity of religious influence is a complex, ever-changing dynamic. It is posited to be under the sway of unconscious psychodynamics, the social psychology of human relationship and group cohesion, the ideological currents within the culture, and the intimate personal experiences and challenges of living. Each contributes to the role that religious sentiment plays within individual experience, motivation, and behavior.

Religion can be viewed as "a system of symbols which acts to establish powerful, persuasive, and long-lasting moods and motivations by formulating conceptions of a general order of existence and clothing these conceptions with such an aura of factuality that the moods and motivations seem uniquely realistic" (Geertz, 1966/1973, p. 90). Religious involvement possesses the potential to be a significant influence in the mental health of a person. Furthermore, religion as a cultural variable needs to be taken into account in keeping with the ethical guidelines of psychologists. The American Psychological Association (1992, p. 1601) mandates that psychologists take an informed view of religion as a dimension of human difference and diversity. The American Psychiatric Association Committee on Religion and Psychiatry (1990) recommended, as well, that the religiosity of an individual be addressed within clinical practice. These ethical guidelines require the development of a knowledge base and competency at all levels of mental health provision: education, training, research, and most important, clinical practice. This book is in part a response to this mandate and contributes to the appreciation of cultural difference and the uniqueness that each client or patient brings to the consulting room.

CONTENTS OF THE BOOK

The purpose of this volume is to address the religious dimension in aspects that are relevant to the clinical practice of psychology. To consider the influence of religion requires us to formulate a series of questions and to ask of the available theory and empirical data, What is the influence of religion as a variable in mental health and psychological treatment? Further inquiry concerns questions such as: What is the nature of Americans' religious beliefs, affiliations, and practices? How has psychology as a discipline and a science considered religious experience? How does religious affiliation affect mental health? How does one distinguish between healthy and pathological beliefs? What do we know about cults? How might a clinician assess the impact of religious participation? How might clinicians address the religious issues in psychotherapy? These are but a sample of the kinds of questions the authors of this volume have addressed.

The aim is to understand rather than to provide a polemic, apologetic, or theoretically sectarian critique. The intent is to present what is known from a number of clinically relevant perspectives. An emphasis is placed on the integration of theory, findings derived from existing empirical data, and discussions of clinical approach and technique. In light of the charge of the book, the range of questions will be circumspect. The intent is not to present a general psychology of religion but to address concerns that are relevant to mental health and to the clinical practice of psychology. The emphasis of this volume is the influence of religion as a variable in the treatment of mental disorders and the clinical process. Issues are discussed in respect to the life of the individual and, secondarily, to the culture at large.

The book does not focus on the religious experiences of particular groups on the basis of sex, race, age, or other sociological categories. It also does not intend to emphasize one particular religious tradition. The extent to which certain chapters draw conclusions or examples exclusively from a particular religious tradition reflects the limitations of the psychological data or theory that are available for scrutiny. Attempts were made to provide commentaries inclusive and respectful of all religious traditions. The Eurocentric bias within the study of American culture is reflected in the paucity of empirical research concerning the unique experiences of many ethnic groups. This is unfortunate in light of the changing cultural and ethnic landscape; however, we should not overstate this limitation. Examples that present Judeo-Christian religious experience may be particularly useful to clinicians because over 86 percent of Americans describe their religious affiliation as Christian and approximately 2 percent as Jewish (Kosmin & Lachman, 1993, p. 3). We conclude this introduction with an overview of the structure and contents of this volume.

Structure

This volume consists of four sections that reflect distinct areas of investigation. The first part, "Religion and Psychology: A Conceptual, Cultural, and Historical Context," provides a theoretical and empirical overview of the domain of religion and applied psychology. It intends to establish a conceptual, historical, and empirical context for the discussion of clinical issues. The second section, "Religion, Mental Health, and Clinical Practice," provides a theoretical and empirical overview of the influence of religion as a variable in mental health promotion, psychopathology, and psychological treatment. It includes a discussion of values in psychotherapy, issues in assessment, and implicit and explicit integration of religious issues in psychotherapy practice and models of practice. "Clinical Practice With Religious People" presents models of psychological intervention with religiously committed clients. Chapters in this section discuss treatment issues and techniques from multiple theoretical orientations. The final section presents a chapter that summarizes the case for the inclusion of religion in the clinical practice of psychology and makes recommendations for graduate education, clinical training, and research to ensure clinical competency.

Descriptive Overview

There are many vantages that point to the necessity of considering religion a variable that is relevant to the clinical practice of psychology. We commence our examination by drawing on the methods of a related discipline—sociology—and its presentation of data. Dean R. Hoge provides an empirical backdrop to our discussion that sheds light on the nature of religion in America. His survey of the data presents religion as a potent institutional force within contemporary life. His analysis suggests that, in this era of technological advance and cultural diversification, the United States is and will continue to be one of the most religious countries in the industrialized world. Clinicians might well take note of the continuing importance of religion and, simultaneously, the subtle changes in the nature of its influence. Hoge notes that there are trends that depict a lessening of institutional authority and a movement away from literal interpretations of scripture. These developments, he notes, may point to increased responsibility on the part of individuals for their beliefs, affiliations, and codes of behavior. As the location of responsibility for faith orientation and morality increasingly shifts from the institution to the individual, people may be faced with ontological, spiritual, and moral challenges that affect mental health. More and more, clinicians may be called on to assist in the exploration of beliefs and values that orient relationships and behavior. This is in keeping with London's observation that psychotherapists may increasingly be called on to "fill a moral vacuum" (1964, p. 171) in modern life.

The demographics concerning patterns of church affiliation and involvement within the life span support Marc Galanter's later chapter discussing charismatic youth groups and James W. Fowler's model of structural developmental faith. These normative developmental patterns of church affiliation may be of diagnostic use to the clinician seeking to understand changes in religious involvement.

Hoge's review of the sociological literature affirms the interrelationship between cultural identity and religious identity. The religious scene in America reflects patterns of immigration and leads to the prediction that religion will continue to play an important role in the lives of Americans. His chapter provides the clinician with a digest of data concerning religious beliefs, church affiliation and involvement, and religious behaviors. This provides abundant support for the contention that religion should be considered in the clinical practice of psychology.

David M. Wulff begins our formal psychological inquiry with a sweeping review of the psychology of religion. His survey finds that some of the most influential psychologists of the 20th century have directed attention to religious experience. He conceptualizes that there are two trends in this examination: the descriptive and the explanatory. The descriptive method accepts religious expression on its own terms and resists the reification into narrow categories of institutional religiosity. The explanatory approach seeks to understand religious experience on the basis of psychological, biological, and environmental constituents. The clinician is faced with resolving the tension that exists within this dialect between a phenomenological appreciation of a patient's religious experience and an explanatory, and potentially reductionistic, assessment of faith experience. Wulff's solution is novel; he advocates developing a comprehensive view that prompts a relativistic stance to religious expression. He recommends that clinicians become as broadly acquainted as possible with various perspectives and cautions against the use of a simple formula to explicate religious experience. Furthermore, he reminds that the appeal of certain theories may reflect the individual's own personal experience of religion. Each of the perspectives that he introduces may provide a heuristic tool for understanding an individual's religious experience.

Hendrika Vande Kemp complements Wulff's survey in demonstrating that not only did a number of prominent psychologists include religious experience in their investigations, but also, as she concludes, "psychology and religion have historically been . . . inextricably intertwined" (p. 72). In addition, she asserts that this enterprise has been and is a legitimate subspecialty of the discipline of psychology. Her thesis is founded not only on theoretical grounds but also primarily on a close inspection of the history of American psychology. Using the tools of an academic historian, Vande Kemp provides evidence that the "integration of psychology and theology/religion" meets the criteria for specialty status.

The clinician seeking to understand the individual with an appreciation of the noetic dimension need not feel that such pursuits lie outside the scope of psychology or on the fringe of the profession. Rather, such an endeavor carries forth the legacy of integration in which clear distinctions between the religious and the psychological are neither found nor presumed. The chapters of Wulff and Vande Kemp point to a rich tradition of scholarship within the psychology of religion and within the profession throughout its development.

Stanton L. Jones's chapter is an example of scholarship that seeks to contribute to the body of integrative literature. In proposing "a constructive relationship for religion with the science and profession of psychology," Jones challenges "the supposed incommensurability of religion and science." Drawing on Barbour's analysis of myths, models, and paradigms, he ably points out the commonalties that religious and scientific paradigms share in their attempts to explain reality in a comprehensive fashion. He identifies six areas of concourse and suggests that differences in the approaches to human knowing are predominantly a matter of degree and emphasis. The differences that exist do not suggest an absolute isolation of the epistemologies of religion and science. His analysis calls for an appreciation of various ways of knowing and the acknowledgment of the values that are implicit in those structures of knowledge. In addition, he advocates a dialectical approach that does not create a barrier to understanding but rather fosters a constructive dialogue. He applies this critique to the practice of psychotherapy and argues for greater attention to philosophical, ethical, and religious dimensions within clinical training. For our purposes, this chapter presents one approach to integration that demands consideration in all areas of the discipline and science of psychology: research, practice, and training.

Edward P. Shafranske reviews the empirical literature on psychologists' religious and spiritual beliefs, affiliations, and practices. His survey suggests that psychologists, as a group, differ from the general population in all aspects of religiosity. He finds that psychologists are less likely to participate in institutional religion and that they report that religion is of lesser personal importance compared with most Americans. In addition, the data suggest that psychologists rarely, if ever, receive graduate education in the psychology of religion or clinical training respective of religious issues. He concludes that this raises a number of concerns regarding psychologists' treatment of religiously committed clients. What impact do the personal beliefs and values of the clinician have on clinical practice respective of religious issues? How do clinicians assess, understand, and use clients' faith commitments in light of their personal eschewing of such commitments? Furthermore, given the lack of education and training in this area, what resources are drawn on to address matters of faith and religious practice within the clinical setting, and on what basis is religion as a variable evaluated? Shafranske's chapter suggests that psychologists, as a group, may rely to a great extent on personal opinion and experience in addressing this dimension of human experience. He recommends that greater attention be placed on the religious dimension in education and in clinical training to ensure expertise in dealing with religious issues in clinical practice.

These chapters build a foundation on which specific issues in clinical practice may be addressed. The backdrop for our continuing discussion has included an appreciation of religion as an important force within society and an invitation to consider this dimension in keeping with the conceptual and historical perspective of dialogue and integration. The chapters that follow present religion as a clinical variable and provide approaches for clinical understanding and intervention.

Theologian James W. Fowler presents faith as a multidimensional construct that is foundational to social relations, personal identity, and the making of personal and cultural meanings. Fowler's theory views faith as a dynamic developmental line that involves challenges, conflicts, and resolutions throughout life. Although not diminishing the sociological features of church affiliation and practice, he broadens the parameters of inquiry to understand the religious experience and faith as ways of knowing. The developmental stages that he presents are patterned operations of knowing and valuing that underlie consciousness and are held to be invariant, sequential, and hierarchical. Psychologists may find an intuitive affinity with Fowler's nuanced consideration of faith development that draws on the constructive, developmental scholarship of Jean Piaget, Erik Erikson, and Lawrence Kohlberg. In this essay, Fowler locates faith-development theory in relation to the work of the American psychologist and philosopher William James. The chapter encourages an appreciation of religious experience in a nonreductionistic and empirical manner. His discussion of conversion amplifies the dynamic turns of commitment and vision that occur in conversion. Furthermore, faith-development theory suggests that neither conversion nor the challenges and conflicts that accompany and proceed changing constructions and relations of self and the Holy are anomalies. He views faith development as necessarily including conversions in ways of knowing; such conversions may be subtle and gentle or may be dramatic turns involving crises of faith and identity.

Clinicians may find in Fowler's approach and stage theory the conceptual tools to better understand the religious aspects of the anxieties, depressions, and dysregulations that are presented clinically. Furthermore, such an appreciation puts in context how trauma and conflict reverberate through every sector of the personality and pose challenges to the core beliefs and identity of the individual. The mental health resources that religious affiliation and belief may provide at a given stage may be lost in the challenges of faith development as one mode of knowing disintegrates leading to the next. For example, the clinician may observe such features in the anomie and confusion of the young adult struggling within the boundary of synthetic–conventional faith and individuative–reflexive faith or in the anxiety of a middle-age adult entering into conjunctive faith.

Fowler concludes his chapter with a personal story that speaks to the heart of this volume: that psychotherapy inevitably involves the faith commitments of both the client and the clinician. His observation of the triadic nature of the therapeutic relationship reminds the clinician of the shared loyalties and implicit dimension of faith that influence the treatment process.

There is substantial literature that has sought to empirically test religion as a variable in mental health and as a correlate to a variety of psychological features. Gorsuch (1984) suggested that there is a boon in the measurement of the psychology of religion that allows for such investigations. This literature, however, poses difficulties in analysis in light of the variety of measures that have been used, the different factors that are collapsed in the scales (e.g., values, beliefs, and practice), noncomparable samples, and the numerous operational definitions establishing the variables in mental health. John Gartner has performed a comprehensive analysis of this literature. His conclusions are of significant value for the clinical community. He presents eleven areas in which religion is associated with mental health—five that are associated with psychopathology and six in which the associations are ambiguous or complex. Following his review, he concludes that the discrepant ways in which mental health is measured account for the inconsistencies in the literature. His chapter presents clinicians with an empirically based understanding of the contributions of religion as a variable in mental health. This review suggests that religion to a great extent appears as a potential resource for mental health. The following chapter amplifies the possibilities of religion serving that aim.

Kenneth I. Pargament locates the import of religion in mental health within the framework of coping. Drawing on theory and a significant body of empirical research, Pargament demonstrates that religion is an important cultural structure through which personal significance can be obtained. He concludes that religion provides both the means and the ends for accomplishing the human task of constructing meaning. He articulates the intersection of religion and mental health in his pointed discussion of external or internal threats to significance. In addition, he defines coping as the search for significance in the face of stressful life situations. Following the lead of anthropologist Geertz (1966/1973), Pargament sees religion as providing some way to cope with "crises of interpretability," in which commonsense attributions cannot provide an explanation or meaning for certain life events.

Individuals often seek consultation from mental health professionals in times of crisis. Pargament's elucidation of the functions that religion provides gives clinicians a unique perspective to understand particular therapeutic aspects of the psychotherapy process. Indeed, psychotherapy participates in the construction and articulation of personal meaning. Pargament sees these institutions of religion and psychology as different, while reflecting that each contributes to the noetic dimension in human experience.

Psychoanalyst W. W. Meissner brings a sophisticated analysis to a difficult issue in clinical assessment: On what basis do therapists determine the valence of a belief in respect to psychosocial status? In other words, how do therapists assess whether holding a particular set of beliefs enhances or impedes mental health? As Pargament has presented, religion provides models of significance that orient cognitions and personal values that determine patterns of coping. Clinicians observe repeatedly in their consulting rooms that patient's modes of coping are often pathological and lead to significant psychological and social impairment. Religious beliefs, affiliations, and practices may be adopted by individuals that serve constructive purposes, in the service of healthy adaptation, or destructive aims, resulting in maladjustment. Meissner establishes a viable model of clinical assessment drawing on the work of Milton Rokeach. Through his proposed system of analysis, clinicians are given conceptual and clinical tools to make appraisals of the pathogenicity of beliefs. His chapter stresses the importance of considering beliefs in terms of adaptation and contraindicates psychotherapists' offering clinical assessments on the sole basis of personal values and prejudices.

Marc Galanter continues the inquiry into the assessment of religious involvement as a force for health or psychopathology. In his chapter he presents an overview of the social psychology of charismatic groups. He finds that alternative religious groups, "cults," and popular self-help movements can be understood through an appraisal of group psychological dynamics, with special attention paid to the process of recruitment, conversion, and group cohesion. His review of the empirical literature, including his own body of work, suggests that charismatic groups appeal to individuals who are alienated from sources of internal and external significance and often suffer from psychological difficulties and, at times, psychiatric illness. He offers data that suggest that affiliation with a charismatic group may offer psychological resources that lead to improvements in psychosocial functioning. He presents in an even-handed manner the potentially adaptive and maladaptive aspects of such involvement. He considers the issue of mind control and offers distinctions between brainwashing and noncoercive group dynamics.

Charismatic groups illustrate many of the salient functions that religion serves concerning an individual's well-being. For many who participate in alternative religious movements, the charismatic group provides the resources for significance that Pargament speaks of, addresses the faith crises within development that Fowler describes, and requires the test of pathogenicity that Meissner offers.

The discussion now turns to explicit clinical concerns as the following chapters consider values in psychotherapy, clinical assessment, and models for addressing religious issues in psychological treatment.

In 1980 Allen E. Bergin sparked a firestorm of intellectual debate and clinical scrutiny with the publication of "Psychotherapy and Religious Values." Over 1,000 mental health professionals, including many prominent clinicians, responded to his thesis that called for an appreciation of the values inherent in the provision of psychotherapy (Bergin, 1985). Complementing London's (1964) presentation of the moral enterprise of psychotherapy and Frank's (1961; Frank & Frank, 1991) appreciation of the quasi-religious aspects of psychological treatment, Bergin initiated a program of research and scholarly writing that explicitly identified faith commitments, moral values, and religion-based life-styles as important clinical variables in mental health and in the provision of psychological services. Bergin with his colleagues, I. Reed Payne and P. Scott Richards, present in their chapter a summary of the contributions of the past decade and set forth a contemporary agenda for the examination of the role of values in applied psychology.

The overarching premise in their work is that values are inevitably expressed within the treatment relationship. They call for the elaboration of mental health values and the recognition of personal and religious values that influence the former. The values that are contained within treatment philosophies and regimens require the identification of their sources and demand empirical investigation of their relationship to mental health. The appreciation of the value-laden nature of psychological intervention further legitimates scholarship that seeks to understand the impact of faith commitments and the moral values and behavioral prescriptions emanating from religious sources as well as those espoused by "secular" psychology. It is through empirical research, including quantitative and qualitative methods, that interventions and behavioral recommendations may be offered more completely on the foundation of science. Also of significance is the issue of client–clinician similarity and its impact on the treatment process. This examination calls into question the notion that clinicians practice, or could ever in fact practice, with the degree of neutrality or objectivity formerly assumed and required. Furthermore, the appreciation of cultural diversity requires additional clarification. Does this ethical guideline mandate a stance that is insufficiently understood? What does it mean to respect another's values that are in conflict with one's own faith and values commitments? Bergin, Payne, and Richards present a historical and conceptual survey of the topic that addresses this question and leads to the further consideration of values in psychotherapy.

Robert J. Lovinger considers the religious dimension in assessment and treatment. His analysis involves a qualitative examination of a client's religiousness and pays particular attention to participation in organized religion. His survey of denominations illustrates the significant differences within religious traditions. While positing the impact of institutional affiliation, he reminds that the influence of religious involvement requires a microanalysis of the individual's unique faith commitment within a particular local congregation. His survey nonetheless provides an introduction to the essential characteristics of the major religious traditions within the United States. In addition, he provides illustrations of the impact of religious affiliation on attitudes and behaviors concerning a wide range of activities. His discussion of the Bible demonstrates the nuances and complexities involved in understanding a client's application of Scripture as a guide for behavior. In addition, Lovinger presents a model in which religious texts and theology might be addressed in psychotherapy. He concludes with the concern—complementing that of Bergin, Payne, and Richards—that psychological treatment may involve a clash of world views, in which respect for autonomy and a clear understanding of professional boundaries are required. Lovinger's chapter, taken with the preceding chapters, illustrates both the necessity of and the complexity in considering the religious dimension in psychological treatment.

Siang-Yang Tan suggests that there are two major models for the inclusion of religious issues within the practice of psychotherapy. These models are differentiated according to the degrees of implicit and explicit integration of religious themes, practices, and resources within psychological treatment. The myriad variations within clinical practice are readily contained within these models. Tan's distinctions between covert and overt influence, between the practice of initiating the consideration of issues of faith and delimiting their discussion, and the inclusion or exclusion of religious and spiritual resources in the psychotherapeutic task clearly demarcate directions in clinical approach and technique.

Implied within his chapter is the responsibility of clinicians to clearly understand the stance toward integration they are taking and to obtain informed consent, particularly in situations in which explicit integration is intended. Tan provides examples of explicit integration within the Christian tradition. The reader might well imagine the explicit integration of an array of religious and spiritual texts and practices culled from the panoply of religious expression. His technical considerations and recommendations can be applied to each instance in which religious or spiritual tradition is to be integrated within treatment. In this discussion readers are faced with the dilemma that is exposed when they consider that psychotherapy is a moral enterprise that is infused with values. That dilemma concerns the fact that the question is not whether to include considerations of world view, religious beliefs, and moral values in psychological treatment but what form such a consideration should take. This point is particularly relevant if you accept London's contention (cf. 1964, p. 156) that the scientific function of psychotherapists is that of manipulators of behavior and their moralistic function is that of a secular priesthood.

The third·major section in this volume presents discussions and examples of clinical practice that involve the treatment of religiously committed clients. Each of the authors was presented with the challenge of articulating approaches within their theoretical orientations to religious issues as presented within treatment. These chapters are not intended to be comprehensive reviews of approach or technique within their respective orientations but to serve as illustrations or models of integration within various forms of psychological treatment. My remarks here are intended to introduce each chapter with an eye to its unique contribution to the discussion of integration.

L. Rebecca Propst presents a cognitive–behavioral approach to treatment. Her discussion suggests that religious beliefs and practices, as exemplars of cognitions and behaviors, indeed influence mental health in their functions as antecedents and reinforcers of thought, behavior, and emotion. She proposes, in taking an explicit approach to integration, that cognitive reframing may include the use of Scripture and theological reflection to shape more adaptive cognitions. Furthermore, she suggests, consistent with Tan, that religious imagery and forms of prayer may be important resources in psychotherapy. She presents the findings of two clinical studies that empirically tested the efficacy of explicit religious interventions in treatment. These studies are examples of the sorts of research that are necessary to further the understanding of the differential effects of explicit integration.

Psychoanalyst Ana-Maria Rizzuto presents a psychoanalytic approach that appreciates what William James (1902/1982, p. 512) referred to as the "hither side" of religious experience and extends Freudian, object-relations, and Winnicottian theory to God representations. She locates religious experience within normal development and considers that "the child needs to find the *psychic means* to form a representation of the phantom and intangible reality of that which the family considers *sacred*" (Chapter 15, this volume, p. 413). This perspective alerts the clinician to contributions of religious influence no matter the faith status or present religious affiliation of the patient. She recommends taking a religious history within the interview process and understands the appearance of religious associations within the context of ever-present psychodynamics that include transference and defense operations. Rizzuto's approach amplifies the multitude of meanings that are disclosed within religious symbolism, language, and experience. She does not attempt to modify religious ideation, as Propst might, but seeks to inquire with the patient about the dynamic meanings and conflicts that are being expressed. Psychoanalytic treatment as presented by Rizzuto exemplifies the implicit approach to integration.

Alvin R. Mahrer finds that a legion of prominent existential–humanistic clinicians and scholars have addressed the domain of ontological meaning. Indeed, many eminent clinicians, such as Viktor Frankl and Rollo May, established the search for meaning as the centerpiece of their therapeutic systems. Mahrer resolves the quandary of how to present such vast literature by providing a more personal description of how a given psychotherapist, at the heart of the tradition, might address the religious and spiritual issues of clients.

In his experiential approach the focus is on the direct and unmediated expression of the essence of the person in the immediacy of the session. Religious material is not placed in a privileged category but is addressed in a manner consistent with all other associations. The exploration of associations to and memories of religious events and beliefs provides opportunities for deepening the potential for "experiencing" in light of the often-powerful affective components of religious experience. Mahrer clearly implicates that the "person" of the therapist is directly available and involved in the therapeutic process; however, the therapist must resist the forces of manipulation in applying undue influence on the client. He indicates that experiential psychotherapy shares a common avenue with religion and spirituality to the extent that each has as its aim the deeper integration and actualization of the person. The values of interest to Mahrer are those that are discovered or constructed within the course of actualizing one's full potential. Unique to this system is its emphasis on the direct experiencing and transformation of the self in each session.

Carl Jung had an abiding interest in religion and made a number of important contributions to the psychological appreciation of the noetic and spiritual dimension in human life. Jungian analyst John Van Eenwyk discusses clinical integration from a contemporary analytical perspective. He presents integration as embracing two separate tracks of discourse in which, like a railroad roundhouse, inquiry can be switched from one linguistic track to the other. Such an approach upholds the integrity of religion and psychology as separate domains of knowledge and avoids reductionism. Analytical psychology shares the psychoanalytic emphasis on unconscious process and transference. Van Eenwyk introduces "active imagination" as a tool for enhancing psychological development and shows how Jung's concepts of agency, intent, and design can be of heuristic value in understanding religious language as depicting forces of conflict and development within the parallel lines of psychology and spirituality.

Transpersonal psychology by definition includes the spiritual dimension in its consideration of well-being. Among the theoretical orientations presented in this volume, it stands out as an exemplar of an explicit integration approach to psychological treatment. In postulating that transpersonal psychotherapy intends to contribute to spiritual realization, resources from diverse spiritual traditions are readily included in the treatment process. Frances Vaughan, Bryan Wittine, and Roger Walsh present a thoughtful and comprehensive introduction to transpersonal psychotherapy. Their presentation locates institutional religious experience and alternative religious involvement within the superseding context of spiritual development. Their presentation of a spectrum of development (i.e., prepersonal, personal, and transpersonal) suggests a human teleology in which transconventional modes of being are anticipated. Psychological consultation may be sought in times of altered states of consciousness or following transpersonal experiences. Vaughan, Wittine, and Walsh discuss the difficult clinical task of distinguishing between genuine experiences of self-transcendence and regressive pathology. In their view psychotherapy not only aims at psychosocial adjustment on the personal level but also serves as a tool, with other spiritual practices, in the development to the farther reaches of human nature (cf. Maslow, 1971).

Marital and family therapy includes modes of treatment derived from each of the aforementioned theoretical orientations taken within the context of systems and structural theories. Len Sperry and Paul Giblin discuss the significant influence that religious orientation has on marital and family attitudes and behaviors. In their view religion plays a crucial role in determining basic beliefs, values, and practices that influence every aspect of family life. This influence is further reinforced to the extent that the couple or family participates in a faith community. Conflicts in relationships, marriages, or families often at their core involve differences of values and beliefs that originate from family and religious upbringing. Considering religious background and current practice may provide the clinician with an important developmental perspective. Sperry and Giblin advocate a detailed assessment of religious background and influence and suggest a timely approach to explicit integration. Within the context of integration they find that theological, scriptural, and ritual resources offer possible sources for healing; however, they affirm—in keeping with Tan's recommendation—a sensitive and informed approach to explicit integration.

Ronald E. Hopson completes our survey of treatment orientations with his presentation of the 12-step program. In terms of sheer numbers, 12-step programs are the most widely used form of intervention in America; as Hopson reports, over 16 million people have participated in one of the over 125,000 separate chapters. Unique to forms of treatment, 12-step programs originated in a religious tradition and continue to rely on spiritual principles. Hopson provides a detailed analysis of the steps and offers a commentary on 12-step programs within the culture and in relationship to psychotherapy. He centers his discussion on the role of faith in the healing process. This is in keeping with Frank's point that healing commences with providing hope in the face of demoralization (cf. Frank, 1961; Frank and Frank, 1991). Contemporary psychology may have much to learn from the constituent elements of 12-step programs.

Edward Shafranske and H. Newton Malony provide closing remarks to this volume in their chapter on the case for the inclusion of religious issues in the clinical practice of psychology. They posit that there are four interrelated factors that provide compelling support for the consideration of religious issues in psychological treatment. These are the professional ideal of cultural inclusion, evidence of religion as a cultural fact, substantive research concerning religion as a variable relevant to mental health, and the appreciation of values in psychological treatment. They recommend a three-pronged approach that includes education, clinical training, and research to ensure clinical competency.

AN INVITATION

Psychoanalyst Erik Erikson (1958/1962) wrote that religion "elaborates on what feels profoundly true even though it is not demonstrable: it translates into significant words, images, and codes the exceeding darkness which surrounds man's existence, and the light that pervades it beyond all discrete comprehension" (p. 21). As we embark on this examination of religion in the clinical practice of psychology, it is perhaps useful to reflect on Erikson's words. For me, Erikson conveys a sense of humility, mystery, respect, and curiosity for this domain in which strands of belief and ritual are woven into a personal use of meaning, and existence is ordained as significant. This volume, in my view, does not intend to reduce people's faith commitments to purely psychological factors but invites an appreciation of the psychological in the religious and the religious dimension within applied psychology.

REFERENCES

American Psychiatric Association Committee on Religion and Psychiatry. (1990). Guidelines regarding possible conflict between psychiatrists' religious commitments and psychiatric practice. *American Journal of Psychiatry, 147,* 542.

American Psychological Association. (1992). Ethical principles of psychologists and code of conduct. *American Psychologist, 47,* 1597–1611.

Barbour, I. (1974). *Myths, models, and paradigms.* New York: Harper & Row.

Berger, P. (1967). *The sacred canopy: Elements of a sociological theory of religion.* Garden City, NY: Doubleday.

Berger, P., & Luckman, L. (1966). *The social construction of reality: A treatise in the sociology of knowledge.* Garden City, NY: Doubleday.

Bergin, A. E. (1980). Psychotherapy and religious values. *Journal of Consulting and Clinical Psychology, 48,* 95–105.

Bergin, A. E. (1985). Proposed values for guiding and evaluating counseling and psychotherapy. *Counseling and Values, 29,* 99–116.

Erikson, E. H. (1958/1962). *Young man Luther.* New York: W. W. Norton.

Frank, J. D. (1961). *Persuasion and healing.* Baltimore, MD: The Johns Hopkins University Press.

Frank, J. D., & Frank, J. B. (1991). *Persuasion and healing* (3rd ed.). Baltimore, MD: The Johns Hopkins University Press.

Gallup, G., Jr. (1995). *The Gallup Poll. Public Opinion 1993.* Wilmington, DE: Scholarly Resources.

Geertz, C. (1966). Religion as cultural system. In M. Banton (Ed.), *Anthropological approaches to the study of religion* (pp. 1–46). London: Tavistock.

Geertz, C. (1973). Religion as a cultural system. In C. Geertz (Ed.), *The interpretation of cultures* (pp. 87–125). New York: Basic Books. (Reprinted from *Anthropological approaches to the study of religion,* pp. 1–46, by M. Banton, Ed., 1966, London: Tavistock)

Gorsuch, R. L. (1984). Measurement: The boon and bane of investigating religion. *American Psychologist, 39,* 228–236.

James, W. (1982). *The varieties of religious experience.* New York: Penguin Books. (Original work published 1902)

Kosmin, B., & Lachman, S. (1993). *One nation under God. Religion in contemporary American society.* New York: Crown.

London, P. (1964). *The mode and morals of psychotherapy*. New York: Holt, Rinehart & Winston.

Maslow, A. (1971). *The farther reaches of human nature*. New York: Van Nostrand.

Parsons, T. (1977). *Social systems and the evolution of action theory*. New York: Free Press.

Weber, M. (1963). *The sociology of religion*. Boston: Beacon Press.

I

RELIGION AND
PSYCHOLOGY:
A CONCEPTUAL,
CULTURAL, AND
HISTORICAL CONTEXT

1

RELIGION IN AMERICA: THE DEMOGRAPHICS OF BELIEF AND AFFILIATION

DEAN R. HOGE

In this chapter my aim is to describe the overall outline of religious life in America today. To accomplish this I need to carry out three tasks. The first is mapping and describing religious behavior, the second is reporting research findings that test important assumptions about religion commonly held by behavioral scientists, and the third is pointing out the relevance of religious change for clinical psychology today.

The topic is laden with definitional problems. Not only are sociologists inconsistent in their concepts and definitions, but the varied and imprecise use of terms by the mass media makes matters worse, as well. Good examples are the varied meanings of the words *cult* and *spirituality*. Some Americans today describe themselves as "spiritual but not religious," and this usually. means that their spiritual beliefs and behaviors are not associated with any traditional church or synagogue. However, these people may study the Bible or the Bhagavad Gita, both of which are eminently religious and traditional. People with this self-description seem to mean they are religious "independents" in the sense of political independents. To compound the problem, the term *spiritual* has such vague and unbounded meanings that it is barely useful, and it fits poorly—if at all—with prevailing psychological theories. One's only option, in face of this confusion, is to set forth the necessary definitions and distinctions at the beginning of any exposition. I will distinguish five entities: religious

21

preference, church affiliation, church involvement, religious belief, and personal religious behavior.

Religious preference is a person's feeling of whether he or she belongs to a religious group. The term *preference* has been in use for only several decades, and its meaning today comes from survey research. Surveys commonly ask, "Do you have a religious preference?" or "What is your religious preference—would you say Protestant, Catholic, Jewish, some other, or none?" The concept of preference is not found in the religious traditions themselves.

Church affiliation is a measure of whether a person belongs to a church or a synagogue in the sense of having his or her name on a membership list (for convenience I use the word *church* generically to include all religious bodies). Being a Protestant or a Jew does not in itself make a person a church member; the person must ask for membership in a particular church or synagogue. There is no general membership. The Catholic situation is unique in that Catholic Canon Law defines a person as a Catholic if he or she was ever baptized Catholic and has never formally joined a non-Catholic religious group. For this reason the Catholic Church has difficulty in estimating the size of its membership, and its only recourses are two: Ask local clergy to estimate how many persons living in the parish (geographically defined) have been baptized Catholic, or ask how many people have registered their name in each parish registry. Each parish has a registry of families who are involved in parish life, a mailing directory of sorts for sending out newsletters and keeping contact. The registry list is a good indication of how many people are interested in parish life and is an approximate analog to church membership rolls among Protestants or synagogue rolls among Jews. An estimated 70% of all baptized Catholics have their names on parish lists.

Church involvement is mainly a matter of church attendance, but it also includes participation in groups or committees in the church, financial contributions to the church, and socialization with other parishioners. No one should assume that church involvement is a direct reflection of religious faith or piety. Rather, it is the result of numerous motives, some religious and some not. For example, single adults seeking mates often participate in churches, and business people seeking clients, visibility, or respectability do the same. Church life provides community support, friendship, religious education for children, and a chance to participate with others in meaningful activities and efforts. Some researchers have attempted to measure the motives for church involvement, but the results have not been clear or convincing.

Religious belief includes belief in God and divine teachings as found in sacred writings. As defined here, it does not include a more general interest in religious questions or religious history, which I will call "religious interest." A religious seeker, for example, might have strong religious interest but few definite beliefs.

Personal religious behavior includes prayer; devotional readings; study of religious texts; meditation; and other behaviors, such as keeping dietary rules, that are seen as spiritually beneficial. It is distinct from church going or ongoing participation groups.

This set of definitions could be expanded further, but it should suffice here. Later I will depict the current religious situation in these terms, and at the end of the chapter I will discuss specific behaviors closely related to religious life, topics that are pertinent to psychologists. But first I need to discuss a widely held assumption today, that of secularization.

THE SECULARIZATION MODEL

Numerous educated people in the United States have a worldview that distinguishes modern scientific truth from everything in the past (often seen as "religious") and dismisses the latter as folk wisdom. They believe that religion is on the wane in the Western urbanized, industrialized nations; science is in a struggle with traditional religion, and in spite of occasional reverses, it will prevail. A person does not need to have a negative evaluation of traditional religion to hold this view. Many believers and admirers of traditional religion fully believe that it is dying because of the onslaught of science and learning. American writers of psychology commonly believe that secularization is moving ahead and that it is inevitable. Among academic disciplines, psychology is relatively disparaging of religion.

In Europe the belief in inevitable secularization is more widely held than it is in the United States, and for good reason: The empirical reality in northern European societies is more supportive. In most of Europe, church going and religious involvement have declined over the past half century and are very low today. Christian churches are nearly empty in northern Europe.

In the United States, the empirical reality is different, and the secularization model does not seem to apply. By most indicators of religious commitment, the United States is far above most modern European nations and on the same level as Ireland and Poland, the two most religious nations in Europe. The vast amount of money Americans donate to their churches constantly dismays European observers. Furthermore, overall church involvement in the United States has not changed measurably since the 1960s. Why is there a high level of involvement in the United States? The question is widely debated (Tiryakian, 1993), but no one has been able to articulate and demonstrate a clear explanation. One approach is to acknowledge the strong religious commitment in the United States but to question its veracity or authenticity, seeing it as no more than one form of social life or community life. Another is to stress the voluntary nature of churches in America, due to the absence of an established church in American history (after about 1800) and the absence of any aristocracy or privileged higher clergy in our past. Yet another is to see the United States' higher level of church going as a result of its immigrant history or its religious diversity. Whatever the reason, the American experience calls the universality of the secularization model into serious question.

The model does not fit the American reality. Either the United States is an exception or (more likely) modern Europe is an exception to a situation of religious stability in most of the world today (Stark & Iannaccone, 1994). Any apparent trends toward secularization in the United States are short-range and self-limiting (Finke & Stark, 1992; Stark & Bainbridge, 1985). The long-range future will see changes in religious institutions but no long-term decline in religious commitment and no disappearance of churches. Religion is a human universal, here to stay in some form or other.

Certain segments of American society have secularized during the last half-century. Most visible is the university system, which was established over two centuries ago under the sponsorship of churches but gradually became autonomous under principles enunciated in the Enlightenment. The scientific establishment has shed its theological and ecclesiastical ties, as have economic institutions (banks and the stock market), most of high culture, and most of the media. But academics and intellectuals should not think that all Americans are as they are.

Assumptions about secularization are so basic to this chapter that I have taken up the question here in the beginning. My main message is that the empirical evidence available—and it is quite substantial—provides no support for the secularization model. Rather, religion should be seen as a constant in human society. It is subject to change, doctrinally and institutionally, just like other elements of culture such as language and family, and we scholars need to devote ourselves to understanding and explaining the changes.

I now turn to the current American situation in religious preference, church affiliation, church involvement, religious belief, and personal religious behavior. Information on all five comes mainly from sociological research, especially public-opinion polls. Some has been obtained from research offices of church bodies.

RELIGIOUS PREFERENCE

The history of the United States has been marked by increasing religious pluralism because of immigration. At the time of the American Revolution the population was almost entirely Protestant. Out of a population of 4 million there were only about 25,000 Catholics and 2,500 Jews.

The first major wave of immigration, from 1840 to 1925, added many Catholics and Jews, and the second wave, which began in 1965 and continues in full force today, is adding many more Catholics, plus some Muslims, Buddhists, and adherents of other Asian religions.

The Gallup Organization has gathered the most extensive data on American religious preferences. In 1992 it estimated the religious preferences of Americans as 56% Protestant, 26% Catholic, 2% Jewish, 7% other; and 9% no preference ("Early 1993 Data," 1993). Within the Protestant group the largest preferences were Baptist (19% of the total population), Methodist (10%), and Lutheran (6%). Reports of polls vary a few percentage points at any one time, so these figures are not precise.

Trends in religious preference have been monitored by the Gallup Organization since 1947. The changes have been a decrease in Protestants (from about 69% to 56%), a decrease in Jews (from about 4% to 2%), an increase in Catholics (from about 24% to 27%), an increase in "other" (from 1% to 4%), and an increase in "none," (from about 5% to 9%; Princeton Religion Research Center, 1990). Other scattered information suggests that Muslims are increasing and now make up between 1.5% and 2% of the population.

The recent trends in religious preference are largely a result of immigration but also partly a result of increased individualism and relativism in some religious groups—trends that induce more and more people to say they have no religious preference. To a small extent, religious trends are a result of differential fertility. All research shows larger family size among more conservative Christians, a factor adding to their growth. Until the mid-1970s Catholics had larger families than non-Catholics, but after that time the differences disappeared.

Future immigration promises to produce more religious diversity and some important shifts in some religious groups. It will certainly augment the number of Catholics in the United States because the majority of immigrants today are Catholics—at least nominally. Estimates vary, but at least two-thirds of the immigrants in the late 1980s were culturally Catholic. Most of these were from Mexico, South and Central America, the Philippines, or Southeast Asia. Not all remain Catholic because thousands switch to conservative and pentecostal Protestant sects. But many immigrants do remain Catholic, and they will become a rising percentage of the Catholic community in the years ahead. Today about 25% to 35% of American Catholics are Hispanic (Deck, 1989).

CHURCH AFFILIATION

Every year Gallup polls ask about church membership. The standard question is: "Do you happen to be a member of a church or synagogue?"

The figure for 1992 was 71% (*Gallup Poll Monthly*, 1993). The figure varied between 67% and 71% during the 1980s, with no visible trend. In the 1940s it was 74%, in the 1950s it was 73%, and in the 1970s it was 70% (Princeton Religion Research Center, 1990). Apparently, the rate of church membership in the total population has dropped slightly since the 1970s. Among Gallup poll respondents who say that their preference is Protestant, 73% claim to be church members; among people saying their preference is Catholic, 82% claim to be church members; among those who say they are Jewish, 58% claim to be synagogue members. (Later we will see that other research has a lower figure for Jews.) Membership is higher in rural areas (77%) than in cities (65%) or suburbs (68%). The Western states are consistently the lowest in church membership, which is a finding in every poll; the explanation is somehow related to the greater individualism, greater transiency, and weaker community ties in the West.

The best data on membership of specific denominations come from the annual *Yearbook of American and Canadian Churches*, published by the National Council of Churches (Bedell, 1994). It compiles membership data and financial data from all religious bodies in the United States who will cooperate, and it makes estimates for the others. Table 1 shows the size of the largest denominations.

The figure for Roman Catholics was compiled from reports from pastors of individual parishes; it is somewhat lower than the estimates made by polling companies (about 62 million). The figure for Muslims is a rough estimate.

The sharpest trends in church membership are in specific denominations, not in the total percentage of the population who are members. The "mainline Protestants," the middle-class denominations that historically were the most dominant, have steadily lost members since the middle 1960s. For example, the Episcopal Church has lost 28% of its membership between 1965 and 1992, the United Church of Christ has lost 23%, the Presbyterians have lost 32%, and the Methodists have lost 19%. In general, the more affluent and more theologically liberal the denomination, the greater the loss. This has occurred even though these well-established denominations had grown more or less consistently throughout previous American history. As a percentage of the total population, they declined from about 45% in the late 1960s to 40% in 1986. In the last century they were "established" culturally, but that is now ending. The decline of mainline Protestant churches has produced self-doubts and a kind of failure of nerve among church leaders.

What caused the decline? A debate has raged for years (Kelley, 1977; Roozen & Hadaway, 1993). The empirical studies that have been done show that numerous changes in the fabric of middle-class Protestant life have contributed to the loss, including smaller families, higher rates of sending children to college, a decline in acceptance of church authority in

TABLE 1
Membership in American Religious Denominations and Groups

Inclusive group	Membership
Baptist churches	
American Baptist Churches in the U.S.A.	1,527,840
National Baptist Convention of America	*3,500,000
National Baptist Convention, U.S.A.	*5,500,000
Southern Baptist Convention	15,232,347
All other Baptist bodies	*1,240,000
Christian Churches (Disciples of Christ)	1,022,926
Christian Churches and Churches of Christ	1,070,616
Churches of Christ	*1,690,000
Eastern Orthodox Churches (combined)	*2,800,000
Episcopal Church in the U.S.A.	2,471,880
Jewish organizations	
Union of American Hebrew Congregations (Reform)	*1,300,000
Union of Orthodox Jewish Congregations of America	*1,000,000
United Synagogues of America (Conservative)	*2,000,000
Church of Jesus Christ of Latter-Day Saints	4,336,000
Lutheran churches	
Evangelical Lutheran Church of America	5,245,177
Lutheran Church—Missouri Synod	2,607,309
All other Lutheran bodies	513,989
Methodist churches:	
United Methodist Church	8,785,135
African Methodist Episcopal Church	*2,210,000
African Methodist Episcopal Zion Church	*1,200,000
All other Methodist bodies	103,130
Muslims	*4,500,000
Pentecostal churches:	
Assemblies of God	2,234,708
All other Pentecostal bodies	*2,000,000
Presbyterian Church (U.S.A.)	3,778,358
Roman Catholic Church	58,267,424
United Church of Christ	1,583,830

Note. Figures were reported to the 1993 *Yearbook of American and Canadian Churches* or estimated by yearbook editors from available information. Inclusive membership includes children and adherents even if not full members.
*Estimated.

matters of doctrinal truth and morality, greater tolerance and acceptance of non-Protestant religions, and greater hesitancy among young adults to trust large institutions in general (Hadaway, 1993; Hoge, Johnson, & Luidens, 1994; Roof, 1993). All research agrees that the mainline Protestant downturns are a result of weak church involvement by young adults, not a result of older people departing.

Meanwhile conservative Protestant denominations have not declined, and a few, such as the Southern Baptist Convention and Assemblies of God, have grown until the most recent years. Their youth have maintained stronger faith and identity, partly because of lower rates of college attendance and lower rates of cross-cultural experiences. However, in the early 1990s some stopped growing. Many independent churches continue to grow.

A large portion of conservative Protestants call themselves "evangelicals." They adhere to a quite literal interpretation of the Bible, and they emphasize conversion and development of a personal relationship with Jesus Christ. Pollsters have tried to estimate their numbers. The Gallup Organization has identified evangelicals by using the question "Would you describe yourself as a Born-Again Christian, or not?" The percentage of Christians who say yes to this has been stable from 1976. In 1987 it was 31% (Gallup & Castelli, 1989, p. 93), and 44% of Protestants and 13% of Catholics said that they are born again. These figures seem unduly high and suggest a larger percentage of evangelicals in the United States than other evidence would indicate. Compared with average Americans, evangelicals are older, less educated, lower in income, and more likely to live in the South. They are more conservative on sexual issues and life-style issues, but they are not different from average Americans in their attitudes on most domestic and foreign-policy issues.

Americans switch denominations readily. Well over a third of Americans change religious affiliations over the course of a lifetime. The main reasons are interfaith marriage and movement from one city to another, with subsequent "church shopping" in the new place. Some people go church shopping even without any residential move if something has made them unhappy with their church, such as an unsettling incident or conflict. When Protestants go church shopping they sample the churches in a half-dozen denominations, and the inevitable result is a high rate of switching. When researchers look at current attitudes of church shoppers, they usually find that denominations are unimportant to the shoppers—within boundaries. Mainline Protestants are comfortable in a number of mainline denominations, and conservatives in a number of conservative denominations. Switching across the boundaries of Protestant/Catholic/Jew is seldom a result of church shopping; when it occurs it is more often due to interfaith marriage.

The Church of Jesus Christ of Latter-Day Saints (Mormon) has been growing for years, and it continues to do so, largely in the West. Its current membership is about 4.3 million. Mormon growth is traceable to its unparalleled missionary energy. It is growing everywhere in the world, and it is especially interesting to cultural analysts, being a product of modern America. Founded in the 1830s in New York and the Midwest, it is thoroughly American in style, culture, organization—a kind of modernized frontier American Protestantism.

The pentecostal churches are also growing. They are very diverse and loosely organized into various denominations. But the largest denomination is the Assemblies of God, which has been growing consistently for several decades.

The Roman Catholic Church has grown consistently and will continue to do so because of today's rapid immigration. The immigrants provide new energies but aggravate the problems of keeping unity and harmony in the church. The huge immigration of Hispanics from Mexico and Latin America—estimated at 300,000 per year in the early 1990s and unlikely to wane in the future—will have a major impact.

The Jewish community today is struggling with the problem of Jewish identity. The threatening trend is that many Jewish young adults have little sense of their Jewishness, and marriage to non-Jews is more and more common. The number of people who tell pollsters that they are Jews is gradually sagging. In recent polls it is 2% or 3%. A 1990 survey of Jews found that 39% are currently synagogue members (Tobin & Berger, 1993). Jews are clearly the most affluent and best-educated religious groups in the nation; they are about 50% higher than Catholics or Protestants in family income and in percent of people who have finished college.

The Muslim community is growing steadily because of immigration. It was estimated at about 3.3 million in 1980, with largest concentrations in California, New York, and Illinois (Stone, 1991). By 1993 its size was roughly 4 million. These people come from very diverse homelands, about 28% from the Middle East and North Africa, about 30% from Eastern Europe, and about 12% from Asia. An estimated 30% of American Muslims are not immigrants but indigenous African Americans. American citizens are just now beginning to recognize Islam as a future major American religious denomination.

Other religious groups in America are much smaller than these. Much media attention has been given to the Unification Church ("Moonies"), to sects such as the Branch Davidians, to new age gatherings, and to Eastern religious groups. But all of these are tiny by comparison with the major religious communities. Media attention was given to new religious movements in the late 1960s and 1970s, and when the attention waned some scholars concluded that the burst of new movements was a temporary product of the 1960s. But an analysis of the demographics of new religious movement indicates that the rapid growth of new movements in the 1960s and 1970s had more to do with liberalization of U.S. immigration laws in 1965, a move that opened the gates to thousands of new immigrants from Asia. Asian religious groups have shown remarkable growth from the late 1960s to today (Melton, 1993; Neusner, 1994). The world today is experiencing new religious energies, with growth and diffusion of many movements from their traditional geographical bases. Whereas in the last century the main diffusion was the spread of Christianity to the non-West, today all religions are spreading in all directions.

CHURCH INVOLVEMENT

The most-cited data on rates of church attendance come from the Gallup Organization, which asks a standard question six or more times a year: "Did you, yourself, happen to attend church or synagogue in the last seven days?" In 1992, 40% said yes, and the figure has been roughly constant since the late 1960s. In the 1950s the rate of attendance was higher; it was 49% in 1955 and again in 1958, then it dropped to the 40% to 42% range in the middle 1960s. The decline in church attendance in the 1960s was disproportionately among Catholics; among Protestants the decline was small. Church attendance is consistently found to be lower in the West than in the rest of the nation.

Church attendance varies widely by religious preference. In 1991, of the persons saying they are Catholic, 51% reported church attendance in the last week; of those saying they are Protestant, it was 45%; of those saying they are Jewish, the figure was about 23% ("Church Attendance Constant," 1992). Within the Protestant category, the more theologically conservative the denomination, the higher the rate of church attendance.

People are inclined to attend church more regularly as they grow older. The age group least likely to attend church weekly is young adults age 18 to 29 years. After age 30 the rate of attendance rises steadily until old age, when physical limits reduce people's ability to get to church.

A modest number of Americans find religious meaning in groups outside of church life. A 1989 survey asked, "In the last two years did you attend a prayer group, Bible study, or other religious group which meets somewhere other than a church?" and "Have you attended a charismatic religious group, that is, one including the gifts of the spirit?" The questions do not explicitly exclude groups that are part of congregational or parish life, but they are useful for a rough indication. Twenty-two percent said they had attended a prayer group or Bible study outside of church, and nine percent had attended a charismatic group (Princeton Religious Research Center, 1990).

The level of involvement by church members, according to all studies, is highly skewed. Churches normally have a small highly committed core group, a larger outer circle of moderately committed members, and an outside circle of uninvolved people. Research on financial giving to churches consistently finds the same pattern—that about 20% of the members give 80% of the contributions.

Another consistent research finding is a high rate of dropping out of church life among youth about 16 to 25 years of age. In a recent survey of baby boomers that asked about their religious histories, over 60% of those who attended church during grade school and high school reported dropping out for a period of at least two years afterward. Among Jews and mainline Protestants the figure was even higher (Roof, 1993, p. 55). This dropping out is usually not an act of rebellion against the family because parents of many religious groups are tolerant of youthful experimentation and prefer that young people follow their own commitments and doubts in religious matters. The most common time of dropping out is when the young person leaves home after high school. Many of the dropouts return to church going later, when they acquire adult roles. Research findings vary on rates of returning, but all studies agree that at least half will return to church going at some time in their lives. Strong predictors of church going among persons in their 30s and 40s are having children of school age and "settling in" to life in one's community (Hoge et al., 1994). The vast majority of Americans want some form of religious education for their children—at least 90% according to surveys—partly because of the element of character education involved. American public schools are perceived to be weak in moral education and character education, but these goals are central to Sunday schools, synagogue schools, and parish-based programs. It is common for parents to send their children to Sunday schools even though they have little interest in church life and church teachings themselves.

RELIGIOUS BELIEF

Levels of religious belief in the United States are steady over the years. No important trends have been found since the 1940s or 1950s in belief in God, belief in an afterlife, or belief in the divine nature of the Bible. The proportion of the population who profess a belief in God has remained at around 95% ever since the question was first asked in 1944. Acceptance of the divinity of Jesus has been virtually unchanged during this time, at about 75% to 77%. Belief in an afterlife has remained at about 75% of the population since 1944 (Greeley, 1989).

One element of religious belief has been changing. Belief in biblical literalism—that the Bible represents the actual Word of God in all instances—has declined over the last three decades. In 1991, 32% of Americans said they believe that the Bible represents the actual Word of God, to be taken literally word for word. In 1963, 65% of Americans held this view, and by 1978 it had fallen to 38%. The survey question gave respondents several options to choose from, and the trend is not toward seeing the Bible as without value; the percentage saying it is "nothing more than an ancient chronicle of myths and precepts" grew only slightly, from 11% in 1963 to 16% in 1991. Rather, the trend was to a view that the Bible is inspired but contains human error. Biblical literalists today are most commonly found among Americans who did not complete high school.

Knowledge of the contents of the Bible is only moderately high. A 1982 survey asked Americans who delivered the Sermon on the Mount, and 42% got the correct answer. It asked the respondent to name the four Gospels—the first four books of the New Testament—and 46% got all four correct. Then it asked where Jesus was born, and 70% got it correct (Greeley, 1989, p. 17). The same questions were asked in an earlier 1954 survey, and the level of knowledge on all three questions was lower in 1954 than in 1982.

In 1991 a nationwide poll asked for agreement or disagreement with a statement about Christ: "The only assurance of eternal life is personal faith in Jesus Christ." It found that 76% agreed completely or somewhat ("Majority Believe," 1991). Women agreed more than men (81% vs. 71%), Blacks more than Whites (95% vs. 74%), and non-college graduates more than graduates (80% vs. 63%).

An interesting set of surveys asked Americans how important a role religion plays in their lives. In 1992, 58% percent said religion is very important in their lives. An additional 29% said it is fairly important, and 12% said it was not very important ("Who Considers Religion Important?" 1993). The questions were first asked in 1952 and 1965, when 75% and 70%, respectively, said religion was very important in their lives. During the 1980s the question was asked repeatedly, with 53% to 56% saying "very important." The 1992 survey found 58%, a slight increase.

Do Americans have confidence in religious leaders? Each year polls ask about confidence in various institutions. The standard question is as follows: "Now I am going to read you a list of institutions in American society. Please tell me how much confidence you, yourself, have in each one—a great deal, quite a lot, some, or very little?" Those saying "a great deal" or "quite a lot" in "church or organized religion" stood at 53% in 1993. It was in the upper 50% or lower 60% in the 1980s and even higher in earlier polls. Public confidence in church leaders has been slipping in recent decades ("Confidence in Organized Religion," 1993), just like the slippage of confidence in most other institutions.

Another area in which religious authority has been declining is specific to Catholics—acceptance of papal authority. It has dropped markedly since first asked in a 1963 survey. At that time 86% of American Catholics said it was "certainly true" or "probably true" that Jesus had handed over authority in the church to Peter and the popes. In 1974 the figure had dropped to 71%, and in 1985 it had dropped to 68%. The weakening of church authority is most advanced among younger Catholics. In 1985, 58% of Catholics age 30 or younger agreed with the statement about Jesus handing over authority, compared with 74% of those over 50 (Hoge, 1987). In the same 1985 survey there was a statement "Under certain conditions, the Pope is infallible when he speaks on matters of faith and morals." Of those age 30 or younger 51% agreed, compared with 74% of those over 50.

PERSONAL RELIGIOUS BEHAVIOR

This section looks at two aspects of the current situation: personal religious behavior as a part of membership in a church and spiritual life outside of traditional religion. In the first category are behaviors such as Bible reading, prayer, personal and family devotions, and participation in special religious groups.

Prayer is an important part of most adults' life. A 1987 poll included this item: "Please tell me how much you agree or disagree with this statement: Prayer is an important part of my daily life." Of those responding, 66% completely or mostly agreed, and 23% disagreed. When polls asked people if they ever pray to God, about 88% say yes, and this figure has been constant since the earliest poll in 1948. People who say they pray often tend to be women more than men, older more than younger, and Blacks more than Whites or Hispanics (Princeton Religious Research Center, 1990).

Researchers have sought to see how many people have religious or mystical experiences. These topics are not very amenable to survey methods because of the layers of interpretation involved, but the findings have some value. In 1984 a nationwide survey asked, "Have you ever felt as though you were very close to a powerful spiritual force that seemed to lift you out of yourself?" and 40% said yes (Greeley, 1989, p. 59).

On all sides there are new spiritual strivings outside of traditional organized religion. They are difficult to describe because of their diversity, but I may note that the most-read book in this field is M. Scott Peck's (1988) *The Road Less Travelled*. The word *spiritual* is used in this literature with a meaning of well-being and health. Thousands of Americans are spiritual seekers and participants in a bewildering array of groups and teachings. The organizations are nonexclusive and institutionally precarious. One segment of the new spirituality is called the New Age movement. It includes such diverse elements as nature religion, teachings from the religion of Native Americans, astrology, the occult, humanistic psychology, and holistic healing. Its extent is difficult to estimate, but a 1990 survey attempted to measure how many people were aware of it. The 1990 survey question did not describe or identify New Age practices but merely asked the respondents if they have heard or read about "the New Age." Nationally, 24% said yes, and among college graduates, the response was 38%. Awareness was higher in the West than elsewhere. Among persons who are aware of the New Age movement, only 18% said they have a favorable opinion of it, whereas 49% were opposed and 33% had formed no opinion. Catholics are more tolerant of New Age beliefs than Protestants ("One in Four," 1991).

The word *movement* in referring to New Age may be misleading because it is really a loose collection of unorganized, competing groups and teachers. Readers of any New Age publication will see advertisements and notices of a remarkable array of healers and teachers. The language of healing is central to the whole thrust—healing the body and mind, and by extension healing the society and the planet. Healing requires love, reconciliation of parts, harmony, and communication, and these themes pervade the wide-ranging spiritualities today.

SOCIAL ISSUES WITH IMPORTANT RELIGIOUS ELEMENTS

From the time of the Puritans, American religion has always aimed to improve the society. For example, religious forces animated the anti-slavery movement in the early 19th century and the prohibition movement at the turn of the century. Recently, religious people spearheaded the civil rights movement and the disarmament movement. But unlike these examples, the majority of religious energies have always been directed to personal behavior—especially alcohol abuse, adultery, and neglect of family responsibilities. The classic repentant sinner in American history has been a man who stopped drinking alcohol, abandoned his female liaisons, and devoted himself to his wife, children, and church. The preponderance of religious concern with personal behavior continues today.

All conservative Christian groups oppose alcohol use, and empirical studies have consistently found that strong religious identification and involvement are associated with lower alcohol use (Benson, 1992; Cochran, Beeghley, & Bock, 1992). The association between religiosity and nonuse is not strong, however; correlations in research studies are usually between .10 and .30. Similar correlations are found between religiosity and nonuse of marijuana and tobacco (Benson, 1992).

Religious groups do not speak with one voice, and every denomination has factions on different sides of personal behavior issues. However, the majority of religious voices are conservative on issues of family, sexuality, personal discipline, and personal responsibility. Empirical studies that have examined correlations between religious commitment and political or social attitudes have found a consistent pattern: Religious commitment does not predict political power issues or foreign-policy issues at all; it is weakly correlated with economic issues such as taxes or minimum wages, but it is strongly correlated with family and sexuality issues. The more conservative the religious group theologically, the more conservative it is on these issues. Prototypically, Baptists, Catholics, pentecostals, and fundamentalists have provided bedrock support for conservatives. On the liberal wing, by contrast, one finds smaller groups composed largely of Unitarian-Universalists, Congregationalists (now United Church of Christ), and Quakers pushing civil liberties, empowerment programs, and environmental causes. To be sure, there are minority splinter groups everywhere, for example, Catholics for a Free Choice, a small association that tries to counter the overwhelming Catholic voice against abortion, or homosexual rights groups in the Baptist and Presbyterian churches.

Because the major denominations are divided on political and moral issues, one would expect that denominational officials charged with monitoring political issues and speaking to them are embattled in their denominations. This is the case in every denomination, as the church spokespeople on Capitol Hill are repeatedly condemned by groups in their own denominations who find their viewpoints to be un-Christian.

The issues that have been most laden with religious elements since the 1960s have been those associated with sex and gender. Earlier, racial prejudice and anti-Semitism were prominent in the discussions in Christian churches, as religious people combatted the most virulent and anti-Semitic and anti-Black expressions in our society. But anti-Semitism has receded dramatically in American society, and anti-Black feelings took on new contours after the civil rights era and the Black Power movements. Neither is prominently talked about in church circles today. The coming decade will see a growing debate over immigration, religious tolerance, and Islam.

The moral attitudes of members in different denominations can be portrayed visually. Roof and McKinney (1987) did so using as a criterion a "New Morality Scale," constructed from attitudes on three issues: support for unrestricted legal abortion, the view that a married person having sexual relations with someone other than the marriage partner is not always wrong, and the view that sexual relations between adults of the same sex are not always wrong (Roof & McKinney, 1987, p. 215). The mean scores of 25 denominations are shown in Figure 1; the scale scores were adjusted to have a mean of zero. The boxes in the figure enclosed families of similar denominations; for example, at the top of the figure three liberal Protestant denominations are enclosed in a box whose horizontal dimension shows the overall mean for the three. Note that Catholics are near the mean, Protestants are arrayed on both sides of the mean, Jews are more liberal than most Protestants, and one Protestant group (Unitarian–Universalists) is far more liberal than any other.

A visible trend in all religious bodies has been in increased individualism and autonomy of members to decide things for themselves. This has been occurring slowly over the decades—but more rapidly among Catholics. It is hard for the pope to convince Catholics about the sinfulness of contraception or the necessity of excommunicating dissident priests who disagree with his moral teachings. It is impossible for Protestant church leaders to enforce discipline on either doctrinal or moral teachings; the most they can do is to keep seminaries and clergy in line. Laity have gained their right (theologically legitimate since the Reformation) to make truly

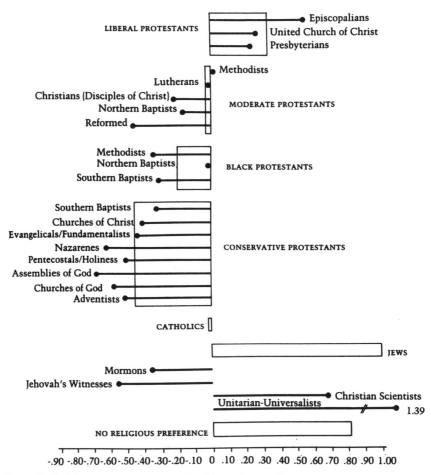

Figure 1. Religious group scores on the New Morality Scale.

moral decisions based on their own experiences and informed conscience. Denominational leaders and offices, more generally, are losing their influence over individual parishioners and special caucuses within the denominations. Like it or not, the laity think for themselves. It is a kind of levelling process, and it has been especially visible since the 1960s. The institutional authority of churches has had to move from the coercive to the persuasive realm (Marty, 1993). As an indication of this, virtually every American denomination, at the highest level, has fallen on fiscal hard times as contributions are reallocated and diverted more and more at the local level.

The Roman Catholic Church is unique in having a large gap between lay opinion and official positions on moral issues. A substantial proportion of laity does not agree with the Church's unchanging positions on the ordination of women, divorce, premarital sex, and birth control. In a 1987 poll of American Catholics, 57% said that "you can be a good Catholic without obeying the Church's teaching on divorce and remarriage," 66% said the same about the Church's teaching on birth control, and 39% on abortion (D'Antonio, Davidson, Hoge, & Wallace, 1989). In a 1990 poll, 40% of American Catholics said that premarital sex is "never wrong." American Catholics are decreasing their level of financial giving to their church. In 1963, Catholics, on the average, contributed 2.2% of their income, but in 1984 the figure was 1.2% (Greeley, 1990).

Today the Jewish community is the most liberal on moral questions relating to sexuality, and the Protestant community is the most conservative. For example, in surveys done from 1982 to 1985 (pooled), a question asked whether premarital sex was always wrong. Among the Jewish respondents, 14% said yes; among the Catholics, 22%; and among the Protestants, 34%. A question asked whether homosexuality is always wrong, and among the Jewish respondents, 45% said yes. Among the Catholics, it was 69%, and among the Protestants, 80%. Respondents approving birth control information being given to teenagers was 99% among Jews, 87% among Catholics, and 86% among Protestants (Greeley, 1989, p. 91).

In 1987, a poll found that evangelical Protestants are more likely than members of other groups to oppose ordaining homosexuals. Only 25% support hiring homosexual clergy, whereas 69% are opposed. The total Protestant community was split, with 47% supporting ordination and 44% opposing. Catholics support ordination of homosexuals by 50% to 44% (Gallup & Castelli, 1989, p. 190). A poll in the same year asked about support for the gay rights movement. Only 3% of the evangelicals supported it, compared with 9% of all other Protestants, 8% of Catholics, 28% of Jews, and 17% of people without a religious preference.

The single issue laden with most religious fervor, pro or con, for the past 20 years has been abortion. America's religious are lined up on both sides of the issue. In the 1980s a new issue arose—homosexuality. It will be contentious throughout the 1990s. Protestant liberals argue that homosexuality is a matter of human rights and dignity before God, whereas conservatives quote the Apostle Paul's letters in the New Testament saying that unrepentant homosexuals are not welcome in the church. In the early 1990s the most common position was that openly active homosexuals are welcome as church members but not as ordained leaders or clergy. Mainline Protestant denominations today are all engaged in study and reflection to decide what their response should be; the laity are too divided to permit denominational bodies to come to peaceful conclusions. Attitudes uncovered by polls on the question are heavily conditioned by theological position—more than denominational membership. Attitudes on the morality of divorce and premarital sex are similarly related to theological position. The Catholic Church has not altered its official ban on church marriages for divorced people although some accommodation is made through liberalized annullment proceedings, which often allow remarriage. Attitudes about alcohol use and marijuana use are religiously freighted, with theological conservatives more opposed.

The most revolutionary social issue for American religion has been the religious role of women. Although women have dominated American Christian churches numerically for hundreds of years, they have been usually excluded from leadership. Most texts were written and interpreted by men, who studied the classics, provided the authoritative views, and held the offices. Women were ordained clergy by most Protestant denominations by the late 1950s, but even in the middle 1990s women clergy do not exist in the Southern Baptist Convention. Roman Catholicism and the Orthodox Churches have consistently excluded women from the priesthood. However, a majority of Catholics would welcome women priests; a 1993 poll of American Catholics found 64% in favor of ordaining women (D'Antonio, Davidson, Hoge, & Wallace, 1996). Of all the students in Protestant seminaries today, about one-third are women, with the percentage inching upward.

Women's issues go beyond ordination to questions of fair participation in denominational offices and boards, inclusive language in church documents, and even rewriting traditional hymns to remove male-oriented language. Mainline denominations have been revising their hymnals, changing lyrics and dropping some irredeemable hymns. For example, "Faith of Our Fathers" has become "Faith of the Ages" for Presbyterians. Translations of the Bible are being scrutinized for sexism, and inclusive-language lectionaries are being published and used.

SUMMARY

Religion in America is as alive as ever, but it is diversifying. Old semiestablished churches are weakening, traditional church authority is weakening, and denominations are losing their influence. Segments of American life, especially higher education and the media, have largely removed themselves from religious influence. The increased level of education, world-consciousness, and individualism in the nation are propelling religious life into new directions. Perhaps most important in the long run is the new wave of immigration.

After the Immigration Reform Act of 1965, immigration surged to very high levels and now promises to alter American society. Immigration is felt more in the West and Southwest than elsewhere and more in urban areas than rural areas. But it will bring unprecedental pluralism and globalization in our religious life. We are living in the second wave of immigration in American history. In a few years Muslims will outnumber Jews in America, and in a few years the new immigrant Catholics will transform American Catholicism. Spanish-speaking Americans will outshadow Blacks as the most prominent minority group.

In traditional church religion, the trend is toward levelling and more consumer option. The authority of the church and its clergy are weaker than ever, and individuals are left to search out spiritual truth, healing, and wholeness from any source available. Church leaders encourage the searching, insofar as it stays within bounds, and gradually churches are becoming more free from dogma, more open to exploration, and less doctrinaire. Church life in some form will remain strong in this new setting because all research shows a strong need among Americans for personal support, family support, religious education for children, and meaningful community life.

Present-day religious trends have relevance for clinical psychologists, though exactly what they are is a matter of guesswork. Let me make three guesses. First, the gradual decline in religious institutional authority will require people to take more responsibility for their own decisions in religious matters. If church teachings are less authoritative than in yesteryear, the individual believer must accept a greater burden in making decisions.

Second, the increased tolerance of religious groups other than one's own will cause a questioning of older stereotypes and social judgments. Yesterday's clear boundaries are vanishing, and we will see more openness to other religious traditions and to new forms of spirituality.

Third, the rapid changes in attitudes on moral questions in the realm of sexuality will trouble many people. Intergenerational tensions are inevitable. Whereas today's grandparents would never have dreamt of cohabitation without marriage, today's middle-age parents are having to face the issue when their children want to do it—and the young adults go ahead without any religious qualms. Changes such as this on moral topics defined by religion will be troublesome within families for years to come.

REFERENCES

Bedell, K. B. (1994). *Yearbook of American and Canadian churches*, Nashville, TN: Abingdon.

Benson, P. L. (1992). Religion and substance use. In J. F. Schumaker (Ed.), *Religion and mental health* (pp. 211–220). New York: Oxford University Press.

Church attendance constant. (1992, March). *Emerging Trends, 14*, 4.

Cochran, J. K., Beeghley, L., & Bock, E. W. (1992). The influence of religious stability and homogamy on the relationship between religiosity and alcohol use among Protestants. *Journal for the Scientific Study of Religion, 31*, 441–456.

Confidence in organized religion down again. (1993, June). *Emerging Trends, 15*, 3.

D'Antonio, W. V., Davidson, J. D., Hoge, D. R., & Wallace, R. A. (1989). *American Catholic laity in a changing church.* Kansas City, MO: Sheed & Ward.

D'Antonio, W. V., Davidson, J. D., Hoge, D. R., & Wallace, R. A. (1996). *Laity American and Catholic: Transforming the church.* Kansas City, MO: Sheed & Ward.

Deck, A. F. (1989). *The second wave: Hispanic ministry and the evangelization of cultures.* New York: Paulist Press.

Early 1993 data show American religiousness may be recovering. (1993, June). *Emerging Trends, 15*, 5.

Finke, R., & Stark, R. (1992). *The churching of America, 1776–1990: Winners and losers in our religious economy.* New Brunswick, NJ: Rutgers University Press.

Gallup, G., & Castelli, J. (1989). *The people's religion: American faith in the 90's.* New York: Macmillan.

Gallup Poll Monthly. (1993). *Report on trends, 331*(4), 36–38.

Greeley, A. W. (1989). *Religious change in America.* Cambridge, MA: Harvard University Press.

Greeley, A. W. (1990). *The Catholic myth: The behavior and beliefs of American Catholics.* New York: Scribners.

Hadaway, C. K. (1993). Church growth in North America: The character of a religious marketplace. In D. A. Roozen & C. K. Hadaway (Eds.), *Church and denominational growth.* (pp. 346–357). Nashville, TN: Abingdon.

Hoge, D. R. (1987). *The future of Catholic leadership: Responses to the priest shortage.* Kansas City, MO: Sheed & Ward.

Hoge, D. R., Johnson, B., & Luidens, D. A. (1994). *Vanishing boundaries: The religion of mainline Protestant baby boomers.* Louisville, KY: Westminster/John Knox.

Kelley, Dean M. (1977). *Why conservative churches are growing* (2nd ed.). New York: Harper & Row.

Majority believe personal faith in Jesus Christ is the only way to assure eternal life. (1991, December). *Emerging Trends, 13*, 2.

Marty, M. E. (1993). Where the energies go. *Annals of the American Academy of Political and Social Science, Issue on Religion in the Nineties, 527*, 11–26.

Melton, J. G. (1993). Another look at new religions. *Annals of the American Academy of Political and Social Science, Issue on Religion in the Nineties, 527*, 97–112.

Neusner J. (Ed.). (1994). *World religions in America: An introduction.* Louisville, KY: Westminster/John Knox.

One in four aware of "New Age." (1991, November). *Emerging Trends, 13*, 2.

Peck, M. S. (1978). *The road less travelled.* New York: Touchstone.

Princeton Religious Research Center. (1990). *Religion in America 1990.* Princeton, NJ: Gallup Organization.

Roof, W. C. (1993). *A generation of seekers: The spiritual journeys of the baby boom generation.* San Francisco: Harper San Francisco.

Roof, W. C., & McKinney, W. (1987). *American mainline religion: Its changing shape and future.* New Brunswick, NJ: Rutgers University Press.

Roozen, D. A., & Hadaway, C. K. (1993). *Church and denominational growth.* Nashville, TN: Abingdon.

Stark, R., & Bainbridge, W. S. (1985). *The future of religion: Secularization, revival, and cult formation.* Berkeley: University of California Press.

Stark, R., & Iannaccone, L. R. (1994). A supply-side reinterpretation of the "secularization" of Europe. *Journal for the Scientific Study of Religion, 33,* 230–252.

Stone, C. L. (1991). Estimate of Muslims living in America. In Y. Y. Haddad (Ed.), *The Muslims in America* (pp. 25–36). New York: Oxford University Press.

Tiryakian, E. A. (1993). American religious exceptionalism: A reconsideration. *The Annals of the American Academy of Political and Social Science, 527,* 40–54.

Tobin, G. A., & Berger, G. (1993). *Synagogue affiliation: Implications for the 1990s* (Research Report) Waltham, MA: Cohen Center Brandeis University.

Wald, K. D. (1987). *Religion and politics in the United States.* New York: St. Martin's Press.

Who considers religion important? (1993, April). *Emerging Trends, 15,* 3.

2

THE PSYCHOLOGY OF RELIGION: AN OVERVIEW

DAVID M. WULFF

No other human preoccupation challenges psychologists as profoundly as religion. Whether or not they profess to be religious themselves—and many do not—psychologists must take religion into account if they are to understand and help their fellow human beings. Factoring in religion, however, is far more easily said than done, for in hardly any other sphere are individuals so cut off from one another. For modern secular psychologists, the great diversity of experiences, conceptions, and practices that constitute "religion" is largely unfamiliar. Moreover, the essential meanings of these phenomena are ultimately derived from their association with a transcendent dimension or realm that, although palpably real to many religious devotees, seems strictly illusory to the secular psychologist. Stripped of the transcendent dimension, religious content can only appear to be deluded superstition and fantasy.

Yet even those psychologists for whom the transcendent is an unquestioned reality may have difficulty penetrating the worlds of other religious people. There is first of all the peculiar resistance of religious experience to expression in discursive language. Inevitably, even the most careful description risks being misunderstood, especially by those who have not had the experience themselves. Furthermore, because religion by definition concerns itself with a shared, ultimate reality, every religious claim implicitly asks for the listener's assent and personal appropriation. Most of us, invested as we are in our own views, respond with spontaneous incredulity, objectifying and thus rejecting the assertion by categorizing it as the other's "religious belief."

Such labeling is not psychologically informative, however, for as social anthropologist Rodney Needham (1972) points out, "believing" designates no distinct and unitary interior state. The many ways in which the word *belief* is used in English, along with the bewildering variety of expressions that serve to translate *believe* into other languages, convinced Needham that belief is not a universal category with a central or essential meaning. It connotes no particular degree of conviction, and although feeling often accompanies belief, it is not part of believing per se. Such feeling as there is will be determined, rather, by the associated circumstances, as in the case of the quite specifiable physical feeling provoked by challenges to a belief. There is likewise no physiognomy of belief, in particular no characteristic tone of voice. Although Needham is content to see the word *believe* continue in its odd-job role in everyday discourse, he urges scholars to cease using the word in their professional writings. What terms they should use instead remains unclear.

In spite of these and still other problems, religion has won the serious attention of some of the 20th century's most influential psychologists, including G. Stanley Hall, William James, Sigmund Freud, Jean Piaget, Erik Erikson, C. G. Jung, B. F. Skinner, Gordon Allport, Erich Fromm, and Abraham Maslow. Other, less widely known psychologists have likewise shown sustained interest in the psychology of religion, some making it their major area of research. Altogether, the literature in this field is far more voluminous than many psychologists would suppose, given its neglect in introductory textbooks and departmental curricula.

That neglect is symptomatic of a century-long struggle for recognition and acceptance. Psychologists, who have long been known for challenging cultural orthodoxies, tend not only to be uninterested in religion but also to harbor genuine antagonism toward it. While thus typically having no desire to study religion themselves, they are often suspicious of the motives and objectivity of those psychologists who do. Scholars in religious studies, on the other hand, worry about the psychologist's proclivity to reduce complex religious phenomena to elemental psychological processes, thereby calling into question both the object of religious faith and the religious community's understanding of the origin and significance of its cherished traditions. When the psychology of religion is taught in departments of religious studies rather than in departments of psychology, as it usually is, the general attitude toward the field is often a pointedly critical one.

Historical factors have also played a major role in the precarious status of the psychology of religion. After a promising inaugural period beginning late in the 19th century, the psychology of religion fell on hard times in the middle of the 1920s. Among the diverse factors responsible for this almost precipitous decline, two major changes stand out. In response to the devastations of World War I and the economic crisis that followed, the religious climate in America shifted dramatically from the liberalism of the social gospel movement to a fundamentalistic, theocentric outlook that rejected as irrelevant all discussion of the human religious consciousness. Interest in subjective religious experience was likewise subverted by the spectacular success of behaviorism and its ideal of an objective and mechanistic science. Although the psychology of religion survived after a fashion, in the forms of pastoral psychology and the psychoanalytic critique of religion, it was not until the decline of behaviorism in the 1950s that basic research in the field was once again systematically undertaken.

The number of active contributors to the field today remains relatively small, yet there is sufficient worldwide interest to support several organizations, including the American Psychological Association's Division 36, Psychology of Religion, which achieved division status in 1975, and such journals as the *Journal of Religion and Health*, founded in 1961, and the *International Journal for the Psychology of Religion*, founded in 1991. The past several decades have also seen the publication of annotated bibliographies (Beit-Hallahmi, 1978; Capps, Rambo, & Ransohoff, 1976; Meissner, 1961; Vande Kemp, 1984), review essays (Gorsuch, 1988; Wulff, 1985), handbooks and collections of essays (Brown, 1973, 1985; Malony, 1977, 1990; Strommen, 1971; Tisdale, 1980), and textbooks of varying comprehensiveness (Argyle & Beit-Hallahmi, 1975; Batson, Schoenrade, & Ventis, 1993; Byrnes, 1984; Crapps, 1986; Meadow & Kahoe, 1984; Paloutzian, 1996; Spilka, Hood, & Gorsuch, 1985; Wulff, 1991).

TWO FUNDAMENTAL TRENDS

From its beginnings, the psychology of religion has been marked by two major trends, one *descriptive* and the other *explanatory*. The descriptive trend, which has most often been advanced by religiously committed scholars, is concerned chiefly with documenting the varieties and types of religious experience, with age or life stage often serving as a significant variable. If the goal of such an undertaking is made explicit, it is usually the fostering of the religious life, especially through religious education and pastoral care. Widely known exemplars of the descriptive approach include Edwin Starbuck, James Pratt, and Allport.

The explanatory trend, which has been promoted primarily by researchers who are suspicious or disdainful of popular piety, seeks to find the origins of religious experience and practice not in a transcendent realm, but in the mundane world of psychological, biological, and environmental events. When the goal is not implicitly the advancement in our knowledge of human experience and behavior, it is explicitly the transforming—if not the elimination—of religion, or at least its most common varieties. The best known representatives of the explanatory trend include James Leuba, Freud, and Skinner. Although James reveals a sustained explanatory interest in *The Varieties of Religious Experience* (1902/1985), this great classic has won its reputation through its contributions to the descriptive literature. Whereas Jung, too, might be thought in some measure to be an explanatory psychologist of religion, he presents himself as a phenomenologist seeking little more than to name and document certain patterns of recurring experience.

With such radically divergent agendas, psychologists of religion are not only attentive to different aspects of religion, but also likely to conceive of religion in starkly contrasting terms. Descriptive psychologists usually identify religion with its experiential core—the inner, subjective states that range from the dramatic ecstasies of the great mystics to the subtle, transcendental moods of the anonymous faithful. Explanatory psychologists, perhaps because they are typically outsiders, usually equate piety with its external expressions, such as creeds and ritual, which they are likely to view as unfounded and irrational.

THE CONCEPT OF RELIGION

In modern Western culture, belief in a divine being or power and regular association with a ritual community are popularly taken to be the primary indicators of a religious person. Social scientists, too, have long used such elements for assessing religiosity, in part because these indicators readily lend themselves to the questionnaire format. Factor analysis of questionnaires sometimes reveals but a single prominent factor, one that emphasizes ideological commitment, or belief, thereby confirming the popular understanding (Wulff, 1991, pp. 210–212).

In the past two or three decades, however, that conception has increasingly been found to be inadequate. As historian of religion Wilfred Smith (1963) points out, our use of the word *religion* is the outcome of a regrettable, centuries-long process of reification. Whereas *religion* seems at first to have designated some greater-than-human power, the feelings in those who have sensed such a power, and the ritual acts they have subsequently carried out, religion now commonly refers to an abstracted, definable, and fixed system of ideas. Smith argues that the noun *religion* and its plural, as well as the names of the various "religions," have largely evolved to serve the needs of outsiders and are thus inherently misleading. In particular, they fail to represent the dynamic personal element in human piety. In their place he proposes that we use the more serviceable terms *cumulative tradition* and *faith*.

Cumulative tradition refers to all of the observable contents—temples, scriptures, myths, moral codes, social institutions, and so on—that are accumulated over time and then passed on to succeeding generations. Faith, an essential and less variable personal quality, encompasses one's orientation toward oneself, other people, and the universe as they are experienced in the light of the transcendent dimension. Not itself directly observable, faith is reflected in the countless forms through which individuals express it outwardly. Belief is only one of these forms, and certainly not the central or universal one it is often assumed to be. Far more important among faith's expressions, Smith says, is individual character.

Sensing themselves that the words *religious* and *religion* fail today to denote certain positive inward qualities and perceptions but, to the contrary, seem increasingly to be associated with prejudicial attitudes, violence, and narrow social agendas, people in various walks of life are choosing to use the terms *spiritual* and *spirituality* instead. Although the adjectives *religious* and *spiritual* have long been used as virtual synonyms, for many today the first suggests nothing more than narrow, dogmatic beliefs and obligatory religious observances, whereas the second calls up the mysterious realm of transcendent experience. The bumper sticker "I'm not religious—I just love the Lord" reflects this growing sentiment, though a spiritual outlook is not necessarily a theistic one.

A few contributors to the psychology of religion, such as Robert Coles in *The Spiritual Life of Children* (1990), have likewise adopted the new rhetoric of spirituality to point beyond the outward and far-from-universal manifestations of belief and ritual. Others, including several of the field's classic contributors, have found a solution in the distinguishing of different types of religion or alternate ways of being religious. Promoted chiefly by descriptive psychologists with a personal investment in religion, these distinctions generally separate authentic, desirable ways of being religious from those that are considered less genuine, less constructive, and hence less desirable.

RELIGION AS A LIABILITY

Among those who begin this overview of the diverse interpretive frameworks in the psychology of religion, there is considerably less interest in drawing such distinctions. Rather, they are largely content to speak of religion as a whole, which to them possesses few if any redeeming qualities. If they do acknowledge that traditional religious belief and practice can yield certain personal or societal advantages, they maintain that science would provide them more consistently and without religion's harmful consequences.

James Leuba: Religion as Irrationality and Pathology

The most dedicated of traditional religion's psychological detractors, as well as one of its best informed and most persuasive, was Leuba, whose numerous publications on the psychology of religion span more than half a century. Leuba challenged traditional theistic religion in several ways. Most directly, he gathered evidence for concluding that mystical experiences may be adequately accounted for in terms of basic principles of psychology and physiology. After demonstrating experimentally, for example, that he could produced the sense of a vague, unseen presence in subjects who were led to expect such an experience, Leuba (1925) argued that the reactions involved are the same essential ones composing our everyday experience of another person's presence. Leuba accounted for more dramatic mystical phenomena in terms of pathological processes, including epilepsy, hysteria, neurasthenia, and narcotic intoxication.

Beyond concluding that the mystic's declarations subsequent to such experience are both naive and illusory, Leuba noted the sheer improbability and pettiness of much religious content and the inhibitory effect that conservative religious views have had on the pursuit of scientific knowledge. In an effort to underscore the unreasonableness of conventional religious beliefs, Leuba gathered questionnaire data showing that eminent scientists and historians are much less likely to believe in God and immortality than their less distinguished colleagues, and that, apart from eminence, the scholars least likely to embrace these beliefs are those most knowledgeable about biological and psychological processes. Among all the scientists who responded to Leuba's questionnaire, the psychologists showed the lowest rate of affirmation (Leuba, 1950).

Although notorious for his thoroughgoing critiques of religion, Leuba was intent on reforming rather than destroying it. As critical of materialistic science as he was of traditional religion, Leuba (1950, p. 136) posited an "intelligent, spiritual urge" toward moral perfection, a tendency he took to be the most fundamental characteristic of human nature. To foster the development of this natural spiritual force, Leuba advocated the founding of religious societies that would use modified forms of ceremony, prayer, confession, and sacred art developed in the light of scientific knowledge and common experience. Although no longer worshiping a social God, members of these societies would reap the essential values—including insight, peace, and moral energy—of the theistic traditions.

B. F. Skinner: Religion as Reinforced Behavior

Whereas Leuba's view of science permitted him to retain some notion of a spiritual impulse, the outlook of the strict behaviorists inclined them to reduce the entirety of religion to mechanistically determined behavior. Exemplary of this trend is Skinner (1953), who maintained that, like all other behaviors, the religious varieties occur because they have been followed by reinforcing stimuli. In many cases, these reinforcements are actively provided by priests and other powerful agents of control. Religious creeds and codes sum up the contingencies of reinforcement that these agents established for their own gain as well as for the benefit of their religious institutions and the larger social order. Religious behaviors not comprehendible in such terms may be understood as the products of adventitious, or accidental, reinforcement. Just as pigeons will come to exhibit nonfunctional but persistent "superstitious" behaviour in response to random reinforcement, so humans will fasten onto odd ritual observances if these behaviors are by chance followed by a reinforcing stimulus.

The exercise of control per se should not offend us, Skinner said, for having rejected the idea of the autonomous individual, he viewed externally based control as inevitable. Yet he is critical of traditional religious forms of it, not only because of the "fictions" used to disguise and maintain them but also because they have historically relied on negative reinforcement or the threat of punishment. Because the techniques of religious control are applied in ways that most reinforce the agent, he said, they tend to be exploitative and highly aversive, sometimes stimulating countercontrol behaviors aimed at undercutting the religious agent's power. It is well, Skinner observed, that religious agencies are today shifting the balance away from aversive measures to more positive ones, for he thought that religion may still be necessary for ordinary people, especially as a means of encouraging them to forgo individual gratification in the present to ensure a better future for all (Wulff, 1991, pp. 123–129).

George Vetter: Religion as Response to Unpredictable Situations

Religion possesses no such redeeming value for Vetter (1958), who dedicated an entire book to the behavioral analysis of religion. More energetically than even Leuba and Skinner, Vetter delineated the various grounds for his negative judgment of religion: the naive conceptions of anthropomorphic deities; the wars and other savageries committed throughout history in the name of religion; the backwardness of religious leaders on social issues; the failure of religious faith to show a consistent empirical relation to moral conduct, either negatively to deceit and criminal behavior or positively to kindness and helpfulness; the correlation of religious institutions in the social and political spheres; and the wealth of resources—including money, time, and human energy—that religious institutions wastefully absorb.

If the only lives improved by religion are those of religious authorities, as Vetter claimed, how are researchers to account for the rise and persistence of religious beliefs and practices among the masses? Recalling Skinner's observations of "superstitious" behavior in randomly reinforced pigeons and N. R. F. Maier's report of stereotypic and nonfunctional behavior when rats were forced to make impossible discriminations, Vetter argued that religious behaviors are the comparable human response to unpredictable and uncontrollable situations.

Two major factors determine what these behaviors will be. First, behaviors that were efficacious in earlier situations will likely recur in ritualized forms under similar circumstances later on. Thus it is, Vetter said, that in situations of need, the gods are frequently addressed as if they were parents. Second, in accord with Guthrie's contiguity theory of learning, behaviors will likely be acquired if they change the associated stimulus complex that triggered them or if they are at least in process when something else changes the situation because in either case they are preserved as the last acts associated with the stimulus complex. Vetter identified two broad classes of religious behavior that meet these criteria: (a) "entreaty" behaviors, such as prayer or meditation, which can be sustained for long periods of time and perhaps even provide sufficient calm to allow simultaneous practical action, and (b) "orgy" behaviors, such as dramatic ceremony, which distract the individual long enough to allow the emotional stress to dissipate on its own.

However effective such behaviors may be in the short run, Vetter strongly objected to them because they are directed, like opiates, to the human sufferers themselves rather than to the external circumstances that are the source of frustration. The problems people face, Vetter argued, can only be solved by systematically applying the problem-oriented methods of science, not the illusory methods of religion. The gradual process of secularization, through which increasing numbers of problems come to be viewed as scientific rather than religious ones, gave Vetter hope that the considerable resources still being spent on religion will in time be reallocated to scientific research, including research on religion itself.

Although behavioral principles, especially those developed by Skinner, retain wide currency among both academic and clinical psychologists, many find their emphasis on individually reinforced response units too molecular and mechanistic to account for such complex behaviors as are found in the religious realm. Social-learning theory, a more cognitive approach that features, global, observational learning, offers a promising alternative, especially in accounting for the transmission of religious tradition from one generation to the next. But apart from a few scholars who have accented the role of imitation in the dynamics of religion (see Wulff, 1991, pp. 134–140), no systematic application of social-learning theory to religious faith and tradition has yet been undertaken.

Sigmund Freud: Religion as Infantile Wish Fulfillment

For many psychologists interested not only in the transmission of religion but also in its origins and dynamics, no theoretical perspective is as fruitful as the psychoanalytic one. Initiated by Freud, the literature on the psychoanalytic interpretation of religion has by today grown to enormous proportions. Over the decades it has also become increasingly diverse, incorporating along the way a variety of contributions based in British object-relations theory, Heinz Kohut's self psychology, and Erikson's ego psychology. Whereas Freud and his immediate followers took an essentially negative view of religion, seeing it as little more than a confluence of infantile or neurotic tendencies, representatives of the revised psychoanalytic perspectives cast religion in a much more favorable light.

For Freud, religion has two outstanding features: fervent belief in a father–god and elaborately detailed obligatory rituals. Noting the seemingly compulsive qualities of these rituals, the aura of inviolability that surrounds religious ideas, and the religious individual's proneness to feelings of guilt and to fear of divine retribution, Freud compared these elements to the obsessive symptoms of neurosis, which he took to be a defense against unacceptable impulses.

Religious beliefs and practices, Freud concluded, have their roots in the universal experiences of childhood. In the early years, the child perceives the parents and especially the father as omniscient and omnipotent; loving, protective care by such powerful figures reassures the terrifyingly helpless child, creating for him or her a virtual paradise. Years later, when the forces of nature and other life circumstances once again arouse deep feelings of vulnerability, the individual's desperate longing for the powerful father finds its fulfillment in the fantasy image of a caring, protective father–god. This longing for the father, which Freud (1913/1953) said "constitutes the root of every form of religion" (p. 148), is marked by ambivalence, however, for as a result of the entanglements of the Oedipus complex, the father is also the object of fear, resentment, and guilt. Obedient submission to God as the projected infantile father finally restores the long-lost relationship.

Religion is thus an illusion, declared Freud (1927/1961), meaning thereby that it is the result of wish fulfillment rather than observation and reason. Furthermore, it is a dangerous illusion, both for the individual and for society. The individual who is introduced to religious dogma at an early age and subsequently discouraged from critically reflecting on it is likely to be dominated by prohibitions of thought and to control impulses through fear-inspired repression. A similar rigidity will result from the aura of sanctity surrounding the laws and institutions of a society that imposes instinctual renunciation through religious sanctions and rewards. Moreover, because its citizens obediently renounce instinctual wishes out of fear rather than reason, a decline in belief in the religious dogmas that serve to justify the cultural prohibitions will throw the society into profound disarray.

Only abandonment of religion and its dogmatic teachings, Freud said, and reliance instead on science and reason will allow individuals and society to grow beyond so infantile a stage. The mature individual will learn to live with the many gaps left by science in our knowledge of reality while facing courageously the helplessness and insignificance that is the lot of us all. Once such maturity is widely attained, Freud said, civilization will cease being oppressive and life will at last become tolerable.

RELIGION AS ASSET

Together, Leuba, Skinner, Vetter, and Freud have fixed on conspicuous aspects of piety that are undeniable still today—the dark, irrational side of religion, which deeply troubles every thoughtful person, religious or not. In work on natural theology, philosopher Alfred North Whitehead (1926) reminds us that

> History, down to the present day, is a melancholy record of the horrors which can attend religion: human sacrifice, and in particular the slaughter of children, cannibalism, sensual orgies, abject superstition, hatred as between races, the maintenance of degrading customs, hysteria, bigotry, can all be laid at its charge. Religion is the last refuge of human savagery. The uncritical association of religion with goodness is directly negatived by plain facts.

Although religion has here and there shown itself capable of being "the main instrument for progress," Whitehead concluded that, on a whole, it has not been so (pp. 37–38).

Psychologists favorably disposed toward religion are no less aware of the sorry history that Whitehead summed up. But chiefly impressed as they are by the more admirable expressions of religion, or at least by its positive potential, they are far less inclined to condemn it sweepingly for the sins of its less reputable devotees. More discriminating in their outlook on religion, they also press for more encompassing definitions of it than Skinner, Vetter, and Freud employed. Some also consider the conceptions of science embraced by these three psychologists to be unnecessarily narrow.

William James: Religion as Way to Human Excellence

James provides a model of a more balanced assessment of religion as well as an implicit critique of the one-sided behavioral approach. At the outset of *The Varieties of Religious Experience* he rejected the very forms of religion that Skinner and Vetter take to be representative: the secondhand "chronic religion of the many," the blindly habitual carrying out of external ritual practices that James (1902/1985, p. 98) said have come to oppose the genuine religious inspiration out of which they have evolved. Only from the uncommon cases of genuine inspiration, however extreme and even "psychopathic" they may appear to be, can one hope to gain insight, he said, into the essential character of religious experience.

Having identified the object of his study, James set about to judge its overall value for human life. Combining common sense with certain philosophic presuppositions and an intuitive "standard of theological probability," James examined with varying degrees of sympathy the lives and thought of a wide range of religious persons. Without a superior intellect, he concluded, those who are temperamentally receptive to religious inspiration will be prone to "holy excesses" and childish conceptions. However, when inspiration and intellect combine in equally large measure, James said, we may expect the attainment of levels of human excellence that are otherwise unobserved. Furthermore, the virtuous saints who heroically achieve these levels will in turn call forth from others unsuspected qualities of goodness and levels of energy that will make the world a better place in which to live. James concluded that religion is "an essential organ of our life, performing a function which no other portion of our nature can so successfully fulfull" (p. 49).

C. G. Jung: Religion as Way to Wholeness

Among those influenced by James was Swiss psychiatrist C. G. Jung (1954/1968), who credits the *Varieties* with giving him insight into "the nature of psychic disturbances within the setting of the human psyche as a whole" (p. 55) Jung may also have derived something of his general understanding of religion from the *Varieties*. Life James, Jung viewed religion as an essential function of the human psyche. From his therapeutic work with hundreds of mostly Protestant patients over a period of 30 years, Jung (1932/1969) concluded that

> Among all my patients in the second half of life—that is to say, over thirty-five—there has not been one whose problem in the last resort was not that of finding a religious outlook on life. It is safe to say that every one of them fell ill because he had lost what the living religions of every age have given to their followers, and none of them has been really healed who did not regain his religious outlook. (p. 334)

By religious outlook, Jung added emphatically, he does not mean subscription to a particular creed or membership in some religious organization.

Jung's distinguishing of original religious experience from the creeds, dogma, and rituals that serve to codify such experience likewise parallels James's approach. But unlike James, Jung ascribed to the derived forms a positive value of their own. They serve, he said, to re-create a limited version of the original experience at the same time that they protect the participants from its potentially overwhelming force. However, such protection is bought at a cost, for creeds set limits on awareness and hence on personal growth. Moreover, religious creeds are vulnerable to the critical probing of reason.

Jung defined religion in accord with its original meaning: It is the experience of what Rudolf Otto called the "numinous," or the Holy. The daunting but fascinating power of the numinous compels one to take it carefully into consideration, on the one hand, while feeling drawn to it in an attitude of devotion and loving abandon, on the other. Because the powers or forces encountered in such experience seem entirely beyond one's comprehension and control, there is a natural tendency to assume that they have invaded one from the outside. According to Jung, however, these forces correspond to dynamic factors that lie within every human psyche, factors that he called *archetypes.*

Acknowledging our profound ignorance about these matters, Jung postulated the existence of a deep, universal layer of the psyche, which he called the *collective unconscious.* The structural elements of his layer are the archetypes, hypothetical entities that, although possessing no specific content or memories, serve nevertheless to reproduce age-old mythic ideas. Corresponding to the typical persons, situations, and processes that have constituted human experience over the millennia, archetypes actively serve to re-create such experiences in the present. The ultimate goal of this complex dynamic is individuation or self-realization, the complex, lifelong process of differentiation and integration that gradually makes the individual whole. When the individuation process lags or fails, as Jung said it has for the great majority of human beings, the outcome is not only individual disorder but social and political upheaval as well.

Historically, according to Jung, individuation has been promoted and guide chiefly by the religious traditions, whose diverse and often puzzling images and rites are thus particularly revealing examples of archetypal expressions. Of special interest are the focal images of these traditions—the gods and saviors as well as certain mythical objects and geometrical shapes—which Jung took to be symbolic expressions of the "self," the most important and least comprehensible of the archetypes. The self, which Jung characterized as the midpoint of the personality, represents the final goal of individuation, the balancing and harmonizing of all the dispositions and qualities of the psyche, both conscious and unconscious. Participation in religious tradition—by engaging in its diverse rituals, telling and retelling its sacred stories, dwelling on its cherished images, and striving to attain its lofty ideals—has served over the centuries to bring about the gradual realization of the self.

Tragically, Jung said, many today have lost the capacity to participate in the images and rites of religion. Thus deprived of adequate symbols for psychic transformation, individuals fall victim to forms of psychoneurosis and psychosis at the same time that whole societies project the neglected archetypes onto other groups and nations, transforming them into dangerous enemies. Yet even persons still engaged by traditional religious images are in a precarious situation today, Jung suggested, for these images remain one-sided and thus preserve a potentially destructive dividedness in the human soul.

To escape widespread discord and destruction and to carry forward the process of individuation, humankind must achieve a new, higher level of consciousness, according to Jung. In taking up this urgent challenge, he argued, psychologists and other students of human nature must consider the full range of human experience, including those experiences we call religious. Although he naturally saw his own psychology as a contribution toward this end, he was anxious that it not become a doctrinal system or creed itself. Unfortunately, it has too often been treated as such, by both proponents and detractors, rather than as a set of observations and tentative proposals offered to the continuing discussion of the nature of the human psyche, as Jung himself represented it.

With the conspicuous exception of academic psychologists, who have by and large ignored Jung's work as both incomprehensible and unscientific, scholars of diverse interests have been stimulated by his extraordinarily wide-ranging synthesis. Among them is a growing number of clinical psychologists and pastoral counselors, some of whom come to Jung by way of the widely popular Myers-Briggs Type Indicator (Myers & McCaulley, 1985), a standardized testing instrument designed to assess individuals in terms of Jung's personality types. In addition to informing clinical practice, Jung's psychology has been embraced as a valuable resource for the critique and renewal of Christianity, the restoration of the feminine to religious tradition, the interpretation of biblical texts, the phenomenological and comparative study of religion, and the fostering of personal spiritual growth (for examples, see Wulff, 1991, pp. 452–456).

Object-Relations Theory: Religion as Therapeutic Relation

For those able to accept Jung's assumption of an inherited collective psyche, no other psychology would seem as serviceable for interpreting historical and textual materials. But Jung's preoccupation with archetypal processes associated with the second half of life and his corresponding neglect of the origins and dynamics of the content of the personal unconscious make his psychology less useful for understanding the content of ordinary, idiosyncratic piety. The advantage for the latter undertaking is possessed by object-relations theory, which expands the psychodynamic approach of Freud in combination with a more positive construction of religion.

Whereas Freud considered religion to be a regressive and illusory effort to satisfy the life and death instincts, the British founders of the object-relations school viewed it as a constructive, if often distorted, system of psychotherapy aimed at bettering personal relationships. Furthermore, in contrast to Freud's exclusive emphasis on the role of the Oedipal father in the dynamics of religion, the object-relations perspective recognizes the influence of both parents, especially the pre-Oedipal mother, if not the influence of other caretakers as well. In so attributing to religious content a more complex derivation, the object-relations framework possesses a double advantage. Just as it is able to take into account a broader range of phenomena in the history of religions, including the remarkable cults of mother–goddesses, so it also proves to be more sensitive to the dynamic composition of God representations in living individuals.

A further advantage derives from Donald Winnicott's (1953) relocating of religion in a transitional realm of experience intermediate between the world of autistic fantasy, where Freud had placed religion, and the world of objective reality, where growing numbers of fundamentalists place it today. Just as a soft blanket or teddy bear helps the young child to move from the hallucinatory omnipotence of infancy toward full acceptance of objective reality, so religion—along with the rest of human culture—eases for all persons this never-completed transition. As Paul Pruyser (1983) noted in his elaborations on Winnicott's provocative suggestion, the repositioning of religion in the intermediate, "illusionistic" realm recognizes its derivation from the mysterious, creative play of human imagining but avoids declaring it sheer illusion. A human construction of reality, just as some scholars now recognize the sciences to be, religion engages in its own way in reality testing.

As Pruyser demonstrated, the three-world schema provides a framework for conceptualizing the distortions to which he says religion is peculiarly prone. Autistic distortions appear when reality testing fails, freeing the religious spirit to fashion fantastic and apocalyptic images with abandon and to promote extravagances of emotionality and obedience. Realistic distortions occur, on the other hand, when illusionistic symbols of transcendence are forced onto the procrustean bed of sensory impressions and literal meanings. Transformed into obligatory dogma and rites, these symbols are stripped of their subtleties and mysteries.

Religion is vulnerable to distortion not only because of its illusionistic character but also because of its natural appeal to neurotic individuals. The latter theme was first enunciated by Ian Suttie (1935/1952), who maintained that, because higher forms of religion are chiefly concerned with improving affective relations with others and thus serve as systems of psychotherapy, they inevitably attract immature and neurotic individuals. Such persons, if not healed in significant measure, end up transforming the tradition into a system of neurotic defensives. Such a dynamic, Suttie argued, is responsible for the deflection of the Christian tradition away from its early emphasis on love and good social relationships toward antipathy, intolerance, and schism.

Viewing religion in like terms but emphasizing individual rather than historical trends, Harry Guntrip (1956) argued that certain predictable distortions in religion will occur when the fundamental need for personal relation to a benign environment is inadequately met from early childhood onward. When the solution is a schizoid denial of the relational need itself, the individual may either reject religion out of hand, because it is about emotional needs and relationships, or reduce it to a passionless philosophy of life. When, however, the deprivation follows an initial satisfactory experience and the reaction is a depressive one instead, the underlying repressed rage and aggression will dispose the individual to feel guilty and sinful and to seek salvation through repentance and conversion. Mature persons, by contrast, will gradually attain the experience of communion, with others and with the Ultimate. This experience, Guntrip said, provides a measure of security and a context for self-realization unavailable anywhere else.

Whereas members of the first generation of object-relations theorists were inclined to make sweeping generalizations about religion as a whole, Boston psychoanalyst Ana Maria Rizzuto (1992, p. 156) carefully delimited the field of psychoanalytic competence to individual religious experience. Influenced in particular by Winnicott, Rizzuto is herself well-known for her clinical studies of the representation of God. These studies and her reflections on them have stimulated the thinking and work of a number of other scholars and clinical practitioners (Finn & Gartner, 1992).

Whether or not one believes in God, Rizzuto (1979) said, one possesses a complex and highly personalized image of God that is derived from early parental experiences, fantasies about the parents, evolving self-representations, and formal or informal religious instruction. Although established early on, this God representation commonly undergoes repeated revision in response to the individual's increasing capacities and the challenges of each successive life crisis. For many individual's, however, it remains essentially unchanged, gradually becoming anachronistic and irrelevant. Yet even in these cases, the God representation lingers in the background, ready when needed to offer "the silent reassurance of an almost imperceptible presence" (p. 203); unlike the blanket or teddy bear, it long retains its potential to function as an illusory transitional object. For the psychology of belief, Rizzuto (1992) remarked, detailing how such complex constructions are transformed in the service of psychic life is the most significant theoretical challenge (p. 158).

Kohut's Self Psychology: Religion as Transformed Narcissism

Two other perspectives akin to the object-relations approach require mention here. One is the self psychology of Kohut, who posits a separate, narcissistic line of libidinous development that, under favorable conditions, promotes the achievement of some of humankind's loftiest goals, including creativity, wisdom, and mystical self-transcendence. Frequently, however, the two early configurations of perfection—the grandiose self and the idealized parental imago—that the infant establishes as consolation for the loss of primary narcissism fail to undergo normal transformation and integration, yielding a variety of psychological disorders.

In the few instances that Kohut's psychology has been applied to religion, it is the symbolic representation of these perfectionistic configurations in the form of divine images that has been featured. New Delhi psychoanalyst Sudhir Kakar (1981), for example, argued that the ithyphallic and androgynous images of the popular Hindu god Shiva serve to reactivate the grandiose self for Hindu men, who are said to be predisposed to a "heightened narcissistic vulnerability" (p. 128) by the peculiar circumstances of traditional Indian childrearing. The infantile grandiose self is similarly discerned in the Christian tradition by Robert Randall (1984), who sees its traces in the claims of certain sects and denominations that they know God's intentions and that they alone possess the way to salvation.

Erik Erikson: Religion as Hope and Wisdom

The other perspective with kinship to object-relations theory is the ego psychology of Erikson. Famous for delineating eight epigenetic stages of psychosocial development, Erikson is also well known for his reflections on religion. Like the British object-relations theorists, Erikson (1950/1963) found religion's deepest roots in the maternal matrix of infancy. And for him, too, this link to the infantile past testifies not to the immaturity of religion, as Freud would have it, but to religion's vital ministrations to the most fundamental needs, fears, and longings of humankind. According to Erikson, religion universalizes trust, the ego quality that comes with the successful resolution of the first, infantile stage of development, just as it provides institutional confirmation for hope, the essential strength or virtue that emerges from this age. While creating a common faith in the trustworthiness of the universe, religion also universalizes mistrust through a shared conception of evil.

Religious tradition likewise offers societal support for the attainment of wisdom, the vital virtue that under favorable circumstances becomes manifest in old age, the final stage of development. The ego quality that issues out of this stage is integrity, a sense of coherence and wholeness that is achieved with the successful synthesis of the seven other ego qualities—hope, will, purpose, competence, fidelity, love, and care—in their most mature forms. Marked by a sense of cosmic order and spiritual meaning, the life of integrity entails acceptance of one's life as it has unfolded and the courageous facing of death.

Among the resources fostering the growth of the ego throughout the eight stages is ritualization, an everyday mode of interpersonal exchange that finds its fullest expression in the religious traditions. Carried out at regular intervals with attentiveness to ceremonial detail, a sense of higher meaning, and a feeling of absolute necessity, ritualization serves, Erikson (1966), said, to modulate impulsivity and excessive control while making familiar and preserving a particular understanding of human existence. Beginning with the numinous element, which finds its ontogenetic source in the daily greeting ceremonial between mother and infant and is most conspicuous later on in religious ritual, each stage develops and integrates some element that, in combination with the others, composes the true forms of adult ritual.

Like the ego qualities and vital virtues, each of the ritual elements possesses a potential antipodal outcome or pathological equivalent. The numinous element is subject to the perversion of idolism, an adulatory attitude aimed at an illusory, narcissistic image of perfection, just as the judicious element may be displaced by self-righteous or moralistic legalism, the dramatic by inauthentic impersonation, the formal by an empty and perfectionistic formalism, the ideological by a fanatic totalism, the affiliative by a narcissistic elitism, the generational by a spurious authorism, and the integral by a coercive dogmatism. In spite of the vulnerability of religion to these and other pathological distortions and its long history of exploiting human weakness, Erikson, too, concluded that it is vital for the attainment of human maturity.

HUMANISTIC PSYCHOLOGY: RELIGION AS BIPOLAR POTENTIAL

In concert with other depth psychologists, Erikson accented religion's grounding in affective and early developmental processes and in that light delineated the various ways in which religion can go awry. In distinct contrast, humanistic psychologists such as Allport, Fromm, and Maslow have featured instead the cognitive side of religion as well as the form and place religion takes in the lives of exceptionally mature or self-actualized persons. Their views will round out this survey of the leading interpretative perspectives in the contemporary psychology of religion.

The humanistic strand in the psychology of religion can be traced to the very beginning of the 20th century, where it is evident, for example, in the work of Leuba. By denying a transcendent realm of supernatural beings while affirming a human urge toward perfection, Leuba identifies himself as a humanist principally in the philosophic sense. Other humanistic psychologists are more open to the theistic hypothesis, if they do not even embrace it in one or another of its forms. Humanistic psychologists are unanimous, however, in their conviction that human beings are born with a range of positive potentialities, the progressive realization of which is among their basic human needs. These psychologists concur, moreover, on the importance and uniqueness of the individual and thus also on the necessity of methods and interpretive frameworks that lend themselves to the study of individuality. Common, too, is the positing of a core of spiritual needs and values, which is often thought to be inadequately developed by conventional religious practices.

Gordon Allport and the Assessment of Religious Orientation

The most influential of the humanists in the psychology of religion is Allport, the renowned personality and social psychologist whose slender book on religion (Allport, 1950) and scales for measuring intrinsic and extrinsic religious orientations continue to shape much thinking and empirical research today. At the heart of Allport's contribution is his depiction of the mature religious sentiment, which in his analysis possesses six distinct traits:

1. It is well differentiated, encompassing and ordering an increasingly complex array of objects, interests, and issues;
2. It is dynamic though derivative, having become an autonomous force in its own right, independent of its origins in organic desires and childhood needs;
3. It is consistently directive, steadfastly sustaining a system of high ethical standards;
4. It is comprehensive, seeking to encompass the totality of human existence within a single, unified framework;
5. It is integral, ever striving to form its diverse elements into a harmonious whole;
6. It possesses a heuristic quality, for in spite of lingering uncertainty and doubt, it embraces religious faith as a working hypothesis that infuses life with energy and conserves fundamental values.

As a religiously committed psychologist who directed much of his own energy into such consequential matters as the effects of mass media, the dynamics of wartime rumor, and the nature of human prejudice, Allport was distressed by the evidence of a consistent, positive association between religiousness and a variety of prejudicial attitudes. Convinced that mature or genuinely religious persons actively oppose such attitudes, Allport and his students set about to develop a measure of religious orientation that would allow them to distinguish mature, intrinsically oriented religious individuals from those who orientation is extrinsic. With such a measure, then, they could test the hypothesis that it is the extrinsically oriented who possess authoritarian, ethnocentric, and other such negative attitudes, whereas the intrinsically oriented actively reject them.

The resulting Allport–Ross Religious Orientation scales—the two orientations provided unexpectedly not to lie on a single dimension—have become sufficiently popular among contemporary empirical researchers to have transformed Allport's distinction into a virtual paradigm. The still-growing literature of intrinsic–extrinsic research does reveal trends of the sort that Allport anticipated. However, the extrinsic scale has been more consistent in this regard than the intrinsic one, which in a few studies has itself proved to be positively correlated with measures of authoritarianism, dogmatism, and prejudice against Blacks and gay men and lesbians. More-over, the conceptual and psychometric problems presented by the I-E scales are serious enough to have led several researchers over the past two decades to urge their colleagues to abandon the distinctions and measures alto-gether (see Wulff, 1991, pp. 228–235).

A different, more constructive challenge to the still-popular I-E scales has been thrown down by Daniel Batson and his collaborators. According to the I-E scale items assembled by Allport, an intrinsically religious person regularly attends church services, reads the Bible and devotional literature, engages in private prayer and meditation, and lives out his or her religious beliefs in everyday life. Noting the omission of three features that Allport had earlier attributed to the mature religious sentiment, or at least to stages of its development—complexity, doubt, and tentativeness—Batson and his associates (1993) have developed a measure of a third religious orientation, quest, which Batson identified as a more mature and flexible religious out-look than the other two.

For Batson, religion is the response an individual gives to existential questions—that is, questions issuing out of one's awareness of the vicissi-tudes of life and death. Of the 12 questions on the current version of the Quest scale, 8 center on the raising of questions or the acknowledgment of doubt and the rest anticipate or report change in religious outlook. On the basis of a multitude of studies using the I-E and Quest scales, Batson and his colleagues (1993) concluded that, of the three orientations, only quest (a) is positively associated with greater open-mindedness, flexibility, and self-acceptance; (b) shows a consistently negative relation to prejudice, even when prejudice is measured covertly or is not proscribed by the in-dividual's religious community; and (c) is positively associated with a style of helpfulness that is responsive to the expressed wishes of the person in need.

Like the I-E scales, the Quest scale has been criticized on both con-ceptual and psychometric grounds. Although some of these criticisms have been addressed by Batson and his associates (1993), fundamental problems remain with all three scales. Each contains items that are either ambiguous in meaning or presuppose certain experiences or forms of religious commitment. Moreover, virtually none of the items gives expression to the basic metaphors used in conceptualizing these three orientations. And even the metaphors themselves are problematic: The I-E metaphors are not only incongruously mixed but also incompatible with those of quest (Wulff, 1992). Metaphors, scholars increasingly emphasize, are not merely rhetorical devices for dressing up prose; rather, they shape our very thinking and give direction to the ways we act. They are also remarkably prevalent in psychology (Leary, 1990).

The absence of the quest metaphor from the Quest scale items, their exclusive focus instead on uncertainty and change, and the finding of evidence that Quest scale scores tend to decline with age (Acklin, 1985) together raise doubts about the scale's validity as a measure of a mature, questing religious faith. Yet Batson's reintroduction of the religiously liberal notion of quest, which some earlier psychologists of religion took to be the only viable option for thinking individuals, constitutes in itself an important contribution to the contemporary literature. Although it is doubtful that it brings empiricists any closer to operationalizing Allport's understanding of the mature religious sentiment—for doubt and questioning are at most residual elements of this sentiment, not the central or important part that the Quest scale makes them into—Batson's contribution to the search for alternatives to the intrinsic and extrinsic orientations does serve the larger goal implicit in Allport's work: an appreciation for the diverse ways in which individuals are religious in today's world.

Erich Fromm

Much in the spirit of Allport's I-E distinction, other humanistic psychologists have put forward basic typologies contrasting mature, constructive, or genuine forms of religion with immature, destructive, and spurious ones. Among them is Fromm (1950), whose writings combine the lasting influences of the Talmudic tradition in which he grew up with the views of Karl Marx, Freud, and 20th-century social psychology and existential phenomenology. As living organisms separated from nature by the evolutionary appearance of self-awareness, reason, and imagination, Fromm wrote, human beings are haunted by an anxious sense of homelessness and isolation as well as by the realization that their strivings will eventually be defeated by death. To avert the madness that these realizations can bring, Fromm said, every individual requires some frame of orientation and an object of devotion. "Any system of thought and action shared by a group" (p. 26) that provides these vital resources is considered by Fromm to be a religion.

Religious traditions or teachings, according to Fromm, tend to fall into two fundamental types, according to whether they foster the development of human potentialities or stifle them. Authoritarian religion entails obedient submission to a power that transcends and dominates humankind. Its self-deprecating mood is marked by sorrow and guilt. Humanistic religion, in contrast, is centered in humankind and its strengths. The mood here is a joyful one, and virtue lies in self-realization, not obedience. Whereas persons of an authoritarian outlook diminish themselves by attributing to God their own most valuable qualities—love, wisdom, and justice—theists of a humanistic bent take God to be a symbol of the higher self, of the powers that may or ought to be realized in their own lives. John Calvin's theology, centering on a demanding and wrathful God, illustrates the authoritarian outlook, whereas the teachings of the Hebrew prophet Isaiah and of Jesus express the humanistic spirit.

According to Fromm, the humanistic character of the early Christian church was soon overwhelmed by the authoritarian spirit of the Roman Empire and the establishment of ecclesiastical authority. The conquering and exploitative pagan hero, rather than the self-sacrificing Christian martyr, became—and remains in our time—the prevailing model, which now threatens humankind with utter destruction. Whereas many today in effect worship the machine and have become impotent and profoundly alienated slaves of technique, Fromm holds out hope for the widespread development of a new, loving character structure embodying the being mode of self-transcendence and growth rather than the having mode of violence and egocentric possession. With it will come, he said, a radically new religiosity of the humanistic type, one fostering the optimal development of such human capacities as reason, compassion, and love, and with them, a more mature sense of relatedness to nature and other human beings.

Abraham Maslow

Deeply influenced by Fromm's reflections on religion, Maslow (1964) was likewise interested in religion's potential association with human excellence. He approached the topic, however, by assembling a group of persons who had attained an exceptional degree of self-actualization and then exploring the characteristics they had in common, including their outlook on religion. Among the 60 prominent historical figures and anonymous contemporaries who seemed to him to be relatively self-actualized, Maslow found conventional piety to be virtually absent. These exceptional individuals were nevertheless not irreligious, for he found that it was "fairly common" for them to report having had mystical experiences—or what Maslow called peak experiences—to dissociate them from traditional religious contexts and interpretations.

Occurring spontaneously in a variety of settings, these peak experiences were marked by profound feelings of integration and wholeness, of self-forgetting fusion with the world, of fully existing in a timeless and deeply satisfying present. Filled with wonder and awe and feeling more fully alive, self-activated, and creative, the subjects of these experiences also reported receiving new insights. The receptive and purposeless "cognition of being" associated with peak experiences opened them to a realm of absolute values, including truth, justice, simplicity, beauty, playfulness, and wholeness. When, in time, peak experiences gave way to the less intense, more voluntary, but equally valuable high-plateau experience, these insights persisted as a continuing sense of illumination.

Underscoring the capacity of peak experiences to revolutionize lives, Maslow charged the religious traditions with having failed to promote such experiences and the values they reveal. In the history of religion, Maslow argued, the private illuminations of acutely sensitive prophets are eventually lost in the process of communicating them to other individuals. The "intrinsic core" of religion—the mystical experience and its revelations—becomes displaced by the verbal formulas, rituals, and organizations that initially served to symbolize and preserve the original insight but that are soon mistakenly taken as objects to be revered in themselves. Like Jung, Maslow thought that the paraphernalia of the religious traditions often serve as a defense against original experience or at least tend to suppress it. They are also divisive, Maslow noted, but the ultimate and deepest split is between the "peakers" and "nonpeakers," those who have and make personal use of core religious experiences and those to whom such experiences remain foreign.

In the spirit of Fromm, Maslow looked to the day when the new humanistic psychology will rescue peak experiences and the ultimate values they reveal from the dead hand of uncomprehending religious tradition, making them widely available in the form of a naturalistic faith. Whether or not such a faith is expressed in traditional form, whether it be theistic or atheistic, he said, it will rely increasingly on empirical facts and become the far goal of all education, if not of every other social institution as well.

On Finding a Viable Point of View

Like all of the other psychologists whose views have been surveyed in this chapter, Maslow silently grounded his analysis of religion first and foremost in his own experience. The only child of Jewish Russian immigrants, Maslow grew up a militant atheist who was contemptuous of his mother's "superstitious" piety. Traditional religious expressions—attending services, praying, reading sacred scriptures—seemed to him an utter waste of time. He was nevertheless capable of being deeply moved—by nature, music, art, and even scientific texts. It is understandable, therefore, that he paints the particular portrait of religion that he does and that he projects for humankind a naturalistic faith much like his own.

Acknowledgment of the role of the "personal equation" in Maslow's and every other psychologist's thinking is not an invitation to reject their theories as mere subjectivity. It would be odd, first of all, if there were a disjunction between what they have personally experienced of religion and what they then make of it in their professional research and writings. Moreover, as Michael Polanyi (1958) argued, the inevitable personal element in scientific knowledge transcends the subjective in so far as it knowingly submits to standards independent of itself (p. 300).

Maslow enthusiastically affirmed the value of such independent testing. Yet feeling a sense of urgency that derived both from the subject matter and from his own impatience, Maslow (1964) confessed to publishing views that more cautious scientists would consider premature, given the relative paucity of supporting data that he had to offer. He hoped that other, more patient researchers would in time subject his ideas to systematic empirical evaluation, separating out those that meet the standards of disinterested scientific testing.

A growing body of research has in fact been inspired by Maslow's writings. Wuthnow (1978) found, for example, that persons who report having peak experiences in a deep and lasting way were more likely than others to say that their lives were very meaningful, that they frequently thought about the purpose of life, that they spent time meditating about their own lives, and that they possessed certain desirable qualities suggesting self-assurance. Together, these findings appear to support Maslow's claim that peak experiences happen more often to self-actualizing persons than to others and that such experiences yield a sense of meaning and purpose.

There is also a modest literature apparently supporting Maslow's claim that self-actualization is hindered by traditional, especially conservative, religious belief and practice, whereas it is promoted by less orthodox practices, such as meditation. In all of these studies, however, self-actualization is assessed by means of the Personal Orientation Inventory, which various sources of evidence suggest would be better conceived as a measure of extraversion, nonconformity, and centeredness in the here and now. Thus it is debatable whether the findings of these studies really apply to Maslow's theories at all (Wulff, 1991, pp. 608–612).

These empirical findings do not in themselves make a strong case for Maslow's perspective on religion. Yet the situation here is not substantially different from what would be found for other perspectives. In these cases, too, the evidence is sufficiently partial and inconclusive to leave the doubtful reader unconvinced. In truth, however, we rarely accept or reject theoretical propositions on the basis of formal empirical evidence. Rather, like the theorists themselves, we look for a fundamental correspondence with our own experience. As Greenberg and Mitchell (1983) remark in their penetrating study of object-relations theories, "Theory stands or falls on how compelling it appears to be, on its underlying vision of human life. Does the theory speak to you? Does it seem to account for your deepest needs, longings, fears?" (p. 407).

The theories that we find most compelling in the psychology of religion will likely be the ones that best account for religion as we experience or understand it. Crucial for psychologists of religion, then, and for clinical practitioners who aspire to a genuine understanding of their clients' religious faith will be the broadest and deepest acquaintance possible with the complex world of religious faith and tradition. Such an acquaintance will make obvious that religion is many things—superstitious habit as well as time-tested procedure, system of control as well as avenue to freedom, neurotic defense as well as impetus to growth, egocentric delusion as well as empathic concern, inchoate intimation as well as articulate world-view. In the face of such diversity, we should be suspicious of any simple formula or typology that aspires to sum it up.

Practitioners should also be wary of the narrowing influences of their own religious views. It may be, as some scholars argue, that those who are not themselves religious, or at least not religious in the usual sense, are destined to remain uncomprehending outsiders, however sympathetic they may be. Yet religious commitment can itself erect barriers to understanding. One may be inclined to construe the other as religiously mistaken, for example, or to assimilate the other's faith to one's own categories or experience. When therapist and client share the same tradition and perhaps even use it as a framework for therapy, such problems as these are largely averted. At the same time, however, the therapist may be blind to dysfunctional aspects of the shared tradition—for example, denigrative views of women or unreasonable ideals of perfection. Sharing a common religious tradition may also foreclose a disinterested evaluation of the origins and dynamics of the client's religious faith.

According to philosopher and psychiatrist Karl Jaspers (1946/1963), the ideal psychotherapist combines, among other qualities, a "profound existential faith" with "scientific attitudes of the sceptic" (p. 808). While possessing a deep sense of a transcendent dimension in all of human experience, such a therapist might well view the particulars of the religious traditions as human constructs that give form to the many faces of the transcendent and provide a mode of human response. From such a perspective, no "religion" is right—and none is sweepingly wrong. When error enters in, it is chiefly in the form of overlooking the human origin of the religious traditions and ascribing too narrow and final a meaning to their contents.

Some version of this perspective has informed the psychology of religion from its very beginnings, and it is arguably a standpoint of great heuristic value for psychotherapy as well. There are nevertheless some who strenuously object to it, either because it assumes a transcendent dimension and takes religious content seriously, on the one hand, or because it rejects the motion of a final, revealed truth and thus relativizes every religious claim, on the other. Critics of the relativistic perspective are right, of course, in saying that it imports into psychology an epistemological outlook that cannot be derived from psychology itself. Yet, as James would argue, some such presuppositions are both inevitable and necessary if psychology is to go about its business. For many in today's pluralistic world, a relativistic perspective on religion offers the most reasonable and comprehensive approach.

The same holds true for an understanding of psychology's pluralism. In this case, too, proponents of a particular theory or method are tempted to view it as absolute—that is, as a privileged means of uncovering universal truths. The recent emergence of the constructivist point of view in psychology (e.g., Danziger, 1990) is now helping psychologists to see more clearly how dependent their knowledge is on historical and contextual factors and thus how limited it is in its generality. Presumably psychologists of religion, too, will undertake to assess the degree to which their concepts and findings are products of social construction. Until they do, clinical practitioners would do well to relativize the field for themselves, by becoming as broadly acquainted as possible with its various perspectives and using each to qualify or contextualize the others. This collection of chapters should serve well toward the achievement of this important goal.

REFERENCES

Acklin, M. W. (1985), An ego developmental study of religious cognition. *Dissertation Abstracts International, 45,* 3926B. (University Microfilms No. 85–03,799)

Allport, G. W. (1950). *The individual and his religion: A psychological interpretation.* New York: Macmillan.

Argyle, M., & Beit-Hallahmi, B. (1975). *The social psychology of religion.* London: Routledge & Kegan Paul.

Batson, C. D., Schoenrade, P., & Ventis, W. L. (1993). *Religion and the individual: A social-psychological perspective.* New York: Oxford University press.

Beit-Hallahmi, B. (1978). *Psychoanalysis and religion: A bibliography.* Norwood, PA: Norwood Editions.

Brown, L. B. (Ed.). (1973). *Psychology and religion; Selected readings.* Baltimore: Penguin.

Brown, L. B. (1985). *Advances in the psychology of religion.* Elmsford, NY: Pergamon Press.

Byrnes, J. F. (1984). *The Psychology of religion.* New York: Free Press.

Capps, D., Rambo, L., & Ransohoff, P. (1976). *Psychology of religion: A guide to informational sources*. Detroit: Gale Research.

Coles, R. (1990). *The spiritual life of children*. Boston: Houghton Mifflin.

Crapps, R. W. (1986). *An introduction to psychology of religion*. Macon, GA: Mercer University Press.

Danziger, K. (1990). *Constructing the subject: Historical origins of psychological research*. Cambridge, England: Cambridge University Press.

Erikson, E. H. (1963). *Childhood and society* (2nd ed.). New York: W. W. Norton. (Original work published 1950)

Erikson, E. H. (1966). Ontogeny of ritualization in man. In J. Huxley (Organizer), A discussion of ritualization of behaviour in animals and man. *Philosophical Transactions of the Royal Society of London: Series B, Biological Sciences, 251* (772), 337–349.

Finn, M., & Gartner, J. (Eds.). (1992). *Object relations theory and religion*. New York: Praeger.

Freud, S. (1953). Totem and taboo: Some points of agreement between the mental lives of savages and neurotics. In J. Strachey (Ed. and Trans.), *The standard edition of the complete psychological works of Sigmund Freud* (Vol. 13, pp. 1–161). London: Hogarth Press and the Institute of Psycho-Analysis. (Original work published 1913)

Freud, S. (1961). The future of an illusion. In J. Strachey (Ed. and Trans.), *The standard edition of the complete psychological works of Sigmund Freud* (Vol. 21, pp. 1–56). London: Hogarth Press and the Institute of Psycho-Analysis. (Original work published 1927)

Fromm, E. (1950). *Psychoanalysis and religion*. New Haven: Yale University Press.

Gorsuch, R. (1988). Psychology of religion. *Annual Review of Psychology, 39,* 201–221.

Greenberg, J. R., & Mitchell, S. A. (1983). *Object relations in psychoanalytic theory*. Cambridge, MA: Harvard University Press.

Guntrip, H. (1956). *Mental pain and the cure of souls*. London: Independent Press.

James, W. (1985). *The varieties of religious experience; A study in human nature*. Cambridge, MA: Harvard University Press. (Original work published 1902)

Jaspers, K. (1963). *General Psychopathology* (J. Hoenig & M. W. Hamilton, Trans.). Chicago: University of Chicago Press. (Revised 4th German edition published 1946)

Jung, C. G. (1968). Concerning the archetypes, with special reference to the anima concept. In H. Read, M. Fordham, & G. Adler (Eds.), *The collected works of C. G. Jung* (Vol. 9, Part I, 2nd ed., pp. 54–72). Princeton, NJ: Princeton University Press. (Original work published 1954)

Jung, C. G. (1969). Psychotherapists or the clergy. In H. Read, M. Fordham, & G. Adler (Eds.), *The collected works of C. G. Jung* (Vol. 11, 2nd ed., pp. 327–347). Princeton, NJ: Princeton University Press. (Original work published 1932)

Kakar, S. (1981). *The Inner world; A psycho-analytic study of childhood and society in India* (2nd ed.). Oxford, England: Oxford University Press.

Leary, D. E. (Ed.). (1990). *Metaphors in the history of psychology.* Cambridge, England: Cambridge University Press.

Leuba, J. H. (1925). *The psychology of religious mysticism.* New York: Harcourt, Brace.

Leuba, J. H. (1950). *The reformation of the churches.* Boston: Beacon Press.

Malony, H. N. (Ed.). (1977). *Current perspectives in the psychology of religion.* Grand Rapids, MI: William B. Eerdmans.

Malony, H. N. (Ed.) (1990). *Psychology of religion: Personalities, problems, possibilities.* Grand Rapids, MI: Baker.

Maslow, A. H. (1964). *Religions, values, and peak-experiences.* Columbus: Ohio State University Press.

Meadow, M. J., & Kahoe, R. D. (1984). *Psychology of religion: Religion in individual lives.* New York: Harper & Row.

Meissner, W. W. (1961). *Annotated bibliography in religion and psychology.* New York: Academy of Religion and Mental Health.

Meyers, I. B., & McCaulley, M. H. (1985). *Manual: A guide to the development and use of the Myers-Briggs type indicator.* Palo Alto, CA: Consulting Psychologists Press.

Needham, R. (1972). *Belief, language, and experience.* Chicago: University of Chicago Press.

Paloutzian, R. F. (1996). *Invitation to the psychology of religion* (2nd ed.). Boston: Allyn & Bacon.

Polanyi, M. (1958). *Personal knowledge: Towards a post-critical philosophy.* Chicago: University of Chicago Press.

Pruyser, P. W. (1983). *The play of the imagination; Toward a psychoanalysis of culture.* Madison, CT: International Universities Press.

Randall, R. L. (1984). The legacy of Kohut for religion and psychology. *Journal of Religion and Health, 23,* 106–114.

Rizzuto, A.-M. (1979). *The birth of the living god: A psychoanalytic study.* Chicago: University of Chicago Press.

Rizzuto, A.-M. (1992). Afterword. In M. Finn & J. Gartner (Eds.), *Object relations theory and religion* (pp. 155–175). New York: Praeger.

Skinner, B. F. (1953). *Science and human behavior.* New York: Macmillan.

Smith, W. C. (1963). *The meaning and end of religion; A new approach to the religious traditions of mankind.* New York: Macmillan.

Spilka, B., Hood, R. W., Jr., & Gorsuch, R. L. (1985). *The Psychology of religion: An empirical approach.* Englewood Cliffs, NJ: Prentice Hall.

Strommen, M. P. (Ed.). (1971). *Research on religious development: A comprehensive handbook.* New York: Hawthorn.

Suttie, I. D. (1952). *The origins of love and hate*. New York: Julian Press (Original work published 1935)

Tisdale, J. R. (Ed.). (1980). *Growing edges in the psychology of religion*. Chicago: Nelson-Hall.

Vande Kemp, H. (1984). *Psychology and theology in Western thought, 1672–1965; A historical and annotated bibliography*. Millwood, NY: Kraus.

Vetter, G. B. (1958). *Magic and religion: Their psychological nature, origin, and function*. New York: Philosophical Library.

Whitehead, A. N. (1926). *Religion in the making*. New York: Macmillan.

Winnicott, D. W. (1953). Transitional objects and transitional phenomena. *International Journal of Psycho-Analysis, 34*, 89–97.

Wulff, D. M. (1985). Psychological approaches. In F. Whaling (Ed.), *Contemporary approaches to the study of religion*, Vol. 2. *The social sciences* (pp. 21–88). Berlin, Germany: Mouton.

Wulff, D. M. (1991). *Psychology of religion: Classic and contemporary views*. New York: Wiley.

Wulff, D. M. (1992). Reality, illusion, or metaphor? Reflections on the conduct and object of the psychology of religion. *Journal of the Psychology of Religion, 1*, 25–51.

Wuthnow, R. (1978). Peak experiences: Some empirical tests. *Journal of Humanistic Psychology, 18*, 59–75.

3

HISTORICAL PERSPECTIVE: RELIGION AND CLINICAL PSYCHOLOGY IN AMERICA

HENDRIKA VANDE KEMP

To explicate the history of *integration*, I will first provide a context for this discussion by presenting definitions of the word *integration* as it contrasts with several illuminating antonyms. Embedded in these definitions are historical facets of the relationship between psychology and the disciplines with which psychologists seek to integrate it. This constitutes a historical model for integration that supplements contemporary models (see Tan, Chapter 13, this volume).[1]

A DIALECTIC WITH DIFFERENTIATION

Organismic psychologists such as Werner (1926/1940) and Allport (1937) characterize integration as a dialectic with differentiation in the

I am grateful to the following persons who facilitated my search for accurate historical and bibliographic details: Ron Braund, Lucy Bregman, Don Browning, Reuven P. Bulka, Gary R. Collins, Dianne C. Grove, David Brian Hickel, Beth Houskamp, Haddon Klingberg, Jr., Steve Levicoff, Kurt Luedke, Leo Marmol, Bruce Narramore, Dan Palomino, Paul Riley, Susan Roberts, Rich Rosengarden, Siang-Yang Tan, and John Tisdale.

[1] The emphasis here will be on American clinical psychology. However, relevant European developments will be included when they impinge closely on American traditions. Portions of this chapter were first presented in my inaugural lecture as professor of psychology, *The Integration of Psychology and Theology: Its Birth and Meaning*, at Fuller Theological Seminary, Pasadena, CA, March 3, 1992, and as part of the symposium, *State of the Art for Psychologists Interested in Religious Issues*, at the 98th Annual Convention of the American Psychological Association, Boston, MA, August 12, 1990.

formation of mental structures. In calculus, integration is the synthetic phase that complements the analytic phase of differentiation in the quest to define as precisely as possible the area under a curve: Accuracy results from increasingly precise differentiation of measurable rectangles, followed by equally meticulous reintegration. From this angle, the process of integration can be thesis or antithesis, but not synthesis: Differentiation of disciplines and modes of inquiry is necessary to the growth of knowledge, but it is a mere phase in the quest for understanding.

Western psychology differentiated out of several disciplines. When the Latin term *psychologia* was first used by Maruic around 1524, it "referred to one of the subdivisions of pneumatology, the science of spiritual beings and substances. Each of the three levels of spiritual beings had its corresponding science, resulting in the subdivisions of natural theology [concerning God], angelology/demonology [concerning the intermediate spirits], and psychology [concerning the human spirit]" (Vande Kemp, 1982a, p. 108). Later in the 16th century, Cassmann coined the term *anthropologia* for the science of persons, which was divided into "psychologia, the doctrine of the human mind; and somatologia, the doctrine of the human body" (p. 109). Von Wolff, in the 18th century, added the distinction between rational and empirical psychology, leading to a theoretical psychometrics (Ramul, 1960) that prepared the way for scientific psychology.

Psychologists trained in the dominant historical tradition of the 20th century may be startled to learn that psychology and religion have historically been this inextricably intertwined. The surprise is perhaps inevitable, as Boring's (1929) monumental history comprises not an objective rendition of psychology's actual roots but a complex of origin myths concocted to bolster the view that psychology was a science unfettered by the bonds of philosophy and theology (see Kelly, 1981; Koch & Leary, 1985; O'Donnell, 1979; Woodward & Ash, 1982).[2] The connection is also inevitable because it is virtually impossible to make a clear distinction between *pneuma* (the spirit, or religious aspect of the person) and *psyche* (the soul, or the psychological). It is one of the ironies of history that "the term 'psychology' gained currency precisely at the time when psychology was about to become anything but 'the study of the soul'" (Lapointe, 1970, p. 645) and that the context in which it gained currency is that of biblical psychology, a later version of psychology as pneumatology and a companion to anthropology. Biblical psychologies were common in the 19th century, with Rauch (1840), Delitzcsch (1855/1867), and Chambers (1900) being

---

[2] Toulmin & Leary (1985) argue effectively that philosophers were as eager as psychologists to have the disciplines disengage, which they did by founding the American Philosophical Association in 1901. Histories that offer an alternative to Boring's, with greater sensitivity to theological and philosophical issues, include Dessoir (1911/1912), Brett (1912–1921), Fay (1939), Klein (1970), Roback (1952), Robinson (1976), and Watson (1963).

its best-known proponents. The minority of biblical psychologists, who distinguish between soul and spirit, are known as trichotomists. The majority, who regard spirit and soul as indistinguishable nonmaterial aspects of the person, are known as dichotomists. The 19th-century emphasis on the problematic trichotomist position may have resulted from the effort clearly to distinguish the domain of theology from that of the new psychology.[3] The connection of psychology and religion is no less inextricable in non-Western traditions. Thus, Müller-Freienfels (1935) asserted that the Hindu psychologists "possessed everything that many people consider the essence of genuine science" (p. 9).

When the notion of dialectic is used with differentiation, integration requires that the increased precision of knowledge gained by the specialty disciplines (the analysis of dialectic and the partial differentials of the calculus) be reintegrated with the knowledge of the other disciplines (to achieve the synthesis of dialectic or the total differential of the calculus).

Opposition to Segregation

Culturally and ethnically, integration opposes segregation or separatism. Christian theologians speak of theology as the "queen of the sciences," but in the complementary quest for knowledge, theologism (Sheldon, 1936) is no less problematic than psychologism (Vande Kemp, 1986). Christian psychologists and theologians are equally called to search for congruence with biblical teaching, in a spirit of liberal education and interdisciplinary cooperation. In scientific circles, the issue is couched in terms of psychology–science and religion–faith as opposing paradigms (see Foster & Ledbetter, 1987). This distinction also is simplistic when one considers the complex historical origins of psychology, which became linked with science when it branched out by adding to its metaphysical concerns (the nature of the soul or of persons) the epistemological questions more familiar to students of psychology's history (Müller-Freienfels, 1935). To use Vico's 17th-century distinction, the old psychology is linked with human science (*Geisteswissenschaft*, literally "spiritual science") and the new psychology with *Naturwissenschaft* ("natural science"; see Leahey, 1987, p. 27).

Even earlier, in the 13th-century universities, natural science was one of the three philosophies (along with metaphysics and ethics) that along with the seven liberal arts (arithmetic, astronomy, geometry, grammar, logic, music, and rhetoric) formed the total curriculum (Klein, 1970; Watson, 1963). Contemporary psychology, with its empirical, logical, and mathematical emphases, draws as much on the liberal arts as it does

---

[3] Discussion of this debate is found in Vande Kemp (1982a,b, 1983b) Titles of biblical psychologies are listed in Vande Kemp (1984) on pp. 55–60 and books on the soul on pp. 41–53.

on natural science and metaphysics. The scholasticism of Aquinas (1225–1274) emerged in response to a medieval version of the science–religion controversy: Siger of Brabant's doctrine of two truths or double truth, which led to his arrest for heresy in 1277 (Leahey, 1987; Klein, 1970). The two truths represented faith and reason as two epistemologies. As articulated by the Arabian philosopher Averroës, "what faith decrees as true may be false in the light of reason, just as what reason finds to be true might be false in the light of faith" (Klein, 1970, p. 163). Aquinas responded with a doctrine of one truth: "there were two paths to the *same* truth, not two truths. . . . Truth was one and came from God" (Watson, 1963, p. 115; for a modern restatement, see Collins, 1977).

The liberally educated scholar recognizes many paths to truth, accepting the multiple epistemologies that are part of the history of knowledge. But positivist scientific psychologists insist on their exclusive method, forcing the Christian psychologist to face a modern version of the scholastic problem, which Christian systematic theologians often resolve by adopting a metaphor used by the theologian Emil Brunner: "We might picture this effort in terms of concentric circles on a target. As the circles move out from the truths of revelation at the personal center (God's self-disclosure in Jesus Christ) to the relatively less personal sphere of knowledge, reason becomes more competent and faith less essential" (Jewett, 1991, pp. 21–22).[4] The closer we move to the center of the circle (i.e., the personal God and the personal creature), the more problematic is the effort to integrate faith and reason. Psychology in this model is quite different from the other sciences because it involves knowing persons as well as objects. Integration must appeal increasingly to revelation and faith as religious psychologists "move from the issues raised for theology by astrophysics, geology, and the like to those raised by history, psychology, and sociology" (p. 22). From this perspective, psychology is best regarded as part of the human sciences, as it was in the tradition of mental and moral science and philosophy,[5] rather than part of natural science or the human-

---

[4] The discussion of this issue is necessarily limited to the Christian perspective because Christianity and related traditions rely in a unique way on a doctrine of revelation and on a personal revealed God. Thus, the Christian theologian does not take belief (faith) to be in contrast to understanding (reason) but integrates them in the assertion attributed to St. Anselm of Canterbury (1033-1109), "I believe in order to understand" (*credo ut intelligam*; see Jewett, 1991, p. 50). Anselm based this on Augustine's (354-430 A.D.) statement, "Unless ye believe, ye shall not understand" (Polanyi, 1958, p. 266n). This belief element becomes central to Polanyi's (1958) theory of "personal knowledge" and is also critical to Kuhn's (1962) understanding of the functioning of scientific paradigms that dictate our observation of data. The notion of God as person providing knowledge of a personal nature is linked to the work of Buber (1922/1937). This leads, in theology, to Brunner's (1938/1943) method of nonpersonalism. See also Footnote 13 on personalism.

[5] In the 19th century it was common to distinguish between mental or intellectual philosophy and moral philosophy. Mental philosophy included "sensation, perception, memory, imagination, and speculations on the nature of the soul," (Scarborough, 1922, p. 277). Moral philosophy included ethics, economics, history, politics, religion, and sociology. Beecher (1831) provides an integrative example.

ities. Integration is not a matter of bringing depth to two linear perspectives (those of religion and science) with a stereoscope, as suggested by Jeeves (1995), but one of bringing the knowledge of a diversity of disciplines to bear on the understanding of the human mind and behavior in all its shifting, kaleidoscopic richness.[6] Psychology then can be to the epistemological disciplines what the Scholastic's common sense (Leahey, 1987) is to the individual mind, allowing one to form perceptions of integrated wholes from the unintegrated impressions provided by the specific senses. Integration in this sense is less adequate to describe the renewed interest in spirituality evident in transpersonal psychology and related traditions: these movements bring with them highly integrated philosophical and theological systems.

Fighting the Forces of Disintegration/Having Integrity

Existentially, integration combats the forces of disintegration, which range from external chaos to internal, psychotic decompensation. Persons fight the incoherence that is the antithesis of both coherence and that object–relational quality of human existence known as coinherence (Williams, 1939).[7] The integrator "holds things together" or works to bring them together again, which is the function of religion based on the root *ligare*.[8] This is the meaning of religion stressed by the psychologist O. H. Mowrer (1966) and the psychiatrist Viktor Frankl (1975). It appears in Christian therapies that stress salvation and redemption (Caruso, 1954/1964; Daim, 1954/1963; de Forest, 1954), tying together the individual's story with the gospel story. And it is present in other narrative traditions, ranging from the parables of Jesus (Sharman, 1917) and the teaching tales of the Suffs (Bayat & Jamnia, 1994), through the therapeutic teaching tales of Erickson (Rosen, 1982) and Friedman (1990), to the narrative method in psychology (Howard, 1991; Lee, 1993).

Integrity is a state of completeness, an unbroken, unimpaired, perfect condition that includes honesty, uprightness, sincerity, and what people generally think of as character. In the Christian theological tradition this immediately suggests the processes of justification and sanctification or experiences of "metanoia," which implies a transformation from outside oneself. White (1952) linked this process of "metanoia, the biblical word for

---

[6] The kaleidoscope metaphor was used by Minuchin (1984) to stress the importance of a systemic perspective, as opposed to an individualistic one, in human relations. I believe a similar perspective is necessary for all psychological studies: Our knowledge is always applied in a highly complex interpersonal and environmental context.

[7] The original doctrine of coinherence in the Catholic church refers to the interrelationship of the three persons of God in the Trinity of Father, Son, and Holy Spirit. Williams extends this notion to the interconnectedness of human existence, a point noted by Laing (1969, p. 5) and discussed further by Vande Kemp (1987).

[8] For a discussion of this somewhat controversial definition of religion, see Vande Kemp (1985a).

change of mind and heart," back to *religare*: "the very word religio, like the Sanskrit yoga, probably means to bind back or together: it is that which should bind a man together by binding him to God—or whatever he may call his ultimate value and the aim of his life" (p. 146).

In the 20th century the attainment of these goals has been linked with character education and psychotherapy, as well as various religious development theories and methods of spiritual growth. We see a growth process in the psychosynthesis of Assagioli (1965/1971), who speaks of parallel spiritual and personal transformation in which people achieve "union with Divine Reality" and "the complete transmutation and regeneration of the personality" (Assagioli, 1956, p. 40). We see growth in Jung's individuation (Goldbrunner, 1946/1955a, 1949/1955b) and in the Sufi's "'stages' of the ascent of God" (Underhill, 1911/1961). The Christian speaks of "the armor of faith" (as described in Ephesians 6 of the Bible, and the psychotherapist speaks of "charactor armor" (Reich 1933/1972), but both are concerned with the person's need to ward off threats to personal existence. Christian integrators generally are concerned that helping professionals address both "anthropocentric" and "theocentric" concerns (Maeder, 1945/1953), a distinction that is less relevant to adherents of Eastern and other nontraditional religions.[9] Theists and nontheists approach these issues differently, but both assume there will be a breakdown when either the spiritual or the psychological is neglected. Progoff (1956), an early spokesman for integration, described the task of a spiritually sensitive psychology as follows: "The ultimate task of the new psychology is to re-establish man's *connection to life*. . . . fundamentally and actually as an evident fact of modern existence" (p. 265).

THE HISTORICAL EMERGENCE OF INTEGRATION

Efforts to reintegrate psychology and theology constituted an immediate response to the alleged emancipation of psychology from theology and philosophy in the mid-to-late 19th century. Such efforts are apparent in Porter's (1868) psychology, Paine's (1872) physiology of the soul, and Müller's (1893) theosophy; in early psychologies of religion such as Boudreaux's (1873) psychological study of God, Alliott's (1855) *Psychology and Theology*, and Brinton's (1876) treatise on the religious sentiment; in pathological interpretations of religion such as Brigham's (1835) focus on excesses of the religious sentiment and Maudsley's (1886) naturalistic explanations of supernatural phenomena; in Christian applications and criticisms of phrenology (Fowler, 1843; Ingalls, 1839; Pierpont, 1850); and

---

[9] The debate around the relationship between spiritual wholeness and psychological healing is far too complex to take up here. An extensive summary is provided in Vande Kemp (1987).

in Kierkegaard's (1849/1941; 1844/1944) classical existential analyses of dread and despair. A century later, at the end of the 20th century, it is clear that these integrative efforts have coalesced into a distinct psychological and interdisciplinary specialty.

The historian is confronted with extensive data to document the assertion that the integration of religion and clinical psychology has emerged as a discrete specialty. In presenting this evidence, I have chosen the categories used both explicitly and implicitly by textbook historians to document the emergence of the larger profession and science of psychology (i.e., the categories that organize the facts of the history of psychology). Each of these developments constitutes a cornerstone in the historical foundation of the integrative discipline. Thus, my claim that integration has attained specialty status is supported by the fact that psychologists have given the name integration to this interdisciplinary task; they have formed professional societies and interest groups devoted uniquely to psychotheological integration; they have developed courses, appointed professors, and designed formal degree programs in integration; they have launched integrative journals, founded laboratories, and designed integrative research programs; they have judged existing textbooks inadequate, written specialized textbooks, and added articles on integration to dictionaries and encyclopedias of psychology; they have founded a clinical tradition, with religion-based therapy models, treatment programs, and psychiatric hospitals as well as accredited internship training; and they have constructed a substantial theoretical literature.[10] Taken together, these developments provide strong justification for the claim that integration is a viable independent specialty within the larger discipline of psychology.

The Naturalization of a Name

The peculiar choice of the common term integration to designate interdisciplinary efforts by theologians and psychologists was first used in reference to psychology and the religious realm in 1953 by Fritz Künkel, founder of We-Psychology and major contributor to Christian education (Johnson, 1990). Künkel established the [Christian] Counseling Center at the First Congregational Church in Los Angeles in the 1940s, and in 1952 he founded the Foundation for the Advancement of Religious Psychology. He described his work after 1943 as "the integration of Christianity and Psychology" (Letter from Fritz Künkel to William Rickel, undated, 1953). The editors of *Pastoral Psychology* adopted this description in a 1953 biographical sketch of Künkel ("The Man of the Month," 1953) and extended

---

[10] Because of space limitations, the historical events documented here must be representative rather than exhaustive, and many significant contributions must be omitted. More extensive discussions can be found in my unpublished historical papers and other works referenced here.

it in 1955 to Gordon Allport, who was depicted as "an outstanding leader in the movement on the integration of psychology and religion" ("The Man of the Month," 1955, p. 59). In 1954, Künkel contributed the opening article on "The Integration of Religion and Psychology" to the *Journal of Psychotherapy as a Religious Process* (Vande Kemp, 1985a, b; Vande Kemp & Houskamp, 1986). Rickel in turn used the term in this journal to describe Paul Tournier, whose work became "the center of a growing movement in several European nations toward the integration of psychotherapy with a religious and spiritual insight into the nature of [persons]" ("Letters," 1954, p. 89).[11] With the publication of Biddle's *Integration of Religion and Psychiatry* in 1955, integration was firmly ensconced as the English title for a movement that dominated the 1960s and 1970s, paving the way for the later emphasis of psychotherapy and spirituality. This usage is specifically linked with existential integrity in Diam (1954/1963).

The Organization of Professional Societies

Two kinds of developments in relation to integration took place in professional societies. First, some organizations emerged specifically for purposes related to integration. The current survivors among these include the Christian Association for Psychological Studies (CAPS), founded in 1953; the (National) Academy of Religion and Mental Health, organized in 1954; and the American Foundation of Religion and Psychiatry, established at Marble Collegiate Church in 1958. A second set of special-interest groups arose within larger organizations. The Friends Conference on Religion and Psychology was organized in 1937 during the World Conference on Religion and Psychology was organized in 1937 during the World Conference of Friends at Swarthmore. The Association for Religious and Value Issues in Counseling arose as an interest group in The American Personnel and Guidance Association in the 1950s. The Person, Culture, & Religion section of the American Academy of Religion was launched in 1973 as the Psychosocial Interpretations in Theology section, an ecumenically diverse group interested in depth-psychological analysis of culture, interpretive (rather than empirical) psychologies of religion, normative

---

[11] Tournier, an internationally acclaimed contributor to Christian psychiatry, wrote in the tradition of personalist psychology, a philosophical and theological movement rooted in the idea that God is a person who relates to humans as people, giving rise to textbooks in personality theory that preceded the classic texts by Allport (1937) and Stagner (1937; see also Bertocci, 1958; Brown, 1929, 1946; Caruso, 1952/1964; Daim, 1954/1963; Driesch, 1926; Guntrip, 1956/1957; Johnson, 1945, 1957; MacMurray, 1936, 1957, 1961; Mounier, 1936/1938, 1946/1956; Stuart, 1938; Vaughan, 1930; Webb, 1918, 1920). In 1947 Tournier joined with Alphonse Maeder (1945/1953) and Jean de Rougement, both members of the Oxford Group, to organize annual International Conferences on the Medicine of the Person (see Tournier, 1951/1960). Tournier has had 21 books translated into English. For a perspective on his life and theories, see Collins (1973), Houde (1990), and Peaston (1972).

implications of depth psychology, and "the critical dialogue between psychology and theology" (Browning, 1982, p. 2).

APA's Division 36 is rooted in several groups. The major, formal group consisted of those Catholic psychologists who met in 1947, under the leadership of W. C. Bier, to form the American Catholic Psychological Association (ACPA), which then began to meet annually in conjunction with APA.[12] In 1970 this group became Psychologists Interested in Religious Issues (PIRI). PIRI attained divisional status in 1976, and in 1993 became The Psychology of Religion, a name change that reflects the heavily scientific emphasis of the division. The history of Division 36 is documented in the ACPA newsletters, the compendia of papers from the annual meetings that were published from 1956 to 1959, the *Catholic Psychological Record*, and the later PIRI newsletters.

A second group coalesced under the sponsorship of Faculty Christian Fellowship, a group of Christian teachers associated with the National Council of Churches. From 1959 to 1962 a group of 7 to 12 people gathered twice a year for in-depth exploration "of the relations between religion and psychology" (Havens, 1968, p. 1). In addition to the discussion published by Havens (1968; Vande Kemp, 1989a), members of this group published a series of psychological articles on Augustine in the *Journal for the Scientific Study of Religion* in 1965 (Bakan, 1965; Clark, 1965; Dittes, 1965; Havens, 1965; Pruyser, 1966; Woolcott, 1966). Much of this work was of a psychodynamic and theoretical/philosophical nature, and PIRI soon provided a natural context for such explorations.

An additional strong presence in APA's Division 36 is the Transpersonal Psychology Interest Group, which first met at the 1980 APA convention. Many participants in this group are members of the Association for Transpersonal Psychology, founded in 1972 by a group within the Association of Humanistic Psychology (Valle, 1989). The basic philosophy of the transpersonal movement is expressed in the works of Maslow (1964, 1968, 1969), who predicted a "fourth psychology, transpersonal, transhuman, centered in the cosmos rather than in human needs and interest, going beyond humanness, identity, self-actualization, and the like" (as cited in Walsh & Vaughan, 1980, p. 20). The movement was christened by

---

[12]Catholics have consistently been at the forefront of integrative work. In 1954, Misiak and Staudt published *Catholics in Psychology: A Historical Survey* to highlight the contributions of Catholic psychologists to scientific psychology. Other overtly Catholic histories include those by Mercier (1897/1918), Brennan (1945), and Vogel (1932). Catholic integrative works are too numerous to itemize, but significant contributions include Barrett (1911, 1921, 1925), Brennan (1941), Dempsey (1956), Gemelli (1953/1955), Goldbrunner (1954/1958), Houselander (1951), Lindworsky (1935/1936), Meseguér (1960), Moore (1948), Morgan (1932), Nuttin, (1950/1962), Terruwe (1955/1959), Vander Veldt & Odenwald (1952), White (1960), Witcutt (1943), Zilboorg (1958, 1962).

Maslow, Frankl,[13] Grof (1976, 1985), and Fadiman (1980). Transpersonal psychologists emphasize the egoic, existential, and transpersonal levels of identity: They regard psychotherapy as a type of awakening to greater identity that is facilitated through "an enhancing of inner awareness and intuition" in both therapist and client" (Wittine, 1992, p. 282) and recognize the therapist's unfolding self and spiritual worldview as cardinal therapeutic variables.

The Appearance of Degree Programs and Professorships

Students can now earn degrees with a focus on the integration of psychology and theology or spirituality. The first APA-accredited integrative doctoral degrees were offered by the Graduate School of Psychology at Fuller Theological Seminary, where the first doctor of philosophy students were enrolled in 1965 and the first doctor of psychology students in 1988.[14] At Fuller, H. Newton Malony served as the first director of programs in the integration of psychology and theology (1977–1990), and Lewis Smedes served from 1990 through 1993 as professor of theology and integration. The Rosemead Graduate School of Psychology at Biola University first enrolled PhD students in 1970 and doctor of psychology students in 1972, in what was the first free-standing school of psychology to be regionally accredited (by Western Association of Schools and Colleges in 1975). More recent doctoral programs include the doctor of psychology at Baylor University, George Fox College Graduate School of Psychology, and Wheaton College (Illinois). A number of integrative master's programs have been established as well, with the earliest of such efforts beginning in 1973 at what is now the Psychological Studies Institute in Atlanta,[15] which offered "the first graduate-level program in counseling with a Christian emphasis established in cooperation with a major state university" (Psychological Studies Institute, 1993, p. 2). Many nonaccredited programs are available as well; a valuative listing of these is available in Levicoff's (1993a) *Name It and Frame It*. In response to the proliferation of such degree programs, the first conference on Christian graduate training in

---

[13] Viktor E. Frankl, a Jewish psychiatrist and concentration-camp survivor, is well-known in Christian as well as transpersonal circles as the founder of logotherapy, which focuses on the search for meaning in human existence. The principles of logotherapy are found in Frankl (1946/1955, 1946/1959, 1965, 1948/1975). *Man's Search for Meaning* (1946/1959) has been published in 24 languages and named by the Library of Congress as one of the ten most influential books in America. More than 120 books and nearly 140 dissertations (in 15 languages) have been written about logotherapy (for early examples, see Bulka, 1979b; Leslie, 1965; Tweedie, 1963; Ungersma, 1961). Frankl's "paradoxical intention" (1946/1955) is also embedded in the current strategic therapy literature on "prescribing the symptom" (see Andolfi, 1979, pp. 124–127).

[14] Addresses for APA-accredited doctoral programs and internships are included in the annual listings in the *American Psychologist.*

[15] The address for PSI is 2055 Mount Paran Road, N.W., Atlanta, GA 30327. The phone number is (404) 233-3949.

professional psychology was held in 1990 (Jones, 1992; Tan & Jones, 1991).[16]

Several nonclinical degree programs also deserve mention because their faculty and graduates have contributed to the clinical integration literature (e.g., Bregman, 1986, 1992; Byrnes, 1984; Capps, 1992; Capps & Capps, 1970; Capps, Capps, & Bradford, 1977; Capps & Fenn, 1992; Capps, Rambo, & Ransohoff, 1976; Clift, 1982; Fenn & Capps, 1992; Klass, 1988; Moore, 1988; Rambo, 1980, 1983). Around 1952, Seward Hiltner, the eminent pastoral theologian (see Aden, 1985), founded a PhD program in religion and personality within the Federated Theological Faculty at the University of Chicago. From 1970 to 1985, the degree was in religion and psychological studies, and leadership was provided by the gifted integrators Don Browning (at that time Alexander Campbell Professor of Religion and Psychological Studies; see Browning, 1973, 1986) and Peter Homans (then professor of religion and psychological studies [formerly professor of religion and personality]; see Homans, 1968, 1970, 1979, 1987).[17] Emory University offers a doctorate in theology and personality, and one can earn a joint master of divinity and master of social work at Union Theological Seminary at Columbia University under the tutelage of scholars such as Ulanov (professor of psychiatry and religion; see Ulanov, 1971, 1981, 1986; Ulanov & Ulanov, 1975, 1982).

Focusing on nontraditional religious approaches, the Association for Transpersonal Psychology (1992) has compiled a listing of more than 130 institutions offering training in transpersonal psychology and related areas.[18] This list includes such fully accredited programs as the MA and PhD offered by the Saybrook Institute, whose faculty includes such well-known figures as Rollo May (1940, 1950, 1953; Caligor & R. May, 1968) and Krippner (1977–1990, 1978); the MA, PhD and PsyD at the California Institute of Integral Studies; the masters and PhD at Duquesne University's Institute of Formative Spirituality (Van Kaam, 1976); the MA and PhD at Maharishi International University; and postdoctoral training for MDs at the University of California, Irvine. Nonaccredited programs are offered at such centers as the Astrology Institute, the Consciousness Research and Training Project, the Deva Foundation, Esalen, Isis Institute, Nyingma In-

---

[16] Most programs of this nature are offered at private educational institutions because of the restrictions inherent in the First Amendment to the American Constitution: "Congress shall make no law respecting an establishment of religion or prohibiting the free exercise thereof." Several Supreme Court decisions in the 1960s and 1970s opened the way for public schools to teach *about* religion, thus creating departments of religious studies, but they cannot support or inculcate a particular religious view (see Michaelsen, 1977).

[17] Since 1985 the degree has been in Psychology and sociology of religion.

[18] This list, which includes full information on accreditation, can be ordered from the *Association for Transpersonal Psychology* at P. O. Box 3049, Stanford, CA 94349 or by calling (415) 327-2066. My examples are intended to convey the range of emphases. Many of these programs may be vulnerable to challenges based on the First Amendment because they appear no less focused on inculcating "religious" traditions than do the Judeo-Christian programs.

stitute, Omega Institute, Psychosynthesis Institute, Samala Retreat, the Taoist Institute, and the Yasodhara Ashram Society. Similar listings are included in *The Common Boundary Graduate Education Guide* (Demetrios, Simpkinson, & Bennet, 1991), which includes not only traditional programs in pastoral counseling and Judeo-Christian clinical psychology but also those that focus on holistic healing, intuition training, psychosynthesis, shamanic counseling, spiritual direction and formation, and transpersonal therapies.

The Establishment of Journals

Several integrative journals have emerged that can be clearly distinguished from the journals focused primarily on pastoral counseling (at the practical theological boundary) or on the psychology of religion (at the research frontier). These include *Inward Light: Journal of the Friends Conference on Religion and Mental Health*, founded in 1937; the *National Catholic Guidance Conference Journal* (now *Counseling and Values*), founded in 1956 and devoted exclusively to the role of religion and values in counseling and psychotherapy; the *Journal of Religion and Health*, founded in 1961 by the Institutes of Religion and Health; *Insight: Quarterly Review of Religion and Mental Health*, founded in 1961 by the Franciscan Fintan McNamee; the *Journal of Psychology and Theology*, established by the Rosemead Graduate School of Psychology in 1973; the *Journal of Psychology and Christianity*, established in 1982 by the Christian Association for Psychological Studies as an extension of its *Bulletin*; and the *Journal of Psychology and Judaism*, launched in 1976 by the [Canadian] Center for the Study of Psychology and Judaism. Jewish psychologists entered the integrative realm relatively late but are developing a unique literature under the leadership of such individuals as Spero (1980, 1985), Ostow (1981), Lovinger (1984, 1990), Meier (1988, 1991), Spiegelman (1993), and Bulka (1979a).[19]

The Journal of Transpersonal Psychology was founded in 1969 and has featured a wide range of authors and transpersonal perspectives that define the field, such as Maslow's (1964) inspirational classic; Assagioli's (1965/1971) psychosynthesis; the lectures of Ram Dass 1975, 1977, 1978); research on altered states of consciousness (Ornstein, 1972, 1973; Tart, 1969, 1975, 1992); reports on LSD-assisted therapy (Grof, 1976; Lake,[20] 1966, 1987); Native American religious practices (Castaneda, 1968, 1987; Nie-

---

[19] The traditions of the psychology of religion and psychoanalysis and religion include many earlier (and classic) works by Jewish writers. See, for example, such works as Ackerman and Jahoda (1950), Bakan (1958), Bookstaber (1950), Freud (1913/1918; 1927/1928; 1939), Fromm (1941, 1950/1931/1963), Grollman (1965), Hirsch (1947), Hoffman (1981), Liebman (1948), Noveck (1956), Reik (1919/1931, 1927/1951, 1957, 1959, 1960, 1961), and Silverstone (1956).

[20] Frank Lake was the founding director of Britain's Clinical Theology Association, which was formed in 1962. Lake reflects the psychological influence of the object-relations school and the theological influence of the Church of England.

hardt, 1961); the psychological aspects of yoga, Buddhism (Zen, Tibetan; see Bennett, 1964), Sufism, Taoism, Hinduism, and other meditative religious traditions (Gyaltshan, 1980; Lichstein, 1988; Naranjo & Ornstein, 1971; Sheikh & Sheikh, 1989); *est* training (see Bartley, 1978); near-death experiences (Grof & Halifax, 1977; Ring, 1980); biofeedback; integrative psychology (Vaughan, 1986); parapsychology (Sinclair, 1962; Ullman & Krippner, 1989); shamanism (Eliade, 1970; Walsh, 1987); existential–phenomenological psychology (Valle & Halling, 1989); and the more familiar humanistic and Jungian traditions (Jung, 1931/1933, 1938, 1958).

The Advent of Laboratories

The psychology of religion (see Wulff; Chapter 2, this volume) represents an early research tradition to which both G. Stanley Hall (Vande Kemp, 1992a) and William James (1902; Gorsuch & Spilka, 1987) were contributors. Psychologists of religion come primarily from personality and social psychology, with both groups exploring clinical issues. Early systematic clinical research is exemplified by the Catholic University of America's *Studies in Psychology and Psychiatry* and the University of Iowa's *Studies in Character* (for individual items in these series see Vande Kemp, 1984, pp. 281–283). A significant empirical clinical tradition is embodied in the various studies of clergy personality and the emerging specialty of clergy assessment that began with the Readiness for Ministry project funded by the Lilly Endowment in the late 1960s and early 1970s at the request of the Association of Theological Schools (ATS) in the United States and Canada (see Schuller, Brekke, Strommen, & Aleshire, 1976; Schuller, Strommen, & Brekke, 1975, 1980). Additional Lilly grants have funded data collection in the areas of Quality of Ministry and Profiles of Ministry (Hunt, Hinkle, & Malony, 1990). Those interested in research relating to the psychology of religion may consult Meissner (1961), Little (1962), Freeman and Freeman (1964), Capps, Rambo, and Ransohoff (1976), Beit-Hallahmi (1978), Vande Kemp (1984), and Wulff (1991), along with sources cited in Hoge (Chapter 1, this volume).

The Emergence of Literature and Textbooks

When one ponders the historical impact of religion on textbooks in the clinically relevant areas of psychology, there are two issues that must be examined. The first is the literature which critiques the secular, non-religious textbooks. The second is the actual production of textbooks focused on religious issues in clinical psychology, the domain of which includes personality theory, psychopathology, psychometrics, and psychotherapy.

Critique of Textbook Treatment of Religion

Recent researchers in psychology and religion have followed Beit-Hallahmi's (1977) suggestion that "one way of measuring the impact and importance of the psychology of religion today is by looking at the treatment given this topic in introductory psychology texts" (p. 381). Results document the fact that current psychology textbooks, whether introductory or advanced, seldom treat religion as a vital personality function (Houde, 1988; Kirkpatrick & Spilka, 1989; Lehr & Spilka, 1989; Ruble, 1985; Shafranske, 1989; Spilka, Amaro, Wright, & Davis, 1981; Spilka, Comp, & Goldsmith, 1981; Vande Kemp, 1976; Vitz, 1989). The current state of affairs is much as that first found by Gordon Allport 50 years ago.

In late 1944, at the request of the Edward W. Hazen Foundation and the American Council on Education, Allport began an inquiry into the treatment of religion in college textbooks as part of a larger study focused on "the place of religion in liberal higher education." This request assumed the importance of religion in culture, the obscuring and denying of this fact by modern thinkers, the importance of textbooks for "inculcating attitudes and convictions inimical to the development of religion," and emphasized the constructive role faculty might play "through a more enlightened study and appraisal of religion as a phase of the culture."[21]

Allport reviewed approximately 50 psychology texts published between 1928 and 1945 (for a listing, see Allport, 1948, or Vande Kemp, 1988, 1989b) and concluded that recent authors have "virtually banished from their pages the essential problems of the *will, conscience, reasoning, . . . self, subjective values,* and the *individual's world view*" (1948, p. 80).[22] Many texts in personality and abnormal psychology accorded religion the "silent-treatment" category; from them, a student "would obtain . . . no idea that religion plays any significant part among the motives or interests of mankind" (p. 82).[23] Allport was amazed that psychologists were more interested in dream activity than prayer activity, even though "the number of people who say their prayers at night is probably greater . . . than the number who can report a dream" (p. 83) and their prayers were far more likely than their dreams to influence human conduct. Ten texts simply listed selected results of statistical research on religion, including Stagner (1937). Five texts emphasized the "instrumental value" of religion (p. 90), especially to the returning members of the armed forces after World War

---

[21] "Exhibit 1. Purpose and Scope of the Survey," in the Allport Archives, Harvard University Library.

[22] One immediately sees a connection with Allport's work in personality theory, where he strongly relies on the personalist emphasis on self (see Footnote 11), and where the concept of *functional autonomy* accounts for the motivational concepts connected to will. Allport's essentially idiographic approach is consistent with this comment as well.

[23] One of these was Maslow and Mittlemann's (1941) *Principles of Abnormal Psychology.* Maslow (1964) corrected this omission with the publication of his well-known *Religions, Values, and Peak Experiences.*

II (Boring, 1945; Child & Van de Water, 1945). Allport was most pleased with Gurnee's (1936) definition of religion, which included the elements of belief, conviction, feeling, and a system of attitudes and overt responses. Allport commended Klein (1944) for his positive approach to religion and his acknowledgment that schizophrenic ideas may be an attempt to approach the ultimate.[24] Allport felt that his own personality text (1937) shared with Klein's the "emphasis upon the importance of an integrative philosophy of life" (Allport, 1948, p. 96) and the inspiration of Eduard Spranger "in characterizing the religious *Weltanschauung* in terms of the unity which confers upon the life that holds it" (p. 96). Allport concluded that the textbooks reflected the implicit attributes of "*determinism, mechanism, environmentalism* and *anti-rationalism*" (p. 97), which together formed the "metaphysical atmosphere of *psychologism*" (p. 97; see also Vande Kemp, 1986). He marveled that "the very authors who in their private lifes are inspired by a purpose, living (as all men must live) by affirmation, loyalty, and a philosophy of life, fail to represent adequately this psychological requirement to their students" (p. 100). Allport's comment on one of the most hostile texts can easily be applied to textbook writers of the 1980s and 1990s: "that the author is gratified by the alleged decline in influence [of religion] is, on the whole, more convincingly demonstrated than the fact of the decline itself" (p. 84). Allport responded to the combined neglect of, and attack on, religion in textbooks by focusing his 1947 Lowell Lectures on the psychology and psychopathology of religion. This led to the publication of his now classic text, *The Individual and His Religion* (1950), a volume inspiring a renewed interest in religion among mainstream psychologists.

Textbooks Focused on Religion

After publishing its research on the treatment of religion in textbooks, the Hazen Foundation invited 13 authors to write on the role of religion in the teaching of their discipline. The chapter on psychology was written by MacLeod (1952), who focused less on teaching itself than on the responsibility of experimental psychologists "to accept the phenomena of religion as a worthy object of scientific curiosity" (p. 5). Rather than view religion as "something secondary to be reduced, something peculiar to be explained away, or something of practical value to be exploited" (p. 12), psychologists should regard it as an area where they might find valid problems of cognition (as belief structures become stable), feelings and

---

[24] The affinity between profound religious experience and psychosis, as attempts at personal reorganization, was emphasized by Boisen (1936, 1955, 1960), the clergyman founder of Clinical Pastoral Education, who suffered five psychotic episodes. A psychotic break was also the stimulus for Mowrer's (1961, 1964, 1966) thesis that real guilt may be the basis for personality disorder and neurosis, a view first asserted by Runestam (1930/1958). Mowrer's emphasis on morality inspired the reality therapy of Glasser (1965).

emotions (with emotions such as courage and serenity involving teleological explanations), and motivation (in goal directedness).[25] MacLeod knew that, for believers, values become regulators of conduct, and religion should be studied scientifically as an area in which psychologists had very few facts and could truly be motivated by curiosity. The method he recommended was psychological phenomenology (see also Vande Kemp, 1989a).

Several critical efforts were also made by the Faculty Christian Fellowship (FCS), which in the early 1960s sponsored semiannual gatherings of theological and psychological scholars. One published effort from FCS was Havens's (1964) *Psychology*, the third volume in the *Faith Learning Studies*, a series designed to examine critically the faith–discipline connection, to suggest directions for future thinking, and to prepare an annotated bibliography.[26] Havens examined the image of a reacting organism versus the *Imago Dei*, psychology's adequacy to assess subjective experience, human freedom, religion as a datum of psychology, transcendental experience, and salvation versus mental health; and he also provided a 60-item bibliography.

Current Christian publishers are intentional in producing textbooks, the earliest including Carter and Narramore's (1979) *The Integration of Psychology and Theology* and Fleck and Carter's (1981) *Psychology and Christianity: Integrative Readings*. More recent efforts include Myers and Jeeves's (1987) *Psychology Through the Eyes of Faith*, published by the Christian College Coalition; Jones's (1986) *Psychology and the Christian Faith: An Introductory Reader*; Heie and Wolfe's (1987) *The Reality of Christian Learning*, produced by the Christian College Consortium; and Philipchalk's (1987) *Psychology and Christianity: An Introduction to Controversial Issues*. Books with a specific clinical focus include Benner's (1987) primer, *Psychotherapy in Christian Perspective* (Benner's, 1985, special journal issue on Christian therapy constitutes a primer as well); Miller and Martin's (1988) *Behavior Therapy and Religion*; Propst's (1988) *Psychotherapy Within a Religious Framework*; Jones and Butman's (1991) *Modern Psychotherapies: A Comprehensive Christian Appraisal*; and Vande Kemp's (1992b) *Family Therapy: Christian Perspectives*.

Texts are also plentiful in the area of transpersonal psychology and its related traditions. Recent texts include a new edition of Tart's (1975,

---

[25] An excellent example of the use of religion to explore and illustrate psychological functions, specifically those of ego psychology, is Paul W. Pruyser's (1968) *A Dynamic Psychology of Religion*, the text for his Dwight Harrington Terry Lectures at Yale. Pruyser carries this further in *Between Belief and Unbelief* (1974).

[26] In Great Britain, similar publications were produced by the Student Christian Movement (SCM) Press. The SCM explored the connections between faith and Christian life through sponsoring study groups, conferences, and publications. SCM publications were popular in the United States as well (see Barry, 1923; Pym, 1922, 1925; Strachan, 1929/1931; Stuart, 1938; Tournier, 1948/1963, 1955/1957; Weatherhead & Greaves, 1931/1932).

1992) classic *Transpersonal Psychologies*; Hixon's (1989) *Coming Home: The Experience of Enlightenment in Sacred Traditions*; Boorstein's (1980) *Transpersonal Psychotherapy*; Wilber, Engler, and Brown's (1986) *Transformations of Consciousness*; Wolman and Ullman's (1986) *Handbook of States of Consciousness*; and other volumes cited above (see also Rowan, 1992; Walsh & Vaughan, 1980).

The Evolution of Praxis

The integrative movement includes a variety of clinical applications and professionalization. One of the first efforts by the clergy to incorporate the healing practices of psychotherapy was Boston's Emmanuel Movement, whose practitioners defined psychotherapy as "the attempt to help the sick through mental, moral, and spiritual methods" (Cabot, 1908, p. 5). When it first emerged in the American literature in 1887 ("Psycho-therapeutic," 1933), the term *psychotherapy* had diverse connotations that blended (and confused) medical, psychical, and spiritual goals. The roots of the term are in the Greek words "'psyche' meaning 'soul' and 'therapist' meaning 'servant' or 'helper'" (Rickel, 1954, p. 97). Several decades passed before definitions of psychotherapy assumed "psychological methods" and the "cure of the mind" (rather than the soul or the body). Bibliographic dictionaries of the early psycho-therapeutic period used extensive cross-referencing and interchanging of terms, often intermingling the "traditionally religious" and the domains of the psychiatrist/alienist. Early reference works treated as synonymous such terms as *Christian Science, Emmanuel Movement, mental healing, faith cure, hypnotism, suggestion, New Thought,* and *psychoanalysis* (Mental Healing, 1910, 1915; for a history of related movements see Weatherhead, 1951). But the Emmanuel Movement faltered within a decade because of the opposition created by the medical establishment, as did a number of later lay analytic movements (see Fleming, 1990; Gifford, 1978; "A New Direction," 1909; Vande Kemp, 1985b).

Clinical Pastoral Education (CPE) and pastoral counseling are a well-known part of the integrative tradition that emerged soon after the fall of the Emmanuel movement. This field has been summarized by Kemp (1947), McNeill (1951), and Clebsch and Jaekle (1964) and critically assessed by Holifield (1983). Generally, the pastoral psychology literature has been derivative, constituting little more than adaptations of Freud, Rogers, and other popular clinical approaches (Vande Kemp, 1984, pp. 157–170). Nonetheless, a few theoretical efforts in this tradition constitute unique theoretical contributions. Among these are Guntrip's (1957) personalist–object-relational *Psychotherapy and Religion*, Hiltner's (1972) psychodynamic *Theological Dynamics*, and Johnson's (1957) "dynamically interpersonal" *Personality and Religion*.

Organizations

Other organizations devoted to religious therapy come and go as fast as blips on a radar screen, as is evident in a quick perusal of "Notes and News" sections of journals in religion and pastoral psychology. As early as 1953 Rickel and Künkel sought to compile a directory of religious therapists ("A Directory," 1954). The *American Association of Religious Therapists* was founded in 1959 but soon vanished. In 1987 the *American Board of Christian Psychology* was founded and lauded by its founders as "the first certification association for Christian workers" (American Board of Christian Psychology, 1987), modeled on the American Board of Professional Psychology. This group also floundered. Currently, Christian counselors may be certified by such legitimate organizations as the American Association of Pastoral Counselors, the Association of Mental Health Clergy, and the National Association of Nouthetic Counselors and other questionable groups such as the American Association of Family Counselors, the American Counselors Society, the American Society of Pastoral Care Professionals, the National Association of Marriage and Family Counselors, the National Christian Counselors Association, and the World Federation of Christian Counselors.[27] One of the largest gatherings of Christian counselors took place in November 1988, when the first International Congress on Christian Counseling in Atlanta was attended by more than 1,100 professionals. The second International Congress attracted more than 2,000 professionals, representing more than 30 countries. The professionalization of Christian psychotherapy was the special focus of the June 1994 conference of the Christian Association for Psychiatrists, Psychologists and Psychotherapists, held in Dalfsen, The Netherlands.[28]

In nontraditional circles, interests in spirituality and psychotherapy has spread beyond the transpersonal psychology movement already mentioned. In 1980 an annual Family Therapy Network Symposium featured a workshop on religion that quickly led to a gathering of "kindred spirits," who organized a 1981 seminar on Integrating Spirituality and Psychotherapy. This truly ecumenical group quickly grew, with further conferences and the founding of a newsletter, *The Common Boundary Between Spirituality and Psychotherapy*. By 1992 this magazine (now *The Common Boundary*) had 25,000 subscribers and included feature articles, special departments, and advertising (Simpkinson, 1992). This group also offers students an award for "an outstanding thesis that addresses the interaction

---

[27] I am grateful to Steve Levicoff (1993a,b) for his thorough investigation into, and assessment of, these organizations, many of which offer legally meaningless "certification." Levicoff's guide is available through the Institute of Religion and Law at P. O. Box 552, Ambler, PA 19002 or by calling (215) 272-4072.

[28] Information on the *Christelijke Vereniging voor Psychiaters, Psychologen, en Psychotherapeuten* [Christian Association for Psychiatrists, Psychologists, and Psychotherapists] may be obtained from its president, Rens Filius, Gouwzee 3, 1423 DS Uithoorn, The Netherlands. Phone 31 29 756-9544. The conference proceedings will be published in European and American editions.

between psychotherapy and spirituality" ("Common Boundary to Offer Dissertation/Thesis Award," 1989).

At the internship level of clinical training, APA-approved predoctoral internships with a traditional religious component are available at Fuller Theological Seminary's Psychological Center and such well-established centers as Pine Rest Christian Mental Health Services and Philhaven Hospital, and the University of Tennessee Professional Psychology Internship Consortium.

Christian Psychiatric Hospitals and Christian Therapy Units

Christian psychiatric hospitals have a long history in the 20th century. The Christian Psychopathic Hospital (in Cutlerville, MI; now the extensive Pine Rest Christian Hospital and Rehabilitation Services) was founded by a group of Reformed protestants in 1910 and is supported financially (though not ecclesiastically) by both the Reformed Church in America (RCA) and the Christian Reformed Church (CRC; "Special Issue," 1980, p. 2). Bethesda Hospital (in Denver, CO), was founded in 1910 by the RCA and CRC as a tuberculosis sanitarium. The transition to private psychiatric facility began in 1948, and a community mental health center was added in 1969 ("Bethesda's Heritage," 1982). In 1945, the Mennonite Mental Health Committee began planning for the first Mennonite mental hospital (Kehler, 1966). The first patients were admitted to Brook Lane Psychiatric Center (Hagerstown, MD) in 1947, and additional centers were soon established, with the earliest ones including Kings View Hospital (Reedley, CA, 1951), Philhaven Hospital (Mt. Gretna, PA, 1952), and Prairie View (Newton, KS, 1954), and later ones including Oaklawn Psychiatric Center (Elkhart, IN, 1963) and Kern View Hospital (Bakersfield, CA, 1966). More recent arrivals on the scene are Christian psychiatric hospitals run by such corporations as Minirth-Meier (Meier, Minirth, & Ratcliff, 1992; Meier, Minirth, & Wichern, 1982), Rapha, and New Life. Many private psychiatric hospitals also feature Christian Therapy Units.[29]

Psychotherapy and Religion: The Theoretical Literature

But what will the doctor do when he sees only too clearly why his patient is ill; when he sees that it arises from his having no love, but only sexuality; no faith, because he is afraid to grope in the dark; no hope, because he is disillusioned by the world and by life; and no understanding, because he has failed to read the meaning of his own existence? . . . *Among all my patients in the second half of life—that is to say, over thirty-five—there has not been one whose problem in the last resort*

---

[29] It is difficult to assess the extent of this movement because individual Christian/spiritual therapy units are often short-lived, there is no separate licensing or credentialing involved, and no national organization for psychologists working on such units.

was not that of finding a religious outlook on life. (Jung, 1931/1933, pp. 225–226, 229; emphasis added)

This quotation by Jung is often cited as the first explicit recognition that religion had a place in psychotherapy. Jung's advocacy of a religious world view is known to most religious psychologists, and his work inspired many early integrators (Goldbrunner, 1946/1955a, 1949/1955b, 1954/1958; Hostie, 1954/1957; Jacobi, 1965/1967; Rudin, 1960/1968; Schaer, 1946/1950; Stern, 1954; White, 1952, 1960). However, Jung was never alone in his positive emphasis on religion in the human psyche. Maeder asserted that "The religiously awakened person brings with him a readiness for working hard, a spiritual agility and open-mindedness to experience, and a practiced self-discipline which are beneficial to the common striving of physician and patient" (Maeder, 1945/1953, p. 158). Ferenczi applied the notion of redemption to psychotherapy, and his "therapeutic genius at 'love' and the process as 'redemption' casts light on the similarity of psychotherapeutic love to that love which permeates the Judeo-Christian tradition" (de Forest, 1954, p. 179). Pfister (1944/1948), a Reformed church pastor, openly debated the positive role of religion with Freud (Freud & Pfister, 1963). A similar debate transpired between Adler and the Lutheran pastor Ernst Jahn (Adler, 1956; Jahn & Adler, 1933). Other books on Christian psychotherapy soon appeared by such authors as Murray (1938), Gregory (1939), Tournier (1944/1966), Daim (1954/1963), Neill (1959), and Ducker (1961, 1964).

Religious therapists have been very strongly influenced by Jung's (1974) approach to dream interpretation, acknowledging the fact that dreams had religious and spiritual meanings long before they attained psychological status (see Vande Kemp, 1981, 1994a,b). Thus, there are strong spiritual and religious themes in such general works as Campbell's (1970) *Myths, Dreams, and Religion* and more specific books on dream interpretation by such writers as Clift and Clift (1984, 1988), von Franz (1986), Fromm (1951), Hillman (1979), Kelsey (1974), Kramer (1993), Krippner (1990), Krippner and Dillard (1988), Meseguér (1960), Sanford (1968), Savary, Berne, & Williams (1984), Schmitt (1984), and Segaller and Berger (1989).

Accompanying the considerable literature on Christian psychotherapy is an even more extensive literature on Christian personality theory (Vande Kemp, 1984, pp. 193–221) and abnormal psychology (Vande Kemp, 1984, pp. 105–111, 223–228). Many of these contributions have been referenced above, especially those by Catholic psychologists and those of Frankl and Tournier (Footnotes 7, 8, and 9) and the volumes printed by the Student Christian Movement Press (Footnote 22). Much of this work was done by eminent psychologists whose names are not usually associated with religion (Vande Kemp, 1983a), such as Dunlap (1946;

Dunlap & Gill, 1933), Guntrip (1957), McDougall (1934), Rank (1941; 1930/1950; see also Griffin, 1990; Progoff, 1956), Rokeach (1964), and Sheldon (1936). Theologians contributed such works as Horton's (1931) *A Psychological Approach to Theology* and Tillich's (1952) classic on anxiety, *The Courage to Be*. Ligon (1935, 1939) documented the results of the extensive Piagetian research undertaken by the Character Research Project at Union College. Ligon's work embodied the essence of the many volumes produced on the topics of Christian education and character research, areas that generally constituted applied work in the psychology of religion extended into the context of religious education (see Vande Kemp, 1984, pp. 175–189 for an extensive listing of books in this area). Well-known to psychologists are the writings arising out of the Character Education Inquiry of 1924–1927 (see Hartshorne & May, 1928; Hartshorn, May, & Maller, 1929; Hartshorne, May, & Shuttleworth, 1930).[30]

A comprehensive review of the literature relevant to clinical psychology and religion would have to include also the biblical psychologies of the 19th century (see Footnote 4) and the related writings on the mind–body problem (McDougall, 1911; Morgan, 1925; Pratt, 1922; Stout, 1931, 1952). The extensive historical literature related to integration is documented in *Psychology and Theology in Western Thought, 1672–1965: A Historical and Annotated Bibliography* (Vande Kemp, 1984), which annotates 1,000 books. Since 1965, this body of literature has grown exponentially, with increased specialization and diversification.

SUMMARY

In this chapter I have noted several definitions of integration in the context of the emergence of 20th-century psychology out of several historical disciplines. I have traced the evolution of the integration of psychology and theology and religion as a clinical specialty by applying the criteria conventionally used by historians of psychology to validate the existence of psychology as a separate discipline. These criteria, as applied in this situation, include the naturalization of a name (psychotherapy for a healing profession, integration for its interface with theology and religion); the organization of professional societies and interest groups; the appearance of advanced degree programs and professorships; the establishment of specialty journals for theory, research, and practice; the advent of laboratories and specialized research programs; the emergence of literature and textbooks (following on research demonstrating the inade-

---

[30] The work of the Character Research Project is ongoing, and related projects are underway at the Character and Competence Research Program of Radcliffe College and The Henry A. Murray Research Center in Cambridge, MA.

quate treatment of religion in mainline psychology textbooks); the evolution of praxis (including special religion-based treatment units and hospitals); internship training and accreditation; and the construction of an independent theoretical literature.

Clearly, when judged by the criteria deemed necessary by historians, the integration of psychology and theology and religion has attained specialty status, and all signs indicate its continued success. What participants in this specialty lack at this point is a systematic awareness of its history. The "20-Year Index" (1993) for the *Journal of Psychology and Theology*; which lists approximately 540 articles, includes only 18 under the topic "Integration (History of)" (p. 42), and only four of these can be regarded as properly historical rather than merely as reviews of recent literature. Perhaps three dozen articles focus on prominent theorists Adler, Allport, Assagioli, Becker, Frankl, Fromm, Goffman, Guntrip, Kelsey, Maslow, R. May, Rogers, Stapleton,[31] and Tillich), with some authors being the subjects of several articles (Kohlberg, Piaget, Kohut, Kierkegaard, Sanford,[32] Tournier, and Winnicott). Eight works are devoted to Freud, reflecting a pervasive bias in historical knowledge that often fails to go beyond Freud's well-known, but highly controversial, works. Ten articles on Jung do reflect efforts to integrate Jungian theory with other works. However, the finest integrative works mentioned in the theoretical section above have received no such attention. All too common in the recent literature are absurd assertions, such as "Carl G. Jung was the first therapist to write about integrating the psychological and the spiritual, and Peck credits this inheritance. But it was Peck [see Peck, 1978, 1983] who first revealed that he integrated his spiritual beliefs into his professional, clinical work" (Simpkinson, 1983, p. 1) or "[Gerald G.] May is the modern pioneer in the field of integrating psychology and spirituality" ("Why a Bibliography?" 1983, p. 6; see G. May, 1982a,b). I hope that the publication of this historical volume will bring about not only awareness of but also appreciation for the rich historical tradition of integration.

REFERENCES

Ackerman, N. W., & Jahoda, M. (1950). *Anti-semitism and emotional disorder: A psychoanalytic interpretation.* New York: Harper.

Aden, L. (Ed.). (1985). Hiltner and pastoral care. *Journal of Psychology and Christianity, 4,* 3–84.

---

[31] Stapleton, sister of former president Jimmy Carter, was a well-known Christian healer. Her work is critically reviewed by Alsdurf & Malony (1980).

[32] Agnes Sanford was another contemporary Christian healer well-known for her powerful prayer ministry. Her work is reviewed by Clark (1989).

Adler, A. (1956). Psychology of religion. In H. Ansbacher & R. Ansbacher (Eds.), *The individual psychology of Alfred Adler* (pp. 460–464). Evanston, IL: Northwestern University Press.

Alliott, R. (1855). *Psychology and theology; or, psychology applied to the investigation of questions relating to religion, natural theology, and revelation.* London: Jackson and Walford.

Allport, G. W. (1937). *Personality: A psychological interpretation.* New York: Holt.

Allport, G. W. (1948). Psychology. In *College reading and religion: A survey of college reading materials* (pp. 80–114). New Haven, CT: Yale University.

Allport, G. W. (1950). *The individual and his religion.* New York: Collier-Macmillan.

Alsdurf, J., & Malony, H. N. (1980). A critique of Ruth Carter Stapleton's ministry of "inner healing." *Journal of Psychology and Theology, 8,* 173–184.

American Board of Christian Psychology. (1987). *New member information.* Copperas Cove, TX: Author.

Andolfi, M. (1979). *Family therapy: An interactional approach* (H. R. Cassin, Trans.). New York: Plenum.

Assagioli, R. (1956). Spiritual development and nervous disease. *Journal of Psychotherapy as a Religious Process, 3,* 30–46.

Assagioli, R. (1971). *Psychosynthesis: A manual of principles and techniques.* New York: Viking. (Original work published 1965)

Association for Transpersonal Psychology. (1992). *1992–1993 listing of schools & programs.* Stanford, CA: Author.

Bakan, D. (1958). *Sigmund Freud and the Jewish mystical tradition.* Princeton, NJ: Van Nostrand.

Bakan, D. (1965). Some thoughts on reading Augustine's Confessions. *Journal for the Scientific Study of Religion, 5,* 149–152.

Barrett, E. J. B. (1911). *Motive-force and motivation tracks, a research in will psychology.* New York: Longmans, Green.

Barrett, E. J. B. (1921). *Psychoanalysis and Christian morality.* [City unknown]: Catholic Theological Society.

Barrett, E. J. B. (1925). *Man: His making and unmaking.* New York: T. Seltzer.

Barry, F. R. (1923). *Christianity and psychology: Lectures toward an introduction.* New York: George H. Doran. (Student Christian Movement, 1923)

Bartley, W. W. (1978). *Werner Erhard—The transformation of a man; the founding of est.* New York: Clarkson N. Potter.

Bayat, M., & Jamnia, M. A. (1994). *Tales from the land of the Sufis.* Boston: Shambala.

Beecher, C. E. (1831). *The elements of mental and moral philosophy, founded upon experience, reason, and the Bible.* Hartford, CT: [No publisher listed].

Beit-Hallahmi, B. (1977). Curiosity, doubt and devotion: The beliefs of psychologists and the psychology of religion. In H. N. Malony (Ed.), *Current per-*

spectives in the psychology of religion (pp. 381–391). Grand Rapids, MI: Eerdmans.

Beit-Hallahmi, B. (1978). Psychoanalysis and religion: A bibliography. Norwood, PA: Norwood Editions.

Benner, D. G. (Ed.). (1985). Christian therapy. Special issue of Journal of Psychology and Christianity, 4(2).

Benner, D. G. (Ed.). (1987). Psychotherapy in Christian perspective. Grand Rapids, MI: Baker.

Bennett, J. G. (1964). A spiritual psychology. London: Hodder & Stoughton.

Bertocci, P. A. (1958). Religion as creative insecurity. New York: Association Press.

Bethesda's heritage. (1982). Unpublished report of task force to the board of trustees. Denver, CO: Bethesda Hospital Association.

Biddle, W. E. (1955). Integration of religion and psychiatry. New York: Macmillan.

Boisen, A. T. (1936). The exploration of the inner world. A study of mental disorder and religious experience. Chicago: Willet Clark.

Boisen, A. T. (1955). Religion in crisis and custom: A sociological and psychological study. New York: Harper.

Boisen, A. T. (1960). Out of the depths: An autobiographical study of mental disorder and religious experience. New York: Harper.

Bookstaber, P. D. (1950). The idea of the development of the soul in medieval Jewish philosophy. Philadelphia: Maurice Jacobs.

Boorstein, S. (1980). Transpersonal psychotherapy. Palo Alto, CA: Science & Behavior.

Boring, E. G. (1929). A history of experimental psychology. New York: Century.

Boring, E. G. (Ed.). (1945). Psychology for the fighting man. Washington, DC: Infantry Journal.

Boudreaux, F. J. (1873). God our father. New York: Catholic Publications Society.

Bregman, L. (1986). Through the landscape of faith. Philadelphia: Westminster.

Bregman, L. (1992). Death in the midst of life: Perspectives on death from Christianity and depth psychology. Grand Rapids, MI: Baker.

Brennan, R. E. (1941). Thomistic psychology: A philosophic analysis of the nature of man. New York: Macmillan.

Brennan, R. E. (1945). History of psychology from the standpoint of a Thomist. New York: MacMillan.

Brett, G. S. (1912–1921). A history of psychology (3 vols.). London: Allen & Unwin.

Brigham, A. (1835). Observations on the influence of religion upon the health and physical welfare of mankind. Boston: Marsh, Capen & Lyon.

Brinton, D. G. (1876). The religious sentiment, its source and aim; a contribution to the science and philosophy of religion. New York: Holt.

Brown, W. (1929). Science and personality. London: Oxford University Press.

Brown, W. (1946). *Personality and religion*. London: University of London.

Browning, D. S. (1973). *Generative man: Psychoanalytic perspectives*. Philadelphia: Westminster.

Browning, D. S. (1982, February). Cited in *Person, Culture, and Religion, 5*(1), 2.

Browning, D. S. (1986). *Religious thought and the modern psychologies: A critical conversation in the theology of culture*. Philadelphia: Fortress.

Brunner, E. (1943). *The divine–human encounter* (A. W. Loos, Trans.). Philadelphia, PA: Westminster Press. (Original work published 1938)

Buber, M. (1937). *I and thou* (R. G. Smith, Trans.). Edinburgh, Scotland: T & T Clark. (Original work published 1922)

Bulka, R. P. (Ed.). (1979a). *Mystics and medics: A comparison of mystical and psychotherapeutic encounters*. New York: Human Sciences.

Bulka, R. P. (1979b). *The quest for ultimate meaning: Principles and applications of logotherapy*. New York: Philosophical Library.

Byrnes, J. F. (1984). *The psychology of religion*. New York: Free Press.

Cabot, R. C. (1908). The American type of psycho-therapy. Psychotherapy: A Course of Reading in Sound Psychology. *Sound Medicine and Sound Religion, 1*(1), 5–12.

Caligor, L., & May, R. (1968). *Dreams and symbols: Man's unconscious language*. New York: Basic Books.

Campbell, J. (Ed.). (1970). *Myths, dreams, and religion*. New York: Dutton.

Capps, D. (Ed.). (1992). *The depleted self: Sin in a narcissistic age*. Minneapolis: Fortress.

Capps, D., & Capps, W. H. (Eds.). (1970). *The religious personality*. Belmont, CA: Wadsworth.

Capps, D., Capps, W. H., & Bradford, G. (Eds.). (1977). *Encounter with Erikson: Historical interpretation and religious biography*. Missoula, MT: Scholars.

Capps, D., & Fenn, R. K. (Eds.). (1992). *The endangered self: Readings bearing on the endangered self in modern society*. Princeton, NJ: Princeton Theological Seminary.

Capps, D., Rambo, L., & Ransohoff, P. (Eds.). (1976). *Psychology of religion: A guide to information sources*. Detroit, MI: Gale Research.

Carter, J. D., & Narramore, B. (1979). *The integration of psychology and theology*. Grand Rapids, MI: Zondervan.

Caruso, I. (1964). *Existential psychology: From analysis to synthesis* (E. Krapf, Trans.). New York: Herder & Herder. (Original work published 1952)

Castaneda, C. (1968). *The teachings of Don Juan: A Yaqui way of knowledge*. Berkeley: University of California.

Castaneda, C. (1987). *The eagle's gift*. New York: Washington Square.

Chambers, O. (1900). *Biblical psychology: A series of preliminary studies* (2nd ed.). London: Simpkin Marshall.

Child, I. L., & Van de Water, M. (Eds.). (1945). *Psychology for the returning serviceman*. Washington, DC: Infantry Journal.

Clark, D. L. (1989). Theory of personality, illness and cure found in the writings of Agnes Sanford and those acknowledging her influence. *Journal of Psychology and Theology, 17*, 236–244.

Clark, W. H. (1965). Depth and rationality in Augustine's Confessions. *Journal for the Scientific Study of Religion, 5*, 144–148.

Clebsch, W. A., & Jaekle, C. R. (1964). *Pastoral care in historical perspective: An essay with exhibits*. Englewood Cliffs, NJ: Prentice-Hall.

Clift, J. D., & Clift, W. B. (1984). *Symbols of transformation in dreams*. New York: Crossroad.

Clift, J. D., & Clift, W. B. (1988). *The hero journey in dreams*. New York: Crossroad.

Clift, W. B. (1982). *Jung and Christianity: The challenge of reconciliation*. New York: Crossroad.

Collins, G. R. (1973). *The Christian psychology of Paul Tournier*. Grand Rapids, MI: Baker.

Collins, G. R. (1977). *The rebuilding of psychology: An integration of psychology and Christianity*. Wheaton, IL: Tyndale House.

Common Boundary to offer dissertation/thesis award. (1989). *Psychologists Interested in Religious Issues Newsletter, 14*(4), 9.

Daim, W. (1963). *Depth psychology and salvation* (K. F. Reinhardt, Trans.). New York: Ungar. (Original work published 1954)

de Forest, I. (1954). *The leaven of love: A development of the psychoanalytic theory and technique of Sandor Ferenczi*. New York: Harper.

Delitzsch, F. J. (1867). *A system of biblical psychology*. (R. E. Wallis, Trans.). Edinburgh, Scotland: T & T Clark. (Original work published 1855)

Demetrios, P. E., Simpkinson, C. H., & Bennet, C. (Eds.). (1991). *The Common Boundary graduate education guide*. Bethesda, MD: Common Boundary.

Dempsey, P. J. R. (1956). *Freud, psychoanalysis, Catholicism*. Chicago: Regnery.

Dessoir, M. (1912). *Outlines of the history of psychology* (D. Fisher, Trans.). New York: Macmillan. (Original work published 1911)

A directory of religious psychotherapists. (1954). *Journal of Psychotherapy as a Religious Process, 1*, 92–93.

Dittes, J. E. (1965). Continuities between the life and thought of Augustine. *Journal for the Scientific Study of Religion, 5*, 130–140.

Driesch, H. A. E. (1926). *The crisis in psychology*. Princeton, NJ: Princeton University Press.

Ducker, E. N. (1961). *A Christian therapy for a neurotic world*. London: Allen & Unwin.

Ducker, E. N. (1964). *Psychotherapy: A Christian approach*. London: Allen & Unwin.

Dunlap, K. (1946). *Religion: Its function in human life, a study of religion from the point of view of psychology.* New York: McGraw Hill.

Dunlap, K., & Gill, D. S. (1933). *The dramatic personality of Jesus.* Baltimore: William & Wilkins.

Eliade, M. (1970). *Shamanism: Archaic techniques of ecstacy.* Princeton, NJ: Princeton University Press.

Fadiman, J. (1980). The transpersonal stance. In R. N. Walsh & F. Vaughan (Eds.), *Beyond ego: Transpersonal dimensions in psychology* (pp. 15–53). Los Angeles: J. P. Tarcher.

Fay, R. W. (1939). *American psychology before William James.* New Brunswick, NJ: Rutgers University Press.

Fenn, R. K., & Capps, D. (Eds.). (1992). *The endangered self.* Princeton, NJ: Princeton Theological Seminary.

Fleck, J. R., & Carter, J. D. (Eds.). (1981). *Psychology and Christianity: Integrative readings.* Nashville, TN: Abingdon.

Fleming, A. (1990). Psychology, medicine, and religion: Early twentieth-century American psychotherapy (1905-1909). *Dissertation Abstracts International, 50*-11B, 5313. (University Microfilms No. DEX-90-08-537)

Foster, J. D., & Ledbetter, M. F. (1987). Christian anti-psychology and the scientific method. *Journal of Psychology and Theology, 15,* 10–18.

Fowler, O. S. (1843). *The Christian phrenologist: Or, the natural theology and moral bearings of phrenology.* Cazenovia, NY: Author.

Frankl, V. E. (1955). *The doctor and the soul: An introduction to logotherapy* (R. Winston & C. Winston, Trans.). New York: Knopf. (Original work published 1946)

Frankl, V. E. (1959). *From death-camp to existentialism: A psychiatrist's path to a new therapy* (I. Lasch, Trans.). Boston: Beacon. (Original work published 1946)

Frankl, V. E. (1965). *The doctor and the soul: From psychotherapy to logotherapy* (2nd ed., R. Winston & C. Winston, Trans.). New York: Knopf.

Frankl, V. E. (1975). *The unconscious god: Psychotherapy and theology.* New York: Simon & Schuster. (Original work published 1948)

Franz, M.-L., von. (1986). *On dreams and death: A Jungian interpretation.* Boston: Shambala.

Freeman, R. S., & Freeman, H. A. (1964). *Counseling: A bibliography (with annotations).* New York: Scarecrow.

Freud, S. (1918). *Totem and taboo; resemblances between the psychic lives of savages and neurotics* (A. A. Brill, Trans.). New York: Moffat, Yard. (Original work published 1913)

Freud, S. (1928). *The future of an illusion* (W. D. Robson-Scott, Trans.). London: Hogarth. (Original work published 1927)

Freud, S. (1939). *Moses and monotheism* (K. Jones, Trans.). New York: Knopf.

Freud, S., & Pfister, O. (1963). In H. Meng & E. L. Freud (Eds.), *Psychoanalysis and faith: The letters of Sigmund Freud and Oskar Pfister* (E. Mosbacher, Trans.). London: Hogarth.

Friedman, E. H. (1990). *Friedman's fables.* New York: Guilford.

Fromm, E. (1941). *Escape from freedom.* New York: Farrar & Rinehart.

Fromm, E. (1950). *Psychoanalysis and religion.* New Haven, CT: Yale University Press.

Fromm, E. (1951). *The forgotten language: An introduction to the understanding of dreams, fairy tales, and myths.* New York: Grove.

Fromm, E. (1963). *The dogma of Christ and other essays on religion, psychology and culture* (J. L. Adams, Trans.). (Original work published 1931)

Gemelii, A. (1955). *Psychoanalysis today* (J. S. Chapin & Attanasio, Trans.). New York: P. J. Kenedy. (Original work published 1953)

Gifford, S. (1978). Medical psychotherapy and the Emmanuel Movement in Boston. In G. E. Gifford (Ed.), *Psychoanalysis, psychotherapy, and the New England medical scene, 1894–1944* (pp. 106–111). New York: Science History Publications/USA.

Glasser, W. (1965). *Reality therapy: A new approach to psychiatry.* New York: Harper & Row.

Goldbrunner, J. (1955a). *Holiness is wholeness* (S. Godman, Trans.). New York: Pantheon. (Original work published 1946)

Goldbrunner, J. (1955b). *Individualism: A study of the depth psychology of Carl Gustav Jung.* London: Hollis & Carter. (Original work published 1949)

Goldbrunner, J. (1958). *Cure of mind and cure of soul.* (S. Godman, Trans.). New York: Pantheon. (Original work published 1954)

Gorsuch, R. L., & Spilka, B. (1987). The varieties in historical and contemporary contexts. *Contemporary Psychology, 32,* 773–778.

Gregory, M. (1939). *Psychotherapy scientific and religious.* London: Macmillan.

Griffin, G. E. E. (1990). Will therapy: Postmodernity and the task of self-creation in the philosophy of Otto Rank. *Dissertation Abstracts International, 51*(2), 985. (University Microfilms No. DEX-90-08-538).

Grof, S. (1976). *Realms of the human unconscious.* New York: Dutton.

Grof, S. (1985). *Beyond the brain: Birth, death, and transcendence in psychotherapy.* Albany: State University of New York.

Grof, S., & Halifax, J. (1977). *The human encounter with death.* New York: Dutton.

Grollman, E. A. (1965). *Judaism in Sigmund Freud's world.* New York: Appleton-Century-Crofts.

Guntrip, H. H. J. S. (1957). *Psychotherapy and religion: The constructive use of inner conflict.* New York: Harper. (Original work published 1956)

Gurnee, H. (1936). *Elements of social psychology.* New York: Farrar & Rinehart.

Gyaltshan, Y. (1980). *Mind in Buddhist psychology* (H. V. Guenther & L. Kawamura, Trans.). Berkeley, CA: Dharma.

Hartshorne, H., & May, M. A. (1928). *Studies in deceit* (2 vols.). New York: Macmillan.

Hartshorne, H., & May, M. A., & Maller, J. B. (1929). *Studies in service and self-control.* New York: Macmillan.

Hartshorne, H., May, M. A., & Shuttleworth, F. K. (1930). *Studies in the organization of character.* New York: Macmillan.

Havens, J. (1964). *Psychology.* New York: Faculty Christian Fellowship.

Havens, J. (1965). Notes on Augustine's Confessions. *Journal for the Scientific Study of Religions, 5,* 141–143.

Havens, J. (Ed.). (1968). *Psychology and religion: A contemporary dialogue.* Princeton, NJ: Van Nostrand.

Heie, H., & Wolfe, D. L. (Eds.). (1987). *The reality of Christian learning.* Grand Rapids, MI: Christian University/Eerdmans.

Hillman, J. (1979). *The dream and the underworld.* New York: Harper & Row.

Hiltner, S. (1972). *Theological dynamics.* Nashville, TN: Abingdon.

Hirsch, W. (1947). *Rabbinic psychology: Beliefs about the soul in rabbinic literature of the Talmudic period.* London: Edward Goldston.

Hixon, L. (1989). *Coming home: The experience of enlightenment in sacred traditions.* Los Angeles: J. P. Tarcher.

Hoffman, E. (1981). *The way of splendor: Jewish mysticism and modern psychology.* Boulder, CO: Shambhala.

Holifield, E. B. (1983). *A history of pastoral care in America: From salvation to self-realization.* Nashville, TN: Abingdon.

Homans, P. (Ed.). (1968). *The dialogue between theology and psychology.* Chicago: University of Chicago.

Homans, P. (1970). *Theology after Freud: An interpretive inquiry.* New York: Bobbs-Merrill.

Homans, P. (1979). *Jung in context: Modernity and the making of a psychology.* Chicago: University of Chicago.

Homans, P. (1987). Psychology and religion movement. In M. Eliade (Ed.), *Encyclopedia of Religion* (Vol. 12, pp. 66–75). New York: Macmillan.

Horton, W. M. (1931). *A psychological approach to theology.* New York: Harper.

Hostie, R. (1957). *Religion and the psychology of Jung* (G. R. Lamb, Trans.). New York: Sheed & Ward. (Original work published 1954)

Houde, K. A. (1988). *The treatment of religion in personality textbooks: Fifty years after Allport.* Unpublished manuscript, Fuller Theological Seminary, Pasadena, CA.

Houde, K. A. (1990). The Christian personality theory of Paul Tournier. *Dissertation Abstracts International, 51*(07B), 3603. (University Microfilms No. DEY-90-33-538)

Houselander, F. C. (1951). *Guilt.* New York: Sheed & Ward.

Howard, G. (1991). Culture tales: A narrative approach to thinking, cross-cultural psychology, and psychotherapy. *American Psychologist, 46,* 187–197.

Hunt, R. A., Hinkle, J. E., & Malony, H. N. (Eds.). (1990). *Clergy assessment and career development.* Nashville, TN: Abingdon.

Ingalls, W. (1839). *A lecture on the subject of phrenology not opposed to the principles of religion; nor the precepts of Christianity.* Boston: Dutton and Wentworth.

Jacobi, Y. (1967). *The way of individuation* (R. F. C. Hull, Trans.). New York: Harcourt, Brace & World. (Original work published 1965)

Jahn, E., & Adler, A. (1933). *Religion and Individualpsychologie. Eine prinzipielle Auseinandersetzung über Menschenführung* [Religion and individual psychology: A fundamental analysis of human conduct]. Vienna: R. Passer.

James, W. (1902). *The varieties of religious experience.* New York: Longmans, Green.

Jeeves, M. (1995, January). *Psychology and Christianity: Partners in understanding human nature.* Lectures presented at the Fuller Symposium on the Integration of Faith and Psychology, Pasadena, CA.

Jewett, P. K. (1991). *God, creation, and revelation: A neo-evangelical theology.* Grand Rapids, MI: Eerdmans.

Johnson, D. (1990). The contributions of Fritz Künkel to the development of a religious psychology. *Dissertation Abstracts International, 51*(05B), 2624. (University Microfilms No. DEX-90-26-682)

Johnson, P. E. (1945). *Psychology of religion.* New York: Abingdon-Cokesbury.

Johnson, P. E. (1957). *Personality and religion.* New York: Abingdon.

Jones, S. L. (1986). *Psychology and the Christian faith: An introductory reader.* Grand Rapids, MI: Baker.

Jones, S. L. (Ed.). (1992). The Rech conference on Christian graduate training in psychology. *Journal of Psychology and Theology, 20,* 1–146.

Jones, S. L., & Butman, R. (1991). *Modern psychotherapies: A comprehensive Christian appraisal.* Downer's Grove, IL: Intervarsity.

Jung, C. G. (1933). *Modern man in search of a soul* (W. S. Dell & C. F. Baynes, Trans.). New York: Harcourt, Brace & World. (Original work published 1931)

Jung, C. G. (1938). *Psychology and religion.* London: Oxford University Press.

Jung, C. G. (1958). *Psychology and religion: West and east.* (R. F. C. Hull, Trans.). New York: Pantheon.

Jung, C. G. (1974). *Dreams.* (R. F. C. Hull, Trans.). Princeton, NJ: Princeton University Press.

Kehler, L. (1966). The Psychiatric Centers. *Mennonite Life, 21*(4), 167–181.

Kelly, B. N. (1981). Inventing psychology's past: E. G. Boring's historiography in relation to the psychology of his time. *The Journal of Mind and Behavior, 2,* 229–241B.

Kelsey, M. T. (1974). *God, dreams, and revelation: A Christian interpretation of dreams.* Minneapolis, MN: Augsburg.

Kemp, C. F. (1947). *Physicians of the soul: A history of pastoral counseling.* New York: Macmillan.

Kierkegaard, S. (1941). *The sickness unto death: A Christian psychological exposition for edification and awakening* (W. Lowrie, Trans.). Princeton, NJ: Princeton University Press. (Original work published 1849)

Kierkegaard, S. (1944). *The concept of dread: A simple deliberation along psychological lines in the direction of the dogmatic problem of original sin* (W. Lowrie, Trans.). Princeton, NJ: Princeton University Press. (Original work published 1844)

Kirkpatrick, L. A., & Spilka, B. (1989, August). *A review and analysis of past and current trends.* Paper presented at the annual meeting of the American Psychological Association, New Orleans, LA.

Klass, D. (1988). *Parental grief: Solace and resolution.* New York: Springer.

Klein, D. B. (1944). *Mental hygiene: The psychology of personal adjustment.* New York: Holt.

Klein, D. B. (1970). *A history of scientific psychology: Its origins and philosophical backgrounds.* New York: Basic Books.

Koch, S., & Leary, D. E. (Eds.). (1985). *A century of psychology as science.* New York: McGraw-Hill.

Kramer, K. (1993). *Death dreams: Unveiling mysteries of the unconscious mind.* Mahwah, NJ: Paulist.

Krippner, S. (Ed.). (1977–1990). *Advances in parapsychological research.* New York: Plenum.

Krippner, S. (Ed.). (1978). *Extrasensory perception.* New York: Plenum.

Krippner, S. (Ed.). (1990). *Dreamtime and dreamwork: Decoding the language of the night.* Los Angeles: J. P. Tarcher.

Krippner, S., & Dillard, J. (1988). *Dreamworking: Using your dreams for creative problem-solving.* Buffalo, NY: Bearly.

Kuhn, T. (1962). *The structure of scientific revolutions.* Chicago: University of Chicago.

Künkel, F. (1954). The integration of religion and psychology. *Journal of Psychotherapy as a Religious Process, 1,* 1–11.

Laing, R. D. (1969). *The politics of the family and other essays.* New York: Pantheon.

Lake, F. (1966). *Clinical theology: A theological and psychological basis to clinical pastoral care.* London: Darton, Longman & Todd.

Lake, F. (1987). *Clinical theology: A theological and psychological basis to clinical pastoral care* (M. H. Yeomans, Abridg.). New York: Crossroad.

Lapointe, F. H. (1970). Origins and evolution of the term "psychology." *American Psychologist, 25,* 640–646.

Leahey, T. H. (1987). *A history of psychology: Main currents in psychological thought* (2nd ed.). Englewood Cliffs, NJ: Prentice-Hall.

Lee, D. J. (1993). *Storying ourselves: A narrative perspective on Christians in psychology.* Grand Rapids, MI: Baker.

Lehr, E., & Spilka, B. (1989). Religion in the introductory psychology textbook: A comparison of three decades. *Journal for the Scientific Study of Religion, 28,* 366–371.

Leslie, R. C. (1965). *Jesus and logotherapy: The ministry of Jesus as interpreted through the psychotherapy of Viktor Frankl.* New York: Abingdon.

Letters from European psychotherapists. (1954). *Journal of Psychotherapy as a Religious Process, 1,* 87–91.

Levicoff, S. (1993a). *Name it and frame it; New opportunities in adult education and how to avoid being ripped off by "Christian" degree mills* (3rd. rev. ed.). Ambler, PA: Institute on Religion and Law.

Levicoff, S. (1993b). The final word. *Christian Counseling Today, 1*(4), 58.

Lichstein, K. L. (1988). *Clinical relaxation strategies.* New York: Wiley-Interscience.

Liebman, J. L. (1948). *Psychiatry and religion.* Boston: Beacon.

Ligon, E. M. (1935). *The psychology of Christian personality.* New York: Macmillan.

Ligon, E. M. (1939). *Their future is now; the growth and development of Christian personality.* New York: Macmillan.

Lindworsky, J. (1936). *The psychology of asceticism* (E. A. Heiring, Trans.). London: Edwards. (Original work published 1935)

Little, L. C. (1962). *Research in personality, character and religious education: Bibliography of American doctoral dissertations, 1885-1959.* Pittsburgh, PA: University of Pittsburgh.

Lovinger, R. J. (1984). *Working with religious issues in psychotherapy.* Northvale, NJ: Jason Aronson.

Lovinger, R. J. (1990). *Religion and counseling: The psychological impact of religious belief.* New York: Continuum.

MacLeod, R. B. (1952). Experimental psychology. In H. N. Fairchild, A. R. Bellinger, et al. (Eds.), *Religious perspectives in college teaching* (pp. 262–285). New York: Ronald. Also published separately by the Edward W. Hazen Foundation, n.d.

MacMurray, J. (1936). *The structure of religious experience.* London: Faber & Faber.

MacMurray, J. (1957). *The form of the personal. Vol. 1. Self as agent.* London: Faber & Faber.

MacMurray, J. (1961). *The form of the personal. Vol. 2. Persons in relation.* London: Faber & Faber.

Maeder, A. (1953). *Ways to psychic health: Brief therapy from the practice of a psychiatrist* (T. Lit, Trans.). London: Hodder & Stoughton. (Original work published 1945)

The man of the month: Fritz Künkel. (1953). *Pastoral Psychology, 4*(33), 8.

The man of the month: Gordon Allport. (1955). *Pastoral Psychology, 6*(52), 59.

Maslow, A. H. (1964). *Religions, values and peak-experiences.* Columbus: Ohio State University.

Maslow, A. H. (1968). *Toward a psychology of being* (2nd ed.). New York: Van Nostrand Reinhold.

Maslow, A. H. (1969). The farther reaches of human nature. *Journal of Transpersonal Psychology, 1,* 2–10.

Maslow, A. H., & Mittlemann, B. (1941). *Principles of abnormal psychology.* New York: Harper.

Maudsley, H. (1886). *Natural causes and supernatural seemings.* London: Kegan Paul, Trench.

May, G. (1982a). *Will and spirit: A contemplative psychology.* San Francisco: Harper & Row.

May, G. (1982b). *Care of mind/care of spirit: Psychiatric dimensions of spiritual direction.* New York: Harper & Row.

May, R. (1940). *The springs of creative living: A study of human nature and God.* New York: Abingdon-Cokesbury.

May, R. (1950). *The meaning of anxiety.* New York: Ronald.

May, R. (1953). *Man's search for himself.* New York: Norton.

McDougall, W. (1911). *Body and mind: A history and defense of animism.* New York: Macmillan.

McDougall, W. (1934). *Religion and the sciences of life, with other essays on allied topics.* London: Methuen.

McNeill, J. T. (1951). *A history of the cure of souls.* New York: Harper.

Meier, L. (1988). *Jewish values in psychotherapy: Essays on vital issues on the search for meaning.* Lanham, MD: University Press of America.

Meier, L. (1991). *Jewish values in Jungian psychology.* Lanham, MD: University Press of America.

Meier, P. D., Minirth, F. B., & Ratcliff, D. E. (1992). *Bruised and broken: Understanding and healing psychological problems.* Grand Rapids, MI: Baker.

Meier, P. D., Minirth, F. B., & Wichern, F. B. (1982). *Introduction to psychology and counseling: Christian perspectives and applications.* Grand Rapids, MI: Baker.

Meissner, W. W. (1961). *Annotated bibliography in religion and psychology.* New York: The Academy of Religion and Mental Health.

Mental Healing. (1910). In A. L. Guthrie (Ed.), *The Reader's Guide to Periodical Literature, 1905-1909* (p. 1446). Minneapolis, MN: H. W. Wilson.

Mental Healing. (1915). In A. L. Guthrie & M. A. Knight (Eds.), *The Reader's Guide to Periodical Literature, 1910-1914* (p. 1649). White Plains, NY: H. W. Wilson.

Mercier, D. F. F. J. (1918). *The origins of contemporary psychology* (W. H. Mitchell, Trans.). New York: P. J. Kenedy. (Original work published 1897)

Meseguér, P. (1960). *The secret of dreams* (P. Burns, Trans.). London: Burns and Oates.

Michaelsen, R. R. (1977). Constitutions, courts and the study of religion. *Journal of the American Academy of Religion, 45,* 291–308.

Miller, W. R., & Martin, J. E. (1988). *Behavior therapy and religion.* Newbury Park, CA: Sage.

Minuchin, S. (1984). *Family kaleidoscope.* Cambridge, MA: Harvard University Press.

Misiak, H., & Staudt, V. (1954). *Catholics in psychology: A historical survey.* New York: McGraw-Hill.

Moore, R. L. (Ed.). (1988). *Carl Jung and Christian spirituality.* New York: Paulist.

Moore, R. V. (1948). *The driving forces of human nature and their adjustment; an introduction to the psychology and psychopathology of emotional behavior and volitional control.* New York: Grune & Stratton.

Morgan, C. L. (1925). *Life, mind, and spirit.* New York: Holt.

Morgan, J. (1932). *The psychological teaching of St. Augustine.* London: E. Stock.

Mounier, E. (1938). *A personalist manifesto* (Monks of St. John's Abbey, Trans.). New York: Longmans, Green. (Original work published 1936)

Mounier, E. (1956). *The character of man* (C. Rowland, Trans.). London: Rocklift. (Original work published 1946)

Mowrer, O. H. (1961). *The crisis in psychiatry and religion.* Princeton, NJ: Van Nostrand Insight.

Mowrer, O. H. (1964). *The new group therapy.* Princeton, NJ: Van Nostrand.

Mowrer, O. H. (1966). *Abnormal reactions or actions? (An autobiographical answer).* Dubuque, IA: William C. Brown.

Müller, F. M. (1893). *Theosophy: Or, psychological religion; the Gifford lectures delivered before the university of Glasgow in 1892.* London: Longmans, Green.

Müller-Freienfels, R. (1935). *The evolution of modern psychology* (W. B. Wolfe, Trans.). New Haven, CT: Yale University Press.

Murray, J. A. C. (1938). *An introduction to a Christian psycho-therapy.* New York: Scribner.

Myers, D. G., & Jeeves, M. A. (1987). *Psychology through the eyes of faith.* New York: Harper & Row.

Naranjo, C., & Ornstein, R. E. (1971). *On the psychology of meditation.* New York: Viking.

Neill, S. C. (1959). *A genuinely human existence: Towards a Christian psychology.* Garden City, NY: Doubleday.

Niehardt, J. G. (1961). *Black Elk speaks: Being the life story of a holy man of the Oglala Sioux.* Lincoln: University of Nebraska.

A New Direction Taken by the Emmanuel Movement. (1909). In *Psychotherapy, A Course of Reading in Sound Psychology, Sound Medicine, and Sound Religion, 1*(3), 4.

Novek, S. (Ed.). (1956). *Judaism and psychiatry: Two approaches to the personal problems and needs of modern man.* New York: National Academy for Adult Jewish Studies of the United Synagogue of America.

Nuttin, J. (1962). *Psychoanalysis and personality: A dynamic theory of normal personality.* (G. Lamb, Trans.). New York: New American Library. (Original work published 1950)

O'Donnell, J. M. (1979). The crisis of experimentalism in the 1920s: E. G. Boring and his uses of history. *American Psychologist, 34,* 289–295.

Ornstein, R. E. (1972). *The psychology of consciousness.* New York: Viking.

Ornstein, R. E. (Ed.). (1973). *The nature of human consciousness: A book of readings.* San Francisco: Freeman.

Ostow, M. (1981). *Judaism and psychoanalysis.* New York: KTAV.

Paine, M. (1872). *Physiology of the soul and instinct as distinguished from materialism; with supplementary demonstrations of the divine communication of the narratives of creation and the flood.* New York: Harper.

Peaston, M. (1972). *Personal living: An introduction to Paul Tournier.* New York: Harper & Row.

Peck, M. S. (1978). *The road less traveled: A new psychology of love, traditional values and spiritual growth.* New York: Simon & Schuster.

Peck, M. S. (1983). *People of the lie.* New York: Simon & Schuster.

Pfister, O. (1948). *Christianity and fear: A study in history and in the psychology and hygiene of religion* (W. H. Johnston, Trans.). London: Allen & Unwin. (Original work published 1944)

Philipchalk, R. P. (1987). *Psychology and Christianity: An introduction to controversial issues.* Lanham, MD: University Press of America.

Pierpont, J. (1850). *Phrenology and the scriptures.* New York: Fowler and Wells.

Polanyi, M. (1958). *Personal knowledge.* Chicago: University of Chicago.

Porter, N. (1868). *The human intellect, with an introduction upon psychology and the soul.* New York: Scribner.

Pratt, J. B. (1922). *Matter and spirit: A study of mind and body in their relation to the spiritual life.* New York: Macmillan.

Progoff, I. (1956). *The death and rebirth of psychology: An integrative evaluation of Freud, Adler, Jung and Rank and the impact of their culminating insights on modern man.* New York: Julian.

Propst, L. R. (1988). *Psychotherapy within a religious framework: Spirituality in the emotional healing process.* New York: Human Sciences.

Pruyser, P. W. (1966). Psychological examination: Augustine. *Journal for the Scientific Study of Religion, 5,* 284–289.

Pruyser, P. W. (1968). *A dynamic psychology of religion.* New York: Harper & Row.

Pruyser, P. W. (1974). *Between belief and unbelief.* New York: Harper & Row.

Psychological Studies Institute. (1993). *Graduate catalog 1994/1995.* Atlanta: Author.

Psycho-therapeutic. (1933). *The Oxford English Dictionary* (Vol. 8; p. 22). Oxford, England: Clarendon.

Pym, T. W. (1922). *Psychology and the Christian life*. New York: George H. Doran. (Student Christian Movement, 1921)

Pym, T. W. (1925). *More psychology and the Christian life*. New York: George H. Doran. (Student Christian Movement, 1925)

Ram Dass. (1975). *The only dance there is*. New York: Doubleday.

Ram Dass. (1977). *Grist for the mill*. Santa Cruz, CA: Unity.

Ram Dass. (1978). *Journal of awakening: The meditator's guidebook*. New York: Doubleday.

Rambo, L. R. (1980). Reflections on the task of integration. *Journal of Psychology and Theology, 8*, 64–71.

Rambo, L. R. (1983). *The divorcing Christian*. Nashville, TN: Abingdon.

Ramul, K. (1960). The problem of measurement in the psychology of the eighteenth century. *American Psychologist, 15*, 256–265.

Rank, O. (1941). *Beyond psychology*. New York: Dover.

Rank, O. (1950). *Psychology and the soul* (W. D. Turner, Trans.). Philadelphia: University of Pennsylvania Press. (Original work published 1930)

Rauch, F. A. (1840). *Psychology; or, A view of the human soul: Including anthropology*. New York: Dodd.

Reich, W. (1972). *Character analysis* (3rd ed.; V. R. Carfagno, Trans.). New York: Farrar, Straus & Giroux. (Original work published 1933)

Reik, T. (1931). *The ritual: Psychoanalytic studies* (B. Douglas, Trans.). New York: Norton. (Original work published 1919)

Reik, T. (1951). *Dogma and compulsion: Psychoanalytic studies of myths and religions* (B. Miall, Trans.). New York: International Universities Press. (Original work published 1927)

Reik, T. (1957). *Myth and guilt: The crime and punishment of mankind*. New York: George Braziller.

Reik, T. (1959). *Mystery on the mountain: The drama of the Sinai revelation*. New York: Harper.

Reik, T. (1960). *The creation of woman: A psychoanalytic inquiry into the myth of Eve*. New York: George Braziller.

Reik, T. (1961). *The temptation*. New York: George Braziller.

Rickel, W. (1954). Editorial. *Journal of Psychotherapy as a Religious Process, 1*, 1–2, 97.

Ring, K. (1980). *Life at death*. New York: Coward, McCann & Geoghegan.

Roback, A. A. (1952). *History of American psychology*. New York: Library.

Robinson, D. N. (1976). *An intellectual history of psychology*. New York: Macmillan.

Rokeach, M. (1964). *The three Christs of Ypsilanti: A narrative study of three lost men*. New York: Knopf.

Rosen, S. (1982). *My voice will go with you: The teaching tales of Milton H. Erickson, M.D.* New York: Norton.

Rowan, J. (1992). *Transpersonal psychotherapy and counseling.* New York: Routledge, Chapman & Hall.

Ruble, R. (1985). How introductory psychology textbooks treat religion. *Journal of the American Scientific Affiliation, 37,* 180–183.

Rudin, J. (1968). *Psychotherapy and religion* (E. Reinecke & P. Bailey, Trans.). Notre Dame, IN: University of Notre Dame. (Original work published 1960)

Runestam, A. (1958). *Psychoanalysis and Christianity* (O. Winfield, Trans.). Rock Island, IL: Augustana. (Original work published 1930)

Sanford, J. A. (1968). *Dreams: God's forgotten language.* Philadelphia: Lippincott.

Savary, L. M., Berne, P. H., & Williams, S. K. (1984). *Dreams and spiritual growth: A Christian approach to dreamwork. With more than 35 dreamwork techniques.* New York: Paulist.

Scarborough, E. (1992). Mrs. Ricord and psychology for women, circa 1840. *American Psychologist, 47,* 274–280.

Schaer, H. (1950). *Religion and the cure of souls in Jung's psychology* (R. F. C. Hull, Trans.). New York: Pantheon. (Original work published 1946)

Schmitt, A. (1984). *Before I wake: Listening to God in your dreams.* Nashville, TN: Abingdon.

Schuller, D. S., Brekke, M., Strommen, M., & Aleshire, D. O. (1976). *Readiness for ministry: Vol. 2. Assessment.* Vandalia, OH: Association of Theological Schools in the United States and Canada.

Schuller, D. S., Strommen, M. P., & Brekke, M. L. (Eds.). (1975). *Readiness for ministry: Vol. 1. Criteria.* Vandalia, OH: Association of Theological Schools in the United States and Canada.

Schuller, D. S., Strommen, M. P., & Brekke, M. L. (Eds.). (1980). *Ministry in America.* New York: Harper & Row.

Segaller, S., & Berger, M. (1989). *The wisdom of the dream: The world of C. G. Jung.* Boston: Shambhala.

Shafranske, E. (1989, August). *The treatment of religion in clinical psychology textbooks.* Paper presented at the annual meeting of the American Psychological Association, New Orleans, LA.

Sharman, H. B. (1917). Records of the life of Jesus. New York: Association.

Sheikh, A. A., & Sheikh, K. S. (Eds.). (1989). *Eastern and Western approaches to healing: Ancient wisdom & modern knowledge.* New York: Wiley-Interscience.

Sheldon, W. H. (1936). *Psychology and the Promethean will: A constructive study of the acute common problem of education, medicine, and religion.* New York: Harper.

Silverstone, H. (1956). *Religion and psychiatry.* New York: Twayne.

Simpkinson, C. H. (1983). Psychiatrist Scott Peck on the road less traveled. *The Common Boundary Between Spirituality and Psychotherapy, 1*(4), 1–2.

Simpkinson, C. H. (1992). History of Common Boundary. *The changing face of Common Boundary.* Chevy Chase, MD: The Common Boundary.

Sinclair, U. (1962). *Mental radio* (Rev. ed.). Springfield, IL: Charles C Thomas.

Special issue. (1980). *Pine Rest Today, 3*(3), 1–8.

Spero, M. H. (1980). *Judaism and psychology: Halakhic perspectives.* New York: KTAV/Yeshiva University.

Spero, M. H. (1985). *Psychotherapy of the religious patient.* Springfield, IL: Charles C Thomas.

Spiegelman, J. M. (1993). *Judaism and Jungian psychology.* Lanham, MD: University Press of America.

Spilka, B., Amaro, A., Wright, G. L., & Davis, J. (1981, August). *The treatment of religion in current psychology texts.* Paper presented at the convention of the American Psychological Association, Los Angeles, CA.

Spilka, B., Comp, G., & Goldsmith, W. M. (1981). Faith and behavior: Religion in introductory psychology texts of the 1950s and 1970s. *Teaching of Psychology, 8,* 158–160.

Stagner, R. (1937). *Psychology of personality.* New York: McGraw-Hill.

Stern, K. (1954). *The third revolution: A study of psychiatry and religion.* New York: Harcourt, Brace.

Stout, G. F. (1931). *Mind and matter.* Cambridge, England: Cambridge University Press.

Stout, G. F. (1952). *God and nature.* Cambridge, England: Cambridge University Press.

Strachan, R. H. (1931). *The authority of Christian experience: A study in the basis of religious authority.* Nashville, TN: Cokesbury. (Student Christian Movement, 1929)

Stuart, G. C. (1938). *The achievement of personality in the light of psychology and religion.* London: Student Christian Movement.

Tan, S.-Y., & Jones, S. L. (1991). Christian graduate training in professional psychology: The Rech conference. *Journal of Psychology and Christianity, 10,* 72–75.

Tart, C. T. (Ed.). (1969). *Altered states of consciousness: A book of readings.* New York: Wiley.

Tart, C. T. (Ed.). (1975). *Transpersonal psychologies.* New York: Harper & Row.

Tart, C. T. (1992). *Transpersonal psychologies: Perspectives on the mind from seven great spiritual traditions.* San Francisco: HarperCollins.

Terruwe, A. A. A. (1959). *The priest and the sick in mind* (C. W. Baars & J. Aumann, Trans.). London: Burns & Oates. (Original work published 1955)

Tillich, P. (1952). *The courage to be.* New Haven, CT: Yale University Press.

Toulmin, S., & Leary, D. (1985). The cult of empiricism in psychology, and beyond. In S. Koch & D. E. Leary (Eds.), *A century of psychology as science* (pp. 594–617). New York: McGraw-Hill.

Tournier, P. (1957). *The meaning of persons* (E. Hudson, Trans.). New York: Harper. (Original work published 1955)

Tournier, P. (1960). *A doctor's casebook in the light of the Bible* (E. Hudson, Trans.). New York: Harper & Row. (Original work published 1951)

Tournier, P. (1963). *The strong and the weak* (E. Hudson, Trans.). Philadelphia: Westminster. (Original work published 1948)

Tournier, P. (1966). *The person reborn* (E. Hudson, Trans.). New York: Harper & Row. (Original work published 1944)

Tweedie, D. F., Jr. (1963). *The Christian and the couch: An introduction to logotherapy.* Grand Rapids, MI: Baker.

Twenty-year index. (1993, Fall). *Journal of Psychology and Theology.* La Mirada, CA: Rosemead Graduate School of Psychology.

Ulanov, A. B. (1971). *The feminine in Jungian psychology and in Christian theology.* Evanston, IL: Northwestern University Press.

Ulanov, A. G. (1981). *Receiving woman: Studies in the psychology and theology of the feminine.* Philadelphia: Westminster.

Ulanov, A. B. (1986). *Picturing God.* Boston: Cowley.

Ulanov, A., & Ulanov, B. (1975). *Religion and the unconscious.* Philadelphia: Westminster.

Ulanov, A., & Ulanov, B. (1982). *Primary speech: A psychology of prayer.* Atlanta: John Knox.

Ullman, M., & Krippner, S. (1989). *Dream telepathy: Experiments in nocturnal ESP* (2nd ed.). Jefferson, NC: McFarland.

Underhill, E. (1961). *Mysticism: A study in the nature and development of man's spiritual consciousness.* New York: Dutton. (Original work published 1911)

Ungersma, A. J. (1961). *The search for meaning: A new approach in psychotherapy and pastoral psychology.* Philadelphia: Westminster.

Valle, R. S. (1989). The emergence of transpersonal psychology. In R. S. Valle & S. Halling (Eds.), *Existential-phenomenological perspectives in psychology: Exploring the breadth of human experience. With a special section on transpersonal psychology* (pp. 257–268). New York: Plenum.

Vande Kemp, H. (1976). Teaching psychology/religion in the seventies Monopoly or cooperation? *Teachings of Psychology, 3,* 15–18.

Vande Kemp, H. (1980). The origin and evolution of the term "psychology": Addenda. *American Psychologist, 35,* 774.

Vande Kemp, H. (1981). The dream in periodical literature 1860-1910. *Journal of the History of the Behavioral Sciences, 17,* 88–113.

Vande Kemp, H. (1982a). The tension between psychology and theology: I. The etymological roots. *Journal of Psychology and Theology, 10,* 105–112.

Vande Kemp, H. (1982b). The tension between psychology and theology. II. An anthropological solution. *Journal of Psychology and Theology, 10,* 205–211.

Vande Kemp, H. (1983a, August). *Great psychologists as "unknown" psychologists of religion.* Paper presented at the meeting of the American Psychological Association, Anaheim, CA.

Vande Kemp, H. (1983b). Spirit and soul in no-man's land: Reflections on Haule's "Care of souls." *Journal of Psychology and Theology*, *11*, 117–122.

Vande Kemp, H. (with H. N. Malony). (1984). *Psychology and theology in Western thought,1672-1965: A historical and annotated bibliography*. Millwood, NY: Kraus International.

Vande Kemp, H. (1985a, November). *Psychotheological integration in the 1950s: The Journal of Psychotherapy as a Religious Process*. Paper presented at the meeting of the American Academy of Religion, Anaheim, CA.

Vande Kemp, H. (1985b). Psychotherapy as a religious process: A historical heritage. *The Psychotherapy Patient*, *1*(3), 135–146.

Vande Kemp, H. (1986). Dangers of psychologism: The place of God in psychology. *Journal of Psychology and Theology*, *14*, 97–109.

Vande Kemp, H. (1987). Relational ethics in the novels of Charles Williams. *Family Process*, *26*, 283–294.

Vande Kemp, H. (1988, August). *Allport on religion before 1950: The archival record*. Paper presented at the meeting of the American Psychological Association, Atlanta, GA.

Vande Kemp, H. (1989a, August). *From preacher's kid to phenomenologist: Robert B. MacLeod and the religious "doctrine of man."* Paper presented at the meeting of the American Psychological Association, New Orleans, LA.

Vande Kemp, H. (1989b, August). *Religion in college textbooks: Allport's historic study*. Paper presented on the annual meeting of the American Psychological Association, New Orleans, LA.

Vande Kemp, H. (1992a). G. Stanley Hall and the Clark school of religious psychology. *American Psychologist*, *47*, 290–298.

Vande Kemp, H. (Ed.). (1992b). *Family therapy: Christian perspectives*. Grand Rapids, MI: Baker.

Vande Kemp, H. (1994a). Psycho-Spiritual Dreams in the Nineteenth Century: I. Dreams of Death. *Journal of Psychology and Theology*, *22*, 97–108.

Vande Kemp, H. (1994b). Psycho-Spiritual Dreams in the Nineteenth Century. II. Metaphysics and Immortality. *Journal of Psychology and Theology*, *22*, 109–119.

Vande Kemp, H., & Houskamp, B. (1986). An early attempt at integration: *The Journal of Psychotherapy as a Religious Process*. *Journal of Psychology and Theology*, *14*, 3–14.

Van Kaam, A. (1976). *The dynamics of spiritual self direction*. Denville, NJ: Dimension.

Vander Veldt, J. H., & Odenwald, R. P. (1952). *Psychiatry and Catholicism*. New York: McGraw-Hill.

Vaughan, F. (1986). *The inward arc: Healing and wholeness in psychotherapy and spirituality*. Boston: Shambhala.

Vaughan, R. M. (1930). *The significance of personality*. New York: Macmillan.

Vitz, P. C. (1989, August). *Bias against religion in public school textbooks.* Paper presented at the meeting of the American Psychological Association, New Orleans, LA.

Vogel, C. L. (Ed.). (1932). *Psychology and the Franciscan school: A symposium of essays.* Milwaukee, WI: Bruce.

Walsh, R. N. (1987). *The spirit of shamanism.* Los Angeles: J. P. Tarcher.

Walsh, R. N., & Vaughan, F. (Eds.). (1980). *Beyond ego: Transpersonal dimensions in psychology.* Los Angeles: J. P. Tarcher.

Watson, R. I. (1963). *The great psychologists: From Aristotle to Freud.* Philadelphia: Lippincott.

Weatherhead, L. D. (1951). *Psychology, religion and healing: A critical study of all the non-physical methods of healing, with an examination of the principles underlying them and the techniques employed to express them, together with some conclusions regarding further investigation and action in this field.* New York: Abingdon.

Weatherhead, L. D., & Greaves, M. (1932). *The mastery of sex through psychology and religion.* New York: Macmillan. (Student Christian Movement, 1931)

Webb, C. C. J. (1918). *God and personality.* London: Allen & Unwin.

Webb, C. C. J. (1920). *Divine personality and human life.* London: Allen & Unwin.

Werner, H. (1940). *Comparative psychology of mental development* (E. B. Garside, Trans.). New York: Harper. (Original work published 1926)

White, V. F. (1952). *God and the unconscious.* Cleveland, OH: World.

White, V. F. (1960). *Soul and psyche: An enquiry into the relationship of psychotherapy and religion.* New York: Harper.

Why a Bibliography? (1983). *The Common Boundary Between Spirituality and Psychotherapy, 1*(4), 6.

Wilber, K., Engler, J., & Brown, D. P. (1986). *Transformations of consciousness: Conventional and contemplative perspectives on development.* Boston: New Science Library.

Williams, C. (1939). *The descent of the dove: A short history of the Holy Spirit in the church.* New York: Oxford University Press.

Witcutt, W. P. (1943). *Catholic thought and modern psychology.* London: Burns, Oates, and Washbourne.

Wittine, B. W. (1992). Basic postulates for a transpersonal psychology. In R. S. Valle & S. Halling (Eds.), *Existential-phenomenological perspectives in psychology: Exploring the breadth of human experience. With a special section on transpersonal psychology* (pp. 269–288). New York: Plenum.

Wolman, B., & Ullman, M. (Eds.). (1986). *Handbook of states of consciousness.* Reinhold, NY: Van Nostrand Reinhold.

Woodward, W. R., & Ash, M. G. (Eds.). (1982). *The problematic science: Psychology in nineteenth-century thought.* New York: Praeger.

Woolcott, P. (1966). Some considerations of creativity and religious experience in St. Augustine of Hippo. *Journal for the Scientific Study of Religion, 5,* 273–283.

Wulff, D. M. (1991). *Psychology of religion: Classic and contemporary views.* New York: Wiley.

Zilboorg, G. (1958). *Freud and religion: A restatement of an old controversy.* Westminster, MD: Newman.

Zilboorg, G. (1962). *Psychoanalysis and religion* (M. S. Zilboorg, Ed.). New York: Farrar, Strauss and Cudahy.

4

A CONSTRUCTIVE RELATIONSHIP FOR RELIGION WITH THE SCIENCE AND PROFESSION OF PSYCHOLOGY: PERHAPS THE BOLDEST MODEL YET

STANTON L. JONES

Religion seems to play a minimal role in the lives of most psychologists in the United States. A 1984 survey of religious preferences of academicians found psychologists to be among the least religious, with fully 50% responding that they had no current religious preference, compared with only about 10% for the general population ("Politics," 1991). Bergin and Jensen (1990) summarized prior research on the religiosity of psychotherapists by saying, "Data from previous surveys indicated that therapists were less committed to traditional values, beliefs, and religious affiliations than the normal population at large" (p. 3). Their survey found clinical psychologists to be the least religious of the major psychotherapy provider groups. Perhaps their most striking finding was that only 33% of clinical psychologists described religious faith as the most important influence in their lives, as compared with 72% of the general population.

In spite of the prominent role that religion plays in many people's lives, religion and religious belief are basically neglected in psychology text-

I wish to gratefully acknowledge the many contributions of Trey M. Buchanan, Richard E. Butman, C. Stephen Evans, Eric L. Johnson, Michael W. Mangis, Robert C. Roberts, Alan C. Tjeltveit, Mark A. Yarhouse, Antonette M. Zeiss, and three anonymous reviewers, who each provided constructive criticisms of the chapter.

Reprinted from *American Psychologist, 49(3)*, 184–199. Copyright 1994 by the American Psychological Association. Reprinted by permission of the author.

books (Kirkpatrick & Spilka, 1989). Similarly, the religious issues and faith of clients are frequently not dealt with by nonreligious psychotherapists (Lovinger, 1984). Many psychologists, academic and applied, do not relate to religion as such; they maintain a stance of neutrality or silence toward it. For many, this is not a hostile stance at all, but rather is the most respectful position one can take toward that which does not personally endorse or understand.

When psychology as a discipline or profession has formally interacted with religion, it has typically been in one of three classic modalities. All three are unidirectional, with psychology being unaffected in any substantive way by the interaction. The first mode is the scientific study of religion by psychologists, referred to as the psychology of religion. The psychology of religion has a long and distinguished history, being one of the major areas of study in the field from the 1880s until the 1930s. Psychology of religion is alive and well today, as demonstrated by the resurgence in publication of psychology of religion textbooks (e.g., Meadows & Kahoe, 1984; Paloutzian, 1983; Spilka, Hood, & Gorsuch, 1985; Wulff, 1991), by the inclusion of a review of the area in the *Annual Review of Psychology* (Gorsuch, 1988), by the recent establishment of the successful *International Journal for the Psychology of Religion*, and by the establishment and growth of Division 36 (formerly Psychologists Interested in Religious Issues, now Psychology of Religion) within the American Psychological Association (APA).

The second major mode in which psychology has interacted with religion has been through supplying useful psychological information to guide the practice of pastoral care (what one might call the psychologizing of pastoral care). Holifield (1983) provided a historical analysis of this process. Beginning almost from the infancy of psychology in America at the end of the last century, clerics have looked to psychology and the related mental health disciplines for insights to guide pastoral care, and psychologists have been unequivocally enthusiastic about providing these insights. Almost every trend and movement in the mental health field has been mirrored in pastoral psychology, as even the most cursory review of courses in pastoral care at seminaries or of pastoral care textbooks will show. Oden (1984), for example, has shown that pastoral care texts prior to 1920 were dominated by references to the historical and theological roots of the pastoral care tradition, whereas after 1920, pastoral care texts came to be dominated by references to the major psychotherapy theoreticians. Today, pastors are vigorously courted by psychologists as referral sources and mental health gatekeepers in almost every community.

The final type of interaction is the use of psychological findings or theories to revise, reinterpret, redefine, supplant, or dismiss established religious traditions. Each of the four major historic paradigms in psychology has been applied to this task. Such applications of psychoanalysis, behaviorism, and humanistic psychology are well known and have been documented by Rolston (1987) and others. An article by Sperry (1988) is a recent example of the current dominant paradigm, cognitivism, being used to redefine religious belief. Sperry essentially argued that the new mentalist paradigm, built on his concept of emergentist mind, provides the basis for a new understanding of religion, or more directly stated, a new religion. Religion should, according to Sperry, be based on biospheric ethics and the teleology of evolutionary cognitive emergentism. This religion, which he noted would easily merge with "antireligious ideologies such as communism or secular humanism" (p. 611), would "have to relinquish reliance on dualistic explanations" (p. 610) and thus be devoid of supernatural beliefs. He suggested that this should not "pose a major obstacle" (p. 610) to modern religion. In short, humanity should review itself as the highest known product of evolution and hence as our own ultimate concern (many theologians would call such a prioritization an attitude of worship). We should thus base our ethics on the promotion of our common good in order to enhance continued evolutionary progress. Sperry, like Freud and Skinner before him, called for his new understanding of religion after a brief period of cognitivist ascendancy (see also Sperry, 1993).

In each of the three modes discussed above, religion is treated as an object, either of study, for education and provision of services, or for reform. Each of these are, at least in some ways, legitimate facets of a relationship between psychology and religion, but as a group they are incomplete. In none of the tree is religion a peer or a partner. This chapter constitutes a call for a different sort of relationship between psychology and religion, a relationship based on mutuality and respect.

In the first major section of this chapter, I argue for an understanding of science and religion that recognizes their differences but also understands the common ground they share. The fundamental thrust of this section is premised on an enlarged understanding of the nature of science and of psychology. A series of articles in the *American Psychologist* over the past decade have paved the way for this current proposal. None has more directly broken ground for this proposal than did O'Donohue's (1989) call for an "(even) bolder model" of understanding clinical psychologists, and indeed all psychologists, as not just practitioners, scientists, or scientist–practitioners, but as "metaphysician–scientist–practitioners" (p. 1460). Because there is no impassable chasm between science and religion, it is inevitable that religion and religious belief will and do relate to the scientific discipline of psychology, and some of the ways in which this is so are explored here. I then explore the way in which interaction occurs between religious belief and the application of psychology in the domain of clinical practice. In the second major section, I expand this analysis beyond the descriptive to the prescriptive by suggesting how religion ought to relate to and have an impact on psychology, both in its more distinctively scientific manifestations and in its professional applications.

The argument I advance is not unique or original, although it has previously not been fully developed for application to the entire discipline of psychology and its relationship with religion. Proposals for alternatives to the "naturalistic" approach to scientific psychology have advanced many of the core ideas in the critique of science that follows, but have not dealt with religion per se. Braybrooke (1987) classified the alterative approaches to disciplined study as falling into two groups. "Interpretative" approaches attempt through phenomenological and qualitative methods to understand the meaning of human action in the context of the meaning systems of the actors (and might include hermeneutic, structuralist, and existentialist approaches to the field). "Critical" approaches also use nontraditional methods of study to make meaning of the subjects of study, but do so from an explicitly value-committed framework (e.g., psychoanalytic, Marxist, or feminist approaches). Neither of these alternative approaches has given rise to a significant literature on its relationship with religion.

On the other hand, many facets of the views of science and religion expressed here have been worked out in more detail by such authors as Ian Barbour (1974, 1990), Holmes Rolston (1987), and Thomas Torrance (1980, 1984), although these authors have tended to be predominantly interested in the relationship of religion with the physical sciences. Furthermore, a diverse community of Christian psychologists have been conducting an isolated dialogue within their community for several decades on "the integration of psychology and theology," a dialogue of remarkable variability in scholarly quality. This dialogue has been encouraged and facilitated by the publication of several journals (e.g., the *Journal of Psychology and Theology* and the *Journal of Psychology and Christianity*) and by a number of books of such relatively prominent psychologists as Malcolm Jeeves (1976), Paul Meehl (Meehl, Klann, Schmieding, Breimeier, & Shroeder-Solmann, 1958), David Myers (1978; Myers & Jeeves, 1987), and Paul Vitz (1977) and by lesser-known authors (e.g., Carter & Narramore, 1979; Evans, 1982; Jones & Butman, 1991; Van Leeuwen, 1985). A similar dialogue is beginning to occur in the context of other traditional faith communities as well, as shown by the development of the *Journal of Psychology and Judaism*, by the publication of a few books (e.g., Rizvi, 1988), and by occasional paper presentations at APA conventions (e.g., Lax, 1993).

ON THE SUPPOSED INCOMMENSURABILITY OF RELIGION AND SCIENCE

The classic formulation of the relationship of religion to science generally, and hence to psychology in particular, is that religion can have no integral relationship to science whatsoever, except perhaps as an object of study. This view has been expressed most tersely in recent times by the National Academy of Sciences in a resolution passed in 1981, which stated that "Religion and science are separate and mutually exclusive realms of human thought whose presentation in the same context leads to misunderstanding of both scientific theory and religious belief" (National Academy of Sciences, 1984, p. 6). The impetus for this resolution was a Louisiana trial regarding the teaching of creationism as science in public school classrooms.

The supposed separateness and exclusivity of religion and science seem to be derived from cherished notions of their incompatibility based on their respective essential natures. Barbour (1974) suggested that science and religion are often regarded as fundamentally incompatible because of the beliefs that (a) science rests on facts and religion on faith, (b) scientific claims are verifiable or falsifiable whereas religious claims are not evaluated by objective experience, and (c) the criteria for choosing between scientific theories are clear and objective whereas the criteria for choosing between religions are ambiguous and subjective.

Some scientists conceive of religion as asking questions solely in the realms of significance, meaning, values, ultimacy, and ethics; these are regarded as making no factual claims on human reality. With this understanding of religion, how can it have any integral relationship with science? However, religion is a multifaceted entity that must be understood from a diversity of perspectives (Gorsuch, 1988). For the purpose of this article, I focus on the cognitive or declarative dimension of religious belief and doctrine. However defined or described, religion usually includes a declarative dimension, whether it is expressed explicitly in formal doctrine (at one extreme) or implicitly and tacitly through the rituals and practices prescribed by the religion (at the other extreme). Every religion asserts or presupposes views of the nature of the universe, the nature of some ultimate reality, the nature of human beings and other beings, the place of humanity in the ultimate scheme of things, and the nature of morality. I focus on that cognitive–declarative dimension of religion in analyzing the relationship of science and religion because it is the dimension of religion most relevant to science. I do not in the process claim that religion is only or even primarily a cognitive phenomenon. It is a presupposition of this article that there is no one entity of religion, but rather that there are religions, and that the present analysis may apply better to some religions than others. Nevertheless, the various religious faiths have enough in common to make a discussion of the relationship of science with religion (singular) meaningful.

Science, on the other hand, has often been viewed in the manner dictated by logical positivists (this has been especially true in the past among psychologists; Krasner & Houts, 1984; Mahoney, 1976; Toulmin &

Leary, 1985). The essence of the positivistic view of science was summarized by Mahoney (p. 130) as asserting that scientific knowledge is grounded in empirical facts that are uninterpreted, indubitable, and fixed in meaning; that theories are derived from these facts by induction or deduction and are retained or rejected solely on the basis of their ability to survive experimental tests; and that science progresses by the gradual accumulation of facts. A growing consensus of scholars today, however, rejects the foregoing as an accurate understanding of science, as I discuss in the next major section. Furthermore, some scholars argue that psychology is not a unitary scientific discipline, but is rather a complex blend of natural and human sciences along with a culturally defined applied disciplinary arm (Koch & Leary, 1985). In short, many aspects of psychology and of science in general defy easy classification according to the logical positivist conceptions of science.

Postpositivistic Philosophy of Science

The traditional or positivistic view of science has been eroding since the late 1950s. Although preceded by a substantial amount of work in the philosophy and sociology of science (Laudan, 1984), the analyses of science promulgated by historian of science Thomas Kuhn (1970) were the first to really catch the attention of the scientific world, and especially the psychological world. Since that time, awareness of postpositivistic, postmodern, or "historicists" trends in the philosophy of science on the part of psychologists has increased (e.g., Bevan, 1991; Gergen, 1985; Gholson & Barker, 1985; Howard, 1985; Manicas & Secord, 1983; O'Donohue, 1989). These trends in understanding science might be summarized as follows.

First, postpositivistic philosophy of science has taught us that data are theory-laden. A simplistic empirical foundationalism or naive realism, the view that empirical data are unsullied and indubitable, is no longer tenable. Philosophers were the first to clearly see this. Results of contemporary perceptual and cognitive psychology clearly support the contention that data are sorted or processed from their first entry into the human organism's sensory equipment. For instance, expectancies have a profound impact on the perceiving process (e.g., the famous Postman studies cited by Kuhn), and these findings have made their way into the philosophy-of-science literature. It is commonly noted that all seeing is "seeing as."

The scientist, according to Toulmin (1962), "does not (and should not) approach Nature devoid of all prejudices and prior beliefs" (p. 45). Without preorienting conceptions of some sort, we cannot perceive data at all; the world would be a "bloomin' buzzin' confusion" (William James's term). We have data precisely because we sort our experience according to dimensions of relevance to our prescientific commitments and the demands of the ongoing scientific task. Koch (1981) said "We cannot discriminate a so-called variable ... without making strong presumptions of philosophical cast about the nature of our human subject matter" (p. 267; see also Tjeltveit, 1989). The nature of psychology, given the complexity, irreducibility, and obscurity of its subject matter, is profoundly shaped by conceptual presuppositions we bring to our areas of study. This theory-ladenness (a term attributed to philosopher of science N. R. Hanson) of the data may be accentuated in the human or behavioral sciences, as I argue later. Recent attention to gender biases in social science might be cited as a case in point (Riger, 1992). So, in counterpoint to the notions that data are uninterpreted, indubitable, and fixed in meaning, contemporary views see data as interpreted (to a greater or lesser extent) and thus not necessarily fixed in meaning.

This assertion should not, however, be taken as an endorsement of relativism or the notion that expectations or theories create data. As Brown (1977) has noted, "we shape our percepts out of an already structured but still malleable material. This perceptual material, whatever it may be, will serve to limit the class of possible constructs without dictating a unique percept" (p. 93). In other words, although reality does not force one and only one structure on our perceptions, there are limits to the degree to which our preexisting conceptions can impose a structure on reality. It is expected that empirical evidence will "show [the scientist] how to trim and shape his ideas further" (Toulmin, 1962, p. 45), rather than theories or percepts leaping forth uncalled from the data (naive realism) or, alternatively, theories or percepts creating data (radical constructivism). This view has been called "critical realism" (Barbour, 1990; Brown, 1977).

Second, the new philosophy of science teaches that scientific theories are underdetermined by facts (Hesse, 1980; Laudan, 1984). Positivistic conceptions of science suggest or imply either that theories are built inductively on data alone and that ideally the data will unequivocally support the theory, or alternatively that we propose theories tentatively and then accept only those that survive critical tests. In either case, the data or facts are presumed to determine the theory. But these assertions have been strongly criticized. Induction is an inadequate description of the process of theory development, as Kuhn (1970) has shown. The data are rarely scrutinized exhaustively before we commit ourselves to a theory. After all, scientists usually believe in their theories before putting them to empirical test; what else would sustain the diligent effort necessary to ever put the theory to the test?

Furthermore, the process of theory "confirmation" is now recognized to be extremely complex and not predicated merely upon the objective data. The "facts" never "pick out one theory uniquely or unambiguously to the exclusion of all its contraries" (Laudan, 1984, p. 15). As a result, falsification of theories by critical tests is now seen as far more difficult than was previously realized. Theories consist of flexible webs of assertions, including major hypotheses, corollaries, and so forth, that can be shifted easily to rebut attempts at theory falsification. For instance, a disconfirming critical test of a personality theory can be dismissed as irrelevant by questioning the operationalization and measurement of the key concepts of the theory, the nature of the studied subject population, the external and internal validity of the experimental manipulations, and so forth. One can never test the central notions of a theory without presuming numerous other ancillary propositions, and thus theories are amazingly resilient to so-called crucial tests (Brown, 1977; Meehl 1978; Wolterstorff, 1984).

Ultimately, the appraising of theories is a highly complex and sophisticated form of value judgment (Howard, 1985, p. 258). Our acceptance of any particular theory is never a result of mechanical methodological operations on the data; rather, empirical and extraempirical factors affect theory acceptance. The extraempirical influences that affect theory choices include what scientists value in a theory (e.g., "epistemic values" such as predictive accuracy and internal coherence; Howard, 1985; Laudan, 1984), the host of nonepistemic values held by the scientist (e.g., feminism, naturalism, and rugged individualism; see Gergen, 1978, 1985), the beliefs of those whom we respect and are trying to emulate, and the contingencies of the scientific social network (e.g., what can get published; Mahoney, 1976). To the extent that this analysis is valid, making explicit the extraempirical determinants of decision making about scientific theories would enhance the honesty of the scientific community and possibly allow us to make more accurate judgments.

Third, numerous attempts have been made to reduce scientific method to a set of concrete, operationalized steps. Although this approach has much to offer in understanding scientific activity, contemporary scholarship suggests that science itself is also a cultural and human phenomenon. As an example of this assertion, note that values—scientific and nonscientific—shape choice of objects of study (Laudan, 1984; O'Donohue, 1989; Sarason, 1984). It has been commonly noted that what is studied as a problem to conquer in modern American culture (e.g., authoritarianism) has been viewed positively in other settings (e.g., Germany in the 1930s). Frequently, our scientific formulations carry implicit within them a pressing value message by the labels we give them and the way we conduct our research (see Gergen, 1978). In the words of Bevan (1991),

> Behind the worlds we construct, coloring both our logic and our rhetoric, are the ideologies that give our world views their dominant cast. Such ideologies are complex and not easily analyzed. . . . As forms of human thought, ideologies permeate virtually every aspect of our mental life, including our science. We ignore them at our intellectual, social, and personal peril. (p. 478)

The variety of extraempirical factors that shape the scientific process are not a chaotic collage of random beliefs, values, and the like. There is a certain cohesiveness to the fundamental commitments we bring to the tasks of life, leading some to characterize our starting points as "world-views":

> Worldview (or vision of life) is a framework or set of fundamental beliefs through which we view the world and our calling and future in it. . . . It is the integrative and interpretive framework by which order and disorder are judged, the standard by which reality is managed or pursued. [It consists of] biophysical, emotional, rational, socio-economic, ethical, and "religious" elements. (Olthuis, 1985, p. 155)

In a very general and fundamental way, a worldview tells us what to expect and not expect to be the case in our world, and as such it forms the ground for all creative human thought and inquiry, for all of our ultimate answers about the nature of our existence. These foundational commitments, presuppositions, or "control beliefs" (Wolterstorff, 1984) are usually tacitly assumed on the basis of faith; they are rarely deliberately produced through rational or empirical inquiry.

How should these types of beliefs and commitments influence the process of doing science? Fletcher (1984) argued for a minimalist approach of only including those assumptions that were absolutely necessary for the conduct of the scientific enterprise and about which there was unanimous assent in the scientific community. In other words, we should only allow those assumptions without which a scientist would be paralyzed (e.g., that our sense experience is trustworthy, that there is a real world out there). Others argue for an explicit and intentionally expanded role for worldview assumptions, including religious beliefs, in scholarly work. O'Donohue (1989), following Lakatos, suggested that "metaphysical sentences," those beliefs that are deeply imbedded in our web of belief and are affected by evidence but not directly testable against experience, "are internal to all the sciences in that they are contained in the hard core and the positive heuristic of a scientific research program. Therefore, there can be no rigid demarcation of science and metaphysics" (p. 1465).

Fourth and finally, the new philosophy of science would teach us, as Kuhn (1970) most effectively pointed out, that science progresses not through the accumulation of bare facts, but through refinement of theories and theory-laden facts that are themselves imbedded in broader conceptual webs (paradigms, research programs, or research traditions; Gholson & Barker, 1985). Although the Kuhnian notion of science progressing by means of cataclysmic revolutions in which incommensurable paradigms supplant one another has been rather thoroughly refuted (Laudan, 1984), Kuhn's argument against the "slow accumulation of facts" understanding of scientific progress is well supported. Scientific progress is real, and change occurs even while fundamental conceptions of the subject matter are undergoing revision.

Commonalities and Distinctions Between Religion and Science

What commonalities do science and religion share? What distinguishes science from that which is not science? Viewing science from a postpositivist perspective reveals the human face of science. Science and the many nonscientific ways of knowing (including religion) are not identical, but "both are creations of the human mind" (Bevan, 1991, p. 476). Scientific knowing differs in degree and emphasis from other forms of human knowing. The work of the scientist is not easily comparable to the practice dimension of religious experience, be it the ecstatic worship of a Pentecostal Christian or the dispassionate meditations of a Zen Buddhist.

Nevertheless, contemporary philosophy of science does not support a radical or categorical separation of science from other forms of human knowing, including religious knowing or belief. The relative differences between them deserve to be carefully observed and maintained, but we cannot justify a failure to explore the interface of religion and science on the basis that religious belief is simply nonscientific. To the extent that science and religion are not "separate and mutually exclusive realms of human thought" (National Academy of Sciences, 1984) but are rather related and somewhat similar human activities, the supposed chasm between the two can begin to be seen in more realistic terms. A careful study of the human face of the postpositivist view of science reveals interesting parallels and similarities between science and the cognitive or declarative dimensions of religion. I would again reiterate that in using the term *religion* in this chapter, I am referring to the cognitive dimension of religious belief.

Subject matter

First, we can note with Barbour (1974) and Rolston (1987) a difference in degree rather than a true dichotomy between the two activities with regard to subject matter, a difference that does not constitute an impassable crevasse between the two activities. Each grapples with real aspects of human experience. Science is more likely to deal with the more sensory, objective, public, quantifiable, and repeatable aspects of experience. Religion is more likely to deal with the more internal, subjective, qualitative, and unmeasurable aspects of human experience and with the nature of the transcendent through revelation, reason, and human experience. These distinctions, however, only hold to a certain point; iron-clad distinctions between the subject matters of two activities are harder to make than one might guess, especially in psychology. Science is not based on pure facts; rather, there is a certain degree of uncertainty and interpretation involved in all human knowing. Certainly, scientists grapple with the abstract, private, ephemeral, and subjective, especially in psychology.

Religion, on the other hand, is not based on blind faith that is insensitive to the contours of reality, but rather is sensitive to certain realities of the human experience. Religion does more than assert things about God; it structures our understanding of the ultimate context of our existence and asserts many things about the nature of human beings. Many assertions about God imply things about the human beings who are to relate to God. Religion commonly grapples with morality, and moral systems necessarily assert or imply things about humans who are supposed to adhere to the system (e.g., a moral system that recommends chastity implies things about the nature of human sexuality). Every religious system presumes to answer the question of the broadest purposes of human existence. Such teleological conceptions are the foundations for the conceptual analysis of human behavior, as the functionalists long ago posited. Finally, every religion attempts to understand the human dilemma, diagnosing our problems and offering an agenda for remediating our difficulties. In each of these cases, religion begins to make factual or quasi-factual assertions about human reality that have implications that can be checked against human experience. Thus, there is substantive overlap in the subject matter of religion and the science of psychology.

Perhaps when each is functioning in its stereotypical modality, as when religion is struggling intuitively or rationalistically with the nature of God and other ultimate realities, and when science is grappling with a narrow slice of the objective, material, impersonal universe (e.g., the behavior of particular acids under extreme conditions of temperature variation), there will be little interpenetration of two forms of human knowing. But when the scientist begins to attempt to weave together discrete bits of empirical knowledge into a grand tapestry to explain and understand vast stretches of reality, she or he passes necessarily into domains of human thought that are also religious (i.e., these realms can be both religious and scientific, although not prototypically either). Prime examples are cosmology, sociobiology, and personality and clinical theory (Rolston, 1987). That the grand unifying theory is still an aspiration of psychological science is suggested by the work of Staats (1991; cf. Fowler, 1990) and others. Science has goals that transcend the mundane description of discrete empirical reality, and religion often has aspirations of saving something about the empirical aspects of human reality.

Accountability to experience

A second area of concourse is that of accountability to rigorously examined human experience. Religion and science should and do each exhibit a certain epistemic humility and hold themselves open to correction and development, at the same time aiming toward verisimilitude—truth-likeness. Scientific theories are meant to have a rather direct and immediate accountability relationship to experience, but as we have seen, there are substantial complications and difficulties in that accountability. Barbour (1974) pointed out that falsifiability is not easy for either science or religion. The criteria for theory acceptance and rejection in science, as I have discussed in passing, are far from clear-cut. Thus, empirical theory testing is part, but not the total sum, of decision making between scientific theories. Furthermore, metaphysical assertions that are not immediately testable in experience are intrinsic to the scientific enterprise (O'Donohue, 1989); scientists normally understand their subject matter in the context of a web of belief, much of which is not directly testable, that they bring to their studies. So, as Kuhn (1970) pointed out clearly, scientists tend to cling to their broad paradigms and scientific revolutions tend to proceed by a new generation bypassing the older generation that fails to change.

Although scientific truth is less directly accountable to experiential testing than was previously imagined, religious truth is not as insulated from experienced reality as its detractors might suggest. People sometimes put their religious beliefs to serious test against reality. Within the Christian tradition, Brunner (1939) said. "The decision about the truth or untruth of the Christian doctrine of man is made in experience" (p. 205). More broadly, Rolston (1987) stated that "religious experience provides a testing of dogmas, confirming or disconfirming them. The history of religion is strewn with abandoned beliefs, largely overcome by more commanding creeds or made implausible by new ranges of experience" (pp. 6–7). With some degree of similarity to the case of science, human experience is relevant to deciding between religions and to making decisions within religious systems. It seems that both religion and science stand in an accountability relationship with experience, although surely epistemic humility and experiential accountability take on a different flavor in the religious realm. "Neither science nor religion arrives at certainties. They at best predict probabilities but religion is looser here than is science and often can predict only a range of possibilities" (Roltson, 1987, p. 28). One interesting area of empirical accountability to reality for religion is the moderate but demonstrable positive contributions of religious devotion to mental health and quality of life (Bergin, 1991; Larson et al., 1992).

Goals

A third commonality between religion and science is that of essential goals; science and religion are related human attempts to make sense out of a very complex existence (Barbour, 1974). A major goal of each is understanding, although the particular form of understanding for each differs (see Toulmin, 1962, for a discussion of understanding in science). Scientific explanations are distinguished by their emphasis on the development of what are commonly called universal mathematical covering laws—theories that attempt to explain by specifying the mathematical-quantitative relationships between naturalistic entities, with the specified relationships being assumed to hold universally whenever comparable conditions apply. Religious explanations typically resort to more poetic, dogmatic, metaphorical, or rationalistic explanatory mechanisms than do scientific explanations (Barbour, 1990). Despite their distinctive styles of explanation, both attempt to foster human understanding: "Religion does claim to be in some sense true as well as useful. Beliefs about the nature of reality are presupposed in all the other varied uses of religious language" (Barbour, 1974, p. 5).

Use of analogical models

Fourth, both religion and science use analogical models rooted in paradigms or worldviews to explain experience (Barbour, 1974). Many scientific psychologists are recognizing the constricting effects of traditional operationalism in science when they try overly rigorously to eliminate nonempirical conceptions from the human activity of science. There is an "as if" quality to much of science, especially at its frontiers. Certainly, however, scientific metaphors are held less tenaciously than their parallels in the religious realm. Even in religion, however, explanatory metaphors evolve.

Human enterprises

A fifth commonality between religion and science is that both are human communal and cultural enterprises subject to the same sorts of human influences that affect all of our activities. Because science and religion are both finely nuanced activities engaged in by human beings, the full scope of neither enterprise is readily reducible to a set of methodological rules or conceptual dogmas. We will never eliminate the human from either set of practices. Hence, a psychological and sociological analysis of the factors shaping each is appropriate. The distinction between shaping each of these activities and exhaustively determining them, however, must be maintained. The extreme conclusions of the "strong programme in the sociology of knowledge" (the view that reduces the determinants of science to social–cultural forces alone; Bloor, 1976; Livingstone, 1988) must be rejected, as should its counterpart in understanding religion (e.g., the reductionistic renderings of religion promulgated by Freud, Skinner, and others; Rolston, 1987).

Passionate devotion

Finally, as Mahoney (1976) noted, science can in fact elicit and inspire the same type of passionate devotion as religion can. Human beings seem to be drawn with religious reverence to some ultimate reality, and certainly science occupies that place in the life of many scientists. The scientific enterprise is sustained by the emotional commitment of its practitioners to both the grand aims of the pursuit of truth and the improvement of the human race, as well as by the more pedestrian dreams of personal advancement, prestige, and prosperity.

A bald assertion that there are no substantial differences between scientific and religious knowing would be ludicrous. The differences are perhaps too many and too obvious to bear mentioning. The objective of this section, however, is to highlight the similarities between the two as a vehicle for breaking down the supposed barriers preventing substantive intercourse between the two. Despite their many differences, scientific and religious attempts at understanding are both exercises of human rationality that are shaped by our preorienting assumptions, are accountable to human experience, are influenced by the human communities of which we are a part, and are attempting to understand aspects of our experienced realities. They are different, but there is not an unbridgeable chasm between the two.

Interaction Between Religion and the Science of Psychology

In the foregoing section, I have argued that religion and science share common ground upon which interaction could take place. I now briefly examine the thesis that such interaction actually does take place on an ongoing basis. Thorough documentation of this thesis would require a separate monograph. Briefly, I would argue that interaction with religious and quasi-religious themes is most frequent and obvious in those arenas in which psychological scientists extend their reach to explain the broadest domains in human behavior and take on the prescriptive function of specifying what it means to be a "healthy" or "normal" or "mature" person. Because these aspects of psychology are generally coterminous with the grand personality theories that are the academic background for the practice of psychotherapy, I leave further discussion of this until the next section.

It may be helpful to explore briefly one concrete example of the intersection of religious concerns with scientific psychological inquiry. Herbert Simon (1990) proposed a new behavior genetics model of altruistic behavior (specifically, the choice to forgo or minimize progeny) that incorporated an explicit cognitive psychological or social learning element as its distinguishing characteristic. Simply put, he suggested that altruistic people are docile—that is, they are adept at social learning of useful skills and proper interpersonal behavior and highly motivated to do what others (society) deem to be good. Docility is made possible by *bounded rationality*, the failure to exercise rigorous rationality in independently evaluating all events for the benefits that those events will contribute to the person's potentialities for genetic propagation, to their personal "fitness." Simon then developed a probabilistic model justifying the continued survival of altruistic behavior in a species.

Simon's (1990) article illustrated the points of connection between the scientific and the religious. Most psychologists would view this article as scientific, on the basis of its publication in *Science* its use of scientific concepts and mathematical formulae. However, Simon's subject matter clearly overlaps with the moral and the religious: He focused on people who choose to forgo progeny, referring to, among others, people who for moral reasons choose chastity as a life commitment or choose to restrain from procreative behavior prior to marriage. Simon clearly meant his hypothesis to be accountable to empirical data, but it is equally clear that it is accountable only in the broadest way imaginable. He invoked such difficult-to-quantify ideas as percentages of altruists in a population, the net cost of altruistic choices, and number of offspring in a population of nonaltruists that is attributable to their altruistic behavior. Clearly, a single critical test of this hypothesis is not likely, and disconfirming evidence could easily be attributed to inadequate measurement of key theoretical terms. His goal was the understanding of behavior that is counterintuitive from his paradigmatic assumptions (but that is easily comprehensible, even rational, from the perspective of certain specific religious traditions). Simon's broad explanatory matrix was explicitly identified as neo-Darwinism or sociobiology. He defined *fitness* as the "expected number of progeny" (p. 1665) one will eventually produce. Simon's model presumes an ultimate context for understanding human action: We are singularly material beings whose greatest advantage comes in maximizing the propagation of our genetic material into succeeding generations. It presumes an understanding of ultimate standards for judging the veracity of human rationality, with the ultimate standard being fitness. The explanatory analogy is that of an animal population in which certain inherited characteristics optimize survivability and in which gene propagation is the highest good. With this standard, clearly antirational behavior, such as the altruistic choice to constrain one's personal propagation, must be explained.

I am not here arguing that Simon's (1990) views were religious in a narrow sense. What I am suggesting, however, is that at the broadest levels many religious traditions would suggest an understanding of the ultimate meaning and context of human action that would be utterly at variance with that assumed by Simon. It is notable that Simon tried to gain understanding of behavior that is inexplicable from his orienting assumptions about meaning and purpose in human life (sexual abstinence), whereas such behavior is rational and quite explicable from other, more traditionally religious paradigm assumptions.

Other examples could be easily explored, including the way in which psychological study of moral development necessarily involves preconceptions (implicit or explicit) about what constitutes morality and moral action, how the study of social effectiveness or skill presupposes a pragmatic or utilitarian standard for the evaluation of human action, and how the study of marital interaction in the paradigm of social exchange theory presupposes the ultimate contexts and motivations for human choice in the most intimate of human relationships. But the clearest examples of the manner in which psychological inquiry and practice intersect with religious understandings of the person come from the applied domains of psychology, to which I turn next.

Interaction Between Religion and the Profession of Clinical Psychology

Psychology is not just a scientific discipline, but a professional discipline as well: The "discipline of psychology includes both its science and its applications" (Flower, 1990, p. 2). I examine the professional practice of psychotherapy as a case example of the relationship between religion and all of the professional application fields of psychology, both because it is the most common form of professional practice of psychology and because it is the domain in which the interrelationship of psychology and religion is most obvious.

London (1986) has made the most persuasive case from within the field of psychology that psychotherapy, in addition to its scientific dimensions, is a moralistic enterprise with substantial religious content. Psychotherapists are not neutral technicians; London characterized them as forming a "secular priesthood" (p. 148). By this, he meant that the mission of reform or healing that psychotherapists embrace is intrinsically a moralistic one. Building upon his analysis, I would argue that three types of factors make this inevitable: (a) factors intrinsic to psychotherapeutic relationships, (b) factors intrinsic to psychotherapeutic theories, and (c) factors intrinsic to the modern culture in which psychotherapeutic services are offered. In each of these areas, psychotherapists are treading on ground shared with both broadly and more narrowly defined religious understandings.

With regard to the factors intrinsic to psychotherapeutic relationships, I would suggest following London (1986, pp. 10–11), that three relationship factors make psychotherapy an intrinsically moral enterprise.

First, clients do not separate psychological and moral phenomena in the way that professionals often do, so that a question such as "Should I vent my anger at my wife?" is not just a question of psychological health. Clients, London argued, interpret therapist reactions to such commonplace choices as moral approbation or disapproval (cf. Meehl, 1959). Clients often do not separate the moral and the religious. Second, therapists are human beings whose values and morals must participate in their human relationship with the client, at the very least in the broad ways in which they evaluate the client as a person (cf. Kelly, 1990). An interesting empirical finding that supports this assertion came from the work of Kelly and Strupp (1992), who found that psychotherapy tends to change client values (although not consistently in the direction of similarity to the values of the therapist) and that therapists tend to rate as more successful those clients whose values regarding personal goals in life change most to match the goals of the therapist, even though other measures did not indicate that these clients did in fact improve more than other clients. Bergin (1991) has documented the undeniable participation of values, including religious values, in psychotherapy. Third, the various ethical codes of our professional bodies exert a normative influence on therapist behavior, impelling a direction to our efforts that a "neutral science" cannot instigate. Going beyond London's comments, I would add, fourth, that it seems that the concerns presented by clients often push the practitioner beyond the limits of what consensually validated scientific research has established. "Given that research supplies only a small fraction of the information needed to completely understand the psychotherapeutic process, we are often compelled to rely on our tacit, background metaphysical notion" (O'Donohue, 1989, p. 1467) for guidance in how to respond to a client. In so doing, we often pass into the moral or religious domain of action (Browning, 1987; London 1986; Tjeltveit, 1989).

The second factor that makes it inevitable that psychotherapy will be a moral enterprise with substantial interrelationship with broad religious understandings is that what many regard to be religious presuppositions are intrinsic to the nature of psychotherapeutic and personality theory. O'Donohue (1989) pointed out the intractable presence of metaphysical presuppositions in all clinical theory. Psychotherapeutic theories embody value assumptions in that each includes explicit or implicit judgments about the nature of the human life that is "good" (healthy, whole, adaptive, realistic, rational, etc.) and "bad" (abnormal, pathological, immature, stunted, self-deceived, etc.). O'Donohue suggested that "therapy programs," or comprehensive views of the person that contain metaphysical assumptions and action principles for psychological or behavioral change,

> influence the problem statement and thereby ontic commitment. Whether a given problem is described in terms of medical/disease en-

tities, behavioral excesses or deficits, unconscious conflicts, or existential problems in living is determined by the therapy program. . . . that
psychologists view a certain state of affairs as problematic is influenced
by our metaphysical views concerning such issues as what constitutes
the good life, human nature, and morality. (p. 1467; see also Tjeltveit,
1989)

Beyond the mere passive containment of metaphysical assumptions, psychotherapy theory systems are inherently prescriptive. London (1986) suggested that psychotherapy usually involves the retrospective repair of past
damage and the prospective planning of how the client will live in the
future; "those that speak to the future are entangled with what, in short,
are problems of salvation. . . . And the arguments which explain and justify
those acts, taken together, total to a moral code" (p. 151). Browning
(1987) argued that theories of psychotherapy necessarily go beyond the
typical limits of scientific theories to answer questions of ultimate meaning
and of human obligation. Any system, he argued, that is used as a guide
to shape, heal, or reform human life cannot avoid metaphysics or ethics.
In this way, psychological theories go beyond the basic scientific need for
a metaphysical infrastructure to a much more extensive set of ethical and
metaphysical commitments. Browning suggested that contemporary scientific models "are modern forms of religious thinking in so far as they attempt to answer our insecurities, give us generalized images of the world,
and form the attitudes we should take toward the value of life, the nature
of death, and the grounds for morality" (p. 120).

Behavior therapy is an excellent specific example of how moralistic
and religious content is intrinsic to therapy theories, even though it seems
the least moralistic and most neutral and scientific of all major approaches.
Woolfolk and Richardson (1984) presented a sophisticated and sympathetic critique of behavior therapy, not as a psychotechnology, but as a
socioculturally based system of belief with deep metaphysical and quasi-
religious commitments. They started with a picture of behavior therapy's
self-image, noting that

virtually all have conceived of [behavior therapy] as a neutral structure,
a body of "objective knowledge" verified by experimental test. Behavior therapy's self-image is that of an applied science, devoid of any
inherent prescriptive thrust or implicit system of values, the essence of
which can be accounted for without reference to any cultural or historical context. (p. 777)

In contrast to this self-image, their conclusion at the broadest level was
that behavior therapy is a worldview of sorts, one that is "closely linked
with the values and patterns of thought characteristic of modernity"
(Woolfolk & Richardson, 1984, p. 777) and is "implicitly predicated on

modern epistemological and ethical assumptions" (p. 778). They suggested that behavior therapy contains "a prescriptive, ideological component: a favored mode of thinking and implicit criteria for making judgments that guide behavior therapists in their activities and also represent a vision of reality underlying those activities that justify and support them" (p. 777). Among the cherished assumptions of behavior therapy are technicism, rationality, amorality, and humanism. Behavior therapy, like all psychotherapy systems, is founded on subtle and often implicit assumptions that overlap with the domain of the moral and religious.

Third and finally, psychotherapy overlaps with the moral and religious because of factors in the contemporary cultural matrix within which psychotherapy is practiced. It seems that psychology is, in American society, filling the void created by the waning influence of religion in answering questions of ultimacy and providing moral guidance. The APA's commitment to promoting human welfare presumes morally laden visions of ultimate human well-being, as do the applied enterprises of the various psychotherapy models (London, 1986; Browning, 1987). The APA's involvement in social and juridical advocacy serves as one example of such a function in contemporary culture (e.g., Bersoff & Ogden, 1991). This perhaps helps to explain the potency of the mental health professions today: They have stepped in to fill the cultural niche vacated by the institutional church and have been in the business of answering questions of ultimacy with the powerful mantle of modern science cast about their shoulders. Kilbourne and Richardson (1984) have argued that therapy and religion each serves the function of establishing a "deep structure" for understanding life through the enactment of myths and ritual, which are given their power through the personal empathy and institutional settings in which they are administered. In addition, they both serve to elevate self-esteem and enhance social integration.

A complicating factor in occupying this cultural niche is the unquestionably high presence of nonreligious and antireligious sentiments among many practicing mental health professionals, as discussed in the opening paragraph of this article (see also Bergin, 1980; Braun, 1981; Richardson, 1991). Mental health professionals are an atypical subpopulation in America today, with lower levels of religious participation and higher levels of agnosticism, skepticism, and atheism than the general population. As Braun noted, this raises the possibility that applied psychologists especially may misunderstand or inappropriately evaluate client religiosity and the place of faith in their lives.

My argument in this section is that there is even more substantial overlap with the moral–religious domain in the applied arena of professional therapeutic psychology than there is with the area of scientific psychology. Browning (1987) has provided an apt summary of this point:

"Traditional religion and modern [therapeutic] psychology stand in a special relation to one another because both of them provide concepts and technologies for the ordering of the interior life" (p. 2).

AN OUTLINE FOR A CONSTRUCTIVE RELATIONSHIP OF RELIGION WITH PSYCHOLOGY AS A SCIENCE AND AS AN APPLIED DISCIPLINE

I have argued that, to this point in its history, psychology has not interacted with religion as a peer. The premise that this noninteractive stance can be justified by the supposed incompatibility of science and religion has been examined and rejected. I have argued that science and religion (broadly speaking) are different, but they are not radically incompatible. Psychology is a prime academic discipline in which we could explore the interface between religion and science. Furthermore, psychology's substantial presence in the helping professions has shifted its institutional identity in the direction of a moral enterprise with considerable overlap with the domain of religious belief. Now I shift my analysis from the descriptive to the prescriptive, using the foregoing arguments as the background assumptions for the proposal. After discussing some foundations for a constructive relationship between psychology and religion or religious belief, I discuss several broad proposals for a constructive relationship between religious belief and scientific psychology, followed by a similar discussion with regard to applied psychology.

Foundations

If data are theory-laden, it follows that there must be sources for the expectations or thought forms we bring to the data. In the natural sciences, the sources for presuppositions about the data one sees in the lab, and about the shape one's theories will take, can come from advances in other scientific areas, from one's socialization history as a scientist in training, from the culture in general, and perhaps occasionally and tangentially from one's religion. It seems likely that psychological scientists carry more presupposed notions of religious origin into the study of persons than natural scientists bring to the study of material subjects (most people having been "lay personality theorists" since birth; see Wegner & Vallacter, 1977). This is descriptively true, but there is also a certain prescriptive validity to this, in that we would be paralyzed in our inquiries if we approached human reality devoid of expectations. We need to approach our subject matter with presuppositions and expectations and to be explicit and accountable in that process. In the human (behavioral, social) sciences, there is good reason to expect any understanding of human data to be profoundly affected by religious presuppositions, in addition to other factors, because religion has so much to say about the human condition.

The various sciences likely differ in terms of the pervasiveness and profundity of the influences that worldview (including religious) assumptions will have on them, with psychology being more permeable to or riddled with influential religious presuppositions than, say, physics, which may contain fewer and weaker extraempirical presuppositions. Is this because psychology is less of a science or a less mature science? Perhaps, but this might have less to do with the relative maturity or purity of the science than it does with the inherent complexity, irreducibility, and inaccessibility of the subject matter of interest. Meehl's (1978) list of 20 intractable difficulties intrinsic to psychological science gives a beginning idea of the difficulties faced in psychological science. For instance, Meehl discussed difficulties in response-class and situation-class taxonomies: How do we divide up the stream of organismic responding and stimulus environment into the most meaningful units? Chemistry has found meaningful joints of nature in molecules, atoms, and subatomic particles; the comparable elemental building blocks of our science are not readily apparent. When taxonomic boundaries are less readily obvious, it would seem that the influence of philosophic and religious presuppositions on the scientist's preconceptions would be more extensive. Does psychology's position as the "most philosophy-sensitive discipline in the entire gamut of disciplines that claim empirical status" (Koch, 1981, p. 267) mean that psychology is really less mature or rigorous as a science or, more radically, does it mean that psychology is necessarily a different type of science that cannot always be judged by adherence to the path hewed out by physics and chemistry? Such issues are beyond the scope of this chapter, but I believe that the answer is probably yes to both halves of the question.

There is a rich tradition of reflection on the problems addressed by psychology in the field of philosophy (see Peters, 1962; Robinson, 1981) and in the field of theology (including practical theology; see Browning, 1987; McDonald, 1982). Alston (1985) has suggested that the philosopher can serve a role as a "concept analysis" consultant in the interacting with the psychological scientist, bringing special analytic skills to bear at the beginning stages of problem formulation on the nature of the questions to be addressed empirically. Theology would serve a similar function, as I develop in the following section.

The explicit incorporation of values and worldviews into the scientific process will not necessarily result in a loss of objectivity or methodological rigor. What is new about this proposal is not the incorporation of assumptions into the process, but rather the proposal that psychological scientists and practitioners be more explicit about the interaction of religious belief and psychology. If scientists, especially psychologists, are operating out of worldview assumptions that include the religious, and if the influence of such factors is actually inevitable, then the advancement of the scientific enterprise would be facilitated by making those beliefs explicitly available for public inspection and discourse. Baumrind (1982) has argued a similar point, suggesting that the relative lack of credibility of the social sciences may be perpetuated in part by our tendency to obscure the values that shape our work. She suggested that social scientists must respond by making their values explicit and deliberately encouraging value pluralism among those active in the discipline. A commitment to explicitness and public accountability about such value matters would seem essential and compatible with the scientific spirit.

With these foundations, I now consider the outlines of how religion could and should interact with scientific and professional psychology.

Three Major Forms of Interaction Between Religion and the Science of Psychology

The first form of interaction is what might be called a *critical–evaluative* mode of functioning, whereby social scientific theories and paradigms are examined and evaluated by the individual scientist for their fit with his or her religious presuppositions. This is somewhat akin at an individual level to Kuhn's phase in scientific progress in which there is acute discontent with a prevailing paradigm and a search begins for new ways to conceptualize the subject. The core task of the psychologist is not to derive the substance of a discipline from divine revelation, religious tradition, or idiosyncratic religious faith, but neither is it to ignore religion in a vain attempt to be totally neutral in doing science.

Religious presuppositions properly operate at very broad and fundamental levels (Wolterstorff, 1984). However, these presuppositions are clear enough to lead us to be skeptical about some theories or paradigms and lean toward others. They are also broad and vague enough to allow a diversity of possible theories to be compatible with them. As a case example, a psychologist is within his or her "epistemic rights" (Plantinga, 1984) to be unconvinced by a radical operant behavioral view of the person because the fundamental behavioristic conception of the subject matter of humanity is so radically opposed to a given religious understanding of persons. Rejecting the paradigm, however, is not synonymous with rejecting the usefulness of the studies emerging from that paradigm, nor does it make one unable to appreciate some elements of the paradigm (after all, a paradigm is not really unintelligible to a person who does not accept it, as Kuhn seemed to have originally hypothesized).

One example of such an evaluative process is my work in evaluating behavior therapy (Jones, 1988). Although I suggested that there is much to commend about behavior therapy, the conclusion of that analysis was that, from the perspective of presuppositions about the person derived from

Christian theism, (a) the presumption of determinism (both in radical behavioral and broadened social–cognitive views) is contrary to a Christian belief in limited human agency; (b) behavior therapy's radical atomism, its decomposition of the self into constituent habits, processes, and behaviors, undermines a reasonable understanding of selfhood; (c) the behavioral views of human motivation and the behavioral understandings and valuing of rationality do inadequate justice to what theists regard as humanity's higher potentialities; and (d) the amorality of the approach fails to reflect a coherent vision of human wholeness or maturity that could be compatible with Christian assumptions about the person. These findings represent challenges for the dialogue between religion and psychology, including possible fruitful areas of discourse that can advance both our religious and psychological understandings of the person.

The critical–evaluative mode for relating science and religion calls for the religious believer to evaluate scientific paradigms carefully in light of her or his most fundamental religious presuppositions, which are of relevance to the scientific paradigm. Such a critical–evaluative mode would also help major models and paradigms to be appropriately self-critical about the assumptions that undergird them. For instance, we are more likely to lapse into ethnocentrism when we are never confronted with ethnic diversity. Thus, the challenge of external evaluation from other perspectives might aid us in self-consciously and critically embracing the presuppositions intrinsic to a particular paradigm. As Browning (1987) has argued, "the clinical psychologies, especially, cannot avoid a metaphysical and ethical horizon and, for this reason, they should critically ground these features of their systems rather than unwittingly lapse into them" (p. xi).

Second, the *constructive* mode of relating religious presuppositions to science should occur when religious belief contributes positively to the progress of science by suggesting new modes of thought that transform an area of study by shaping new perceptions of the data and new theories. It is vital to point out that religiously influenced worldviews will not "actually contain [the scientist's] theories" (Wolterstorff, 1984, p. 77) and are not the source of the data by which we evaluate our theories, but our worldviews do influence what we see as the data and what form we expect a theory to take. An example of this is the contribution of Eastern forms of mediation to contemporary behavioral medicine, in which various forms of relaxation practices are among the most effective modes of intervention (Bernstein & Carlson, 1992; Carlson & Hoyle, 1993). Religious scientists will not function as scientists or scholars if they remain perpetually in a passive mode, passing judgment on scientific paradigms by the standards of their religious presuppositions. Rather, they must constructively contribute to the progress of human understanding by putting their suppositions to the test and seeing if they actually contribute to the progress of human knowing.

To the best of my knowledge, there are no clear examples of traditionally religious systems giving rise to major productive scientific paradigms within psychology, although there is a very long history of attempts to interrelate psychology and religion (Vande Kemp, 1984). Perhaps the closest we could get to the model would be the way the quasi-religious view of persons behind the Rogerian person-centered counseling model has produced a tremendous spate of empirical studies of therapist–client relationships, resulting in a deepened understanding of psychotherapy process. The nontraditionally religious foundations of existential psychology and of Jungian analytic psychology seem indisputable, but these systems have had negligible scientific impact upon the field. Similarly, the transpersonal psychology movement has clear roots in the wave of experimentation with consciousness-altering techniques, largely derived from the Eastern religions, that began in the 1960s (Goleman, 1980; Hutch, 1985; Tisdale 1994; Walsh & Vaughn, 1980). As I argued earlier, nontraditionally religious suppositions are fundamental to many positive scientific contributions in the field (e.g., the earlier discussion of Simon, 1990).

Philosopher Alvin Plantinga (1984; Plantinga & Wolterstorff, 1983) has argued that there is no compelling reason for individuals who believe in God not to include the existence of God among the fundamental worldview assumptions brought to the scholarly, scientific task. Plantinga (1984) asserted (and his suggestions for Christian philosophers were meant for all traditionally religious scholars):

> The Christian philosopher quite properly starts from the existence of God, presupposes it in philosophic work, whether or not he can show it to be probable or plausible with respect to premises accepted by all philosophers, or most philosophers, or most philosophers at the leading centers of philosophy. (p. 261)

Albert Ellis and B. F. Skinner, among others, have explicitly made naturalism (to the exclusion of belief in God and the transcendent) a part of the fundamental commitments they bring to the scientific task. If disbelief in the supernatural can suitably be among the control beliefs of some scientists, it would seem that belief in God and related beliefs about human persons could be allowable for others as a part of their control beliefs. "To insist on the objectivity of a science in terms of its separateness from the life experiences, intentions, values, and world views of the persons who create that science is to deny its fundamental character as a human activity" (Bevan, 1991, p. 477).

Although the truth value of the religion that is used to guide prescientific presuppositions will not itself be measured by its fruitfulness in inspiring scientific psychological studies, the truthfulness of the presuppositional conceptions derived from the religious beliefs will be partially tested by the empirical findings. For example, if a Christian understanding of persons suggested that a certain type of existential anxiety was an inevitable part of the human condition (perhaps following the tradition of Søren Kierkegaard; Evans, 1990), then perhaps a therapeutic program to understand, accept, and grow through that anxiety would increase the effectiveness of existing anxiety treatment programs. The failure of such a program to demonstrate empirical utility (assuming a definition of utility compatible with the conception of the phenomenon itself) would not seriously challenge the central truths of Christianity, but would challenge the alleged implications of this religion regarding human anxiety, leading to a productive interchange between science and religion regardless of the outcome of empirical findings.

This brings me to the third form of interaction. The relationship between science and religion must be dialogical and not unilateral. I opened this chapter by criticizing strongly the type of unilateral relationship that psychology has cultivated toward religion in the past. These roles should not be simply reversed, with religion dictating to the science of psychology (or any science). The relationship between the two must be dialogical (Barbour, 1990; Browning, 1987) or dialectical (Evans, 1982, p. 141). New findings in cosmology, sociobiology, philosophy, anthropology, sociology, and even psychology should infuse and affect the religious enterprise. Just as changing from a geocentric to a heliocentric vision of existence had a number of effects on religious belief, as have other scientific discoveries and revolutions, so also religion must be prepared to change as it engages in a constructive dialogue with psychology.

This commitment to a dialectical relationship between religion and science helps to address the two major concerns that some might raise regarding the dialogical relationship between religious worldview assumptions and the conduct and evaluation of science: (a) that such a move could lead to a "religious imperialism" of religion over science, or (b) that scientific progress could be impeded by the fragmentation of scientific psychology into competing religious camps. Does the present critique open the door to a religious psychology in which the dogmatic assertions of systematic theology replace the attempt to test our beliefs against reality, or in which science could degenerate into unproductive and endless squabbling about the relative merits of the assumptions of different religions as the starting point for psychological science? Although such an outcome may be possible, a commitment to modesty about the influence of control beliefs, to the value of pluralism for enhancing our understanding, and to the possibilities of testing our assertions against reality can prevent both of these undesirable outcomes from occurring. A willingness to establish such a dialogical relationship with religion will necessarily presume the willingness of scientists and professionals to become theologically and philosophically literate and for theologians and philosophers to become scientifically and professionally literate.

Three Major Implications for the Relationship Between the Profession of Psychology and Religion

What are the implications of the present argument for a respectful and productive interrelationship of religion or religious belief with the discipline of applied psychology, particularly with the profession of therapeutic psychology? First, there should be vastly more attention given in clinical training to the philosophical, ethical, and religious dimensions of human psychology and of professional practice. Bergin (1991), London (1986), and O'Donohue (1989) have paved the way for the present proposal by arguing, respectively, for enhanced efforts in clinical training directed at increasing the awareness of practitioners in training to the value, moral, and metaphysical dimensions of clinical theory and practice. I would echo their call for such enhancements and argue for the explicit extension of such efforts to expanded education in the religious domain.

As London (1986, p. xi) noted, since the publication of the first edition of his book in 1964, hardly any movement has occurred in increasing the awareness and competence of psychotherapists in training with regard to matters ethical, philosophical, or religious. A recent survey reported that 85% of clinical psychologists describe themselves as having little or no training in psychology and religion (Shafranske & Malony, 1990). A substantial fraction of coursework in graduate programs in applied psychology should be devoted to religious traditions, religious and moral dimensions of professional practice, and the philosophical and theological parentage of contemporary systems of thought. Contemporary instruction in history and systems of psychology is a start, but only a start, toward this goal. Only with this sort of preparation can psychologists be aware of their inevitable interaction with the religious. As London (1986) has said, such concerns.

> would be better handled if, to begin with, therapists became more vividly aware of their own moral investments and thought more about those of their clients. Students of therapy are too often encouraged to view their clients, themselves, and their work exclusively in terms of dynamics, drives, impulses, defenses, relationships, contingencies, and stimulus–response systems. Too little attention has been paid to consonant and conflicting ideologies, philosophies, and moral codes which are important to therapists' and patients' lives. (pp. 11–12)

As suggested by Tan (1993), there is now a substantial and growing body of literature that can serve as a resource in the training of the next generation of applied psychologists (e.g., Lovinger, 1984, 1990; Malony, 1988; Miller & Martin, 1988; Propst, 1988; Stern, 1985; Tjeltveit, 1986; Worthington, 1988, 1989, 1991). These resources can be of use in expanding the competencies of psychologists already in practice as well, an enhancement urged by the recent American Psychological Association

(1992) revision of its *Ethical Principles of Psychologists and Code of Conduct*, which in its new form mandates that psychologists should view religion as one facet of those human differences that require special attention, sensitivity, and training (Standard 1.08). Division 36 of the APA has for a number of years offered a continuing education workshop on working with religious issues in psychotherapy.

As a corollary to this first point, I would argue that the sectarian or religiously committed programs that require faculty or student compatibility with the religious stance of the institution or attempt to be sensitive to and serve the religious needs of their constituencies serve important functions in the field of professional psychology and in the entire discipline. Promotion of diversity (cf. Baumrind, 1982; Bergin, 1991; Tan, 1993) is served both by the creation of the heterogeneous environments of nonsectarian institutions and of the more focused environments of religiously committed schools, in much the same way that the advancement of women is served both by the complete integration of women into mainline academic programs and by the creation of special women's studies programs (Marsden, 1992; Riesman, 1993). Sectarian programs also raise the visibility of religious influences in applied psychological training, and they guarantee that a plurality of explicitly religious identities will be visible as professional subdisciplines develop. Baylor University (Baptist), Brigham Young University (Church of Jesus Christ of Latter Day Saints), Fuller Graduate School of Psychology (Christian Evangelical), and Rosemead Graduate School of Psychology (Christian Evangelical) are some of the schools that currently offer doctoral level APA-accredited professional training within an institutional context that requires, to greater or lesser degrees, at least some modicum of religious conformity to an explicit tradition. In other words, these institutions and others (perhaps explicity embracing alternative religious paradigms or purposely representing religious pluralism) can serve as valuable resources for the whole of applied psychology.

Second, there should be greater honesty in public relations by practitioners about the value-ladenness of the mental health enterprise. If it is true (a) that psychotherapeutic practice is influenced by the religious, moral, metaphysical, and philosophical commitments of practitioners and theoreticians (Bergin, 1991; Tjeltveit, 1989); (b) that mental health practitioners are disporportionately nonreligious compared with the general public (Bergin & Jensen, 1990); and (c) that psychotherapy often involves changes in client values (including the moral and religious; Kelly, 1990), then a cultivated public image of psychotherapeutic practice as a value-neutral enterprise is a misrepresentation of reality. Practitioners who are explicit about their value and religious commitments often hear complaints from former clients of "secular" practitioners that the client presumed that religious and moral neutrality would be maintained by the practitioner, only to perceive later that a religious and moral agenda was being pressed by the therapist.

Two areas of contemporary empirical research are relevant to this point. First, despite the frequent claims about a supposedly negative relationship between mental health and religious belief and practice (e.g., Albee, 1991; Ellis, 1980), and despite the frequent negative stereotypes of religious belief and practice that are so much a part of the mental health subculture—such as those in the *Diagnostic and Statistical Manual of Mental Disorders* (3rd ed., rev.; American Psychiatric Association, 1987; Richardson, 1993)—the best contemporary research suggests a neutral to mildly positive relationship between the two variables (Bergin, 1991; Larson et al., 1992; also see Richardson, 1985, 1992, for reviews of research related specifically to new or "cult" religions).

Furthermore, there is beginning evidence that religious clients actually do respond better to therapy that is adapted to their religious values and concerns (Propst, Ostrom, Watkins, Dean, & Mashburn, 1992). Also, Kelly and Strupp (1992) found that "salvation," an explicitly religious value, was the only single client–therapist value that they studied on which therapists and clients significantly differed (due largely to the nonreligiosity of the therapists in the study) and found it to be the only variable on which patient–therapist similarity significantly predicted the outcome of therapy. Their tentative conclusion was an extremely provocative one: "This suggests that patient–therapist similarity on religious values may serve as a *matching variable*" (p. 39), meaning that patient–therapist similarity on religious values may be one of the best predictors we have of successful outcome and thus a variable on which client and therapist ought to be matched. We might therefore be acting in the best interest of clients by directing them to therapists of similar religious commitments. The finding of Propst et al. (1992) that religious adaptation of the treatment approach was more important than the personal religious commitment of the therapist may soften the implications of Kelly and Strupp's finding.

Rather than recommitting ourselves to an impossible value neutrality, we should instead recognize that one cannot intervene in the fabric of human life without getting deeply involved in moral and religious matters. It thus seems incumbent on practitioners in our field to press for greater explicitness about this as we present our profession to the public. In addition, much more research in this area is needed.

Finally, greater thought should be put into the development of accountability relationships for individual practitioners, given the sensitivity of their work. At this time, supervisory and consultation relationships tend to focus on the technical aspects of applied practice; we need to join more explicitly in peer accountability in the moral–religious dimensions of our work. Psychologists whose background beliefs are identifiable with an established religious tradition should establish formal accountability relationships of some sort with that group in order to articulate that tradition more responsibly. Practitioners whose religious presuppositions are more idiosyncratic will need to develop more creative accountability linkages with like-minded individuals or persons who are of a compatible spirit so that practitioners with similar religious presuppositions can be helped to articulate that perspective responsibly while respecting the rights of their clients.

CONCLUSION

Psychological scientists and practitioners are human beings. As such, our activites and efforts as scientists and practitioners are connected to all dimensions of our personhood, including our religious beliefs and commitments, whether those beliefs and commitments are traditional and explicitly codified or nontraditional and implicit. Even in conducting scientific investigations, we act out of the entire web of our understandings of the world, others, and ourselves. Our religious beliefs (broadly understood) help to shape the contours of that web of belief.

My main objectives in this article have been (a) to demonstrate that no hard barrier separates the domain of religious thought and commitment from that domain of human activity that we call science, although at the same time I have argued that science and religion are quite different and should not be confused or overidentified; (b) to stimulate a greater awareness within the psychological community of the importance and pervasiveness of religious beliefs and commitments to the scientific and professional objectives of contemporary psychology; and (c) to encourage an increased awareness and unprecedented explicitness in discussing the part that religious beliefs (broadly defined) play in our scientific and professional activities, including specific proposals for relating religious belief with the science and profession of psychology. Psychology could be enriched by a more explicit exploration of the interface of religion with its scientific and applied activities.

McFall (1991) has recently called for a radical recommitment to advancing clinical psychology as an applied science, and he strongly rejected any compromise that would contaminate science with pseudoscience. His commitment to documented quality of care and of the protection of the public from speculative intervention methods is laudable. Is the present proposal opposed to his initiative? No. Rather, I would argue that in the pursuit of empirical documentation of quality of care, we must not lose our understanding of how science and professional practice (derived from scientific and quasi-scientific models) are infused with metaphysical, moral, and religious beliefs. If psychological research and practice are going to be maximally effective in understanding and improving the human condition, psychologists would be well-advised to explicitly explore the connections of their work with the deepest levels of our human commitments. Even if we think about our religious beliefs as biases that we bring to psychological science and practice, we must come to realize first that such biases are intrinsic to our professional activities, in that it is our biases that allow us to perceive and understand anything at all, and second, that the most limiting and dangerous biases are those that are unexamined and hence exert their effect in an unreflective manner.

REFERENCES

Albee, G. W. (1991). Opposition to prevention and a new credal oath. *The Scientist Practitioner, 1,* 30–31.

Alston, W. (1985). Conceptual analysis and psychological theory. In S. Koch & D. Leary (Eds.), *A century of pscyhology as science* (pp. 594–617). New York: McGraw-Hill.

American Psychiatric Association. (1987). *Diagnostic and statistical manual of mental disorders* (3rd ed., rev.). Washington DC: Author.

American Psychological Association. (1992). Ethical principles of psychologists and code of conduct. *American Psychologist, 47,* 1597–1611.

Barbour, I. (1974). *Myths, models, and paradigms.* New York: Harper & Row.

Barbour, I. (1990). *Religion in an age of science: The Gifford lectures, 1989–91* (Vol. 1). New York: Harper Collins.

Baumrind, D. (1982). Adolescent sexuality: Comment on William's and Silka's comments on Baumrind. *American Psychologist, 37,* 1402–1403.

Bergin, A. (1980). Psychotherapy and religious values. *Journal of Consulting and Clinical Psychology, 48,* 95–105.

Bergin, A. (1991). Values and religious issues in psychotherapy and mental health. *American Psychologist, 46,* 394–403.

Bergin, A., & Jensen, J. (1990). Religiosity of psychotherapists: A national survey. *Psychotherapy, 27,* 3–7.

Bernstein, D. A., & Carlson, C. R. (1992). Progressive relaxation: Abbreviated methods. In P. M. Lehrer & R. Woolfolk (Eds.), *Principles and practices of stress management* (2nd ed., pp. 53–87). New York: Guilford.

Bersoff, D., & Ogden, D. (1991). APA amicus curiae briefs: Furthering lesbian and gay male civil rights. *American Psychologist, 46,* 950–956.

Bevan, W. (1991). Contemporary psychology: A tour inside the onion. *American Psychologist, 46,* 475–483.

Bloor, D. (1976). *Knowledge and social inquiry.* London: Routledge & Kegan Paul.

Braun, J. (1981). Ethical issues in the treatment of religious persons. In M. Rosenbaum (Ed.), *Ethics and values in psychotherapy* (pp. 131–162). New York: Free Press.

Braybrooke, D. (1987). *Philosophy of social science*. Englewood Cliffs, NJ: Prentice Hall.

Brown, H. (1977). *Theory, perception, and commitment: The new philosophy of science*. Chicago: University of Chicago Press.

Browning, D. S. (1987). *Religious thought and the modern psychologies*. Philadelphia: Fortress.

Brunner, E. (1939). *Man in revolt*. (O. Wyon, Trans.). Philadelphia: Westminster.

Carlson, C. R., & Hoyle, R. H. (1993). Efficacy of abbreviated progressive muscle relaxation training: A quantitative review of behavioral medicine research. *Journal of Consulting and Clinical Psychology, 61*, 1059–1067.

Carter, J., & Narramore, B. (1979). *The integration of psychology and theology*. Grand Rapids, MI: Zondervan.

Ellis, A. (1980). Psychotherapy and atheistic values: A response to A. E. Bergin's "Psychotherapy and human values." *Journal of Consulting and Clinical Psychology, 48*, 635–639.

Evans, C. S. (1982). *Preserving the person: A look at the human sciences*. Grand Rapids, MI: Baker. (Original work published 1977)

Evans, C. S. (1990). *Søren Kierkegaard's Christian psychology*. Grand Rapids, MI: Zondervan.

Fletcher, G. (1984). Psychology and common sense. *American Psychologist, 39*, 203–213.

Fowler, R. D. (1990). Psychology: The core discipline. *American Psychologist, 45*, 1–6.

Gergen, K. (1978). Toward generative theory. *Journal of Personality and Social Psychology, 36*, 1344–1360.

Gergen, K. (1985). The social constructionist movement in modern psychology. *American Psychologist, 40*, 266–275.

Gholson, B., & Barker, P. (1985). Kuhn, Lakatos, and Laudan: Applications in the history of physics and psychology. *American Psychologist, 40*, 755–769.

Goleman, D. (1980). Perspectives on psychology, reality, and the study of consciousness. In R. N. Walsh & F. Vaughan (Eds.), *Beyond ego: Transpersonal dimensions in psychology* (pp. 29–35). Los Angeles: Tarcher.

Gorsuch, R. (1988). Psychology of religion. *Annual Review of Psychology, 39*, 201–221.

Hesse, M. (1980). *Revolutions and reconstructions in the philosophy of science*. Bloomington: Indiana State University Press.

Holifield, E. B. (1983). *A history of pastoral care in America: From salvation to self-realization*. Nashville, TN: Abingdon.

Howard G. (1985). The role of values in the science of psychology. *American Psychologist, 40*, 225–265.

Hutch, R. (1985). Who is it that we treat?: The interface between religion and therapy. *Pastoral Psychology, 33*, 152–160.

Jeeves, M. (1976). *Psychology and Christianity: The view both ways*. Downers Grove, IL: InterVarsity.

Jones, S. (1988). A religious critique of behavior therapy. In W. Miller & J. Martin (Eds.), *Behavior therapy and religion: Integrating spiritual and behavioral approaches to change* (pp. 139–170). Newbury Park, CA: Sage.

Jones, S., & Butman, R. (1991). *Modern psychotherapies: A comprehensive Christian appraisal*. Downers Grove, IL: InterVarsity.

Kelly, T. (1990). The role of valules in psychotherapy: A critical review of process and outcome effects. *Clinical Psychology Review, 10*, 171–186.

Kelly, T., & Strupp, H. (1992). Patient and therapist values in psychotherapy: Perceived changes, assimilation, simiarlity, and outcome. *Journal of Clinical and Consulting Psychology, 60*, 34–40.

Kilbourne, B., & Richardson, J. (1984). Psychotherapy and new religions in a pluralistic society. *American Psychologist, 39*, 237–251.

Kirkpatrick, L., & Spilka, B. (1989, August). *Treatment of religion in psychology texts*. Paper presented at the 97th Annual Convention of the American Psychological Association, New Orleans.

Koch, S. (1981). The nature and limits of psychological knowledge. *American Psychologist, 36*, 257–269.

Koch, S., & Leary, D. (Eds.). (1985). *A century of psychology as science*. New York: McGraw-Hill.

Krasner, L., & Houts, A. (1984). A study of the "value" systems of behavioral scientists. *American Psychologist, 39*, 840–850.

Kuhn, T. (1970). *The structure of scientific revolutions* (2nd ed.). Chicago: University of Chicago.

Larson, D. B., Sherill, K. A., Lyons, J. S., Craigie, F. C., Jr., Thielman, S. B., Greenwold, M. A., & Larson, S. S. (1992). Associations between dimensions of religious commitment and mental health reported in the *American Journal of Psychiatry* and *Archives of General Psychiatry*: 1978–1989. *American Journal of Psychiatry, 149*, 557–559.

Laudan, L. (1984). *Science and values: The aims of science and their role in scientific debate*. Berkeley: University of California Press.

Lax, W. D. (1993, August). *Narrative, deconstruction, and Buddhism: Shifting beyond dualism*. Paper presented in the 101st Annual Convention of the American Psychological Association, Toronto, Ontario, Canada.

Livingstone, D. (1988). Changing scientific concepts. *Christian Scholar's Review, 17*, 361–380.

London, P. (1986). *The modes and morals of psychotherapy* (2nd ed.). Washington, DC: Hemisphere.

Lovinger, R. (1984). *Working with religious issues in therapy*. New York: Jason Aronson.

Lovinger, R. J. (1990). *Religion and counseling: The psychological impact of religious belief*. New York: Continuum.

Mahoney, M. (1976). *Scientist as subject*. Cambridge, MA: Ballinger.

Malony, H. N. (1988). The clinical assessment of optimal religious functioning. *Review of Religious Research, 30*, 3–17.

Manicas, P., & Secord, P. (1983). Implications for psychology of the new philosophy of science. *American Psychologist, 38*, 399–412.

Marsden, G. R. (1992). *The secularization of the academy*. New York: Oxford University Press.

McDonald, H. (1982). *The Christian view of man*. Westchester, IL: Crossway.

McFall, R. M. (1991). Manifesto for a science of clinical psychology. *The Clinical Psychologist, 44*, 75–88.

Meadows, M., & Kahoe, R. (1984). *Psychology of religion*. New York: Harper & Row.

Meehl, P. (1959). Some technical and axiological problems in the therapeutic handling of religious and valuational materials. *Journal of Counseling Psychology, 6*, 255–259.

Meehl, P. (1978). Theoretical risks and tabular asterisk: Sir Karl, Sir Ronald, and the slow progress of soft psychology. *Journal of Consulting and Clinical Psychology, 46*, 806–834.

Meehl, P., Klann, R., Schmieding, A., Breimeier, K., & Schroeder-Slomann, S. (1958). *What, then, is man?: A symposium of theology, psychology, and psychiatry*. St. Louis, MO: Concordia.

Miller, W. R., & Martin, J. (Eds.). (1988). *Behavior therapy and religion: Integrating spiritual and behavioral approaches to change*. Newbury Park, CA: Sage.

Myers, D. G. (1978). *The human puzzle: Psychological research and Christian belief*. New York: Harper & Row.

Myers, D. G., & Jeeves, M. A. (1987). *Psychology through the eyes of faith*. San Francisco: Harper Collins

National Academy of Sciences. (1984). *Science and creationism: A view from the National Academy of Sciences*. Washington, DC: Author.

Oden, T. C. (1984). *The care of souls in the classic tradition*. Philadelphia: Fortress.

O'Donohue, W. (1989). The (even) bolder model: The clinical psychologist as metaphysician–scientist–practitioner. *American Psychologist, 44*, 1460–1468.

Olthuis, J. (1985). On worldviews. *Christian Scholars Review, 14*, 153–164.

Paloutzian, R. F. (1983). *Invitation to the psychology of religion*. New York: Scott, Foresman.

Peters, R. (Ed.). (1962). *Brett's history of psychology*. New York: Macmillan.

Plantinga, A. (1984). Advice to Christian philosophers. *Faith and Philosophy, 1*, 253–271.

Plantinga, A., & Wolterstorff, N. (Eds.). (1983). *Faith and rationality: Reason and belief in God*. Notre Dame, IN: University of Notre Dame Press.

Politics of the professoriate. (1991, July–August). *The Public Perspective*, pp. 86–87.

Propst, R. L. (1988). *Psychotherapy in a religious framework: Spirituality in the emotional healing process.* New York: Human Sciences Press.

Propst, L., Ostrom, R., Watkins, P., Dean, T., & Mashburn, D. (1992). Comparative efficacy of religious and nonreligious cognitive–behavioral therapy for the treatment of clinical depression in religious individuals. *Journal of Consulting and Clinical Psychology, 60,* 94–103.

Richardson, J. T. (1985). Pyschological and psychiatric studies of new religions. In L. B. Brown (Ed.), *Advances in the psychology of religion* (pp. 209–223). New York: Pergamon Press.

Richardson, J. T. (1991). Cult/brainwashing cases and freedom of religion. *Journal of Church and State, 33,* 55–74.

Richardson, J. T. (1992). Mental health of cult consumers: Legal and scientific controversy. In J. Schumaker (Ed.), *Religion and mental health* (pp. 223–244). New York: Oxford University Press.

Richardson, J. T. (1993). Religiosity as deviance: Negative religious bias in and misuse of the *DSM-III. Deviant Behavior, 14,* 1–21.

Riesman, D. (1993). Quixotic ideas for educational reform. *Society, 30(3),* 17–24.

Riger, S. (1992). Epistemological debates, feminist voices: Science, social values, and the study of women. *American Psychologist, 47,* 730–740.

Rizvi, S. A. A. (1988). *Muslim tradition in psychotherapy and modern trends.* Lahore, Pakistan: Institute of Islamic Culture.

Robinson, D. (1981). *An intellectual history of psychology* (Rev. ed.). New York: MacMillan.

Roston, H. (1987). *Science and religion: A critical survey.* Philadelphia: Temple University Press.

Sarason, S. (1984). If it can be studied or developed, should it be? *American Psychologist, 39,* 477–485.

Shafranske, E.P., & Malony, H. N. (1990). Clinical psychologists' religious and spiritual orientations and their practice of psychotherapy. *Psychotherapy, 27,* 72–78.

Simon, H. (1990). A mechanism for social selection and successful altruism. *Science, 250,* 1665–1668.

Sperry, R. W. (1988). Psychology's mentalist paradigm and the religion/science tension. *American Psychologist, 43,* 607–613.

Sperry, R. W. (1993). The impact and promise of the cognitive revolution. *American Psychologist, 48,* 878–885.

Spilka, B., Hood, R., & Gorsuch, R. (1985). *The psychology of religion.* Englewood Cliffs, NJ: Prentice Hall.

Staats, A. (1991). Unified positivism and unification psychology: Fad or new field? *American Psychologist, 46,* 899–912.

Stern, M.E. (Ed.). (1985). *Psychotherapy and the religiously committed patient.* New York: Haworth Press.

Tan, S. Y. (1993, January). *Training in professional psychology: Diversity includes religion*. Paper presented at the midwinter conference of the National Council of Schools of Professional Psychology, La Jolla, CA.

Tisdale, J. R. (1994). Transpersonal psychology and Jesus' Kingdom of God. *Journal of Humanistic Psychology, 34,* 31–47.

Tjeltveit, A. C. (1986). The ethics of value conversion in psychotherapy: Appropriate and inappropriate therapist influence on client values. *Clinical Psychology Review, 6,* 515–537.

Tjeltveit, A. C. (1989). The ubiquity of models of human beings in psychotherapy: The need for rigorous reflection, *Psychotherapy, 26,* 1–10.

Torrance, T. F. (1980). *Christian theology and scientific culture*. Belfast, Northern Ireland: Christian Journals Limited.

Torrance, T. F. (1984). *Transformation and convergence in the frame of knowledge: Explorations in the interrelations of scientific and theological enterprise*. Belfast, Northern Ireland: Christian Journals Limited.

Toulmin, S. (1962). *Foresight and understanding*. San Francisco: Harper.

Toulmin, S., & Leary, D. (1985). The cult of empiricism in psychology and beyond. In S. Koch & D. Leary (Eds.). *A century of psychology as science* (pp. 594–617). New York: McGraw-Hill.

Vande Kemp, H. (1984). *Psychology and theology in Western thought (1672–1965): A historical and annotated bibliography*. Mill Wood, NY: Kraus.

Van Leeuwen, M. S. (1985). *The person in psychology: A contemporary Christian appraisal*. Grand Rapids, MI: Eerdmans.

Vitz, P. (1977). *Psychology as religion: The cult of self-worship*. Grand Rapids, MI: Eerdmans.

Walsh, R. N., & Vaughan, F. (Eds.). (1980). *Beyond ego: Transpersonal dimensions in psychology*. Los Angeles: Tarcher.

Wegner, D. M., & Vallacter, R. R. (1977). *Implicit psychology*. New York: Oxford University Press.

Wolterstorff, N. (1984). *Reason within the bounds of religion* (2nd ed.). Grand Rapids, MI: Eerdmans.

Woolfolk, R., & Richardson, F. (1984). Behavior therapy and the ideology of modernity. *American Psychologist, 39,* 777–786.

Worthington, E. L. (1988). Understanding the values of religious clients: A model and its application to counseling. *Journal of Counseling, 35,* 166–174.

Worthington, E. L. (1989). Religious faith accross the life span: Implications for counseling and research. *The Counseling Psychologist, 17,* 555–612.

Worthington, E. L. (1991). Psychotherapy and religious values: An update. *Journal of Psychology and Christianity, 10,* 211–223.

Wulff, D. (1991), *Psychology of religion: Classic and contemporary views*. New York: Wiley.

5

RELIGIOUS BELIEFS, AFFILIATIONS, AND PRACTICES OF CLINICAL PSYCHOLOGISTS

EDWARD P. SHAFRANSKE

Religion as an influence in the United States is an undeniable fact. A review of the literature by Hoge (Chapter 1, this volume) and an inspection of recent survey data find that the majority of the population declare themselves, in some fashion, to be religious (Barna, 1992; Clark, 1994; Gallup, Jr., 1994; Hastings & Hastings, 1994; Kosmin & Lachman, 1993; Princeton Religious Research Center, 1990; Spiritual America, 1994). For example, a 1993 Gallup poll found that 93% indicated a religious preference and that in response to the question, "How important would you say religion is in your own life?" 59% reported "very important" and 29% reported "fairly important" (Gallup, Jr., 1994, p. 72). Sixty-three percent of respondents to a 1990 survey agreed "that religion can answer all or most of today's problems" (Smith, 1992, p. 367), and 57% reported that they pray at least once a day (Hastings & Hastings, 1994, p. 445). In addition, people appear to place a great deal of confidence in religious institutions; church or organized religion ranked second, only to the military, in ratings of confidence (Hastings & Hastings, 1994, p. 313). These data suggest that the majority of Americans affiliate and involve themselves in organized religion and find this involvement important. These reports of salience and confidence, as well as affiliation, may suggest that the beliefs and values fostered by religious institutions serve as important influences in the lives of many Americans. The empirical literature suggests that re-

149

ligious involvement in many instances influences attitudes and behaviors in both the political and the social arenas (Kosmin & Lachman, 1993; Gartner, Chapter 7, this volume). Religion appears to be a significant cultural institution, providing meaning, affiliation, and support for many individuals.

Having established the relevance of religion for the general population, I turn now to an examination of the religious beliefs, affiliations, and practices of psychologists and a discussion of clinical training and the use of religious interventions. This inquiry is required in light of the value-laden nature of psychotherapeutic work (Bergin, 1980, 1985, 1991; Jensen & Bergin, 1988). This is particularly the case in psychotherapy in which the treatment is based on the development of an interpretive understanding of behavior through a given psychological hermeneutic. In this regard, the clinician's personal values, beliefs, and faith commitment (couched in part in the form of therapeutic orientation) may enter into the clinical discourse, shape technical interventions, and yield behavioral prescriptions. It seems reasonable to assume that preprofessional experiences and the ongoing personal life of the clinician are often a source of influence. Culture, history, family, values, and beliefs continue to shape the backdrop on which therapeutic values are expressed in both subtle and overt ways in the conduct of psychotherapy. In addition, should psychologists agree with Frank and Frank (cf. 1991, p. 52) that psychotherapy essentially involves persuading patients to transform their personal meanings, then the beliefs and values of the clinician are an even more salient feature of the treatment process. The following review of selected literature will provide an inspection of the beliefs, affiliations, and practices of psychologists.

ATTITUDES, BELIEFS, AND PRACTICES

Before I examine the findings specific to psychologists, it is useful to consider education as a factor that influences the salience of religion. Salience, in this instance, refers to the importance that one places on religion.

Education

Education appears to significantly affect the importance that one places on religion. Although religious preference may not be significantly affected, a 1993 Gallup poll found that college graduates reported lower salience compared with people who had not attended college (Gallup, Jr., 1994, p. 72). Interestingly, however, there was no significant difference between those who obtained postgraduate education compared with college graduates (See Table 1). Consistent with these findings, Beit-Hallahmi (1977) found in his comprehensive review of the literature that scientists

TABLE 1
Salience of Religion

	Very important %	Fairly important %	Not very important %	No opinion %
National sample[a]	59	29	12	<1
Education				
Postgraduate	50	35	15	<1
College graduate	51	35	35	<1
College incomplete	56	33	11	<1
No college	64	29	7	<1
Psychologists[b]				
Salience of religion	26	22	51	0
Salience of spirituality	48	25	26	0

[a]1993 Gallup poll, Gallup, Jr. (1994); [b]random sample of APA members listing degrees in clinical psychology or counseling psychology (N = 253), Shafranske (1995).

and academicians are less religious than the rest of the population. A more recent survey ("Politics," 1991, p. 87; see Figure 1) found that 30% of all faculty members reported no religious affiliation in contrast to 5% of the general population (Gallup, Jr., 1994, p. 72). Psychologists hold religion to be less important compared with the general population. These findings suggest that differences between psychologists and the general population may be in part the result of the factor of higher education.

Attitudes and Beliefs

My discussion begins with an examination of psychologists' attitudes toward religion and their religious beliefs. A distinction will be maintained between religious attitudes and beliefs and religious preferences, affiliations, and practices. This division allows for institutional involvement to be considered as a separate factor.

Leuba (cited in Wulff, 1991, p. 205) conducted two important early studies of scientists' religious beliefs. He found that physical scientists were the most likely to "believe in a God who answers prayers" and psychologists were generally the least likely. In his 1914 study, 50% of the "lesser physical scientists" and 34% of the "greater physical scientists" held this belief as compared with 32% of the "lesser psychologists" and 13% of the "greater psychologists." His 1933 replication produced the following results: 43% of the "lesser physical scientists," 17% of the "greater physical scientists," 12% of the "lesser psychologists," and 2% of the "greater psychologists" held this belief. He thus found that the features of eminence and academic discipline appear to be related to religious belief. Similar trends were reported respective of beliefs concerning immortality.

Question: **What is your present religion?**

Religious preference of faculty by department

Percent saying "none"

Department	Percent
All faculty	30%
Anthropol./Archaeol.	65%
Philosophy	55%
Zoology	53%
Physiology/Anatomy	52%
Gen./Oth. biol. sci.	51%
Psychology	50%
Educ. foundations	50%
Electrical engineering	49%
Sociology	49%
French lang./lit.	48%
Educ. psych./counseling	47%
Bacteriol./Molec. Biol./Virology/Microb.	47%
Gen./Oth. Soc. Sci.	47%
Art	44%
Spanish lang./lit.	44%
Archit./Design	42%
English lang./lit.	41%
Botany	41%
History	39%
Earth sciences	38%
Biology	36%
Poli. sci./Govt.	36%
Law	35%
Math./Stat.	35%
Geography	34%
German lang./lit.	33%
Other fine arts	33%
Physics	33%
Other health fields	33%
Multidisciplinary fields	31%
Economics	30%
Educ. admin.	30%
Gen./other humanities	29%
Dramatics and speech	28%
Aeronaut./Astronaut. engin.	28%
Medicine	27%
Biochemistry	26%
Chemistry	25%
Chemical engineering	25%
Elementary/Secondary educ.	23%
Gen./Oth. physical sci.	23%
Music	21%
Gen./Oth. educational	21%
Business/Commerce/Manag.	21%
Journalism	21%
Physical/Health educ.	19%
Other foreign language	18%
Dentistry	16%
Mechanical engineering	16%
Agriculture/Forestry	15%
Library science	13%
Nursing	12%
Civil engineering	11%
Soc. work/Soc. welfare	9%
Gen./Other engineering	9%
Vocational/Technical	6%
Home economics	4%
Industrial arts	**
Religion/Theology	**

Figure 1. Percentage of faculty with no religious preference, by department. Copyright *The Public Perspective*, a publication of the Roper Center for Public Opinion Research, University of Connecticut, Storrs. Reprinted by permission.

Beit-Hallahmi (cf. 1977, p. 381) concluded that contemporary American psychology seems to consider religion marginal and considered personal beliefs to contribute to this status. Ragan, Malony, and Beit-Hallahmi (1980) found that psychologists were less religious as compared with the general population. However, more recent surveys by Shafranske and Malony (1990a, 1990b) and Bergin and Jensen (1990) suggest that attitudes toward religion may not be as different from the general population's attitudes as previously assumed and that psychologists do not perceive religious beliefs in an entirely negative light. Distinctions need to be made between valuing religion as a force in human existence; personal religious and spiritual beliefs; and preference, affiliation, and involvement in a formal religious body. Data culled from a number of recent national surveys will be the primary focus of my examination of psychologists' attitudes, beliefs, and practices.

The findings should be read with the understanding that the return rates ranged from 41% to 59%. Although these return rates are not unusual, it is acknowledged that the nonrespondents may hold dissimilar views from those reported. Shafranske and Malony (1990a) investigated this in comparing salience between the participants and the nonparticipants. When compared with nonparticipants, the participants evidenced a greater affinity and receptivity to religious and spiritual issues than actually exists within the larger psychologist population. On its face it may be reasonable to assume that those who find religion to be relevant are more likely to dedicate the time to complete and return a survey instrument that concerns religion than those who do not. The conclusions should therefore be read with this caveat in mind.

A general finding is that psychologists view religion as valuable. For example, Shafranske and Malony (1990a, p. 73) reported that 53% of the respondents indicated religion was valuable, 33% were neutral, and 14% rated this as undesirable. Sixty-five percent reported that spirituality was personally relevant, and 59% disagreed with the statement "Whether I turn out to be religious/spiritual or not doesn't make much difference to me." Bergin and Jensen (1990, p. 5) found that 65% of the psychologists and 77% of the total psychotherapist sample agreed or strongly agreed with the statement "I try hard to live my life according to my religious beliefs," and 68% endorsed the item "Seek a spiritual understanding of the universe and one's place in it" (p. 6). Lannert (1992), in a study of internship training directors found that the majority reported that spirituality was personally relevant. The results of a 1995 study of psychologists possessing doctoral degrees in counseling or clinical psychology found that, although 48% reported the salience of religion to be fairly to very important, 73% indicated that spirituality was fairly to very important (See Table 1). This finding suggests that the noetic domain is of importance to the majority of psychologists; however, institutional forms of religious sentiment are less likely to be endorsed. These studies taken together, although using different modes of questioning, suggest that psychologists value the religious dimension. They may be somewhat more similar to the general population than previously assumed, particularly in terms of noninstitutional expressions of spirituality.

Beliefs

Looking at the content of beliefs, the surveys suggest a wide range of religious beliefs. These studies found that roughly 40% endorsed a personal, transcendent God orientation; 30% an orientation that affirms a transcendent dimension in all nature; 26% the position that all ideologies are illusion, although they are meaningful; and 2% the position that all ideologies are illusion and are irrelevant to the real world (See Table 2).

Affiliation and Practice

One aspect of religiosity is preference for and affiliation with religion. Within the professorate, psychologists rank among the least likely to affiliate with religion ("Politics," 1991, p. 87); 50% list their religious prefer-

TABLE 2
Ideological Orientations

Ideological statement	1990[a]		1995[b]	
	N	%	N	%
There is a personal God of transcendent existence and power whose purposes will ultimately be worked out in human history.	121	29.6	60	23.9
There is a transcendent aspect of human experience which some persons call God but who is not immanently involved in the events of the world and human history.	42	10.3	34	13.6
There is a transcendent or divine dimension which is unique and specific to the human self.	38	9.3	17	6.8
There is a transcendent or divine dimension found in all manifestations of nature.	85	20.8	78	31.1
The notions of God or the transcendent are illusory products of human imagination; however, they are meaningful aspects of human existence.	106	25.9	59	23.5
The notions of God or the transcendent are illusory products of human imagination; therefore, they are irrelevant to the real world.	8	2.0	3	1.2
No Response	9	2.2	0	0

Note. [a]random sample of members of APA Division 12 (Clinical Psychology; N = 409), Shafranske & Malony (1990); [b]random sample of APA members listing degrees in clinical psychology or counseling psychology (N = 253), Shafranske (1995).

ence as "none" (See Figure 1). Each of the surveys found that psychologists, although receptive to religious and spiritual beliefs, are less likely to affiliate and become involved in organized religion. Ragan et al. (1980) found a "de-emphasis on overt religious behavior" (p. 211).

The relative eschewing of religious affiliation is of interest in light of the fact that the majority of psychologists come from religious backgrounds that are similar to the general population. Henry, Sims, and Spray (1973), Shafranske and Malony (1990a), and Shafranske (1995) indicate that psychologists were most often raised in families in which the feature of religiosity was similar to the general population (see Table 4). Although there are differences in the religious bodies in which affiliation took place, the rates of affiliation were similar. Over 95% reported to have been raised within a particular religion, regardless of their degree of involvement. This was in contrast to current affiliation with organized religion that was just over 70%, regardless of involvement, and under 50% if the criteria included regular participation (see Table 3). Lannert (1992, p. 80) reported similar results in her study of internship training directors; 72% indicated that they identified with or participated in a particular religion. The survey data suggest that, although they may value religiousness in general, psychologists personally participate in religion to a lesser extent than the general population.

The 1990 study indicated that fewer than one in five subjects agreed that organized religion was the primary source of their spirituality (Shaf-

TABLE 3
Affiliation and Involvement in Organized Religion

	1990[a]		1991[b]		1992[c]		1995[d]	
Degree of affiliation	N	%	N	%	N	%	N	%
Active participation, high level of involvement	74	18.1	31	11.5	9	11.4	40	16.1
Regular participation, some involvement	93	22.7	62	23.0	19	24.1	53	21.3
Identification with religion very limited, or no involvement	121	29.6	93	34.4	29	36.7	73	29.3
No identification, participation, or involvement with religion	91	22.2	53	19.6	17	21.5	51	20.5
Somewhat negative reaction to religion[e]	—	—	24	8.9	4	5.1	22	8.8
Disdain or very negative reaction to religion	29	7.1	7	2.6	1	1.3	10	4.0
No response	1	.2	0	0	0	0	4	1.6

Note. [a]random sample of members of APA Division 12 (Clinical Psychology), Shafranske & Malony (1990); [b]random sample of members of APA Division 29 (Psychotherapy), Derr (1991); [c]random sample of training directors listed in the 1990–1991 directory published by the Association of Psychology Internship Centers (APIC), Lannert (1992); [d]random sample of APA members listing degrees in clinical psychology or counseling psychology, Shafranske (1995); [e]in the Shafranske & Malony (1990) study, only one category was given: "Disdain and negative reaction to religion"; these results are presented under the "Disdain or very negative reaction to religion."

TABLE 4
Past and Present Religious Affiliations

| | Affiliation | | | |
| | Childhood | | Present | |
Religion	N	%	N	%
Roman Catholic	90	22.0	57	13.9
Jewish	83	20.3	64	15.6
Methodist	48	11.7	23	5.6
Protestant	44	10.8	9	2.2
Episcopal	22	5.4	21	5.1
Baptist	20	4.9	9	2.2
Presbyterian	20	4.9	23	5.6
No religion	12	2.9	122	29.8
Lutheran	11	2.7	8	2.0
Christian	7	1.7	4	1.0
Church of Latter Day Saints	7	1.7	2	.5
Mennonite	6	1.5	1	.2
Congregational	5	1.2	3	.7
Unitarian Universalist	4	1.0	18	4.4
Other (1% or less of sample)	30	7.3	45	10.9

Note. Data are from a random sample of members of APA Division 12 (Clinical Psychology), Shafranske & Malony (1990)

ranske & Maloney, 1990a). The majority of the subjects characterized their spiritual beliefs and practices as an "alternative spiritual path which is not a part of an organized religion." Lanner (1992, p. 82) found that 50% agreed with the item "My spirituality is a personal stance neither rooted in religion nor any particular organization/movement." For some the eschewing of organized religion may be in response to negative experiences in the past or socialization away from institutional involvement. Survey data were highly variable in the self-report of negative religious experiences, and no definitive conclusion can be reached (Derr, 1991; Lannert, 1992; Shafranske & Molony, 1990a; See Table 3).

These data suggest that psychologists appreciate the religious dimension and hold religious beliefs, and many value the dimension of spirituality. Although most had been "raised within a religion," the majority do not actively participate within organized religion.

Clinical Practice

It is of note that, despite the attention that was placed on religious experience starting with William James and by a number of prominent scholars throughout the history of American psychology, as Wulff (1991) concluded, "now and then evidence points to a genuine antagonism toward religion among typical psychologists" (p. 34). He further suggested, taking up an argument raised by Bellah (1970), that academicians have not allowed that religion can be approached with a scholarly attitude but rather hold that religion is something that can only be preached (cf. Wulff, 1991, p. 36; see also Lehman & Shriver, 1968). In addition, psychology and religion may be seen as paradigms that offer systems of significance and compete as institutions of influence within the polity. Such a view may account for the finding, that will be discussed later, that religious issues are rarely discussed within the graduate education and clinical training of a psychologist and the finding of scant references to religion in psychology textbooks (Kirkpatrick & Spilka, 1989; Shafranske, 1989). Such a view suggests that professional attitudes may be less influenced by scientific principles and scholarly training as much as by personal beliefs.

Relevance

The findings of Shafranske and Malony (1990a, 1990b), Derr (1991), Lannert (1992), and Shafranske (1995) suggest that psychologists, in general, view spiritual and religious issues to be relevant in their work as clinicians. The majority of psychologists report that spirituality is relevant in their professional life (Shafranske, 1995; Shafranske & Malony, 1990). The findings suggest that clinicians appreciate the religious and spiritual dimensions of their clients' experiences.

Furthermore, it appears that often religious factors may influence the selection of clients and therapists. Henry et al. (1973) reported that their "findings showed that psychotherapeutic religiocultural congruence involves an affinity between the patient's current commitments and the therapist's religiocultural origins" (p. 221). They found that patients and therapists were remarkably similar.

Practice

The attitudes and behaviors of the psychologists indicated a wide variance in respect to the manner in which religious and spiritual aspects were clinically addressed. Although the majority find religious issues to be relevant in clinical practice, most clinicians agreed with the statement "Psychologists, in general, do not possess the knowledge or skills to assist individuals in their religious or spiritual development." (Shafranske & Malony, 1990). Approximately one third of these clinicians expressed personal competence in counseling clients regarding religious issues and matters of spirituality.

Table 5 presents the explicit religious interventions that are used by psychologists. It is observed that, as the counseling interventions become more explicitly religious and participatory in nature, the frequency of behavior declines. The data suggested that the majority of the subjects ap-

TABLE 5
Therapists' Use of Interventions of a Religious Nature

Behaviors	1990[a]		1995[b]	
	N	%	N	%
Know clients' religious backgrounds	372	91	82	42
Pray with a client	30	7	8	3
Use religious language or concepts	235	57	58	26.6
Use or recommend religious or spiritual books	129	32	18	7
Recommend participation in religion	147	36	—	—
Recommend leaving a religion	—	—	3	1.3

Note. [a]Random sample of members of APA Division 12 (Clinical Psychology), Shafranske & Malony (1990); [b]Random sample of APA members listing degrees in clinical psychology or counseling psychology, Shafranske (1995).

peared cognizant of the religiousness of their clients and used to some extent religious language and concepts. The data suggested that, although psychologists may possess opinions regarding their clients' religiousness or share in the belief orientation, they tend to not participate or actively seek to influence their clients' lives in this regard. The 1990 survey (Shafranske & Malony, 1990a) found that 73% disagreed that it would be appropriate for a psychologist to recommend to a client to leave his or her religion if he or she assessed it to be a hindrance to his or her psychological growth (see Table 5).

Attitudes and behaviors regarding interventions of a religious nature were primarily influenced by the clinician's personal view of religion and spirituality rather than by his or her theoretical orientation in psychology. The subject's personal experience of religion significantly correlated with his or her attitudes and behaviors regarding interventions of a religious nature. Shafranske and Malony (1990) found a positive correlation between affiliation and participation in organized religion and the performance of the aforementioned interventions ($r = .27$). The more negatively the subject viewed the religious experiences in his or her past the less likely he or she was utilizing interventions of a religious nature ($r = .16$). The type of religiousness also influenced the therapist's view of his or her competence to provide counseling regarding these religious and spiritual issues. Therapists whose predominant religiousness was assessed as ends orientation (Batson & Ventis, 1982) expressed the highest degree of competence in knowledge and skills, $F (2, 398) = 8.39, p < .001$.

Education and Training

The findings of this review suggested that the majority of the clinicians viewed religious and spiritual issues as relevant in their practice of clinical psychology and to varying degrees used interventions of a religious nature. It was important, therefore, to assess the educational and training opportunities that prepare psychologists to deal with these issues. The surveys have found that over 90% indicate that education and training in religious issues rarely or never occurs (Shafranske, 1995; Shafranske & Malony, 1990a).

In the area of training, Lannert's study (1992) indicated that considerably more attention is being placed on religious issues. Seventy-two percent of the clinical-training directors reported that they "examined case studies in which spiritual/religious issues were integrated into the case," and 75.9% said that spiritual or religious value issues were addressed in clinical case presentations and 59.5% in initial intakes. These findings may reflect the heightened sensitivities of clinicians involved in directing clinical training or may suggest a more recent sea change within the field. Furthermore, these data are interesting in light of the fact that less than 20% reported that they had a working knowledge of the psychology of religion.

Other educational experiences were investigated by Shafranske and Malony (1990). Approximately 10% of the subjects had some degree of theological training; 10% were current members of APA Division 36, Psychology and Religion. The degree of background in the area of psychology and religion was also assessed by asking the subjects to note which, if any, of three seminal texts in the field (as selected by the 1987 Executive Committee of APA Division 36) and one popular text they had read. Thirty-eight percent of the 1990 sample and 21.6% of Lannert's sample (1992, p. 84) had read William James's *Varieties of Religious Experience*, 19% had read Gordon Allport's *The Individual and His Religion*, 3% had read Paul Pruyser's *A Dynamic Psychology of Religion*, and 33% had read the best-selling book M. Scott Peck's *The Road Less Traveled*. Sixty-five percent (N = 228) had read at least one of the above mentioned books. Lannert (1992, p. 84) reported that 43.2% of her sample had read Carl Jung's *Modern Man in Search of Religious Experience*. These data suggest that psychologists, in general, receive limited education and training in the area psychology and religion. However, 54% rated the psychology of religion as desirable in the education of a clinical psychologist, and 62% indicated that clinical supervision and training in dealing with religious and spiritual issues with clients was desirable (Shafranske & Malony, 1990a, p. 77).

CONCLUSION

Psychologists appear to value the role that religion serves in human existence. The majority hold religious beliefs and affiliate to some extent with organized religion. It appears that psychologists may be more similar than dissimilar to the general population in their religious views and faith commitments.

Psychologists appear to consider the religious dimension of their clients in their clinical practice. The extent to which religious issues are addressed and the nature of the techniques that are used are primarily determined by their personal religious commitments than by clinical training. Education and training within the area of psychology and religion appears to be very limited; the vast majority report that religious issues were rarely, if ever, addressed.

The conclusion that the approach clinicians bring to understanding the religiosity of their clients is primarily based on personal convictions rather than on graduate education and clinical training point to the need for the profession to reflect on its fundamental attitudes toward religion as a variable in mental health and in the clinical practice of psychology. Research efforts need to be extended to identify the values that are inherent in psychological treatment, the influences of religiocultural match on treatment process and outcome, and the effects of implicit and explicit integration of religious considerations within psychological services.

REFERENCES

Allport, G. (1950). *The individual and his religion; A psychological interpretation.* New York: Macmillan.

Barna, G. (1992). *What Americans believe: An annual survey of values and religious views in the United States.* Ventura, CA: Regal Books.

Batson, C., & Ventis, L. (1982). *The religious experience. A social psychological perspective.* Oxford, England: Oxford University Press.

Beit-Hallahmi, B. (1977). Curiosity, doubt, and devotion: The beliefs of psychologists and the psychology of religion. In H. N. Malony (Ed.), *Current perspectives in the psychology of religion* (pp. 381–391). Grand Rapids, MI: Eerdmans.

Bellah, R. (1970). Confessions of a former establishment fundamentalist. *Bulletin of the Council on the Study of Religion, 1*(3), 3–6.

Bergin, A. E. (1980). Psychotherapy and religious values. *Journal of Consulting and Clinical Psychology, 48,* 95–105.

Bergin, A. E. (1985). Proposed values for guiding and evaluating counseling and psychotherapy. *Counseling and Values, 29,* 99–116.

Bergin, A. E. (1991). Values and religious issues in psychotherapy and mental health. *American Psychologist, 46,* 394–403.

Bergin, A. E., & Jensen, J. P. (1990). Religiosity of psychotherapists: A national survey. *Psychotherapy, 27*(1), 3–7.

Clark, C. S. (1994, November). Religion in America. *CQ Researcher, 4,* 44.

Derr, K. (1991). *Religious issues in psychotherapy: Factors associated with the selection of clinical interventions.* Unpublished doctoral dissertation, University of Southern California, Los Angeles.

Frank, J. D., & Frank, J. B. (1991). *Persuasion and healing* (3rd ed.). Baltimore, MD: The Johns Hopkins University Press.

Gallup, G., Jr. (1994). *The Gallup poll. Public opinion 1993.* Wilmington, DE: Scholarly Resources.

Hastings, E., & Hastings, H. (Eds.). (1994). *Index to international public opinion: 1993-1994.* Westport, CT: Greenwood Press.

Henry, W., Sims, J., & Spray, S. (1973). *Public and private lives of psychotherapists.* San Francisco: Jossey-Bass.

James, W. (1902). *The varieties of religious experience; A study in human nature.* Cambridge, MA: Harvard University Press.

Jensen, J. P., & Bergin, A. E. (1988). Mental health values of professional therapists: A national interdisciplinary survey. *Professional Psychology: Research and Practice, 19,* 290–297.

Kirkpatrick, L., & Spilka, B. (1989). *The treatment of religion in psychology textbooks: A review of past and current trends.* Paper presented at the convention of the American Psychological Association, New Orleans, LA.

Kosmin, B., & Lachman, S. (1993). *One nation under God: Religion in contemporary American society.* New York: Crown Trade Paperbacks.

Lannert, J. L. (1992). *Spiritual and religious attitudes, beliefs, and practices of clinical training directors and their internship sites.* Unpublished doctoral dissertation, University of Southern California.

Lehman, E. C., Jr., & Shriver, D. W., Jr. (1968). Academic discipline as predictive of faculty religiosity. *Social Forces, 47,* 171–182.

Peck, M. S. (1978). *The road less traveled.* New York: Simon & Schuster.

Politics of the professorate. (1991, July-August). *The Public Perspective,* pp. 86–87.

Princeton Religious Research Center. (1990). *Religion in America.* Princeton, NJ: American Institute of Public Opinion.

Pruyser, P. (1968). *A dynamic psychology of religion.* New York: Harper & Row.

Ragan, C., Malony, H. N., & Beit-Hallahmi, B. (1980). Psychologist and religion: Profession factors associated with personal belief. *Reviews of Religious Research, 21*(2), 208–217.

Shafranske, E. (1989). *The treatment of religion in clinical psychology textbooks.* Paper presented at the convention of the American Psychological Association, New Orleans, LA.

Shafranske, E. (1995). *Religiosity of clinical and counseling psychologists.* Unpublished manuscript.

Shafranske, E., & Elkins, D. (1987). *Religiosity and psychotherapy: A comparison of California and Wyoming psychologists.* Paper presented at the convention of the California State Psychological Association, Coronado, CA.

Shafranske, E., & Gorsuch, R. (1985). Factors associated with the perception of spirituality in psychotherapy. *Journal of Transpersonal Psychology, 16*, 231–241.

Shafranske, E. P., & Malony, H. N. (1990a). Clinical psychologists' religious and spiritual orientations and their practice of psychotherapy. *Psychotherapy, 27*(1), 72–78.

Shafranske, E. P., & Malony, H. N. (1990b). California psychologists' religiosity and psychotherapy. *Journal of Religion and Health, 28*(3), 219–231.

Smith, T. (1992). The polls: Poll trends. Religious beliefs and behaviors and the televangelist scandals of 1987-1988. *Public Opinion Quarterly, 56*, 360–380.

Spiritual America. (1994, April 4). *U. S. News and World Reports*, pp. 48–59.

Wulff, D. (1991). *Psychology of religion. Classic and contemporary views*. New York: Wiley.

II

RELIGION, MENTAL HEALTH, AND CLINICAL PRACTICE

6

PLURALISM AND ONENESS IN RELIGIOUS EXPERIENCE: WILLIAM JAMES, FAITH-DEVELOPMENT THEORY, AND CLINICAL PRACTICE

JAMES W. FOWLER

In this chapter I will explore some of the principal similarities and differences between the depiction of the motions and emotions of faith and religious experience as set forth in the faith-development approach and the approach to those matters found in Jamesian philosophy and psychology of religious experience. This dialogue sets forth an understanding of religious experience that is sensitive to the nuances of an evolving faith throughout the life of the person. Such a perspective allows the clinician to view the faith dimension as an essential feature of human experience that complements other lines of development. Furthermore, the faith-development approach, as I will present, offers a model through which the faith experiences and crises, which often parallel and contribute to psychological complaints, may be understood. I first turn to the confluence of thinking in the works of William James and in my works as a foundation to present an overview of stages of faith.

Portions of this chapter were presented in "The William James Award Lecture," APA Division 36 (Psychology of Religion), given at the annual meeting of the APA on August 14, 1994, and "Faith Development Theory and Psychodynamic Perspectives: Some Theoretical and Practical Reflections" presented at the annual meeting of the American Psychiatric Association on May 25, 1993. A shortened and altered version of this material will appear in chapter 3 of the author's forthcoming book, *Faithful change: The personal and public challenges of postmodern life* (Abingdon Press, 1996).

JAMES AND *THE VARIETIES OF RELIGIOUS EXPERIENCE*

In writing *The Varieties of Religious Experience*, James (1902/1961) combined remarkable capacities for finding descriptive accounts of various aspects of religious experience with an ongoing process of assessment based on his primary philosophical methods and commitments. His commitment to the sense of a "pluralistic universe" allowed him to honor difference, variety, and multiplicity with regard to types and excellences of religious experience. His commitment to pragmatism allowed him to reshape the question of the "truth" of religious experiences, practices, and beliefs. Instead of addressing questions of truth epistemologically, metaphysically, or theologically, his analysis consistently sought to appraise the veridical character of religious experience by assessing its impact on the intensity of human action and on the shaping of human welfare. James clearly valued religion and religious experience for the zest, the drive, the inspiration it provided for the heroic and strenuous life. Inclined to melancholy and vocational indecision in his early life, he valued the ebullient energy and higher sense of purpose religion provided for many. While admiring the equanimity and poise of the "one-born" type of person and the optimistic rationality of the "healthy-minded," James distrusted their blindness to the presence of real and pervasive evil in nature and the human community. Over their shallow optimism and bland idealism, he favored the subconscious ferment and emotional upheaval of the "twice-born" type.

Like the 19th-century German theologian, Friedrich Schleiermacher, James saw the essence of religion in feeling—the feeling of solemnity, the feeling of seriousness, the feeling of relatedness to transcendence or what he called the *more*. James's own existential search gives compelling power to his wrestling with the pragmatic questions of religion's truth and usefulness, as well as its plurality of manifestations. His personal questions fuel his investigations of conversion, saintliness, and mysticism. His courageous commitment to a nonreductionistic examination of the topics of psychology of religion appropriately leads, in the end, to his bringing his readers face to face with the mystery that lies on the "father side" of religious experiences and their practical consequences. James does, indeed, anticipate Freud with his suggestion that

> the *more* with which in religious experience we feel ourselves connected is on its *hither* side the subconscious continuation of our conscious life. . . . At the same time, the theologian's contention that the religious man is moved by an external power is vindicated, for it is one of the peculiarities of invasions from the subconscious region to take on objective appearances, and to suggest to the Subject an external control. In the religious life the control is felt as "higher"; but since . . . it is primarily the higher faculties of our own hidden mind

which are controlling, the sense of union with the power beyond us is a sense of something, not merely apparently, but literally true. (pp. 396–397)

James leaves us with a sketch of his own "overbeliefs," as he calls them, which expresses the conviction that

> confining ourselves to what is common and generic, we have in *the fact that the conscious person is continuous with a wider self through which saving experiences come*, a positive content of religious experience which, it seems to me, *is literally and objectively true as far as it goes*. (p. 398)

When people commune with the wider self—which for James, plunges them "into an altogether other dimension of existence from the sensible and merely "understandable" world—they are affected and changed. He says,

> When we commune with it, work is actually done upon our finite personality, for we are turned into new men and consequences in the way of conduct follow in the natural world upon our regenerative change . . . [T]hat which produces effects within another reality must be termed a reality itself, so I feel as if we had no philosophic excuses for calling the unseen or mystical world unreal. (p. 399)

Having thus removed the excuse for dismissing the reality of an unseen dimension, James proceeds to use the name God for it.

> We and God have business with each other, and in opening ourselves to his influence our deepest destiny is fulfilled. The Universe, as those parts of it which our personal being constitutes, takes a turn genuinely for the worse or for the better in proportion as each one of us fulfills or evades God's demands . . . God is real since he produces real effects. (pp. 399–400)

My brief characterization of James's classic is merely intended as a reminder of some of his characteristic concerns, his passion, and the flavor of his conclusions. I have found it bracing to re-enter his thought world and its social–historic location. His phenomenological accounts of conversion experiences, of the aspects of saintly existence, and of mystical rapture are juicy beyond compare with most of what is found in the faith-development literature. The foci and questions fueling the two projects have significant differences. There are also significant similarities I want to point to as well. To make these comparisons, I need to offer a brief review of faith-development theory; its underlying distinctions of faith, belief, and religion; and the sweep of the developmental stages of faith.

FAITH, SELFHOOD, AND THE MAKING OF MEANING

Faith-development theory and research have focused on a multidimensional construct for faith that sees it as foundation to social relations, to personal identity, and to the making of personal and cultural meanings (Fowler, 1980, 1981, 1986, 1987, 1989, 1991). My claim is that faith is a generic feature of human beings. To make this claim credible, I must take some care to distinguish faith from two related patterns of human action that are often treated as synonymous with faith; belief and religion. Belief, in the modern period, has come increasingly to mean the giving of intellectual assent to propositional statements that codify the doctrines or ideological claims of a particular tradition or group. Although belief may be an aspect of a person's or a group's faith, it is only a part. Faith includes unconscious dynamics as well as conscious awareness. It includes deep-seated emotional dimensions as well as cognitive operations and content. Faith is both more personal and more existentially defining than belief, understood in this modern sense.

Religion, as distinguished from faith, may be though of as a cumulative tradition composed from the myriad beliefs and practices that have expressed and formed the faith of individuals in the past and present. The components of a cumulative tradition can include art and architecture; symbols, rituals, narrative, and myth; scriptures, doctrines, ethical teachings, and music; practices of justice and mercy; and much more. Elements from a cumulative tradition can be the source of awakening and forming for the faith consciousness of individuals in the present. A current generation's drawing on and being formed by elements from a cumulative tradition make for a reciprocity of mutual vitalization and commitment. In the long evolution of humankind, the tie between faith and religion has generally been inextricable. It is only in the modern period, where many people have separated themselves from religious communities and religious faith, that religious faith needs to be distinguished from faith in a more generic and universal sense.

Faith, understood in this more inclusive sense, may be characterized as an integral, centering process, underlying the formation of the beliefs, values, and meanings, that (a) gives coherence and direction to people's lives; (b) links them in shared trusts and loyalties with others; (c) grounds their personal stances and communal loyalties in a sense of relatedness to a larger frame of reference; and (d) enables them to face and deal with the limit conditions of human life, relying on that which has the quality of ultimacy in their lives.

The foregoing characterization of faith is meant to be as formal as possible. It aims to include descriptions of religious faith as well as the less explicit faith orientations of individuals and groups who can be described as secular or eclectic in their belief and values orientations. This non-content-specific characterization of faith correlates with the formal intent of the descriptions of the stages of faith. The stages aim to describe patterned operations of knowing and valuing that underlie consciousness. The varying stages of faith can be differentiated in relation to the degrees of complexity, of comprehensiveness, of internal differentiation, and of moral inclusiveness that their operations of knowing and valuing manifest. In continuity with the constructive developmental tradition, faith stages are held to be invariant, sequential, and hierarchical.

Stages of Faith: An Overview

In the following descriptions of the faith stages, I want to acknowledge the complex interplay of factors that must be taken into account if people are to begin to understand faith development. These include biological maturation, emotional and cognitive development, psychosocial experience, and religio-cultural influences. Knowledge of brain functioning in cognitive and emotional behavior opens a rich field for inquiry regarding neurophysical dynamics underlying faith. Because development in faith involves aspects of all these sectors of human development, movement from one stage to another is not automatic or assured. People may reach chronological and biological adulthood while remaining best defined by structural stages of faith that would most commonly be associated with early or middle childhood or adolescence (see Table 1 for a summary of the stages).

Primal Faith (Infancy)

A prelanguage disposition of trust forms in the mutuality of one's relationships with parents and other caregivers to offset the inevitable anxiety and mistrust that result from the succession of cognitive and emotional experiences of separation and self-differentiation that occur during infant development. Experiences combining to form this trusting disposition include body contact and care; vocal and visual interplay; ritualized interactions associated with early play, feeding, and tending; and the development of interpersonal affective attunement in the infant's relations with caregivers. Factors such as these activate prepotentiated capacities for finding coherence and reliability in self and primal others, for forming bonds of attachment with them, and for shaping a predisposition to trust the larger value and meaning commitments conveyed in parental care. Anxiety and mistrust have their own developmental pattern of emergence that caregivers' consistency and dependability help to offset. (Erikson, 1963; Fowler, 1989; Stern, 1985).

Primal faith (infancy): A prelanguage disposition of trust forms in the mutuality of one's relationships with parents and other caregivers to offset the anxiety that results from separations that occur during infant development. The incorporative self.

Intuitive–projective faith (early childhood): Imagination, stimulated by stories, gestures, and symbols and not yet controlled by logical thinking, combines with perception and feelings to create long-lasting images that represent both the protective and the threatening powers surrounding one's life. The impulsive self.

Mythic–literal faith (childhood and beyond): The developing ability to think logically helps one order the world with categories of causality, space, and time; to enter into perspectives of others; and to capture life meaning in stories. The imperial self.

Synthetic–conventional faith (adolescence and beyond): New cognitive abilities make mutual perspective taking possible and enable one to integrate diverse self-images into a coherent identity. A personal and largely unreflective synthesis of beliefs and values evolves to support identity and to unite one emotional solidarity with others. The interpersonal self.

Individuative–reflexive faith (young adulthood and beyond): Critical reflection on one's beliefs and values, using third-person perspective taking; understanding of the self and others as part of a social system; the internalization of authority; and the assumption of responsibility for making explicit choice of ideology and lifestyle open the way for critically self-aware commitments in relationships and vocation. The institutional self.

Conjunctive faith (early midlife and beyond): The embrace of polarities in one's life, an alertness to paradox, and the need for multiple interpretations of reality mark this stage. Symbol and story, metaphor and myth (from one's own traditions and others') are newly appreciated (second, or willed naïveté) as vehicles for expressing truth. The interindividual self.

Universalizing faith (midlife and beyond): Beyond paradox and polarities, individuals in this stage are grounded in a oneness with the power of being. Their visions and commitments free them for a passionate yet detached spending of self in love, devoted to overcoming division, oppression, and violence, and in effective anticipatory response to an inbreaking commonwealth of love and justice.

Table 1. Stages of Faith and Selfhood.

Intuitive–Projective Faith (Early Childhood)

From the time children begin to use language to communicate about self and objects in the world, there can be seen the emergence of a style of meaning making based on an emotional and perceptual ordering of experience. Imagination, not yet disciplined by consistent logical operations, responds to story, symbol, dream, and experience. It attempts to form images that can hold and order the mixture of feelings and impressions evoked by the child's encounters with the newness of both everyday reality and the penumbra of mystery that surrounds and pervades it. Death becomes a conscious focus as a source of danger and mystery. Experiences of power and powerlessness orient children to a frequently deep existential concern about questions of security, safety, and the power of those on whom they rely for protection.

From psychodynamic perspectives this stage begins with the time of first self-consciousness. Standing on one's own two feet, being aware of being seen and evaluated by others, and being attentive to standards for how things are supposed to be make the child especially sensitive to the twin polarities of pride and shame (Emde, Johnson, & Easterbrooks, 1987; Erikson, 1963; Kegan, 1984; Nathanson, 1992). At about this time, children undertake the construction of their first representations of God. Ana-Marie Rizzuto's research (1981) suggests that these earliest God representations are populated with the dominant emotional characteristics children have experienced in their relations with those all-powerful ones on whom they feel absolutely dependent, namely the *imagoes* of their parents. Where defenses such as splitting and dissociation have been necessitated by parental or other abuse or neglect, either God is likely to undergo splitting as well or the child constructs images of the "bad" self as being the deserving recipient of the inevitable—and deserved—punishment of a demanding but justifiably angry God. Where inadequate mirroring in the previous stage has resulted in an empty or incoherent sense of self and where conditions of worth and esteem are such that the child must suppress his or her own processing of truth and experience, the forming of a "false self" is often seen (Kohut, 1977; Miller, 1987; Winnicott, 1971).

Mythic–Literal Faith (Middle Childhood and Beyond)

Though the emotive and imaginal funding of the previous stage is still operative in this newly emerging stage, concrete operational thinking (Piaget) makes possible more stable forms of conscious interpretation and shaping of experience and meanings. Operations of thought can now be reversed, which means that cause and effect relations are now more clearly understood. Simple perspective taking emerges to ensure that the differentiation of one's own experiences and perspectives from those of others becomes a dependable acquisition. The young person constructs the world in terms of new linearity and predictability. Although still a potent source of feelings, the previous stage's store of images gets "sealed over," and its episodic, intuitive forms of knowing are subordinated to more logical and prosaic modes.

In this mythic–literal stage the child, adolescent, or adult does not yet construct the interiority—the feelings, attitudes, and internal guiding processes—of the self or others. Similarly, one does not construct God in particularly personal terms or attribute to God highly differentiated internal emotions and interpersonal sensitivities. In making sense of the larger order of things, therefore, this stage typically structures the ultimate environment—the cosmic pattern of God's rule or control of the universe—along the lines of simple fairness and moral reciprocity. God is constructed on the model of a consistent, caring, but just ruler or parent. Goodness is rewarded; badness is punished. In gathering its meanings, this stage employs narrative. Story (and stories) are as close as the mythic–literal stage comes to reflective synthesis. In this stage the use of symbols and concepts remains largely concrete and literal. The mythic–literal stage begins to wane with the discovery that this is not a "quick payoff universe (i.e., evil or bad people do not necessarily suffer for their transgressions," and often "bad things happen to good people"). The term *11-year-old atheists* has been coined for children, who in having this latter experience, temporarily or permanently give up belief in a God built along the lines of simple cosmic moral retribution.

Synthetic–Conventional Faith (Adolescence and Beyond)

Accompanying the exploding physical, glandular, and sexual changes brought on by adolescence, there can also be revolutions in cognitive functioning and in interpersonal perspective taking. With the emergence of early formal operational thinking, a young person's thought and reasoning take wings. Capable of using and appreciating abstract concepts, young people begin to think about their thinking, to reflect on their stories, and to name and synthesize their meanings.

This period is punctuated by the emergence of mutual interpersonal perspective taking. "I see you seeing me; I see the me I think you see." And the obverse can also be appreciated: "You see you according to me; you see the you think I see." This capacity can make youths acutely sensitive to the meanings they seem to have to others and the evaluations those meanings imply. Identity and personal interiority—one's own and others—become absorbing concerns. Personality, both as style and substance, becomes a conscious issue. From within this stage, youth construct the ultimate environment in terms of the personal. God representations can be populated with personal qualities of accepting love, understanding, loyalty, and support during times of crisis. During this stage youths are prepared to develop attachments to beliefs, values, and elements of personal style that link them in conforming relations with the most significant others among their peers, family, and other nonfamily adults. Identity, beliefs, and values are strongly felt, even when they contain contradictory elements. However, they tend to be espoused in tacit, rather than explicit, formulations. At this stage one's ideology or worldview is lived and asserted; it is not yet a matter of critical and reflective articulation.

One decisive limit of the synthetic–conventional stage is its lack of third-person perspective taking. This means that in its dependence on significant others for confirmation and clarity about one's identity and meaning to them, the self does not yet have a transcendental perspective from which it can see and evaluate self–other relations from a perspective outside them. In the synthetic–conventional stage the young person or adult can remain trapped in the "Tyranny of the They."

Individuative–Reflective Faith (Young Adulthood and Beyond)

For this stage to emerge, two important movements must occur, together or in sequence: First, the previous stage's tacit system of beliefs, values, and commitments must be critically examined. The assumptive configuration of meanings assembled to support one's selfhood in its roles and relations must now be allowed to become problematic. Evocative symbols and stories by which lives have been oriented will now be critically weighed and interpreted. Second, the self, previously constituted and sustained by its roles and relationships, must struggle with the question of identity and worth apart from its previously defining connections. This means that individuals must take into themselves much of the authority they previously invested in others for determining and sanctioning their goals and values. It means that definitions of the self that are dependent on roles and relationships with others and with groups must now be regrounded in terms of a new quality of responsibility that the self takes for defining itself and orchestrating its roles and relations.

At the heart of this double movement in the transition to the individuative–reflective stage is the emergence of third-person perspective taking. This capacity generally emerges out of the conflict of voices of external or internalized authorities. With its transcendental view of one's self–other relations, the third-person perspective allows one a standpoint from which conflicting expectations can be adjudicated and one's own inner authorization can be strengthened.

To sustain their reflective identities individuals at this stage compose (or ratify) meaning frames that are conscious of their own boundaries and inner connections and are aware of themselves as worldviews. Using its capacities of procedural knowing and critical reflection, the individuative stage "demythologizes" symbols, rituals, and myths, typically translating their meanings into conceptual formulations. Frequently overconfident in their conscious awareness, people at this stage attend minimally to unconscious factors that influence their judgments and behavior. This excessive confidence in the conscious mind and in critical thought can lead to a kind of second narcissism in which the now clearly bounded, reflective self overassimilates "reality" and the perspectives of others into its worldview.

Conjunctive Faith (Early Midlife and Beyond)

The name of this stage implies a rejoining or a union of that which previously has been separated. The name comes from Nicolas of Cusa (1401–1464) who wrote about what he called the *coincidentia oppositorum*, the "coincidence of opposites" in our apprehensions of truth. The confident clarity about the boundaries of self and faith that the individuative stage worked so hard to achieve must be relativized in the move to the conjunctive stage. The executive ego, which claims authority for its own decisions and selectively affirms values and beliefs that it finds acceptable, must come to terms with the fact that its confidence is based in part at least on illusion or on seriously incomplete self-knowledge. People are many selves: they have a conscious mind, but they also are a great deal of patterned action and reaction that is largely unconscious. Those powerful and important unconscious aspects of selfhood are personal, social, cultural, and perhaps archetypal in origin. People are driven and pushed, as well as funded, from underneath by motives, desires, and hungers—and lures of spirit—that are difficult to recognize and integrate.

In the transition to the conjunctive stage one begins to make peace with the tension arising from the realization that truth must be approached from a number of different directions and angles of vision. Faith must learn to maintain the tensions between these multiple perspectives, refusing to collapse them in one direction or another. In this sense, faith must begin to come to terms with indissoluble paradoxes: the strengths found in apparent weakness; the leadership that is possible from the margins of societies and groups, but not from the center; and the immanence and the transcendence of God.

Conjunctive faith exhibits a kind of epistemological humility. The realities that religious rituals, symbols, and metaphors seek to bring into reach spill over in excess and recede behind them in simultaneous disclosure and concealment. This stage marks a movement beyond the demythologizing strategy of the individuative stage. Acknowledging the multidimensionality and density of symbols and myth, people at the conjunctive stage learn to enter into symbolic realities, allowing them to exert their illuminating and mediating power. In what Paul Ricoeur (1967) called a "second" or a "willed" naïveté, people at the conjunctive stage manifest a readiness to enter into the rich dwellings of meaning that true symbols, ritual, and myth offer. As a correlate of these qualities, this stage exhibits a principled openness to the truths of other religious and faith traditions.

Until recently, only the Jungian traditions, among analytic perspectives, provided very much help in the transition to the conjunctive stage. Although Jung may have underestimated the wily resistances and cunning conservatism of the personal unconscious and its defenses, his teachings about the midlife process of individuation have much to commend them. His notions and teachings about how to work at integrating such archetypal complexes as the shadow, the contrasexual element, the wise elder, and the archetype of the self itself are important. Transition to the conjunctive stage involves the embrace of what Carlyle Marney once called a necessary "ego leak." It requires methods of meditation and therapy that nurture a safe permeability of the defensive membrane that separates the conscious from the nonconscious.

Universalizing Faith (Midlife and Beyond)

This stage involves individuals moving beyond the paradoxical awareness and embrace of polar opposites that are hallmarks of the conjunctive stage. The structuring of this stage derives from the radical completion of a process of decentration from self that proceeds throughout the sequence of stages. From the nondifferentiation of self and objects in the earliest phases of infancy to the naive egocentrism of the intuitive–projective stage, each successive stage marks a steady widening in social perspective taking. Gradually the circle of "those who count" in faith, meaning making, and justice has expanded until, at the conjunctive stage, it extends well beyond the bounds of social class, nation, race, gender, ideological affinity, and religious tradition. In universalizing faith, this process comes to a kind of completion. In the previous stage, people continue to live in the tension between their rootedness in and loyalties to their segment of the existing order, on the one hand, and the inclusiveness and transformation of their visions toward a new ultimate order, on the other. The conjunctive self is a tensional self.

People found in the universalizing stage are relatively rare. What I am going to say about the qualities they exhibit may remind some of James's discussion of "Saintliness" in Lectures 11–15 in *The Varieties of Religious Experience*. Psychodynamically, the self in this universalizing stage moves beyond usual forms of defensiveness and exhibits an openness that is based on groundedness in the being, love, and regard of God. I need to say that such individuals continue to be finite creatures. They have blind spots and inconsistencies, and they still exhibit some distorted capacities for relations with others. On the other hand, if they have done the work of healing and reintegration that the previous stages require, they cannot be confused with those dangerously charismatic figures who exhibit the kind of manipulative dissociations and psychotic pseudo-authority we have seen in the Jonestown and Waco tragedies. A good test for distinguishing the authentic from the dangerously charismatic copy is whether the leader requires regressive dependence and relinquishing of self responsibility among his or her followers. Similarly, the authentic spiritually of the universalizing stage avoids polarizing the world between the "saved" and the "damned." Their approaches to personal and social reform are as concerned with the transformation of those they oppose as with the bringing about of justice and reform.

SOME SIMILARITIES BETWEEN JAMES AND FAITH-DEVELOPMENT THEORY

In this section, I intend to demonstrate some affinities that are shared between the ideas James expressed in *The Varieties of Religious Experience* and faith-development theory. Such an examination, while acknowledging differences, helps relate current thinking within the Jamesian tradition.

Both Mean to Be Nonreductionistic and Are Indirectly Apologetic

Earlier I likened James to Schleiermacher in relation to his focus on feeling and emotion. James's psychology of religion also shows a relatedness to Schleiermacher with regard to its forceful address to "the cultured among the despisers" of religion. Of course, James is writing in such a way that his text, appearing just after the cresting of the revivalist period in late 19th-century America, would have broad popular appeal. However, the text was written for a university audience, and in psychology it aimed to counter the emerging positivist passion for making psychology an exclusively laboratory science. At the time of his writing, James was increasingly defining himself as a philosopher. As such, he makes a strong case for honoring the *sui generis* character of religious experience. Although he anticipates Freud's account of religion based on the projection of unconscious needs, James's account affirms the indispensability of this activating role of the "subconscious," as he calls it. He pointedly insists on leaving open the question of how the subconscious dynamics of people's experiences of the Holy may connect them with a genuine transcendence.

Faith-development theory is grounded in a conviction that humans have evolved into an ontological vocation for responsiveness to God. This approach claims that the orientation to centers of value, the constructing of meaning as the context for relationships and life projects, is generic to human beings. Like the works on faith by Paul Tillich (1957) and H. Richard Niebuhr (1960, 1989), which so influenced me in my early theological work, faith-development theory may be said to have an apologetic aim of demonstrating that this central act of meaning making, of shared commitment to centering values, and joint living by core stories is indispensable and integral to human survival and flourishing. Like James, I have sought to make this case in ways that commend the research and theory to university audiences. Also like James, I have written to and addressed a wider audience from this perspective. Both perspectives aim to be non-reductionistic; both are indirectly apologetic.

Each Approach Is Empirical, Though in Different Senses of the Term

A central characteristic of pragmatist philosophy is that it puts conceptual categories at risk in relation to the dynamic contours of experience. This is the sense, I believe, in which James's *Varieties* may be said to be both pragmatist and empirical. Through the use of case accounts and texts of autobiography and biography, he builds up shared experience of dimensions of religious life. Then he retrieves categories from religious and psychological traditions and both fills them and reworks them to convey and order his rich, reflective sense of their role in religion and in the lives of those who experience them. Unlike Max Weber, who claimed that he was not "religiously musical," James had an acute ear and feel for the nuances and emotions of religious experience. His own vicarious participation in the experiences he recounts from others—despite his disclaimers of any significantly original personal experiences of his own—makes his empirical method one full of the risk and passion of his own involvement. The reader participates, through James, in the "strenuous mode" of reconstructing and evaluating experience.

Faith-development theory and research can also rightfully claim to be empirical, in some ways that overlap with James. But in other respects, it is empirical in more typical social scientific senses of the term. The stage theory had its origins in my joint leadership of intensive group experiences where participants were invited to share their life and faith pilgrimages with one another in an unusual context of intense leisure. The hermeneutical framework of Erikson's psychosocial development theory initially helped me order what I was hearing. Later, teaching a course at Harvard Divinity School called "Theology as the Symbolization of Experience," I broadened the interpretive framework to include the works of Freud, Jung, Durkheim, Bellah, and eventually, Piaget and Kohlberg. With grant money, during the decade of the 1970s I was able to work with students and a research team that helped me carry out three major waves of empirical work. We used semi-structured interviews, on which we based the analyses that led to successive phases of reconstruction and elaboration of the stages of faith. While increasingly detailed and clarified description of stages and transitions emerged from this empirical and constructive process, the theory was also being presented to university audiences and gatherings of professionals in religious education, ministry, and pastoral care. The empirical evidences of resonance and dissonance with the reflective experience of these professionals has been a significant factor for me as the primary author of this work. And, like James, the personal quest for orientation and truth about these matters has been a continuing source of motivation and energy in this project. Each of these approaches is empirical, though in different senses of the term.

Both Point to a Generic Unity Underlying the Many Manifestations of Religion and Faith

James's contention for a pluralistic universe is well known, and the very title, *The Varieties of Religious Experience* advertises his commitment to the honoring of difference. In a subsequent place I will say more about James and pluralism. Here, however, as I enumerate similarities between James and faith-development theory, I want to emphasize an underlying unity each of these approaches finds behind the diversity. "The pivot round which the religious life, as we have traced it, revolves," said James (1902/1961) in his *Conclusions*, "is the interest of the individual in his private personal destiny" (p. 381). Destiny here, I take it, refers not only to people's ultimate destiny, as in concern for what becomes of people after death, but also to the question of the unfolding of lives and the meaning and purpose of striving. James poses the question: "Is there, under all the discrepancies of the creeds, a common nucleus to which they bear their testimony unanimously?" He gives an affirmative answer:

> The warring gods and formulas of the religious do indeed cancel each other, but there is a certain uniform deliverance in which religions all appear to meet. It consists of two parts:
> 1. An uneasiness; and
> 2. Its solution.
> 1. The uneasiness, reduced to its simplest terms, is a sense that there is *something wrong about us* as we naturally stand.
> 2. The solution is a sense that *we are saved from the wrongness* by making proper connection with the higher powers. (p. 303)

This statement manifests James's commitment to the twice-born paradigm as fundamental and generic for human beings. In this he confirms the puritan and evangelical heritage mediated through his father and renders the Emersonian and Unitarian influences of the Transcendalist movement secondary. Religion, in all its guises and manifestations, is fundamentally about concern for one's personal destiny and finding an adequate solution for the fundamental *dis-ease* of human existence found in its natural form.

For the faith-development perspective, the generic unity underlying the many manifestations of religion and faith has to do with the supposed universal need for meaning and orientation in life, in face of its ultimate limits and conditions, and secondarily, the sense of meaning and significance for the expenditures of one's life energies and capacities for commitment. Fundamental, then, are the making or finding of life meaning and sustaining networks of valuing and commitment. Both perspectives point to a generic unity underlying the great variety of religious and faith orientations.

Each Combines A Pragmatist and Functional Approach With Normative Evaluative Criteria

In keeping with his pragmatist orientation, James consistently focuses his eye on the differences in life and living that religious experiences and convictions tend to make. With his passion for the strenuous life, for the zest and energy that make for an audacious engagement with the challenges of life, he often temporarily seems to subordinate questions of the moral worth of religious experience to questions of its vividness, vitality, and impact. On the whole, however, truth, in relation to religious experience, consists in the combination of its vividness and power to transform a life and the linking of its subject more clearly in his or her unique relation to the "higher powers." In a fine, unpublished dissertation, Brian James Mahan (1989) has identified three criteria he finds in James for the functional truth of religious experiences and their impacts. These are (a) responsiveness to immediate luminousness, (b) philosophical reasonableness, and (c) moral helpfulness. For James no substantive content of religious experience or belief can qualify as truth unless all three of these criteria are met in the assessment of its functional shaping of the lives of persons. (pp. 136–141).

Faith-development theory also takes a functionalist approach that it combines with normative criteria. Its primary attention rests on the patterning of knowing and valuing by which persons compose and commit to meanings and to the ways their faith perspectives shape their patterns of relating and interpreting experience. The functionalism of faith-development theory is much more related to individual's ways of construing and interpreting experience than it is to the energy and motivation for action they engender. However, it does argue, on the bases of aesthetic, rational, and ethical criteria, that the constructive patterns of the later stages of faith and more adequate, more "true," than those employed in earlier stages. Each combines a pragmatist and functional approach with normative evaluative criteria in its approach to religion and faith.

SOME DIFFERENCES BETWEEN JAMES AND FAITH DEVELOPMENT THEORY

As much as faith development theory agrees with elements of the psychological perspective that William James brought to the understanding of religious experience, there are important differences that must be highlighted.

Two Different Types of Address to Pluralism in Faith and Religious Experience

James asked in his *Conclusions*, "Ought it to be assumed that in all persons the mixture of religion with other elements should be identical? Ought it, indeed, to be assumed that the lives of all persons should show identical religious elements?" (p. 378). In answer to his own question he wrote:

> The divine can mean no single quality, it must mean a group of qualities, by being champions of which in alternation, different people may all find worthy missions. Each attitude being a syllable in human nature's total message, it takes the whole of us to spell the meaning out completely. So a "god of battles" must be allowed to be the god for one kind of person, a god of peace and heaven and home, the god for another. We must frankly recognize the fact that we live in partial systems, and that parts are not interchangeable in the spiritual life. If we are peevish and jealous, destruction of the self must be an element of our religion; why need it be one if we are good and sympathetic from the outset? If we are sick souls, we require a religion of deliverance; but why think so much of deliverance, if we are healthy-minded? (pp. 378–379)

The varieties of faith and religious experience, for James, seem to be equivalent to the variety of personality types and patterns of need. This likely means that from James's point of view, the stage theory of faith development might present a far too confining frame, a Procrustean bed, into which to force the rich welter of various types of religious people. His accounts of the differing expressions of sainthood and its distortions, alone, suggest the range and variations of religious personality that attracted his interest. However, he does give some hint of interest in evolutionary or developmental perspectives, or at least characterizations of higher degrees of religious experience. He wrote: "Unquestionably, some persons have the completer experience and the higher vocation, here as in the social world. . . ." But then he adds, ". . . for each person to stay in their own experience, whate'er it be, and for others to tolerate them there, is surely best" (p. 379).

Faith-development theory deals with what I have sometimes called "vertical pluralism." The same person, across a life cycle, may well construct his or her faith perspective in a predictable range of three to seven different stages. In any average group of adults, one may find individuals in any of the stages from the mythic–literal to the conjunctive or universalizing stages. In this sense, faith-development theory is a "reception theory." It shows the range and variations of ways in which people appropriate religious traditions or correlate meanings with eclectic or secular ideological perspectives. Faith-development theory offers an implicit model of evolving selfhood, constituted by its characteristic patterns of construing self and the self–other, self–world, and self–ultimate relations.

The Feeling Self and the Construing Self

Given James's account of the self in *Psychology*, we should not expect that he would give an essentialist or substantivist account of the self. Nor does he, like George Herbert Mead (1934), provide a social and relational account of the self. For James I might transform Decartes's famous statement to read "I feel, therefore I am" or, more adequately, "I am moved by the flow of my affections toward centers of value that capture my will and focus my passions." Like Jonathan Edwards, James might say, "The will is as its strongest motive is." James uses the term *feeling* in sense broad enough to include both the perceptive and the cognitive processes that it orients and presses into its service, but clearly, it is feeling that is fundamental for motivation and orientation. Cognitive processes follow feeling and attempt to bring to consciousness, thought, and word, what one has experienced so powerfully.

Faith-development theory stands in a tradition in which cognition and affection or emotion tend to be distinguished and theoretically separated. Piaget (1971) acknowledged that one always observes the presence and influence of affections in thought and action, but his theory clearly privileges cognition and the modes of discursive rationality that can balance and guide the emotions. In contrast to Piaget and Kohlberg, in my work I have tried from the beginning to include the role of emotion and valuing in the construing activity by which a person finds or makes meaning and grounds the self in its relatedness to others, a self, and to an ultimate environment. This has meant arguing for a "logic of conviction"—a kind of reasoning in faith—as more primal than Piaget's "logic of rational certainty." It may be said that James privileges the self as constituted by its life-shaping feelings and affections, with cognitive processes giving account and elaborating their meanings in derivative ways. The faith-development approach, however, privileges patterns of construing as constitutive of the self but tries to incorporate the affections and valuing into the patterns of construal I call stages.

Development and Conversion: Contrast in the "Once-Born/Twice-Born" Distinction

From a superficial standpoint, it would seem obvious that James's psychology of religious transformation is centered in conversion and the "twice-born" orientation, whereas faith-development theory is centered in the progressive movement of one stage to another in an expansive working out of the "once-born" orientation. But the situation is more complex than that. In *Stages of Faith* I characterize conversion as "a significant recentering of one's previous conscious or unconscious images of value and power, and the conscious adoption of a new set of master stories in the commitment to reshape one's life in a new community of interpretation and action" (Fowler, 1981, pp. 281–282). In that definition, and in the account I give of conversion experiences in the book, one can detect the lines of transformation that James, with his imagery of the rupture of the hard rind of the subconscious and "the expulsive power of a new affection," paints more vividly. The major difference lies in situating the conversion phenomena in a sequence of developmental stages that have to do with structuring of faith, whereas conversion—for me and for James—has to do with dramatic or gradual shifts in the contents of faith. Put more vividly, James—and faith-development theory, when dealing with conversion—address the question of the heart's attachments, its resting place, and its dynamic relation to an animating source of value and power. James, however, I may say crudely, is more interested in the quantitative impact of conversion—the power of a new direction and the energy of a new centering loyalty and affection. I alternatively, am clearly more interested in the impact of a new set of affections and their object on the overall process of making and sustaining life-orienting meanings. The interest is more qualitative, in the sense that conversion may occur at different stages for the same or different people and may be interpreted and integrated in quite different ways depending on a person's present stage or transition.

Grounding Convictions and Overbeliefs

Put alongside each other, *The Varieties of Religious Experience and Stages of Faith* have some striking similarities and some vivid differences. Both books, despite the undergirdings they share in considerable scholarly research, are personal books. The authorial voice in each book is a personal voice. *The Varieties of Religious Experience* was prepared as a set of lectures. One can almost hear the sibilant intake of breath and the rise and fall of a voice close at hand as one reads it. Many parts of *Stages of Faith* were lectured repeatedly before finding integrated form in a final written version. In writing this volume, I experienced frequently the presence of past audiences, recognizing the need for a narrative or an explanation from the remembrance of frowning brows or glazed eyes at particular junctures.

By virtue of personal voice and a certain existential passion, both James and I convey, I think, the conviction that the subject matter is important, for us and for our readers. Each of us uses the text to weave a holding environment where transactions between the souls of persons and a reality or realities on the further side of human experience can be explored and honored as intrinsically valuable and indispensable in human experience. Separated by nearly 80 years, both books address the reader with rich maps of essential areas of human experiencing and with a certain pressure to locate themselves in recognition and decision. Both books, in complex ways, combine empirical descriptiveness with an undeniable normativity.

Both James and I rely on the convictions James called "overbeliefs" to resolve intrinsic tensions between science and faith. James finds the linkage with God in the self's relation to its own "transmarginal" or "subconscious" depths. Straightforwardly, he affirms that the sense of an objective and truly "other" entity encountered in religious experience can be identified with aspects of people's subconscious self. With some intellectual sleight of hand, James—in the spirit of his essay, "The Will To Believe"—leaves standing the conviction that through this encounter with aspects of people's subconcious mind, they are (or may well be) experiencing relatedness to the "more"—the higher powers on the further side of religious experience. This conviction, left standing because no other way accounts for the data of experience, gives James's pluralistic universe its complex, but final, integrity. This is not a static integrity but an integrity in the midst of process—the process of the self and the process of myriad humans and other organisms embracing and experiencing relatedness in a great variety of ways.

For me, a straightforwardly expressed conviction affirms a oneness that encompasses and preserves the expanding manyness of the manifold processes of nature and history. I, a theologian at base, affirm the priority in being, valuing, and power, of God. My anthropology affirms that humans have evolved with prepotentiated capacities that underlie the structuring activities of faith and that equip people for their ontological callings to relatedness and partnership with God. Also processial, but less radically than James, I see the self as being constituted in fundamental ways by this ontological vocation—which, of course, humans may embrace, neglect, or struggle against.

The structure and temper of people's overbeliefs help explain why James struggles between the once-born and the twice-born pattern of experience as normative and why my theory dominantly attends to a kind of once-born series of transforming reconfigurations of the ongoingly dynamic relationships of faith. I am glad that one of these options does not have to be negated in the study of religious experience and faith to embrace and affirm the other.

RELEVANCE FOR THE CLINICAL PRACTICE
OF PSYCHOLOGY

Let my turn briefly to the explicit concerns of this book—religion and the clinical practice of psychology. As put forth in my introduction to this chapter, faith-development theory, complemented by the Jamesian tradition, allows for an appreciation of faith experience as a foundational development process in the life of the individual. In a therapeutic relation James's work may help one identify a once-born or twice-born person; it may invite attention to similarities and differences of conversion experiences or particular forms of melancholy or levels of energy.

Faith-development theory serves diagnostic aims by providing a framework to characterize qualitatively different ways of constructing self, others, and self–other relations, including one's relation with God. It offers some precision to knowledgeable therapists in identifying the stage or transition that best characterizes a given help seeker's way of making meaning. An understanding of the dimension of faith may amplify the range of meanings involved in a patient's presenting complaints and psychological difficulties. Crises of faith may accompany psychological turmoil. Furthermore, faith-development theory suggests that the therapeutic relationship exists within a broader cultural matrix that includes the faith commitments of both participants, the patient and the therapist, whether implicitly held or explicitly disclosed. A personal note may illustrate this contention.

I find it important to recognize that the relational structure of the therapeutic alliance between therapist and help seeker is triadic rather than merely dyadic. Part of this triadic structure was symbolized for me by the conspicuous presence, in one psychiatrist's office where I spent considerable time at one point in my life, of the complete works of Sigmund Freud. These, along with diplomas and certificates, and the peculiar postures of two of us assumed while communicating, reminded us both that our involvement with each other occurred in a particular tradition, with its canon of normative literature and practices. These things symbolize a faith we shared, albeit from different angles of commitment, that consistent and conscientious following of procedures evolved in that tradition would bring relief for the inner burdens and pain that I carried and make possible new degrees of personal healing, reintegration, and eventually, self-understanding. At the same time I was not required to relinquish my life commitments to values and beliefs formed in my family and my involvements in a religious tradition and in the practices and disciplines of my work in the university. Some of these would be re-examined and altered in the course of the work we did, but at no time was I required to deny or devalue them. I also was not disturbed in my conviction that my life had been, and could continue to be, involved in a project of responsiveness to God. I cannot speak directly for my partner in this work, for the rules of the practice we engaged in did not allow for direct communication of the convictions he holds about what it is that sustains and collaborates with the shared intention to find truth and release from distorting illusions and fantasies in the therapeutic relation. But almost from the first, I felt a confidence, which grew in depth and intensity, that he strongly believed that his careful listening to me, his spare comments and questions to me, and our looking together deeply at certain relations and experiences in my life would bring about new degrees of inner freedom and release of constricted energies and would make possible a more whole-hearted investment of myself in the relations and tasks about which I cared most.

In any relation where two people are working together in depth of mutual trust to bring about healing and wholeness for the help seeker, there is a "third body" constituted by the focal trusts and loyalties that each of them bring to the encounter. There is a third body constituted by their relationship that involves the respective beliefs, values, and commitments they each bring to the partnership. In these reflections I am simply trying to say that we work in relations where faith—your faith, the help seeker's faith, and the third body of shared trusts and loyalties that both constitute the relation and emerge in importance as it proceeds—is present and a vital factor in healing. The triadic shape of this relationship needs to be acknowledged, honored, and cared for. This volume clearly aims at acknowledging, honoring, and caring for the often-hidden dimension, the often-unspoken, implicit dimension of faith that informs the construction of the self and influences the clinical practice of psychology.

REFERENCES

Emde, R., Johnson, W., & Easterbrooks M. (1987). The do's and don'ts of early moral development: Psychoanalytic tradition and current research. In J. Kagan & S. Lamb (Eds.), *The emergence of morality in young children* (pp. 245–276). Chicago: University of Chicago Press.

Erikson, E. H., (1963). *Childhood and society* (2nd ed.) New York: Norton.

Fowler, J. (1980). Faith and the structuring of meaning. In J. W. Fowler & A. Vergote (Eds.), *Toward moral and religious maturity* (pp. 51–85). Morristown, NJ: Silver Burdett.

Fowler, J. W. (1981). *Stages of faith: The psychology of human development and the quest for meaning.* San Francisco: Harper & Row.

Fowler, J. (1986). Dialogue toward the future in faith development studies. In C. Dykstra & S. L. Parks (Eds.), *Faith development and Fowler* (pp. 275–301). Birmingham, AL: Religious Education Press.

Fowler, J. (1987). *Faith development and pastoral care*. Philadelphia: Fortress Press.

Fowler, J. (1989). Strength for the journey: Early childhood development in selfhood and faith. In D. Blazer (Ed.), *Faith development and early childhood* (pp. 1–36). Kansas City, MO: Sheed and Ward.

Fowler, J. (1991). *Weaving the new creation*. San Francisco: Harper San Francisco.

James, W. (1961). *The varieties of religious experience*. New York: Collier Books. (Original work published 1902)

Kegan, J. (1984). *The nature of the child*. New York: Basic Books.

Kohut, H. (1977). *The restoration of the self*. Madison, CT: International Universities Press.

Mahan, B. J. (1989) *The ethics of belief: An interpretation and evaluation of William James's notion of spiritual judgment*. Unpublished doctoral dissertation, University of Chicago.

Mead, G. H. (1934). *Mind, self, and society*. Chicago: University of Chicago Press.

Miller, A. (1981). *The drama of the gifted child*. New York: Basic Books.

Nathanson, D. L., (1992). *Shame and pride: Affect, sex, and the birth of the self*. New York: Norton.

Niebuhr, H. R. (1960). *Radical monotheism and western culture*. New York: Harper Torchbooks.

Niebuhr, H. R. (1989). *Faith on earth*. New Haven, CT: Yale University Press.

Piaget, J. (1971). *Insights and illusions of philosophy* (W. Mays, Trans.) New York: World, Median Books.

Ricoeur, P. (1967). *The symbolism of evil* (E. Buchanan, trans.). Boston: Beacon Press.

Rizzuto, A-M. (1981). *The birth of the living God: A psychoanalytic study*. Chicago: University of Chicago Press.

Stern, D. (1985). *The interpersonal world of the infant*. New York: Basic Books.

Tillich, P. (1957). *Dynamics of faith*. New York: Harper & Row.

Winnicott, D. W. (1971). Playing and reality. New York: Basic Books.

Wulff, D. M. (1991). *Psychology of religion: Classic and contemporary views*. New York: Wiley.

7

RELIGIOUS COMMITMENT, MENTAL HEALTH, AND PROSOCIAL BEHAVIOR: A REVIEW OF THE EMPIRICAL LITERATURE

JOHN GARTNER

At first glance, one cannot help but be confused by the research on the relationship between religion and mental health, where mixed and even contradictory findings appear to be the rule. In an often-cited meta-analysis of results across studies, Bergin (1983) found that studies distributed themselves much as one would predict by chance: 23% manifested a negative relationship between religion and mental health, 30% found no relationship, and 47% found a positive relationship.

The results are consistent with previous literature reviews, prompting more than one reviewer (e.g., Levin & Vanderpool, 1987; Sanua, 1969) to assert that the data provide little or no basis for positing any relationship between religion and mental health. Spilka and Werme (1971), alternatively, have argued that "the inconsistency of empirical findings has led some reviewers (Argyle, 1959; Scott, 1961) to conclude that no relationship exists [between religion and mental health]. However, it seems more likely that the inconsistencies testify to methodological complexities" (p. 463).

Seventeen years after Spilka and Werme made that statement, many of those "methodological complexities" have yet to be defined. In this

This chapter is based in large part on a previous paper: Gartner, J., Larson D., & Allen, G. (1991). Religious commitment and mental health: A review of the empirical literature. *Journal of Psychology and Theology, 19,* 6–25.

review I searched for patterns when studies were divided according to what aspect of mental health they were studying and how they were measuring it.

I reviewed approximately 200 recent studies on the relationship between religious commitment and psychopathology as well as a half dozen previous review articles. I made a computer search of *Psychology Abstracts* for the period from 1979 to 1989 for all articles that contained both the letters *religi* and any one of 30 terms denoting psychopathology or an aspect of it (e.g., anxiety). All research reports or review articles were photocopied. As a second step, all relevant research reports or review articles cited in these articles were also obtained and included in the final pool.

Although it would be desirable for the purposes of this chapter to define *religious commitment*, there are marked differences in the psychology of religion over how to define and measure *religion*, and the studies I reviewed reflected these different methods and views. To be comprehensive it is necessary to integrate findings from studies that used different measures of religious commitment. These include comparing members of religious organizations to nonmembers, measuring degree of participation in religious activities (e.g., frequency of church attendance), measuring attitudes concerning the importance or salience of religious experience (i.e., religiosity), measuring belief in traditional religious creeds (i.e., orthodoxy), and examining a variety of religious typologies that compare one religious type to another (e.g., intrinsic vs. extrinsic). I also attempted to discover patterns across studies in the way religious commitment is measured and the results obtained. The review is divided into the following three sections: (a) a review of the literature suggesting that religion is associated with mental health, (b) a review of the literature suggesting that the relationship between religion and mental health is ambiguous or complex, and (c) a review of the literature suggesting that religion is associated with psychopathology (see Table 1).

A REVIEW OF THE LITERATURE SUGGESTING THAT RELIGION IS ASSOCIATED WITH MENTAL HEALTH

Physical Health

In a comprehensive review, Levin and Vanderpool (1987) found that:

> Twenty-two out of 27 studies found the frequency of religious attendance to be significantly associated with health in a positive direction, and in four studies reporting insignificant associations, the authors presented data revealing strong salutary trends for attendance. In

TABLE 1
The Relationship Between Religious Commitment and Mental Health

Religion associated with mental health
Physical health
Mortality
Suicide
Drug use
Alcohol abuse
Delinquency and criminal behavior
Divorce and marital satisfaction
Well-being
Outcome
Depression
Ambiguous or complex associations between religion and mental health
Health
Anxiety
Psychosis
Self-esteem
Sexual disorders
Intelligence/education
Prejudice
Religion associated with psychopathology
Authoritarianism
Dogmatism, tolerance of ambiguity, and rigidity
Suggestibility and dependence
Self-actualization
Temporal lobe epilepsy

short it seems clear that frequent attendance is a protective factor against a wide range of illness outcomes. (p. 590)

This is inconsistent with past reviews (Argyle & Beit-Hallahmi, 1975; Larson, 1985) and the findings of additional studies that I reviewed (Gottlieb & Green, 1984; Jenkins, 1976; Larson et al., 1988).

Although the unanimity of the findings above is impressive, the findings do not support decisive conclusions regarding the health benefits of religious commitment. Few studies control potential confounding or mediating variables. For example, health-promoting behavior may be a key moderating variable in this health effect. Gottlieb and Green (1984) found that the differences in the physical health of religious attenders were accounted for by their lower rates of smoking and drinking. However, studies of heart disease (Comstock & Partridge, 1972) and blood pressure (Graham, 1978; Larson et al., 1988) that controlled for smoking levels still found the religion–health connection. Moreover, it is not inconsistent with the hypothesis that religious commitment promotes health—if indeed it does so—by fostering health-promoting behavior.

A more serious confound is that physical health may support religious attendance rather than the other way around. People who are sick or disabled may attend church less frequently because of their decreased ability to function. The only study (Levin & Markides, 1986) that controlled for this factor found that the correlation between religious attendance and health became insignificant when controlling for activity limitation among older subjects. Clearly, more such controlled studies are needed.

Longevity

As a group, religiously committed individuals live longer. Consistent with the general physical health effect, all of the studies reviewed by Larson (1985) and Levin and Vanderpool (1987), as well as those I was able to find, confirm a positive relationship between religious participation and longevity (Berkman & Syme, 1979; Comstock & Lundin, 1967; Comstock & Partridge, 1972; Comstock & Tonascia, 1977; Helsing & Sklo, 1981; House, Robbins, & Metzner, 1982; Reynolds & Nelson, 1981; Zuckerman, Kasl, & Ostfeld, 1984). This effect may be stronger for men than women (Larson, 1985).

Suicide

In their 1975 review, Argyle and Beit-Hallahmi report mixed results on the relationship between religion and suicide. Three small-scale clinical studies failed to find a relationship between religious beliefs or feelings and suicide attempts. However, the one large-scale study they reviewed (Comstock & Partridge, 1972) found that those who did not attend church were four times more likely to kill themselves than were frequent church attenders.

In my review, all of the 12 studies I found reported a negative relationship between religiosity and suicide. Religious subjects reported experiencing fewer suicidal impulses (Minear & Brush, 1980–1981; Paykel, Myers, Lindenthal, & Tanner, 1974; Reynolds & Nelson, 1981) and reported more negative attitudes toward suicidal behavior (Bascue, Inman, & Kahn, 1982; Hoelter, 1979; Stillion, McDowell, & Shamblin, 1984). Furthermore, a decline in church attendance has been found to predict suicide rates nationwide (Martin, 1984; Stack, 1983a) more powerfully than other factors such as unemployment (Stack, 1983a). Across nations, differences in both religious commitment (Stack, 1983b), as measured by percentage of religious book production, and "religious integration" have been found to predict suicide rates (Breault & Barkey, 1982).

Drug Use

In their 1976 review of the literature, Gorsuch and Butler found 20 studies that examined the relationship between religion and drug use. They found that

> Whenever religion is used in an analysis, it predicts those who have not used an illicit drug regardless of whether the research is conducted prospectively or retrospectively and regardless of whether the religious variable is defined in terms of membership, active participation, religious upbringing, or the meaningfulness of religion as viewed by the person himself. (p. 127)

In my review of the more recent literature, I found the same results. Of the studies I reviewed, 11 out of 12 found the same negative relationship between various measures of religious commitment and drug use (Adlaf & Smart, 1985; Burkett, 1977; Burkett & White, 1974; Galanter & Buckley, 1978; Guinn, 1975; Hasin, Endicott, & Lewis, 1985; Hays, Stacey, Widaman, & DiMatteo, 1986; Hundleby, 1987; Newcomb & Bentler, 1986; Nicholi, 1985; Query, 1985). There is evidence that church attendance may be more strongly associated with drug abstinence that other religious variables such as religious feelings (Adalf & Smart, 1985) or parental religiosity (Burkett, 1977)

Alcohol Abuse

Early research on the relationship of religion to alcohol abuse focused on differences between religious denominations. As Argyle and Beit-Hallahmi (1975) report, Jews have been consistently found to have the lowest rate of alcoholism and Catholics the highest. Protestants are in the middle, although higher rates of alcoholism have been found, paradoxically, in Protestants raised in conservative denominations or homes that typically discourage alcohol use (Argyle & Beit-Hallahmi, 1975). This led some to hypothesize that religious traditions that modelled controlled drinking were the best protection against alcoholism.

Argyle and Beit-Hallahmi (1975) found a negative relationship between personal religiosity or church attendance and drinking in the four studies that they reviewed. In our review, six of the seven studies we found confirmed that those with a higher level of religious involvement are less likely to use or abuse alcohol (Burkett, 1977; Burkett & White, 1974; Coombs, Wellisch, & Fawzy, 1985; Globetti & Windham, 1967; Gottlieb & Green, 1984; Hasin et al., 1985). The one study that found no difference compared levels of fundamentalism in addicted as opposed to nonaddicted DWI (driving while intoxicated) offenders (Mookherje, 1986).

In our study (Gartner, Hohman, Larson, Canino, & Allen, 1988) of over 2,000 randomly selected individuals in Puerto Rico, we found that people who claimed no religious affiliation had a higher rate of alcoholism. However, this effect dropped out when controlling for gender, inasmuch as men were more likely both to drink and to claim no religious affiliation. Nonetheless, in the other two studies that controlled for gender, the negative relationship between religious participation and alcohol use (Burkett & White, 1974) and abuse (Hasin et al., 1985) was sustained.

Delinquency and Criminal Behavior

The consensus of most early review articles was that research had failed to support the expected negative relationship between religion and delinquency (Lea, 1982; Sanua, 1969) or, at the very least, results were mixed (Argyle & Beit-Hallahmi, 1975). Across studies delinquents were found to be no less religious in their beliefs than nondelinquents (Argyle & Beit-Hallahmi, 1975; Lea, 1982; Sanua, 1969). It was also found that the rate of church attendance in a community failed to correlate with the crime rate (Sanua, 1969).

However, personal church attendance was found to correlate negatively with delinquency in five of the six studies reviewed by Argyle and Beit-Hallahmi (1975). In other words, whereas religious attitudes did not differentiate delinquents from nondelinquents, religious behavior did. This is consistent with the finding reported above, namely that church attendance proved to have the strongest association with drug use, compared with other religious variables.

The seven additional studies I found all confirmed the negative relationship between delinquency and religious commitment (Albrecht, Chadwick, & Alcorn, 1977; Burkett & White, 1974; Higgins & Albrecht, 1977; Nye, 1958; Robins, 1974; Rohrbaugh & Jessor, 1975; Stark, Kent, & Doyle, 1982), and once again the relationship was stronger with church attendance than with other religious variables (Albrecht et al., 1977). Thus, although in one sense these might be interpreted as mixed results, closer examination reveals that a consistently negative relationship has been found between religious commitment and delinquency when looking at religious participation and not simply religious attitudes.

In two recent studies (Ames, Larson, Gartner, & O'Connor, 1990; Young et al., 1990), the recidivism rates of federal prisoners participating in a prison fellowship ministry program were found to be substantially lower than those of controls, both one year and ten years after release from prison. These studies were able to control for most demographic factors known to be associated with recidivism including sex, age, race, and seriousness of crime. The study's main weakness was that prisoners were self-selected to participate in the program, making this a correlational rather than experimental design.

Divorce and Marital Satisfaction

In a previous article, Larson (1985) reviewed the literature on religion, divorce, and marital satisfaction. All of the five studies reviewed found a negative relationship between church attendance and divorce (Caplow, 1983; Jackson, 1972; McCarthy, 1979; Scanzoni, 1977; Shrum, 1980).

These findings raise the question of whether religious people remain in unhappy marriages out of obedience to religious proscriptions against divorce. Although this must unquestionably be true in some individual cases, as a group the religious report a higher level of marital satisfaction. All seven of the studies reviewed by Larson found a positive relationship between religiosity, usually measured by church attendance, and self-reported marital satisfaction (Burchinal, 1957; Burgess & Cottrell, 1939; Caplow, 1983; Glen & Weaver, 1978; Hunt & King, 1978; Locke, 1951; Schumm, Bollman, & Jurich, 1982). One study, found, in fact, that church attendance predicted marital satisfaction better than any of the other eight variables included in their regression model (Glen & Weaver, 1978). Indeed, subjects from long-lasting marriages rank religion as one of the most important "prescriptions" for a happy marriage (Sporawski & Houghston, 1978).

It is possible, however, that, because some religious individuals believe that divorce is not a religiously acceptable option, they must evaluate their marriages more highly out of cognitive dissonance. However, I have no data on this question.

Well-Being

Several studies have examined the relationship between religious commitment and well-being. Although well-being has been assessed by a variety of methods, they are most frequently self-report scales that ask subjects to assess their personal level of internal comfort and life satisfaction. Based primarily on the research of Moberg (1965), early review articles (e.g., Argyle & Beit-Hallahmi, 1975; Stark, 1971) reported a relationship between religious participation and well-being for elderly populations. Debates ensued as to whether church attendance in fact increased well-being for the elderly or was simply an index of their overall level of functioning. Failing to attend church could be a sign of failing health and loss of functioning. However, my current review found six studies that studied a wide variety of populations, two of which were elderly (Moberg, 1965; Rogalski & Paisey, 1987). They all reported a positive relationship between religious commitment and well-being (Beckman & Houser, 1982; Decker & Schultz, 1985; Guy, 1982; Moberg, 1965; Paloutzian & Ellison, 1982; Rogalski & Paisey, 1987).

In addition, several large-scale epidemiological studies have examined the overall rate of psychological distress in the general population. They have consistently found a negative relationship between religious participation and psychological distress (Lindenthal, Myers, Pepper, & Stern, 1970; Stark, 1971).

Mental Health Outcome

A fundamental problem with the literature in this area is that the vast majority of the studies are correlational (Warren, 1977) and that they rarely take measurements at more than one point in time. Therefore, it is difficult to know if religious commitment plays any causal role in mental health. There is an obvious need for well-controlled outcome studies in this field. Inasmuch as religious commitment is a difficult variable to manipulate, one can study the effect of religious participation or interventions, sometimes using quasi-experimental designs, which at the very least include a repeated measurement. This allows researchers to study what might better approximate the causal effect of religious commitment.

I did find six such studies, all of which demonstrated improvement in psychological functioning following religious participation or a religious intervention. Lower rates of rehospitalization were noted in schizophrenics who attended church (Chu & Klein, 1985) or were given supportive aftercare by religious housewives and ministers (Katkin, Zimmerman, Rosenthal, & Ginsburg, 1975). Following participation in religious worship, a significant reduction in diverse psychiatric symptoms has been noted on both self-report inventories (Finney & Maloney, 1985; Griffith, Mahy, & Young, 1986; Morris, 1982) and biofeedback measures (Elkins, Anchor, & Sandler, 1979). Finally two studies of "cults" have found that converts report lower levels of psychological distress immediately subsequent to their conversion (Galanter, Rabkin, Rabkin, & Deutsch, 1979) as well as four years afterward (Ross, 1985).

Depression

Overall, the preponderance of evidence suggests that religiosity is associated with lower levels of depression. Four studies found a negative relationship between religious commitment and depression (Brown & Lowe, 1951; Hertsgaard & Light, 1984; Mayo, Puryear, & Richeck, 1969; McClure & Loden, 1982). The only study that found higher levels of depression in religious subjects was conducted with Tibetan adolescents (Gupta, 1983) and thus may represent the influence of cross-cultural variables. Finally, one study found that infrequent church attenders were twice as likely to be clinically depressed, but the effect became statistically insignificant when controlling for education, caring from spouse, health, and income (Spendlove, West, & Stanish, 1984).

A REVIEW OF THE LITERATURE SUGGESTING THAT THE RELATIONSHIP BETWEEN RELIGION AND MENTAL HEALTH IS AMBIGUOUS OR COMPLEX

Anxiety

Sanua (1969) reported in his review that the literature "points out that the religious person may at times show greater anxiety and at times less anxiety" (p. 1206). In a more recent review, Bergin (1983) found that "contradictions [in results in research on religion and psychopathology] continued in studies of manifest anxiety" (p. 123). This finding is consistent with my review. I found the following in my literature review: (a) four studies that reported that religious subjects were more anxious (Gupta, 1983; Hassan & Khalique, 1981; Spellman, Baskett & Byrne, 1971; Wilson & Miller, 1968); (b) three studies that found religious subjects to be less anxious than nonreligious subjects (Hertsgaard & Light, 1984; Williams & Cole, 1968) or less anxious after participation in religious pilgrimage (Morris, 1982); and (c) three studies that found no relationship between anxiety and religiosity (Brown, 1962; Epstein, Tamir, & Natan, 1985; Heintzelman & Fehr, 1976).

One possible explanation is that there may be different forms of religiosity that are differentially related to anxiety. De Figueiredo and Lemkau (1978) found that anxiety-derived somatic symptoms were negatively associated with public religious participation but positively associated with private religiosity. Bergin, Masters, and Richards (1987) found intrinsic religiosity to be correlated with lower anxiety, whereas extrinsic religiosity was associated with higher levels of anxiety.

A growing literature has developed around the relationship between religious commitment and one particular form of anxiety, death anxiety. Inasmuch as religion promises an afterlife, some investigators have explored whether such beliefs reduce fear of death. Six studies found less fear of death in religiously committed subjects (Aday, 1984–1985; Richardson, Berman & Piwowarski, 1983; Smith, Nehemkis, & Charter, 1983–1984; Tobacyk, 1983; Westman & Canter, 1985). Three studies found more fear of death in religiously committed groups (Beg & Zilli, 1982; Dodd & Mills, 1985; Florian, Kravetz, & Frankel, 1984). Five studies found no relationship between religious commitment and death anxiety (Dhawan & Sripat, 1986; Kunzendorf, 1985–1986; Mahabeer & Bhana, 1984; Muchnik & Rosenheim, 1982; Rosenheim & Muchnik, 1984–1985). Two studies found a curvilinear relationship between religious commitment and death anxiety, so that the moderately religious were the most anxious and the very religious and nonreligious were the least anxious (Downey, 1984; McMordie, 1981). Finally, two studies found that the religiously committed were more anxious about some aspects of death but less anxious about others (Florian & Kravitz, 1983; Hoelter, 1979).

Psychosis

Research has failed to support a clear relationship between religion and psychosis, although it was once part of clinical lore that psychotics were disproportionately preoccupied with religious concerns (Walters, 1964). Across studies, the level of religious commitment in schizophrenics has been found to be lower than that in the general population (Cothran & Harvey, 1986; Walters, 1964). Furthermore, religious commitment has been found to correlate negatively with psychoticism (Francis & Pearson, 1985). The frequency of religious delusions has been found to correlate strongly with the rate of religious commitment in the culture at large, suggesting that general cultural factors, more than the effect of individual religious commitment, determines the content of delusions (Ahmed & Naeem, 1984; Argyle & Beit-Hallahmi, 1975; Walters, 1964).

These findings are consistent with contemporary research perspectives on schizophrenia. This research points primarily to a genetic link in the disorder, with penetrance influenced by the environment, which would make a link with religious commitment less likely. Although higher rates of schizophrenia have been noted in Catholics (Buckalew, 1978; Burgess & Wagner, 1971; Murphy & Vega, 1982), the most likely explanation is a genetic loading for schizophrenia in some Catholic ethnic groups. Further research on this connection is clearly needed.

Self-Esteem

In a previous review (1983) I found mixed results in the literature on religion and self-esteem. Of the 18 studies reviewed, 4 found the religiously committed to be lower in self-esteem, 8 found no differences between groups, and 6 found the religiously committed to be higher in self-esteem. Since conducting that 1983 review, I have found one additional study reporting a negative relationship between religiosity and self-esteem (Beit-Hallahmi & Nevo, 1987), two additional studies that failed to find any relationship between religiosity and self-esteem (Bahr & Martin, 1983; Weltha, 1969), and one study reporting a positive relationship (Meisenhelder, 1986).

Once again, we need to ask "What type of religious commitment is associated with self-esteem?" Benson and Spilka (1977), for example, found that self-esteem was associated with loving images of God and negatively associated with punitive God images. Wickstrom and Fleck (1983) found self-esteem to be negatively associated with consensual religiosity.

In addition, there are special issues in assessing self-esteem in religious populations (Gartner, 1983). As Watson, Hood, Morris, and Hall (1985) have said, "The language of sin and self esteem are at least partially incompatible, and this must explain some of the empirical inconsistencies" (p. 116). It is possible that conservative Christian beliefs about the depravity of humankind may be confused with the psychological trait of self-esteem when these tests are administered to conservative religious populations.

Sexual Disorders

It is commonly stated in the sex therapy literature that traditional religious backgrounds and beliefs contribute to sexual dysfunction. Clearly, more research is needed, for I was able to find little data on this issue. One study (Hoch, Safir, Peres, & Shepher, 1981) did find that male sex therapy patients came from more traditionally religious homes than did normal controls. However, another (Cole, 1986) failed to find such a difference.

Intelligence and Education

Using data from five national surveys, Roozen (1979) found a weak positive association between education and religious participation. This is consistent with the findings of The Princeton Religious Research Center (1982) and the General Social Survey (1982–1984). In contrast, "a number of early American studies found a negative correlation between intelligence and measures of religious conservatism" (Argyle & Beit-Hallahmi, 1975, p. 93). It seems, therefore, that religious participation is positively associated with education, but religious conservatism, possibly because of its association with lowered social class, is negatively associated with measures of intellectual achievement. For example, in his review Dittes (1969) reports that six studies found a negative relationship between religious conservatism and intelligence and that one study found a positive relationship between intelligence and religious participation. On a denominational basis, Jews consistently score highest on measures of education and intelligence (Argyle & Beit-Hallahmi, 1975).

Prejudice

Although early studies seemed to suggest that religious people were more prejudiced, the relationship between religious commitment and prejudice has proven to be more complex. For example, numerous studies have replicated the finding that there is a curvilinear relationship between church attendance and prejudice (Dittes, 1969; Gorsuch & Aleshire, 1974); for example, the least-prejudiced people are those who attend church often and those who never attend. The most prejudiced are those who attend church with moderate frequency.

Furthermore, intrinsic religiosity and committed religiosity have been found to have a negative relationship with prejudice, where as extrinsic and consensual forms of religiosity have been found to have a positive relationship to prejudice (Batson, 1986; Dittes, 1969; Gorsuch & Aleshire, 1974; Herek, 1987).

A REVIEW OF THE LITERATURE THAT SUGGESTS THAT RELIGION IS ASSOCIATED WITH PSYCHOPATHOLOGY

Authoritarianism

Every major review article in this area notes that "the positive correlation between religiosity and authoritarianism has been reported in many studies" (Sanua, 1969, p. 1208). I found three such recent studies (Beit-Hallahmi & Nevo, 1987; Dubey, 1986; Hassan & Khalique, 1981).

The findings, however, may be more specific and limited. In four of the five studies Stark (1983) reviewed, there was no relationship between authoritarianism and religious participation. One study found a positive relationship, and Stark (1983) found a negative relationship for Catholics and conservative Protestants. Thus, a general relationship between religiosity and authoritarianism seems unlikely.

Argyle and Beit-Hallahmi (1975) found that all five of the studies that they reviewed found a relationship between authoritarianism and religious conservatism. Thus, it may be measures of religious orthodoxy and not religious commitment that have been correlated with authoritarianism. However, there may be a tautological problem inasmuch as it could be argued that the F scale is, in part, a conservatism scale (Hyman & Sheatsley, 1954). Hogan & Emler (1978) have, in fact, argued that the F scale is designed to pathologize working-class conservative values:

> Given the scale's correlation with social class, there is more reason to believe that it measures working-class political ideology (than pathology). The net result of the study by Adorno and his associates is that it has allowed the representatives of one group (middle class academic liberals) to stigmatize the beliefs of another (working class conservatives) as pathological. This public hostility of liberal social scientists toward working class political ideology is of course scandalous; it is itself, moreover, an expression of prejudice. (p. 505).

Thus, while the relationship between religious conservatism and authoritarianism has been well established, more research may be needed to understand how to interpret that relationship.

Dogmatism, Tolerance of Ambiguity, and Rigidity

Closely related to studies of the authoritarian personality have been attempts to study closed mindedness and "rigidity." Partially in response to the criticism that the F scale only measured right-wing closed mindedness, Rokeach (1960) developed the Dogmatism scale to study closed mindedness independent of ideology.

Some relationship has been found between orthodoxy and dogmatism (McNeel & Thorsen, 1985). One study found that degree of social contact with people outside one's own religious circle was the best predictor of dogmatism (Wilson, 1985).

Religiosity has been found to correlate with inability to tolerate ambiguity (Hassan & Khalique, 1981). Converts have been found to be the least able to tolerate ambiguity (Ullman, 1982). Those who cannot tolerate ambiguity have reported being most satisfied with less autonomous and open church contexts (Pargament, Johnson, Echemendia, & Silverman, 1985). Finally, one study found a relationship between religiosity and a measure of rigidity (Hassan & Khalique, 1981).

Suggestibility and Dependence

After reviewing 13 studies, Argyle and Beit-Hallahmi (1975) concluded that "there is a fairly strong correlation between religiosity and suggestibility" (p. 199). Similar results are reported in a review by Dittes (1969). The strength of the evidence lies not only in the unanimity of the findings but also in the diversity of measures used to measure suggestibility, which include psychological tests, psychomotor and behavior measures, and studies of placebo effects.

Argyle and Beit-Hallahmi (1975) also found three studies that show the religious to be more dependent and submissive. I found an additional study (Tennison & Snyder, 1968) that was consistent with these results. In contrast, I also found one study that reported a negative relationship between dependency and committed religiosity (Wickstrom & Fleck, 1983).

Self-Actualization

As I reported in an article in 1981, 15 studies have found a negative relationship between religious commitment and self-actualization (Bertoch,

1969; Gibb, 1968; Graff & Ladd, 1971; Hjelle, 1975; Jansen, Gravey, & Bonk, 1972; Kennedy, Heckler, Kohler, & Walker, 1977; LaBach, 1969; Lee & Piercy, 1974; Lindskoog & Kirk, 1975; Pellegrin, 1970; Reglin, 1976; Reynolds, 1968; Schroeder, 1970; Stewart & Webster, 1970; Webster & Stewart, 1969).

All of these studies used the Personal-Orientation Inventory (POI) to measure self-actualization. Gartner (1981) expressed concern that the POI is based on assumptions that may penalize a subject holding traditional religious beliefs. For example, one is rated as lower in self-actualization if one endorses the item "I am orthodoxly religious." In a similar fashion, points are deducted for belief in the "inherence of evil in human nature" and "the beneficial value of repentance," "restraint of impulse," and "self sacrifice." Consistent with this suspected antireligious bias in the POI, Watson, Morris, and Hood (1990) found that religion correlated positively with self-actualization when the religious items from the POI were removed. Thus, although these findings on religion and self-actualization appear consistent, there is reason for great caution in interpreting them—that is, if they can be interpreted at all.

Temporal Lobe Epilepsy

Since the 19th century, the clinical literature has reported hyper-religiosity, (i.e., religious rumination, symptoms of guilt, obsessiveness, and scrupulosity) as an associated feature of temporal lobe epilepsy (Fedio, 1986; Hopping, 1984; Knudsen & Bolwig, 1986; Sorenson & Bolwig, 1987). Two studies have found temporal lobe epilepsy patients to report more religious feelings or concerns than normal and psychiatric controls (Bear, 1982; Stark-Adamec, Adamec, Graham, Hicks, & Bruun-Meyer, 1985), although one failed to differentiate temporal lobe epilepsy from other seizure disorders (Tucker, Novelly, & Walker, 1987). There is tentative but intriguing evidence that at least some religious experience may be mediated by temporal lobe activity (Makarec & Persinger, 1985; Persinger, 1984; Persinger & Makarec, 1987).

CONCLUSION

One of my major conclusions is that the discrepant ways in which mental health is measured account for many of the discrepancies in the findings. Most of the results linking religious commitment and psychopathology have been obtained with what are called "soft variables." Soft variables are defined as paper and pencil personality tests. Such tests endeavor to infer from responses some "underlying" theoretical intrapsychic characteristic of mental health. These hypothetical traits are measured indirectly by items that test writers suspect, on the basis of theory and psychometric investigation, to be signs of that trait. Typically, such tests are of limited psychometric reliability and validity. Negative associations have been found between religious commitment and aspects of mental health that fit this definition, such as self-actualization, authoritarianism, dogmatism, tolerance of ambiguity, rigidity, and suggestibility.

In contrast, most of the studies that found a positive relationship between religion and mental health used what are referred to as "hard variables," that is "real-life" behavior events that can be directly observed and reliably measured and are of unquestionable validity: physical health, mortality, suicide, drug use, alcohol abuse, delinquency, and divorce. Donahue and Bergin (1983) report a similar finding; they state that most of the articles that link religion to psychopathology used "intrapsychic" measures, whereas most of the studies linking religion to mental health used "behavioral" measures.

This is not a completely new observation. In their 1975 review, Argyle and Beit-Hallahmi concluded that "concerning religion and neurosis ... the findings can be summed up in two generalizations: that religiosity is related to personal inadequacy in students, according to *psychological tests and inventories* [italics added]; and that participation in public religious activities is positively related to personal adjustment in the adult population, especially among the elderly" (p. 130). What has not been sufficiently considered, however, are the implications of these findings. It may not be, as Argyle and Beit-Hallahmi suggest, that religious commitment is bad for college student and good for older adults but that psychological tests and inventories produce different results than other methods of measuring mental health.

Hard and soft variables can be distinguished on another dimension, however. Hard variables are value-neutral or reflect consensually held values. All would agree, for example, that suicide is a negative outcome. On the other hand, soft variables sometimes reflect an implicit value bias as to what constitutes mental health. Indeed, many of these tests implicitly reflect the "non-theistic" (Bergin, 1983) orientation of authors who define mental health in their own image (Bergin, 1983; Gartner, 1981, 1983, 1985; Watson et al., 1985). In some obvious cases, such as the POI, a test of self actualization, and the Ego Strength scale of the Minnesota Multiphasic Personality Inventory (MMPI) the endorsement of items such as "I am orthodoxly religious" will subtract points from your score. Often, however, the value is more subtle. On a wide variety of psychological tests, traits such as self-discipline, altruism, humility, obedience to authority, and conventional morality are weighted negatively, whereas self-expression, assertiveness, and a high opinion of oneself are weighted positively. Moreover, the psychometric proof that one of these tests is valid is that it has been found to correlate with another test that shares the same implicit values.

We also found that the measure of religious commitment used affects the results obtained. In general, measures of actual religious behavior (i.e., measures of religious participation such as church attendance) were more powerfully related to mental health than were attitude scales measuring religiosity. This was particularly true when the relationship between religious commitment and mental health was a positive one. Once again the suggestion seems to be that measures of actual behavior have proven more powerful and valid than paper and pencil tests.

There is another, perhaps competing explanation for this pattern of findings, other than the hard and soft variable explanation. It may be that religion, especially in its more traditional forms, provides a socially reinforced structure that paradoxically provides protection from many psychiatric ills and temptations to act out impulses but at the same time limits the development of more autonomous forms of higher personality development. In that sense, religion is a structure that provides both a floor, which prevents its adherents from falling too low, and a ceiling, which prevents them from riding too high. Consistent with this, being nonreligious is associated with disorders of impulse control—that is problems of "under control" (e.g., alcohol and drug use, antisocial behavior, and suicide), whereas religious participation is associated with problems of "overcontrol" (e.g., rigidity and authoritarianism).

A similar conclusion was drawn by Batson and Ventis (1982), who, like myself, found that the way mental health is measured had a dramatic impact on the pattern of relationships found in the literature between religion and mental health. They found that religion was positively associated with an absence of psychiatric illness but negatively associated with measures of mental health (usually measured by personality tests) that they defined as measures of personal competence and control, self-acceptance, self-actualization, open-mindedness, and flexibility.

In his recently published edited volume titled *Religion and Mental Health*, Schumaker (1992) also wrestles with this same paradox:

> Some people have depicted religion as destructive to mental health on the grounds that it breeds intolerance, prejudice, personality constriction, self-denigration, dependency and hypersuggestibility, diminished sense of autonomy, loss of critical thinking ability, and so forth. . . . I would argue that the above categories of behavior are better understood as predictable side effects of religion. . . . [However] in my view irreligion (as well as most improvised religions) divest people of certain age-old pathways to psychological health. (p. 65).

In spelling out what these pathways are, Schumaker cites a number of contemporary scholars of the scientific study of religion in making the point that religion has provided a "web of meaning" and a "moral net." Now that "religion no longer serves as a traditional linchpin . . . our culture lacks a center ... and this has predisposed contemporary people to the angst, despair and unceasing yearning so prevalent today" (p. 64).

A well-known saying in the Middle Ages was "a bad king is better than no king." It meant that the violent anarchy of civil war and crime that resulted from the absence of structure was worse than almost any structure, no matter how repressive it might be. Simply put, when the moral net dissolves, chaos erupts. In society today, without the moral net of religion, on almost every measure the level of impulse control has deteriorated, so that people are now no longer shocked by stories of serial killings, drive-by shootings, pedophilia, and so on. Conversely, to the degree that the moral net of religion is intact, the data unquestionably show a reduction in almost every form of acting out.

Alternatively, although societal structure is essential, it can also be repressive. While the moral net might rescue one man from falling, it might snare another who is progressing in a healthy autonomous way along a path outside the boundaries of what is normally accepted. Those who are more educated and have more mature personalities (as measured by psychological tests) are far less likely to be religious in the traditional sense. Could it be that both the best and the worst of society fall outside the religious moral net? The agnostic professor and the recidivist criminal may have one thing in common: They don't go to church very often. The crucial difference perhaps is that the professors have presumably adopted a nontraditional moral net, be it the ethics and methods of their discipline, liberalism, or something else. For a large portion of society the waning of religion has left only a dangerous vacuum. Only history will tell what will fill that vacuum and whether it will represent an advance or a decline for civilization.

REFERENCES

Aday, R. H. (1984–1985). Belief in afterlife and death anxiety: Correlates and comparisons. *Omega Journal of Death and Dying, 15,* 67–75.

Adlaf, E. M., & Smart, R. G. (1985). Drug use and religious affiliation, feelings, and behavior. *British Journal of Addiction, 80,* 163–171.

Adorno, T. W., Frenkel-Brunswick, E., Levineson, D. J., & Sanford, R. N. (1950). *The authoritarian personality.* New York: Harper & Row.

Ahmed, S. H., & Naeem, S. (1984). First rank symptoms and diagnosis of schizophrenia in developing countries. *Psycholopathology. 17,* 275–279.

Albrecht, S. L., Chadwick, B. A., & Alcorn, D. S. (1977). Religiosity and deviance: Application of an attitude behavior contingent consistency model. *Journal for the Scientific Study of Religion, 16,* 263–274.

Ames, D., Larson, D., Gartner, J., & O'Connor, T. (1990, August). *Participation in a Volunteer Prison Ministry Program and Recidivism*. Paper presented at the annual meeting of the American Psychological Association, Boston.

Argyle, M. (1959). *Religious behavior*. Glencoe, IL: Free Press.

Argyle, M., & Beit-Hallahmi, B. (1975). *The social psychology of religion*. London: Routledge & Kegan Paul.

Bahr, H. M., & Martin, T. K. (1983). "And thy neighbor as thyself": Self-esteem and faith in people as correlates of religiosity and family solidarity among Middletown High School students. *Journal for the Scientific Study of Religion, 22*, 132–144.

Bascue, L. O., Inman, D. J., & Kahn, W. J. (1982). Recognition of suicidal lethality factors by psychiatric nursing assistants. *Psychological Reports, 51*, 197–198.

Batson, C. D. (1986). Religious orientation and overt versus covert racial prejudice. *Journal of Personality and Social Psychology, 50*, 175–181.

Batson, C. D., & Ventis, W. L. (1982). *The religious experience*. Oxford, England: Oxford University Press.

Bear, D. M. (1982). Interictal behavior in hospitalized temporal lobe epileptics: Relationship to idiopathic psychiatric syndromes: *Journal of Neurology, Neurosurgery, and Psychiatry, 45*, 481–488.

Beckman, L. J., & Houser, B. B. (1982). The consequences of childlessness on the social-psychological well-being of older women. *Journal of Gerontology, 37*, 243–250.

Beg, M. A., & Zilli, A. S. (1982). A study of the relationship of death anxiety and religious faith to age differentials. *Psychologia, 25*, 121–125.

Beit-Hallahmi, B., & Nevo, B. (1987). Jews in Israel: The dynamics of an identity change. *International Journal of Psychology, 22*, 75–81.

Benson, P. L., & Spilka, B. P. (1977). God-image as a function of self-esteem and locus of control. In H. N. Malony (Ed.), *Current perspectives in the psychology of religion* (pp. 209–224). Grand Rapids, MI: Eerdmans.

Bergin, A. E. (1983). Religiosity and mental health: A critical revaluation and meta-analysis. *Professional Psychology: Research and Practice, 14*, 170–184.

Bergin, A. E., Masters, K. S., & Richards, P. S. (1987). Religiousness and mental health reconsidered: A study of an intrinsically religious sample. *Journal of Counseling Psychology, 34*, 197–204.

Berkman, L. F., & Syme, S. L. (1979). Social networks, host resistance, and mortality: A nine-year follow-up study of Alameda County residents. *American Journal of Epidemiology, 109*, 186–204.

Bertoch, M. R. (1967). *A study of the relationship of counseling theory concepts to the self concepts and values of counselors in training*. Doctoral dissertation, Boston University, MA.

Breault, K. D., & Barkey, R. (1982). A comparative study analysis of Durkheim's theory of egoistic suicide. *Sociological Quarterly, 23*, 321–331.

Brown, L. B. (1962). A study of religious belief. *British Journal of Psychology, 53,* 259–272.

Brown, D. G., & Lowe, W. L. (1951). Religious beliefs and personality characteristics of college students. *Journal of Social Psychology, 33,* 103–129.

Buckalew, L. W. (1978). A descriptive study of denominational concomitants in psychiatric diagnosis. *Social Behavior and Personality, 6,* 239–242.

Burchinal, L. G. (1957). Marital satisfaction and religious behavior. *American Sociological Review, 22,* 306–310.

Burgess, E. W., & Cottrell, L. S. (1939). *Predicting success or failure in marriage.* New York: Prentice Hall.

Burgess J. H., & Wagner, R. L. (1971). Religion as a factor in extrusion to public mental hospitals. *Journal for the Scientific Study of Religion, 10,* 237–240.

Burkett, S. R. (1977). Religion, parental influence, and adolescent alcohol and marijuana use. *Journal of Drug Issues, 7,* 263–273.

Burkett, S. R., & White, M. (1974). Hellfire and delinquency: Another look. *Journal for the Scientific Study of Religion, 13,* 455–462.

Caplow, T. (1983). *All faithful people.* Minneapolis: University of Minnesota Press.

Chu, C., & Klein, H. E. (1985). Psychological and environmental variables in outcome of Black schizophrenics. *Journal of the National Medical Association, 77,* 793–796.

Cole, M. (1986). Socio-sexual characteristics of men with sexual problems. *Sexual and Marital Therapy, 1,* 89–108.

Comstock, G. W., & Lundin, F. E. (1967). Parental smoking and perinatal mortality. *American Journal of Obstetrics and Gynecology, 98,* 708–718.

Comstock, G. W., & Partridge, K. B. (1972). Church attendance and health. *Journal of Chronic Disease, 25,* 665–672.

Comstock, G. W., & Tonascia, J. A. (1977). Education and mortality in Washington County, Maryland. *Journal of Health and Social Behavior, 18,* 54–61.

Coombs, R. H., Wellisch, D. K., & Fawzy, F. I. (1985). Drinking patterns and problems among female children and adolescents: A comparison of abstainers, past users, and current users. *American Journal of Drug and Alcohol Abuse, 11,* 315–348.

Cothran, M. M., & Harvey, P. D. (1986). Delusional thinking in psychotics: Correlates of religious content. *Psychological Reports, 58,* 191–199.

Cox, W. F. (1985). Content analysis of the dogmatism scale from a biblical perspective. *The High School Journal, 68,* 197–204.

Dhawan, N., & Sripat, K. (1986). Fear of death and religiosity as related to need for affiliation. *Psychological Studies, 31,* 35–38.

Decker, S. D., & Schultz, R. (1985). Correlates of life satisfaction and depression in middle-aged and elderly spinal cord-injured persons. *American Journal of Occupational Therapy, 39,* 740–745.

De Figueiredo, J. M. & Lemkau, P. V. (1978). The prevalence of psychosomatic symptoms in a rapidly changing bilingual culture: An exploratory study. *Social Psychiatry, 13,* 125–133.

Dittes, J. E. (1969). Psychology of Religion. In G. Lindzey & E. Aronson (Eds.), *The handbook of social psychology* (pp. 602–659). Reading, MA: Addison-Wesley.

Dodd, D. K., & Mills, L. L. (1985). FADIS: A measure of the fear of accidental death and injury. *The Psychological Record, 35,* 269–275.

Donahue, M. J. (1985). Intrinsic and extrinsic religiousness: Review and meta-analysis. *Journal of Personality and Social Psychology, 48,* 409–419.

Donahue, M. J., & Bergin, A. E. (1983, August). Religion, personality and lifestyle: A meta-analysis. Paper presented at the annual meeting of the American Psychological Association, Anaheim, CA.

Downey, A.M. (1984). Relationship of religiosity to death anxiety of middle-aged males. *Psychological Reports, 54,* 811–822.

Dubey, R. S. (1986). Authoritarianism in Indian leaders. *Psychological Research Journal, 10,* 16–23.

Elkins, D., Anchor, K. N., & Sandler, H. M. (1979). Relaxation training and prayer behavior as tension reduction techniques. *Behavioral Engineering, 5,* 81–87.

Epstein, L., Tamir, A., & Natan, T. (1985). Emotional health state of adolescents. *International Journal of Adolescent Medicine and Health, 1,* 13–22.

Fedio, P. (1986). Behavioral characteristics of patients with temporal lobe epilepsy. *Psychiatric Clinics of North America, 9,* 267–281.

Finney, J. R. & Malony, H. N. (1985). An empirical study of contemplative prayer as an adjunct to psychotherapy. *Journal of Psychology and Theology, 13,* 284–290.

Florian, V., & Kravetz, S. (1983). Fear of personal death: Attribution, structure, and relation to religious belief. *Journal of Personality and Social Psychology, 44,* 600–607.

Florian, V., Kravetz, S., & Frankel, J. (1984). Aspects of fear of personal death, levels of awareness, and religious commitment. *Journal of Research in Personality, 18,* 289–304.

Francis, L. J., & Pearson, P. R. (1985). Psychoticism and religiosity among 15-year-olds. *Personality and Individual Differences, 6,* 397–398.

Galanter, M., & Buckley, P. (1978). Evangelical religion and meditation: Psychotherapeutic effects. *Journal of Nervous and Mental Disease, 166,* 685–691.

Galanter, M., Rabkin, R., Rabkin, J., & Deutsch, A. (1979). The "Moonies": A psychological study of conversion and membership in a contemporary religious sect. *American Journal of Psychiatry, 136,* 165–170.

Gartner, J. (1981, April). *Anti-religious value assumptions in psychological testing: The personal orientation inventory.* Paper presented at the meeting of the Christian Association of Psychological Studies, San Diego, CA.

Gartner, J. (1983). Self-esteem tests: Assumptions and values. In Craig Ellision (Ed.), *Your better self: Psychology, Christianity and self-esteem* (pp. 98-110) New York: Harper & Row.

Gartner, J. (1985). Religious prejudice in psychology: Theories of its cause and cure. *Journal of Psychology and Christianity, 4,* 16–23.

Gartner, J., Hohmann, A., Larson, D., Canino, G., & Allen, G. (1988, November). *Psychiatric, psychosocial and health services utilization characteristics of frequent church attenders.* Paper presented at the meeting of the American Public Health Association, Boston.

General Social Survey (1982–1984). Chicago: National Opinion Research Center, University of Chicago.

Gibb, L. L. (1968). Home background and self-actualization attainment. *Journal of College Student Personnel, 9,* 49–53.

Glen, N. D., & Weaver, C. N. (1978). A multivariat, multi-survey study of marital happiness. *Journal of Marriage and the Family, 40,* 269–282.

Globetti, G., & Windham, G. (1967). The social adjustment of high school students and the use of beverage alcohol. *Journal of Applied Social Psychology, 2,* 1–16.

Gorsuch, R. L., & Aleshire, D. (1974). Christian faith and ethnic prejudice: A review and interpretation of research. *Journal for the Scientific Study of Religion, 13,* 281–307.

Gorsuch, R. L., & Butler, M. C. (1976). Initial drug abuse: A review of predisposing social psychological factors. *Psychological Bulletin, 83,* 20–137.

Gottlieb, N. H., & Green, L. W. (1984). Life events, social network, life-style, and health: An analysis of the 1979 national survey of personal health practices and consequences. *Health Education Quarterly, 11,* 91–105.

Graff, R. W., & Ladd, C. E. (1971). POI correlates of a religious commitment inventory. *Journal of Clinical Psychology, 27,* 502–504.

Graham, T. W. (1978). Frequency of church attendance and blood pressure evaluation. *Journal of Behavioral Medicine, 1,* 37–43.

Griffith, E. E., Mahy, G. E., & Young, J. L. (1986). Psychological benefits of Spiritual Baptist "mourning," II: An empirical assessment. *American Journal of Psychiatry, 143,* 226–229.

Guinn, R. (1975). Characteristics of drug use among Mexican American students. *Journal of Drug Education, 5,* 235–241.

Gupta, A. (1983). Mental health and religion. *Asian Journal of Psychology Education, 11,* 8–13.

Guy, R. F. (1982). Religion, physical disabilities, and life satisfaction in older age cohorts. *International Journal of Aging and Human Development, 15,* 225–232.

Hasin, D., Endicott, J., & Lewis, C. (1985). Alcohol and drug abuse in patients with affective syndromes. *Comprehensive Psychiatry, 26,* 283–295.

Hassan, M. K., & Khalique, A. (1981). Religiosity and its correlates in college students. *Journal of Psychological Researches, 25,* 129–136.

Hays, R. D., Stacy, A. W., Widaman, K. F., & DiMatteo, M. R. (1986). Multistage path models of adolescent alcohol and drug use: A reanalysis. *Journal of Drug Issues, 16,* 357–369.

Heintzelman, M. E., & Fehr, L. A. (1976). Relationship between religious orthodoxy and three personality variables. *Psychological Reports, 38,* 756–758.

Helsing, J. K., & Sklo, M. (1981). Mortality after bereavement. *American Journal of Epidemiology, 114,* 45.

Herek, G. M. (1987). Religious orientation and prejudice: A comparison of racial and sexual attitudes. *Personality and Social Psychology Bulletin, 13,* 34–44.

Hertsgaard, D., & Light, H. (1984). Anxiety, depression, and hostility in rural women. *Psychological Reports, 55,* 673–674.

Higgins, P. C., & Albrecht, G. L. (1977). Hellfire and delinquency revisited. *Social Forces, 55,* 952–958.

Hjelle, L. A. (1975). Relationship of a measure of self-actualization to religious participation. *Journal of Psychology, 89,* 179–182.

Hoch, Z., Safir, M., Peres, Y., & Shepher, J. (1981). An evaluation of sexual performance: Comparison between sexually dysfunctional and functional couples. *Journal of Sex and Marital Therapy, 7,* 195–206.

Hoelter, J. (1979). Religiosity, fear of death and suicide acceptability. *Suicide and Life-Threatening Behavior, 9,* 163–172.

Hogan, R., & Embler, N. (1978). The bias in contemporary psychology. *Social Research, 45,* 478–534.

Hopping, M. (1984). Psychic seizures: A diagnostic challenge. *Bulletin of the Menninger Clinic, 48,* 401–417.

House, J. S., Robbins, C., & Metzner, H. L. (1982). The association of social relationships and activities with mortality. *American Journal of Epidemiology, 116,* 123–140.

Hundleby, J. D. (1987). Adolescent drug use in a behavioral matrix: A confirmation and comparison of the sexes. *Addictive Behaviors, 12,* 103–112.

Hunt, R. A., & King, M. B. (1978). Religiosity and marriage. *Journal for the Scientific Study of Religion, 17,* 403.

Hyman, H., & Sheatsley, P. (1954). The authoritarian personality: A methodological critique. In R. Christie & M. Jhoda (Eds.), *The authoritarian personality,* Glencoe, IL: Free Press.

Jansen, D. G., Gravey, F. J., & Bonk, E. C. (1972). Personality characteristics of clergymen entering a clinical training program at a state hospital. *Psychological Reports, 31,* 878.

Jackson, J.J. (1972). Marital life among Blacks. *The Family Coordinator, 34,* 24–28.

Jenkins, C. D. (1976). Recent evidence supporting psychological and social risk factors for coronary disease. *New England Medical Journal, 294,* 987–994.

Katkin, S., Zimmerman, V., Rosenthal, J., & Ginsburg, M. (1975). Using volunteer therapists to reduce hospital readmissions. *Hospital and Community Psychiatry, 26,* 151–153.

Kennedy, E. C., Heckler, V. J., Kohler, F. J., & Walker, R. E. (1977). Clinical assessment of a profession: Roman Catholic clergymen. *Journal of Clinical Psychology, 33*(1), 120–128.

Knudsen, H. C. & Bolwig, T. G. (1986). The relationship between epilepsy and personality: Reality or myth. *Nordisk Psykiatrisk Tidsskrift, 40*, 337–343.

Kunzendorf, R. (1985–1986). Repressed fear of inexistence and its hypnotic recovery in religious students. *Omega Journal of Death and Dying, 16*, 23–33.

LaBach, P. (1969). *Self-actualization in college students: Interrelationships of self-actualization, personal characteristics and attitudes in the subcultures of liberal arts freshmen and seniors*. Unpublished doctoral dissertation, Kent State University, Kent, Ohio.

Larson, D. B. (1985). Religious involvement. In G. Rekers (Ed.), *Family building* (pp. 121–147). Ventura, CA: Regal Books.

Larson, D. B., Koenig, H. G., Kaplan, B. H., Greenberg, R. F., Logue, E., & Tyroler, H. A. (1988). *The impact of importance of religion and frequency of church attendance on blood pressure status*. Manuscript submitted for publication.

Lea, G. (1982). Religion, mental health, and clinical issues. *Journal of Religion and Health, 21*, 336–351.

Lee, R., & Piercy, F. P. (1974). Church attendance and self-actualization. *Journal of College Student Personnel, 15*, 400–403.

Levin, J. S., & Markides, K. S. (1986). Religious attendance and subjective health. *Journal for the Scientific Study of Religion, 25*, 31–40.

Levin, J., & Vanderpool, H. (1987). Is frequent religious attendance really conducive to better health?: Toward an epidemiology of religion. *Social Science Medicine, 24*, 589–600.

Lindenthal, J. J., Myers, J. K., Pepper, M. P., & Stern, M. S. (1970). Mental status and religious behavior. *Journal for the Scientific Study of Religion, 9*, 143–149.

Lindskoog, D., & Kirk, R. E. (1975). Some life history and attitudinal correlates of self-actualization among evangelical seminary students. *Journal for the Scientific Study of Religion, 14*, 51–55.

Locke, H. J. (1951). *Predicting adjustment in marriage*. New York: Holt, Rinehart & Winston.

Mahabeer, M., & Bhana, K. (1984). The relationship between religion, religiosity and death anxiety among Indian adolescents. *South African Journal of Psychology, 14*, 7–9.

Makarec, R., & Persinger, M. A. (1985). Temporal lobe signs: Electroencephalographic validity and enhanced scores in special populations. *Perceptual and Motor Skills, 60*, 831–842.

Martin, W. T. (1984). Religiosity and United States suicide rates, 1972–1978. *Journal of Clinical Psychology, 40*, 1166–1169.

Mayo, C. C., Puryear, H. B., & Richek, H. G. (1969). MMPI correlates of religiousness in late adolescent college students. *Journal of Nervous and Mental Disease, 149*, 381–385.

McCarthy, J. (1979). Religious commitment, affiliation and marriage dissolution. In R. Wuthnow (Ed.), *The Religious dimension: New directions in quantitative research* (p. 190). San Diego, CA: Academic Press.

McClure, R. F., & Loden, M. (1982). Religious activity, denomination membership and life satisfaction. *Psychology, A Quarterly Journal of Human Behavior, 19,* 13–17.

McMordie, W. R. (1981). Religiosity and fear of death: Strength of belief system. *Psychological Reports, 49,* 921–922.

McNeel, S. P., & Thorsen, P. L. (1985). A developmental perspective on Christian faith and dogmatism. *The High School Journal, 68,* 211–220.

Meisenhelder, J. B. (1986). Self-esteem in women: The influence of employment and perception of husband's appraisals. *Image Journal of Nursing Scholarship, 18,* 8–14.

Minear, J. D., & Bruch, L. R. (1980–1981). The correlations of attitudes toward suicide with death anxiety, religiosity, and personal closeness to suicide. *Omega Journal of Death and Dying, 11,* 317–324.

Moberg, D. O. (1965). Religiosity in old age. *Gerontologist, 5,* 78–87.

Mookherjee, H. N. (1986). Comparison of some personality characteristics of male problem drinkers in rural Tennessee. *Journal of Alcohol and Drug Education, 31,* 23–28.

Morris, P. A. (1982). The effect of pilgrimage on anxiety, depression and religious attitude. *Psychological Medicine, 12,* 291–294.

Muchnik, B., & Rosenheim, E. (1982). Fear of death, defense-style and religiosity among Israeli Jews. *Israeli Journal of Psychiatry and Related Sciences, 19,* 157–164.

Murphy, H. B. M., & Vega, G. (1982). Schizophrenia and religious affiliation in Northern Ireland. *Psychological Medicine, 12,* 595–605.

Newcomb, M. D., & Bentler, P. M. (1986). Cocaine use among adolescents: Longitudinal associations with social context, psychopathology, and use of other substances. *Addictive Behaviors, 11,* 263–273.

Nicholi, A. M. (1985). Characteristics of college students who use psychoactive drugs for nonmedical reasons. *Journal of American College Health, 33,* 189–192.

Nye, F. I., (1958). *Family relationships and delinquent behavior.* New York: Wiley.

Paloutzian, R. F., & Ellison, C. W. (1982). Loneliness, spiritual well-being, and the quality of life. In L. A. Peplau & D. Perlman (Eds.), *Loneliness: A sourcebook of current theory research and therapy* (pp. 224–237). New York: Wiley.

Pargament, K. I., Johnson, S. M., Echemendia, R. J., & Silverman, W. H. (1985). The limits of fit: Examining the implications of person-environment congruence within different religious settings. *Journal of Community Psychology, 13,* 20–30.

Paykel, E. S., Myers, J. K., Lindenthal, J. J., & Tanner, J. (1974). Suicidal feelings in the general population: A prevalence study. *British Journal of Psychology, 124,* 460–469.

Pellegrin, V. B. H. (1970). *A descriptive study of a midwestern sample of Episcopal clergy and seminarians categorized according to various criteria*. Doctoral dissertation, University of Kansas, Lawrence.

Persinger, M. A. (1984). People who report religious experiences may also display enhanced temporal-lobe signs. *Perceptual and Motor Skills, 58*, 963–975.

Persinger, M. A., & Makarec, R. (1987). Temporal lobe epileptic signs and correlative behaviors displayed by normal populations. *Journal of General Psychology, 114*, 179–195.

The Princeton Religious Research Center. (1982). *Religion in America*. Princeton NJ: Author.

Query, J. N. (1985). Comparative admission and follow-up study of American Indians and Whites in a youth chemical dependency unit on the north central plains. *International Journal of the Addictions, 20*, 489–502.

Reglin, R. (1976). *A study of self-actualization factors in individuals with a conservative evangelical religious background*. Doctoral dissertation, United States International University, San Diego. CA.

Reynolds, E. N. (1968). *Interpersonal risk and self-actualization in four religious groups*. Doctoral dissertation, Case Reserve University, Cleveland, OH.

Reynolds, D. K., & Nelson, F. L. (1981). Personality, life situation, and life expectancy. *Suicide and Life Threatening Behavior, 11*, 99–110.

Richardson, V., Berman, S., & Piwowarski, M. (1983). Projective assessment of the relationships between the salience of death, religion, and age among adults in America. *The Journal of General Psychology, 109*, 149–156.

Robins, L. N. (1974). *Deviant children grow up*. Huntington NY: Krieger.

Rogalski, S., & Paisey, T. (1987). Neuroticism versus demographic variables as correlates of self-reported life satisfaction in a sample of older adults. *Personality and Individual Differences, 8*, 397–401.

Roozen, D. A. (1979). The efficacy of demographic theories of religious change: Protestant church attendance, 1952–1968. In D. R. Hoge & D. A. Roozen (Eds.), *Understanding church growth and declines 1950–1978* (pp. 90–110). New York: The Pilgrim Press.

Rohrbaugh, J., & Jessor, R. (1975). Religiosity in youth: A control against deviant behavior. *Journal of Personality, 43*, 136–155.

Rokeach, M. (1960). *The open and closed mind*. New York: Basic Books.

Rosenheim, E., & Muchnik, B. (1984–1985). Death concerns in differential levels of consciousness as functions of defense strategy and religious belief. *Omega Journal of Death and Dying, 15*, 15–24.

Ross, M. (1985). Mental health in Hare Krishna devotees: A longitudinal study. *American Journal of Social Psychiatry, 5*, 65–67.

Sanua, V. D. (1969). Religion, mental health, and personality: A review of empirical studies. *American Journal of Psychiatry, 125*, 1203–1213.

Scanzoni, J. H. (1977). *The Black family in modern society* (2nd ed.). Chicago: Chicago University Press.

Schroeder, B. L. (1970). *An examination of the characteristics of students and faculty in a small Black denominational college*. Doctoral dissertation, University of Texas, Austin.

Schumaker, J. F. (Ed.). (1992). *Religion and mental health*. Oxford, England: Oxford University Press.

Scott, E. M. (1961). Presumed correlation between religion and mental health. *Guild of Catholic Psychiatrists Bulletin, 8*, 113–121.

Schumm, W. R., Bollman, S. R., & Jurich, A. P. (1982). The marital conventionalization argument: Implications for the study of religiosity and marital satisfaction. *Journal of Psychology and Theology, 10*, 237.

Shrum, W. (1980). Religion and marital instability: Change in the 1970's? *Review of Religious Research, 21*, 125–147.

Smith, D. R., Nehemkis, A. M., & Charter, R. A. (1983–1984). Fear of death, death attitudes, and religious conviction in the terminally ill. *International Journal of Psychiatry in Medicine, 13*, 221–232.

Sorensen, A. E., & Bolwig, T. G. (1987). Personality and epilepsy: New evidence for a relationship? A review. *Comprehensive Psychiatry, 28*, 369–383.

Spellman, C. M., Baskett, G. D., & Byrne, D. (1971). Manifest anxiety as a contributing factor in religious conversion. *Journal of Consulting and Clinical Psychology, 36*, 245–247.

Spendlove, D. C., West, D. W., & Stanish, W. M. (1984). Risk factors in the prevalence of depression in Mormon women. *Social Science Medicine, 18*, 491–495.

Spilka, B., & Werme, P. H. (1971). Religion and mental disorder: A research perspective. In M. Strommen (Ed.), *Research on Religious development: A comprehensive handbook* (pp. 461–481). New York: Hawthorn.

Sporawski, M. J., & Houghston, M. J. (1978). Prescriptions for happy marriage adjustments and satisfaction of couples married 50 or more years. *Family Coordinator, 27*, 321–327.

Stack, S. (1983a). The effect of the decline in institutionalized religion on suicide, 1954–1978. *Journal for the Scientific Study of Religion, 22*, 239–252.

Stack, S. (1983b). The effect of religious commitment on suicide: A cross-national analysis. *Journal of Health and Social Behavior, 24*, 362–374.

Stark, R. (1971). Psychopathology and religious commitment. *Review of Religious Research, 12*, 165–176.

Stark, R., (1983). Beyond Durkheim: Religion and suicide. *Journal for the Scientific Study of Religion, 22*, 120–131.

Stark, R., Kent, L., & Doyle, D. P. (1982). Religion and delinquency: The ecology of a lost relationship. *Journal of Research in Crime and Delinquency, 19*, 4–24.

Stark-Adamec, C., Adamec, R. E., Graham, J. M., Hicks, R. C., & Bruun-Meyer (1985). Complexities in the complex partial seizures personality controversy. *The Psychiatric Journal of the University of Ottowa, 10*, 231–236.

Stewart, R. A. C., & Webster, A. C. (1970). Scale for theological conservatism and its personality correlates. *Perceptual and Motor Skills, 30*, 867–870.

Stillion, J. M., McDowell, E. E., & Shamblin, J. B. (1984). The suicide attitude vignette experience: A method for measuring adolescent attitudes toward suicide. *Death Education, 8*, 65–79.

Tennison, J. C., & Snyder, W. U. (1968). Some relationships between attitudes toward the church and certain personality characteristics. *Journal of Counseling Psychology, 15*, 187–189.

Tobacyk, J. (1983). Death threat, death concerns, and paranormal belief. *Death Education, 7*, 115–124.

Tucker, D. M., Novelly, R. A., & Walker, P. J. (1987). Hyperreligiosity in temporal lobe epilepsy: Redefining the relationship. *Journal of Nervous and Mental Disease, 175*, 181–184.

Ullman, C. (1982). Cognitive and emotional antecedents of religious conversion. *Journal of Personality and Social Psychology, 43*, 183–192.

Warren, N. C. (1977). Empirical studies in the psychology of religion; an assessment of the period 1960–1970. In N. Maloney, (Ed.), *Current perspectives in the psychology of religion* (pp. 93–100). Grand Rapids, MI: Eerdmans.

Walters. (1964). Religion and psychopathology. *Comprehensive Psychiatry, 101*, 24–35.

Watson, P. J., Hood, R. W., Morris, R. J., & Hall, J. R. (1985). Religiosity, sin and self-esteem. *Journal of Psychology and Theology, 13*, 116–128.

Watson, P. J., Morris, R. J., & Hood, R. W. (1990). Intrinsicness, self-actualization, and the ideological surround. *Journal of Psychology and Theology, 18*, 40–53.

Webster, A. C., & Stewart, R. A. C. (1969). Psychological attitudes and beliefs of Ministers. *Anvil Quarterly, 1*, 11–16.

Weltha, D. A. (1969). Some relationships between religious attitudes and the self-concept. *Dissertation Abstracts International, 30*, 2782B.

Westman, A. S., & Canter, F. M. (1985). Fear of death and the concept of extended self. *Psychological Reports, 56*, 419–425.

Wickstrom, D. L. , & Fleck, J. R. (1983). Missionary children: Correlates of self-esteem and dependency. *Journal of Psychology and Theology, 11*, 226–235.

Williams, R. L. & Cole, S. (1968). Religiosity, generalized anxiety, and apprehension concerning death. *Journal of Social Psychology, 75*, 111–117.

Wilson, R. W. (1985). Christianity biased and unbiased dogmatism's relationship to different Christian commitments. *High School Journal, 68*, 334–338.

Wilson, W., & Miller, H. L. (1968). Fear, anxiety and religiousness. *Journal for the Scientific Study of Religion, 7*, 111.

Young, M., Gartner, J., O'Connor T., Larson, D., Wright, K., Ames, D. & Rosen, B. (1990, August). *Participation in a volunteer ministry program and recidivism:*

A *ten year follow-up*. Paper presented at the meeting of the American Psychological Association, Boston.

Zuckerman, D. M., Kasl, S. V., & Ostfeld, A. M. (1984). Psychological predicators of mortality among the elderly poor. *American Journal of Epidemiology, 119,* 410–423.

8

RELIGIOUS METHODS OF COPING: RESOURCES FOR THE CONSERVATION AND TRANSFORMATION OF SIGNIFICANCE

KENNETH I. PARGAMENT

Long before the rise of clinical psychology, religious thinkers and practitioners pondered the human condition, the nature of suffering, and the coming to terms with the human's lot in life. It seems strange then that psychologists have largely overlooked the answers of the religious world to these fundamental existential questions. Perhaps psychologists' peculiar neglect of religion reflects the belief that it is in some sense a competitor to psychology, vying with it for the hearts and minds of those they serve. Perhaps psychologists simply underestimate the power of religion in the lives of many people; after all, psychologists as a group tend to be far less religious than those that they study and with whom they work (Beit-Hallahmi, 1977; Shafranske, Chapter 5, this volume). Whatever the cause, psychological and religious communities have had, for the most part, little to do with each other, in spite of what they share—a commitment to personal well-being.

This chapter takes a different position: Psychologists have much to gain by learning about, learning from, and working with the religious world in the effort to promote mental health (Pargament & Maton, in press). This is not to say that religion cannot at times threaten, disrupt, or even

---

The material in this chapter will be presented in more extensive form in the forthcoming book *The Psychology of Religion and Coping* (Guilford Press).

destroy the things people care about most. Certainly it can. But much has already been written about the negative side of religious life. Here, I will shift focus from the negative to some of the positive psychological contributions that religion can make to coping with life's most stressful moments. To begin with, it is important to consider a few of the assumptions and key terms that will guide this discussion.

THE SEARCH FOR SIGNIFICANCE

In this chapter I assume that people are goal-directed beings, engaged in an effort to find and hold on to whatever they may define as significant in living. The capacity to envision goals and take the steps to realize them, many have argued, is one of the most distinctively human attributes (Rotter, 1954; Rychlak, 1981). However, the significance people reach toward is by no means uniform. It changes with time and circumstance, and it varies across people. Much of the richness and complexity of behavior follows from the human propensity to seek out different types of significance. That significance may be material (e.g., a house), physical (e.g., health), social (e.g., intimate relationships), psychological (e.g., meaning), or spiritual (e.g., closeness with God). Although this discussion will focus mostly on prosocial forms of significance, significance is not necessarily good; people may pursue destructive ends (e.g., drugs) as well as constructive ones.

Religion as a Search for Significance

I also assume that religion is involved in the search for significance; in fact, religion has been defined as a search for significance in ways related to the sacred (Pargament, 1992). Implicit in this definition is religion's dual role: (a) It prescribes what people should strive for, and (b) it prescribes the path people should take to reach these goals. In short, religion is concerned with both the ends and the means of significance. What makes religion unique, however, is its focus on the sacred. Unlike other personal and social institutions, the religious world wraps its search for significance in higher powers; deities; ultimacy; and the beliefs, experiences, rituals, and institutions associated with these transcendent forces. People are called religious when the sacred is a part of their deepest values and when the sacred is involved in the way they build, maintain, and change these values (Pargament, 1992). From the religious perspective, then, objects of significance are not simply "goals," and the methods to attain significance are not simply "instruments" or "tools." For example, if people are told to seek a more just world, it is not because social justice is a value in and of itself but because God has asked humankind to remake the world in the divine image of fairness and benevolence. By their association with the sacred, many seemingly secular means and ends can take on a sacred power of their own.

Conservation and Transformation: Methods of Coping for Significance

Significance is occasionally threatened by external or internal crisis and transition. These are the times that call for coping. Coping refers to the search for significance in the face of stressful life situations. In an effort to attain and maximize significance, the individual draws on one of two types of coping mechanisms: conservational or transformational.

Conservational coping involves attempts to preserve or protect significance in the face of threat, challenge, or loss. The Amish who maintain a distinctive dress, language, and way of life, the Christians who reinterpret life's trials and tribulations as opportunities to grow closer to Jesus in his suffering, or the Jewish concentration camp inmates who persisted in practicing their faith despite the imminent danger to their lives all have tried to conserve something of significance, be it a culture, a feeling of comfort and intimacy with God, or the religion itself. Conservation appears to be the first and perhaps strongest tendency in coping. Even children, Piaget (1954) once observed, "resist every new accommodation" (p. 353).

There are times, however, when people can no longer preserve or protect what they care about most deeply. It may be a bereaved parent stripped of what is most precious in his or her life; a soldier who went to war to protect freedom and democracy only to find himself or herself totally disillusioned by war's end; or an accident victim forced to abandon his or her plans for a career, marriage, and children. In each of these instances, the task of coping shifts from conservation to transformation; difficult as it may be, new sources of significance must be found to replace lost or inadequate significant objects. After a transformation of significance has taken place, the focus of coping returns once again to conservation and the protection of newfound significance. In this sense conservation and transformation are complementary, interdependent processes that help guide and sustain the person throughout the life span.

The Religion and Coping Connection

Following the tragic bombing of a federal office building in Oklahoma City in May 1995, the nation came together to mourn the victims. Religion was a central part of the process, as is shown by this newspaper account: "Lines two miles long began forming some six hours before yesterday's prayer service honoring the victims of Wednesday's blast. . . . People from throughout the region traveled to the fairgrounds arena to pay their respects. Nearby buildings and several churches with large-screen television opened their doors as 'overflow' praying sites" (Jacobs, 1995, 3A). One woman who had come to the service has this to say: "This just isn't for the people here, it's for the people of Oklahoma. That's why I am here. It brings everyone back to God. Prayer is the answer" (Jacobs, 1995, 3A). Now, the old saying that there are no atheists in foxholes is not totally accurate. There are people who doubt or disbelieve in a higher power before and after crisis. One survivor of a concentration camp commented, "I never believed in God. Not before the Holocaust, not during my stay in the camps and not afterwards. I didn't need the Holocaust as proof of God's nonexistence. I was never in doubt that He didn't exist" (Brenner, 1980, p. 96). However, empirical evidence does indicate that religion is often intimately involved in life's most stressful moments (e.g., Bulman & Wortman, 1977; Koenig, George & Siegler, 1988; Lindenthal, Myers, Pepper, & Stein, 1970; McRae, 1984; Segall & Wykle, 1988–1989).

Several empirical studies have also shown a clear relationship between general indicators of religiousness and religious coping, and adjustment to crisis (e.g., Koenig et al., 1992; McIntosh, Silver, & Wortman, 1993; Park, Cohen, & Herb, 1990). Less clear, however, is what it is about religion that makes a difference. Measures of average church attendance, frequency of prayer, or religious commitment do not speak to the functions of religion. They also do not specify the mechanisms that affect adjustment. In times of crisis, general religious beliefs and practices have to be translated into more specific ways of coping, and it is these specific forms of religious coping that may have the most important implications for the resolution of the crisis.

Recently, investigators have begun to take a closer look at various methods of religious coping. The results have been promising. Consistent with coping theory, measures of religious coping have emerged as stronger predicators of adjustment to life crisis than general indicators of religiousness (see Pargament, 1995, for review). Moreover, as I will note later, measures of religious coping methods have been found to predict adjustment over and above the effects of nonreligious coping. In this chapter, I take a functional look at some of these religious coping methods. Specifically, I focus on a few of the many roles religion can play in the conservation and transformation of significance. Although it is important to recognize that religion can, at times, impede the coping process (in essence, making bad matters worse), my emphasis here will be on the helpful roles of religion in understanding and dealing with stressful situations.

Religious Methods of Coping for the Conservation of Significance

Philosopher Harald Höffding (1914) once wrote that "the innermost tendency of all religion, is the axiom of the conservation of value" (p. 209). Social scientists have echoed this view; religion has typically been described as a source of psychological and social stability. And on close inspection, religion can be found to indeed provide its members with a variety of mechanisms to help them conserve whatever is of significance in times of trouble.

Religious Prevention

One way to conserve significance is by preventing those events that pose a threat to it. Religious institutions and systems of belief and practice often serve important preventive functions. The behaviors to be avoided are clearly and unmistakably marked by religious signs that read "taboo," "profane," or "sinful." Labelled in this fashion, the problems of today—drug abuse, promiscuity, violence, and injustice—become more than misbehaviors or psychosocial disorders. They represent transgressions against the holy and carry with them heavy spiritual penalties, as the New Testament states: "For the wrath of God is revealed from heaven against all ungodliness and unrighteousness of men who hold the truth in righteousness" (Romans 1: 18).

Injunctions against these types of behaviours may be expressed through religious institutions as well as through religious beliefs. Through their clergy, leaders, and special programs, many churches and synagogues discourage their members (and, in some cases the larger community) from taking a wrong turn and encourage them to stay on the right path. For example, one survey of a congregation in a large Western city revealed that half of the churches had provided drug or alcohol education programs to their youth within the past three years (Lorch, 1987). Other congregations have been involved in preventive programming for problems ranging from homelessness, cancer, and hypertension to unemployment, divorce, and racism (see Pargament, Maton, & Hess, 1992, for a review).

Empirical evidence suggests that religious beliefs, practices, and institutions can be effective in their preventive role. For example, Seventh Day Adventists, a group that discourages the consumption of coffee and meat, have lower mortality rates from bowel, prostate, and breast cancer than the general population. In a similar vein, the Amish, who have strong sanctions against sex outside of marriage, have lower rates of cervical cancer (see Jenkins, 1992). Furthermore, religious involvement, defined and measured in a variety of ways, has been tied to a reduced risk of suicide, drug and alcohol abuse, and family breakup (see Payne, Bergin, Bielema, & Jenkins, 1992, for a review).

Religious Support

The Bible says, "They confronted me in the day of my calamity: but the Lord was my stay" (Psalms 18: 19). Not all negative events can be prevented or avoided, but religion tries to assist in the conservation of significance after calamity strikes as well as before. Spiritual support represents one important religious conservational mechanism. The individual may look for support most directly from God (see Maton, 1989). In fact, many people report that they turn to the divine for help in crisis. For example, 60% of one adult sample faced with a recent negative life event reportedly coped by putting their faith in God (McRae, 1984). In an interview study of African-American caregivers to relatives with dementia, 65% spontaneously mentioned faith and prayer as ways in which they coped with their situation (Segall & Wykle, 1988–1989). Another study by Shrimali and Broota (1987) illustrates how stress may activate a search for religious support and comfort. These researchers compared a group of patients in India who were about to undergo major surgery with a group about to have minor surgery and a control group. Prior to surgery the major surgery patients reported more anxiety and beliefs in God than the other two groups. Afterward, anxiety levels and beliefs in God among the major surgery patients decreased to the same level as that of the other groups.

Although other family members, friends, and associates may come and go, God can be seen as an everpresent partner, continually available for emotional assistance and guidance in times of trouble. This collaborative type of spiritual coping must be distinguished from the deferral of personal responsibility to religious authority, the style of religious coping so criticized by mental health professionals. Research indicates that people who involve God more as a partner in coping with stress have lower levels of anxiety (Schaefer & Gorsuch, 1991), better physical and mental health (McIntosh & Spilka, 1990), and greater psychosocial competence (Hathaway & Pargament, 1991; Pargament et al., 1988).

Religious support may be sought only from God but also from the multitude of individuals and institutions associated with the divine. In 1991, there were over 545,000 clergy in the United States and over 350,000 religious congregations (Jacquet & Jones, 1991). More so than human and health service systems, religious organizations have a widely recognized right to reach out to people in times of transition and trouble. In turn, many people in distress prefer to seek help from their clergy or religious congregation than from mental health professionals, and many feel less social stigma in the process (Chalfant et al., 1990). Although the deepest of angers is often reserved for clergy and congregational members who fail to live up to the expectations of the individual in crisis (e.g., Horton, Wilkins, & Wright, 1988), there is evidence that members can derive support from clergy, fellow members, and institutional involvement as well. For example, in a study of 16 terminally ill cancer patients, Gibbs and Achterberg-Lawlis (1978) found that those who reported greater emotional support from their church also reported less difficulty in sleeping. In another study of members of Christian mainline churches coping with a major negative life event, reports of support from the clergy and church were associated with better psychological status and outcomes of the event (Pargament, et al., 1990). O'Brien (1982) investigated a sample of mostly African-American chronic dialysis patients and found that frequency of church attendance was tied to less alienation, more and better-quality interactions with others, and greater compliance with treatment. In short, religious institutions and their members appear to be significant sources of support for many people. As "vehicles for the knowledge and service of God" (Carroll, Dudley, & McKinney, 1986, p. 7), religious institutions extend the scope of religious assistance from a vertical-spiritual plane to a horizontal–interpersonal dimension.

Ritual Purification

That people occasionally transgress comes as no surprise to the religions of the world. Virtually every tradition provides mechanisms to help people find their way back to a more faithful life. Through rituals of purification, it is believed, the impurity and sinfulness associated with acts of transgression are removed and the breach between the individual and the sacred is repaired. The rituals may involve punishment, sacrifice, isolation, or repentance as well as the use of water, ashes, oil, blood, or fire. Rituals occur throughout the life cycle—from the baptismal immersion of Christian newborns, to the annual liturgy of atonement of Jews on Yom Kippur, to the final cleansing offered to unconfessed Roman Catholics in purgatory before they can enter heaven (Paden, 1988). In fact, few people go through life without participation in a purification ritual of some kind or another.

In spite of their embeddedness in the lives of many people, relatively little attention has been paid to religious rituals by psychologists and mental health professionals. However, rituals may offer one way of coping with difficult life situations. In this vein, Lilliston and Klein (1989) found that college students who reported a discrepancy between their actual selves and the selves they felt they ought to be were more likely to use religion in coping than students with less of an "actual–ought" discrepancy. They conclude that, for these people, crisis elicits an attempt "to live more fully in accord with the religion they have chosen" (pp. 8–9).

Purification rituals may serve important psychological as well as spiritual functions. The ritual of reconciliation, for instance, is nicely designed to produce feelings of relief and comfort. Tension is momentarily increased by admissions of personal shortcomings and flaws. However, when the confession is greeted with acceptance and forgiveness rather than criticism and condemnation, the individual may feel a lifting of burdens and respite from distress. Pennebaker and his colleagues have conducted a series of studies that points to the beneficial effects of confession, although not of the specifically religious kind. In one study, they asked one group of students to write about the most traumatic event they had ever experienced and another group to write about a set of unimportant topics (Pennebaker & Beall, 1986). Those who wrote about the traumatic event were further subgrouped into those asked to describe only the facts associated with the trauma (trauma–factual), those told to describe only the emotions associated with the trauma (trauma–emotional), and those asked to write about both the facts and emotions tied to the trauma (trauma–combination). Immediately after writing about the trauma, students in the trauma-emotional and trauma-combination groups reported themselves to be the most upset. However, the same two groups also reported fewer illnesses, less illness-related restriction in activity, and fewer visits to a health center over the following six months. Confession appeared to lead to short-term upset but better physical health over the long term.

How well these findings apply to religious confession is another question. It could be argued, however, that the forgiveness offered by a religious authority would only add to the relief effect accompanying such intimate self-disclosure. Two studies of religious coping with significant negative events among church members (Pargament et al., 1990) and with the death of a close friend among college students (Park & Cohen, 1993) suggest this may be the case. Confession, participation in religious rituals, and efforts to live a better life in response to the crises were assessed in these studies through a subscale titled Religious Good Deeds. Among church members, good deeds were associated with more positive adjustment on the three measures of outcome. Among the college students, good deeds were associated with greater event-related distress but more personal growth. Preliminary as these results are, they suggest that rituals of purification may assist an individual in coming to terms with critical life experiences.

Religious Reframing

Any religion, anthropologist Clifford Geertz (1966) wrote, must provide some way to cope with "crises of interpretability," those events that profoundly shake the sense that life is meaningful or comprehensible. In fact, virtually every religious system offers its members a set of cognitive reframing mechanisms to help individuals conserve a sense of meaning in life in the face of what may seem to be senseless, unbearable, or unjust (e.g., Capps, 1990). Religious reframing may focus on the negative event, the individual, or the sacred.

Reframing the Situation. Looking back on the process of helping her parents with Alzheimer's disease, one caregiver commented: "I would not have given up this period to care for my parents for anything. There has been . . . lots of frustration. But I'm learning for the first time to take each day at a time. This illness is teaching me to gain strength from the Lord" (Wright, Pratt, & Schmall, 1985, p. 34). From a religious perspective, negative events may take on a new dimension and a different meaning. Painful as the situation may be, it is not senseless; rather it is part of God's plan for the individual. Perhaps the event is God's way of preventing a more terrible situation from occurring. Perhaps it is God's way of encouraging self-examination on the individual's part. Perhaps it is an opportunity for the person to grow spiritually. And surely, it is believed, God will not push the person beyond endurance. These types of religious reappraisals of the situation are not uncommon. Among groups faced with serious medical problems, attributions of the event to God's will are more common than any other explanation (Bulman & Wortman, 1977; Pargament & Sullivan, 1981). Other studies have found that those who are more religiously committed are more likely to reframe negative events as challenges and opportunities to grow than their less committed counterparts (Pargament, et al., 1992; Wright et al., 1985).

Armed with the knowledge that the event is a part of a larger divine plan and that God will not give the person more than can be handled, the individual may be more able to reaffirm and sustain the belief that life has meaning and that suffering is indeed "sufferable" (Geertz, 1966). Several studies have found this type of religious reframing of the situation to be associated with better adjustment. More specifically, attributions of negative events to God's will, God's love, or God's purpose have been related to more positive outcomes for cancer patients (Jenkins & Pargament, 1988), college students coping with the death of a loved one (Grevengoed & Pargament, 1987; Park & Cohen, 1993), and church members faced with a significant negative event (Pargament et al., 1990).

Reframing the Individual. A second form of religious reframing focuses on the person rather than on the situation. In this type of reframing, calamity and misfortune are accepted as tragedies; however, they are attributed to human forces rather than to divine ones. Consider the following explanation that a chaplain in Vietnam arrives at for the war and its suffering: "One cannot be immersed in sin and at the same time expect to feel the loving presence of God. . . . God indeed checked out of our lives in Vietnam because we 'checked out' on Him" (Mahedy, 1986, p. 131). By reframing Vietnam as a spiritual problem, one brought on by people themselves, the chaplain is able to preserve his belief in a loving, caring God. The concept of Karma within Hinduism illustrates a similar reframing mechanism. According to this tradition, negative events in life are reflections of past deeds from earlier incarnations rather than punishments from God. If pain and sorrow are encountered, Hindus should look to themselves, not God, as the responsible party. At first glance, this may appear to be a particularly harsh form of coping, a process of "blaming the victims" for their woes. However, implicit in this type of reappraisal is opportunity—chance to atone for one's sins, to purify oneself, and to achieve some kind of redemption in this life or subsequent ones. Thus, explanations of negative events in terms of human sinfulness may not necessarily be maladaptive. A few studies have been conducted on this topic (see Watson, Hood, Morris, & Hall, 1985; Watson, Morris, & Hood, 1987). For example, Dalal and Pande (1988) studied patients from India who had been hospitalized with major injuries following an accident. Most of these patients were Hindu, male, and lower middle class. Causal attributions of the accident to Karma, they found, were related to greater psychological recovery at one and three weeks after the accident.

Reframing the Sacred. The third and least common type of religious reframing involves the reappraisal of the sacred. Ordinarily, people implicate the divine in negative situations only as a last resort. And when the divine is tied to a negative event it is usually in tandem with a reframing of the person. If the event is a punishment from God, the punishment is one that is deserved rather than random or malicious. We hear this type of reframing in the advice of one woman to a friend who had recently been diagnosed with cancer: "Surely, there's something in your life which is displeasing to God. . . . You must have stepped out of His will somewhere. These things don't just happen" (Yancey, 1977, p. 13). The cost of this form of appraisal—a personal sense of sinfulness and a punitive image of God—would seem to be high. In fact, a few studies indicate that attributions of negative events to an angry or punishing God are associated with poorer outcomes (Grevengoed & Pargament, 1987; Pargament et al., 1990). The steep costs of these appraisals may account for the relatively small number of people who hold God responsible for crises in life (Bearon & Koenig, 1990; Croog & Levine, 1972; Pargament et al., 1990). For instance, one sample of heart-attack victims was less likely to attribute the illness to a punishment from God than to any other causal factor (Croog & Levine, 1972). It is important to note that the feeling of being punished by God may pass fairly quickly in the process of coping with crisis. In this regard, among those heart-attack patients who initially saw their illness as a punishment from God, only one third held a similar view 1 year later (Croog & Levine, 1972). Nevertheless, one might still wonder why people (even though few in number) would turn to such a harsh interpretation of themselves and God (even if short-lived). Negative though it may be, the notion of a punitive God allows for the possibility of some security and control in life. By living within God's laws, penalties can be avoided. Only when people transgress by stepping outside of the moral boundary will they be subject to punishment. Finally, I should note, the belief in a punitive God may be preferable to an even bleaker alternative—the idea of a world without God, one in which there is no explanation for the bad things that happen and one in which life has no meaning at all.[1] Whether it is by a reframing of the situation, the person, or the sacred, much of the power of religion is located in its capability to find meaning in those situations that confound, baffle, and shake people's most basic assumptions about the world.

Religious Methods of Coping for the Transformation of Significance

Although psychologists have generally viewed religion more as a defender of the status quo than as a force for change, if one looks carefully, one can find that religion is often a part of those times when people make the most dramatic transformation of their lives. Virtually every religious tradition provides its adherents with exemplars—from Siddhartha Gautama to Moses to Jesus Christ—who were stripped of their senses of direction only to find a new purpose in living. Accounts of religious transformation can be found today as well. Below I consider two of the ways religion is involved in this process of fundamental change: religious rites of passage and religious conversion.

Religious Rites of Passage

The human life span is punctuated by important turning points: transitions from womb to birth, from childhood to adolescence, from single to married status, and from life to death. As many writers have noted, these transitions often take on a transcendent character, eliciting feelings of uneasiness, awe, and fear as they remind people of the powerful but unseen forces moving inexorably beneath the surface of day-to-day experience. These turning points are disorienting and disconcerting, for in the shift from one status to another, old roles, expectations, and values must be given up and replaced with new ones. The religions of the world have developed a number of rites of passage that mark these critical periods, acknowledge their transcendental nature, and ease their members through the transition.

Although their content varies dramatically (from fasting and ceremonial dance to special meals and immersion in liquid), rites of passage share a basic structure, one made up of three phases: preparation and sep-

---

[1] A few other religious reframing mechanisms deserve brief mention. Another form of person-centered reframing focuses on the inability of the individual to understand negative situations rather than human responsibility for these situations. Religious reframing of the sacred may also be accomplished by first splitting the sacred into the forces of good and the forces of evil and then attributing misfortune to the latter (e.g., the devil, Satan). In addition, the sacred may be reframed by redefining God's powers to intervene directly in the world. From this perspective, the divine is unable to prevent pain or erase it. Nevertheless, God feels compassion for human suffering and offers solace and hope to people in the midst of their trials.

aration, transition, and incorporation (van Gennep, 1960). Perhaps no turning point is more enveloped in religion than death, so let's briefly consider how religious rites of passage unfold for this final transition.

Even before a death occurs, many religious groups prepare the dying and their survivors for the event. Prior to a death, it is customary for the Amish to make, wash, and clean the funeral clothing for their loved ones (Bryer, 1979). Proper meditation in the last moments of life, popular Buddhist belief holds, facilitates the passage of the dying from this world to the next (Long, 1975). Final confession among Roman Catholics is said to serve a similar function. Death itself is marked through religious rituals that underscore the separation of the living from the dead and the bereaved from the rest of the community. In some traditions, the bodies of the dead are quickly removed from the home; mention of the dead is taboo; and those in grief cut their hair, wear special dress, and go into seclusion to signify their changed status (Rosenblatt, Walsh & Jackson, 1976).

Religious rites are also prominent immediately after the death, which is a period of transition—according to many faiths—between death and the afterlife. Religious funeral services commonly include prayers and rituals designed to speed the passage of the deceased into the hereafter. For example, the Islamic faith speaks of a "trial of the grave" that determines whether the dead will go to hell or paradise; to "tip the scales" of judgment in this momentous decision, Muslims traditionally whisper to the dead answers to the questions the angels may pose about their lives (Chidester, 1990). Although this type of practice may seem odd by Judeo-Christian standards, it should be noted that 71% of people in the United States believe in an afterlife (Gallup & Castelli, 1989).

Funeral ceremonies facilitate transitions for the living as well as the dead. In contrast to stereotypic views about religion as a way to deny negative events, most religious traditions encourage the bereaved to face the fact that a death has occurred. Many funeral rites—the viewing of the body, procession to the gravesite and shoveling of dirt onto the casket in the grave—force the mourner to behave publicly in ways that acknowledge rather than deny the power and weight of the moment. However, funeral ceremonies also offer solace, support, and solidarity to the bereaved as they are being confronted with the reality of death. Loved ones gather around those in mourning to soothe them and shield them from excesses of anger or despair. Clergy provide a similar function in their funeral eulogies and personal ministrations to survivors. And in the coming together of a larger group of witnesses at the funeral, the community reasserts its own solidarity in the face of the loss of one of its members (Durkheim, 1915).

The involvement of religion in death does not end with the funeral ceremony. Many religious groups provide their members with final bereavement ceremonies that symbolize the incorporation of the deceased into the afterlife (van Gennep, 1960). Memorial candles, special anniversary

Masses, prayers for the dead, and anniversary graveside services are some of the rites offering reassurance that the loved one is now safely and securely at rest. These final ceremonies serve other purposes as well: They symbolize the end of the period of mourning, the reintegration of the bereaved into the community, and the incorporation of the spiritual essence of the departed into the lives of the survivors. It is unfortunate that within Western culture, final ceremonies have become a less common part of the mourning process. The support and sympathy, so plentiful immediately after the death, may come to an end with the funeral service; ironically, the mourners may be left to fend for themselves during the subsequent period of bereavement, a time potentially more stressful than the time of initial shock and loss. A study by Rosenblatt et al. (1976) suggests that the loss of final ceremonies may come at some cost to our culture. They studied ethnographic descriptions of 78 cultures and found that those cultures with final ceremonies reported fewer grief-related problems including physical illness, suicidal behavior, nightmares, and work-related troubles.

The involvement of religion in death illustrates the dual character of all religious rites of passage: confrontative and supportive. These rites encourage people to face the fact that an important change has taken place. Old sources of significance that gave meaning and purpose to life must be given up, and new sources of identity and value must be found. But rites of passage are not simply confrontative, they are supportive as well. The members of a religious tradition come together to remind one another than their lives are part of a greater continuity and to offer spiritual, psychological, and social reassurance and guidance at a time when significance is being transformed.

Religious Conversion

Theologians, psychologists, and sociologists have been fascinated by accounts of religious conversion for many years. In their review of the social scientific literature on this topic, Snow and Machalek (1984) noted that, although any number of definitions have been offered, "the notion of radical change remains at the core of all conceptions of conversion" (p. 169). People speak of religious conversion when fundamental change is called for, when small changes seem insufficient for the problems of living because the problem seems to be life itself. Instead, the individual seeks a transformation, or in religious language "rebirth or new life."

What precipitates a religious conversion? A history of uneasiness and stress seems to be one important factor. Several studies have shown higher levels of emotional distress (Galanter, 1980), the encounter with more major negative life events (Kox, Meeus, & Hart, 1991), and lengthier histories of tension and conflict (Deutsch, 1975; Schwartz & Kaslow, 1979) among religious converts than various nonconvert control groups. As important as stress may be, however, it is not a sufficient condition for conversion. Significant numbers of people who do not convert also report high levels of distress (e.g., Kox et al., 1991). Religious converts not only experience stress but also experience a sense of personal futility in dealing with stress. The usual attempts at coping have failed, often dramatically, and demonstrate to individuals the limits of their personal power and their own self-centered strivings. Consider, for example, the conversion account of Asa Candler, Jr. (1951), son of the founder of Coca-Cola:

> One afternoon my chauffeur was driving me home. I was about three quarters drunk at the time. I was unusually troubled in my soul. Suddenly I heard a voice, just as clearly as I have ever heard anyone. . . . The voice said to me, 'You must get rid of your *self*; you must renounce your *self*; you must reject your *self*. (p. 55)

Giving up and *self-surrender* are terms commonly found in the narratives of religious conversion. The terms should not be confused with total helplessness or fatalism, for in the case of religious conversion, the individual has someone to surrender to—namely, the sacred. What makes a religious conversion religious is the incorporation of the sacred into the individual's identity. As a result, the convert reports a new sense of self. Listen to the words of one convert as reported by Edward Starbuck (1899), a pioneer in the study of religious conversion: "All at once light and peace came into my soul as gently as the sun coming up on a June morning. Heaven and earth seemed to meet. All was love. . . . I laughed that now I was the child of God, and the equal of any other creature. The best things in the world were for me as well as for anyone else" (p. 119).

Of course, people may come to identify with different types of sacred objects. In the case of a spiritual conversion, the self becomes identified with a higher power or spiritual force. In the case of a religious group conversion, the self attaches sacred power to a religious leader, group, or mission. Personal identity is then organized around devotion to the leader or the activities of the group. In the case of a universal conversion, the whole of humanity takes on a sacred quality, and the self becomes identified with the larger world as well as with the desire to move the world closer to an ideal transcendent vision. Leo Tolstoy, Mahatma Gandhi, and Martin Luther King, Jr. illustrate this latter type of religious conversion.

Be it a spiritual force, a religious group, or humanity, the conversion to the sacred represents a radical transformation, a response to a profound sense of uneasiness with the world, with one's own capacity to deal with the world, and with one's direction for living. Through the incorporation of the sacred into the self, these tensions may be alleviated. With self-centeredness replaced by a new source of significance and personal futility replaced by a new source of power, the religious convert feels radically transformed, now able to pursue newfound goals with newfound vigor (see Zinnbauer & Pargament, 1995).

Some psychologists may find this description of religious conversion overly positive, particularly in light of vivid accounts of forcible conversion of psychologically vulnerable people to cults and its negative aftereffects. In fact, some groups have been involved in misleading and coercive practices. For example, the Family of the Unification Church was widely criticized in the 1970s for its deceptive recruiting practices. Potential converts were invited to participate in seemingly nonreligious programs with titles such as "Creative Community Workshop" that served as a forum to present the principles of the Church. Furthermore, unbeknownst to the potential converts, other participants in the workshops were, in fact, members of the Church instructed to respond to any doubts or fears with affection and support. Only after the potential converts had become more committed to the group was the identity of the Church revealed (Galanter, 1989). Even stronger concerns about coercion and manipulation arise from the dramatically violent endings to the lives of members of some nonconventional religious groups (e.g., the People's Temple at Jonestown, the Branch Davidians at Waco, and the Order of the Solar Temple in Switzerland).

Alarming as these examples are, they may be the exception rather than the rule. J. Gordon Melton (1986), author of the *Encyclopedia Handbook of Cults in America*, argues against the notion that most religious group converts are unsuspecting victims of nonconventional groups. By virtue of their unusual appearance and practices, he notes, many groups cannot cloak their identities. Furthermore, some nonconventional groups put their potential members through several tests before they are invited to join the group, a few groups ask new recruits to sign an "informed consent" in which they acknowledge that they are participating in a church-related activity, and a few avoid efforts to recruit new members entirely. In addition, of those who attend a church-sponsored recruitment program, only a small percentage actually join. Melton points out that far from being unsuspecting, many new converts experiment with a variety of religious practices and groups before they select one to join. And most who do join a nonconventional religious group will return to their religion of origin within two years.

This is not to say that the convert does not experience personal, as well as social pressures. However, there is a difference between pressure, and coercion and deception. The perception of the convert-as-victim ignores the active dimension of coping, the fact that even within a larger field of personal and social forces, the individual continues to make choices and decisions. Rather than victims, many converts might be described as "seekers" (cf. Richardson, 1985)—people willing to experiment with radical transformation in the search for significance.

Not all psychologists share this view. Conversion has been likened to an addiction (Simmonds, 1977), a symptom of family dysfunction (Schwartz & Kaslow, 1979), and a schizophrenic decompensation (Wooten & Allen, 1983). Although there is some evidence that at least some converts show more signs of psychopathology (e.g., Witztum, Greenberg, & Buchbinder, 1990) and authoritarian tendencies (Shaver, Lenauer, & Sadd, 1980) than others, empirical studies are not entirely consistent with this negative portrait.

For example, Levine and Salter (1976) interviewed 106 converts to nine nontraditional religious groups (e.g., Hare Krishna, Divine Light, and Scientology). Asked why they remained in the group, the converts spoke of psychological and interpersonal benefits, including a sense of self-confidence, greater calm, closer friendships, and a higher sense of purpose in living. After interviewing a random subsample of 11 members in more detail, the authors concluded: "While it could be said that many were unhappy before they joined, and a disproportionate number were manifesting psychiatric symptoms, psychiatric diagnoses could not be applied to the majority of cases" (p. 414). Galanter, R. Rabkin, J. Rabkin, and Deutsch (1979) followed a group of potential converts through a series of workshops to introduce them to the Unification Church. Those who joined reported less neurotic distress after they became affiliated than before their membership. Galanter noted that these findings could be partially attributable to the desire of converts to present their religious transformation in a positive light. However, because the distress scores of new affiliates were still greater than those of established members, Galanter suggested that long-term membership may actually be associated with a reduction in distress levels. These positive results are tempered by the finding that both long-term members and those who continued with the workshops scored lower on a measure of psychological well-being than a nonmember comparison group. On the other hand, Latkin, Hagan, Littman, and Sundberg (1987) found that members of the Rajneeshpuram community in Oregon showed less depression and greater self-esteem than the general population. Paloutzian (1981) was able to collect some psychological measures in a group of nonconverts and in samples of people who had converted to Christianity within the previous five days, the previous month, one to six months, and six months or longer. As a group, the converts reported significantly greater purpose in life than nonconverts. Moreover, fears of death sharply declined among the convert groups over the six-month period following conversion. Finally, a number of studies point to sharp declines in drug and alcohol abuse following religious group conversion (e.g., Galanter & Buckley, 1978; Robbins, 1969).

When and why religious conversion takes a dramatically dysfunctional turn are critical questions for psychological study. Nevertheless, the current literature warns against equating religious conversion with psychotic breakdown or self-destruction. Though religious conversion may not be a panacea, it is often accompanied by emotional relief, greater self-confidence and self-control, less estrangement from others, and a clearer sense of direction in living.

THE EXTRAORDINARY POWER OF RELIGION

I hope the illustrations of these conservational and transformational coping mechanisms convey some sense of the rich and varied resources religion brings to the search for significance. However, an important question remains. Does religion add anything in the way of coping beyond what the secular world already provides its members? It could be argued that religious methods of coping are functionally redundant. After all, numerous groups apart from religious communities care deeply about prevention. Support can be gained from many sources other than spiritual and congregational ones. Religions are not the only groups that offer rites of passage, as every psychologist who has survived the trials and tribulations of graduate school can attest. Even conversion is not restricted to the religious world; people can convert to other objects as well, from political movements to psychotherapeutic orientations.

A few investigators have tested whether religious methods of coping add anything above and beyond secular approaches to coping with life stresses. For example, one study of 586 members of mainline Christian churches dealing with serious negative life events found that both religious and nonreligious forms of coping accounted for unique proportions of variance in several measures of adjustment to the events (Pargament et al., 1990). Similar results have been found in studies of high school students making the transition to college (Maton, 1989) and college students coping with the stresses of the Persian Gulf War (Pargament et al., 1994). Religion, these results suggest, adds another dimension to the coping process. But what? What's so special about religion anyway?

Part of the unique power of religion may lie in its capability to respond to so many needs in so many different ways. The abstract, symbolic, and mysterious character of most religious traditions may frustrate its adherents at times. However, it is just these qualities that allow religions to bend and flex with changing times, circumstances, and needs. In their writings, social scientists may have underestimated the diversity and flexibility of religious life. For Sigmund Freud, religion offered a shelter from destructive human impulse and a precarious world. For anthropologist Clifford Geertz, religion is largely a system that provides meaning in life. Sociologist Emile Durkheim spoke of religion as a source of social integration. Others have viewed religion primarily in terms of self-esteem, self-actualization, and personal growth. Although arguments have gone back and forth about the most essential functions of religion, they may only obscure the more critical point: Religion serves diverse purposes in life. These purposes are not simply conservational. At times, religion is involved in transforming the character of significance. Religion offers mechanisms with the potential not only to sustain the world but also to destroy it and re-create it.

Important as the versatility of religion is, I may be sidestepping the most unique characteristic of religion. It is the sacred that makes the religious search for significance so distinctive and so potentially powerful. Seemingly secular goals can take on special significance, positive or negative, when cloaked in sacred garb; Creativity and growth become ways to fan the divine spark within, fostering social justice is said to advance God's kingdom on earth, internecine conflicts intensify when redefined as holy wars. From the religious perspective, the sacred is a goal in itself, one that cannot be reduced to other psychological or social ends. "It is the ultimate Thou whom the religious person seeks most of all" (Johnson, 1955, p. 70). Measures of spiritual motivation have been tied to distinctive attitudes and behavior (Pargament et al., 1990; Welch & Barrish, 1982).

Means as well as ends can be wrapped in the sacred as I have shown in the illustrations of religious conservation and transformation. Although these mechanisms are diverse, they offer a counterpoint to traditional secular approaches to coping. Much of everyday life is taken up with attempts to master big and little problems. Efficacy, agency, and control are guiding principles in coping, particularly in Western culture, which stresses the value of individualism and achievement. Unfortunately, however, not all problems are controllable. Faced with the insurmountable, Western culture has less to say or offer. The language of the sacred—forbearance, mystery, suffering, hope, finitude, surrender, divine purpose, and redemption—and the mechanisms of religion become more relevant here. At the risk of overexaggerating, it might be said that Western culture (and along with it psychology) helps people gain control of their lives, whereas religion helps people come to grips with the limits of their control.

In fact, several studies indicate that religious forms of coping are especially helpful to people in uncontrollable, unmanageable, or otherwise difficult situations (Bickel, 1992; Maton, 1989; Park et al., 1990; Siegel & Kuykendall, 1990; Williams, Larson, Buckler, Heckmann, & Pyle, 1991). For instance, in a 2-year longitudinal study of a community sample, Williams et al. (1991) found that attendance at religious services buffered the effects of increased numbers of undesirable life events on subsequent psychological distress. Maton (1989) reported that spiritual support was tied to less depression and greater self-esteem among those who had suffered the death of a child in the past two years. Similar relationships were not found for those whose child had died more than two years prior to the study. Bickel (1992), working with a sample of Presbyterian church members, found that a collaborative religious coping style buffered the effects of perceived uncontrollable stress on depression; a more self-directed coping style, alternatively, exacerbated these same effects as the perception of uncontrollable stress increased. These studies suggest that the sacred is particularly helpful in the worst of times. Vested with unlimited strength and compassion, the sacred offers a source of solace, hope, and power when other resources have been exhausted and people must look beyond themselves for help.

What's so special about religion? The extraordinary power of religion lies in the melding of the sacred with the human in the search for significance. Psychologist Paul Johnson (1955) put it more eloquently:

> It is because man is a finite person with infinite possibilities that he ventures upon the religious quest. He is naturally finite, yet he learns of infinite possibilities which he cannot reach alone. . . . Religious learning is the discovery of ultimate resources to meet infinite longings of the finite spirit. (pp. 64–65)

PSYCHOLOGY AND THE RESOURCES OF RELIGION: SOME IMPLICATIONS

Underlying this chapter has been the assumption that psychologists have much to gain from looking beyond their own borders to the broader world around them. When they do, they find that religious beliefs, practices, and institutions are more alive and well than they might have guessed on the basis of their own religious commitments. Furthermore, they find that religion has the capacity to build, sustain, and rebuild human lives, individually and collectively, in many ways. And, finally, they discover a number of new opportunities for interaction between psychological and religious communities. One opportunity is to work within the religious world helping clients access their religious resources or strengthen them (e.g., Bergin, 1988; Pargament et al., 1991). Methods of religious coping could be judiciously incorporated into the process of psychotherapy. Another opportunity is to work with the religious world as partners assisting people in their search for significance. For example, mental health and religious communities have pooled their resources in collaborative attempts to solve problems of homelessness, physical illness, or mental illness (e.g., Cohen, Mowbray, Gillette, & Thompson, 1991; Eng & Hatch, 1991). A third opportunity is to draw from the religious world, creating new psychoreligious resources to help people who may or may not be involved in traditional religious life. Recent uses of ritual, forgiveness, and meditation in psychotherapy and 12-step programs illustrate some of the approaches that draw on religious methods of coping and extend them to a larger population (e.g., Hebl & Enright, 1993; Imber-Black, Roberts & Whiting, 1988).

Interaction between psychology and religion must rest on a respect for the differences as well as the similarities between the two disciplines. Clergy should not be mistaken for psychologists. And churches and synagogues should not be mistaken for mental health centers. The missions and values of the two systems are, in important ways, distinctive. However, psychological and religious communities are joined by their commitment to the well-being of those they serve. Clearly, both groups must wrestle with the points of commonality and divergence in their visions of the world before they can work together effectively. But there may be much to gain in this process. I hope it is clear from this chapter than psychologists do not have a monopoly on helpful methods of coping, be they conservational or transformational. The same is true of the religious world. By recognizing the strengths and limitations of each tradition, both communities may multiply their own resources and enhance their value to people searching for significance.

REFERENCES

Bearon, L. B., & Koenig, H. G. (1990). Religious cognitions and use of prayer in health and illness. *Gerontologist, 30*, 249–253.

Beit-Hallahmi, B. (1977). Curiosity, doubt, and devotion: The beliefs of psychologists and the psychology of religion. In H. Malony (Ed.), *Current perspectives in the psychology of religion* (pp. 381–391). Grand Rapids, MI: Eerdsman.

Bergin, A. E. (1988). Three contributions of a spiritual perspective to counseling psychotherapy, and behavior change. *Counseling and Values, 33*, 21–31.

Bickel, C. (1992), *Perceived stress, religious coping styles, and depressive affect.* Unpublished doctoral dissertation. Loyola College, Columbia, Maryland.

Brenner, R. R. (1980). *The faith and doubt of Holocaust survivors.* New York: Free Press.

Bryer, K. B. (1979). The Amish way of death: A study of family support systems. *American Psychologist, 34*, 255–261.

Bulman, R. J., & Wortman, C. B. (1977). Attributions of blame and coping in the "real world": Severe accident victims react to their lot. *Journal of Personality and Social Psychology, 35*, 353–363.

Candler, A. G., Jr. (1951). Self-surrender. In D. W. Soper (Ed.), *These found the way: Thirteen converts to Protestant Christianity* (pp. 51–62). Philadelphia: Westminster.

Capps, D. (1990). *Reframing: A new method in pastoral care.* Minneapolis, MN: Fortress Press.

Carroll, J., Dudley, C., & McKinney, W. (1986). *Handbook for congregational studies*. Nashville, TN: Abingdon Press.

Chalfant, H. P., Heller, P. L., Roberts, A., Briones, D., Aguirre-Hochbaum, S., & Farr, W. (1990). The clergy as a resource for those encountering psychological distress. *Review of religious Research, 31*, 305–313.

Chidester, D. (1990). *Patterns of transcendence: Religion, death and dying*. Belmont, CA: Wadsworth.

Cohen, E., Mowbray, C. T., Gillette, V., & Thompson, E. (1991). Preventing homelessness: Religious organizations and housing development. *Prevention in Human Services, 11*, 169–186.

Croog, S. H., & Levine, S. (1972). Religious identity and response to serious illness: A report on heart patients. *Social Science and Medicine, 6*, 17–32.

Dalal, A. K., & Pande, N. (1988). Psychological recovery of accident victims with temporary and permanent disability. *International Journal of Psychology, 23*, 25–40.

Deutsch, A. (1975). Observations of a sidewalk Ashram. *Archives of General Psychiatry, 32*, 166–175.

Durkheim, E. (1915). *The elementary forms of the religious life*. New York: Free Press.

Eng, E., & Hatch, J. W. (1991). Networking between agencies and Black churches: The lay health advisor model. *Prevention in Human Services, 11*, 123–146.

Galanter, M. (1989). *Cults: Faith healing and coercion*. Oxford, England: Oxford University Press.

Galanter, M. (1980). Psychological induction into the large-group: Findings from a modern religious sect. *American Journal of Psychiatry, 137*, 1574–1579.

Galanter, M., & Buckley, P. (1978). Evangelical religion and meditation: Psychotherapeutic effects. *Journal of Nervous and Mental Disease, 166*, 685–691.

Galanter, M., Rabkin, R., Rabkin, J., & Deutsch, A (1979). The "Moonies": A psychological study of conversion and membership in a contemporary religious sect. *American Journal of Psychiatry, 136*, 165–170.

Gallup, G., Jr., & Castelli, J. (1989). *The people's religion: American faith in the 90's*. New York: Macmillan.

Geertz, C. (1966). Religion as a cultural system. In M. Banton (Ed.), *Anthropological approaches to the study of religion* (pp. 1–46). London: Tavistock.

Gibbs, H. W., & Achterberg-Lawlis, J. (1978). Spiritual values and death anxiety: Implications for counseling with terminal cancer patients. *Journal of Counseling Psychology, 25*, 563–569.

Grevengoed, N., & Pargament, K. (1987). *Attributions for death: An examination of the role of religion and the relationship between attributions and mental health*. Paper presented at the Society for the Scientific Study of Religion, Louisville, KY.

Hathaway, W. L., & Pargament, K. I. (1990). Intrinsic religiousness, religious coping, and psychosocial competence: A covariance structure analysis. *Journal for the Scientific Study of Religion, 29*, 423–441.

Hebl, J. H., & Enright, R. O. (1993). Forgiveness as a psychotherapeutic goal with elderly females. *Psychotherapy, 30,* 658–667.

Höffding, H. (1914). *The philosopy of religion.* London: Macmillan.

Horton, A. L., Wilkins, M. M., & Wright, W. (1988). Women who ended abuse: What religious leaders and religion did for these victims. In A. L. Horton & J. A. Williamson (Eds.), *Abuse and religion: When praying isn't enough* (pp. 235–246). Lexington, MA: Lexington Books.

Imber-Black, E., Roberts, J., & Whiting, R. (Eds.). (1988). *Rituals in families and family therapy.* New York: Norton and Co.

Jacobs, D. (April 24, 1995). Service attracts overflow crowds. *Toledo Blade,* p. A3.

Jacquet, C., Jr., & Jones, A. M. (1991). *Yearbook of American and Canadian churches 1991.* Nashville, TN: Abingdon Press.

Jenkins, R. (1992). Toward a psychosocial conceptualization of religion as a resource in cancer care and prevention. In K. Pargament, K. Maton, & R. E. Hess (Eds.), *Religion and prevention in mental health: Research, vision, and action* (pp. 179–194). New York: Haworth Press.

Jenkins, R. & Pargament, K. (1988). Cognitive appraisals in cancer patients. *Social Science and Medicine, 26,* 625–633.

Johnson, P. E. (1955). *Psychology of religion.* Nashville, TN: Abingdon Press.

Koenig, H. G., Cohen, H. J., Blazer, D. G., Pieper, C., Meador, K. G., Shelp, F., Goli, V., & DiPasquale, B. (1992). Religious coping and depression among elderly, hospitalized medically ill men. *American Journal of Psychiatry, 149,* 1693–1700.

Koenig, H. G., George, L. K., & Siegler, I. C. (1988). The use of religion and other emotion-regulating coping strategies among older adults. *Gerontologist, 28,* 303–310.

Kox, W., Meeus, W., & Hart, H. (1991). Religious conversion of adolescents: Testing the Lofland and Stark model of religious conversion. *Sociological Analysis, 52,* 227–240.

Latkin, C. A., Hagan, R. A., Littman, R. A., & Sundberg, N. D. (1987). Who lives in Utopia? A brief report on the Rajneeshpuram research project. *Sociological Analysis, 48,* 73–81.

Levine, S. V., & Salter, N. E. (1976). Youth and contemporary religious movements: Psychosocial findings. *Canadian Psychiatric Association Journal, 21,* 411–420.

Lindenthal, J. J., Myers, J. K., Pepper, M. P., & Stein, M. S. (1970). Mental status and religious behavior. *Journal for the Scientific Study of Religion, 9,* 143–149.

Lilliston, L., & Klein, D. G. (1989). *A self-discrepancy reduction model of religious coping.* Paper presented at the American Psychological Association. Boston, MA.

Long, J. B. (1975). The death that ends death in Hinduism and Buddhism. In E. Kubler-Ross (Ed.), *Death: The final stage of growth* (pp. 52–72). Englewoods Cliffs, NJ: Prentice Hall.

Lorch, B. R. (1987). Church youth alcohol and education programs. *Journal of Religion and Health, 26(2)*, 106–114.

Mahedy, W. P. (1986). *Out of the night: The spiritual journey of Vietnam vets.* New York: Ballantine Books.

Maton, K. I. (1989). The stress-buffering role of spiritual support: Cross-sectional and prospective investigations. *Journal for the Scientific Study of Religion, 28,* 310–323.

McIntosh, D. N., Silver, R. C., & Wortman, C. B. (1993). Religion's role in adjustment to a negative life event: Coping with the loss of a child. *Journal of Personality and Social Psychology, 65,* 812–821.

McIntosh, D. N., & Spilka, B. (1990). Religion and physical health: The role of personal faith and control. In M. L. Lynn & D. O. Moberg (Eds.), *Research in the social scientific study of religion* (Vol. 2; pp. 167–194). Greenwich, CT: Jai Press.

McRae, R. R. (1984). Situational determinants of coping response: Loss, threat, and challenge. *Journal of Personality and Social Psychology, 46,* 919–928.

Melton, J. G. (1986). *Encyclopedic handbook of cults in America.* New York: Guilford.

O'Brien, M. E. (1982). Religious faith and adjustment to long-term hemodialysis. *Journal of Religion and Health, 21,* 68–80.

Paden, W. E. (1988). *Religious worlds: The comparative study of religion.* Boston: Beacon Press.

Paloutzian, R. F. (1981). Purpose in life and value changes following conversion. *Journal of Personality and Social Psychology, 11,* 1153–1160.

Pargament, K. I. (1992). Of means and ends: Religion and the search for significance. *International Journal for the Psychology of Religion, 2,* 201–229.

Pargament, K. I. (1995). *In the dust of our trials: Methods of religious coping with major life stressors.* Paper presented at the American Psychosomatic Society, New Orleans, LA.

Pargament, K. I., Ensing, D. S., Falgout, K., Olsen, H., Reilly, B., Van Haitsma, K. & Warren, R. (1990). God help me (I): Religious coping efforts as predicators of the outcomes to significant negative life events. *American Journal of Community Psychology, 18,* 793–824.

Pargament, K. I., Falgout, K., Ensing, D. S., Reilly, B., Silverman, M., Van Haitsma, K., Olsen, H., & Warren, R. (1991). The congregation development program: Data-based consultation with churches and synagogues. *Professional Psycholoyg: Research and Practice, 22,* 393–404.

Pargament, K. I., Ishler, K., Dubow, E., Stanik, P., Rouiller, R., Crowe, P., Cullman, E., Albert, M., & Royster, B. J. (1994). Methods of religious coping with the Gulf War: Cross-sectional and longitudinal analyses. *Journal for the Scientific Study of Religion, 33,* 347–361.

Pargament, K. I., Kennell, J., Hathaway, W., Grevengoed, N., Newman, J., & Jones, W. (1988). Religion and the problem-solving process: Three styles of coping. *Journal for the Scientific Study of Religion, 27,* 90–104.

Pargament, K. I., & Maton, K. I. (in press). Religion in American life: A community psychology perspective. In J. Rappaport & E. Seidman (Eds.), *Handbook of community psychology*. New York: Plenum Press.

Pargament, K. I., Maton, K. I., & Hess, R. E. (Eds.). (1992). *Religion and prevention in mental health: Research, vision and action*. New York: Haworth.

Pargament, K. I., Olsen, H., Reilly, B., Falgout, K., Ensing, D. S., & Van Haitsma, K. (1992). God help me (II): The relationship of religious orientations to religious coping with negative life events. *Journal for the Scientific Study of Religion, 31*, 504–513.

Pargament, K. I., & Sullivan, M. (1981). *Examining attributions of control across diverse personal situations: A psychosocial perspective*. Paper presented at the American Psychological Association, Los Angeles.

Park, C. L., & Cohen, L. C. (1993). Religious and nonreligious coping with the death of a friend. *Cognitive Therapy and Research, 17*, 561–577.

Park, C. L., Cohen, L. C., & Herb, L. (1990). Intrinsic religiousness and religious coping as life stress moderators for Catholics versus Protestants. *Journal of Personality and Social Psychology, 59*, 562–574.

Payne, I. R., Bergin, A. E., Bielema, K. A., & Jenkins, P. H. (1992). Review of religion and mental health: Prevention and the enhancement of psychosocial functioning. In K. I. Pargament, K. I. Maton, & R. E. Hess (Eds.), *Religion and prevention in mental health: Research, vision and action* (pp. 57–82). New York: Haworth.

Pennebaker, J. W., & Beall, S. (1986). Confronting a traumatic event: Toward an understanding of inhibition and disease. *Journal of Abnormal Psychology, 95*, 274–281.

Piaget, J. (1954). *The construction of reality in the child*. New York: Basic Books.

Richardson, J. (1985). The active vs. passive convert: Paradigm conflict in conversion/recruitment research. *Journal for the Scientific Study of Religion, 24*, 163–179.

Robbins, T. (1969). Eastern mysticism and the resocialization of drug users: The Meher Baba cult. *Journal for the Scientific Study of Religion, 8*, 308–317.

Rosenblatt, P. C., Walsh, H. P., & Jackson, D. A. (1976). *Grief and mourning in cross-cultural perspective*. New Haven, CT: HFAR.

Rotter, J. B. (1954). *Social learning and clinical psychology*. Englewood Cliffs, NJ: Prentice Hall.

Rychlak, J. E. (1981). *Introduction to personality and psychotherapy*. Boston: Houghton-Mifflin.

Schaefer, C. A., & Gorsuch, R. L. (1991). Psychological adjustment and religiousness: The multivariate belief-motivation theory of religiousness. *Journal for the Scientific Study of Religion, 20*, 448–467.

Schwartz, L. L., & Kaslow, F. W. (1979). Religious cults, the individual and the family. *Journal of Marital and Family Therapy, 5*, 15–26.

Segall, M., & Wykle, M. (1988–1989). The Black family's experience with dementia. *The Journal of Applied Social Sciences, 13(1)*, 170–191.

Shaver, P., Lenauer, M., & Sadd, S. (1980). Religiousness, conversion, and subjective well-being: The "healthy-minded" religion of modern American women. *American Journal of Psychiatry, 137*, 1563–1568.

Shrimali, S., & Broota, K. A. (1987). Effect of surgical stress on belief in God and superstition: An in situ investigation. *Journal of Personality and Clinical Studies, 3*, 135–138.

Siegel, J. M., & Kuykendall, D. H. (1990). Loss, widowhood, and psychological distress among the elderly. *Journal of Consulting and Clinical Psychology, 58*, 519–524.

Simmonds, R. B. (1977). Conversion or addiction: Consequences of joining a Jesus Movement group. *American Behavioral Scientist, 20*, 909–924.

Snow, D. A., & Machalek, R. (1984). The sociology of conversion. *Annual Review of Sociology, 10*, 167–190.

Starbuck, E. D. (1899). *The psychology of religion*. New York: Scribner.

van Gennep, A. (1960). *The rites of passage* M. B. Vizedom and G. L. Caffee, Trans. Chicago: University of Chicago Press.

Watson, P. J., Hood, R. W., Jr., Morris, R. J., & Hall, J. R. (1985). Religiosity, sin, and self-esteem. *Journal of Psychology and Theology, 13*, 116–128.

Watson, P. J., Morris, R. J., & Hood, R. W., Jr. (1987). Antireligious humanistic values, guilt, and self esteem. *Journal for the Scientific Study of Religion, 26*, 535–546.

Welch, M. R., & Barrish, J. (1982). Bringing religious motivation back in: A multivariate analysis of motivational predicators of student religiosity. *Review of Religious Research, 23*, 357–369.

Williams, D. R., Larson, D. B., Buckler, R. E., Heckmann, R. C. & Pyle, C. M. (1991). Religion and psychological distress in a community sample. *Social Science and Medicine, 32*, 1257–1262.

Witztum, E., Greenberg, D., & Buchbinder, J. T. (1990). "A very narrow bridge": Diagnosis and management of mental illness among Bratslav Hasidim. *Psychotherapy, 27*, 124–131.

Wootton, R. J., & Allen, D. F. (1983). Dramatic religious conversion and schizophrenic decompensation. *Journal of Religion and Health, 22*, 212–220.

Wright, S., Pratt, C., & Schmall, V. (1985). Spiritual support for caregivers of dementia patients. *Journal of Religion and Health, 24*, 31–38.

Yancey, P. (1977). *Where is God when it hurts*. Grand Rapids, MI: Zondervan.

Zinnbauer, B., & Pargament, K. I. (1995). *Spiritual Conversion: A study of religious change among college students*. Paper presented at the Society for the Scientific Study of Religion in St. Louis, MO.

9

THE PATHOLOGY OF BELIEFS AND THE BELIEFS OF PATHOLOGY

W. W. MEISSNER

Freud recognized the power of religious beliefs and belief systems when he called them "illusions, fulfillments of the oldest, strongest and most urgent wishes of mankind" (1927/1961, p. 30). However, for Freud, as is well-known, such illusions were essentially neurotic—residues of infantile dependence creating powerful gods to which man could turn for support and reassurance in the face of the painful difficulties of life and the irreducible disillusionments of loss and ultimately death. In the half century and more since Freud's death, the psychoanalytic understanding of religious beliefs and their role in psychic life has advanced well beyond his agnostic and pessimistic outlook (Jones, 1991; Meissner, 1978, 1984b; Rizzuto, 1979; Spero, 1992). In a sense, Freud's (1927/1961) observations and analysis of religious beliefs were not incorrect as far as they went; the problem is that they did not go far enough. They limited their scope to a rather confined perspective on religious experience and tried to encompass the aspect of religious belief that fit Freud's model of obsessional neurosis and his rather negative view of human existence as mired in infantility and neurotic dependence.

PATHOLOGY IN BELIEF SYSTEM

The question of pathology in religious belief systems has multiple dimensions. One dimension concerns the role a given system of belief plays in the intrapsychic economy of the mental life of the individual believer. Any belief can become a vehicle for expression of neurotic forces and conflicts in the person's psychic makeup, whether as symptoms or as character pathology. On this level the focus falls on the pathological organization of beliefs as it operates in the patient's personality, prescinding from the question of pathological components within the belief system itself. Should the patient be caught up in endless and guilt-ridden self-accusations and tormented convictions that because of the person's sinfulness he or she is condemned to an eternity of damnation in hell, the person's scrupulosity would not necessarily force psychologists to conclude that there was anything pathological about the particular religious beliefs the person embraced. Psychologists would be more likely to locate the pathology in the person's neurotic use of the belief system—for example, in the service of unconscious guilt motives (Meissner, 1991).

Another dimension of the question of pathology and belief system pertains to the extent to which pathological derivatives are found in the belief system itself, regardless of the neurotic use any given patient might make of it. This aspect of the question reaches beyond the Freudian *status questionis*. Freud's argument might be read as focused more on the infantile motivations giving rise to religious beliefs and the neurotic usages to which religious beliefs might be put rather than on the pathological structure of the beliefs themselves—or we might conclude that he presumed that all religious beliefs were pathological without ever bothering to consider the question I am concerned with here.

Belief systems can be classified as pathological or not. Deciding when a given system of belief is in itself pathological is not an easy matter. Objective criteria are difficult to establish, and subjective criteria—that is, from within the context of any given system, or within the perspective of the individual believer's mind's eye—are lacking, so that from a subjective perspective no beliefs would be regarded as pathological. If the only criteria to which we can appeal, then, are relative, their position would be analogous to that of the clinician trying to evaluate the delusional system of a paranoid patient. The patient's delusion is true and valid within its own context; any judgment of pathology requires that psychologists evaluate it from a vantage point outside the delusional system and in the context of some other frame of reference. I do not mean to imply that religious beliefs and paranoid ideas both qualify as psychotic delusions, but nonetheless there are similarities of structure and process that underlie both phenomena, raising the question of how they differ and how they can be discriminated.

Any question of reality testing or of the truth value of the belief system is not relevant in this context. Freud (1939/1964) recognized this aspect of religious beliefs but remained convinced that the truth was an ancient one that had returned from the repressed. He commented:

> What has returned from oblivion asserts itself with peculiar force, exercises an incomparably powerful influence on people in the mass, and raises an irresistible claim to truth against which logical objections remain powerless: a kind of "credo quia absurdum." This remarkable feature can only be understood on the pattern of the delusions of psychotics. We have long understood that a portion of forgotten truth lies hidden in delusional ideas, that when this returns it has to put up with distortions and misunderstandings, and that the compulsive conviction which attaches to the delusion arises from this core of truth and spreads out onto the errors that wrap it round. We must grant an ingredient such as this of what may be called *historical* truth to the dogmas of religion as well, which, it is true, bear the character of psychotic symptoms but which, as group phenomena, escape the curse of isolation.

There are echoes of this phylogenetic argument from *Totem and Taboo* (1912–1913/1955). I shall return to the question of the discrimination of the pathological from the nonpathological in belief systems later.

Pathology versus Truth Value

The distinction between the pathological quality of a given belief system and its truth value is poorly maintained in traditional discussions of this subject. The question regarding pathology asks whether the belief system contains in its formulations or in the substance of its assertions material that reflects processes or influences that would have a deleterious effect on the health, psychological well-being, character structure, or life adjustment of the believer. The question regarding truth value asks whether the assertions of the belief system are true, that is, whether they reflect the veridical structure and integration of real forces and entities existing in the real world. These questions are not synonymous.

Let me take one religious belief fairly widely accepted in Christian religions, namely the belief in a final judgment by God when an ultimate disposition will be made of all humans, assigning them for all eternity to the beatitude of heaven or the torment of hell. The doctrinal basis for this belief is found in the famous eschatological discourse in Mt 25: 31–46, which echoes many of the messianic themes of Palestinian Judaism of the first century—particularly, the conditions of the return of the Messiah in glory at the time of the parousia (Meissner, 1993, 1995). The belief, therefore, is an ancient one spanning more than one religious tradition.

Penetration of this belief with pathological elements might cast this mythological day of judgment in terms of a severe, judgmental, harsh, unloving, and punishing God who dooms large numbers to a final punishment for their inadequacies, failures, and sins. One would have little difficulty recognizing the ultimate superego projection, perhaps deriving from the internalization of a punitive and judgmental father figure. Furthermore, the damnation is to a condition of abandonment and hopeless pain and torture that applies with unmitigated viciousness punishment for each and every crime of humanity. Can one recognize here the projection of unresolved guilt and destructive aggression onto a cosmic mythological state? I would argue that these formulations would at least qualify as candidates for evaluation as pathological beliefs. But what does that conclusion tell people about the validity of the belief?

To take another example—one that I have previously proposed (Meissner, 1978) and that A. Grümbaum disputed (1993)—Holy Communion in the celebration of the Catholic mass is a ritual recalling and repetition of Christ's action at the Last Supper offering bread and wine to his disciples as symbolizing His body and blood. The sacramental doctrine proposes that wine and bread in the ritual sacrifice of the Mass represent the "real presence" of Christ to His church and to His faithful believers. How can the truth value of this belief be assessed? I would contend that there is no real test applicable to ascertain its validity. It is believed in virtue of faith or not at all. But what, more accurately, is the belief? The doctrinal content goes no further than assertion of the real presence—but in what sense? There's the rub! Theologians will argue interminably over that question. The doctrine of Trent, cited by Grünbaum, appeals to the Aristotelian–Thomistic analysis in terms of substance and accidents to explain the belief. Although the accidents accounting for sensory experience remain unchanged, the substance is transformed into the body and blood of Christ—transubstantiation; thus, what looks and tastes like bread or wine has been transformed sacramentally into Christ.

However, the explanation is far from satisfactory. Not only are the terms of the analysis outdated, but also the analysis implies a kind of ontological presence that identifies wine and blood, bread and flesh, as though there were no consideration of metaphoric, symbolic, and mythological usage in question. If transubstantiation on these terms is what is in question as intrinsic to the belief, then Grünbaum's change of an immunizing strategy flying in the face of reason becomes plausible. However, that is not the basis or substance of the belief. The explanation was no more than a historical effort to lend intelligibility to the doctrine of real presence—one that had to be cast in terms of the only frame of reference available to the council fathers (Schillebeeckx, 1963, 1968). The implicit translation of "real" presence into "ontological" presence would make communion an act of cannibalism. Therefore, there is no test of the validity of the doctrine of real presence, and even if one insisted on a test for the validity of the historical explanation (not the same as the doctrine), one would still seek in vain for a valid test.

What, then, is the truth value of such beliefs? Do these propositions enunciate a state of affairs that had validity and veracity? Are they for real? There are no empirical tests to satisfy our need for verification. There are also no means for demonstrating the falsity of these assertions. On what basis would one deny their validity? They serve either as prophetic expressions of a state of affairs not to be realized until the end of time in the final divine disposition of the world and mankind or as untouchable by any imaginable scientific test. Real presence of Christ in the Eucharist was never intended or proposed as a matter of real perception or experience. If we accept the ideas, we accept them on the basis of faith. If we do not accept the ideas, we reject them on the basis of no faith. From the perspective of scientific or psychoanalytic understanding, there is no resource that would allow the matter to be solved. We can say no more than that we simply do not know. Therefore, a determination of the pathological standing of any religious belief implies nothing, neither pro nor con, about the truth value of the propositions in question. If we accept or reject them (i.e., their validity as true statements), it must be on some other ground. Unfortunately, Freud seems to have made truth value the test of pathogenicity.

Moreover, at this juncture the present analysis parts company from Grünbaum's, and by implication Freud's, approach. Challenging this view, which is essentially the same argument proposed by Hans Küng (1979, 1984), Grünbaum (1993) poses an insoluble dilemma. With regard to Küng's argument on personal immortality, he writes that

> [Küng (1979) contends that "the glory of eternal life is completely new, unsuspected and incomprehensible, unthinkable and unutterable" (p. 220). But, again, if the very domain of eternal life is avowedly "incomprehensible," what does it mean to believe in it? And how could Küng possibly take the "unutterable" on faith? (p. 229)

And again, "Küng and Meissner's own insistence that the content of some cardinal religious utterances is incomprehensible renders belief in them meaningless. Thus, it becomes imperative to explain *psychologically* what stake such theists have in paradoxically demanding credulous assent to those utterances" (p. 301). Grünbaum apparently refuses to allow the religious or theological mind the prerogative of determining its own proper basis of assent; if assent is not generated on his terms of scientific positivism, it has no intelligibility and any assent is spurious. But this is exactly the point at issue: On what grounds is the content of religious faith judged unintelligible or delusional? Is there only one standard of truth, or is there a truth of scientific method and a truth of religious belief? To take the doctrine of transubstantiation literally and subject it to chemical analysis would miss the point. No chemical analysis can answer the question of real presence.

Psychologists, psychiatrists, and psychoanalysts have a frame of reference allowing them to assess the pathology in belief systems according to diagnostic criteria familiar to them on clinical grounds. I do not refer to diagnosis in its most restrictive and narrow sense, as in the process of attaching descriptive diagnostic labels, such as those from the *Diagnostic and Statistical Manual of Mental Disorders* (1994), but to the more difficult and subtly demanding process of assessing the degree to which any aspect of the patient's behavior or thinking contributes to a pattern of meaningful life experience and adaptive functioning or does not do so. To the extent that a patient's religious belief system involves content or principles that prevent or subvert effective and adaptive functioning or contribute to personality disturbances or symptomatic disruptions, psychologists, psychiatrists, and psychoanalysts would judge that system to be psychiatrically pathological. This is a judgment about the belief system itself and not simply about the disturbed usage or involvement of the patient with it. In terms of an expanded criterion of delusional pathology, I would think that the Jonestown massacre, the politicized destructiveness of Islamic fundamentalism, the fratricidal strife of Hindu and Moslem, and the sectarian ravings of Rabbi Kahane and Ayatollah Komeini could all be classified as pathological. In making such a judgment, psychologists prescind from any conclusion regarding the religious validity or truth value of the beliefs in question. That judgment does not belong to the psychoanalyst, but to the theologian.

Delusion Versus Illusion

Although the distinguished between "illusion" and "delusion" on the basis of their connection with reality, Freud did not keep the distinction clear when it came to religious illusions. An illusion was not simply an error, even though it might be a false belief; its defining characteristic was derivation from wishes. Illusions were not necessarily false nor in contradiction to reality, but when the did contradict reality they became delusions. Freud (1927) wrote: "We call a belief an illusion when a wish-fulfillment is a prominent factor in its motivation, and in doing so we disregard its relation to reality, just as the illusion itself sets no store by verification" (p. 31). But he regarded religious beliefs as contradicting reality and, therefore, as delusions. On the contrary, I am arguing that Freud had no legitimate basis for declaring religious beliefs delusional, that is, as violating reality. Because there was no basis for the decision regarding the contradiction or lack of contradiction with reality, Freud would have had to presume—contrary to his own foundation—that religious beliefs were delusional precisely because they were wish fulfillments.

Within the continuum of subjective, transitional, and objective understanding of religious ideas (Meissner, 1984b, 1990), Freud takes his stand unreservedly at the subjective or intrapsychic pole of experience and correspondingly minimizes the objective or extrapsychic dimension. At the subjective pole of the dialectic, religious ideas and beliefs have no external validity, no objective reality, no degree of verifiable truth but are purely products of the inner world and the dynamics of wish fulfillment.

The question of the distinction between delusion and illusion is taken a step further by Grünbaum (1987, 1993) who argued that Freud's concept of mass delusion is not congruent with the notion of delusion found in psychiatric usage. Standard usage links delusion with hallucination insofar as there is no demonstrable fact corresponding to the content of the belief, just as in a hallucination there is no external stimulus corresponding to the perception (Hinsie & Campbell, 1970). However, current psychiatric usage adds a contextual note stressing the lack of sociocultural fit. A later edition adds:

> Delusion—a false belief that is firmly maintained even though it is contradicted by social reality. While it is true that some superstitions and religious beliefs are held despite the lack of confirmatory evidence, such culturally engendered concepts are not considered delusions. What is characteristic of the delusion is that it is not shared by others; rather it is an idiosyncratic and individual misconception or misinterpretation ... in the area of his delusion he no longer shares a consensually validated reality with other people. (Campbell, 1981; as cited in Grünbaum, 1987, p. 174; als. 1993, p. 286).

Grünbaum's objections raise some critical questions. Is it correct to say that—regardless of how primitive, superstitious, irrational, or unrealistic a belief may be—as long as a belief is culturally shared, it would not be regarded as delusional? How do we establish that a given idea is part of a social reality? Does one count adherents? Does one need to have a majority of the population to regard a belief as socially accepted? What does one regard as social reality in pluralistic societies such as the United States, where there are such radically divergent and incompatible belief systems held by various contending and politically oppositional groups—secular humanists, the Moral Majority, evangelicals, various religious groupings, abortionists, right-to-life groups, and on and on? What judgment can be made regarding the strikingly maladaptive and pathological shared beliefs of certain cult groups, such as the Temple of God cult that extinguished itself so gruesomely at Jonestown or the more recent episode of the Branch Davidians that ended so murderously in Texas? In dictionary terms these belief systems would not be regarded as delusional, whereas in Freud's terms they would represent forms of mass delusion, presumably paranoid. Grün-baum (1993) seems troubled by the notion that pathological ideas might not qualify as delusions because they are culturally endorsed (e.g., Ayatol-lah Khomeini's view of President Carter as Satan, a view consensually endorsed by his coreligionists); here Grünbaum takes his stand with Freud.

Belief Systems as Pathological

In focusing on pathology within belief systems, I shift from an individual to a group analysis insofar as belief systems involve shared meaning and significance within the religious group. The structure of any system of beliefs is not always dictated by the demands of logic and rationality. Belief systems in general can deviate from the path of reason and realism in both formal organization and content; that is, specific beliefs may express the pathological derivatives of unconscious fantasy systems that are in themselves unrealistic or reflect distortion by pathological forces. Pathology in belief systems can be found in more or less organized religious groups, but such pathological systems can often be more easily identified in certain cults, sects, and other deviant religious groups (Pruyser, 1977). Pathological beliefs are more likely to be found in such deviant religious groups because of the dynamic forces underlying the splitting off and formation of such groups. The process often involves a more or less rebellious or antinomian sequence by which the newly formed group splits off from the parent group and sets itself in opposition to the group of origin. I have described this process in terms of the "cultic process" (Meissner, 1984a, 1987, 1995). Similar aspects of the cultic process can often be identified in the origins of more established church groups or in their structure and functioning.

The issue raised by Freud, whether all religious beliefs systems are forms of mass delusion—and, therefore, pathological—is crucial. To put it in other terms, if a belief system is determined by or expressive or an unconscious fantasy system, does that mean that it is thereby pathological? In Freud's eyes, the most powerful, and therefore the worst, illusions belonged to religion. Religious beliefs were set in opposition to reality and provided one important vehicle for withdrawal from painful remedy. His attack on religion was uncompromising. He wrote:

> It regards reality as the sole enemy and as the source of all suffering, with which it is impossible to live, so that one must break off all relations with it if one is to be in an way happy. The hermit turns his back on the world and will have no truck with it. But one can do more than that; one can try to re-create the world, to build up in its stead another world in which its most unbearable features are eliminated and replaced by others that are in conformity with one's wishes. But whoever, in desperate defiance, sets out upon this path to happiness will as a rule attain nothing. Reality is too strong for him. He

becomes a madman, who for the most part finds no one to help him in carrying through his delusion. It is asserted, however, that each one of us behaves in some respect like a paranoic, corrects some aspect of the world which is unbearable to him by the construction of a wish and introduces this delusion into reality. A special importance attaches to the case in which this attempt to procure a certainty of happiness and a protection against suffering through a delusional remoulding of reality is made by a considerable number of people in common. The religions of mankind must be classed among the mass-delusions of this kind. No one, needless to say, who shares a delusion ever recognizes it as such. (Freud, 1930/1961, p. 81).

Clearly, for Freud, if a belief system was based on wish fulfillment it had to be pathological.

The issue of truth value is also relevant here. The definition of delusion requires that the belief be maintained despite contradictory evidence. The problem in evaluating religious belief systems is that not only is there no convincing evidence for them, but also there is also no convincing evidence contradictory to them. One might think of the almost universal belief in an afterlife; there is no evidence that contradicts such a conclusion. There is no good evidence to support it either. Therefore, when there is no evidence to support or contradict a belief, there are no grounds on which to determine whether it is delusional, whether it has negative or positive truth value. In the Freudian system, however, if there is no evidence pro or con, it must be delusional.

The understanding of the notion of delusion seems split dichotomously between subjective and objective polarities. Freud's criteria are essentially subjective—that is, delusions are basically wish fulfillment that do not correspond to reality as a matter of subjective experience. The psychiatric view is more objective—the criteria of delusional belief rest on the extent to which the belief fails to correspond with validating external evidence or is not congruent with a shared social or cultural reality. I would argue for a third alternative, encompassing both of these criteria. If we were to assume the vantage point of an ideally objective and independent observer, we would probably take the wishful or fantasy-derived aspect of a given belief into consideration and conclude that the particular belief could be regarded as delusional in the degree to which it prescinded from, contradicted, or was impervious to qualification by demonstrable objective evidence or realities. There is always the question of the consensual validation of extrinsic and objective evidence, however, which requires some degree of resolution before this criterion could provide a possible basis for the determination of delusional beliefs.

From this ideal vantage point, one can also make some evaluation of the cultural and social contexts within which a belief system functions. I would argue, for example, that regardless of the passion and conviction of the participants, an impartial outside observer would have little difficulty in assessing the internecine slaughter and paranoid-like, prejudicial attitudes between Irish Catholics and their Protestant brethren or the hate-filled, fanatical, blindly destructive rage of Moslem fundamentalists and their Jewish antagonists as beyond the pale of rational, reasonable, non-pathological thought processes. Likewise, the deadly slaughter of the Jonestown massacre and the fanatical and suicidal Armageddon mentality of the Branch Davidians in the Waco debacle do not speak of reasoned and adaptive psychic processes. They are rather the products of delusional convictions reeking of destructive narcissistic and aggressive, omnipotent and grandiose, suicidal and homicidal, drive distortions. The intensity of the fanatical emotions accompanying the convictions of such protagonists is a clear index of their pathological import. Psychologists' assessment would most likely take into consideration the psychological needs and emotionally disturbed states of rage and fear as contributing influences shaping the relevant belief systems in a delusional form. Moreover, even though in each instance there is a high degree of consensual validation of the beliefs within each group, there is little or no consensus regarding the validity and acceptability of the group convictions in the larger social and cultural matrix. The group beliefs in that sense are deviant. This might be the perspective of the impartial observer, but it is certainly not the perspective of the cult members.

The criteria of such judgment may be more complex and problematic than those implied in either Freud's or the usual psychiatric assessment. Such polarized criteria may not be sufficient for the assessment of living human situations in which beliefs, values, attitudes and commitments play such a vital and determinative role. The criteria psychologists seek, therefore, are neither exclusively subjective or objective—that is, they may be both inclusively subjective and objective. To follow the implications of this view, religious belief systems would fall within the realm of transitional conceptualization (Meissner, 1990) and would not be subject simply to the criteria of either objective or subjective validation. In these terms, religious beliefs would remain open to both subjective and objective interpretation, neither one without the other. In this sense, belief systems cannot be restrictively regarded as delusional and therefore implicitly pathological. In summary, belief systems may be pathological without being delusional, but if they are delusional they are also presumably pathological.

Pathological Criteria

I have previously argued (Meissner, 1992) that the criteria of pathology in belief systems can be formal and material. Formal aspects include qualities such as openness versus closedness, broadness versus narrowness and perspective, and degrees of rigidity versus degrees of flexibility—to name a few. One can distinguish between the belief system, as an aspect of consensual group ideology and identity, and the personalized and individualized version of the belief system of the individual believer. These are not synonymous. Belief systems, as they come to be individually internalized, always bear the stamp of the individual's personality, so that the beliefs carry a quotient of meaning derived from the individual's psychic world and to that extent are idiosyncratic and open to drive-derivative determinants, including wish fulfillment. The group belief system, however, represents either a consensus mutually sustained by the members or an impersonal dogmatic code to which the members accede by reason of their commitment to the group and membership in it. The element of wish fulfillment at this level is not a group dynamic but secondary to individual dynamics.

The degree of openness or closedness of a belief system may reflect levels of defensive need operating within the group structure. A belief system would represent all the beliefs, sets, expectancies, or hypotheses—conscious and unconscious—that a group of believers at a given time accepts as true of the world in which they live.[1] In every group there is a corresponding set of disbeliefs containing elements in one degree or another rejected as false. This constellation of beliefs and disbeliefs can be characterized for any religious group as open or closed. The system is formally open when the degree of rejection of disbeliefs is low, when the degree of communication within parts of respective belief systems and between beliefs and disbeliefs is high, and when there is little discrepancy in the degree of differentiation between beliefs and disbeliefs. The system is open materially—that is in terms of content, when the specific content of central beliefs pertains to a view of the world, or the immediate context of interaction, as basically friendly or when authority and the role of authority figures is regarded as relative and egalitarian rather than absolute, and correspondingly, that evaluations of people, both within and outside the group, are not based on their agreement or disagreement with authority.

In contrast, the more a belief system becomes closed, the more it formally involves a high degree of rejection of disbeliefs, relatively strong isolation of parts within and between systems, a high degree of differentiation and discrepancy between beliefs and disbeliefs, and relatively little differentiation within the disbelief system. Materially, the view of the world dictated by the belief system tends to seem threatening, authority tends to be viewed as absolute and authoritarian, the authority of religious leaders is unquestioned and unquestionable, the role of the members tends to be defined in terms of submission and obedience, and the criterion for accep-

---

[1] This is a paraphrase of Rokeach's (1960) description of an individual belief system as "all the beliefs, sets, expectancies, or hypotheses, conscious and unconscious, that a person at a given time accepts as true of the world he lives in" (p. 33).

tance or rejection of others is the degree to which they agree or disagree with these authorities (Rokeach, 1960).

Closed belief systems reflect underlying needs to compensate for feelings of inadequacy and self-hate by excessive concerns over power and status. There arises a cognitive confusion among individual members between information and the source of the information, which fosters a tendency to bring closure to systems of thought and belief. Overidentification with an absolute authority standing behind the belief system serves to defend against feelings of loneliness and isolation. Rokeach (1960) also points to a positive aspect of such closure:

> Closed belief systems provide a systematic cognitive framework for rationalizing and justifying egocentric self-righteousness and the moral condemnation of others. Thus, the more closed the belief–disbelief system, the more do we conceive it to represent, in its totality, a tightly woven network of cognitive defenses against anxiety. Such psychoanalytic defense mechanisms as repression, rationalization, denial, projection, reaction formation, and overidentification may all be seen to have their representation in the belief–disbelief system in the form of some belief or in the form of some structural relation among beliefs. Indeed, we suggest that, in the extreme, the closed system is nothing more than the total network of psychoanalytic defense mechanisms organized together to form a cognitive system and designed to shield a vulnerable mind. (pp. 69–70)

Such defensive and distorting mechanisms are familiar in the mind of the individual believer (Meissner, 1991), but analogous pathological processes may be at work in the genesis and sustaining of beliefs and ideologies within religious group structures. This view of the closed mind can be recognized as close to identifiably pathological states of mind. However, adherence to a relatively closed religious belief system would not necessarily be regarded as pathological in its own right. We would not necessarily conclude that the believer's acceptance of such a closed system was an index of the person's own psychopathology. Nonetheless, there is continuity between these characterological and relatively normal configurations of adaptation to environmental stress and more pathological resolutions. Psychologists can envision, for example, a spectrum of states of mind stretching from the delusions of the psychotic paranoid to the relatively normal and culturally assimilated attitudes of the closed mind and sharing similar attitudes and mechanisms. The differentiation of degrees of pathogenicity in this continuum is a matter of degrees of intensity and relative adaptiveness to a sociocultural context. These considerations lead psychologists into an ill-defined area between the pathological and the normal. In terms of this argument, it would be a mistake to attribute the dynamics of individual wish and need to group dynamics and consensual belief systems.

CHARACTERISTICS OF RELIGIOUS BELIEF SYSTEMS

At this point I would like to briefly consider some of the characteristics of religious belief systems and the role that they play in psychic economy. Belief systems are general social phenomena constituting a significant and central aspect of group culture. Society directs considerable energy to the maintenance and support of institutions and structures that represent and stabilize its common beliefs. Belief systems are important for maintaining the vitality of the group. They are also important for young people becoming participating members of the group and sharing in its culture. Answering this continuing need in social structures, an emergent need in young people for ideological commitment is born out of the uneasiness of vague inner states and the conflicts of emergent but unresolved identity. Thus, society provides belief systems, or what Erikson (1959, 1962) calls "ideologies," in part in response to the inner need of youth for ideological commitment.

The introduction of the term *need* adds a new dimension to the consideration of belief systems psychoanalytically. Contemporary psychoanalytic thinking about religion, following the lead of Winnicott and Erikson (1962), has shifted the ground of the discussion from a focus on belief systems as wish fulfillments to their role as need fulfillments. If they can be regarded as answering powerful human wishes—infantile wishes, as Freud (1927/1961) would have insisted—they also in some fundamental sense respond to the basic human needs. Winnicott (1971) reshaped the psychoanalytic purview by his notion that illusion is not simply a matter of wish fulfillment, but that there is a basic human need for illusion that can be satisfied in no other way. Religious belief systems would qualify as a major area of illusion. Connecting such illusory areas of human experience with fundamental psychic needs offers a degree of legitimacy and acceptability to the role of religious belief in psychic economy that is not carried by regarding them restrictively as wish fulfillments. The shift from wish to need stakes out a fundamental divergence between classical psychoanalytic view of religion and more contemporary post-Freudian views (Jones, 1991; Meissner, 1984b).

Religious systems of belief constitute a particular type of cognitive process that from a formal perspective, prescinding from content, organizes the understanding of some aspect of reality in terms of a coherent explanation. The explanation is not supported scientifically at all points by explicit evidence—adherence to the explanation is urged on other grounds. It is this aspect of the cognitive organization that distinguishes belief systems from scientific theories, or correlatively, belief from knowledge. The belief system, therefore, requires assent from those who accept it, not on the basis of evidence demonstrating its validity, but on the basis of inner needs that the belief system satisfies and responds to. Religious belief systems answer to some of the most basic and fundamental needs and inse-curities in individuals—insecurities about the meaning of life and the confrontation with death. These questions are met with a vacuum of evi-dence and lie beyond the reach of scientific method. The religious belief system supplies an answer, but the answer is accepted, at least in part, on emotional grounds and in response to basic needs. The extent to which the belief system may reflect pathogenic aspects would depend on the path-ological quality of the needs to which it answers.

The more closed a given belief system may be, the more one sees a rigidity in adherence to it, the greater one sees the insistence on main-taining the totality of the belief system with all its parts, and the greater one sees the degree of intolerance to other conflicting beliefs. The closed belief system is characterized by rigidity and dogmatism; rigidity has to do with the resistance to change in single beliefs, whereas dogmatism refers to resistance to change in the belief system as such. The more dogmatic a system of beliefs, the more at risk is the total belief system rather than single beliefs. The degree of dogmatism or of closedness is associated with a need to adhere to the belief system as a whole, whose respective parts are interdependent. No single part of the whole can be challenged or ques-tioned without posing a threat to the whole system. This attitude is based on the intensity of the inner needs that generate and sustain the belief system. The underlying intensity of need and insecurity can be very great indeed, and to this extent the individual needs the support and security of a complete, totally integrated, unshakable, and unquestionable view of his world and its meaning. If doubt is cast on any portion of the belief system, doubt can be cast on any other portion, and this threatens the cohesiveness and solidarity of the group as well as the inner psychic stability of the individual believer. This threat can reach psychotic proportions, in which it is equivalently the threat of inner disintegration, loss of self, and psychic death.

The argument draws psychologists inexorably to ask how the closed (pathological) religious belief system differs from a paranoid delusional sys-tem. The paranoid system is characterized by the need to bring all data into congruence with the delusion and the need to maintain it in the face of contradictory evidence. There is, thus, an analogy between the paranoid delusional system and closed belief systems, particularly in the degree to which such basic, fundamental, and pathological needs are involved. It is not surprising, considering the nature of the motivational issues, that in this area more than others one finds a greater degree of rigidity and dog-matism. But in the interest of clarifying one's understanding, one must ask what it is that distinguishes systems of religious belief from paranoid de-lusions. To be clear about the question, given that both are pathological, it is a question not about pathology or nonpathology but about truth value;

a belief is delusional only to the extent that it violates the canons of realistic verification.

Religious belief systems are complex cognitive organizations that explain in a coherent fashion fundamental and existential questions involving the origin of the universe, the relationship between the universe and the deity, the meaning of human existence, and the conditions of salvation. If one looks at any coherent religious tradition, it represents a continuing and historically embedded effort to conceptualize and understand these related questions. The earlier parts of the Judeo-Christian tradition, for example, were more of a retelling of the story of God's salvific action in Israelite history with only minimal attempts to theologize this history. Later parts of the tradition took the form of prophetic reflections on the history of divine intervention, particularly on the Exodus and the subsequent desert experience that formed a central aspect of the Jewish historical and religious experience. The prophetic reflection was interpretive and more explicitly theological. When Freud (1927/1961) referred to such religious ideas as "illusions," the stress fell on the role of human wishes in generating and maintaining such ideas; they differ from delusions that are essentially in contradiction with reality.

The distinction between illusions and delusions is slippery, however, because delusions are not without their kernel of historical truth, and religious ideas may at times override apparently contradictory ideas. Waelder (1951) referred to the Hebrew belief that they were the chosen people as a collective delusion—evidence to the contrary was rationalized in terms of the belief system. Religious belief systems are formed in some degree in response to the basic human needs, but the degree of closedness and resistance to change by experience is a function of the degree to which the belief system serves a defensive function in preserving the believer from inner psychic insecurity and dread. The greater the intensity of that underlying anxiety, the greater is the tendency for those who adhere to the belief system to regard the system as a whole without differentiation of its parts and to feel that preservation of the parts is essential to the preservation of the whole. This is reflected in an increased rigidity and dogmatism and a reluctance to even question any part of the complex of moral and speculative positions that compose the system. This would in some degree be an index of pathogenicity. In the current re-examination and reconsideration of basic moral positions among religious groups, particularly the sensitive area of sexual morality and its attendant issues of contraception and abortion, part of the problem has to do with this form of pressure toward closedness and rigidity. The problem is complicated by the more general shift from a climate of belief, which demands adherence to established doctrine (closed), to a greater emphasis on personal realization and grasp of religious truth in its historical and emergent dimensions (open).

SCHREBER CASE

It may help to examine some specific belief systems in these terms. The first system I have in mind is the theocosmological system formulated by Judge Schreber, the subject of one of Freud's most famous cases. Schreber's system has particular interest, not only because of Freud's (1911/1958) connection with the case, but also because it has served as a paradigmatic example of a paranoid delusional system.

The case of Daniel Paul Schreber and Freud's analysis of it are sufficiently well-known so that I need only touch on a few central points for this discussion. Schreber was a prominent jurist who had enjoyed a rather distinguished political career. He was a candidate for the Reichstag in the autumn of 1884, but soon after his election he began to experience hypochondriacal delusions and had to be hospitalized. He was discharged in the following year and then appointed to the Leipzig Landgericht. He functioned reasonably effectively in this office until 1893, when he was elevated to the more prestigious Court of Appeals. In October of the same year, he was appointed as presiding judge of the court, but in the month following he again decompensated and had to be readmitted to the hospital. Altogether, Schreber spent 13 of the 27 years following his initial breakdown in mental asylums. His *Memoirs of My Nervous Illness* (Schreber, 1903/1955) is a remarkable document, written between 1900 and 1902, recounting the development of his illness and describing graphically his elaborate delusional system. The *Memoirs* were published in 1903, but did not come to Freud's attention until 1910; they provided him with ripe material for his germinating ideas about paranoia.

Schreber's delusions were bizarre and elaborate. His physician at the Leipzig Clinic had been Flechsig, the famous neuropsychiatrist. Schreber had originally admired and esteemed Flechsig but later on felt, as a part of his persecutory delusions, that Flechsig was performing "soul murder" on him, although Schreber never explained what he meant by the term. Freud interpreted this powerful persecutor as a substitute for an important figure in the patient's emotional life prior to his illness: A once loved and honored object became a hated and feared persecutor. In terms of his libidinal hypothesis, Freud speculated that the reason for the paranoid delusion was the wish–fear of sexual abuse by Flechsig and that the precipitating cause of the illness was an outburst of homosexual libido. Later in the course of his illness, Schreber developed the delusion that he was being transformed into a woman by the power of God, that his genitalia were changing into those of a woman, and that he was developing breasts.

The place of the divinity in these delusions was very special. In Schreber's view, God consisted purely of nerves; he was convinced that God was changing his body by influencing his own nerves. The nerves of God had a creative capacity, possessing all of the properties of human nerves to a greatly intensified degree. They could transform into any kind of object in the created world through the rays that emanated from the Deity. After the work of creation, God had withdrawn to an immense distance and left the world to its own meager devices. God's activities were restricted to drawing to himself the souls of the dead. Schreber felt that he was selected by God for a special mission and that, consequently, God worked his power on Schreber's nerves to give them the character of female "nerves of voluptuousness," transforming his body into a female body. Schreber was able to reconcile himself to this sexual transformation by bringing it into harmony with the higher purposes of God. God demanded femaleness from him in connection with his special mission in the world, in which he was to be God's special agent, to save and redeem God's creation. He was the chosen messenger of God, selected to carry out the special mission of saving the world by means of this subordination to the divine will and the transformation of his body into that of a woman. Only in this way was the world to be saved from imminent and complete destruction. Schreber was to become the wife of God, and after divine impregnation he would give birth to a new race of men and, thus, become the redeemer of the world. Consequently, Schreber developed an elaborate theocosmology in which he developed his ideas of God's special relation to the world and his own special relation to God.

Briefly, Schreber identified his God with the sun, but following a Zoroastrian pattern, divided this God into an upper God called Ormuzd and a lower God called Ahriman.[2] In this ancient tradition, Ormuzd was the good divinity who created the world and guided it, and Ahriman was the Evil Spirit who entered into universal conflict with the Good Spirit for the control of the world and men's souls. Schreber's God seemed to combine these attributes of good and evil, reflecting according to Freud's hypothesis Schreber's ambivalence toward both the physician Flechsig and his father (Meissner, 1976; Niederland, 1974; Westphal, 1990). Schreber's relation to God included a mixture of blasphemous criticism and mutinous insubordination, on the one hand, and reverent devotion, on the other. He felt that God was incapable of learning anything by experience and that, because he only knew how to deal with corpses, did not understand living men. Freud speculated that God stood for Schreber's distinguished father; the sun thus became the symbol of the father, and the conflict with God could be construed as representing the infantile conflict with the father whom the patient loved and to whom he was forced to submit. It was the Oedipal threat of the father, namely, the threat of castration, that provided the basic material for Schreber's wishful fantasy of transformation into a woman. Part of Schreber's delusional system was his belief in the

---

[2] Spelled "Ariman" and "Ormuzd" in Freud (1911) and Schreber (1903/1955). See the discussion of this in connection with Zoroastrianism below.

imminent destruction of the world, interpreted by Freud in terms of the withdrawal of cathexis from the environment, so that the expected end of the world became a projection of the patient's inner catastrophe. The libido thus liberated was attached to the ego in the form of self-aggrandizement and megalomania.

The Projective System

The major emphasis in Freud's consideration of Schreber's pathology fell on the projective system. Moreover, later studies have exquisitely documented the relation between specific elements in Schreber's projective delusions and detailed aspects of what he must have experienced as a child, particularly the persecution at the hands of his father (Niederland, 1974; Schatzman, 1973). In this sense, Schreber's projective system preserves and extrapolates his pathological relationship to his father. The price of relation with the father, therefore, was subjugation and submission, just as the price of becoming the special agent and instrument of God's divine purposes for redemption of the world was transformation into a woman. Schreber's projective system was founded on recognition and acceptance by, and special relationship to, the projected father figure of God.

The projective system can thus be seen as an attempt to redeem and salvage Schreber's damaged narcissism. Within the delusional system he retained a grandiose and narcissistically embellished position as the agency of divine purpose. His self-esteem and his impaired sense of inner value and worth were in this fashion generously restored. The important element, however, was the transformation into a woman. On one level, the transformation offered the potentiality for redeeming the narcissistic loss experienced through his failure to generate healthy children; his wife's many miscarriages were narcissistic injuries for him. On another level, the transformation into a woman established and consolidated his underlying identification with his mother.

In terms of the paranoid process (Meissner, 1978, 1986), the projective system has a derivative relation to the patterning of introjects around which the sense self is organized. The roots of the projective system must be sought in the patterning of introjects, even as the structure of the projective system is a response to the undermined and deprived narcissism embedded in the introjective economy. In Schreber's case, his early developmental experiences left him with a crippled sense of himself as valueless, humiliated, evil, unlovable, and ultimately worthy only of sadistic subjugation and cruel restraint. Around this nuclear formation was erected a context of object relatedness defined by the emerging sense of self based on the central introjects.

The introjective economy rests in crucial ways on the introjections received from both parents. The dominant element in the traditional view of the Schreber case is the introjection of the aggressive and punitive father figure. Identification with the aggressor, formed around this paternal introject, is the basis for the persecutory projection. But other elements are also present. Although there is very little direct knowledge of Schreber's mother, one can infer that she must have been a woman whose character contained strong depressive and masochistic elements. Sustaining a relationship with her severely sadistic and authoritarian husband would have suggested strongly masochistic elements in her own character structure.

In a powerful and convincing manner, Schreber identified himself with the castrated figure of the mother–victim. His delusional system realized the ultimate in victimized subjugation to the power of the father–God. Close and extensive study of paranoid pathology indicates that the combined elements of identification with the aggressor and identification with the victim are persistent and central elements in the introjective economy of paranoid patients. In one aspect at least, the paranoid process can be seen as a reinforcement of the victim introject as a means of defending against the aggressive and victimizing introject (Meissner, 1976). Permutations in the dynamics of these introjects provide the basis for some of the complex manifestations of the paranoid process.

Consequently, the projective system serves an important function in the preservation of a sense of self. The sense of self in the paranoid individual is derived from the pathogenic introjects that do not allow for the establishment or organization of an authentic sense of self meaningfully related to real objects. To sustain the pathological sense of self related to these introjects, the ego must organize a projective system allowing for a substitute relatedness of the pathological self and providing it with a sense of meaningful belongingness within the system of projective relations.

Schreber's Delusions as Beliefs

The dynamics of this delusional system have been exhaustively analyzed elsewhere (Freud, 1911/1958; Meissner, 1976; Niederland, 1974; Westphal, 1990), but my focus here is on the belief system itself. Why do I call it pathological? First of all, it is an idiosyncratic system entirely personal in derivation and connected with no current or consensual religious tradition or organized religious group. It has, therefore, no culture within which it can articulate itself; it incorporates elements of an ancient tradition with respect to the divine names and their essential duality, but it has no real connection with that or any other religious tradition. The conviction of the imminent end of the world is common to many cultic, especially millennarian, beliefs and was even part of the early Christian kerygma in the form of the expectation of the imminence of the parousia in which the triumphant Christ would return in glory—a belief the Christian tradition had to learn to temper as time wore on (Meissner, 1995).

Other details carry the stamp of unreality and delusional wish fulfillment, especially the "nerves" and the sexual transformation that so graphically express the sexual dynamics along with powerful themes of narcissistic grandiosity and self-enhancement. Elevation to the status of God's wife and redeemer of the world would do very nicely in satisfying unresolved grandiose narcissistic desires of a quite primitive and pathological order.

It is of interest to compare Schreber's delusional system with the belief system of Zoroastrianism. Schreber was apparently influenced by the current resurgence of interest in ancient Iranian religion. The influence was strongly felt in the work of his contemporary Nietzsche (1844–1900) in his *Also Sprach Zarathustra* (1954). Zoroastrianism was the dominant religion in ancient Persia for over a millennium, only to be submerged in the rise of Islam. The dating of Zarathustra's life is uncertain, extending anywhere from the 10th to the 5th century B.C., but he probably came from eastern Iran. One tradition says that he converted the father of Darius the Great, who became the protector of the new faith. At about the age of 30 the prophet received, in an ecstatic shamanic vision, his inspired revelation of the great god Ahura Mazda, the spirit of good, not unlike other sky gods of the Vedic or Mesopotamian religions of the second millennium B.C. Opposed to Ahura Mazda was the principle of evil, the god Angra Mainyu. In later formulations these principles of good and evil were called Ormazd and Ahriman, the terms used by Schreber. The cosmic struggle between good and evil would be resolved only at the end of time in the final judgment, when the dead would be resurrected and the evildoers banished to eternal punishment (Eliade, 1978).

Early Zoroastrianism was more concerned with ethical principles and behavior but over the centuries evolved an elaborate historical and cosmological view of the universe. The primal separation of good and evil resulted from the choice of Ahura Mazda, who created all things by thought alone—a form of *creatio ex nihilo*. Ethically, mankind was called to imitate the deity, because each person possessed the freedom to choose between good and evil in the world. Zarathustra preached the final overthrow of the *daeves*, the evil spirits, through the power of Ahura Mazda, in which the world would be transfigured and renewed (Eliade, 1978). The world as presently constituted would be destroyed and replaced, definitively and once and for all regenerated. The prophet set himself against the myths of cyclic cosmic regeneration and proclaimed the final *eschaton*.

History was divided into four periods or eras. In the first, Ahura Mazda created the angelic spirits and the prototypes of all creatures, including Angra Mainyu. The second era saw the existence of the primeval Man and the primeval Ox (the prototype of all animals), but, in the third, Angra Mainyu launched an attack against them and destroyed them. From the seeds of the primeval beings came humans and animals, leaving a mixture of good and evil in the world. Angra Mainyu's legendary life exemplified the constant struggle of every believer in Mazda against the demons, the forces of evil, to gain salvation. This and the faith in supernatural light are Mazdaist characteristics.

In the final era, Zarathustra's mission was to lead to the final divine victory abetted through the work of a semidivine savior. The universe would then be saved and restored to a state of purification. However, the origin of the principle of evil from the creator creates a dilemma for Zoroastrian theologians—how can the principle of evil come from the principle of good? One solution was offered by Zurvanism, namely that both Ahura Mazda and Angra Mainyu issued from a first principle, Zurvan (infinite time), the Supreme Being who dwells in an eternal state beyond the conflicts and ambiguities of the temporal world. The work of redemption begun by Zarathustra was continued by the priests of Mazda through ecstatic spiritual illuminations, particularly from the divine flame springing from the forehead of Mithra, the solar god, and is absorbed in the *haoma* ceremony in which the "drink of immortality" carries the sacred fluid, "at once igneous, luminous, vivifying and spermatic" (Eliade, 1978, p. 315).

This is enough to make a rough comparison of this ancient religious tradition with the delusions of Schreber. Ormazd and Ahriman occupy much the same position as Ahura Mazda and Angra Mainyu. The mission is much the same—the salvation of the world from the forces of evil. The prophet in both cases is chosen by God to carry the mission of redemption and transformation of the world. The transfiguration of the prophet of Mazdaism took place through the achievement of ecstatic illumination and vision. The transfiguration of Schreber took place through nerves of voluptuousness transforming the good judge into a woman. The lines of communication in both cases involved illuminating rays emanating from the deity. God himself withdrew to a great distance after the work of creation, not unlike the hidden Zurvan of late Zoroastrianism; he would communicate with chosen, gifted individuals to intervene in the destiny of the world. He communicates only with the dead to purify their spiritual parts and reunite them to himself. Those who pass through the purification enter the state of bliss, in which they learn the "basic language" spoken by God Himself. For both, God came to be identified with the sun.

The parallels between these thought systems are striking. I would even venture to think, allowing for differences in time, space, and culture, that Schreber's and Zarathustra's belief systems might be close to interchangeable. If Schreber's delusions were presented to mid-first millennium Iranians, he might have passed for a prophet and his delusions would have been the stuff of divinely inspired illumination. By the same token, if Zarathustra were to be transported to late 19th-century Germany and had pronounced his prophetic vision, he would very likely have suffered the same fate as Schreber.[3] How then, does one draw a line between the theo-cosmological delusions of Schreber and the belief system of Zoroastrian Mazdaism? Schreber's *Memoirs* (1903/1955) read in part like an elaborate theological tract. His delusional system is a highly evolved and systematized attempt to organize and understand his experience. The organized doctrine of the prophet represents a similar attempt to interpret human experience and give it meaning in terms of a divinely instituted plan and guidance. Both delusional and belief systems reach certain untestable conclusions that cannot be contradicted by available evidences—Freud's (1927/1961) "mass delusions."

How would one go about disproving Schreber's delusion that he was being transformed into a woman? We can recognize that a delusional sys-tem is in conflict with reality as we interpret it, but how does one go about proving that our interpretation is sane and that the delusional one is insane and in contradiction to reality? Ultimately we cannot. We can resort to an appeal to consensus or to practical and adaptive exigencies that are consequent to our interpretation rather than the delusional one, but these are not matters of evidence. The delusional system as well as the belief system is maintained on the basis of a prior emotional commitment or necessity, not on the basis of evidences. The illusion sets no store by ver-ification. Even the delusion of change of sex is not *a priori* to be presumed as delusional. Given the assumption that Ormazd has the power to change anything as he wishes, transformation into a woman would not be beyond his power. If Schreber were found to undergo anatomical and hormonal changes, what would one say? Miraculous? Certainly beyond the range of normal experience. In summary, one cannot demonstrate the falseness of a belief within the confines of the delusional system. All one can say is that there is no evidence to support the claim, just as there is no evidence to refute it.

The apologetic argument tries to establish the truth value of a given religious belief system. It bases its arguments on biblical accounts, or some other form of special revelation, as its data base, but this is in effect an appeal to a historically antecedent belief system. Apologetics ultimately relies on an acceptance through faith beyond the reach of reason. But this brings one closer to the element or elements distinguishing delusional from belief systems. The delusional system is created anew by the psychotic in response to inner idiosyncratic needs and serves to isolate the person from communal participation in inverse proportion to the degree of develop-ment of the person's pseudocommunity. The needs underlying the person's delusional system are inherently pathological. The religious belief system, in contrast, is not created anew but stems from a tradition that is in some

---

[3] Nietzsche's aphoristic writing in this name were regarded as a product of a deranged mind.

degree institutionalized and has a significant history. The content of the system, therefore, is not idiosyncratic but answers to common needs and shared concerns of the community. Contrary to the effect of a delusional system, the belief system serves to unite the believer with a community of believers, and this social interaction is an important component of the support that the community offers to the emerging sense of identity (Erikson, 1959). The pathogenicity of underlying needs in such circumstances would be minimized.

Thus, whereas the paranoid delusional system is divisive, exclusive, and built out of the fabric of distrust, the belief system rests on shared conviction, mutual support, and trust. As Erikson (1959) commented:

> The psychological observer must ask whether or not in any area under observation religion and tradition are living psychological forces creating the kind of faith or conviction which permeates a parent's personality and thus reinforces the child's basic trust . . . in the world's trustworthiness. . . . All religions have in common the periodical child-like surrender to a Provider or providers who can dispense earthly fortune as well as spiritual health . . . the need for clearer self-delineation and self-restriction; and finally, the insight that individual trust must become a common faith, individual mistrust a commonly formulated evil, while the individual's need for restoration must become part of the ritual practice of many, and must become a sign of the trustworthiness of the community. (pp. 64–65)

Putting it in these terms makes it clear that one cannot discriminate the truth value of delusional from belief systems on the grounds of underlying needs, inner structure, relation to reality, or—a point that deserves emphasis—on the grounds of underlying mechanisms. The mechanisms of introjection, projection, and cognitive construction that characterize the paranoid process (Meissner, 1978, 1986) are detectable in both contexts. These elements are graphically portrayed in the Schreber case (Meissner, 1976). Certainly the Christian doctrine of hell and diabolic influence provides ample scope for the projection of hostile impulses—whether this belief be regarded as enunciating a kernel of truth or not. However, even here the projection serves to underline a common peril and reinforces ties to the community. The mechanisms of belief, here projections and introjections, tend to support the individual's participation and membership in the community, whereas the identical mechanisms in paranoia tend to isolate and exclude the individual from the real community of objects—the delusional network of suspicious and hostile interactions in a paranoid pseudocommunity is a far cry from meaningful sharing in the community of belief of one's fellows. These issues all pertain to the determination of pathogenicity in a given belief system; the truth value can only be determined on other grounds.

CLINICAL IMPLICATIONS

It is not the business of psychiatrists, psychologists, and psychotherapists to stand in judgment on their patients' beliefs and religious convictions (American Psychiatric Association Committee on Religion and Psychiatry, 1990), but it remains part of their mission as caregivers and healers to recognize and help their patients come to terms with the pathological and maladaptive aspects of their religious commitments and investments. Their scientific vantage point enables them to discriminate those aspects of their patients' beliefs that are supportive, mature, reasonable, and psychologically adaptive, as opposed to those aspects that are destructive; misleading; misguided; and needlessly productive of guilt, anxiety, depression, and despair. To the extent that psychiatrists, psychologists, and psychotherapists can approach their religious patients with respect for their needs and struggles with the vicissitudes of human existence, and with respectful reverence for the beliefs by which they guide their lives and hopes, caregivers can use their therapeutic skills more effectively to enable patients to lead more satisfying and religiously fulfilled lives.

If Judge Schreber had presented himself in a modern consulting room or clinic, psychologists or psychiatrists would have no call to question his delusional beliefs or pass judgment on them. Even the delusional conviction that he was changing into a woman would not require any evaluation other than diagnostic, regardless of its inherent psychological interest. If his delusion led him to seek a sex change operation, a mental health professional might intervene, perhaps on the grounds of the self-destructive effects of such a course. But he or she could still not pass judgment on the truth value of the proposition that God was changing his sex. The questions of the truth value of his belief system would actually not concern professionals. They would be intensely concerned with the quality of his life, the effectiveness and meaningfulness of his object relations, the degree to which his beliefs contributed to a psychologically mature and responsible capacity to meet the exigencies of his life and career, and the way in which they facilitated his adaptation to the challenges and demands of his life. The hallmark of Schreber's pathology was the degree to which his beliefs had a destructive and maladaptive influence on his life and work.

By the same token, were psychiatrists to be transported in H. G. Wells's time machine to the middle of the first millennium B.C. and find themselves in ancient Persia, they might well find themselves interviewing a believer in the cult of Zoroastrianism. They would have exactly the same concerns and interests. But the likelihood is that the Zoroastrian would find that his or her belief reinforced the bonds of communion with the prevailing religious group within his or her culture and that this provided many significant and meaningful involvements and engagements in his life, as well as providing a set of beliefs that gave the person hope and solace in the face of the many hardships and vicissitudes of life. The belief system would bind the person to his or her social reference group and would consolidate and support his or her individual sense of identity and belonging.

A further technical point can be made. If it does not fall within the purview of one's therapeutic role to judge the truth value of any patient's beliefs, this does not mean that these same beliefs may not be subjected to therapeutic processing. When a religious patient conveys his or her religious beliefs, therapists are interested in the meaning of the person's beliefs to the person and the role they play in the person's life experience. More is to be gained from a careful and detailed exploration of the content and meaning of such beliefs, because through them the patient tells the therapist something vital about the person's self. To the extent that they act as religiously determined equivalents to the paranoid construction of the paranoid process, careful and empathic exploration of the details of such a conceptual system can yield valuable information about the patient's inner world and the person's sense of self in all the rich complexity of the aggressive and victimized, the narcissistically superior and inferior, aspects of the person's introjective organization. When these configurations are pathological, they become the focus of meaningful therapeutic work. The therapeutic emphasis falls not on the belief system, on its truth or falsity, but on its pathogenicity and the degree to which it reflects the underlying pathogenicity of the patient's self-system (Meissner, 1986).

REFERENCES

American Psychiatric Association. (1994). *Diagnostic and statistical manual of mental disorders* (4th ed.). Washington, DC: Author.

American Psychiatric Association Committee on Religion and Psychiatry (1990). Guidelines regarding possible conflict between psychiatrists' religious commitments and psychiatric practice. *American Journal of Psychiatry, 147,* 542.

Campbell, R. J. (Ed.). (1981). *Psychiatric dictionary* (5th ed.). Oxford, England: Oxford University Press.

Eliade, M. (1978). *A history of religious ideas: Vol. 1. From the stone age to the Eleusinian mysteries.* Chicago: University of Chicago Press.

Erikson, E. H. (1959). *Identity and the life cycle.* New York: International Universities Press.

Erikson, E. H. (1962). *Young man Luther.* New York: Norton.

Freud, S. (1955). Totem and taboo. In J. Strachey et al. (Ed. and Trans.), *The standard edition of the complete psychological works of Sigmund Freud* (Vol. 13, pp. vii–162). London: Hogarth Press. (Original work published 1912–1913)

Freud, S. (1958). Psycho-analytic notes on an autobiographical account of a case of paranoia (*dementia paranoides*). In J. Strachey et al. (Ed. and Trans.), *The standard edition of the complete psychological works of Sigmund Freud* (Vol. 12, pp. 1–82). London: Hogarth Press. (Original work published in 1911)

Freud, S. (1961). The future of an illusion. In J. Strachey et al. (Ed. and Trans.), *The standard edition of the complete psychological works of Sigmund Freud* (Vol. 21, pp. 1–56). London: Hogarth Press. (Original work published 1927)

Freud, S. (1961). Civilization and its discontents. In J. Strachey et al. (Ed. and Trans.), *The standard edition of the complete psychological works of Sigmund Freud* (Vol. 21, pp. 57–145). London: Hogarth Press. (Original work published 1930)

Freud, S. (1964). Moses and monotheism. In J. Strachey et al. (Ed. and Trans.), *The standard edition of the complete psychological works of Sigmund Freud* (Vol. 23, pp. 1–137). London: Hogarth Press. (Original work published 1939)

Grünbaum, A. (1987). Psychoanalysis and theism. *The Monist, 70,* 152–192.

Grünbaum, A. (1993). *Validation in the clinical theory of psychoanalysis: A study in the philosophy of psychoanalysis.* Madison, CT: International Universities Press.

Hinsie, L. E. & Campbell, R. J. (Eds.). (1970). *Psychiatric dictionary* (4th ed.). Oxford, England: Oxford University Press.

Jones, J. W. (1991). *Contemporary psychoanalysis and religion: Transference and transcendence.* New Haven, CT: Yale University Press.

Küng, H. (1979). *Freud and the problem of God* (Rev. ed.). New Haven, CT: Yale University Press.

Küng, H. (1984). *Eternal life?* Garden City, NY: Doubleday.

Meissner, W. W., S. J. (1976). Schreber and the paranoid process. *Annual of Psychoanalysis, 4,* 3–40.

Meissner, W. W., S. J. (1978). *The paranoid process.* New York: Aronson.

Meissner, W. W., S. J. (1984a). The cult phenomenon: Psychoanalytic perspective. *Psychoanalytic Study of Society, 10,* 91–111.

Meissner, W. W., S. J. (1984b). *Psychoanalysis and religious experience.* New Haven, CT: Yale University Press.

Meissner, W. W., S. J. (1986). *Psychotherapy and the paranoid process.* Northvale, NJ: Aronson.

Meissner, W. W., S. J. (1987). The cult phenomenon and the paranoid process. *Psychoanalytic Study of Society, 12,* 69–95.

Meissner, W. W., S. J. (1990). The role of transitional conceptualization in religious thought. In J. H. Smith & S. A. Handelman (Eds.), *Psychoanalysis and religion* (pp. 95–116). Baltimore, MD: Johns Hopkins University Press.

Meissner, W. W., S. J. (1991). The phenomenology of religious psychopathology. *Bulletin of the Menninger Clinic, 55,* 281–298.

Meissner, W. W., S. J. (1992). The pathology of belief systems. *Psychoanalysis and Contemporary Thought, 15,* 99–128.

Meissner, W. W., S. J. (1993). Christian messianism. *Psychoanalytic Study of Society, 18,* 391–413.

Meissner, W. W., S. J. (1995) *The cultic process*. Manuscript in preparation.

Meissner, W. W., S. J. (1995). *The Kingdom come: Psychoanalytic perspectives on the messiah and the millenium*. Kansas City, MO: Sheed and Ward.

Niederland, W. G. (1974). *The Schreber case: psychoanalytic profile of a paranoid personality*. New York: Quadrangle/The New York Times.

Nietzsche, F. (1954). Thus spoke Zarathustra. In W. Kaufman (Ed.), *The portable Nietzsche*. New York: Viking Press.

Pruyser, P. W. (1977). The seamy side of current religious beliefs. *Bulletin of the Menninger Clinic, 41*, 329–348.

Rizzuto, A. M. (1979). *The birth of the living God*. Chicago: University of Chicago Press.

Rokeach, M. (1960). *The open and closed mind*. New York: Basic Books.

Schatzman, M. (1973). *Soul murder: Persecution in the family*. New York: Random House.

Schillebeeckx, E., O. P. (1963). *Christ the sacrament of the encounter with god*. New York: Sheed and Ward.

Schillebeeckx, E., O. P. (1968). *The eucharist*. New York: Sheed and Ward.

Schreber, D. P. (1955). *Memoirs of my nervous illness*. (I. MacAlpine & R. A. Hunter, Trans.) Cambridge, MA: Bentley. (Original published 1903)

Spero, M. H. (1992). *Religious objects as psychological structures: A clinical integration of object relations theory, psychotherapy, and judaism*. Chicago: University of Chicago Press.

Waelder, R. (1951). The structure of paranoid ideas. *International Journal of Psycho-Analysis, 32*, 167–177.

Westphal, M. (1990). Paranoia and piety: Reflections on the Schreber case. In J. H. Smith & S. A. Handelman (Eds.), *Psychoanalysis and religion* (pp. 117–135). Baltimore, MD: Johns Hopkins University Press.

Winnicott, D.W. (1991). *Playing and reality*. New York: Basic Books.

10

CULTS AND CHARISMATIC GROUP PSYCHOLOGY

MARC GALANTER

Within the many expressions of religious affiliation and belief, the emergence of contemporary cults pose a number of issues for the clinician. The activities of contemporary cults confront psychologists with a variety of troubling and poorly explained phenomena. These include the adoption of deviant life styles, the disruption of nuclear families, and tragic events such as those at Jonestown and Waco. These raise the question of whether the study of contemporary groups of this type might shed light on certain issues addressed by psychology—in particular, the impact of zealous group settings on individual psychopathology and on social behavior. Furthermore, the clinician may be called on by family members seeking understanding or consultation regarding a child, sibling, or parent who has joined a charismatic group. Clinicians may have the opportunity of treating patients who present a history of involvement in a charismatic group. An understanding of the psychological aspects of group initiation, affiliation, and lifestyle, in addition to related psychiatric considerations, may better prepare clinicians to understand their patients and to provide consultation and appropriate intervention.

This chapter is based in part on the following articles by the author: Galanter (1982), Galanter (1990), and Galanter et al. (1991).

269

Because the term *cult* typically connotes a deviant religious orientation and is often used pejoratively, I will instead adopt the term *charismatic group* here. This allows for consideration of a variety of political and non-religious movements, in addition to the religious groups that use group psychology typically seen in religious cults.

There are four aspects that appear as constituent characteristics of charismatic groups. These features appear in religious groups, political groups, and many other institutions that maintain authority through the use of related group psychology procedures. Members of such groups typically (a) adhere to a consensual belief system, (b) sustain a high level of social cohesiveness, (c) are strongly influenced by group behavioral norms, and (d) impute charismatic or divine power to the group or its leadership (Galanter, 1978, 1981; Weber, 1922/1963). I shall first examine circumstances of membership in the group and then review the underlying psychology that maintains participation in these charismatic groups. This will include a discussion of the psychiatric concomitants of such group affiliation. Finally I will provide three case examples.

CIRCUMSTANCES OF MEMBERSHIP

One remarkable feature of charismatic groups concerns the circumstances of membership. Unlike the members of mainstream religions who most often affiliate with a religious institution or tradition on the basis of their family of origin's involvement, entry into a zealous religious sect often involves a dramatic conversion. Conversion plays a crucial role in the process of entry in which a previously unsatisfactory life circumstance is left for the transforming promise of a new lifestyle and social and personal identity. A comprehensive understanding of the process of initiation and affiliation includes an examination of the antecedents to joining, the process of conversion, and the psychological dynamics that encourage and structure assimilation into active membership in the group.

Antecedents to Joining

I will begin by examining the circumstances surrounding engagement into some recent "youth cults." These groups are of particular interests in light of the fact that charismatic groups often target their solicitation to adolescents and young adults. As I will show, such groups offer unique psychological appeal to youth as they address the anxieties and difficulties of that developmental epoch.

It has been often observed that adolescence and young adulthood pose considerable psychological challenges, including the establishment of identity, the consolidation of values, the development of meaningful relationships and work, and the necessity of appropriately expressing sexuality (Blos, 1962; Erikson, 1968). Charismatic groups appear to offer succor and the promise of resolution of many of these developmental conflicts, particularly in respect to identity and participation in a viable peer group. Such groups may also hold particular appeal to youth or other members of society who are socially alienated or suffer from psychiatric complaints.

Psychological distress is a frequent antecedent to joining these groups. On the basis of interviews with members, ex-members, and relatives, a number of clinicians have described the members themselves as emotionally disturbed. One investigator described them as predominantly depressed, inadequate, or borderline antisocial youths (cf. Etemad, 1978), and others have characterized them as lonely, rejected, and sad (cf. Levine & Salter, 1976). In addition, inductees often have limited social ties before joining a sect. Their preoccupations with purpose and destiny are closely associated to a dissatisfaction with interpersonal relations, leading to loneliness and a sense of alienation. Some adolescents who join are described as using these sects to reduce a sense of personal "incompleteness," often at a time of normal crisis (Nicholi, 1974). These characteristics point to difficulties in mastering developmental challenges and, for some, more serious psychiatric problems.

Considerable attention has been directed to the social and family backgrounds of people who join a "cultic" sect. Self-reports indicate that many sect members come from troubled families that evidence disturbed interpersonal relationships (Deutsch, 1975; Nicholi, 1974). Schwartz and Kaslow (1979) reported patterns of "overly enmeshed families" (Minuchin, Montalvo, & Guerney, 1967) in their studies of the families themselves. They observed that for sect members the group represented a solution to the conflicts aroused by society's demand for autonomy. Because taking responsibility for one another is the hallmark of enmeshed families, these young people had been uncomfortable with entering an adult world that valued personal autonomy.

Most reports have characterized members as coming from middle- and upper-middle-class families. In two cults that my associates and I studied, the majority of members had attended college, as had one or both of their parents (Galanter & Buckley, 1978; Galanter, Rabkin, J., Rabkin, R., & Deutsch, 1979). The same was true in a study of young people who had left charismatic sects (Singer, 1978). It appears that the features of adolescent developmental failure, personal and interpersonal distress, and family conflict, in conjunction with the pressing societal demand for self-sufficiency, may predispose certain youth to a receptivity to affiliation with a charismatic group. Suchan affiliation marks a departure from a negative life circumstance to one offering stability and identity.

The Conversion Experience

One compelling feature of charismatic groups is that entry is often marked by a dramatic experience of conversion. In 1902, Willam James (1902/1929) wrote about religious conversion as a process through which an individual, "divided and consciously wrong, inferior and unhappy," becomes "unified and consciously right, superior and happy" (p. 186) as a consequence of achieving a hold on his or her religious reality. It may otherwise be described as a process by which a person comes to adopt an all-pervasive world view. The taking of a new world view and personal identity marks an attempt to solve departmental challenges and, for some, is a curative agent for serious psychiatric maladies.

The issue of sudden conversion as a pseudosolution for dealing with extreme and disintegrating conflict was raised before the emergence of recent charismatic sects. On the basis of his study of religious converts, Salzman (1953) observed that this sudden process might precipitate or be part of a psychotic process. Another researcher (Roberts, 1965) reported higher scores on a neuroticism scale (although no report of psychosis) for sudden converts than for individuals experiencing a more gradual conversion. These observations suggest that a discernible state of dysphoria may indeed be compatible with sudden conversion experiences. This may be particularly the case for youth, who may have suffered through a prolonged period of dysphoria and alienation and find themselves unable to meet the challenges of the entry into adulthood.

The potential restitutive function of conversion, however, has also been emphasized. It has been likened to the crystallizing role of an "experience of significance" that may occur at the onset of delusion formation; nonetheless, delusion formation per se generally occurs in the face of disruption of a consistently pathological and much more severe nature. Whatever the magnitude of the preceding disruption or dysphoria, such religious experiences may be considered as part of the coping system that provides ego integration for the individual (cf. Pattison, Labins, & Doerr, 1973). This has also been emphasized with regard to people in the contemporary youth culture who are experiencing various degrees of psychiatric disruption. Nicholi (1974), for example, studied a series of relatively well-adapted college student converts who reported feeling considerable existential despair before their conversion. He reported that they found an enhanced sense of purpose and an improvement in their relations with peers following their conversion experiences. These reports may suggest a potentially stabilizing effect of conversion and affiliation.

Transcendental or mystical experiences are often important in the conversion process, as noted by both James (1902/1929) and Freud (1921/1955). The importance of transcendental experiences in conflict resolution, even to the point of precipitating acute hallucinatory episodes in both nonpsychotic (Jacobsen, 1964; Sterba, 1968) and psychotic (Sedman & Hopkinson, 1966) individuals, has also been emphasized. These experiences are also integral to continuing group membership for many members of charismatic sects. These events may provide powerful affective experiences that mobilize affiliation with others who have experienced similar phenomena.

Explanatory models for the appearance of psychotic-like transcendental phenomena in the context of religious experience have not yet been developed. It should be noted, however, that rather striking perceptual phenomena are regularly reported among members of these sects. For example, 30% of the 119 members of one group reported hallucinatorylike experiences during their meditation (Galanter & Buckley, 1978). Clearly, such phenomena should make a considerable impact on psychologists' understanding of pathologic as well as normal mental processes. They may, perhaps, help psychology understand the nature of certain contexts that can precipitate hallucinatory states in those who are designated as mentally ill.

Another feature of entry into charismatic groups is the influence of active solicitation and evangelization. Several groups of researchers have investigated the role of active recruitment by religious sects. Lofland and Stark (1965; Lofland, 1977) proposed a model for this phenomenon based on their observations of a small millenarian Christian group. They emphasized the acutely felt tension experienced by the convert in the context of religious problem solving, which leads to acquiring the role of "religious seeker." The encounter with the cult then becomes a turning point in the person's life. Close ties are developed to other members as they shower the convert with affection—a phenomenon noted by other observers (Clark, 1979; Levine & Salter, 1976). Some investigators (Adams & Fox, 1972; Glock & Stark, 1965; Gordon, 1974; Simmonds, Richardson, & Harder, 1976) have stressed the importance of early contacts with the group in relieving an inductee's feelings of meaninglessness and deprivation. The induction apparently occurs through psychological engagement rather than coercion.

In a controlled study (Galanter, 1980), for example, I found intense social ties and ideologic commitments among the majority of persons who stayed beyond the first two days of a noncoercive three-week induction sequence. Nonetheless, only 9% of the 106 who began the sequence actually joined, and a third of these dropped out within four months. Thus, at least early on, these affiliative ties may be subject to change. It appears that the active engagement by the group with the potential convert plays an important role in the process of conversion. A related feature of conversion lies in the potential positive effects of this newly gained affiliation.

The Psychiatric Impact of Joining Charismatic Sects

Individual members of contemporary charismatic sects generally state that joining the group has had a positive effect on their psychological state. Interviewers describe reports of new strength and "spiritual resources" as well as reduced "self-hatred" (Nicholi, 1974). Increased feelings of calm and happiness and a capability for better relationships are also noted (Levine & Salter, 1976; Wilson, 1972).

In one series of controlled studies, we (Galanter, 1980, 1981; Galanter & Buckley, 1978; Galanter et al., 1979) measured the psychological impact of conversion to the Divine Light Mission and the Unification Church. Structured self-reports of representative samples of members of these groups indicated considerable amelioration of emotional state, referred to as a "relief effect," on joining. We found that this improved state was maintained over the course of long-term membership defined minimally as two to three years. It is interesting, however, that despite the reported improvement, long-term members' scores on the psychological General Well-Being Schedule (Dupuy, 1973) were slightly below those of an age- and sex-matched sample from the general population. This was compatible with our finding of even lower scores on psychological well-being for a representative sample of nonmembers who registered for the sects' workshops before joining (Galanter, 1980). Members' current level of psychological well-being was correlated with the intensity of their social affiliation with other members and their espousal of the group ideology, indicating that there may be an implicit inclination among charismatic group members to sustain their affiliations with the group so as to maintain their enhanced emotional state. The salient feature concerns seeming beneficial effects offered by the cohesiveness of the group.

When cohesiveness is strong, participants work to sustain the commitment of their fellow members, to protect them from threat, and to ensure the safety of shared resources. This can lead to the members' psychotherapeutic benefit, as Pattison (1977) and others (Galanter, 1989a; Kilbourne & Richardson, 1984; Levine, 1983) have pointed out.

The impact of group cohesiveness on the psychological status of members was evident in a study of a Hindu-oriented charismatic sect, the Divine Light Mission (Galanter, 1978; Galanter & Buckley, 1978). Young adult members of the group we studied reported appreciable psychiatric problems before joining. For example, 30% had sought professional help, and 9% had been hospitalized for emotional disorders. Furthermore, their self-reports reflected a considerable relief in neurotic distress after they became affiliated with the Divine Light Mission. Their responses also demonstrated an intense social cohesiveness in the group that was highly correlated with the degree of symptom relief evidenced by individual members. Cohesive forces based on family and community ties operate in a similar fashion in a wide variety of indigenous mental healing rituals, both in preindustrial societies, as in Zar ceremonies of Northeast Africa (Kennedy, 1967), and in the United States, as in Espiritismo among Puerto Rican immigrants (Singer & Borrero, 1984).

In conclusion, there appears to be a biologically grounded inclination among individuals to coalesce into such groups, particularly when ties to other sources of affiliation are weakened. It appears that, for some, entry into the social matrix of the charismatic group may provide significant resources that bolster psychological functioning and produce an improved sense of well-being. This effect may be particularly significant for members whose dissatisfaction with their previous life status was most pronounced.

LIFESTYLE AND GROUP COHESION

Charismatic groups can profoundly shape the thinking and behavior of their members. The psychological forces brought to bear on the preexisting disposition and psychology of recruits is crucial to the process of initiation into the group. As has been previously reported, group cohesion plays a significant role in the functioning and attraction of the sect.

Group cohesiveness is defined as the product of all the forces that act on members to keep them engaged in a group (Cartright & Zander, 1962). In this section I will discuss the interrelated features of communal living; shared beliefs, experiences, and practices; and codes of behavior that contribute to the social cohesiveness of charismatic groups. I will conclude with a discussion of systems theory that illuminates the reciprocal reinforcement patterns that maintain the group structure.

Communal Living

Communal living is characteristic of many charismatic sects, both contemporary ones and those in previous centuries, such as the Shakers and the first communities of the Church of Jesus Christ of Latter-Day Saints (Mormons). In contemporary sects, members often live together in an institutional setting or in smaller private residences. For example, in the Divine Light Mission, 20% of the 119 members lived in communal ritual residences with stringent behavioral norms, 50% with other members in smaller informal private residences, and the remaining 30% independently (Galanter & Buckley, 1978). Communal living strengthens the bonds of affiliation and, as shown through systems theory, provides a boundary between the group and the larger surrounding society.

Sect members frequently refer to one another as family, as do charismatic groups directed primarily toward therapeutic purposes. Ofshe (1976) studied patterns of relating in Synanon, a self-help group that was initiated for the treatment of drug abusers. Shared residential facilities and economic resources and a familylike atmosphere underlay a considerable degree of intimacy within this group, which was manifest in patterns of social intercourse, in structured group communications (the "games"), and in informal socialization. Both self-help drug-treatment programs and formally constituted religious groups may be characterized by common beliefs, behavioral norms, and residence. These characteristics suggest the importance of the group structure for the maintenance of the affiliation. Each of these characteristics sustains the integrity of the group and reinforces continued participation.

Shared Belief

Shared belief, a second force in the charismatic group, was evident in our studies on the psychological well-being of longstanding Unification Church members (Galanter et al., 1979). Measures of social cohesiveness and religious belief accounted for a large portion of the variance in well-being, and items that measured religious belief were the highest ranking predictors of well-being. This suggests the additional role of belief as a force in charismatic groups. It may also reflect the importance of a set of beliefs held by healers and their patients about illness and treatment. Kleinman and Gale (1982) found this explanatory model to be an important component of the effectiveness of indigenous healing in their cross-cultural studies of shamanistic treatment. The acquisition of shared beliefs is a subject of particular interest concerning charismatic groups. The issue is most often framed in terms of thought control or brainwashing.

Thought Control

The issue of thought control or brainwashing in sects has been raised in both the popular press and the scientific literature (Clark, 1978; Etemad, 1978; Simmonds et al., 1976; Ungerleider & Wellisch, 1979). Lifton (1961) studied the characteristics of this process as applied by Chinese Communists to Western prisoners of war during the Korean conflict. Richardson and Stewart (1977) drew on a number of these traits in their study of the Jesus movement. The acquisition of shared beliefs comes under the influence of group cohesion, self-enhancing beliefs and attributions, the charisma of the leader, and the insulation of the group from the outside world.

For example, a shared belief that members' work is devoted to some grand plan (whether revealed or not) and is the basis for the mystical manipulation of members' activities provides reinforcement for beliefs. That all planned and observed events are rationalized on the basis of the group's mysticized goals further establishes support for the group's beliefs.

The sect may also have a sacred science, whose unquestioned dogma can explain all facets of life, thus effectively eliminating the difference between the sacred and secular spheres. In addition, the possession of such beliefs may enhance a members' esteem, a feeling that they possess special knowledge or share in a manifest destiny unique within the culture.

Further, milieu control, for example, entails establishing constraints over all facets of communication; the degree of such control varies among religious sects, usually being contingent on members' proximity to one another in residential and work arrangements. The charismatic leaders' influence within the group establishes the validation of the beliefs within the sect, often within the exclusive control of the leader. The insulation of the group from the surrounding culture and alternative viewpoints, together with the group dynamics influenced by the charismatic leader, conjoin to shape and reinforce the shared validation of beliefs. One can acquire a better understanding of the ability of certain groups to define the norms for consensual validation by becoming familiar with the psychological literature on cognitive dissonance and attribution theory (Bem, 1967; Festinger, Ricker & Schacter, 1973; Galanter et al., 1979; Hardyck & Braden, 1962; Proudfoot & Shaver, 1976). For example, beliefs are reinforced through cognitive dissonance following a prolonged period of sacrifice and commitment; the more adverse the consequences of holding beliefs, the more likely the beliefs will be maintained. Suffice it to say, psychological group dynamics play an essential role in belief commitment, perhaps one that is more important than the content of the beliefs themselves.

An overview of the many cultlike belief systems currently found on the American (and often the international) scene is helpful to the clinician in placing specific sects in perspective. The belief systems are generally confusing to the outsider, and many are based on transcendental and mystical experiences. Some are drawn from unfamiliar Eastern traditions; others embellish established religions to the point of reconstructing doctrine. Singer (1978) divided the many cult orientations into nine types, although many typologies are possible.

One common orientation is based on neo-Christian ideas, as illustrated by the True World, an evangelical sect associated with the Pentecostal movement (Hardyck & Braden, 1962). This group accepts the Bible as the literal word of God, and members have been observed to speak in tongues and believe in personal prophecy and faith healing. Groups based on Eastern religions typically emphasize meditation and transcendent experiences. The most common Eastern orientations are based on Hindu concepts, as in the Divine Light Mission and the Hare Krishna movement (Nagy & Spark, 1973); some are based on Zen Buddhism or other Sino-Japanese practices. Soka Gakkai (Kumasaka, 1966), for example, is a Buddhist sect that originated in Japan and now has headquarters in major American cities; the belief system emphasizes religious chanting and a positive attitude but does not impose extensive behavioral restrictions on followers.

Not all charismatic large groups in America are religiously oriented. Some emphasize contemporary psychology as an ideological perspective, to the point of a charismatic commitment. Groups such as Synanon (Ofshe, 1976) and Erhard Seminar Training (est; Simon, 1978) are examples. Although mystification may enhance the attraction of an ideology to its members, a group is more likely to elicit a positive response in the outsider if its beliefs are comprehensible in terms of the outsider's own world view.

Politically oriented or racially based groups such as the People's Temple, or perhaps the Italian Red Brigades, became well-known through the popular press. Less familiar groups are based on witchcraft, Satanism, spiritualism, and an outer space orientation. Each in their own way is formed around similar group dynamics and reinforcements for holding shared beliefs and maintaining group cohesion. The term *autism*, typically applied to an individual's cognitive framework, may have its own counterpart on a group level in this context. It would apply when ideas different from those consensually validated by the society become entwined in the members' coping system. In such circumstances there is a closed system in which validation, support, and identity are isolated from the more inclusive culture. The orbit of the group becomes the only source of affiliation and reality.

Shared Experiences and Practices

Shared experiences and practices provide additional elements that contribute to group cohesion. The shared experience of altered states of consciousness can be a potent force operating in the charismatic group. It is frequently described by modern cult members (Galanter, 1989b; Needleman & Baker, 1978) and is typically elicited in an intense group experience. In addition to the function of group cohesion, altered states of consciousness in relation to religious conversion can serve as the basis for the converts' attributing a new construction of reality to their life (Proudfoot & Shaver, 1976). In Divine Light Mission and Unification Church samples, for example, my associates and I found that experiences of altered consciousness were significantly correlated with the improved affective status experienced by members on conversion (Galanter et al., 1979). There are also parallels to the ceremonies of indigenous mental healers (Favazza & Faheem, 1983): Descriptions date back half a century to the observations of Leighton and Leighton (1941) among Navajo shamans. Emetics and even hot pokers were used by Navajos to induce transcendent states during rites for treatment of major mental illnesses (Kaplan & Johnston, 1964). Such experiences establish a common and unique ground for affiliation and group identity formation.

Codes of Conduct

In addition to providing affiliation, charismatic groups establish codes of conduct that regulate individual and social behavior. Such external regulation, within the context of an insulated sect, furnishes group support to the management of psychological difficulties concerning control. The behavioral norms of many sects appear to reflect reaction formation against current attitudes toward sexual permissiveness. These norms are often sustained only by adopting a number of ritualized group defenses. Harder, Richardson, and Simmonds (1976), for example, studied courtship, marriage, and family style in one segment of the Jesus movement. They described the members' express avoidance of situations that might be sexually charged and outlined the specific sect regulations regarding courtship and bodily pleasures. Dating, for instance, was considered inappropriate because it might lead to temptations and possible transgressions. Similar transformations in peoples' attitudes on joining a sect were reflected in the study of Unification Church members mentioned earlier, of whom 76% indicated that they should "very much" avoid thinking about sex, although only 11% reported feeling this way before joining (Galanter et al., 1979). Group psychology, therefore, plays an important role in the management of drive expression and other areas of conflict.

Charismatic Leader

Charismatic groups often form around the magnetism of a charismatic leader. The ability to inspire hope or fear combined with a dynamic presence in an important aspect of the leader's authority and influence in the formation and maintenance of the charismatic group. The group, as well, participates in the creation of the charisma of the leader. Through forces of projection and idealization, members impute wisdom and at times deification to the leader. Considerable psychological influence becomes located in the person of the charismatic leader.

The idiosyncrasies of each group's leader may, of course, be translated into behavioral norms for the group. Some leaders are apparently unstable. Deutsch (1980) reviewed the impact of the psychotic behavior of one charismatic sect leader from a psychiatric perspective. Because of the grandiose role vested in this leader, members' reality testing was suspended in the face of the proclamations he presented to them. The leader had a paradoxical appeal that apparently heightened his charismatic attraction. When necessary, rationalizations emerged so that his bizarre commands might be perceived as reasonable and then accepted. As observed in Jonestown and Waco, the influence of the group leader, together with the forces of group cohesion, poses significant psychological dynamics and control over individuals.

Social Control

In the charismatic group, the forces of group cohesiveness, shared belief, altered consciousness, codes of conduct, and the appeal of a leader operate to compel behavioral conformity and modulate affect without overt coercion. To understand this process of social control, it is useful to contrast it with the influence of brainwashing.

Brainwashing was described by Lifton (1961) among prisoners of the Korean War who were forcibly confined by the Communist Chinese. In both brainwashing and charismatic groups, those directing the process maintain control over the "context of communication" to prevent the expression of perspectives contrary to their own. In the brainwashing setting, however, participants are imprisoned and physically coerced. There is no physical coercion in charismatic groups. Instead, the psychological forces described above allow members to attribute new meaning and values to their experiences by means of social reinforcement of compliance.

How does this reinforcement take place? Findings on the role of these forces (Galanter, 1978, 1989a; Kilbourne & Richardson, 1984; Wenegrat, 1989) suggest the operation of a "relief effect" in the psychiatric impact of charismatic groups. That is to say, both recruits and long-term members experience a relief from emotional distress when they feel more closely affiliated with the group; a decline in affiliate feelings, on the other hand, can result in greater distress. Such an effect, likely grounded in biologically based inclinations to affiliation (Galanter, 1978) and mediated by the social context, can serve as an operant reinforcer for regulating behavior (Ferster, 1958). Members who act in accordance with the group's expectations are reinforced by enhanced well-being; when they reject the group's behavioral norms they experience the negative reinforcement of increased distress. This also serves to enhance the likelihood of members' maintaining affiliation with the group and compliance with its expectations for behavior. It takes place both informally and in structured rituals. In Alcoholics Anonymous (AA), a modern healing group, for example, Rodin (1985) pointed out that members' compliance is regularly reinforced by their peers at meetings. This is done by means of the verbal expressions of approval and demonstrations of affection routinely made by members to reward speakers during a chapter meeting.

Because the operant reinforcement of approved behaviors can engage members into compliance with the group and restructure their perceptions of the world around them, it can also serve as the basis for a remission in recruits' pathological perceptions. The enhanced well-being inherent in the affiliation process can then contribute to the relief of major psychopathology, as illustrated by the following case history.

A 24-year-old technician with no history of mental illness became increasingly isolated over the course of a year after beginning to smoke marijuana. He felt that his coworkers were conspiring to have him arrested for drug possession. He then moved into a secluded rural setting, where he soon came to believe that his "soul was moving out" of him and that he saw flying saucers nearby. Soon he felt he was going out of his mind. At this point he met several members of an Eastern cultic group, who invited him to spend time at their communal residence. After two months of meditation and daily attendance at their religious services, he was no longer anxious or delusional, reporting that he was "at peace with himself." A year later, he had had no recurrence in symptoms and was still involved in the group's activities.

The intense cohesiveness of the charismatic group in combination with its ability to influence members' beliefs can yield relief in psychopathology. The support of the group and the provision of routine and consistent tasks and role expectations may provide a measure of stability that socially alienated or mentally ill people desire. It can also generate psychiatric syndromes, however. This is particularly true when an individual becomes alienated from a cohesive group but still accepts its belief system. The potent impact of such estrangement, even to the point of inducing psychotic symptoms, is illustrated below.

A 16-year-old boy whose family belonged to a neo-Christian isolated cult was admitted to the hospital because he was hearing voices. Both the patient and others reported that he had never experienced psychiatric difficulties until fellow members caught him smoking marijuana; the members insisted that he was tainted by the devil because he had violated the group's religious injunction against smoking marijuana. Very soon after this experience, the boy became alienated from the group and ran off to stay at the home of a relative not affiliated with the cult. Over the course of a month he became increasingly guilty and anxious about having left the group and then began to hallucinate the voice of the Devil telling him he had betrayed the cult. His symptoms remitted during a one-month hospitalization that provided supportive milieu treatment only. In addition to the powerful influence of group cohesion, the charisma of the sect leader played a significant role. Leaving or being expelled from one's primary, and in these cases exclusive, source of affiliation, belief, and lifestyle poses significant threat to psychological cohesion and mental functioning.

I found that the maintenance of affiliation within a charismatic group is based on powerful group psychology dynamics. The establishment of group cohesion in which beliefs and behaviors are socially regulated and reinforced, together with the influence of a charismatic leader, provides a high degree of structure and contributes to maintaining the affiliation. The nature of dynamics of group cohesion is further illuminated through the application of systems theory.

Psychology of the Charismatic Group: A Systems Perspective

Alternative religious sects, as I have shown, derive their influence primarily from psychological processes related to the establishment and maintenance of group cohesion. My discussion to this point has emphasized the member in relation to the group. A complementary view of dynamics concerns the psychology of the group as an entity in its own right. Group psychology theorists such as Bion (1959) and Ezriel (1950) have pointed out that certain issues gain expression in the group, irrespective of the intentions of the individual members. Puzzling individual behaviors, they explain, may be manifestations of obligate themes within the group, such as dependency and fight–flight patterns. In this regard it is as if the group supersedes the members of group as a collective.

If the charismatic group is to be conceptualized as a functioning whole, systems theory may serve as a useful model. This theory was developed by Von Bertalanffy (1974) and first applied in the study of relationships among components of complex biological systems. The approach, however, has also been applied to a number of other areas relevant to the issues addressed here, such as individual personality structure (Allport, 1965; Von Bertalanffy, 1974) and group organization (Baker, 1970; Miller & Rice, 1967).

From the perspective of systems theory, an aggregate of interacting components is considered a system. In studying the system, the relationships among components are emphasized, rather than the effect of each component directly on another. An open system is one that is in active exchange with its environment (primarily in the form of interpersonal exchanges). In this respect, the group's environment is the broader society in which it is lodged, which has a contradictory set of beliefs and is often hostile to the group.

Some characteristics of an open system may be related to our knowledge of charismatic groups. Open systems, for example, are characterized by boundary control (Baker, 1970; Miller & Rice, 1967), by means of which the potential components of the system (people and beliefs, in this case) are either defined as part of the system or kept outside it. In the charismatic group, this is particularly important because of conflicts between the group's perspectives and those of the general population. Thus, individuals' acceptance of unusual beliefs may be puzzling in terms of their antecedent personalities; the panoply of ideologies outlined in this chapter bears little obvious relationship to the psychological or social needs of one group's individual members as distinguished from those of another group's individual members. With regard to systems needs, however, such ideologies do serve as a cognitive basis for the group's boundary control function—to differentiate the group's own members from nonmembers (see Figure 1).

Boundary control, like functions of the open system, may help to explain puzzling behaviors observed among members of charismatic large groups. For example, some observers of these groups (Clark, 1979; Singer, 1978) have described the glazed and withdrawn look of certain sect members. Although this responses may appear pathologic when observed in a given individual, it may be quite adaptive for sustaining membership in the group. It may facilitate the members' avoidance of influence from outsiders and can thus be understood as a component of the group's boundary control function, evinced as a demand characteristic of the group. Although such responses may be engendered through membership in the group, they may emerge only in settings that threaten the group's integrity. Thus, an observer who is perceived as antagonistic to the group would be more likely to report this response than one who is not.

This may help to explain the puzzling discrepancies between reports of different observers of these groups, who may be studying them in different contexts relative to the "safe" boundaries of the group. Clark (1979) and Singer (1978), for example, have dealt frequently with people leaving sects and have addressed the ill effects of membership. From this perspective, they have observed affective constriction and stereotyped behavior associated with membership. On the other hand, Ungerleider and Wellisch (1979) and my associates and I (Galanter & Buckley, 1978; Galanter et al., 1979), in conducting studies, established a positive working relationship with active, committed group members and often addressed the more

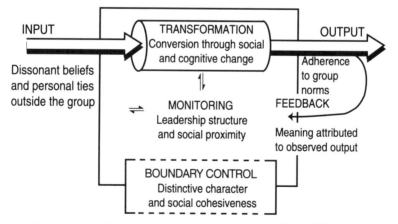

Figure 1. The charismatic large group as an open system. From "Charismatic religious sects and psychiatry," by M. Galanter, 1982, *American Journal of Psychiatry, 139*, p. 1545. Copyright 1982, American Psychiatric Association. Used with permission of the publisher.

constructive aspects of membership in the sect. Neither Ungerleider and Wellisch nor we reported such observations. Members may thus have responded on the basis of whether or not the investigators were perceived as trusted figures who were no threat to the safe boundaries of the group. This illustrates the influence of the subject's own expectations, drawn from group-related attitudes, on the psychiatric phenomena that are observed. In the psychiatric assessment of these groups and their members, the observer's objectivity may not be sufficient to ensure an accurate clinical perspective. One must be cautious about generalizing from a given set of clinical or research contacts and consider that informants in the member's family and community (outside the group's boundaries) as well as those among the membership (within the group boundaries) may have different and equally relevant perspectives to offer.

For charismatic groups, boundary control is facilitated by the development of the group's distinctive character, whether in dress, custom, or ideology. It is also ensured if the group develops a fearfulness of outsiders and their beliefs. As noted above, members have been reported to experience relief of neurotic distress on joining a group. When variables related to social cohesiveness were examined to ascertain which of them were correlated with this relief, the variable most highly correlated with it was suspiciousness toward outsiders. It predominated over positive feelings toward the sect's own members as a component of this psychological relief effect. This may help to explain the case with which a defensive "paranoia" may emerge among certain sect members who are pressed by family or strangers to give up their ties to the group. It may be characterized by seemingly persistent delusional thinking regarding outsiders, in the absence of other psychotic symptoms, and may be born out of close association with others who have similar "delusions" (i.e., other members). These shared beliefs—particularly when paranoid in orientation—may be of considerable practical importance; they may serve as the basis for the highly deviant actions undertaken by some groups.

Another characteristic of open systems is transformation of input from the environment into output, which then is returned to the environment (Allport, 1965; Weber, 1922/1963). This can be used as a model for the charismatic group's religious conversion practices. They consist of transforming outsiders' attitudes and affiliative feelings (primarily among recruits) into ones compatible with those of the group (primarily among converts), which helps ensure the group's homeostasis (Ezriel, 1950). In addition to maintaining a needed level of group membership, conversion is perceived as a legitimization of the group's own ideology, thereby consolidating the commitment of its longstanding members.

All open systems must observe and regulate their own operations, a process called monitoring (Allport, 1965; Miller & Rice, 1967). This is accomplished by an individual leader or a hierarchical structure that defines work assignments and goals, interpreting them in relation to the group's ideology. The close interpersonal bonds and the physical proximity of the members of a charismatic group tend to ensure regulation of deviancy and implementation of group norms. They determine the basis for the consensual validation of members' perception of reality. The group may thus be expected to establish a milieu that promotes transcendental experiences, such as meditation and group prayer. The use of transcendental experience to enhance group religious commitment has been observed in cultural settings as varied as classical bacchanals and voodoo sects.

Most of the religious sects I have mentioned posit a significant role for their group in shaping the course of future events. This is important to the group because of the feedback it produces. Feedback is a function of the open system wherein a portion of its output returns to the system, serving to regulate the group's operation and maintain homeostasis. In this way, the group's behavior validates its own perspectives. Thus, the very undertaking of a grandiose scheme may be perceived as evidence of the divine powers of a charismatic leader. The zeal observed in new recruits is similarly understood as feedback that validates the group's ideology. Such feedback also plays a role in reinforcing behavior and supporting the commitment and self-esteem of individual members. Having presented our theoretical and research-based understandings of charismatic group process, I turn now to three illustrations.

CASE EXAMPLES

The impact of group forces is felt at each stage of membership in a charismatic group, from induction to stabilization to departure. The first case illustration, concerning the Unification Church, demonstrates the psychological forces at work in the church's evolution before it became more established in the general community.

The Unification Church

One recruitment format used by the Unification Church is the structured workshop series. In studying this recruitment setting (Galanter, 1980), I found that a sizable portion of participants (29%) agreed to stay beyond the weekend for which they were initially invited and that 9% joined after the entire three-week experience. Analysis of self-report data revealed that those who stayed beyond the first weekend—even those who did not later join—had become highly involved in the group process. This occurred both on the level of social cohesiveness and in terms of accepting the group's creed. Those who later joined the group, however, had experienced greater psychological distress before the workshops and felt less cohesive ties to friends and family outside the group. This suggests that people who demonstrate a modicum of interest in a charismatic group can easily become engaged on interpersonal and cognitive levels. Long-term engagement, however, may require the fertile soil of psychological distress and alienation.

Once a person joins a charismatic group, his or her behavior is typically subject to its control. This was evident in the marked decline in heavy drug and alcohol use effected by the Unification Church in its recruits, which continued in long-term members (Galanter et al., 1979). It was also illustrated by the nature of the engagement and marriage rituals of the Unification Church, because the norms espoused in these rituals deviated greatly from those of the U.S. middle class. For example, Reverend Moon himself selected the mates for almost all Church members. A large majority of Unification Church fiancés and fiancées (87%) reported that they felt no preference at all for a particular individual at the time Moon chose their mate for them, reflecting their compliance on a cognitive level. The affective impact of the aforementioned "relief effect" was evident in the distress associated with noncompliance; those contemplating severing their engagement were the most severely depressed subgroup of members.

In a three-year follow-up study of the engaged members, despite the remarkable deviant nature of the cult's marital customs, almost all (95%) were still active in the Unification Church and were married to fellow church members (88%). The members' commitment could be understood by recourse to the model of the pincer effect; on the one hand, the Church, like other charismatic groups, created distress by ordering deviant behaviors; on the other hand, it provided relief when members complied and maintained their commitments to the group.

Members' commitment to a charismatic group is remarkably persistent, even after they leave the group. For example, three years after their departure from the Unification Church, ex-members still maintained a considerable fidelity toward the group, although most of them were well-adjusted in the general community (Galanter, 1983). A sizable majority still cared strongly for the members they knew best and reported that they "got some positive things" out of their involvement with the group. This fidelity is evidence of the potential of a charismatic group for continuing its influence even after a member departs, as I shall show among self-help groups who operate along similar lines.

It is useful to consider how charismatic groups operate as social systems to understand why they elicit certain puzzling behaviors in their members. As members become part of the social system of the group, they become entrained in the system's need to assure its own stability. The behavior of individuals which may appear pathological, may reflect no more than responses induced in the group to assure its integrity. For example, one function of social systems is boundary control—protection from external disruptions. Such self-protectiveness is frequently seen in charismatic groups, often to the point of paranoia. It was evident in our findings on the Divine Light Mission (Galanter, 1978), where the single item that correlated most highly with improvement in a member's neurotic distress on joining was suspiciousness of outsiders; outsiders might undermine a recruit's commitment to the group. Similarly, a cult may implicitly suggest that members close themselves off from any outsider's influence. Because of this, some members may even manifest behavior something like dissociative phenomena when they feel that they are vulnerable. This is evident in the affective constriction and stereotyped behavior that Clark (1979) and Singer (1978) described as possibly meeting criteria for a dissociative disorder.

Christian Psychiatry

The psychology of charismatic groups can be highlighted by looking at related social phenomena that lie within the cultural mainstream but benefit as well from the qualities of this unique social phenomenon. Two examples of these are the Christian Psychiatry movement and AA. These also illustrate the role of charismatic group psychology in movements that operate within the mainstream, in a productive manner.

We will first examine what I call Christian Psychiatry. Christian Psychiatry is a broad-based national movement of psychiatrists who are evangelical Christians. Although most of adherents are not formally affiliated among themselves, the orientation of this movement is expressed in beliefs espoused by the Christian Medical and Dental Society, which has recently counted 7,500 health professionals among its members, 260 of whom are psychiatrists or physicians in psychiatry residency training. Applicants must sign a statement acknowledging "the final authority of the Bible as the word of God . . . , the presence and power of the Holy Spirit in the work of regeneration . . . , [and] the everlasting blessedness of the saved and the everlasting punishment of the lost."

We surveyed a sample of Christian Psychiatrists (Galanter, Larson, & Rubenstone, 1991) and found that in terms of demographics and practice variables, the respondents were similar to psychiatrists overall, but they were more strongly religiously oriented than the population overall. This latter difference, however, should be considered in light of a comparable, perhaps greater, disparity in belief between psychiatrists in general and the overall population. Whereas 56% of psychiatrists have been found to be agnostic or atheist (American Psychiatric Association, 1975), only 5% of the general public do not believe in God or a higher power (Religion in America, 1985). Psychiatrists' general lack of concern for religious matters is also evident in a review of major psychiatric journals conducted by Larson, Pattison, Blazer, Omran, & Kaplan (1989), which revealed that only

3% of published articles include a quantified religious variable. This is a rather small percentage considering how widespread religious belief is and the degree to which it can affect the cognitive issues relevant to both psychopathology and psychotherapeutic rehabilitation. The discrepancy between psychiatrists' beliefs and those of their patients is also underlined by a recent study by Kroll and Sheehan (1989) that found that 95% of a group of hospitalized psychiatric patients believed in God and a comparably large proportion espoused related religious beliefs.

The Christian Psychiatrists' incorporation of religious belief into treatments used in psychiatric practice is, however, a step beyond sensitivity to patients' beliefs. In taking such a step, the practitioner must depart from the norms for treatment learned in the officially sanctioned specialty training. This alteration may be understood by recourse to a model for religious influence described here. An intense religious experience of members was found in our study to yield relief from emotional distress, initially serving as a nidus for engaging commitment; indeed, 95% of the respondents said they had had "born again" experiences. Typically, such events were followed by a decline in distress and symptoms, an experience also reported by our respondents. Beliefs shared by a fundamentalist religious reference group were then acquired. This reference group provides a cognitive framework for behavior change. Our respondents came to espouse a set of strongly held beliefs, rooted in the Bible and promoted by born-again Christians; these shared beliefs legitimized their adoption of new standards of behavior. Finally, these converts became engaged in a cohesive group that sustains their involvement with the movement and that determined the consensual norms they adopted. For our respondents, measurements of cohesiveness revealed that it was quite high, comparable to what we found in the charismatic, cultic youth movements described above. This illustrates the dynamics of conversion in belief and subsequent affiliation in a cohesive group that profoundly shapes and reinforces behavior.

Alcoholics Anonymous

A perspective on charismatic groups can help explain more explicitly how zealous self-help movements achieve their widespread, generally positive clinical impact by means of psychotherapeutic factors often described as nonspecific (Frank, 1973). Such an understanding is crucial in light of the fact that over 12 million people in the United States now belong to self-help organizations, a figure that has doubled in the past decade (Brown, 1988). An appreciable portion of these individuals have joined zealous groups that address psychiatric problems ranging from kleptomania to schizophrenia.

The popularity of AA is illustrative of this. A worldwide membership of more than 1.5 million (General Service Office of Alcoholics Anonymous, 1987) testifies to the ability of AA to engage alcoholics and help them change their longstanding behaviors. AA's group process suggests that its operation as a charismatic group accounts for much of this success, as evident in the psychological forces described above. For example, the 12 steps of AA recovery, central to its belief system, are zealously espoused by its members. Members are highly cohesive and meet frequently—generally daily for the first three months. They form a mutually protective "social cocoon" (Rudy, 1986) and, like members of new religious movements, avoid outsiders if they threaten the group's ethos, which in this case is total abstinence.

The emergence of AA parallels the rise of charismatic religious groups in a number of ways. Bill W., its founder, was experiencing great despair when he had a revelatory experience that was clearly religious in nature:

> All at once I found myself crying out, "If there is a God, let Him show Himself!" Suddenly the room lit up with a great white light. . . . It seemed to me in my mind's eye that I was on a mountain and that a wind, not of air, but of spirit was blowing. (Thomsen, 1975, pp. 220–221)

Bill went on from this experience to preach to other alcoholics, and as with cultic groups described above, the forces of shared belief and group cohesiveness have become central in the engagement process of AA (Eckhardt, 1967; Trice & Roman, 1970). Furthermore, the program's evolution from these early origins to a large organization parallels the development of rituals and bureaucracy described by Weber for charismatic religions (Galanter, 1989a; Trice & Beyer, 1986).

These cases illustrate the psychological dynamics that are common to charismatic groups. In each, processes of conversion and affiliation, sustained through the cohesion of the group, influence significantly the identity, world view, and practices of the members.

PSYCHIATRIC AND PSYCHOLOGICAL INTERVENTION

The evaluation, diagnosis, and treatment of patients is a complex, clinical task. The complexity of this assignment is furthered in circumstances in which experiences fall within the intersection of psychiatric symptoms, on the one hand, and normative religious experience within a given religious group, on the other. This is further complicated by the fact that psychiatric difficulties can coexist with ecstatic spiritual experiences and normative religious affiliation and practice.

Our nomenclature for psychopathology raises certain problems in a clinical understanding of charismatic groups. In the first place, it was developed as a typology of mental illness rather than of social adaption.

Charismatic group experience, however, is essentially normal in certain contexts, as illustrated by the high incidence of hallucinatory phenomena reported by nonpsychotic individuals in the context of religious experience (Christensen, 1963; Galanter & Buckley, 1978; James, 1902/1929; Sedman & Hopkinson, 1966). The nomenclature was also developed specifically to describe the phenomena of individual behavior, whereas the zealous group phenomena mentioned here must be understood in relation to the demand characteristics of a group context. The demand characteristics in a psychological setting are cues, both implicit and explicit, that communicate what behavior is expected. This suggests that psychologists shift their focus from the psychology of the individual alone and consider also the psychology of the large group, which would also allow for more effective use of their diagnostic terminology in relation to individual members, for whom it is appropriate. As Lovinger (Chapter 12, this volume) points out, individual behavior needs to be assessed in terms of its normative status within the specific religion.

Returning to the perspective of individual psychology, however, the conversion experience is sometimes fraught with considerable turmoil, yielding a clinical picture that might be compatible with a diagnosis of pathology. The application of this diagnosis might rest on whether or not the clinician sees the individual's response as a maladaptive reaction with impairment of function, as specified in the definition of this syndrome. More commonly, the experience would be considered adaptive, particularly for certain isolated individuals (Shapiro, 1977) should their psychosocial functioning reflect increased effectiveness.

When conversion is characterized by transcendental experiences and the acceptance of a highly deviant belief system, the phenomenology may appear to mimic a brief reactive psychosis that includes an apparent stressor and the absence of previous major psychopathology. The diagnosis of pathology in this case may rest on the degree to which the experience conforms with a social reference group, rather than occurring in relative social isolation. The taking of a detailed history, as well as consultation with family members with the consent of the patient, is essential to assess the psychological status of the individual before induction into the charismatic group. A finding may be obtained that suggests the presence of a psychiatric illness that has been inadequately ameliorated or covered up by involvement in the group. Ultimately, psychologists must assess the extent to which a religious conversion leads a given patient either toward more constructive behavior and stable social behavior or toward a bizarre and destructive adaptation (Levin & Zegans, 1974).

Treatment of present or former members of charismatic groups requires a sensitive and respectful understanding of the beliefs and the affiliations of the patient. Both the adaptive and the maladaptive aspects of group membership need to be appreciated. Particular attention should be placed on the antecedents to joining the group as these reflect points of conflict or vulnerability that may not have been sufficiently addressed. Psychiatric and psychological treatment does not have as its aim the critique of religious faith and affiliation; however, psychological aspects of charismatic group involvement must not be considered off-limits for investigation. Rather, an examination is required that respects the autonomy of the patient and assesses mental status and behavior in respect to the normative practices of a given sect and the psychosocial functioning of the individual.

This issue can become particularly difficult for family members who equate "deviant" religious practice and disassociation from their normative group experience as de facto evidence of the presence of mental disorder. Controversy, both legal and psychiatric, exists over psychiatric and psychological intervention that is designed to "deprogram" an individual. The mental incompetency of the adult member must be evaluated and legally established in circumstances in which nonvoluntary treatment is recommended. Furthermore, the aim of such treatment would be primarily to reorient the subject to think for himself or herself and be independent of the cult leader. Objective criteria for evaluating the mental state of sect members must be developed to ascertain what levels of intervention, if any, are warranted. We also need models to relate current psychiatric terminology of our knowledge of the psychology of these groups.

Finally, an understanding of charismatic groups may increase our knowledge of aspects of healing processes that may be enlisted by the mental health community. The influence of group cohesion and the effects of beliefs on mental health and the amelioration of psychological distress require further study. Furthermore, an inspection of charismatic groups may provide useful information regarding the potential of religious institutions and other group movements to effect changes in psychological status.

REFERENCES

Adams, W. P., & Fox, R. J. (1972). Maintaining Jesus: The new trip. *Society, 9*, 50–56.

Allport, G. W. (1965). An open system for personality. In G. Lindsey & C. S. Hall (Eds.), *Theories of personality, primary sources in research* (pp. 231–239). New York: Wiley.

American Psychiatric Association. (1975). *Psychiatrists' viewpoints on religion and their services to religious institutions and the ministry: A report of a survey conducted by the task force on religion and psychiatry.* Washington, DC: Author.

Baker, F. (1970). General systems theory, research, and medical care. In A. Sheldon, F. Baker, & C. P. McLaughlin (Eds.), *Systems and medical care* (pp. 1–26). Cambridge, MA: Massachusetts Institute of Technology Press.

Bem, D. J. (1967). Self-perception: An alternative perception of cognitive dissonance phenomena. *Psychological Review, 74,* 183–200.

Bion, W. R. (1959). *Experiences in groups.* New York: Basic Books.

Blos, P. (1962). *On adolescence: A psychoanalytic interpretation.* New York: Free Press.

Brown, P. L. (1988, July 16). *Troubled millions heed call of self-help groups. The New York Times,* p. A1.

Cartright, D., & Zander, A. (Eds.). (1962). *Group dynamics: Research and theory.* Evanston, IL: Row Peterson.

Christensen, C. W. (1963). Religious conversion. *Archives of General Psychiatry, 9,* 207–216.

Clark, J. G., Jr. (1978). Problems in referral of cult members. *National Association of Private Psychiatric Hospitals Journal, 9*(4), 27–29.

Clark, J. G., Jr. (1979). Cults. *Journal of American Medical Association, 242,* 279–281.

Deutsch, A. (1975). Observations on a sidewalk ashram. *Archives of General Psychiatry, 32,* 166–175.

Deutsch, A. (1980). Tenacity of attachment to a cult leader: A psychiatric perspective. *American Journal of Psychiatry, 137,* 1569–1573.

Dupuy, H. (1973). *The psychological section of the current health and nutrition examination survey* (DHEW Publication No. 74-1214). Rockville, MD: National Center for Health Statistics.

Eckhardt, W. (1967). Alcoholic values and Alcoholics Anonymous. *Quarterly Studies of Alcoholism, 28,* 277–288.

Erikson, E. H. (1968). *Identity: Youth and crisis.* New York: Norton.

Etemad, B. (1978). Extrication from cultism. *Current Psychiatric Therapy, 18,* 217–223.

Ezriel, H. (1950). A psychoanalytic approach to group treatment. *British Journal of Medical Psychology, 23,* 59–74.

Favazza, A. R., & Faheem, A. D. (1983). Indigenous healing groups. In H. I. Kaplan & B. J. Saddock (Eds.), *Comprehensive group psychotherapy* (pp. 63–70). Baltimore, MD: Williams & Wilkins.

Ferster, C. B. (1958). Control of behavior in chimpanzees and pigeons by time out from positive reinforcement. *Psychology Monographs, 461.*

Festinger, L., Ricker, H. W., & Schacter, S. (1973). When prophecy fails. In R. I. Evans & R. M. Rozelle (Eds.), *Social psychology in life* (pp. 257–268). Boston: Allyn and Bacon.

Frank, J. (1973). *Persuasion and healing.* New York: Schocken.

Freud, S. (1955). Group psychology and the analysis of the ego. In J. Strachey (Ed.), *The standard edition of the complete psychological works of Sigmund Freud* (pp. 69–143). London: Hogarth. (Original work published 1921)

Galanter, M. (1978). The "relief effect": A sociobiological model for neurotic distress and large-group therapy. *American Journal of Psychiatry, 135,* 588–591.

Galanter, M. (1980). Psychological induction into the large-group: Findings from a contemporary religious sect. *American Journal of Psychiatry, 137,* 1574–1579.

Galanter, M. (1981). Sociobiology and informal social controls of drinking. *Journals on Studies of Alcohol, 42*(1), 64–79.

Galanter, M. (1982). Charismatic religious sects and psychiatry. *American Journal of Psychiatry, 139,* 1539–1548.

Galanter, M. (1983). Unification Church ("Moonie") dropouts: Psychological readjustments after leaving a charismatic religious group. *American Journal of Psychiatry, 140,* 984–988.

Galanter, M. (1989a). *Cults: Faith, healing and coercion.* Oxford, England: Oxford University Press.

Galanter, M. (Ed.). (1989b). *Cults and new religious movements: A report of the American Psychiatric Association.* Washington, DC: American Psychiatric Press.

Galanter, M. (1990). Cults and zealous self-help movements: A psychiatric perspective. *American Journal of Psychiatry, 147,* 543–551.

Galanter, M., & Buckley, P. (1978). Evangelical religion and meditation: Psychotherapeutic effects. *Journal of Nervous Mental Disorders, 166,* 685–691.

Galanter, M., Larson, D., & Rubenstone, E. (1991). Christian psychiatry: The impact of evangelical beliefs on clinical practice. *American Journal of Psychiatry, 148,* 90–95.

Galanter, M., Rabkin, J., Rabkin, R., & Deutsch, A. (1979). The "Moonies": A psychological study. *American Journal of Psychiatry, 136,* 165–170.

General Service Office of Alcoholics Anonymous. (1987). *World A.A. directory.* New York: A. A. World Services.

Glock, C. Y., & Stark, R. (1965). *Religion and society in tension.* Chicago: Rand McNally.

Gordon, D. (1974). The Jesus people: An identity crisis. *Urban Life and Culture, 3,* 159–178.

Harder, M. W., Richardson, J. T., & Simmonds, R. (1976). Life style: Courtship, marriage and family in a changing Jesus movement organization. *International Review of Modern Sociology, 6,* 155–172.

Hardyck, J. A., & Braden, M. (1962). Prophecy fails again: A report of a failure of replicate. *Journal of Abnormal Social Psychology, 65,* 136–141.

Jacobsen, E. (1964). *The self and the object world.* New York: International Universities Press.

James, W. (1929). *The varieties of religious experience.* New York: Modern Library. (Original work published 1902)

Kaplan, B., & Johnson, D. (1964). The social meaning of the Navajo psychopathology. In A. Kiev (Ed.), *Magic, faith, and healing* (pp. 203–229). New York: Free Press.

Kennedy, J. G. (1967). Nubian Zar ceremonies and psychotherapy. *Human Organization, 4*, 185.

Kilbourne, B., & Richardson, J. T. (1984). Psychotherapy and new religions in a pluralistic society. *American Psychologist, 39*, 237–251.

Kleinman, A., & Gale, J. G. (1982). Patients treated by physicians and folk healers: A comparative outcome study in Taiwan. *Culture, Medicine and Psychiatry, 6*, 405–423.

Kroll, J., & Sheehan, W. (1989). Religious beliefs and practices among 52 psychiatry inpatients in Minnesota. *American Journal of Psychiatry, 146*, 67–72.

Kumasaka, Y. (1966). Soka Gakki: Group psychology study of new religiopolitical organization. *American Journal of Psychiatry, 20*, 462–470.

Larson, D. B., Pattison, E. M., Blazer, D. G., Omran, A. R., & Kaplan, B. H. (1989). Systematic analysis of research on religious on religious variables in four major psychiatric journals, 1978-1982. *American Journal of Psychiatry, 143*, 329–334.

Leighton, A., & Leighton, D. (1941). Elements of psychotherapy in Navajo religion. *Psychiatry, 4*, 515–523.

Levine, S. (1983). Alienated Jewish youth and religious seminaries. In D. A. Halperin (Ed.), *Psychodynamic perspectives on religion, sect, and cult* (pp. 267–276). Boston: John Wright PSG.

Levine, S. V., & Salter, N. E. (1976). Youth and contemporary religious movements: Psychological findings. *Canadian Psychiatric Association, 21*, 411–420.

Levin, T. M., & Zegans, L. S. (1974). Adolescent identity crisis and religious conversion: Implications for psychotherapy. *British Journal of Medical Psychology, 47*, 73–82.

Lifton, R. J. (1961). *Thought reform and the psychology of totalism.* New York: Norton.

Lofland, J. (1977). Becoming a world-saver revisited. *American Behavioral Scientist, 20*, 805–818.

Lofland, J., & Stark, R. (1965). Becoming a world-saver: A theory of conversion to a deviant perspective. *American Sociological Review, 30*, 862–875.

Miller, E. J., & Rice, A. K. (1967). *Systems of organization.* London: Tavistock.

Minuchin, S., Montalvo, B., & Guerney, B. J. R. (1967). *Families of the slums.* New York: Basic Books.

Nagy, I. B., & Spark, G. (1973). *Invisible loyalties.* New York: Harper & Row.

Needleman, J., & Baker, G. (Eds.). (1978). *Understanding new religions.* New York: Seabury Press.

Nicholi, A. M. I. (1974). A new dimension of the youth culture. *American Journal of Psychiatry, 131*(4), 369–401.

Ofshe, R. (1976). Synanon: The people business. In C. Y. Glock & R. N. Bellah (Eds.), *The new religious consciousness* (pp. 116–137). Berkeley: University of California Press.

Pattison, E. M., Labins, N. A., & Doerr, H. A. (1973). Faith healing: A study of personality and function. *Journal of Nervous and Mental Disease, 157*(6), 367–409.

Pattison, M. (1977). A theoretical-empirical base for social systems therapy. In *Current perspectives in cultural psychiatry* (pp. 217–254). New York: Tavistock.

Proudfoot, W., & Shaver, P. (1976). Attribution theory and the psychology of religion. *Journal for the Scientific Study of Religion, 14*, 317–330.

Religion in America. (1985). Gallup report 236. Princeton, NJ: Gallup Organization.

Richardson, J. T., & Stewart, M. (1977). Conversion process models and the Jesus movement. *American Behavioral Scientist, 20*, 819–838.

Roberts, F. J. (1965). Some psychological factors in religious conversion. *British Journal of Social Clinical Psychology, 65*, 185–187.

Rodin, M. B. (1985). Getting on the program: A biocultural analysis of Alcoholics Anonymous. In L. Bennett & G. M. Ames (Eds.), *The American experience with alcohol: Contrasting cultural perspectives* (pp. 41–58). New York: Plenum Press.

Rudy, D. R. (1986). *Becoming alcoholic: Alcoholics Anonymous and the reality of alcoholism.* Carbondale: Southern Illinois University Press.

Salzman, L. (1953). The psychology of religious and mystical conversion. *Psychiatry, 16*, 177–187.

Schwartz, L. L., & Kaslow, F. W. (1979). Religious cults, the individual and the family. *Journal of Marital and Family Therapy*, April, 15–26.

Sedman, G., & Hopkinson, G. (1966). The psychopathology of mystical and religious conversion experiences in psychiatric patients: I, II. *Confinia Psychiatrica, 9*, 1–19, 65–77.

Shapiro, E. (1977). Destructive cultist. *Family Physician, 15*, 80–83.

Simmonds, R. B., Richardson, J. T., & Harder, M. W. (1976). A Jesus movement group: An adjacent checklist assessment. *Journal for the Scientific Study of Religion, 15*, 323–337.

Simon, J. (1978). Observations on 67 patients who took Erhard Seminars Training. *American Journal of Psychiatry, 135*, 686–691.

Singer, M. (1978). Therapy with ex-cult members. *National Association of Private Psychiatric Hospitals Journal, 9*(4), 14–18.

Singer, M., & Borrero, M. G. (1984). Indigenous treatment for alcoholism: The case of Puerto Rican spiritualism. *Medical Anthropology: Cross-Cultural Studies in Health and Illness, 8*, 246–273.

Sterba, R. (1968). Remarks on mystic states. *American Imago, 25*, 77–85.

Thomsen, R. (1975). *Bill W* (pp. 220–221). New York: Harper & Row.

Trice, H. M., & Beyer, J. M. (1986). The routinization of charisma in two movement organizations. In B. M. Staw & B. L. Cummings (Eds.), *Research in organizational behavior* (Vol 8, 113–164).

Trice, H. M., & Roman, P. M. (1970). Sociopsychological predictors of affiliation with Alcoholics Anonymous: A longitudinal study of "treatment success." *Social Psychiatry, 5,* 51–59.

Ungerleider, J. T., & Wellisch, D. K. (1979). Coercive persuasion (brainwashing), religious cults, and deprogramming. *American Journal of Psychiatry, 136,* 279–282.

Von Bertalanffy, L. (1974). General systems and psychiatry. In S. Arieti (Ed.), *American handbook of psychiatry* (2nd ed.; Vol. 1; pp. 1095–1117). New York: Basic Books.

Weber, M. (1963, 1922). *The sociology of religion.* Boston: Beacon Press.

Wenegrat, B. (1989). Religious cult membership: A sociobiologic model. In M. Galanter (Ed.), *Report on cults and new religious movements* (pp. 193–210). Washington, DC: American Psychiatric Association.

Wilson, W. P. (1972). Mental health benefits of religious salvation. *Diseases of the Nervous System, 33,* 382–386.

11

VALUES IN PSYCHOTHERAPY

ALLEN E. BERGIN, I. REED PAYNE, and P. SCOTT RICHARDS

The purpose of this chapter is to discuss the relationship between values and psychotherapy. The major premise is that a value-free or value-neutral approach to psychotherapy has become untenable and is being supplanted by a more open and more complete value-informed perspective (Bergin, 1991). Interest regarding the place of value issues in psychotherapy has accelerated in the past decade or two. Religious and spiritual values in particular have been extensively addressed in the therapeutic context, although mainstream psychology is only beginning to show awareness of this formerly taboo area (Bergin, 1980a). Biases and stereotypes against religiosity are giving way to empirical findings showing positive relationships between mental health markers and committed religiosity. Prevalence of religious and spiritual beliefs and practices is high among the American public and stronger among mental health professionals than had been assumed.

A clear consensus on some values, of both clinical and traditional origins, among mental health professionals gives evidence of a potential common value foundation (Jensen & Bergin, 1988). However, diversity concerning many other values among clients and therapists challenges the profession to honor individual integrity and provide an ethical experience where growth and change can occur within one's value framework. Given the empirical findings that there may be movement in therapy of client values toward therapist values (Beutler & Bergan, 1991), though not consistently (Kelly & Strupp, 1992), it is essential that relevant values become explicit so informed choice is possible and autonomy remains a reality. Opening the values domain widely to include the religious and spiritual raises new issues regarding professional training and competence to deal respectfully with such dimensions of human experience. According to psychology's revised ethical guidelines (APA, 1992), responsiveness to religious diversity has become not only an opportunity but also an obligation. This is not to disparage traditional training or standard therapeutic approaches, which must continue to be regarded as foundational to any therapeutical endeavor. Rather, we suggest that integrative advances will continue to bring together techniques derived from standard as well as religious and spiritual resources.

This value-laden enterprise holds exciting promise but not without concerns and cautions. Disputes over values will continue, requiring even greater tolerance and understanding. Value awareness, issues of boundaries, skill and training, autonomy of clients, and respect for individual values tax psychologists' capacities in conducting this secular and moral encounter ethically and productively.

BACKGROUND, HISTORY, AND ISSUES

At one time, theorists, researchers, and psychotherapists believed that values could be kept out of psychological theory, research, and practice (Patterson, 1958). It was assumed that therapists could be a "blank slate;" an objective, scientific technician; or a nonjudgmental, nonevaluatory listener and facilitator. The major psychotherapy orientations, referred to by Bergin (1980a) as clinical pragmatism and humanistic idealism, were developed under this assumption.

Beginning in the late 1940s and continuing into the 1960s and 1970s, the belief that values could be kept out of psychological theory, research, and practice was challenged theoretically and empirically (Beutler, 1972; Kessell & McBrearty, 1967; Patterson, 1958). By the late 1970s to early 1980s, it was widely agreed that it was impossible to keep values completely out of psychological work (Bergin, 1980a, Beutler, 1979; Howard, 1985; Patterson, 1989). Despite the growing awareness that values are embedded in psychological theories, research, and practice, these value assumptions remained largely hidden behind technical and theoretical language.

In addition, the fact that the major psychological and psychotherapeutic orientations contained implicit world views and value assumptions that conflicted with the beliefs and value assumptions of theistic and spiritual perspectives was widely disregarded. Psychology's long-standing historical bias against theistic and spiritual perspectives continued and remained unchallenged and, by many, unrecognized.

Bergin's (1980a) article attempted to clarify the situation. It (a) documented the growing interest in and concern with values issues (particularly spiritual values) among helping professionals; (b) made explicit many of the value assumptions that had been implicitly embedded in the major therapeutic orientations of the profession; (c) explicitly described the beliefs and value assumptions of a theistic and spiritual world view; (d) showed where the value assumptions of clinical pragmatism and humanistic idealism conflict with the value positions of the theistic and spiritual perspective; (e) confronted the profession with its long-standing negative bias against religious and spiritual values; (f) challenged psychologists and therapists to be more open about their values and less subtly coercive with clients; (g) encouraged therapists to be more culturally sensitive and respectful toward clients who approach life from diverse value perspectives, including theistic and spiritual ones; and (h) called for an infusion or restoration of theistic and spiritual values into mainstream psychology and psychotherapy, on the basis of careful scholarship and a program of empirical research.

This appeal to respect the spiritual orientations of the majority of clients, and to restore theistic perspectives into clinical psychology, met with resistance from some (e.g., Ellis, 1980; Seligman, 1988; Walls, 1980) because many professionals held stereotypical views about religion and theistic people (i.e., that religion and belief in God is irrational, less mature, or damaging). Just as women and various racial and ethnic minority groups had to confront helping professionals with the stereotypes they held, religious professionals (see Bergin, 1980b; Collins, 1977; Strommen, 1984; Vitz, 1977) had to confront professionals' deeply held stereotypes and prejudices toward theistic and spiritual beliefs and people.

Despite scattered opposition, more than 1,000 professional people responded to Bergin's (1980a) article, and many prominent individuals endorsed its general themes without necessarily agreeing with every specific value. Among these people were well-known leaders in psychology and psychiatry, such as Ellen Berscheid, Karl Menninger, Hans Strupp, Robert Sears, Albert Bandura, and Carl Rogers (Bergin, 1985). Their support instituted a powerful endorsement to proceed, and as a result, many people were encouraged to pursue these issues further (Bergin, 1988a, 1988b, 1991).

An empirical evidence has accumulated, the simplistic, culturally encapsulated stereotype that religiously devout people are more emotionally disturbed or less rational and intelligent than less religious people has given way to a more thoughtful, culturally sensitive perspective that affirms the beneficial aspects of theistic and spiritual beliefs and values, while acknowledging that some beliefs and practices can be used in harmful, dysfunctional ways (Bergin, 1991; Richards, 1991; Richards, Smith, & Davis, 1989). With this more balanced understanding, the door has been opened to a consideration of how such beliefs, values, and practices can be approached therapeutically to enhance clients' well-being (Bergin, 1988a, 1988b, 1991; Bergin & Payne, 1991; Payne, Bergin, & Loftus, 1992; Richards & Potts, 1995).

Although these developments represent a step forward, they also create a new dilemma of whether some values may be universal as opposed to being culture-specific or situation-specific. Current guidelines and recommendations for multiculturally sensitive therapy are problematic because they implicitly advocate an ethically relativistic therapist stance that suggests the world views and values of different cultures are equally valuable and true. Although it is important for therapists to be tolerant of differences and to respect clients' rights to hold values that differ from their own, an ethically relativistic position implies that therapists should agree with all client values or accept clients' values as equally good or valid. This extreme position is a world view or value assumption itself. Both Kitchener (1980) and Bergin (1980c) have discussed why an ethically relativistic stance is logically inconsistent with the goals of behavior (and other) therapies because whenever therapists advocate and pursue specific goals of change (which all therapists do) they cease to be relativists. The relativistic position creates other problems in the therapeutic situation because it sometimes becomes clear that clients' values have negative emotional or physical consequences. Therapists who adopt a relativistic stance cannot logically challenge destructive client values because all values are assumed to be equally worthwhile.

It has been shown that a majority of helping professionals believe that peoples' values and lifestyles have an impact on mental health and emotional functioning and that some values do more to promote mental health than others (Jensen & Bergin, 1988). Thus, therapists should acknowledge that they are value agents and endorse values and lifestyles they believe enhance mental health (London, 1986; Lowe, 1976); however, this should be based on evidence and open professional debate.

Advocating or promoting certain mental health values must be done sensitively and with regard and respect for the client's right to disagree and differ from the therapist. An explicit and nonrelativistic therapist stance about values, along with a tolerance for differences, is advocated, therefore, instead of an implicit and relativistic therapist stance (Bergin, 1985, 1991).

Despite the increased recognition of the importance of values, including spiritual ones, the profession still has much room for progress in this domain. A great deal of confusion, uncertainty, and ambiguity about how to actually handle value issues during psychotherapy still exists. APA itself contributes to this confusion by sending mixed messages and adopting double standards for dealing with value issues. APA ethical standards advocate respect and tolerance for cultural and individual differences, but then APA endorses and advocates some value positions (e.g., regarding abortion and sexual behavior) that demonstrate insensitivity to the cultural beliefs and values of many people (e.g., Richards, 1993). We hope this chapter will be step forward by bringing about a greater awareness of (a) value and valuing issues; (b) empirical and theoretical import of value integration in an eclectic approach to therapy; (c) diversity needs balanced by mental health universals pertaining to practice and training; and (d) cautions as we explore this domain of personal beliefs and assumptions, a uniquely human endeavor.

ATTENDING TO THE CLIENT'S VALUES AND ENGAGING THE THERAPIST'S VALUES

A client already confused about what is important and how to obtain more satisfaction in life will find even greater perplexity with a therapist who denigrates values that may be tenaciously held by the client and central to his or her existence. The secularization of life and the humanistic elevation of the individual to the ultimate position of meaning poses a special dilemma for those who see life in terms of the sacred and transcendent and in terms of social responsibility rather than self-focus.

Kudlac (1991) stated "From a languaging perspective, it is not necessary for the therapist to subscribe to the same beliefs held by the client; however, to be able to fully enter into a conversation, these beliefs must be addressed" (p. 281). In the context of family therapy and family systems, Kudlac added "If God is part of the problem-organized system, then God must be part of the solution" (p. 284).

Experiencing empathy for clients, knowing something of their struggle and identifying with their dilemmas, depends on comprehending their beliefs, their moral framework, and their assumptive world. This understanding is approximated by being open to the client's perceptions and taking the position of being informed by the client. Therapists are often urged to set aside their filters, abandon censoring schemas, and place their own values and priorities in temporary abeyance while absorbing the other's constructs of reality, hoping to appreciate the client's world and grasp the essence of their problems before engaging the therapist's own values in the process. If clients invoke religious and spiritual conceptions, so much the better—if that is what and how they think. While some therapists are reluctant to introduce or initiate religious and spiritual concerns, should they shrink from them when they occur? We think not. Values are pertinent to the nature of being human (Harari, 1989). Helping people clarify their own values may be the most important aspect of therapy (Smiley, 1985).

Havenarr (1990) takes psychotherapeutic theories to task for not acknowledging that the systems of beliefs, values, and behavioral patterns inherent in various cultures play an important role in psychotherapy. Psychotherapeutic and anthropological research between 1936 and the 1980s has shown common beliefs about illnesses and cures shared by both therapist and patient are central factors in determining illness behavior and outcomes of psychotherapy. Havenarr, therefore, proposes that psychotherapy promotes healing by culture. Values, commonalities, language, and expectations all become relevant.

The therapy process, as it incorporates the valuing dimension, raises several issues (Bergin, 1991) about how to proceed. For instance, increased disclosure of relevant therapist values or valuing processes becomes essential. Informing clients of therapists' educated opinions and of alternatives is important but should also be balanced by respectful patience and noninterference, even when bad choices are being made. Therapists participate in goal setting, including judgments of how to effectively modify the disorder and maintain lasting change. With the client, they must mutually establish the goals of therapy. "Therapist experience and conviction can be helpful, but wisdom and self-restraint are equally relevant" (Bergin, 1991, p. 397). The client's move from initial dependency to eventual independence requires trust in the therapeutic frame of reference, stimulation of guided growth, clarification and testing of value choices, and a gradual decrease in external advice and nurturance while increasing autonomy and maturity.

On the issue of value similarities and difference, an intermediate range of values similarity between client and therapist may help predict positive outcomes. Goldsmith and Hansen (1991) suggest the proposition that values of medium centrality offer therapists optimal possibilities for effective interventions. Martinez (1991) observed that clients more often rated their improvement higher when their religious values initially differed from their therapist or when therapists were more conservative than the clients. But the therapist's rating of client improvement was related to initial dissimilarity only when the client's initial religious orientation was less conservative than the therapist's. Value convergence was not related to client self-improvement ratings. Although many clinicians and researchers concede that counseling is a value-laden enterprise, the nature of the values that most influence process and outcome in therapies is unclear (Beutler & Bergan, 1991).

Within the basic beliefs or meaning systems of an individual, several value agenda items might be therapeutically addressed, without dislodging core constructs. Illustrative of these possibilities are value clarification, which places the client in the driver's seat with a better grasp of his or her commitments and valuing process; value ordering, which may assist with a self-examination of priorities; value realization, which calls attention to a congruence or lack thereof between what one does and what is said to be valued; value discovery, which alludes to the unconscious or subconscious holding of values expressed indirectly through behaviors and verbalizations but without awareness; and value enhancement, which implies the reach toward more effective means of implementing values.

RELIGION AND MENTAL HEALTH

The research on religion and mental health provides some empirical justification for viewing religious and spiritual values of clients as a possible resource in therapy. Support for this position is demonstrable in the cumulative relationships between religiosity and mental health markers (Bergin, 1991; Larson et al., 1992).

Early research relating mental health with religiosity asked the question "Is the person religious?" The relationships between religion measures and pathology measures were sometimes equivocal, sometimes negative. As research has gained sophistication and awareness of biases, the question has become "How is the person religious?" (Payne, Bergin, Bielema, & Jenkins, 1991). This was prompted by Allport and Ross's (1967) analysis of intrinsic and extrinsic religiosity. The intrinsic orientation is characterized as involving sincere commitment that functions as a central motivation in a person's life. Intrinsic individuals internalize their beliefs and live by them with less regard for external consequences. In contrast, the extrinsic orientation is more utilitarian. Religion is therefore used to obtain status, security, sociability, and self-justification. Recent and extensive research on this dual dimension of religiosity has shown, with few exceptions, that positive mental health indexes are generally aligned with intrinsicness, and extrinsicness is paired with less healthy and sometimes pathological or negative correlates (Donahue, 1985).

A more recent review by Masters and Bergin (1992) also concluded that intrinsic religiousness is positively related to mental health. But what is it about being intrinsically religious that is beneficial? The authors suggest that at the base of this effect is a sense of purpose and meaning in life. Also, it is possible that strength of conviction to these world views is equally important.

It is hypothesized that beneficial mental health consequences are an outcome of congruence or behaving in synchrony with one's religious values (Pargament, Steele, & Tyler, 1979), whereas acting contrary to personal values results in dissonance, with consequences of guilt, anxiety, despair, or alienation (Mickleburgh, 1992). If commitment is, then, all important, what are the ramifications of particular types of commitment? Donahue (1989) argues that theology may be important to the psychology of religion and that relevant cognitive structures and religious beliefs need to be understood in terms of their association with various outcomes.

Relevant to therapeutic thinking is a study examining the lifestyles and mental health of religious students (18–21 years old) at a major university, which found disciplined and emotionally interdependent lifestyles associated with better mental health (Bergin, Stinchfield, Gaskin, Masters, & Sullivan, 1988). Individuals deviating from their moral standards appeared more disturbed than those who followed their beliefs. Self-justification for deviation also related to pathology. These findings are contrary to the notion that religiousness is negatively related to mental health (Albee, 1991; Ellis, 1980).

During a 3-year follow-up study (Masters, Bergin, Reynolds, & Sullivan, 1991) 8 homogeneous samples of intrinsically religious-oriented students became even more intrinsic. Experiences of doing missionary work over a 2-year period were associated with higher (a) self-esteem, (b) purpose in life, (c) social consciousness, and (d) spirituality. Religious orthodoxy was again found to be compatible with mental health.

A review of studies relating religion and mental health (Payne et al., 1991) noted numerous positive correlates between certain religious measures (e.g., intrinsic) and mental health variables such as a sense of well-being, self-esteem, family relations, sexual conduct and adjustment, and abstinence from alcohol and drugs. These positive relationships may possibly emanate from (a) an overlap or correlation of mental health values and religious values; (b) some forms of religiosity being congruent with growth, achievement, stability, family cohesion, and self-actualization; (c) some religiously encouraged developmental patterns may be prosocial; and (d) a sense of destiny, purpose, and transcendent meaning may provide continuity and guidance over time.

In general, the recent literature amply supports the therapeutic potential of healthy spiritual commitments. Religion emerges as a promising ally.

PREVALENCE OF RELIGIOUS AND SPIRITUAL COMMITMENT

What is the extent of religious and spiritual commitment and how do clients and therapists compare? In a sample of psychiatric patients, Kroll and Sheehan (1989) found that 95% believed in God. Gallup surveys show that 95% of Americans believe in a universal spirit or God and as many as 87% claim to pray (Religion in America, 1985). One third of the U.S. population endorses religious commitment as the most important dimension of their lives. Religion was considered a very important factor for another one third of the population. Bergin and Jensen (1990) suggest that for this two thirds of the population, secular approaches to psychotherapy may provide an alien values framework. The majority of the population probably prefers an orientation to therapy that is sympathetic or at least sensitive to their spiritual perspectives.

Findings from the national survey by Bergin and Jensen (1990) of 425 therapists representing 59% of the sampling of clinical psychologists, psychiatrists, clinical social workers, and marriage and family therapists show that a large proportion (80%) claim some type of religious preference. The largest group in this survey consisted of Protestant, at 38%. The second largest group consisted of agnostic, atheistic, humanistic, or none, at 20%. If one uses attendance at religious services as a measure of religiosity, regular attenders accounted for 41%, whereas occasional attenders or nonattenders totaled 59%. Another measurement of therapists' religiousness was assessed by the Religious Orientation scale (Allport & Ross, 1967). Results categorized 100 respondents as intrinsically religious, 20 as extrinsically religious, 102 as proreligious (high on both extrinsic and intrinsic), 89 as nonreligious (low in both extrinsic and intrinsic), and 106 as not having responded. By these measures, 54% are classified as religious, which is consistent with another earlier estimate of 50% by Ragan, Malony, and Beit-Hallahmi (1980).

The Gallup poll estimates 91% of the public shows a denominational religious preference, which is higher than the 80% of the professional sample in the Bergin and Jensen (1990) survey. Another comparison based on religious attendance and lifestyle commitment shows a surprising similarity between 41% of therapists who attend services regularly and 40% of the public who are regularly attenders. The Bergin and Jensen survey also noted that 77% of therapists attempt to live according to their religious beliefs, compared with 84% of the general public.

The foregoing information is important because it shows that a large proportion of the therapists' clientele approach life from a religious and spiritual perspective, while therapists also have considerably more interest than they show in professional contexts. If therapists are going to be culturally sensitive to and respect our clients' values, they need to acknowledge that clients' religious values are every bit as important as their racial, ethnic, gender, or cultural background; and they need to be more comfortable with their own spirituality at the same time.

VALUES AMONG PSYCHOTHERAPISTS

A national interdisciplinary value survey of clinical psychologists, marriage and family therapists, social workers, and psychiatrists was also conducted to assess the degree of value consensus (Jensen & Bergin, 1988).

Values already present in theory and application, as expressed by mental health practitioners, were carefully selected across several content areas. Pilot work and refinements resulted in these value themes: (a) competent perception and expression of feelings, (b) freedom/autonomy/responsibility, (c) integration/coping ability, (d) self-maintenance/physical fitness, (e) self-awareness/growth, (f) human relatedness/interpersonal commitment, (g) mature frame of orientation, (h) forgiveness, (i) regulated sexual fulfillment, and (j) spiritual/religiosity (p. 291).

Findings of this survey supported the consensus believed to exist in the literature with the first seven themes. The eighth theme of forgiveness had substantial but slightly less consensus, whereas themes nine and ten (sex and religion) yielded considerable diversity. Through an analysis of demographic variables it was seen that the values psychotherapists endorse for mental health are a result of both professional concepts and traditional values. Jensen and Bergin (1988) note high agreement with traditional values such as self-control, forgiveness of others, work satisfaction, and family commitment. The more clinically labeled values concerning psychological autonomy, communication skills, self-awareness, and interpersonal affection also received high endorsement.

Data (Jensen & Bergin, 1988) also showed that one's personal orientation and lifestyle influenced concepts of mentally healthy behavior. For example, higher scores on religiosity corresponded with greater likelihood of the therapist endorsing religious values as important to psychotherapy and mental health. Professionals in their first marriages regarded marital values more highly than other groups. Psychiatrists and older therapists valued self-maintenance and physical fitness more than did nonphysicians and younger professionals. Dynamic therapists felt that self-awareness and growth values were more salient to mental health and psychotherapy than did behavior therapists. The areas of nonconsensus, sex and religion, are the same areas where therapists and client values tend to differ the most. Nonreligious therapists diverge on these points from most other therapists and clients as well.

For the sake of coherence and viability there is an ethical and professional need for articulated values having consensual validation to serve as goals, objectives, and purposes overarching the practice of psychotherapy. Equally viable is the need to be open to individual value differences.

The process of making implicit values explicit in therapy has been expressed as an important step by Bergin (1985, 1991), Lovinger (1984), and Tan (1988, 1993). Bergin's point is that greater personal freedom in the therapeutic environment may actually be the outcome of making values explicit. Open deliberation then becomes a possibility and hidden agendas obscuring implicit values no longer dominate with their subtle influences.

Tan (1993) goes further in making personal values of both the client and the therapist explicit by using religiously derived techniques in the therapeutic process when appropriate and agreed on. He cautioned "Such an explicitly religious approach to therapy should be conducted in a clinically sensitive, ethically responsible, and professionally competent way" (p. 7).

Shapiro (1990) concludes that considerable therapeutic benefits are available if therapists become aware of their own values and the degree to which this is revealed to their patients. Authorization for therapists to attend to their own values as well as those of their clients is found in the concepts of pluralism and diversity.

VALUES, DIVERSITY, AND PROFESSIONAL TRAINING

In APA's ethical principles update (1992), principle D addresses the issue of diversity with respect to rights and dignity:

> Psychologists accord appropriate respect to the fundamental rights, dignity, and worth of all people. They respect the rights of individuals to privacy, confidentiality, self-determination, and autonomy, mindful that legal and other obligations may lead to inconsistency and conflict with the exercise of these rights. Psychologists are aware of culture, individual, and role differences, including those due to age, gender, race, ethnicity, national origin, religion, sexual orientation, disability, language, and socioeconomic status. Psychologists try to eliminate the effect on their work of biases based on those factors, and they do not knowingly participate in or condone unfair discriminatory practices. (p. 3)

This general principle defines diversity more broadly than in previous versions. In doing so, diversity has come to include strange bedfellows, of which religion may appear to be the strangest—in an otherwise liberal mind-set. According to this ethical principle, professionals in psychology should no longer exercise the option of ignoring, denigrating, or blatantly doing battle with the spiritual realm of human diversity. APA (1992) standards further state in *Ethical Principles of Psychologists and Code of Conduct*, Section 1.08 (Human Differences):

> Where differences of age, gender, race, ethnicity, national origin, religion, sexual orientation, disability, language, or socioeconomic status significantly affect psychologists' work concerning particular individuals or groups, psychologists obtain the training, experience, consultation, or supervision necessary to ensure the competence of their services, or they make appropriate referrals. (p. 5)

This principle puts new light on the therapeutic process. Religion is now a legitimate part of human diversity and must be afforded the same consideration in therapy as all other forms of diversity.

Training and supervision of professional psychologists dealing with religious diversity have been recently articulated (Tan, 1993). Guidelines suggested by Tan for those providing services and therapy to religious people include:

1. Provide systematic training on religious diversity and religious issues and values. Both formal and informal avenues of instruction are detailed. The model is the same as for other diversity issues.

2. Provide exposure or course work in psychology of religion with its social-psychological and empirical foundations relevant to psychotherapy, religion, and health.

3. Encourage open-mindedness of supervisors in exploring religious issues as they arise in treatment and assessment. Openness to utilizing spiritual resources is suggested. Countertransference issues in the religious context of therapy should be addressed.

4. More training and supervision in prevention and community psychology skills is needed. Working more directly with religious leaders and lay counselors may be important to prevention and maintenance.

5. Networking with other schools and programs where an integration of faith and psychology has been attempted would provide support and direction. Fuller Theological Seminary's Graduate School of Psychology and Rosemead School of Psychology at Biola University are cited as two examples. Resources and expertise can be usefully shared.

Since August 1990, Division 36 of APA has sponsored a continuing education workshop at the annual convention of "Psychotherapy With Religiously Committed Clients" conducted by Shafranske, Tan, and Lovinger.

The workshop has focused on six points in helping the participants (Tan, 1993):

1. Identify religious themes within client presentation.
2. Recognize the potential influence of religious and cultural application on the client's perception of his or her psychological difficulties.
3. Understand the sources of resistance and support of the psychotherapeutic process that have their origin in religion.
4. Use the religious world view of the client to support therapeutic change and use interventions of a religious nature.
5. Identify systems of support within religious traditions.
6. Consult with religious professionals with a clearer understanding of their perspective.

Tan alludes to a "growing body of literature" that can be used in the training of professional psychologists who might choose to work with religiously committed clients (Bradford & Spero, 1990; Lovinger, 1984, 1990;

Malony, 1988; Miller & Martin, 1988; Propst, 1988; Shafranske, 1990; Spero, 1985; Stern, 1985; Worthington, 1989, 1991). Other useful resources include Bergin (1980a, 1991), Jones (1994), Tan (1993), Tjeltveit (1986), Vachon and Agresti (1992), and Worthington (1988).

O'Donohue (1989) proposes an "(even) Bolder Model" of clinical training that recognizes the clinical psychologist as "metaphysician-scientist-practitioner." O'Donohue sees metaphysical statements as internal to all the sciences. Issues of abnormality are interwoven with judgments about human nature, morality, the good life, and so on. O'Donohue suggests people's beliefs are influenced by religious commitments. Similarly, Tjeltveit (1992) argues for the therapist's functioning as an ethicist in the value laden process of therapy.

Jones and Wilcox (1993) document why this is so in their suggestion that theories in psychology are "under-determined by the data" and metaphysical assumptions influence the general view of psychology's subject matter, choice of problem statements, and the types of hypotheses generated and commitment to psychological theories. In this framework, values become an integral part of psychological theories and are in fact locked into the assumptions forming the backdrop of the theories, as has been eloquently stated earlier by Frank and Frank (1991), Szasz (1978), and others. The psychotherapy process thus incorporates values out of necessity because of the integral tie to "ultimate meaning and human obligation." Jones and Wilcox (1993) stated,

> psychotherapeutic theories embody values, in that each includes explicit or implicit judgments about the nature of human life that is 'good' (healthy, whole, realistic, rational) and that is 'bad' (abnormal, pathological, immature, stunted, self-deceived). (p. 42)
>
> While we maintain fidelity to our faith commitments, this leads us to treat psychotherapy systems with respect as systems of hypotheses about various facets of human experience, and to have a spirit of humility that while our faith framework is nonnegotiable, the hypotheses we generate from it are not infallible and need to be tested empirically and conceptually. (p. 58)

Methods of ascertaining values are outlined by several writers (Browning, 1987; Jones & Butman, 1991; Roberts, 1987, 1991) in attempting to understand the implicit values, metaphors, and virtues in various psychotherapy systems. These "views of ultimacy" and "ethics" are deeply embedded and need to be understood in relationship to other values regarding compatibility, goodness of fit, or acceptability. Tjeltveit (1991) suggests that Christian ethics appropriately add to and challenge psychological explanations of what is good, right, or virtuous in psychological, ethical, and religious realms connected with therapy. Other religious systems could also be invoked here as well. Regardless of the particular ethical or religious background, the issue is one of how to integrate the plethora of therapeutic procedures emanating from diverse sources.

INTEGRATING SPIRITUAL AND SECULAR THERAPIES

Payne et al. (1992) have reviewed attempts to integrate spiritual and standard psychotherapy techniques where findings are organized around the cognitive–behavioral, psychodynamic, existential–humanistic, and health psychology perspectives. Integrative efforts are developed from the strategy of applying traditional approaches to spiritual concerns as well as deriving psychotherapeutic techniques from the religious and spiritual traditions. Empirical and theoretical approaches have produced effective and creative strategies dealing with therapeutic issues of spiritual and religious importance. The following summarizes importance themes from Payne et al. (1992).

In the psychodynamic realm, attitudes toward integration have been generally regarded with animosity and philosophical antitheses, but attitudes have begun to change (Lovinger, 1984). Shafranske (1988) takes an object-relations approach to understanding unconscious determinants of religious experience and illustrates a harmony between analytical and spiritual perspectives. Other broad spectrum efforts to understand meaningful interaction between religion and psychoanalysis continue (Smith & Handelman, 1990).

Combining behaviorism with spiritual strategies as reported by Miller and Martin (1988) demonstrates a variety of successful applications in dealing with pathology. Friedman et al. (1984) and Thoresen (1987) provide impressive data over an extended period that give evidence of the effectiveness of spiritual–behavioral intervention with coronary patients. Spiritual aspects are singled out as contributing to the physical and behavioral effects noted. Spiritual goals and health goals are coordinated and tailored to individual subjects. Martin and Carlson (1988) advance the notion that certain health problems are related to spiritual deficits, and optimal health may be somewhat dependent on spiritual as well as social and behavioral factors. In reference to their research methods, the authors stated

> we proceed systematically to program into their daily lives the prayer, meditation, worship time, rest, and loving time with family that are clearly prescribed by their religion. In this way, their rule-governed (belief-mediated) behavior system is tapped, to lay the foundation better and to enhance the effectiveness of the primary behavioral contingency-management therapy deemed necessary to change their health and disease risk behaviors. (p. 88)

Combining traditional psychotherapy with religious content is seen in Propst's (1980) successful study of cognitive–behavioral therapy (CBT) using religious imagery. A later study by Propst, Ostrom, Watkins, Dean, and Mashburn (1992) inspired by a National Institute of Mental Health collaborative research program on depression (Elkin, 1994; Elkin et al., 1989) used two forms of cognitive–behavioral treatment, one with religious content and one without. Lower rates of post-treatment depression and better adjustment scores were measured for the religious content CBT treatment and pastoral counseling treatment groups compared with the control group and standard CBT treatment group. Nonreligious therapists obtained the best results using religious content.

Aust (1990) outlines an approach in dealing with maladaptive hyperreligiosity by using religious sources that often portray opposition to the pathology expressed. In contrast, but with similar objectives, the technique of "joining the resistances" outlined by Lovinger (1979) is in good therapeutic tradition and applicable to problems encountered in working with fervently religious clients, as an alternative to ignoring, avoiding, or depreciating client's religious values.

Differential forms and uses of prayer have been recognized. Inappropriate uses of prayer are identified by Finney and Malony (1985). Four types of prayer noted by Paloma and Pendleton (1989) show that certain approaches to prayer may yield better results than others. A study by Byrd (1988) incorporated a controlled design where prayer was used by coronary care patients assigned randomly to a prayer group and no-prayer group, with the prayer group having a statistically better outcome. Imagery integrated with religious concepts has been found effective (Lovinger, 1984; Propst, 1980; Worthington, 1978). Aust (1990) points to the importance of using imagery with which the client is familiar and allowing clients to select their own imagery to maximize effectiveness.

It would be impossible to address the integration of therapy techniques without considering forgiveness as a process of frequent concern. Even with its centrality to both standard and spiritual therapies, forgiveness is surprisingly lacking in definition and structure. Many have addressed this issue (Bergin, 1980a; Brandsma, 1985; Donnelly, 1982; Hope, 1987; Lovinger, 1990; Worthington, 1990), but there is no clear agreement regarding how it can be effectively applied.

Worthington (1990) describes an approach to marriage counseling aimed at helping committed Christian couples. Assumptions set forth in the approach are consistent with cognitive–behavioral counseling theory, as well as strategic family therapies, and are eclectic in nature. Content of the sessions is specifically Christian. Techniques used include prayer, Bible exposition, and teaching from Christian sources when concordant with the values of the clients. The counselor functions from a value-informed perspective rather than a value-free or value-neutral relationship.

Service is mentioned as a necessary step toward wholeness and reconciliation (Little & Robinson, 1988; Lovinger, 1984). Little and Robinson have developed a systematic approach (moral-reconation therapy) to reclaim antisocial and drug abuse clientele. Paying back society, self-assessment, being responsible for one's own treatment and treatment of others, tolerating delays in gratification, and so on are prescribed on an individual basis with promising results.

The surge of interest in psychotherapy integration over the past 15 years (Norcross & Goldfried, 1992) is accounted for, in part, by the lack of differential effectiveness of various forms of therapies (Arkowitz, 1992). Dissatisfaction with a singular therapeutic approach is evidenced in the Jensen, Bergin, and Greaves (1990) data that show 68% of mental health workers, including psychologists, prefer an eclectic position. The eclectic inclusion of religious and spiritual domains in psychotherapy has the potential of requiring therapists to rethink their constructs of human nature and to attend to individual beliefs and assumptions as possible enhancers or resistance to change. Arkowitz (1992) calls for an emphasis that "directs us to look primarily at the individual's mental representations or self-schemas that may bear on change, and at the relationships among various self-schemas in order to predict change" (p. 13).

Although Arkowitz is addressing resistance to change as an intrapersonal conflict among aspects of the self, it is a small step to insert religious and spiritual concepts of the self as an important inclusion and significant part of self-schemas and mental representations that may hinder or help in the process of change. The integrative hope is to glean benefits from all relevant sources, acknowledging that no one resource is all-encompassing. The ironic discovery psychologists make, finally, in the pursuit of integration is the enlarged possibility for addressing diversity. Meaningful therapeutic integration is not limiting, restrictive, or exclusive. It includes and accounts for the diverse range of human experience and commitment. At the same time, unity is sought in the sense of overarching principles or abstractions that explain, guide, predict, and describe phenomena that may seem diverse but are undergirded by important connections common to being human.

As psychologists progress, theories of pathology and change will grow in sophistication so as to encompass diversity in a context of sociality, universal meaning, common genesis, and freedom of expression. Individuality (diversity) may be enhanced by the social context (unity and integration). The personal actualization often promoted by traditional therapies may continue to be valued but found to depend on integrative or unifying principles that arise from universals common to the great religious traditions that have emerged during thousands of years of social evolution (Campbell, 1975). Diversification looks ahead to the future for new ways of knowing and doing. Unification looks to the past, to psychologists' origins and threads of connectedness. Creative balance between diversifying interests and unifying interests will ultimately characterize the successful enterprise of psychotherapy (Jones, 1994; Mahoney, 1991).

CONCERNS, CAUTIONS, AND CAVEATS

Informed consent and open agreement between client and therapist regarding the relevance of values and religious issues in the therapy transaction are foundational (Lewis & Epperson, 1991) and crucial to an effective therapeutic alliance. Brace (1992) regards respect for clients' welfare and respect for their self-determination as two essential principles. A therapist needs to be open to an assessment of religious and spiritual needs even though he or she may not initiate such topics. Avoiding religious issues or routinely redirecting spiritual concerns in therapy is no more justifiable than refusing to deal with the death of a family member or fears of social encounters. Religious and spiritual concerns can be initiated by the client, but therapists are always in a position to approve or disapprove, to be open or closed to the concern, or to show interest or lack of interest in the experiences and perceptions of the client as they take on spiritual meanings. Can there be a separation, in practice, between one's professional and personal values (Beutler, Machado, Neufeldt, 1994, p. 240)? Although it is a given that assumptions, constructs, and values may change in therapy, the question of how these changes will come about is critical. Only with deep respect for autonomy and for a person's beliefs and values can therapy proceed safely in the change process.

Ethical problems associated with value conversion of the client are delineated by Tjeltveit (1986) and include reduction of client freedom, failure to provide adequate information regarding therapy, and violation of the therapeutic contract, all of which are threats to client autonomy. It is argued that efforts need to be made to minimize the ethical problems associated with value conversion and to reduce its occurrence. Toward these ends, therapist training, therapist–client matching, referral, informed consent, and changing roles are possible solutions.

It is not uncommon to hear of secular therapists advising traditionally religious clients to give up some aspect, or even all, of their religious commitment on the grounds that one's beliefs and practices are inhibiting the therapeutic progress. Such advice may present a threat to some individuals' sense of identity and integrity. Although some changes in values may be therapeutic, an assault on the client's core values is likely to be harmful (Bergin et al., 1988). This is not to say that therapists should be inhibited or prevented from entering into any aspect of the client's life that is important for treatment, but it does suggest that empathic sensitivity to the client's core issues of religiosity would be essential to avoiding harmful consequences.

Similarly, religiously zealous therapists, "do-gooders" with a self-righteous agenda of how everyone should be, pose an equivalent problem. Pressures applied to convert are inappropriate in therapy, although clients may need help in exploring issues relevant to faith commitments. Arguments over doctrine seem out of line, although clarifications may be crucial (Lovinger, 1984, 1990). Challenging the truth of a client's faith can be abusive. However, these abuses need not characterize the spiritual strategy any more than traditional therapy. A sensitive line exists between exploring and even critiquing values, faith, beliefs, and spiritual constructs while pursuing psychological integrity in either spiritual or secular orientations and examining these highly individualized perspectives with preemptive judgments.

Lack of information regarding the particular life orientation represented by a client's beliefs and a lack of therapist training or skill may result in therapy being uncomfortable and questionable when the focus concerns spiritual, moral, or religious values. Referrals need to be considered under these circumstances. Sometimes a closer liaison with a client's ecclesiastical leader can obviate the problem.

Additional therapeutic cautions are warranted.

1. Religion is often misused to avoid addressing personal issues or accepting responsibility for behavior. On the other hand, religious concepts may promote a client's feelings of control, self-esteem, and meaning. There is a traditional concern about increasing guilt and stress resulting from acute awareness of moral imperfections when religion is misapplied.

2. Skill and training in the use of religious and spiritual techniques must be considered in this enterprise as well as in traditional psychotherapy (Sollod, 1992). Few psychologists feel confident or trained in the addressing of religious issues in matters of spirituality. Shafranske and Malony (1990) noted in their survey that only one third of the psychologists expressed a sense of competence in this regard.

3. The issue of autonomy seems universally applauded by traditional therapists and prioritized in numerous ways. However, Jones and Butman (1991) assert that service to others and relationship with God may have a higher priority for many than an egocentric self-actualization approach. The therapist must consult the values of the individual rather than assume autonomy to be the choice or priority of ultimate value.

4. Boundary issues will always plague those who are bold enough to take on religious and spiritual matters and personal values of the client. Psychotherapists have been accused of establishing a secular priesthood (London, 1986). Although there is often overlap in functions of ecclesiastical leaders and therapists, roles need to be defined and boundaries adhered to if mutual respect and comfort are to prevail. Mutual referrals and mutual involvement are needed, but psychologists have been reluctant to refer clients to pastoral counselors or ecclesiastical leaders because of confidentiality, mistrust, and assumed value differences. Of concern is helping the client understand that the therapist does not assume ecclesiastical responsibility even though spiritual matters may be the focus.

Evangelical Christians represent the feelings of many religiously conservative groups in the fear that secular therapists may (a) neglect religious concerns; (b) deal with religious belief events as pathological or psychological; (c) fail to discern religious language and ideas; (d) presume that religious clients share nonreligious cultural norms (e.g., living together, premarital sex, and divorce); (e) promote therapeutic conduct that contradicts their own particular sense of morals (e.g., abortion and homosexual conduct); or (f) make presumptions, explanations, and suggestions that their account of revelation is not valid epistemology (Worthington, 1986).

DIRECTIONS FOR THE FUTURE

Psychologists' deepening and progressive focus on values is long overdue. It is not uncommon for neglect and avoidance to be turned into obsessive concern, as if to compensate or balance the scales. Applauding psychology's self-conscious awareness of humankind as a valuing entity with notions of fairness and unfairness, constructs of what relationships should be or can be, and commitments to various principles and goals must be countered by a keen wariness born of historical warnings and pessimistic caution that this too could turn against the profession.

Diversity itself, with all its trouble and divisiveness, may be psychologists' best bet to prosper in facing value dilemmas. In facing up to conflicting and incompatible values, destructive values, and consensual values, diversity calls into question one-sidedness or quick and impulsive solutions. Unity may be feasible in broad strokes, adopting general guidelines and mutually beneficial principles, but on specifics there will always be diversity in a free society. Diversity may actually be the hallmark of freedom and personal agency. This need not deter therapists from continuously assessing which values are destructive and which are conducive to growth. On a social level and on a personal level, value clarification and value choice are the essence of being human.

Sometimes at odds with one another and sometimes together, psychologists choose to do what they think best, using a wide range of changing criteria to guide their tentativeness and uncertainty. They divide themselves on grounding assumptions (faith), but often on other less profound bases and always with an eye toward some notion of truth or integration, however fragmented and incomplete. Regardless of how tentative or determined their "faith" may be, it now seems clear that therapies of the future will prosper only as they are able to adapt to and simultaneously analyze the diverse narratives and personal constructions with which clients meet their worlds.

Thus, the zeitgeist in the past decade or so has been fertile for psychological conceptualization beyond traditional "scientific" constraints. In a review of journal articles from 1987 through 1993 from the PSYCLIT Database, we found 6,138 articles on "values." A further search of the combination of "values and psychotherapy" revealed 198 journal articles.

Interest in the religious and psychospiritual domains are represented primarily outside the mainstream of psychological literature in quality publications combining religious and psychological themes: *International Journal for the Psychology of Religion, Journal of Judaism and Psychology, Journal of Psychology and Christianity, Counseling and Values, Journal of Psychology and Theology,* and *Journal for the Scientific Study of Religion.* Gradually these issues and research findings are filtering into mainstream psychology (Bergin & Garfield, 1994), of which this book is one example.

Dispute over values, typified by Bergin (1980a) and Ellis (1980), is, perhaps, historically definitive in setting a point of demarcation for the infusion of values in psychotherapy. If cognitive psychology can be regarded as a fourth force in the field, it might not be unreasonable to depict the value emphasis with its religious and spiritual influences as a fifth force, at least in the realm of personality and psychotherapy. The above trends support this tentative assertion. Underlining this movement is the concern for wholeness, for integration, for a unification of conceptual and practical strategies for change. Secularization of psychotherapy can no longer be promoted without question. Value-free therapy is no longer viable (Owen, 1986). In saying this, there is no promotion of a particular value or set of values but only the ethical imperative of dealing openly with ones own values as therapists and those of the clients.

Professional malaise and lassitude, or even the hostility sometimes encountered when addressing these issues, cannot be explained by an elitist or condescending pronouncement that these aspects of human nature are not scientific. Science is defined by methodology, not by content, and many of these areas have been studied scientifically. No, the reason for this neglect lies elsewhere. Among the reasons is the clear but discomforting factor of value judgment—the preferencing process. Aside from the investigative problems, which are numerous, the fact remains that a large number of influential psychologists have chosen (for one reason or another) to exclude issues of purpose, meaning, values, and spiritual and religious constructs or experiences from their theorizing about human behavior. Others (Bevan, 1991; O'Donohue, 1989; Olthius, 1985; Wolterstorff, 1984) have recognized the profound influence of "control beliefs," foundational commitments, a world view, and ideologies on their creative thought, scientific inquiry, and ultimate answers.

Jones (1994) observes that "Psychology's previously non-interactive stance toward religion was premised on an outmoded understanding of science and an overly narrow professionalism" (p. 184). Consequently he calls for an explicit and constructive working relationship between psychology and religion, noting differences as well as commonalities. A case is made that psychotherapeutic practice "is influenced by . . . religious, moral, metaphysical and philosophical beliefs" (p. 196) and if the connections between psychologists' work and their deepest human commitments are to be understood, these aspects must be examined and appreciated. In a general sense, combined efforts have stopped short of recognizing the salient roles of spiritual and religious values, purposes, and meanings as important determinants and regulators of human behavior. Only when these factors of the human equation are included will there be a possibility of a relevant, comprehensive, and integrated theory of human personality.

SUMMARY AND CONCLUSION

It can be stated that the therapy relationship inevitably includes the transmission of values. The importance of recognizing one's values, both as therapist and as client, must be addressed. Evolution of the infusion of values in psychotherapy has been referenced and highlighted. The past decade or two have been especially productive and provocative regarding values' issues in psychotherapy. Among the six emerging themes currently identified in the *History of Psychotherapy* (Freedheim, 1992) are pluralism, contextualism, and therapeutic alliance—themes elaborated in this chapter.

It has been shown that values are an essential aspect of the therapeutic enterprise. Certain religious and spiritual values may promote mental health, whereas others may not. It is the work of the next decade to more clearly specify the impact of given values. How to do this effectively and ethically are challenges psychologists must accept. Recommendations for training in professional programs must be forthcoming to prepare professionals handling diversity and all its ramifications. Guidelines for ethical thinking and conduct when dealing with value issues in psychotherapy must be more carefully articulated. Several trends are identified:

1. There is a growing respect for individual values and recognition of their integral therapeutic import. This represents a vast resource for health and growth that is just beginning to affect the field of psychotherapy.
2. Research findings on therapist values rescue therapists from the false assumption that professionals are totally out of step with mainstream society, yet significant differences exist. There are trends among professionals that reflect values and realigned thinking congruent with some of the more traditional values expressed in society (Bergin & Jensen, 1990; Jensen & Bergin, 1988). How therapist values affect clients is of significant interest.
3. Both theoretical and empirical work have moved therapists toward integration of psychology and religious values. Research findings have identified not only areas of compatibility but also relationships between certain kinds of religious values and mental health.
4. Diversity now includes religious and spiritual issues. The diversity thrust, then, has opened the door for inclusion of such values, and it demands a careful consideration of these values when dealing with individuals in the therapeutic mode.
5. There has been a proliferation of articles (research and theory) regarding the role of values in psychotherapy. This accelerated with the 1980 values debate (Bergin & Ellis) and has piqued the interest of professionals throughout the world.

We can conclude that the effort to integrate value concerns into the theory and practice of psychotherapy has been more than a passing fancy. Relevance is shown for explicit strategies and techniques as well as for assumptions of personality and psychopathology. Empirical studies and a body of clinical observations have added legitimacy to the inclusion of a variety of value issues. Areas can now be approached that were formerly taboo. Therapists' claim to be open to any client concern is closer to fact as they find ways of addressing all kinds of values in therapy. All this is not without caution and sensitivity to potential abuses; but it is consistent with the emergent eclectic and integrative climate. A rapprochement is being achieved between traditional therapeutic systems and approaches emphasizing the diversity of values and religious issues that clients bring to their therapists. Whether buttressed by phenomenology, humanism and existentialism, cognitive–behavioral thinking, or psychodynamic narratives, the valuing experience of each person remains a reality—determining and directing, to a large extent, both the essence of being human and the nature of change.

REFERENCES

Albee, G. W. (1991). Opposition to prevention and a new creedal oath. *The Scientist Practitioner*, *1*(4), 30–31.

Allport, G. W., & Ross, J. M. (1967). Personal religious orientation and prejudice. *Journal of Personality and Social Psychology*, *5*, 432–443.

American Psychological Association (1992). Ethical principles of psychologists and code of conduct. *American Psychologist*, *41*, 1597–1611.

Arkowitz, H. (1992). Psychotherapy intervention: Bringing psychotherapy back to psychology. *The General Psychologist*, *28*(2), 11–17, 20.

Aust, C. F. (1990). Using the client's religious values to aid progress in therapy. *Counseling and Values*, *34*, 125–129.

Bergin, A. E. (1980a). Psychotherapy and religious values. *Journal of Consulting and Clinical Psychology*, *48*, 95–105.

Bergin, A. E. (1980b). Religious and humanistic values: A reply to Ellis and Walls. *Journal of Consulting and Clinical Psychology*, *48*, 642–645.

Bergin, A. E. (1980c). Behavior therapy and ethical relativism: Time for clarity. *Journal of Consulting and Clinical Psychology*, *48*, 11–13.

Bergin, A. E. (1985). Proposed values for guiding and evaluating counseling and psychotherapy. *Counseling and Values*, *29*, 99–116.

Bergin, A. E. (1988a). Three contributions of a spiritual perspective to counseling, psychotherapy, and behavior change. *Counseling and Values*, *33*, 21–31.

Bergin, A. E. (1988b). The spiritual perspective is ecumenical and eclectic (rejoinder). *Counseling and Values*, *33*, 57–59.

Bergin, A. E. (1991). Values and religious issues in psychotherapy and mental health. *American Psychologist*, *46*, 394–403.

Bergin, A. E., & Garfield, S. L. (Eds.). (1994). *Handbook of psychotherapy and behavior change*. New York: Wiley.

Bergin, A. E., & Jensen, J. P. (1990). Religiosity of psychotherapists: A national survey. *Psychotherapy*, *27*, 3–7.

Bergin, A. E., & Payne, I. R. (1991). Proposed agenda for a spiritual strategy in personality and psychotherapy. *Journal of Psychology and Christianity*, *10*, 197–210.

Bergin, A. E., Stinchfield, R. D., Gaskin, T. A., Masters, K. S., & Sullivan, C. E. (1988). Religious life styles and mental health: An exploratory study. *Journal of Counseling Psychology*, *35*, 91–98.

Beutler, L. E. (1972). Value and attitude change in psychotherapy: A case for dyadic assessment. *Psychotherapy*, *9*(4), 262–267.

Beutler, L. E. (1979). Values, beliefs, religion and the persuasive influence of psychotherapy. *Psychotherapy, 16*, 432–440.

Beutler, L., & Bergan, J. (1991). Value change in counseling and psychotherapy: A search for scientific credibility. *Journal of Counseling Psychology, 38*, 16–24.

Beutler, L. E., Machado, P. P. P., & Neufeldt, S. A. (1994). Therapist variables. In A. E. Bergin & S. L. Garfield (Eds.), *Handbook of psychotherapy and behavior change* (pp. 229–269). New York: Wiley.

Bevan, W. (1991). Contemporary psychology: A tour inside the onion. *American Psychologist, 26*, 475–483.

Brace, K. (1992). Nonrelativist ethical standards for goal setting in psychotherapy. *Ethics and Behavior, 2*, 15–38.

Bradford, D. T., & Spero, M. H. (Eds.). (1990). Psychotherapy and religion [Special issue]. *Psychotherapy, 27*(1).

Brandsma, I. M. (1985). Forgiveness. In D. G. Benner (Ed.), *Baker encyclopedia of psychology.* Grand Rapids, MI: Baker Book House.

Browning, D. S. (1987). *Religious thought and the modern psychologies.* Philadelphia: Fortress.

Byrd, R. C. (1988). Positive therapeutic effects of intercessory prayer in a coronary care unit population. *Southern Medical Journal, 31*, 826–829.

Campbell, D. T. (1975). On the conflicts between biological and social evolution and between psychology and moral tradition. *American Psychologist, 30*, 1103–1120.

Collins, G. R. (1977). *The rebuilding of psychology: An integration of psychology and Christianity.* Wheaton, IL: Tyndale House.

Donahue, M. J. (1985). Intrinsic and extrinsic religiousness: Review and meta-analysis. *Journal of Personality and Social Psychology, 48*(2), 400–419.

Donahue, M. J. (1989). Disregarding theology in the psychology of religion: Some examples. *Journal of Psychology and Theology, 17*, 324–335.

Donnelley, D. (1982). *Putting forgiveness into practice.* Allen, TX: Argus Communications.

Elkin, I. (1994). The NIMH treatment of depression collaborative research program: Where we began and where we are. In A. E. Bergin & S. L. Garfield (Eds.), *Handbook of psychotherapy and behavior change* (4th Ed.; pp. 114–139). New York: Wiley.

Elkin, I., Shea, T., Watkins, J., Imber, S., Sotsky, S., Collins, J., Glass, D., Pilkonis, P., Leber, W., Docherty, J., Fiester, S., & Parloff, M. (1989). National Institute of Mental Health treatment of depression collaborative research program: General effectiveness of treatments. *Archives of General Psychiatry, 35*, 837–844.

Ellis, A. (1980). Psychotherapy and atheistic values: A response to A. E. Bergin's "Psychotherapy and religious values." *Journal of Consulting and Clinical Psychology, 48*, 635–639.

Finney, J. R., & Malony, H. N. (1985). Contemplative prayer and its use in psychotherapy: A theoretical model. *Journal of Psychology and Theology, 13*, 172–181.

Frank, J. D., & Frank, J. B. (1991). *Persuasion and healing* (3rd ed.). Baltimore: The Johns Hopkins University Press.

Freedheim, D. K. (Ed.). (1992). *History of psychotherapy.* Washington, DC: American Psychological Association.

Friedman, M., Thoresen, C. E., Gill, J. J., Powell, L. H., Ulmer, D., Thompson, L., Price, V. A., Rabin, D. D., Breall, W. S., Dixon, R., Levy, R., & Bourge, E. (1984). Alteration of Type A behavior and reduction in cardiac recurrences in postmyocardial infarction patients. *American Heart Journal, 108*, 237–248.

Gallup Organization. (1985). *Religion in America* (Report No. 236). Princeton, NJ: Author.

Goldsmith, W. M., & Hansen, B. K. (1991). Boundary areas of religious clients' values: Target for therapy. *Journal of Psychology and Christianity, 10*, 224–236.

Harari, C. (1989). Humanistic and transpersonal psychology: Values in psychotherapy. *Psychotherapy in Private Practice, 7*, 49–56.

Havenarr, J. M. (1990). Psychotherapy: Healing by culture. *Psychotherapy and Psychosomatics, 53*, 8–13.

Hope, D. (1987). The healing paradox of forgiveness. *Psychotherapy, 24*, 240–244.

Howard, G. S. (1985). The role of values in the science of psychology. *American Psychologist, 40*, 255–265.

Jensen, J. P., & Bergin, A. E. (1988). Mental health values of professional therapists: A national interdisciplinary survey. *Professional Psychology: Research and Practice, 19*, 290–297.

Jensen, J. P., Bergin, A. E., & Greaves, D. W. (1990). The meaning of eclecticism: New survey and analysis of components. *Professional Psychology: Research and Practice, 21*(2), 124–130.

Jones, S. L. (1994). A constructive relationship for religion with the science and profession of psychology. *American Psychologist, 49*(3), 184–199.

Jones, S. L., & Butman, R. (1991). *Modern psychotherapies: A comprehensive Christian appraisal.* Downers Grove, IL: InterVarsity.

Jones, S. L., & Wilcox, D. A. (1993). Religious values in secular theories of psychotherapy. In E. L. Worthington, Jr. (Ed.), *Psychotherapy and religious values* (pp. 37–61). Grand Rapids, MI: Baker Book House.

Kelly, T. A., & Strupp, H. H. (1992). Patient and therapist values in psychotherapy: Perceived changes, assimilation, similarity, and outcome. *Journal of Consulting and Clinical Psychology, 60*, 34–40.

Kessell, P., & McBrearty, J. F. (1967). Values and psychotherapy: A review of the literature. *Perceptual and Motor Skills, 25*, 669–690. (Monograph Supplement 2-U25).

Kitchener, R. F. (1980). Ethical relativism and behavior therapy. *Journal of Consulting and Clinical Psychology, 48,* 1–7.

Kroll, J., & Sheehan, W. (1989). Religious beliefs and practices among 52 psychiatric inpatients in Minnesota. *American Journal of Psychiatry, 146,* 67–72.

Kudlac, K. E. (1991). Including God in the conversation: The influence of religious beliefs on the problem-organized system. *Family Therapy, 18*(3), 277–285.

Larson, D. B., Sherrill, K. A., Lyons, J. S., Craigie, Jr., F. C., Thielman, S. B., Greenwold, M. A., & Larson, S. S. (1992). Associations between dimensions of religious commitment and mental health reported in the American Journal of Psychiatry and Archives of General Psychiatry: 1978-1989. *American Journal of Psychiatry, 149,* 557–559.

Lewis, K. N., & Epperson, D. L. (1991). Values, pre-therapy information, and informed consent in Christian counseling. *Journal of Psychology and Christianity, 10,* 113–131.

Little, G. L., & Robinson, K. D. (1988). Moral reconation therapy: A systematic step-by-step treatment system for treatment resistant clients. *Psychological Reports, 62,* 135–161.

London, P. (1986). *The modes and morals of psychotherapy* (2nd ed.). New York: Hemisphere.

Lovinger, R. J. (1979). Therapeutic strategies with "religious" resistances. *Psychotherapy: Theory, Research and Practice, 16,* 419–427.

Lovinger, R. J. (1984). *Working with religious issues in psychotherapy.* New York: Jason Aronson.

Lovinger, R. J. (1990). *Religion and counseling: The psychological impact of religious belief.* New York: Continuum.

Lowe, C. M. (1976). *Value orientations in counseling and psychotherapy: The meanings of mental health* (2nd ed.). Cranston, RI: Carroll Press.

Mahoney, M. J. (1991). *Human change processes.* New York: Basic Books.

Malony, H. N. (1988). The clinical assessment of optimal religious functioning. *Review of Religious Research, 30,* 3–17.

Martin, J. E., & Carlson, C. R. (1988). Spiritual dimensions of health psychology. In W. R. Miller & J. E. Martin (Eds.), *Behavior therapy and religion: Integrating spiritual and behavioral approaches to change* (pp. 57–110). Newbury Park, CA: Sage.

Martinez, F. I. (1991). Therapist client convergence and similarity of religious values: Their effect on client improvement. *Journal of Psychology and Christianity, 10,* 137–143.

Masters, K. S., & Bergin, A. E. (1992). Religious orientation and mental health. In J. F. Schumaker (Ed.), *Religion and mental health* (pp. 221–232). Oxford, England: Oxford University Press.

Masters, K. S., Bergin, A. E., Reynolds, E. M., & Sullivan, C. E. (1991). Religious life styles and mental health: A follow-up study. *Counseling and Values, 35,* 211–224.

Mickleburgh, W. E. (1992). Clarification of values in counseling and psychopathology. *Australian and New Zealand Journal of Psychiatry, 26*, 391–398.

Miller, W. R., & Martin, J. E. (Eds.). (1988). *Behavior therapy and religion: Integrating spiritual and behavioral approaches to change.* Newbury Park, CA: Sage.

Norcross, J. C., & Goldfried, M. R. (Eds.). (1992). *Handbook of psychotherapy integration.* New York: Basic Books.

O'Donohue, W. (1989). The (even) bolder model: The clinical psychologist as metaphysician-scientist-practitioner. *American Psychologist, 44,* 1460–1468.

Olthuis, J. (1985). On worldviews. *Christian Scholars Review, 14,* 153–164.

Owen, G. (1986). Ethics of intervention for change. *Australian Psychologist, 21,* 211–218.

Paloma, M., & Pendleton, B. (1989). Exploring types of prayer and quality of life: A research note. *Review of Religious Research, 31,* 46–55.

Pargament, K. I., Steele, R. E., & Tyler, F. B. (1979). Religious participation, religious motivation and individual psychosocial competence. *Journal for the Scientific Study of Religion, 18,* 412–419.

Patterson, C. H. (1958). The place of values in counseling and psychotherapy. *Journal of Counseling Psychology, 5,* 216–223.

Patterson, C. H. (1989). Values in counseling and psychotherapy. *Counseling and Values, 33,* 164–176.

Payne, I. R., Bergin, A. E., Bielema, K. A., & Jenkins, P. H. (1991). Review of religion and mental health: Prevention and the enhancement of psychosocial functioning. *Prevention in Human Services, 2,* 11–40.

Payne, I. R., Bergin, A. E., & Loftus, P. E. (1992). A review of attempts to integrate spiritual and standard psychotherapy techniques. *Journal of Psychotherapy Integration, 2,* 171–192.

Propst, L. R. (1980). The comparative efficacy of religious and non-religious imagery for the treatment of mild depression in religious individuals. *Cognitive Therapy and Research, 4,* 167–178.

Propst, L. R. (1988). *Psychotherapy in a religious framework: Spirituality in the emotional healing process.* New York: Human Sciences Press.

Propst, L. R., Ostrom, R., Watkins, P., Dean, T., & Mashburn, D. (1992). Comparative efficacy of religious and nonreligious cognitive-behavioral therapy for the treatment of clinical depression in religious individuals. *Journal of Consulting and Clinical Psychology, 60,* 94–103.

Ragan, C., Malony, H. N., & Beit-Hallahmi, B. (1980). Psychologists and religion: Professional factors and personal belief. *Review of Religious Research, 21,* 208–217.

Richards, P. S. (1991). Religion devoutness in college students: Relations with emotional adjustment and psychological separation from parents. *Journal of Counseling Psychology, 38,* 189–196.

Richards, P. S. (1993). The treatment of homosexuality: Some historical, contemporary, and personal perspectives. *AMCAP Journal (Association of Mormon Counselors and Psychotherapists), 19,* 29–45.

Richards, P. S., & Potts, R. (1995). Using spiritual interventions in psychotherapy: Practices, successes, failures and ethical concerns of Mormon psychotherapists. *Professional psychology: Research and practice, 26*, 163–170.

Richards, P. S., Smith, S. A., & Davis, L. F. (1989). Healthy and unhealthy forms of religiousness manifested by psychotherapy clients: An empirical investigation. *Journal of Research in Personality, 23*, 506–524.

Roberts, R. C. (1987). Psychotherapeutic virtues and the grammar of faith. *Journal of Psychology and Theology, 15*, 191–203.

Roberts, R. C. (1991). Mental health and the virtues of community: Christian reflections on contextual therapy. *Journal of Psychology and Theology, 19*, 319–333.

Seligman, L. (1988). Invited commentary: Three contributions of a spiritual perspective to counseling psychotherapy, and behavior change (Allen E. Bergin). *Counseling and Values, 33*, 55–56.

Shafranske, E. P. (1988, November). *The contributions of object relations theory in Christian Counseling.* Paper presented at the International Convention of Christian Psychology, Atlanta, GA.

Shafranske, E. P., & Malony, H. N. (1990). Clinical psychologists' religious and spiritual orientations and their practice of psychotherapy. *Psychotherapy, 27*, 172–178.

Shapiro, E. (1990). Tools of the trade: The use of the self in psychotherapy. *Group, 14*, 170–172.

Smiley, H. (1985). Values and empowerment. *Hakomi Forum, 3*, 10–13.

Smith, J. H., & Handelman, S. A. (Eds.). (1990). *Psychoanalysis and religion.* Baltimore: The Johns Hopkins University Press.

Sollod, R. N. (1992). Letter to the editor. *The Scientist Practitioner, 2*(1), 33.

Spero, M. H. (Ed.). (1985). *Psychotherapy of the religious patient.* Springfield, IL: Charles C Thomas.

Strommen, M. P. (1984). Psychology's blind spot: A religious faith. *Counseling and Values, 28*, 150–161.

Szasz, T. S. (1978). *The myth of psychotherapy: Mental healing as religion, rhetoric, and repression.* Garden City, NY: Doubleday.

Stern, E. M. (Ed.). (1985). *Psychotherapy and the religiously committed patient.* New York: Haworth Press.

Tan, S. Y. (1988, November). *Explicit integration in psychotherapy.* Invited paper presented at the International Congress on Christian Counseling, Atlanta, GA.

Tan, S. Y. (1993, January). *Training in professional psychology: Diversity includes religion.* Paper presented at the National Council of Schools of Professional Psychology midwinter conference on Training in Professional Psychology, La Jolla, CA.

Thoresen, C. (1987, June). *Development and modification of Type A behavior patterns.* Paper presented at San Diego State University summer symposium, "Type A Coronary Prone Behavior Pattern: A Comprehensive Look," CA.

Tjeltveit, A. C. (1986). The ethics of value conversion in psychotherapy: Appropriate and inappropriate therapist influence on client values. *Clinical Psychology Review, 6,* 515–537.

Tjeltveit, A. C. (1991). Christian ethics and psychological explanations of "religious values" in therapy: Critical connections. *Journal of Psychology and Christianity, 10,* 101–112.

Tjeltveit, A. C. (1992). The psychotherapist as Christian ethicist: Theology applied to practice. *Journal of Psychology and Theology, 20,* 89–98.

Vachon, D. O., & Agresti, A. A. (1992). A training proposal to help mental health professionals clarify and manage implicit values in the counseling process. *Professional Psychology: Research and Practice, 23,* 509–514.

Vitz, P. (1977). *Psychology as religion: The cult of self-worship.* Grand Rapids, MI: Eerdmans.

Walls, G. B. (1980). Values and psychotherapy: A comment on "Psychotherapy and religious values." *Journal of Consulting and Clinical Psychology, 48,* 640–641.

Wolterstorff, M. (1984). *Reason within the bounds of religion* (2nd ed.). Grand Rapids, MI: Eerdmans.

Worthington, E. L., Jr. (1978). The effects of imagery content, choice of imagery content, and self-verbalization on the self-control of pain. *Cognitive Therapy and Research, 2,* 225–240.

Worthington, E. L., Jr. (1986). Religious counseling: A review of published empirical research. *Journal of Counseling and Development, 64,* 421–431.

Worthington, E. L., Jr. (1988). Understanding the values of religious clients: A model and its application to counseling. *Journal of Counseling Psychology, 35,* 166–174.

Worthington, E. L., Jr. (1989). Religious faith across the life span: Implications for counseling and research. *The Counseling Psychologist, 17,* 555–612.

Worthington, E. L., Jr. (1990). Marriage counseling: A Christian approach to counseling couples. *Counseling and Values, 34,* 3–15.

Worthington, E. L., Jr. (1991). Psychotherapy and religious values: An update. *Journal of Psychology and Christianity, 10,* 211–223.

12

CONSIDERING THE RELIGIOUS DIMENSION IN ASSESSMENT AND TREATMENT

ROBERT J. LOVINGER

Assessment and treatment occur in a context comprising many complex influences that must be considered in order to maximize accuracy and efficacy. Although it is now recognized that ethnic, socioeconomic, and cultural influences bear upon treatment and assessment, religion is one influence that is often overlooked in spite of its transection of these three other influences. It is the religious dimension in assessment and treatment that is the subject of this chapter.

In spite of Ellis's (1980) assertions, religion is not related to dysfunction in any simple, linear fashion. Bergin's (1983) survey found essentially no relationship between religious affiliation and pathology. Rather, those with strong religious belief or no belief show lower levels of distress than those with moderate levels of belief (Ross, 1990). (For an extensive review of these influences, see Matthews, Larson, & Barry, 1993.) For the diagnostician or therapist encountering definite religious factors in a client, the ordinary evaluative and therapeutic tasks are complicated by considering the nuances of the client's religious sentiments. Most clients have been exposed to religion in childhood, and that exposure colors many clients' work in therapy, often in subtle ways.

For example, a client came to see me as her second marriage was collapsing. Her first marriage, of 12 years duration, had been to an abusive husband, whereas her second marriage was to a man who was not abusive and was more loving. As a child, she had been exposed to her father's abusive sexuality: whenever he decided to have sex with her mother, the children were roughly sent out of the house. What was happening was explicit (and noisy), although she did not recall having seen anything. At one point in therapy she and her husband agreed that they were not going to have sex. Then a rapprochement in their relationship occurred and they wound up going to bed. In the next therapy session she described this, with a touch of sarcasm, as "The Plan." I thought I recognized this, so I inquired. She made a reference to the biblical plan for women embodied in the phrase, "Women submit to your husband" in the King James translation of St. Paul's letter to the Ephesians. She resented feeling pressured under this dictum, although she had been willing to have sex at the time.

Had I not recognized the allusion to "The Plan," an exploration might not have been initiated. Being ready and able to hear religious imagery allows the diagnostician or therapist to be aware of another dimension of the client's life, one that is of at least conventional significance to over 90% of the American population, and of much more importance to a sizable minority (Paloutzian & Kirkpatrick, 1995).

DENOMINATIONS

Overview

The approach described in this chapter looks at clients in a denominational framework. Denominations differ widely, as does their impact on the person's attitudes, values, and worldview. For example, Cochran and Beeghley's (1991) study of attitudes toward premarital and extramarital sex and toward homosexuality demonstrated wide denominational differences. Denominations have central qualities that they impart to their members, or that attract those who find these qualities important.

The United States is, in a sense, a religious "supermarket." Some locales have a "house" brand; so for example, if you live in Utah, it is the Church of Jesus Christ of Latter-day Saints. If you are a Seventh-day Adventist, you might feel uncomfortable there, but most people can find a wide range of vehicles for religious expression. Southern California has a wider choice than a small town in the rural South. Overall, some 30% of the population have tried other religions (Roof, 1989). There are denominational differences: Jews are least likely to switch, followed by Catholics, Baptists, Lutherans, Methodists, Episcopalians, and Presbyterians.

Babchuk and Whitt (1990) found that the Episcopalian, Methodist, and Presbyterian denominations have lower rates of retention of adolescent members into their adulthood (in the middle to upper 50% range), whereas those raised as Catholics, Jews, or in conservative churches (Fundamentalist, Pentecostal, etc.) have higher retention rates (in the middle 80% range). Baptists and Lutherans were in the middle 70% range. Greer and Roof (1992) found that those members of more liberal denominations were more likely to value a private, individually structured religiousness than were members of conservative churches. Thus, at least among Protestant denominations, conservatism was inversely related to individualism in religious expression. People in conservative churches seek more authoritative answers, leading to less independence in religious thought and practice. These differences are relative and changes are continuing.

If all that is known about a client's religious affiliation is that it is Protestant, Jewish, or Catholic, this is much too general. For the therapist to work with clients from the perspective of their denominational frame, the therapist must consider what the clients grew up with, what denomination they are now members of, the particular qualities of the specific denomination, and differentiations within that denomination.

In the next section, I will examine specific denominational groups in more detail, but let me illustrate some of the issues here. The Episcopal Church has three main divisions: the "High Church" is associated with the Anglican (English Catholic) Church, with more emphasis on ritual and sacrament; the "Broad Church" is more middle of the road; and the "Low Church" is more austere and Protestant in character. All those within these diverse modes of practice are considered Episcopalians and are generally accepted within the denomination. Individuals who value ritual are likely to emphasize public expression of faith whereas those in a more austere church are more likely to prize the internal, meditative aspects. This does not necessarily imply an external or internal orientation in one or the other. Thus, even to say that a person is Lutheran, Episcopalian, or Methodist says less than one would suspect. To specify within a denomination will narrow the range, but for many clients even more specificity may be needed for a sufficient understanding of their experience.

Fundamentalist, Pentecostal, Holiness, and Evangelical are terms that are sometimes used interchangeably by outsiders, but although these churches are all theologically conservative, distinctions exist that are important to members (Ammerman, 1987). The Fundamentalist movement is less than a century old and began as a conservative reaction against a liberal Protestant interpretation of the Bible and Christian life in this country (Marty, 1986a). Fundamentalism is based on a few basic principles (fundamentals), including a (selectively) literal interpretation of the Bible (Ammerman, 1987), the divinity of Jesus, his salvific death, and other similar core concepts. However, whereas Fundamentalists subscribe to orthodox Christian principles, orthodox Christians are distinguishable from Fundamentalists on such dimensions as prejudice (Kirkpatrick, 1993). Kirkpatrick suggested that, in addition to specific beliefs, fundamentalism relates to boundary maintenance.

Evangelical, from "good news" in Greek, refers to an effort to spread the "good news" of the salvific death of Jesus through active outreach efforts. Pentecostal churches may use the word holiness in their title, but Holiness churches do not use the word Pentecostal in their name. Typically Holiness and Fundamentalist worship is much more reserved and less emotionally expressive than a Pentecostal service. For example, speaking in tongues (glossolalia) is typically disapproved of in Holiness and Fundamentalist churches. In contrast to the Methodist or Episcopal church, Fundamentalist and Holiness churches are quite individualistic, typically loosely federated, but very wary about accepting another church's theology or practice as valid (Ammerman, 1987). In general, it seems that the very authoritative stance toward doctrine taken by most churches in this group is attractive to people who are seeking certainty and reassurance in the answers provided, and strict behavioral controls. Nevertheless there are differences between each subgroup and we will return to these later.

People with an individual spirituality are not easily located in the denominational approach, although if there was a specific church affiliation in the family of origin, this may give some clues as to earlier influences on what the client presents. If an individual spirituality is the main dimension of a client's religious life, a careful and sensitive exploration is needed. A striking expression of this was noted by Bellah, Madsen, Sullivan, Swidler, and Tipton (1985) in *Habits of the Heart*. One person interviewed was named Sheila who described her personal religiousness—she had faith but did not go to church—as "Sheilaism." She tries to love herself and believes that God promotes taking care of others. Greer and Roof (1992) noted that

> we do not have good measures of Sheila-like religiosity, which is all the more ironic considering that some of the most interesting, potentially significant religious and spiritual developments in the country today are to be found outside the narrow confines of institutional religion. (p. 347)

Greer and Roof added a short Privatism scale to the 1988 General Social Survey and found somewhat higher rates of Privatism for men than women, Whites than Blacks, younger than older, and those with more education and jobs with higher prestige. They also found that Nones (no affiliation) had highest levels of Privatism, followed by Jews, liberal Protestants, Roman Catholics, moderate Protestants, and Fundamentalist Protestants. Thus it is possible to touch only on some of the main features of the many shades of attitude and practice, even within denominations.

Buddhism has several variants and is a very interesting form of spirituality, but is beyond our scope here. The Eastern religions tend to be nontheistic and are very different from Christianity and Judaism, which are the primary foci in this chapter. Normative Islam is growing in the

United States, so I will comment both on the Nation of Islam and standard Islamic practice.

Specific Denominational Groups

Each denomination briefly summarized here has its own history and distinctive features. (Fuller details are available in several sources: Ammerman, 1987; Hunter, 1983; Lippy & Williams, 1988; Lovinger, 1984, 1990; Marty 1986a, 1986b, 1991; Roof & McKinney, 1987.) The denominations will be summarized within related groups, with some individual features noted as well. This taxonomy is one of convenience; some distinctions will seem obvious, as between Judaism and Catholicism, but others will be less so, as between Fundamentalism and Evangelicalism. The distinctions I have made here are informed by differentiations readily made by members of each denomination.

Judaism

Christianity arose out of a Jewish matrix, and although Judaism and Christianity share an overlapping ethical code, it is an error to construe Jewish concepts or practices in Christian terms and categories without verifying the reality of the apparent similarities. Judaism is a religious culture that, like Catholicism, can saturate the lives of its adherents. It emphasizes correct behavior (orthopraxis), but not correct belief (orthodoxy), which characterizes normative Christianity. Appropriate satisfactions and pleasures are a religious duty, whereas asceticism for its own sake is regarded as ingratitude to God.

Study and argument (even with God) is a path to knowledge and correct practice. Jews are three to five times as likely to be members of literary groups as are Catholics or Protestants (Rigney & Hoffman, 1993). Judaism does not regard itself as the only path to salvation; that is available to anyone who conforms to a minimum standard of behavior. Home and family are the central foci of Jewish life and of much religious practice. The synagogue (or temple) also serves as a community center and study hall.

European (Ashkenazic) Judaism has four main divisions or streams. Modern Orthodoxy is the descendent of normative Rabbinic Judaism and retains much of the traditional practice regarding diet, dress, worship, relations between husbands and wives, Sabbath practices, and so forth. The Hasidic (ultra-orthodox) movement, which arose in the 17th Century, attempted to reinfuse joy and energy into Jewish worship and practice but now has the character of a sect with even more devotion to the specifics of study, worship, and practice. The Reform movement arose in Germany to adapt traditional Jewish life to opportunities that were opening as the ghetto restrictions diminished. The Conservative movement was a counterreaction to the Reform movement: It moved toward the middle ground between Reform and Orthodox Judaism. The Mediterranean Jewish community (Sephardic) is different in many practices that depend, in part, on the specific country of origin but is considered part of Judaism. The comments that follow mainly describe European Judaism.

Although men and women are not traditionally equal in Judaism in the modern sense, women are typically powerful figures in their families, and jokes about Jewish mothers reflect the reality of their influence on their children's development in the family crucible. Fathers also have very significant roles, although they are likely to come into play later. Tight (and sometimes too tight) family bonds are a frequent feature as is an emphasis on education and achievement. A major concern of many families is assimilation, and because Jews make up less than three percent of the U.S. population, there are both real and dynamic factors at work in behavior, affect, and ideation.

Alcohol and food are interstitial features of family life; moderation in alcohol use is emphasized, but overeating is more likely a problem. Identity as a Jew is not easily maintained without family or social support, sometimes leading to syncretistic practices, such as a Christmas tree used as a "Chanukah bush" (Roiphe, 1989). In therapy, Jewish clients are likely to find free association and introspection plausible and comfortable.

Jewish clients will easily identify themselves as Jewish without showing the usual indicators, such as synagogue attendance or ritual observance. A Christian therapist may misread this as hypocrisy. Fear of enmeshment with the therapist, although a problem to be dealt with in treatment, also has cultural and family roots. A certain disputatious quality is partly a cultural characteristic as is a ready emotional intensity. "Paranoid" fear of the therapist or others, also a problem to be dealt with in treatment, has a historical reality as well. The therapist has to tread sensitively in untangling these threads.

Catholicism

The Eastern Orthodox and Roman Catholic churches are the two main branches arising from the Great Schism in 1054 and, more permanently, the Crusaders' sack of Constantinople. Whereas the Eastern Orthodox Church has approximately maintained its numbers in the past century, it has decreased in relative size compared with the growth of the Roman Catholic Church in the United States, which now comprises approximately 20% of the population. A smaller group of more than three-quarters of a million Eastern Rite (Byzantine Catholic or Uniate) congregants are under the sway of the Roman Catholic Church although their liturgy has a distinct admixture of Eastern Orthodox practice.

The Roman Catholic Church has a highly sacramental and ceremonial worship ritual and liturgy. It is hierarchical in organization but the myth of Catholic monolithic structure should have been laid to rest by even a casual perusal of the popular media. There are significant demographic facets. Commonly there are generational differences (Rigney & Hoffman, 1993); those who came to maturity at or before Vatican II are more likely to feel comfortable with an older, more authoritative practice, whereas the younger Catholic is more likely to define morality independently. They are less likely, for example, to follow church teachings than to follow their conscience on such matters as artificial contraception and abortion. Rigney and Hoffman (1993) also found that Catholics do not differ from others in attitudes toward intellectualism, although they were even lower than Fundamentalist Protestants in membership in literary groups.

There are typically ethnic and regional influences in Catholicism. Catholics of Italian extraction will typically differ from Irish Catholics in attitudes toward marriage, alcohol, family relations, emotional expressiveness, and comfort in self-disclosure. The nearer people are to their immigrant origins, the more marked these influences are likely to be. Priests in Eastern Rite Catholicism are not allowed to marry in this country, a Roman imposition that has produced resentment (Garrett, 1988).

The Catholic saturation of the life of the youngster typically leads to lifelong effects, and sometimes to jokes about being a "recovering Catholic." The general emphasis on an intellectual belief structure, plus the early introduction to church rituals and sacraments can lead to puzzling and disturbing experiences. Children taking First Communion are required to go to confession (Sacrament of Reconciliation or Penance). At age seven or eight, children frequently do not understand what this means. I have heard some as adults report having made up a sin to have something to confess; at their next confession, they then really had something to confess.

Older adults may sometimes confuse free association with confession and express that their therapy is not valid because they have not "told everything": For Catholics, a confession that is not complete (actually just mortal sins) lacks efficacy. But resistance is the bread and butter of therapy, so the therapist may have to explain to a client that not saying everything only means there is something to explore.

Shame, guilt, and confusion are not infrequent sequelae reported in therapy, along with ridicule of doctrine, priests, nuns, or brothers. When prior experiences with hypocritical or pompous clergy have been significant, a latent or overt skepticism toward the therapist may be a common problem in therapy. Inhibition or dysfunction regarding bodily pleasure (e.g., sexuality), gratification in personal achievement, or an anxiety-deflecting ritual are sometimes distinctive features in Catholic clients, although this is not restricted to Catholic clients. With less sophisticated clients, one may have to deal with whether the therapist has the "authority" to hear confession. In spite of ample adult sophistication, some clients (and their therapists) may be surprised by the emergence of very young feelings, thoughts, or reactions in the deeper phases of therapy.

The Eastern Orthodox Church is less centralized, less intellectual, more mystical, and has a more expressive liturgy than the Roman Church. To some degree the Eastern Rite Catholic Church is similar although it is under the control of the Roman Church, a control that has been insensitive in the past. These churches, because of their decentralized quality tend to have stronger ethnic affiliations and more variability in many matters.

Mainline Protestantism

A word about terminology is apropos here. *Church* refers to a religious group that sees itself in interaction with society, as do all the mainline churches. *Sect* defines a religious group that arose within a church but has separated itself to a greater or lesser degree from the wider society. This includes many Fundamentalist churches. *Cults* are religious groups that do not arise within a church but also are separate from the larger society. The Mormon church (Latter-day Saints) arose as a cult and eventually made the transition to functioning as a Church. Although *cult* is a disparaging term in its general usage, sociologically it does not carry this connotation; indeed there are several cults within the Roman Catholic Church that are just groups with a special interest in some facet of Catholic life, worship, or thought.

Mainline, sometimes a term of approval and sometimes deprecation, refers primarily to the Episcopal, Presbyterian and Reformed, Lutheran and Methodist churches. Some Baptist groups are also within this category. Once these churches represented significant sectors of American society but now, except for the Lutheran churches, and some Baptist churches, they are in notable membership declines (Lovinger, 1990). Except for the Methodist church that arose out of the Church of England (Episcopal), these churches are rooted in the Protestant Reformation.

Mainline churches tend toward diversity of thought and practice within each denomination, thus they are generally more accepting of a range of variations. Some individual Methodist congregations are more conservative than is the norm since the United Methodist Church brought together some disparate congregations. Similarly, the mainstream of Lutheran practice seen in the recently merged Evangelical Lutheran Church of America differs from the more conservative Lutheran Church-Missouri Synod and the even more conservative Wisconsin Synod.

The diversity that characterizes the mainline churches suggests that a full range of personality characteristics is to be expected. However the doctrinal rigidity and biblical literalism characteristic of the Fundamentalist or Evangelical churches are not normative and represent some particular issue for the client. Certain Pentecostal practices (e.g., glossolalia or speaking in tongues, healing) have entered some mainline churches so several characteristics that once distinguished between the two groups no longer do so as reliably. Although the presence of such practices in, for example, a Methodist or Presbyterian client would no longer connote extreme divergence from normative practice, it is still not common. Southern and Northern churches within the same denomination differ notably. Typically, Southern churches are likely to be more conservative in doctrine and expected behavior, but a good deal of any particular congregation's traits depends on the character of the pastor.

The Episcopal, Lutheran, and Methodist churches have an episcopal form of governance (i.e., supervised by a bishop or superintendent) although they also have local boards of trustees or directors. Presbyterian and Reformed churches are governed by a board of elders (trustees), whereas Baptist churches are congregationally regulated, even though they may be affiliated with regional or national groups. The Baptist movement is quite individualistic and many local churches can and do ordain their own ministers. My impression is that the more mainstream Baptist churches are less likely to do this.

Clients from this background will reflect what is typical of clients in general. Methodists are likely to be somewhat more cheerful and less ideological, whereas Lutherans may range from approximately this point to a rather rigid, dogmatic stance if the person's background arises from the Missouri or Wisconsin synod. Social action interests are more common among adherents in this group than among many Fundamentalists.

New Scripture Churches

Most denominations have additional writings that supplement the Bible. Judaism has the Talmud and the writings of the great medieval sages. The Roman Catholic Church has Canon law, papal encyclicals, and other writings. However, the Church of Jesus Christ of Latter-day Saints (Mormon or LDS) and the Christian Science church both venerate writings that are decisively formative for them.

Except for their reliance on their own new Scriptures, the Church of Jesus Christ of Latter-day Saints and the Christian Science church could hardly be more different. Mormon theology and practice emphasizes the perfection of one's life by following the commandments of God. The church is operated by a lay ministry. Emphasis is placed on missionary action, service, and work. God is a loving deity who provides, and this is concretized through mutual support for all within the community who are in need. If a person is able, repayment is expected. All this makes Mormon life attractive, so it is no surprise that in the thirty years from 1955 to 1985, membership in the Latter-day Saints grew over 200% (Lovinger, 1990). In Utah, for every five converts, there were two dropouts (Bahr & Albrecht, 1989), a 60% retention rate. They also found among the disaffiliated that many were marginal to begin with. Thus losses were found among those that would have been expected to leave any denomination.

Mormons are very family oriented; they expect early marriage and frown on celibacy. Coffee, tea, tobacco, alcohol, and pre- or extramarital sex are prohibited. Although husbands and wives make varying accommodations within individual families, normative practice places men as leaders in their families. Psychotherapy, as a contrivance of the material world may have acceptance, but the leader of the local ward or branch will be concerned that a non-Mormon therapist might undermine Mormon teachings.

There is a strong emphasis on conformity to accepted practice, and certain parts of Mormon religious practice are closed to non-Mormons. In therapy, there may be a subtle we–they quality, and marked shame or guilt over violating practice or doctrine, even in thought. The restricted role for women is likely to offend therapists not steeped in the full range of Mormon life. In addition to countertransference problems, the therapist must be aware that there can be considerable painful social, familial, and personal costs to clients who undergo major change in outlook as a result of therapy.

Christian Science holds that the nature of reality is spiritual, whereas matter is evil and illusory, and illness is due to incorrect thinking (Simmons, 1991). This leads to an entire system of healing provided by Christian Science practitioners, recognized by the IRS as a legitimate medical expense. Setting broken bones is the only acceptable material medical intervention; ordinary treatment of illnesses involves prayer and the effort to help the ill person correct their erroneous thinking. Because matter is illusory and thought is crucial, treatment does not even require the physical presence of the practitioner. For children, this highly abstracted representation may well be experienced as a doomed sense of abandonment (Simmons, 1991). When Simmons entered psychotherapy, this cut all his ties to the church: "if medicine was considered incompatible with Christian Science, mental health services were unspeakable. They used mortal mind to treat the disease of mortal mind, instead of trying to eradicate that 'illusory' mind" (p. 146).

The few Christian Science clients whose treatment I have some knowledge of evinced a curious emotional vacuity. Those raised within the church have an intense attachment to its doctrines so they are unlikely to be seen in therapy. Conversely, those who do enter treatment are leaving or have left. The therapist may have to deal with the client's expectation of having to believe in the therapist's theoretical system or applied techniques, a stance not compatible with increasing personal freedom. The emotional emptiness I have seen makes engagement in a therapeutic relationship more than usually difficult so there may be slow progress early in therapy.

Millennial Churches

The Seventh-day Adventists and Jehovah's Witnesses subscribe to the description in the Book of Revelation of a 1,000-year struggle between Christ and Satan during which Christ will rescue his followers and Satan will be destroyed (see the next section, on Fundamentalist, Evangelical, Holiness, and Pentecostal churches for more detail). The Seventh-day Adventist movement began, as did Latter-day Saints and Christian Science, in the 19th Century. It is distinctive in holding to Saturday Sabbath observance, not eating meat unless butchered according to scriptural requirements, and also prohibiting tobacco, alcohol, seductive clothing, union membership, and pre- or extramarital sex (Rayburn, personal communication, November 17, 1993). In spite of a foreboding theology, Adventists value hard work and success but are very motivated to do what is right, to strive for perfection, to avoid errors, and are concerned about what others may think of them as Christians. In seeking therapy they are likely to be concerned about either a judgmental therapist or an attack on their religion, but will be cooperative if they perceive that this will not occur (Rayburn, personal communication, November 17, 1993).

The founder of Jehovah's Witnesses was influenced by Adventist theology but the Witnesses' theology has a darker, more apocalyptic coloration. They qualify as a sect because (a) they vigorously promote an end-of-the-world vision in which only they will be saved (Botting & Botting, 1984), (b) they actively oppose anything more than minimal contact with "worldly" people, and (c) they strongly disapprove of postsecondary school education unless it is vocationally oriented. They distinguish between Christendom (all other Protestant and Catholic churches) and Christians (themselves). Those baptized members who are insufficiently active may be required to disaffiliate. If a member's behavior is sufficiently deviant (e.g., smoking, having oral sex, or having one's own interpretation of the Bible), the member may be disfellowshipped, a terribly painful punishment for most former members.

As a group, Jehovah's Witnesses have experienced considerable persecution, often taken as a testimony to the truth of their position. Their construction of Christian doctrine differs considerably from the standard view, such that contemporaneous hostility, even in theologically sophisticated people, occurs (e.g., Hoekema, 1972). Because Jehovah's Witnesses is a closed society, information is difficult to secure except from disaffected former members or hostile outsiders. Nevertheless, in the 30 years from

1955 to 1985, membership in Jehovah's Witnesses grew nearly 300% (Lovinger, 1990). Considerable disaffection occurred when prophecies of Armageddon (universal conflict and destruction) failed to occur, as happened in 1975.

Whereas current members are unlikely to seek psychotherapy, former members may do so. These clients will have grown up in, or entered a society that is very tightly knit, devoted to right thinking as dictated by the central office in Brooklyn, and extremely patriarchal. There are very strong prohibitions against pre- and extramarital sex, masturbation, the independent interpretation of the Bible, or contact with the disfellowshipped (even if they are family members). Misbehavior by a child can seriously threaten the parents' standing in the local Kingdom Hall (*church* is a rejected term and seen as part of the world's problems; Botting & Botting, 1984).

Fundamentalist, Evangelical, Holiness, and Pentecostal

Although each of these deserves a separate section, the limits of space and their theological similarities allow their review together here. These churches tend to be very individualistic, often not tightly associated with larger church bodies, and inclined toward schism. For Fundamentalists, dispensational premillennialism is a key differentiation from most churches outside this group (Ammerman, 1987). Dispensational refers to the concept of time being formed into periods or dispensations. Christ is expected to return and "rapture" his followers, which will be followed by a 1,000-year reign of the anti-Christ and a time of "Tribulations." The Rapture will occur when Christ returns to remove all of his followers from this world without the rest of the world knowing it. Then God's army will defeat Satan's forces at Armageddon and the millennium will begin (hence premillennial). This is expected soon. There are variants on the millennial theme based on whether the period of peace is expected to occur before or after Christ's return.

Creationism as an alternative to evolution is a common theme as part of the selectively literal treatment of Scripture. Ammerman (1987) has described Fundamentalist churches as sectarian in avoiding more than minimal contact with the larger society, so many Fundamentalists regard someone like Jerry Falwell as a "left-winger." Despite this, some Fundamentalists are moving to act politically on the wider American scene in furtherance of specific aims and goals. This includes continued efforts to promote creationism, oppose abortion, restore prayer in public schools, censor or purge offensive reading material, suppress pornography, install their own school board candidates, and elect political representatives who support their agenda. Because of their theological similarity to Evangelicals, it may not be easy to distinguish between the two.

Whereas the strict behavioral and conceptual control demanded by Fundamentalist churches may seem oppressive to outsiders, members are provided with continuing reassurance of their safety, importance, and eventual reward, plus firm assurance and guidance about important decisions and choices (Ammerman, 1987). Children are raised to adhere to these standards and are often polite, agreeable, and achievement-oriented; adults (many of whom came to Fundamentalism in adolescence or later) often report considerable life improvement.

However, Capps (1992) has persuasively argued that the "religious legitimation of the physical punishment of children is widely known to be a centerpiece of certain conservative and fundamentalist theologies" (p. 7). It is based on the generally held religious view

> that the child enters this world with a distorted or wayward will. It is therefore the responsibility of parents to break . . . the child's natural will that he or she will then be able to respond to parental guidance and live in conformity with the superior will of God. (Capps, p. 3)

Capps discussed the serious effects of the abuse implicit in this position, and the intensification of feelings of shame, doubt, emotional detachment, and the separation of religious thought from the rest of the person's ideational abilities.

Despite the theology, Fundamentalists are generally cheerful and optimistic. Sethi and Seligman (1993) contrasted congregations divided into fundamentalist (Orthodox Jews, Calvinists, and Muslims), moderate (Conservative Jews, Catholics, Lutherans, and Methodists) and liberal (Unitarians and Reform Jews) groups and found very significant differences in members' personal optimism and in the optimism of the preaching and liturgy. Although Sethi and Seligman did not study Protestant Fundamentalists, their results are entirely consistent with Ammerman's (1987) observations. Most Fundamentalists are very wary of nonchurch based or nonapproved counseling or therapy, having been warned of the negative attitude of therapists toward religion. For these clients, erotically tinged transferences would be very hard to tolerate and the therapist may have to give at least a general forewarning that emotional reactions may occur but do not imply what they would mean in ordinary life. Similar difficulties with anger are likely.

Most of Fundamentalist theology would be acceptable to Evangelicals who differ primarily in their willingness to compromise with or accommodate to the larger society (Ammerman, 1987). Evangelicalism was once the dominant religious theme in American society (Hunter, 1983). With the rise of modern society, characterized by increasing urbanization, technological specialization, job-related mobility, and the diffusion of scientific findings into the general culture, a revelation-oriented, belief-demanding, literal acceptance of Scripture and traditional belief and practice is under increasing pressure. The massive network of modern secular belief, supported by powerful, empirically based views of reality and by increasingly robust, rapid, and effective technologies, forces some accommodation in the Evangelical religious system. The alternatives of withdrawal or massive resistance are not feasible for most, who must earn a living from modern society (Hunter, 1983).

Nevertheless, this accommodation has not been easy although it has led to a recognition of pluralism and the bare possibility of alternate paths to truth. Ellison and Sherkat (1993) have found empirical support for an increased awareness in Evangelicals of the need for autonomy in thought in their children to help them resist the pervasive images of sexuality, violence, and drugs. Similarly, Wilcox (1989) found that although Evangelicals were more likely to support the Moral Majority than were Catholics or mainline Protestants, support came from only about 60% of Evangelicals.

Like Fundamentalists, Evangelicals emphasize Bible reading; the Devil as a real personage; church volunteer work and attendance; tithing; and a personal conversion and relationship to Jesus as Lord and Savior. In all these aspects, Evangelicals differ markedly from liberal Protestants and Catholics (Hunter, 1983), who are typically much less likely to emphasize these activities. More than four fifths of the Evangelicals receive much consolation from their beliefs, and that is notably, and in some cases dramatically, higher than the other groups Hunter surveyed. As their name suggests, Evangelicals evangelize or proselytize, seeking to convert others to their faith position. The Fundamentalists in the church Ammerman (1987) studied were similarly eager for converts but not as active in seeking people out, preferring to witness an attractive style of spiritual and family life.

The Holiness movement arose from within the Methodist tradition. They saw baptism as justification (removal of Original Sin) and the first blessing. A person could work toward sanctification or spiritual perfection and the eradication of sin (the second blessing). When the movement precipitated out as a group of churches, they saw holiness or perfection as a much more rapid process than did the Methodists. The Pentecostal movement arose within Holiness churches and saw "baptism in the Holy Spirit" or "being slain in the Spirit" (Poloma & Pendleton, 1989) as the third blessing, accompanied by the "gifts of the Spirit," which included speaking in tongues, teaching, healing, prophecy, and miracles.

Worship in Holiness churches is decorous and restrained, whereas much physical and vocal activity is evident in Pentecostal churches. However, this is changing as some Pentecostal practices have been diffusing through mainline churches or appearing as the Charismatic movement in American Roman Catholic churches. Poloma and Pendleton have suggested that these practices may revitalize religious institutions.

African American Churches

There are three main African American religious groupings: Protestant, Catholic, and the Nation of Islam. The Nation of Islam had a considerable rise among African Americans under Elijah Muhammad. Many Whites were disturbed by the Nation of Islam's extreme stance vis-à-vis Whites. However, when Elijah Muhammad died and his son assumed the mantle of leadership, he changed the name to the American Moslem Mission and led the group into a normative Islamic attitude toward Whites and others. Louis Farrakhan did not accept this change and reconstituted the Nation of Islam.

The African American churches, primarily Protestant, were very important havens for African Americans both before and after the Civil War; they were one institution that Whites did not control. Along with the National Association for the Advancement of Colored People (NAACP), African American "churches became important centers of social protest and group solidarity" (Roof & McKinney, 1987, p. 13) during the civil rights struggle in the 60's. These churches also provided significant services (e.g., meals service, community education, public health education) that would ordinarily be performed for the White community by secular organizations (Chaves & Higgins, 1992).

African American Protestants have strong ties to their churches. Their attendance at worship services is second only to that of conservative White Protestants, and their membership in church-related groups exceeds all other groups surveyed (Roof & McKinney, 1987). In worship, there is a distinctive style of preaching, and my impression is that the usually restrained and decorous style in mainline White Protestant churches is not the norm in mainline Protestant African American churches. The congregation is more participatory and expressive.

Suspicion or fear of the therapist or others in the social environment, which is a problem to be dealt with in treatment, has both a present and historical reality. Many African Americans are more likely to seek counseling from the pastor, church counselor or priest (if Catholic) than to go to an agency or private therapist. If the church is unable to provide the needed help, denial is a not-infrequent alternative. Related to this is a tendency to acknowledge problems when they are identified, but not explore them. The therapist may need to be more active in bringing this to a client's attention to educate them to the benefits of exploration. Those African American clients who do come for therapy may express the concept that suffering is a message from God to change one's ways. This takes sensitive handling.

For many clients who have achieved middle-class status, adaptation to living in a largely White residential community has entailed presentation of a proper, well-behaved, untroubled facade to fend off common criticisms and stereotypes. Therapeutic exploration of perceived deficits and failings may be experienced as a particularly sharp threat to a highly adaptive facade, especially if the therapist is White.

Islam

The image of Islam is, for many people in this country, colored by its association with the Middle-East conflict, Arab terrorism, and the distrust of Iran (which is not an Arab state). Added to this are reports of the subjugation and control of women (extensive in Saudi Arabia, and to lesser-to-much-lesser degrees in other Islamic countries) and accounts of the practice of genital mutilation (by no means universal in Arab countries nor restricted to them). Consequently, a highly negative picture of Islam has developed. Ironically, compared with the Old and New Testament, the Qur'an (Koran) is clearer and firmer in declaring equality between men and women, in the requirement to provide charitable aid (2½% of one's total net worth, not 10% of annual income), and the necessity for modest dress in both men and women. In addition to the Qur'an, there is a codified set of practices embedded in the *Shari'a* and a specially protected status (*dhimmi*) for both Christians and Jews as peoples who adhere to books of Scripture. The rejection of Whites or any ethnic group, as practiced by the Nation of Islam, is prohibited in normative Islam. Devotion to the family, self-control, and diligent work, all leading to a modest, dignified, but satisfying life are characteristic of Islam both in this country and around the world.

In the United States, Islam may function in at least three forms: one arising from African American sources and bifurcated into the Nation of Islam or the American Moslem Mission, whereas the third springs from Muslims who have emigrated to the United States or are the children of immigrants (Haddad & Lummis, 1987). The Nation of Islam deviates from normative Islam (Lovinger, 1990) in its attitudes towards Whites, whereas the American Moslem Mission is closer to traditional Islamic values. But both may exhibit a praxis subtly influenced by the Protestant or Catholic backgrounds of their adherents. Immigrant Muslims or their children will be affected by customary differences in praxis in their home countries as well as separations due to theology (e.g., Sunni vs. Shi'i).

Whereas some Muslims have assimilated an American identity and are adaptable in thought and practice, many others are more strict in their practice, and others are deeply committed to the worldwide Islam movement. For the latter two segments there is a "striving to realize an Islamic order" (Haddad & Lummis, 1987, p. 18). The traditional view of everything as God's will is countered by a recent trend of holding humans to be capable of rationality and responsible for their behavior. This revision of traditional Islamic teaching also runs counter to mystical Sufi practices of the 19th century. This modern view is certainly consistent with cognitive interventions.

In Islamic tradition, prayer services are conducted by the *imam*, a nonordained leader. In Muslim countries, specialized functions are performed by *shaykhs* (religious leaders), *qadis* (judges) and *'alims* (theologians), but in the United States these services are often undertaken by the *imam* (Haddad & Lummis, 1987). Also atypically, the *imam* in this country handles marital and family problems and this occupies much of his work. Many *imams* are not trained in either Islamic law or counseling but this may alter as Islamic communities expand and adapt to the peculiar American society they exist in. Thus some Islamic practices will come to resemble the common activities of pastors and priests.

Sufism is a mystical spiritual discipline in Islam that has resemblances to psychoanalytic ego psychology (Shafii, 1985). Employing regular meetings with the Sufi guide, or *pir*, and music, dance, chanting, seclusion, individual and group meditation, and poetry reading, the goal is awareness of reality through self-knowledge (including unconscious ideas and motives). In actual application it seems quite different from dynamic psychotherapy as practiced in the West, but the comparison may be useful in helping a person of traditional Muslim background understand the therapy process.

THE BIBLE

Because the Bible undergirds much of the development of religious life in this country, and may be introduced by the client in therapy, a little background may be helpful. (I will discuss its use in treatment later.) Whereas many are likely to think that the power of the Bible resides in being the "word of God," in fact its capacity for authority is centered more in the power of its narrative, vividness of imagery, clarity of demand, balance between satisfaction and restraint, and its uncompromising, vibrant portrayal of real individuals, families, and emotions. The apparent simplicity of the text conceals complex depths beneath a literary style whose conventions and allusions modern readers no longer recognize (Alter, 1981; Josipovici, 1988).

Translations

The Bible was written over a long period in a language very dissimilar from English and originating from a different understanding of the world. Because of this, translations are influenced by text variations in the manuscripts, uncertainties about meanings of rare words, and loss or misunderstanding of contexts that would make idiomatic and specific historical references clearer. In addition, denominational theologies and traditions shade translations according to interpretational requirements.

Thus if a particular text excerpt is important to the client and related to a specific therapeutic issue it helps to compare several different translations (Lovinger, 1984; Lovinger, 1990). One example of the problems with translations comes from George Lamsa (1985), a Syrian Christian minister who grew up in an area that spoke Aramaic, the common language at the time of Jesus. It is now thought that many of the Gospels were either originally written in Aramaic or written in Greek by Aramaic-speaking authors.

Lamsa suggested that the Greek texts of the Gospels made errors in translating some Aramaic idioms. One of the most famous is "sooner a camel will go through the eye of a needle than a rich man will get into heaven." The implication is that it is impossible. However the word for camel and the word for rope in Aramaic are so close that it takes a native speaker to know the difference. If you say "sooner a rope will go through the eye of a needle than a rich man will get into heaven," a very different image is created because a rope could go through the eye of a needle if some changes are made. Some materialism will have to be stripped off, but it is possible.

Language Qualities of the Bible

Humor and word play in the Bible are common and well worth considering. The first man was Adam, or *adom* in Hebrew, and he was made from the earth or the dust. In Hebrew the word for earth is *adomah* so his name would translate as "Dusty" or "Earthy," but not "Rocky." Another example is *manna*, synonymous with help from heaven. Apparently there are insects in that region that exude a sweet, sticky residue that is edible. The Israelites picked this up and they went to Moses and said "*man-hu*," meaning "what's that?" In other words, manna means "whatzit." One final example is Sarah, Abraham's wife, who is infertile. When she is old God comes and says to Abraham that Sarah is going to have a child. Sarah laughs at the thought of having a child in her old age, but she becomes pregnant and gives birth to Isaac or, in Hebrew, *Yitzhak*, derived from the Hebrew verb "to laugh."

The use of language in the Bible also illustrates the directness of the relationship of people to God. The Authorized or King James version contains some beautiful language, but it often misses the pungent, immediate quality of the Bible's language. There is no "thou" in Hebrew, only a very direct "you." Jesus calls God "*abba*" which in Aramaic means "daddy," connoting a direct availability open to everyone. At one point while Abraham was camped, God appears in the form of three men to announce the doom of Sodom and Gomorrah. Abraham protests by raising the possibility of the innocent being destroyed with the guilty. A long exchange ensues during which God, who originally agreed not to destroy these cities if there were fifty innocent people, finally agrees to spare the cities if there are only ten such people. People are not punished for arguing with God or for being angry; they are punished for their behavior.

Aspects of Biblical Literature

The Bible's literary structure is diverse and different from modern styles. First, there is not the pride of authorship that we find in modern writing. The tradition was to either attribute writings to more ancient figures or to have no author at all. Although tradition sometimes attributes authorship in books of the Bible in the Old Testament, the texts themselves are usually silent. The Gospels have names attached, as do Paul's letters, but with several, authorship is not certain. What was important was the message, not the author.

Hebrew, a concrete, earthy language, did not lend itself to abstractions: Issues, such as the explanation of evil would be dealt with in story form rather than in an abstract essay. There are reasons to think that Job is not a real character but an attempt to discuss the problem of evil. Similarly, the Book of Jonah can be understood as an exploration of the prophetic calling and the nature of God. The use of narrative to discuss an issue is clearest in the story of Ruth. The story of Ruth, a Moabite woman, was written at a time when the Jews and the people of Moab were actually in conflict. Ruth marries one of Naomi's two sons and another woman (Orpah) marries the other. The sons were named Mahlon and Chilion which mean "Sickness" and "Wasting," the biblical equivalent of naming children Cancer and AIDS. This clearly indicates that the Book of Ruth is not intended to be a historical narrative. Ruth leaves her people to go with Naomi after her husband dies and eventually becomes the grandmother of King David. By showing an enemy woman as an ancestor of King David, this story probably opposed a move at one time in Jewish history to force men to divorce their foreign wives.

There are other qualities in the narratives that are worth knowing about. For example, characters may be introduced with a single comment and then dropped. Sarah is introduced relatively early in the story, where the narrator announces that she is barren and says no more. This is not the modern way of fictional character development. The Bible is often less direct. Character is the center of surprise in the Bible (Alter, 1981), as people change in personality and their behavior becomes unexpected. Jacob first exploits his brother's weakness to secure Esau's birthright, but changes greatly later. There is a complex quality to the character of biblical figures.

No one in the Bible is presented as perfect. They get angry, make mistakes; they can be argumentative, love some people, and hate others; sometimes they act deceitfully and sometimes generously; in other words they are human. Clients who have a strong need to idealize one figure or another may be saying that some quality in that person is especially meaningful to them.

Miracles are described so as to be frequently recognizable as natural events. The crossing of the Red Sea was actually over the Sea of Reeds, a shallow sea. A strong wind, as described in Exodus, would alter the water level and might make a crossing quite easy. Miracles, then, were understood as events that happened when they did as signs to people. A client much concerned with biblical miracles may also be expressing a need for a kind of rescue in the face of apparent helplessness or hopelessness.

Lastly, parables are stories that are supposed to make a point. The parable of the prodigal son is one of the more famous into which many meanings have been read. These include that Christianity has displaced Judaism, but one could infer a message about God's love, parental love, and favoritism, jealousy among brothers, and what jealousy does to people (Josipovici, 1988). It is important to be aware that interpretations are attributed to biblical texts, not always inherent in them.

ASSESSMENT OF RELIGIOUS FACTORS IN PSYCHOTHERAPY

Clinical assessment is important in the conduct of therapy because it leads to significant treatment decisions affecting both strategy and tactics. The denominational orientation provides a context for an assessment. As an example, I worked with a young woman in her senior year in college who was a Methodist. She was concerned because she felt she was out of alignment with her peers because they were interested in the inerrancy of the Bible and the gifts of the spirit whereas she was interested in world hunger and social justice. Among Protestant denominations, Methodists are most likely to express their faith through social justice concerns, but at that time such fundamentalist issues were quite unusual among Methodists. This young woman was entirely mainstream for Methodism; hence I hypothesized that her presenting "religious" problem screened a poor emotional connection.

Religious coping styles also influence organization of affect. Kaiser (1991) compared Pargament's three religious problem-solving styles (*self-directing*, or seeing the self, not God, as responsible to work out problems; *collaborative*, or seeing God as a partner; *deferring*, or submitting to God's omnipotent power) with guilt about sex, hostility, and conscience. Guilt was negatively related to self-directing measures whereas collaborative or submitting styles were positively related to Kaiser's guilt measures.

One form of religious behavior that may be misunderstood is "speaking in tongues." Originally this was described in the Book of Acts as an intense religious experience around the time of the Jewish holiday known as the Feast of Weeks or the Pentecost (in Greek). Churches that value this form of expression adopted the name (i.e., the Pentecostal churches). Thus it is common to see glossolalia in many Pentecostal churches, but although it has spread, many churches do not foster this aspect of worship.

If a client talks about communication with the Holy Spirit, or being bathed in the Holy Spirit, it is very easy to think that this person is seriously disturbed. But they may be expressing nothing more than a common practice in their denomination. If somebody talks about direct communication with God or Satan, this is more likely pathological.

Similarly, reports of mystical experiences have sometimes been taken as pathognomic for psychosis. Stifler, Greer, Sneck, and Dovenmuehle (1993) found that although psychotic inpatients and members of contemplative or mystical religious orders were higher than a noninstitutional sample on Hood's mysticism scale, they were clearly discriminable on personality measures.

Based on clinical experience, 10 markers of probable religious pathology are offered below, followed by 5 indices of likely mature religious adjustment. A recent empirical study of coping difficulties is also discussed.

Markers of Pathology

1. *Self-Oriented Display:* For some people, being religious is not merely something that is within them, but is an exhibition of one's religious adherence. Clients who produce a significant self-oriented display are using their religion primarily for its ability to satisfy narcissistic needs.

2. *Religion as Reward:* Clients who see religion as a constant aid in the ordinary difficulties in life are easy to mock or parody. I have heard ministers talk about "Parking-Space Christians," congregants who recount events where they were looking for a parking space in the downtown area: They pray for a parking space and there it is. I think that frequently this says that a person feels so needy and so empty in their life that this kind of experience is very important to them emotionally and substitutes for the satisfaction of human relationships.

3. *Scrupulosity:* Scrupulosity is an intense focus on the avoidance of sin or error. In some people this has obsessive-compulsive features. Issues of control of one's impulses and motives may be present but the therapist should also keep in mind the possibility of a history of physical or sexual

abuse. Scrupulosity, if undertaken in a way that significantly affects other people, can express a good deal of hostility either as a primary or additional motive. If hostility is being expressed, it may be very hard to access because the client is only following God's rules, thus avoiding personal responsibility.

4. *Relinquishing Responsibility:* Or "the devil made me do it." Even in nonreligious terms, clients feel accountable for what they could not really have responsibility for, or do not feel answerable for what they should be responsible. For example, an adult who was abused as a child may well take blame for the adult's behavior.

5. *Ecstatic Frenzy:* This is seen in some churches, not as part of the regular practice, but as an idiosyncratic expression. This needs careful evaluation as it may be an ominous indicator: Such intense, unregulated emotional expression may herald a progressive process of decompensation.

6. *Persistent Church-Shopping:* Clients who can never find a church that satisfies them for more than a few months or a year are signaling serious difficulties in maintaining stable relationships. There may be severe narcissistic vulnerability to real or imagined rebuffs, major difficulties in maintaining object permanence, or intense needs for the kinds of energizing they may experience in a worship service (Shafranske, 1991). It is also important to pay attention to repetitive time patterns that may indicate an anniversary reaction to some event in the client's past.

7. *Indiscriminate Enthusiasm:* This seems similar to ecstatic frenzy except in terms of where and how it is expressed. There are certain generally accepted constraints on social behavior. For example a person has had a transformative religious experience and attempts to share this with others. If other people are similarly responsive, there is no problem. If there are clear, persistent responses indicating that the person's enthusiasm is unwelcome, this begins to verge onto the pathological. If the behavior is persistent and begins to impair relationships or one's work, it begins to resemble an addiction.

8. *Hurtful Love in Religious Practice:* Sometimes characterized as *Christian love* to the client, this term has been associated with unnecessarily hurtful, damaging, or very painful experiences with others and may generate confusion in the client as to what love is and how it is expressed. Another manifestation of hurtful love, often found in Jewish families, is

the self-sacrificing parent who demands a constant return on what has been done for the child.

9. *The Bible as a Moment-to-Moment Guide to Life:* This may be related to relinquishing responsibility. Some clients want the Bible to be not only a form of spiritual guidance and a way to live with others, but as a resource for ordinary questions about daily living. The concrete, behavioral prescriptions that the Bible presents may lend themselves to this view, but the therapist has to judge whether the client is surrendering ordinary self-direction (Pruyser, 1977) in emphasizing a passive stance in giving oneself over to God.

10. *Possession:* Skeptical therapists are not likely to take reports of or questions about spirit or demon "possession" seriously, and when such phenomena are reported by clients this may lead to a too-ready assumption of a delusional or paranoid psychosis. One has to also consider hysteria, multiple personality disorder, dissociative reactions, and borderline disorders. Some therapists who work with a number of multiple personality disordered clients may be too ready to accept accounts of satanic ritual involvement that may only be the psychic representation of parental torture. I worked with a borderline client who feared being possessed by the Devil (Lovinger, 1985). He felt tormented by his relationship with his father. Here, as elsewhere, such feelings have to be explored.

Indices of Mature Adjustment

1. *Awareness of Complexity and Ambiguity:* The Bible and its derivative literature, plus various church and synagogue traditions, are complex and sometimes quite ambiguous because they reflect the ambiguities of human existence. A person with a mature adjustment should have some recognition of the complexities that exist within most, if not all denominations. The therapist should not be misled if the client comes from a very conservative or Fundamentalist denomination and presents a religious issue as being seen only one way in his or her church. There is usually more "wiggle room."

2. *Choice in Religious Affiliation:* The "supermarket" selection in American religious life presents the religious person with a vast range of options. If the person continues in their parents' religious affiliation, the therapist needs to listen carefully to see if this is a commitment, or if this is an

affiliation with no special investment. Where the person has experimented with, or at least considered some alternatives, their eventual choice is more likely to represent a more mature choice. The therapist must, however, be aware of a propensity for "church-shopping."

3. *Value-Behavior Congruence:* It's not always possible to practice your values and ideals yet there should be some reasonable congruence. A person's concern for an issue is not infrequently the site of a personal conflict: A client who is concerned about world hunger but contributes very little to charity is a clear example of such a conflict. To characterize this as hypocrisy would overlook the conflicted ambivalence.

4. *Recognition of Shortcomings:* Although we all fall short of our values at times, they should redirect our striving. Recognizing such failings within a religious framework without excess self-punitive reproaches or adjusting your standards to be consistent with what you are actually doing seems a marker of maturity for most people.

5. *Respect for Boundaries:* Religious enthusiasm inflicted on other people rather than offered or witnessed to them suggests that the person may need to make everybody the same because they are afraid of their own doubts, questions, and uncertainties.

Empirical Measures of Religious Adjustment

Pargament and his associates (1993) have been conducting an extensive research program on religious coping for a number of years. They looked at 3 dimensions comprising 11 scales that they thought were "Red Flags" of problems in religious coping. To evaluate the effectiveness of religious ideation or practice in coping, they asked, "how do we know whether religion is part of the problem or part of the solution?" (p. 3). These four to five item scales are listed below with a single item from each as an example.

Wrong Direction

1. *Self-Sacrifice:* Decided to devote all of my time to my religion.
2. *Self-Worship:* Decided to start caring about me and stop caring about God.
3. *Religious Apathy:* Stopped caring after God showed me how futile life is.

Wrong Road

4. *God's Punishment:* Believed God was punishing me for my sins.
5. *Religious Passivity:* Let the church handle the situation for me.
6. *Religious Vengeance:* Prayed that God would punish the real sinners.
7. *Religious Denial:* Was not bothered at all because it was God's will.

Against the Stream

8. *Interpersonal Religious Conflict:* Felt that the church did not support me in my time of need.
9. *Conflict With Church Dogma:* Disagreed with my clergy about faith, God, and religion.
10. *Anger at God:* Felt angry that God did not hear my prayers.
11. *Religious Doubts:* Had difficulty gaining comfort from my religious beliefs.

Administering the scales to 245 people who had suffered recent losses, major illnesses, or injuries they correlated these scales with measures of self-esteem, trait anxiety, and problem solving skills. Whereas seven of their anticipated "red flags" performed largely as predicted, two scales, Self-Sacrifice and Religious Denial, were associated with more positive outcomes, and Religious Passivity and Religious Vengeance had mixed outcomes.

As Pargament and his associates noted, although some of these scales seem to involve surrender of personal agency and efficacy, it is important to understand their personal meaning to the individual. Denial did not mean denial of the event, but of its negative emotional impact. These results are of sufficient moment that they deserve replication.

The two scales with positive outcomes do not cut across the five items discussed previous as Indices of Mature Adjustment. However, the 10 Markers of Pathology have three dimensions that appear to parallel the 11 scales that Pargament et al. (1993) investigated. These are Scrupulosity and Relinquishing Responsibility, which seems to parallel Religious Vengeance; and The Bible as a Moment-to-Moment Guide to Life, which appears to resemble Religious Passivity. Neither the Vengeance nor the Passivity scales showed significant correlations with Pargament's mental health and coping measures, but Passivity was associated with more positive religious outcomes and Vengeance was associated with a more negative mood. Perhaps one difference is that the Passivity scale reflects nonagency in circumstances where this may be appropriate as in death, loss, or serious illness, whereas The Bible as a Guide dimension saturates a person's thinking on events ranging from trivial to significant.

PSYCHOTHERAPY

Initial Obstacles

There are numerous initial obstacles in therapy, some apparently practical (Lovinger, 1978), but many more clearly related to the problems that bring the client to treatment (Freud, 1913). Issues of the fee, the initial relationship, defining the parameters of the work and the nature of the problem, all contribute to the problem of developing a therapeutic alliance. As will be described below, religious issues can pose special, additional problems and opportunities.

A client may ask "Are you a Christian (or saved)?" For clients out of a Fundamentalist, Evangelical, Holiness, or Pentecostal background being born a Christian is not enough, even if the therapist is serious in her or his religious beliefs and practices. If they ask directly, I tell clients the truth, although I prefer to explore the question's meaning if the client will tolerate it. Although honesty is desirable, the therapist need not tell the client any more than they ask for. When I say to clients that I am Jewish, this usually goes well, because at least I identify with some religion. Many clients have been warned about the antireligious attitude of therapists. So if a client reveals this fear, informing the client that this is not your role may get the therapy past this initial hurdle until the client can experience therapeutic neutrality directly.

Pruyser (1979) noted several other obstacles. Some clients may want someone just like themselves, a wish that may mask grandiosity, narcissism, resistance, or an awareness of personal doubts. Pruyser delineated several patterns. Legalists emphasize the right thing to do, which, as a guide to conduct, defends against terror. The supralegalists are similar to the legalists but also seek deeper, more profound rules. The Orthodox highly value the right beliefs, which may allow them to align with, and share power with a transcendent authority. The supraorthodox seeks ultimate truth embedded within popular truth. For others, the aesthetic component in religion is primary, whereas those that emphasize the symbolic or sacramental participate in the power of the transcendent.

Another question that may come up quickly is, "why has my faith failed me?" The assumption that one's faith has failed to prevent the client from having emotional problems is not uncommon in some very conservative churches (Ammerman, 1987). One may ask if that is what faith is supposed to do. Faith should improve the client's relationship with God. If it has done that, faith has not failed the client, but the client has expected more from his or her faith than it could deliver (Lovinger, 1991). If therapy can help resolve relationships with people, it may help the client's relationship with God. An intervention like this can answer these initial concerns.

Although psychotherapy with religious clients is not essentially different from nonreligious clients, it does present special problems. Countertransference, collisions in values that are personal or represent competing worldviews, and special knowledge about particular religious cultures are among the considerations that affect treatment.

The Client's Religious Issues

Many clients whose religious lives are implicated in their difficulties have misunderstood the Scripture they rely on or have distorted their theology. An example was given above of a young Methodist woman who felt out of alignment with her peers on religious issues. As another example, it is commonly thought that masturbation is forbidden in the Bible, but it is never mentioned as such. This prohibition is derived from the story of Judah, one of the 12 sons of Jacob. Judah had three sons, and the oldest married a woman named Tamar, but died young, without children. The next surviving son is required to marry his brother's wife to continue the brother's name. Onan practices coitus interruptus, or in the biblical circumlocution, he spilled his seed on the ground. Masturbation, sometimes called onanism, was interpreted as forbidden. Although this is a plausible interpretation, the Bible does not say anything directly about masturbation. In any case, this passage does not pertain to women, although the prohibition is sometimes applied to them.

Homosexuality appears to be a much clearer issue. It is mentioned twice in the Old Testament: "If a man lies with a male as one lies with a woman, the two of them have done an abhorrent thing; they shall be put to death—their bloodguilt is upon them" (Lev. 20:13; Levine, 1989, p. 138). Lesbian relations are not mentioned in the Old Testament but it is forbidden for men or women to have sexual intercourse with animals, so women were not entirely overlooked regarding sexuality.

It has been argued that male homosexuality in the Old Testament referred to ritual sexual activities. Later, in Greek and Roman times, the common paradigm of a homosexual relationship (frequently involving slavery) was between an adult male and young boy. Would Saint Paul have prohibited a modern adult homosexual relationship? We do not know, but that was not what he was talking about (Scroggs, 1983).

Surprisingly, homosexuality was not a matter of great concern to biblical writers in the same way that idolatry, incest, or the mistreatment of strangers was. A simple frequency count yields some surprising results. Harassing or mistreating strangers was prohibited 36 times in the first five books of the Bible. Male homosexuality was mentioned twice in the Old Testament and twice in the New Testament (which also contains a vague statement about improper behavior in women).

Arguing or directly confronting a client's belief is not likely to be therapeutically effective, and even if it is, the client's autonomy may be impaired. Furthermore, most religious clients approach the Bible with deadly seriousness: If the therapist appears to mock specific biblical precepts, this may damage the therapy relationship.

THE THERAPIST

The Therapist's Personal Background

Almost all therapists have had some exposure to religion. Presently affiliated therapists either have continued (perhaps with modification) a religious affiliation from their youth, or have acquired one as an adult. Nonaffiliated therapists may have grown up in a home where Easter and Christmas (or the equivalent) were the extent of religious activity, if that. Their parents were often not antireligious, but they probably were not exactly interested either. The therapist-to-be may have had an ordinary religious training (Sunday school, catechism class), but this did not have a special effect.

Formerly affiliated therapists either grew up with a religious background or acquired one, but they are no longer active. They may joke about their "past" as "recovering Fundamentalists" or "recovering Catholics," but it is not usually very significant in their present lives. Another group of therapists are Anti-affiliated and they display their distaste for religious faith, regarding it as neurotic, controlling, immature, or unscientific. Finally there are converted therapists, who as an adult or adolescent have accepted Jesus as their personal savior. This final group differs from the presently affiliated therapist in the intensity and exclusivity of their self-definition.

All of the positions that I have described can refract the client's material that is produced in therapy in at least three ways: countertransference, value clashes, and failure to grasp meanings through misunderstanding of the cultural or denominational context.

Treatment

Treatment of clients with religious issues has been commented on at points in this chapter. Although general principles of treatment will not be discussed here, special techniques with clients who present these types of issues will be addressed.

Problems Tied to Specific Biblical Texts

The material about the Bible in the section on denominations is aimed at giving therapists who are not biblical scholars some alternative, more flexible ways to approach these apparently forbidding texts by seeing them as having many modes of understanding, differing voices, styles, and literary qualities, as well as having complexities of meaning and context, and problems in translation.

If a client presents an issue anchored to some specific text, some tools are available to the therapist to loosen the issue. The following sequence of steps can be useful:

1. If possible, I try to explore what the specific textual point means to clients and when it first became an issue.
2. If necessary, I may then ask clients to show me the text if I am not familiar with it, without being surprised if they cannot find it.
3. If they do find it, I find it helpful to read the larger section in which it is embedded, to see if the context offers any help in expanding our understanding.
4. If the issue remains in place, I would look to comparing alternate translations, which sometimes differ dramatically (Lovinger, 1984, pp. 228-229).
5. Parallel to these steps, it may be useful to consult various sources, some of which are given at the end of the chapter. An Analytical Concordance may help in finding a specific word and all the places it appears in the Bible, plus its various translations. This may provide help in developing alternatives through use of contextual clues. Other sources include bibles that have explanatory notes appended. The Anchor Bible is a very scholarly, nondenominational series, but the explanatory notes may contain more about the technical problems in translation than applied issues. Other biblical translations are sponsored by one or more church or synagogue groups and contain some denominational perspectives or biases. This does not impair their utility but caution is needed. For some clients only their own denominationally approved source has authority—at first.

There are several sources that compare or assemble biblical excerpts dealing with specific issues (anger, love, sex, pleasure, children, parents, marriage, etc.) and, although these sources do not "solve" the therapeutic problem, they do give the interested therapist material that raises alternate viewpoints (Coyle & Erdberg, 1969; Lovinger, 1984; Lovinger, 1990).

Religious Imagery and Individual Theology

Religious imagery can appear in several ways. Its value is exemplified in the following three vignettes. One client had a dream about her children taking art lessons from a man named Priest. She was having an affair as her marriage was breaking down and when I explored this, I found that her lover had been in a seminary. Drawing her attention to the parallel between her dream content and her life increased her willingness to give notice to her thoughts and dreams.

Another example was a client described above: a young Methodist woman who wanted to become a minister but whose ambition was to become a bishop in the Methodist church. She reported a dream in which she was in a play that had appeared in high school called *Annie Get Your Gun*. In the dream she is standing next to a large wheel that, through association, she tied to her desire to be a "big wheel."

For the individual, her or his theology is a theory about the nature of God, the world, and people in their interrelations. Some clients have a rather developed theology that may nevertheless be informative as to their inner life. The client just mentioned above was the middle of three children, an older sister and a younger brother. She had many issues with her parents and her older sister but the younger brother was not significant in her life. While she was going through a series of interviews required of ministerial candidates, I asked her about her theology. She told me that she knew all the right things to say in these interviews, but that Jesus was an empty figure for her; her theological concerns were with God the Father. When I pointed out the parallels between that and her own family constellation, she became quite agitated and asked if her theology was wrong. I said "no, but it does suggest that you should be thoughtful about your theology." We continued to work in therapy before she left for the seminary, and later Jesus became more significant to her.

In these and other similar instances the clients' life experiences are reflected in their religious imagery. Thoughtful consideration of this material can illuminate ongoing issues during therapeutic inquiry.

Resistance and Transference

Resistance may appear as distrust, fear of a loss of faith, or in other forms in the initial contact. Although it is never useful to label resistance to the client, who will feel attacked or criticized, there are certain things that can help. If a client indicates distrust or wariness, I support the feelings as reasonable; trust is an outcome, not a precondition for therapy. The religious client who has been required to come for some reason may openly express distrust or may indicate that a religious healing is what is desired. I would reply, "Well, that's understandable, but since you are here, perhaps we can talk for a while. Even if you are only here for this one session, maybe I can be of some help to you, although I cannot provide you with the kind of healing that is so important to you."

Another occasion for resistance is the development of erotic feelings in the religious client toward the therapist. This may be especially troubling for clients from a very conservative background. When the therapist and client are the same sex, this may be even more troubling, appearing to be homosexual. What may be at work in either instance is that the client is expressing feelings of love or affection for the therapist and is using the idiom of sexuality. Here the therapist may have to open the topic first, and perhaps sooner than he or she may think is therapeutically optimal, or the client may flee.

Physical and emotional abuse is all too frequently present in the history of clients in treatment. There are some people who have grown up where one or both parents are abusive and the children know it. That is painful and it has serious consequences, but it is not mystifying, and the person is not confused about what happened. But you also see clients who grow up in abusive environments in which the parents present as sweet and loving but the child is full of anger and resentment. It often takes a good deal of work to help the client recognize what really happened to them because they have been mystified. Sometimes this is presented to children as "Christian love," which further confounds the client's efforts to understand. An equivalent process can occur in Jewish families, sometimes framed as parental self-sacrifice.

A history of abuse not only impairs relationships but may lead the client to particular kinds of transference reactions. Whereas there is an underlying distrust and fear of intimacy, this may be overlaid with openness, trust, and cooperativeness. Intense difficulties with anger, sometimes linked to biblical injunctions to forgive and be meek, may also be seen.

One of the most common bases for suppression of anger is the statement by Jesus (Mark 12:31; Matt. 19:19), "love your neighbor as yourself." This is frequently taken as always respond with kindness and acceptance to the harmful behavior of others. However when Jesus was talking, his audience knew that he was referring to a section in Leviticus, Chapter 19. It reads "you shall not hate your kinsmen in your heart. Reprove your neighbor but incur no guilt because of him. You shall not take vengeance or bear a grudge against your kinfolk. Love your neighbor as yourself. I am the Lord" (Jewish Publication Society, 1967, p. 217).

To understand this variously interpreted statement, it is important to know that in ancient times the heart was considered the seat of both the intellect and the emotions. Because Hebrew had no generic words for *humanity*, the use of different words (*neighbor, kinsman, brother*) connotes general meaning. Thus, you shall not keep hateful feelings within but should speak up, because if you do not speak up you are participating in a sin. This does not demand that you have to like your neighbor, but instead you are responsible to object when something wrong is occurring. When Jesus calls this the great commandment, a plausible interpretation relates this to communal responsibility and resistance to injustice.

Sexual abuse is likely to present even more difficulties in treatment. Some clients with this history have been subjected to the demand to forgive their abuser(s), again based on New Testament texts on forgiveness. If this is supplemented by reference to the commandment to "honor your father and your mother," it is important to realize that *honor* comes from a word meaning "to make heavy," or weighty, or "to glorify," so this commandment most likely meant to act to bring credit to your parents, a task within the bounds of mortal possibilities. Although coming to terms in therapy with past abuse and reducing or resolving its effects is a very valuable therapeutic goal, it cannot meaningfully occur through fiat but only through a process. To forgive someone who has not asked for it or acknowledged the wrong may be understood as condoning, and perhaps perpetuating the behavior.

Countertransference

I once supervised a student who was working with a woman who had grown up in a Christian Science home. The client was quite detached emotionally, had little impact on her children's behavior, felt quite isolated and socially deprived, and during some good therapy she began to make progress. Then the therapist went on summer vacation but returned to find that the client had converted and accepted Jesus as her personal savior. Her depression was lighter but the therapist was very upset. I pointed out that the client finally had a connection with someone.

The therapist's countertransference was unrelieved. I was not able to help but she talked to another supervisor who explored it with her. The therapist was Jewish, the younger of two siblings; the first born was a son. This is important in many Jewish families and in this family this boy was called "the Messiah." Once she could connect her antagonism to Jesus (*Christ* means "Messiah" in Greek) with her anger at her parents and her brother she was able to continue her work with the client. My failure to adequately explore this with the therapist was supervisory countertransference.

Values Clashes and Worldviews

Although values were briefly discussed at the beginning of this chapter, it will be worthwhile to reconsider them in the context of therapy (Bergin, 1980a, 1980b).

1. Most people express their religious life through a faith community, whereas psychotherapy focuses on the individual. Even marital and family therapy rarely considers the larger community. Competing interests exist from the beginning: Therapy typically considers individual growth and personal resolution to be primary goals (even if the treatment unit is a family), but a faith community is less likely to do so, especially if it negatively affects the larger group's goals or cohesiveness.

2. For therapists, a typical goal of treatment is to increase personal autonomy, emotional expressiveness, and to reduce symptomatic behavior or conflict-based inhibitions. In child-rearing, these values often lead to practices that diverge from those arising from certain religious frameworks, which emphasize obedience, and communal standards and goals.

3. For many therapists, values and standards are best developed from within, based on the needs and decisions of the person and others with whom the individual is emotionally connected. Judaism, Christianity, and Islam emphasize revealed values and standards that the member is called to assent and enact. That the ideal outcomes of either worldview may not differ all that much is a separate issue; the processes of development are quite different and a potential source of conflict. A simple resolution for these clashes is far from easy but therapists need to be aware that such conflicts are often embedded in their work.

Consultation and collaboration between therapists and clergy can be very effective, in many cases allowing a therapist both to get to the heart of presenting religious problems and to improve a client's relationship with his or her clergy. If a client has a serious alcohol problem and is strongly affiliated with a specific church that is ardently opposed to any alcohol use, the therapist may want to consider eventually asking the client's permission to talk to the minister. Although some ministers may pound the pulpit about alcohol abuse, they know that their congregants are human beings. They are often more flexible in private consultation or collaboration.

Referral to a minister or priest if a client is struggling with a spiritually complex issue may be very useful. It is helpful to develop a connection with receptive members of the clergy; once the therapist makes clear that she or he is not interested in attacking the congregant's faith, local clergy are likely to be quite cooperative. They may need the therapist to set some boundaries about what can and cannot be discussed, as well as presenting the therapist's perception of the issues.

SUMMARY

The assessment and treatment of clients for whom religion is a significant facet of their lives adds an obvious complexity to an already complex task. To the therapist willing to listen to these matters, such material offers therapeutic opportunities for grasping the meaning and course of the client's past and present difficulties, as well as ways to intervene. The approach taken here considers the client within a denominational framework as informing the therapist about the probable nature of the past and present influences that form the present situation. And the Bible, which is often seen as a monolithic, impenetrable structure, is considered as much more flexible in meaning, and having qualities of humor, depth, and awareness of the human condition, than many individuals are ordinarily aware of. It too, used properly, can aid the therapeutic enterprise.

The assessment of the client's religious practices and ideation needs to be considered in the context of what is normative for the person's denomination. Also, there are obstacles to treatment related to the client's religious issues that can arise throughout the therapy process. I am offering suggestions for avoiding or handling them as well as sources of further information, listed after the references.

REFERENCES

Ammerman, N. T. (1987). *Bible believers: Fundamentalists in the modern world.* New Brunswick, NJ: Rutgers University Press.

Alter, R. (1981). *The art of biblical narrative.* New York: Basic Books.

Babchuk, N., & Whitt, H. P. (1990). R-order and religious switching. *Journal for the Scientific Study of Religion, 29,* 246–254.

Bahr, H. M., & Albrecht, S. L. (1989). Strangers once more: Patterns of disaffiliation from Mormonism. *Journal for the Scientific Study of Religion, 28,* 180–200.

Bellah, R. N., Madsen, R., Sullivan, W. M., Swidler, A., & Tipton, S. M. (1985). *Habits of the heart: Individualism and commitment in American life.* Berkeley, CA: University of California Press.

Bergin, A. (1980a). Psychotherapy and religious values. *Journal of Consulting and Clinical Psychology, 48,* 95–105.

Bergin, A. (1980b). Religious and humanistic values: A reply to Ellis and Walls. *Journal of Consulting and Clinical Psychology, 48,* 642–645.

Bergin, A. (1983). Religiosity and mental health: A critical re-evaluation and meta-analysis. *Professional Psychology: Research and Practice, 14,* 170–184.

Botting, H., & Botting, G. (1984). *The Orwellian world of Jehovah's Witnesses.* Toronto: University of Toronto Press.

Capps, D. (1992). Religion and child abuse: Perfect together. *Journal for the Scientific Study of Religion, 31,* 1–14.

Chaves, M., & Higgins, L. M. (1992). Comparing the community involvement of black and white congregations. *Journal for the Scientific Study of Religion, 31,* 425–440.

Cochran, J. K., & Beeghley, L. (1991). The influence of religion on attitudes toward nonmarital sexuality: A preliminary assessment of reference group theory. *Journal for the Scientific Study of Religion, 30,* 45–62.

Coyle, F. A., Jr., & Erdberg, P. (1969). A liberalizing approach to maladaptive fundamentalist hyperreligiosity. *Psychotherapy: Theory, Research and Practice, 6,* 140–142.

Ellis, A. (1980). Psychotherapy and atheistic values: A response to A. E. Bergin's "Psychotherapy and religious values." *Journal of Consulting and Clinical Psychology, 48,* 635–639.

Ellison, C. G., & Sherkat, D. E. (1993). Obedience and autonomy: Religion and parental values reconsidered. *Journal for the Scientific Study of Religion, 32,* 313–329.

Freud, S. (1913). Further recommendations on the technique of psychoanalysis. In *Collected papers of Sigmund Freud.* New York: Collier.

Garrett, P. D. (1988). Eastern Christianity. In *The encyclopedia of the American religious experience* (Vol. 1, pp. 325–344). New York: Charles Scribner's Sons.

Greer, B. A., & Roof, W. C. (1992). "Desperately Seeking Sheila": Locating religious privatism in American society. *Journal for the Scientific Study of Religion, 31,* 346–352.

Haddad, Y. Y., & Lummis, A. T. (1987). *Islamic values in the United States.* New York: Oxford University Press.

Hoekema, A. A. (1972). *Jehovah's witnesses.* Grand Rapids, MI: W. B. Eerdmans.

Hunter, J. D. (1983). *American evangelicalism: Conservative religion and the quandary of modernity.* New Brunswick, NJ: Rutgers University Press.

Jewish Publication Society. (1967). *The Torah: The five books of Moses* (2nd ed). Philadelphia: Author.

Josipovici, G. (1988). *The book of God: A response to the Bible.* New Haven: Yale University Press.

Kaiser, D. L. (1991). Religious problem-solving styles and guilt. *Journal for the Scientific Study of Religion, 30,* 94–98.

Kirkpatrick, L. E. (1993). Fundamentalism, Christian orthodoxy, and religious orientation as predictors of discriminatory attitudes. *Journal for the Scientific Study of Religion, 32*, 256–268.

Lamsa, G. M. (1985). *Idioms in the Bible explained and a key to the original Gospels.* New York: Harper & Row.

Levine, B. A. (1989). *The JPS Torah Commentary: Leviticus.* New York: Jewish Publication Society.

Lippy, C. H., & Williams, P. W. (1988). Encyclopedia of the American Religious Experience. New York: Charles Scribner's Sons.

Lovinger, R. J. (1978). Obstacles in psychotherapy: Setting a fee in the initial contact. *Professional Psychology, 9*, 350–352.

Lovinger, R. J. (1984). *Working with religious issues in therapy.* Northvale, NJ: Jason Aronson.

Lovinger, R. J. (1985). Religious issues in the psychotherapy of a borderline patient. In M. H. Spero (Ed.), *Psychotherapy of the Religious Patient* (pp. 181–207). Springfield, IL: Charles C Thomas.

Lovinger, R. J. (1990). *Religion and counseling: The psychological impact of religious belief.* New York: Continuum.

Lovinger, R. J. (1991, August). *I have faith—Why do I still have problems?* Paper presented at the annual meeting of the American Psychological Association meeting, San Francisco.

Marty, M. E. (1986a). *Protestantism in the United States: Righteous empire.* New York: Charles Scribner's Sons.

Marty, M. E. (1986b). *Modern American religion: Vol. 1. The irony of it all, 1893–1991.* Chicago: University of Chicago Press.

Marty, M. E. (1991). *Modern American religion: Vol. 2. The noise of conflict, 1919–1941.* Chicago: University of Chicago Press.

Matthews, D. A., Larson, D. B., & Barry, C. P. (1993). *The faith factor: An annotated bibliography of clinical research on spiritual subjects.* Rockville, MD: National Institute for Healthcare Research.

Paloutzian, R. F., & Kirkpatrick, L. A. (1995). Introduction: The scope of religious influences on personal and societal well-being. *Journal of Social Issues, 51*, 1–11.

Pargament, K. I., Stanik, P., Crowe, P., Ishler, K., Freidel, L., Possage, J., Rouiller, R., Ward, M., & Weinborn, M. (1993, August). *Red flags and religious coping: Identifying some religious warning signs among people in crisis.* Paper presented at the annual meeting of the American Psychological Association Convention, Toronto, Canada.

Poloma, M. M., & Pendleton, B. F. (1989). Religious experiences, evangelism and institutional growth within the Assemblies of God. *Journal for the Scientific Study of Religion, 28*, 415–431.

Pruyser, P. (1977). The seamy side of current religious beliefs. *Bulletin of the Menninger Clinic, 41*, 329–348.

Pruyser, P. (1979). *The psychological examination: A guide for clinicians.* New York: International Universities Press.

Rigney, D., & Hoffman, T. J. (1993). Is American Catholicism anti-intellectual? *Journal for the Scientific Study of Religion, 32,* 211–222.

Roiphe, A. (1989). Taking down the Christmas tree. *Tikkun, 4,* 58–60.

Roof, W. C. (1989). Multiple religious switching: A research note. *Journal for the Scientific Study of Religion, 28,* 530–535.

Roof, W. C., & McKinney, W. (1987). *American mainline religion: Its changing shape and future.* New Brunswick, NJ: Rutgers University Press.

Ross, C. E. (1990). Religion and psychological distress. *Journal for the Scientific Study of Religion, 29,* 236–245.

Scroggs, R. (1983). *The New Testament and Homosexuality.* Philadelphia: Fortress Press.

Sethi, S., & Seligman, M. E. P. (1993). Optimism and fundamentalism. *Psychological Science, 4,* 256–259.

Shafii, M. (1985). *Freedom from the self: Sufism, meditation and psychotherapy.* New York: Human Sciences Press.

Shafranske, E. (1991, March). *God representation as the transformational object.* Paper presented at the Spring meeting of the Division of Psychoanalysis, American Psychological Association, Chicago, IL.

Simmons, T. (1991). *The unseen shore: Memories of a Christian Science childhood.* Boston: Beacon Press.

Stifler, K., Greer, J., Sneck, W., & Dovenmuehle, R. (1993). An empirical investigation of the discriminability of reported mystical experiences among religious contemplatives, psychotic inpatients, and normal adults. *Journal for the Scientific Study of Religion, 32,* 366–372.

Wilcox, C. (1989). Evangelicals and the Moral Majority. *Journal for the Scientific Study of Religion, 28,* 400–414.

APPENDIX
SELECTED GENERAL SOURCES FOR THERAPIST AND CLIENT

Cole, W. G. (1959). *Sex and love in the Bible*. New York: Association Press.

Kosnik, A., Carroll, W., Cunningham, A., Modias, R., & Schulte, J. (1977). *Human Sexuality: New Directions in American Catholic Thought*. Mahwah, NJ: Paulist Press.

Patai, R. (1960). *Family, love and the Bible*. London: MacGibbon and Kee.

Pruyser, P. W. (1974). *Between belief and unbelief*. New York: Harper and Row.

Stacey, D. (1977). *Interpreting the Bible*. New York: Hawthorn Books.

13

RELIGION IN CLINICAL PRACTICE: IMPLICIT AND EXPLICIT INTEGRATION

SIANG-YANG TAN

This chapter focuses on the actual use of religion in clinical practice. More specifically, I will describe two major models for integrating religion and psychotherapy: an implicit, more covert integration and an explicit, more overt integration. Before going into a detailed description and discussion of these two models and the ethical issues involved in their practice, I will provide a brief review of the literature relevant to religion and clinical practice.

In recent years, the topic of religion and psychotherapy or clinical practice has received significant attention, both in the general psychological literature,[1] including a special issue of *Psychotherapy* (vol. 27, no. 1, Spring 1990) on "Psychotherapy and Religion," as well as in the more specifically Christian literature focusing on the integration of religious or Christian faith and psychotherapy or counseling (e.g., Tan, 1993a; Worthington, 1993). As Jones (1994) recently pointed out, the integration of faith and psychotherapy, or more broadly, psychology, is also occurring in

---

[1] See, for example, Beit-Hallahmi, 1975; Bergin, 1980a, 1980b, 1983, 1988a, 1988b, 1991; Bergin & Jensen, 1990; Bergin & Payne, 1991; Ellis, 1980; Jones, 1994; Kelly, 1995; Lovinger, 1984, 1990; Miller & Martin, 1988; Payne, Bergin, & Loftus, 1992; Quackenbos, Privette, & Klentz, 1986; Spero, 1985; Spilka, 1986; Stern, 1985; Tan, 1993b; Walls, 1980; Worthington, 1986, 1988, 1989, 1991.

other faith communities, such as in Jewish (e.g., Meier, 1988; see also *Journal of Psychology and Judaism*), Muslim (e.g., Rizvi, 1988), and Buddhist (e.g., Lax, 1993) contexts. Vande Kemp (this volume; see also Vande Kemp, 1984) has provided a historical perspective on religion and clinical psychology in America, pointing out an interest in religion and clinical practice that was evident many years ago. She also noted that a magazine called *The Common Boundary* (between spirituality and psychotherapy), which came out of a seminar on "Integrating Spirituality and Psychotherapy" organized in 1981, had 5,000 subscribers by 1992 (Simpkinson, 1992). Demetrios, Simpkinson, and Bennet (1991) recently published *The Common Boundary Graduate Education Guide* which has information on programs ranging from more traditional ones in Judeo–Christian clinical psychology and pastoral counseling, to those on shamanic counseling, holistic healing, intuition training, psychosynthesis, spiritual direction and formation, and transpersonal therapies (see also *Journal of Transpersonal Psychology*). These observations point to the renewed attention that religious issues have received within the psychological community.

Although religion still seems to play a somewhat minimal role in the lives of most psychologists (Jones, 1994), there has been some change in the past decade or so. Surveys conducted by Bergin and Jensen (1990), as well as by Shafranske and Malony (1990), have indicated that professional therapists, including clinical psychologists, appear to be personally more religious or spiritually oriented today, but religion is still not as significant to them as it is to the general population. Shafranske and Malony found that 71% of the clinical psychologists they surveyed were affiliated with an organized religion, with 41% attending religious services regularly. However, about 85% of them indicated that they had little or no training in the area of psychology and religion. It is not surprising, therefore, that 68% of them felt it was inappropriate for a psychologist to pray with a client, and 55% said it was inappropriate to use religious scripture or texts in therapy.

Bergin and Jensen (1990) concluded that a majority of the general population would probably prefer an approach to psychotherapy and counseling that is at least sensitive, if not sympathetic, to a spiritual perspective. The importance of religion for many clients was noted, and they emphasized the need for "a careful reeducation of therapists whose conceptual/ clinical frameworks have room only for secular and naturalistic constructs" (p. 7).

Worthington (1991) has pointed out that psychotherapists will have to deal with religious issues in psychotherapy much more in the next 30 years, partly because religious people have become more vocal about their religious beliefs and practices in recent years, and many have demanded explicitly religious therapists or counselors from their own distinctive religious groups. Religiously committed clients, especially Christian clients, seem to prefer more explicit forms of religiously oriented therapy that include the use of spiritual resources like prayer and sacred texts or Scripture where appropriate (Tan, 1993b).

Further, the recently revised Ethical Principles of Psychologists and Code of Conduct of the American Psychological Association (APA, 1992) mandate that psychologists view religion as one of the several significant dimensions of human differences or diversity which may require special training, experience, consultation, or supervision in order to ensure the competence of the services they render, or else they should make appropriate referrals (p. 1601, Standard 1.08).

Religion in clinical practice is therefore a crucial area for psychologists to develop competence in, both from a professional or clinical point of view, as well as from an ethical perspective. Clinical training in professional psychology should include religion as one dimension or facet of human diversity (Tan, 1993b). Division 36 of the APA therefore recently offered an annual continuing education workshop, from 1990 to 1993, at the APA Annual Convention, on "Psychotherapy With Religiously Committed Clients." It was conducted by Edward Shafranske, PhD, from Pepperdine University; Siang-Yang Tan, PhD, from Fuller Theological Seminary; and Robert J. Lovinger, PhD, from Central Michigan University. The workshop was designed to help participants (a) to identify religious themes within client presentation; (b) to recognize the potential influence of religious and cultural affiliation on clients' perceptions of their psychological problems; (c) to understand the sources of resistance and support of the psychotherapeutic process that have their origin in religion; (d) to use the religious world view of the client to support therapeutic change and employ interventions of a religious nature; (e) to identify systems of support within religious traditions; and (f) to consult with religious professionals with a clearer understanding of their perspectives.

However, as Tan (1993b) has pointed out, there still are strong critics of religion in the mental health field (e.g., see Albee, 1991; Ellis, 1980; Seligman, 1988). Ellis (1992), in the past a strident critic of religion, has recently clarified his current views, which are not as critical of regular religion as they are of dogmatic, absolutist, devout "religiosity." Despite such critics and their criticisms of religion or certain types of religion, there are others in the mental health field who have arrived at more favorable conclusions about religion and mental health including religion in clinical practice as well as community psychology and prevention (e.g., Bergin, 1983, 1991; Bjorck, 1992; Jones, 1994; Larson et al., 1992; Pargament, 1990; Payne, Bergin, Bielema, & Jenkins, 1991; Payne, Bergin, & Loftus, 1992; Rosik, 1992; Sollod, 1992; Tan, 1991, 1993b).

IMPLICIT AND EXPLICIT INTEGRATION OF RELIGION IN CLINICAL PRACTICE

There are two major models of integrating religion and clinical practice: implicit and explicit integration. *Implicit integration* of religion in clinical practice refers to a more covert approach that does not initiate the discussion of religious or spiritual issues and does not openly, directly, or systematically use spiritual resources like prayer and Scripture or other sacred texts, in therapy. The therapist practicing from an implicit integration model or perspective can still be a religious person who shows respect and caring for the client, while maintaining values, including religious values, that are consistent with the therapist's own religious convictions and beliefs. Such a therapist may even pray quietly for the blessing and healing of his or her clients, but the therapist will not pray explicitly or out loud with clients. Respect for clients' religious values and issues is consistent with an implicit integration model. That is not to say that religious issues are not dealt with in implicit integration. Religious and spiritual issues may be dealt with or interpreted when they are brought up for discussion by the client. However, if clients want to pursue their religious or spiritual issues more explicitly, including the use of their spiritual resources like prayer and sacred texts, the implicit integration therapist will probably not be comfortable doing so, and therefore will usually refer such clients to other competent therapists who practice more from an explicit integration model or perspective. It should be noted that a particular therapist may be comfortable and competent practicing both implicit *and* explicit integration in psychotherapy, depending on the client's needs and interests. In other words, for some clients, for example those who are not religious or who are not interested in exploring spiritual issues further or using religious resources explicitly, the therapist might adopt an implicit integration model. For other clients who are more religiously oriented and want to pursue a direct and open religiously oriented therapy, the therapist might adopt an explicit integration model.

Explicit integration of religion in clinical practice or psychotherapy refers to a more overt approach that directly and systematically deals with spiritual or religious issues in therapy, and uses spiritual resources like prayer, Scripture or sacred texts, referrals to church or other religious groups or lay counselors, and other religious practices. It emphasizes the spirituality of both the therapist and client as foundational to effective therapy and human growth and healing. It integrates psychological therapy with some degree of spiritual guidance or direction in the therapeutic context (Tan, 1988, 1990). The therapist practicing from an explicit integration model or perspective is usually a religious person himself or herself, and is comfortable with not just praying for clients but praying with clients aloud and systematically in therapy sessions where appropriate. However, it is not essential for a therapist to be religious in order to practice explicit integration in therapy. Such a therapist nevertheless needs to be sensitive to and respectful of clients' religious issues and resources, and comfortable with and open to facilitating discussion of religious issues and use of spiritual resources. Propst, Ostrom, Watkins, Dean, and Mashburn (1992) recently found that nonreligious therapists who used religiously oriented cognitive–behavioral therapy (including religious imagery treatment) with depressed religious (Christian) clients actually had the best treatment effect. There is also some evidence that religiously oriented cognitive–behavioral therapy with depressed religious clients produces better therapeutic results (Propst, 1980; Propst et al., 1992) but this finding is not consistent in the research literature (e.g., Johnson, 1990; Pecheur & Edwards, 1984).

Religious clients, and orthodox Christians in particular, seem to prefer the use of prayer and Scripture in therapy (Gass, 1984), and to prefer therapists who have similar religious values (Dougherty & Worthington, 1982; Worthington & Gascoyne, 1985) although this latter finding has been somewhat challenged more recently (see Wyatt & Johnson, 1990). Religious clients, however, do have concerns about being misunderstood by a secular therapist who might pathologize or ignore religious or spiritual issues, fail to comprehend religious ideas or terminology, and negate revelation as a valid source of truth (Worthington & Scott, 1983). For such clients, a more explicit integration approach in therapy may be more appropriate and helpful. Kelly and Strupp (1992) recently suggested that patient–therapist similarity on religious values may function as a matching variable, but "any matching of patients with therapists by religious orientation would involve not so much the therapist's personal religious convictions as their ability to understand and deal sensitively with their patients' specific religious values" (p. 39).

Explicit integration of religion in clinical practice should be practiced in a clinically sensitive, ethically responsible, and professionally competent way as Tan (1988, 1990, 1993b) has emphasized. This model or approach can be abused or misused, and therapists may unethically impose their religious values and spiritual interventions on clients. Some ethical guidelines are needed (see Tan, 1994), and Nelson and Wilson (1984) have suggested at least three: It is ethical for therapists to use or share their religious faith in therapy (a) if they are dealing with clinical problems that would be helped by spiritual or religious intervention, (b) if they are working within the client's belief system (as long as they do not impose their own religious values on the client), and (c) if they have carefully defined the therapy contract or informed consent agreement to include the use of religious or spiritual interventions and resources. It is therefore important for a therapist to address the religious dimension sensitively in the first intake interview with a client to determine the appropriateness of an implicit or explicit approach to integration. A helpful question to ask in the context of gathering other demographic and personal data is something like, "What is your religious affiliation or religion, if any?" If interest in religion is shown by the client, then the therapist can follow up with another question like, "Are religious or spiritual issues and resources (e.g., prayer) important for you and me to address explicitly or openly in our sessions together?" If the client shows no interest at all in religion or spiritual issues, then the therapist has to respect the client's preferences. Goals for therapy, including whether spiritual issues and resources are important to the client, need to be clarified in the first session, so that an appropriate contract for therapy can be agreed upon, preferably in writing. Informed consent on the part of the client to engage in psychotherapy with the therapist should therefore, where necessary, include clarification of how the therapist and client will deal with religious issues in therapy. An explicit integration approach in particular should be agreed upon before it is used. However, if a therapist feels he or she is not adequately trained or is uncomfortable using an explicit integration approach in therapy, then he or she should, ethically speaking, refer a religiously committed client who requests such an approach to another more religiously oriented therapist who has more training or experience in an explicit integration model.

The two models of implicit and explicit integration of religion in clinical practice should not be conceptualized as mutually exclusive. It may be more helpful to view them as two ends of a continuum of integration whereby a therapist can be relatively more or less explicit, or more or less implicit, in dealing with religious issues and using spiritual resources in therapy. Again, as was pointed out earlier, the needs and interests of the client should come first. Also, the theoretical orientation and clinical preferences of the therapist play a crucial role in what model he or she eventually chooses to use, or where on the continuum between implicit and explicit integration he or she decides to be. Some therapists will be comfortable with both models as well as different points on the continuum, depending on the clients and the clinical problems and needs with which they present.

Payne et al. (1992) recently reviewed attempts to integrate spiritual and standard psychotherapy techniques, some of which I will describe later on in this chapter. Payne et al. pointed out that explicit forms of integration seem to be more easily adopted by therapists practicing from cognitive–behavioral and humanistic–existential schools. Psychodynamic schools, especially psychoanalytic ones, seem to have more difficulty with explicit integration, although object relations approaches to therapy have apparently made some significant advances in this area (e.g., Finn & Gartner, 1992), and psychoanalytically oriented therapists have also begun to deal with religion more directly (e.g., Jones, 1991; Randour, 1993; Smith & Handelman, 1990).

EXPLICIT INTEGRATION: USE OF RELIGIOUS AND SPIRITUAL RESOURCES IN PSYCHOTHERAPY

A key characteristic of explicit integration is the open and systematic use of religious or spiritual resources in psychotherapy, including the following three major ones described by Tan (1988, 1990): prayer, Scripture or sacred texts, and referral to religious groups.

Prayer

Prayer can be broadly defined not only as talking with God (or the Divine) but it also includes other ways of focusing attention on God or experiencing the Divine (Johnson, 1987). Prayer can be used by a therapist at different times (e.g., before, during, or after the therapy session, at the beginning or end of the therapy session, or any time during the session, etc.), and in different ways or forms (e.g., quiet, meditative prayer; general prayer aloud with the client; specific prayer aloud for the client; inner healing prayer or prayer for healing of memories; etc.). Finney and Malony (1985a, 1985b, 1985c) have published several helpful articles on Christian prayer, and more specifically, the use of contemplative prayer in psychotherapy. They define contemplative prayer as a process in which full attention is given toward relating to God in a passive, nondemanding, nondefensive, and open way. They emphasized that such prayer should only be used in psychotherapy if spiritual development is a goal of treatment, and therefore it should not be used simply as a technique for anxiety reduction or desensitization (Finney & Malony, 1985b), as Payne et al. (1992) have pointed out. Similarly, Johnson (1987) has cautioned Christian therapists in particular not to use prayer only as a technique, but to be true to the biblical teaching of prayer as a way of life for the believer in relationship with God. The therapist should also be sensitive to the whole range of the prayer experience which includes not only asking for healing or help in petition for oneself or intercession for others, but also confession, thanksgiving, and praise or worship of God.

Inner Healing Prayer

A specific form of prayer during therapy sessions is prayer for healing of memories or inner healing prayer. Inner healing prayer is particularly relevant in situations where the client has suffered past hurts or childhood traumas (e.g., involving neglect or deprivation, sexual and physical abuse, rejection, abandonment, harsh criticism or sarcasm, etc.) that are still unresolved and very painful emotionally. Such traumatic memories can continue to bother the client, often paralyzing him or her in the form of psychological symptoms like depression or anxiety, and poor or conflictual interpersonal relationships. Seamands (1985) has written a helpful book from a Christian perspective on how to conduct prayer for healing of memories. In such a prayer the clinician uses guided imagery of Jesus walking back into the past with the client and healing and comforting the client in the midst of the traumatic event being experienced again in imagery. The use of such prayer within the context of ongoing sessions of counseling does not ignore the complexities and depth of human problems and sufferings. In other words, inner healing prayer is not a panacea, but it can be a helpful intervention for religiously committed, especially Christian, clients who suffer from traumatic memories. Propst (1988) has described a similar religiously oriented cognitive–behavioral therapy that makes use of such religious guided imagery.

Although several authors like Seamands (1985) and Propst (1988) have emphasized the guided imagery part of inner healing prayer, there is a danger of imposing the preferred imagery, script, or agenda of the therapist onto the client. Some clients are not good at imagery, whereas others may not like the guided imagery suggested by the therapist. Some therapists and pastoral counselors who make frequent use of healing of memories seem to like to suggest that the client visualize Jesus hugging him or her as a sign of his love and healing grace toward the client. Although this particular image may be helpful to many clients, it can not only be unhelpful but may even be damaging to some clients—for example those who have had a long history of sexual abuse, and for whom any physical touch or hugging, even in imagery, may be initially experienced as further trauma or abuse. I suggest therefore an approach to inner healing prayer for the healing of memories that does not place as much emphasis on guided imagery or any other script from the therapist, but places more emphasis on prayer and waiting upon God. It stresses prayer more than imagery per se. The seven steps of inner healing prayer, from a Christian perspective, that I have described elsewhere (Tan, 1992b, pp. 10–11; see also Tan & Ortberg, 1995a, 1995b) are as follows:

1. Start with prayer for God's healing for the client, and protection during the session.
2. Conduct brief relaxation training to help the client relax as deeply as possible (e.g., by taking some slow, deep breaths; using calming self-talk like "Relax, Take it easy, Let go of all tension, etc."; and visualizing pleasant, enjoyable, peaceful, and serene scenes, like lying on the beach in Hawaii, or watching a beautiful sunset, or taking a walk in the countryside).
3. Ask the client to go back to the past traumatic event in imagery (if possible) and relive it. If the client has trouble visualizing it, then ask him or her to describe it verbally, with

eyes still closed, even though no clear images are being experienced. The therapist may find it helpful to say to the client something like, "Can you try to put yourself back to when you were a child? Can you imagine this particular painful event happening to you again? (Or at least verbally describe it again?)" The client is therefore encouraged to relive the painful scenario without denying the reality of what actually happened. This can be a very intensely emotional and painful time, with much crying on the part of the client. Some clients, however, do not respond as emotionally. Sufficient time should be given for the client to reexperience the pain and not try to run away from it or block it. The therapist should be gentle and supportive, periodically asking the client, "What's happening? What are you experiencing now?"

4. After enough time has gone by, the therapist will then pray again, and ask for God to come and minister his healing grace and love to the client in whatever way is appropriate or needed. No specific guided imagery is provided, unless it appears to be necessary.

5. In step five, there is a period of waiting in quiet contemplative or receptive prayer for God to minister to the client in the context of the painful, traumatic memory. The therapist asks the client periodically, "What's happening? What are you experiencing or feeling now?" Clients do not always respond by saying that they are experiencing healing imagery like seeing Jesus being at their side or putting his hand on their shoulder, or hugging them, although some clients have experienced such images and have reported feeling comforted and healed or helped by them. Other clients have reported other healing or helpful experiences like recalling particular verses from the Bible, or a song or hymn, or a sensation of being flooded with the warmth of God's love and grace toward them. There are still other clients for whom the process of inner healing prayer is not experienced in any dramatic way, but there is often a peace that they sense deep within. Even if they do not experience anything, the therapist and client already acknowledge beforehand that prayer is basically communion with God and waiting upon God. It is not result-centered or experience-seeking per se. There is a letting go of control, and trust in a God who truly cares and works things out in good time.

6. After enough time has passed, the session of inner healing prayer is then closed with a prayer, usually by both the ther-

apist and the client (unless the client is too shy to pray aloud, in which case the therapist can end with a short prayer, usually of thanksgiving).

7. This final step involves debriefing and discussion with the client about his or her experience of inner healing that has just occurred. Also, as Seamands (1985) has pointed out, eventually, inner healing needs to deal with forgiveness. Forgiveness by the client of those who have hurt him or her, and letting go of bitterness and resentment, is usually a process that takes time (e.g., Smedes, 1984).

Inner healing prayer can therefore be a very helpful part of explicit integration. Adequate time should be allocated for this intervention, with some therapists suggesting a 2-hour block for the initial session in which inner healing prayer is conducted.

Prayer for Deliverance

One other form of prayer should be briefly mentioned, which Christian or other religious therapists in particular have referred to as prayer for deliverance or "exorcism." The problem of evil is a thorny one, and the area of the demonic is not easy to deal with, because many therapists deny the existence of such spiritual phenomena, and others have religious convictions that evil and the demonic are real and have to be dealt with if they are manifested in therapy (see Peck, 1983, 1993). It is beyond the scope of this chapter to go into further detail, except to point out that some helpful literature is now available on differential diagnosis between mental illness and demonization by evil spirits or so-called demon possession (e.g., Bufford, 1988; see also Beck & Lewis, 1989; Page, 1989a, 1989b; Wilson, 1989). This is an area where therapists may need to refer certain clients to pastors, pastoral counselors, or other religious leaders who may have more expertise and experience dealing with situations of apparent demonization.

Potential Misuses of Prayer

There are potential abuses or misuses of prayer in psychological treatment including dangers associated with superficial inner healing approaches to prayer (see Alsdurf & Malony, 1980; Malony, 1987). However, although prayer can be used as a defense or escape from exploring painful issues more deeply in therapy, it can also be used in a religiously meaningful and therapeutically helpful way. Nevertheless, prayer is not always appropriate to use in psychotherapy (e.g., with nonreligious clients, unless they are open to or request prayer). Also, at times even religiously committed clients may be struggling with bitterness or resentment toward God, or may be having crises of faith, so that they do not want to engage in prayer or use any spiritual resources at the present time.

Scripture or Sacred Texts

The use of Scripture or sacred texts is a second major example of employing religious or spiritual resources in psychotherapy. As with prayer, sacred texts like the Bible can be misused or abused in therapy, especially if the therapist uses specific passages or verses in an authoritarian way to almost "force" a client to "repent" from wayward behaviors, or in a simplistic way to deal with complex problems which require more than a few proof-texts to resolve (see Johnson, 1987). There may also be different interpretations at times of the same Scriptures by the therapist and client, with an obvious requirement on the part of the therapist to deal sensitively and delicately with such differing views. Despite the dangers of misusing or abusing the Scriptures or sacred texts in therapy, such texts can be used in constructive and helpful ways with religiously committed clients who hold them to be authoritative and divinely inspired. These clients often respond more positively to cognitive restructuring (of distorted or dysfunctional thinking) based on the Scriptures rather than only on reasoning or empirical verification (cf. Tan, 1987; see also Craigie & Tan, 1989). In fact Ellis (1993) has recently acknowledged the Judeo–Christian Bible as a self-help book that has probably helped more people make more significant changes in personality and behavior than all professional therapists put together!

There are some helpful resources that can aid in the appropriate use of the Bible or sacred texts in psychotherapy. For example, Backus (1985) has described how the Scriptures and biblical truth can be used in Christian cognitive restructuring or "misbelief therapy" with religious, Christian clients (see also McMinn, 1991; Propst, 1988; Tan & Ortberg, 1995a, 1995b; Wright, 1986). He has also coauthored a widely used self-help book containing many scriptural references which can be used to help clients think more biblically and appropriately in common areas of struggle such as depression, anxiety, and anger (Backus & Chapian, 1980; see also Thurman, 1989). Ward (1977) has similarly provided helpful Bible studies that can be assigned as homework tasks for clients to complete in between sessions. Such completed Bible studies that are specially relevant to the personal needs and problems faced by the client can then be openly discussed with the therapist at subsequent sessions (also see Collins, 1988, 1993).

Referral

The third major spiritual resource that can be explicitly used in psychotherapy is referral of the client to church, parachurch, or other religious groups within the belief system of the client. These organizations can be used for fellowship and the facilitation of further personal and spiritual growth and healing of the person. Such religiously oriented groups can be a source of deep caring for the client, expressed through interaction, support, and often prayer for each other. They may even help the client in the separation process that is part of the termination phase of therapy. Examples of helpful groups include small groups, bible study groups, recovery groups, prayer groups, fellowship groups, religiously oriented or Christ-centered 12-step programs, youth groups, and so forth. Lay or paraprofessional counselors who are carefully selected, trained, and supervised are another resource often available in religious groups or churches, and clients can also be referred to them for ongoing support and help, especially if finances are a problem because such lay counseling or peer helping is usually provided without charge (Tan, 1991, 1992a; see also Sturkie & Tan, 1992, 1993).

EXPLICIT INTEGRATION: DEALING WITH SPIRITUAL ISSUES IN PSYCHOTHERAPY

Psychotherapists often see clients who are seeking help for problems in living that involve spiritual and moral issues or causes (Crabb, 1987; White, 1987; see also Menninger, 1973; Mowrer, 1961). Such issues are dealt with openly and directly in explicit integration of religion in psychotherapy. A proper and adequate assessment of the client's religious functioning and spirituality should be made as far as possible before intervening directly to discuss or deal with spiritual and religious issues. Malony's (1988) religious status interview is a helpful one to use for conducting such a religious assessment.

In fact, Peck (1993) has recently suggested that all psychiatry residents in their first month of training should be taught how to routinely take a spiritual history, in addition to a more general history and a mental status exam. Some of the simple and obvious questions he listed for possible use in obtaining a spiritual history include the following:

> What religion were you raised in? What denomination? Are you still in that same religion? The same denomination? If not, what religion do you adhere to, and how did the change come about? Are you an atheist? An agnostic? If you are a believer, what is your notion of God? Does God seem abstract and distant, or does God seem close to you and personal? Has this changed recently? Do you pray? What is your prayer life like? Have you had any spiritual experiences? What were they? What effect did they have upon you? (p. 251)

A number of particular religious or spiritual issues may surface in therapy. They include broad concerns like the search for meaning or direction in life (cf. Welter, 1987), fear of death, and the need for clarification of values, as well as more specific issues like doubts, sins or moral failures, struggles with guilt, bitterness, and an unforgiving spirit, spiritual dryness, and even possible demonization. "Toxic faith" (Arterburn & Felton, 1991) or religious addiction (Booth, 1991) are also spiritual problems with which the therapist may have to deal. The therapist needs to proceed gently and respectfully, however, and avoid imposing his or her convictions on the client. White (1987) has cautioned that if religious or spiritual issues are confronted too soon, some aspects of the client's faith might be affected negatively. Even if it is appropriate or timely to deal with spiritual issues openly in therapy, the therapist should be sensitive to the client's pace, as well as respect the client's freedom of choice and responsibility in making personal decisions. In a situation where supportive therapy may be needed in order to prevent or retard disintegration in a severely disturbed client, the therapist should refrain from confronting the client's religious convictions or beliefs, even if they may appear to be somewhat neurotic or unhealthy, until a later time when the client is more stabilized emotionally and able and willing to engage in such discussion or caring confrontation.

Lovinger (1984, 1990) has discussed a number of helpful ways of working with religious issues in therapy in general (see also Kelly, 1995), and has provided good summaries of the major Christian denominations as well as other major religions like Judaism and Islam. He has also described several examples of countertransference that might occur in conducting therapy with religiously committed clients, which therapists need to guard against. They include having extended "philosophical" discussions with no therapeutic aim, arguing with clients about their doctrine, failing to explore thoroughly why a client has had a significant shift in religious orientation, especially toward the therapist's denomination, and so forth (Lovinger, 1984).

EXPLICIT INTEGRATION: INTRAPERSONAL INTEGRATION AND THE DEVELOPMENT OF SPIRITUALITY IN THERAPIST AND CLIENT

The intrapersonal integration (i.e., a person's own appropriation of faith and integration of psychological and spiritual experience) and especially the spiritual development of the therapist himself or herself are seen as crucial, even though they may not be absolutely necessary, for effective explicit integration of religion in psychotherapy to occur (Tan, 1988,

1990). From a Christian perspective, the following spiritual disciplines are helpful for developing mature faith and deep Christlike spirituality: the inward disciplines of meditation, prayer, fasting and study; the outward disciplines of simplicity, solitude, submission, and service; and the corporate disciplines of confession, worship, guidance, and celebration (Foster, 1988; see also Willard, 1988).

As the therapist grows in his or her own spirituality, he or she can be more effective in facilitating the spiritual growth and development of the client, through the therapy process, as well as encouraging the client to read about and use the spiritual disciplines. Although it is generally true that a therapist can only bring a client as far as he or she has gone psychologically and spiritually, it is not always the case. There are therapists who believe that the grace of God can work in the therapeutic situation and relationship in such a way that the client can grow beyond where the therapist is, or both the client and therapist may even experience greater depths of spirituality and wholeness.

Religiously oriented therapists often believe that the ultimate goal of therapy includes facilitating the spiritual growth of clients, especially those who are religiously committed. Benner (1988) has noted that although psychotherapy is very much a spiritual process, with psychotherapy and spiritual direction or guidance being related activities, psychotherapy is nevertheless still somewhat discrete from spiritual direction. However, he acknowledged that it is possible for a therapist who is well trained or experienced in both psychotherapy and spiritual direction to provide an integrated psychospiritual therapy to clients desiring such an explicit integration approach. One notable example from the Roman Catholic tradition of such an integrated approach to therapy has been explicated by Tyrrell (1982) as "Christotherapy." A number of Protestant Christian approaches have already been cited earlier in this chapter. Explicit integration of religion in psychotherapy is therefore an integrated psychospiritual approach that attempts to provide both effective psychotherapeutic help as well as spiritual guidance to clients so that they can grow as whole persons. The therapist who practices explicit integration, however, does not try to assume all of the roles or functions of pastor or ecclesiastical leader, in addressing spiritual and religious issues openly in therapy. Referral to pastors or ecclesiastical leaders may be necessary at times, just as they may need to refer to mental health professionals (Payne et al., 1992).

TOWARD THE FUTURE

It may be interesting to note that Jerome Frank over a decade ago concluded that the most gifted therapists, who obtain extraordinary therapeutic outcomes with clients, may have telepathic, clairvoyant, or other parapsychological abilities and what he termed "healing power" (Frank, 1982, p. 31). He called for more research on such phenomena, which seem to be somewhat related to spirituality. Similarly, Marks (1978) challenged researchers to study further the faith and religious processes involved in faith healing because of its powerful effectiveness when it works.

The three major dimensions of explicit integration just described are not exhaustive, but merely illustrative of the many interventions or techniques that can be used in such a model or approach to integrating religion in clinical practice. Payne et al. (1992) have reviewed specific techniques like the use of prayer, forgiveness, and scriptural reference or imagery, as well as attempts to integrate spiritual and standard psychotherapy techniques in the cognitive–behavioral, psychodynamic, existential–humanistic, and health psychology areas. Worthington, Dupont, Berry, and Duncan (1988) found that the five most widely used spiritual guidance techniques by seven Christian mental health professionals or counselors were: assigning religious homework, quoting scripture, interpreting scripture, discussing the client's faith, and prayer during the therapy session. Forgiveness of others, forgiveness of God, religious imagery, and rededication were the other techniques mentioned. They also found that session helpfulness was related to the use of forgiveness of others or God, and engagement in religious homework.

Moon, Willis, Bailey, and Kwasny (1993) recently used a list of 20 Christian spiritual guidance techniques (see Exhibit 1) and surveyed Christian psychotherapists, pastoral counselors, and spiritual directors regarding their self-reported use of them. They found that across all three professional identity groups, the most commonly used techniques were spiritual history, discernment, forgiveness, solitude or silence, intercessory prayer, and teaching from Scripture. The techniques least likely to be used were praying in the Spirit, deliverance, and healing. They pointed out that previous research done by Ball and Goodyear (1991), DiBlasio and Benda (1991), Jones, Watson, and Wolfram (1992), and Worthington et al. (1988) also found that instruction in forgiveness, prayer (in different forms), and teaching and quoting Scripture were techniques frequently employed by religious Christian mental health practitioners. Interestingly enough, Moon et al. (1993) reported that doctoral level religious mental health practitioners were less likely to use such explicit spiritual guidance techniques than were masters' level practitioners, providing some support for Winger and Hunsberger's (1988) earlier finding of a negative correlation between the use of religious techniques and level of graduate education among 127 male clergy. Moon, Bailey, Kwasny, and Willis (1991) in a previous study of training in the use of Christian or spiritual disciplines as counseling techniques within religiously oriented graduate training programs (see Tan & Jones, 1991 regarding Christian graduate training programs in professional psychology), found that journal keeping, forgiveness, healing, and discern-

Techniques
Concrete meditation
Abstract meditation
Intercessory prayer
Contemplative prayer
Listening prayer
Praying in the Spirit
Scripture: counselor pro-active
Scripture: client pro-active
Confession
Worship
Forgiveness
Fasting
Deliverance
Solitude/silence
Discernment
Journal keeping
Obedience
Simplicity
Spiritual history
Healing

ment were the techniques most likely to be taught, but noted they were not often incorporated into a course syllabus or given much formal lecture time. Graduate-level training in the use of explicit integration techniques therefore is in need of greater attention and development. Moon et al. (1993) suggested that it may be time to develop seriously specialized education and certification in religious counseling or therapy.

Payne et al. (1992) have also pointed out that even with populations that are not particularly religiously oriented, integrative applications of spiritual resources with such populations as alcoholics (Brown, Peterson, & Cunningham, 1988a, 1988b, 1988c) and antisocial persons in moral reconation therapy (Little & Robinson, 1988) have been shown to be fruitful. Further research is needed, especially in matching problems and clients with particular techniques and therapists (Payne et al., 1992; see also Worthington, 1991).

In conclusion, religion in clinical practice is an important area in which clinicians need better training and more experience (Tan, 1993b). Two major models of implicit and explicit integration have been described, with an emphasis on explicit integration approaches that seem particularly relevant to the needs and preferences of religiously committed clients. Above all, both explicit and implicit integration should be practiced in a clinically sensitive, ethically responsible, and professionally competent way.

Further research is also needed to evaluate or validate the efficacy of therapeutic interventions of a religious nature.

REFERENCES

Albee, G. W. (1991). Opposition to prevention and a new creedal oath. *The Scientist Practitioner, 1*(4), 30–31.

Alsdurf, J. M., & Malony, H. N. (1980). A critique of Ruth Carter Stapleton's ministry of "inner healing." *Journal of Psychology and Theology, 8,* 173–184.

American Psychological Association. (1992). Ethical principles of psychologists and code of conduct. *American Psychologist, 47,* 1597–1611.

Arterburn, S., & Felton, J. (1991). *Toxic faith: Understanding and overcoming religious addiction.* Nashville, TN: Thomas Nelson.

Backus, W. (1985). *Telling the truth to troubled people.* Minneapolis: Bethany House.

Backus, W., & Chapian, M. (1980). *Telling yourself the truth.* Minneapolis: Bethany House.

Ball, R. A., & Goodyear, R. K. (1991). Self-reported professional practices of Christian psychotherapists. *Journal of Psychology and Christianity, 10,* 144–153.

Beck, J. R., & Lewis, G. R. (1989). Counseling and the demonic: A reaction to Page. *Journal of Psychology and Theology, 17,* 132–134.

Beit-Hallahmi, B. (1975). Encountering orthodox religion in psychotherapy. *Psychotherapy: Theory, Research and Practice, 11,* 357–359.

Benner, D. G. (1988). *Psychotherapy and the spiritual quest.* Grand Rapids: Baker.

Bergin, A. E. (1980a). Psychotherapy and religious values. *Journal of Consulting and Clinical Psychology, 4,* 95–105.

Bergin, A. E. (1980b). Religious and humanistic values: A reply to Ellis and Walls. *Journal of Consulting and Clinical Psychology, 48,* 642–645.

Bergin, A. E. (1983). Religiosity and mental health: A critical reevaluation and meta-analysis. *Professional Psychology: Research and Practice, 14,* 170–184.

Bergin, A. E. (1988a). The spiritual perspective is ecumenical and eclectic (rejoinder). *Counseling and Values, 33,* 57–59.

Bergin, A. E. (1988b). Three contributions of a spiritual perspective to counseling, psychotherapy, and behavior change. *Counseling and Values, 33,* 21–31.

Bergin, A. E. (1991). Values and religious issues in psychotherapy and mental health. *American Psychologist, 46,* 394–403.

Bergin, A. E., & Jensen, J. P. (1990). Religiosity of psychotherapists: A national survey. *Psychotherapy, 27,* 3–7.

Bergin, A. E., & Payne, I. R. (1991). Proposed agenda for a spiritual strategy in personality and psychotherapy. *Journal of Psychology and Christianity, 10*(3), 197–210.

Bjorck, J. P. (1992). [Letter to the editor]. *The Scientist Practitioner, 2*(1), 33–34.

Booth, L. (1991). *When God becomes a drug: Breaking the chains of religious addiction and abuse*. New York: Jeremy P. Tarcher/Perigee Books.

Brown, H. P., Peterson, J. D., & Cunningham, O. (1988a). An individualized behavioral approach to spiritual development for the recovering alcoholic/addict. *Alcoholism Treatment Quarterly, 5*, 177–191.

Brown, H. P., Peterson, J. D., & Cunningham, O. (1988b). A behavioral/cognitive spiritual model for a chemical dependency aftercare program. *Alcoholism Treatment Quarterly, 5*, 153–166.

Brown, H. P., Peterson, J. D., & Cunningham, O. (1988c). Rationale and theoretical basis for a behavioral/cognitive approach to spirituality. *Alcoholism Treatment Quarterly, 5*, 47–59.

Bufford, R. K. (1988). *Counseling and the demonic*. Dallas: Word Books.

Collins, G. R. (1988). *Christian counseling: A comprehensive guide* (rev. ed.). Dallas: Word.

Collins, G. R. (1993). *The biblical basis of Christian counseling for people helpers*. Colorado Springs, CO: NavPress.

Crabb, L. J. (1987). *Understanding people: Deep longings for relationship*. Grand Rapids: Zondervan.

Craigie, F. C., & Tan, S. Y. (1989). Changing resistant assumptions in Christian cognitive–behavioral therapy. *Journal of Psychology and Theology, 17*, 93–100.

Demetrios, P. E., Simpkinson, C. H., & Bennet, C. (Eds.). (1991). *The Common Boundary graduate education guide*. Bethesda, MD: Common Boundary.

DiBlasio, F. A., & Benda, B. B. (1991). Practitioners, religion and the use of forgiveness in the clinical setting. *Journal of Psychology and Christianity, 10*, 166–172.

Dougherty, S. G., & Worthington, E. L. (1982). Preferences of conservative and moderate Christians for four Christian counselors' treatment plans. *Journal of Psychology and Theology, 10*, 346–354.

Ellis, A. (1980). Psychotherapy and atheistic values: A response to A. E. Bergin's "Psychotherapy and religious values." *Journal of Consulting and Clinical Psychology, 48*, 635–639.

Ellis, A. (1992). My current views on rational–emotive therapy (RET) and religiousness. *Journal of Rational–Emotive and Cognitive–Behavior Therapy, 10*, 37–40.

Ellis, A. (1993). The advantages and disadvantages of self-help therapy materials. *Professional Psychology: Research and Practice, 24*, 335–339.

Finn, M., & Gartner, J. (Eds.). (1992). *Object relations theory and religion: Clinical applications*. New York: Praeger.

Finney, J. R., & Malony, H. N. (1985a). An empirical study of contemplative prayer as an adjunct to psychotherapy. *Journal of Psychology and Theology, 13*, 284–290.

Finney, J. R., & Malony, H. N. (1985b). Contemplative prayer and its use in psychotherapy: A theoretical model. *Journal of Psychology and Theology, 13*, 172–181.

Finney, J. R., & Malony, H. N. (1985c). Empirical studies of Christian prayer: A review of the literature. *Journal of Psychology and Theology, 13*, 104–115.

Foster, R. J. (1988). *Celebration of discipline* (Rev. ed.). San Francisco: Harper San Francisco.

Frank, J. D. (1982). Therapeutic components shared by all psychotherapies. In J. H. Harvey & M. M. Parks (Eds.), *The Master Lecture Series: Vol. 1. Psychotherapy research and behavior change* (pp. 5–37). Washington, DC: American Psychological Association.

Gass, S. C. (1984). Orthodox Christian values related to psychotherapy and mental health. *Journal of Psychology and Theology, 12*, 230–237.

Johnson, C. B. (1987). Religious resources in psychotherapy. In D. G. Benner (Ed.), *Psychotherapy in Christian perspective* (pp. 31–36). Grand Rapids: Baker.

Johnson, W. B. (1990). *The comparative efficacy of religious and nonreligious Rational–Emotive Therapy with religious clients.* Unpublished doctoral dissertation, Graduate School of Psychology, Fuller Theological Seminary, Pasadena, CA.

Jones, J. W. (1991). *Contemporary psychoanalysis and religion.* New Haven: Yale University Press.

Jones, S. (1994). A constructive relationship for religion with the science and profession of psychology: Perhaps the boldest model yet. *American Psychologist, 49*, 184–199.

Jones, S. L., Watson, E., & Wolfram, T. (1992). Results of the Rech conference survey on religious faith and professional psychology. *Journal of Psychology and Theology, 20*, 147–158.

Kelly, E. W., Jr. (1995). *Spirituality and religion in counseling and psychotherapy.* Alexandria, VA: American Counseling Association.

Kelly, T. A., & Strupp, H. H. (1992). Patient and therapist values in psychotherapy: Perceived changes, assimilation, similarity, and outcome. *Journal of Consulting and Clinical Psychology, 60*, 34–48.

Larson, D. B., Sherrill, K. A., Lyons, J. S., Craigie, F. C., Jr., Thielman, S. B., Greenwold, M. A., & Larson, S. S. (1992). Associations between dimensions of religious commitment and mental health reported in the American Journal of Psychiatry and Archives of General Psychiatry: 1978–1989. *American Journal of Psychiatry, 149*, 557–559.

Lax, W. D. (1993, August). *Narrative, deconstruction, and Buddhism: Shifting beyond dualism.* Paper presented at the annual convention of the American Psychological Association, Toronto, Ontario, Canada.

Little, G. L., & Robinson, K. D. (1988). Moral reconation therapy: A systematic step-by-step treatment system for treatment resistant clients. *Psychological Reports, 62*, 135–161.

Lovinger, R. J. (1984). *Working with religious issues in therapy*. Northvale, NJ: Jason Aronson.

Lovinger, R. J. (1990). *Religion and counseling: The psychological impact of religious belief*. New York: Continuum.

Malony, H. N. (1987). Inner healing. In D. G. Benner (Ed.), *Psychotherapy in Christian perspective* (pp. 171–179). Grand Rapids: Baker.

Malony, H. N. (1988). The clinical assessment of optimal religious functioning. *Review of Religious Research, 30*, 2–17.

Marks, I. M. (1978). Behavioral psychotherapy of adult neurosis. In S. L. Garfield & A. E. Bergin (Eds.), *Handbook of psychotherapy and behavior change* (2nd ed., pp. 493–547). New York: Wiley.

McMinn, M. (1991). *Cognitive therapy techniques in Christian counseling*. Dallas: Word.

Meier, L. (1988). *Jewish values in psychotherapy*. New York: University Press of America.

Menninger, K. (1973). *Whatever became of sin?* New York: Hawthorn Books.

Miller, W. R., & Martin, J. E. (Eds.). (1988). *Behavior therapy and religion: Integrating spiritual and behavioral approaches to change*. Newbury Park, CA: Sage.

Moon, G. W., Bailey, J. W., Kwasny, J. C., & Willis, D. E. (1991). Training in the use of Christian disciplines as counseling techniques within religiously oriented graduate training programs. *Journal of Psychology and Christianity, 10*, 154–165.

Moon, G. W., Willis, D. E., Bailey, J. W., & Kwasny, J. C. (1993). Self-reported use of Christian spiritual guidance techniques by Christian psychotherapists, pastoral counselors, and spiritual directors. *Journal of Psychology and Christianity, 12*, 24–37.

Mowrer, O. H. (1961). *The crisis in psychiatry and religion*. Princeton, NJ: D. Van Nostrand.

Nelson, A. A., & Wilson, W. P. (1984). The ethics of sharing religious faith in psychotherapy. *Journal of Psychology and Theology, 12*, 15–23.

Page, S. H. T. (1989a). Exorcism revisited: A response to Beck and Lewis and to Wilson. *Journal of Psychology and Theology, 17*, 140–143.

Page, S. H. T. (1989b). The role of exorcism in clinical practice and pastoral care. *Journal of Psychology and Theology, 17*, 121–131.

Pargament, K. I. (1990). God help me: Toward a theoretical framework of coping for the psychology of religion. *Research in the Social Scientific Study of Religion, 2*, 195–224.

Payne, I. R., Bergin, A. E., Bielema, K. A., & Jenkins, P. H. (1991). Review of religion and mental health: Prevention and the enhancement of psychosocial functioning. *Prevention in Human Services, 9*(2), 11–40.

Payne, I. R., Bergin, A. E., & Loftus, P. E. (1992). A review of attempts to integrate spiritual and standard psychotherapy techniques. *Journal of Psychotherapy Integration, 2*, 171–192.

Pecheur, E., & Edwards, K. J. (1984). A comparison of secular and religious versions of cognitive therapy with depressed Christian college students. *Journal of Psychology and Theology, 12*, 45–54.

Peck, M. S. (1983). *People of the lie: The hope for healing human evil.* New York: Simon & Schuster.

Peck, M. S. (1993). *Further along the road less traveled.* New York: Simon & Schuster.

Propst, R. L. (1980). The comparative efficacy of religious and non-religious imagery for the treatment of mild depression in religious individuals. *Cognitive Therapy and Research, 4*, 167–178.

Propst, R. L. (1988). *Psychotherapy in a religious framework: Spirituality in the emotional healing process.* New York: Human Sciences Press.

Propst, R. L., Ostrom, R., Watkins, P., Dean, T., & Mashburn, D. (1992). Comparative efficacy of religious and nonreligious cognitive–behavioral therapy for the treatment of clinical depression in religious individuals. *Journal of Consulting and Clinical Psychology, 60*, 94–103.

Psychotherapy. (1990). Psychotherapy and religion [Special issue]. *27* (1).

Quackenbos, S., Privette, G., & Klentz, B. (1986). Psychotherapy and religion: Rapprochement or antithesis? *Journal of Counseling and Development, 65*, 82–85.

Randour, M. L. (Ed.). (1993). *Exploring sacred landscapes: Religious and spiritual experiences in psychotherapy.* New York: Columbia University Press.

Rizvi, S. A. A. (1988). *A Muslim tradition in psychotherapy and modern trends.* Lahore, Pakistan: Institute of Islamic Culture.

Rosik, C. H. (1992). [Letter to the editor]. *The Scientist Practitioner, 2*(1), 34–35.

Seamands, D. (1985). *Healing of memories.* Wheaton, IL: Victor Books.

Seligman, L. (1988). Invited Commentary: Three contributions of a spiritual perspective to counseling, psychotherapy, and behavior change (Allen E. Bergin). *Counseling and Values, 33*, 55–56.

Shafranske, E. P., & Malony, H. N. (1990). Clinical psychologists' religious and spiritual orientations and their practice of psychotherapy. *Psychotherapy, 27*, 72–78.

Simpkinson, C. H. (1992). *History of Common Boundary: The changing face of Common Boundary.* Chevy Chase, MD: The Common Boundary.

Smedes, L. (1984). *Forgive and forget.* San Francisco: Harper Collins.

Smith, J. H., & Handelman, S. A. (Eds.). (1990). *Psychoanalysis and religion.* Baltimore: Johns Hopkins University Press.

Sollod, R. N. (1992). [Letter to the editor]. *The Scientist Practitioner, 2*(1), 33.

Spero, M. H. (Ed.). (1985). *Psychotherapy and the religious patient.* Springfield, IL: Charles C Thomas.

Spilka, B. (1986). Spiritual issues: Do they belong in psychological practice? Yes—but! *Psychotherapy in Private Practice, 4*, 93–100.

Stern, E. M. (Ed.). (1985). *Psychotherapy and the religiously committed patient.* New York: Haworth Press.

Sturkie, J., & Tan, S. Y. (1992). *Peer counseling in youth groups.* Grand Rapids: Youth Specialties/Zondervan.

Sturkie, J., & Tan, S. Y. (1993). *Advanced peer counseling in youth groups.* Grand Rapids: Youth Specialties/Zondervan.

Tan, S. Y. (1987). Cognitive–behavior therapy: A biblical approach and critique. *Journal of Psychology and Theology, 15*(2), 103–112.

Tan, S. Y. (1988, November). *Explicit integration in psychotherapy.* Invited paper presented at the International Congress on Christian Counseling, Atlanta, Georgia.

Tan, S. Y. (1990). Explicit integration in Christian counseling [an interview]. *The Christian Journal of Psychology and Counseling, V* (2), 7–13.

Tan, S. Y. (1991). *Lay counseling: Equipping Christians for a helping ministry.* Grand Rapids: Zondervan.

Tan, S. Y. (1992a). Development and supervision of paraprofessional counselors. In L. VandeCreek, S. Knapp, & T. L. Jackson (Eds.), *Innovations in clinical practice: A sourcebook: Vol. 11* (pp. 431–440). Sarasota, FL: Professional Resources Exchange.

Tan, S. Y. (1992b). The Holy Spirit and counseling ministries. *The Christian Journal of Psychology and Counseling, VII* (3), 8–11.

Tan, S. Y. (1993a). Religious values and interventions in lay Christian counseling. In E. L. Worthington, Jr. (Ed.), *Psychotherapy and religious values* (pp. 225–241). Grand Rapids: Baker.

Tan, S. Y. (1993b, January). *Training in professional psychology: Diversity includes religion.* Paper presented at the National Council of Schools of Professional Psychology (NCSPP) Mid-Winter Conference on "Clinical Training in Professional Psychology," La Jolla, California.

Tan, S. Y. (1994). Ethical considerations in religious psychotherapy: Potential pitfalls and unique resources. *Journal of Psychology and Theology, 22,* 389–394.

Tan, S. Y., & Jones, S. L. (1991). Christian graduate training in professional psychology: The Rech Conference. *Journal of Psychology and Christianity, 10*(1), 72–75.

Tan, S. Y., & Ortberg, J., Jr. (1995a). *Coping with depression.* Grand Rapids, MI: Baker.

Tan, S. Y., & Ortberg, J., Jr. (1995b). *Understanding depression.* Grand Rapids, MI: Baker.

Thurman, C. (1989). *The lies we believe.* Nashville, TN: Thomas Nelson.

Tyrrell, B. J. (1982). *Christotherapy II.* New York: Paulist Press.

Vande Kemp, H. (1984). *Psychology and theology in western thought (1672–1965): A historical and annotated bibliography.* In collaboration with H. Newton Malony. Milwood, NY: Kraus International.

Walls, G. B. (1980). Values and psychotherapy: A comment on "Psychotherapy and religious values." *Journal of Consulting and Clinical Psychology, 48,* 640–641.

Ward, W. O. (1977). *The Bible in counseling.* Chicago: Moody Press.

Welter, P. R. (1987). *Counseling and the search for meaning.* Waco, TX: Word Books.

White, F. J. (1987). Spiritual and religious issues in therapy. In D. G. Benner (Ed.), *Psychotherapy in Christian perspective* (pp. 37–46). Grand Rapids: Baker.

Willard, D. (1988). *The spirit of the disciplines.* San Francisco: Harper & Row.

Wilson, W. P. (1989). Demon possession and exorcism: A reaction to Page. *Journal of Psychology and Theology, 17,* 135–139.

Winger, D., & Hunsberger, B. (1988). Clergy counseling practices, Christian orthodoxy and problem solving styles. *Journal of Psychology and Theology, 16,* 41–48.

Worthington, E. L., Jr. (1986). Religious counseling: A review of published empirical research. *Journal of Counseling and Development, 64,* 421–431.

Worthington, E. L., Jr. (1988). Understanding the values of religious clients: A model and its application to counseling. *Journal of Counseling, 35,* 166–174.

Worthington, E. L., Jr. (1989). Religious faith across the life span: Implications for counseling and research. *The Counseling Psychologist, 17,* 555–612.

Worthington, E. L., Jr. (1991). Psychotherapy and religious values: An update. *Journal of Psychology and Christianity, 10*(3), 211–223.

Worthington, E. L., Jr. (Ed.). (1993). *Psychotherapy and religious values.* Grand Rapids: Baker.

Worthington, E. L., Jr., Dupont, P. D., Berry, J. T., & Duncan, L. A. (1988). Christian therapists' and clients' perceptions of religious psychotherapy in private and agency settings. *Journal of Psychology and Theology, 16,* 282–293.

Worthington, E. L., Jr., & Gascoyne, S. R. (1985). Preferences of Christians and non-Christians for five Christian counselors' treatment plans: A partial replication and extension. *Journal of Psychology and Theology, 13,* 29–41.

Worthington, E. L., Jr., & Scott, G. G. (1983). Goal selection for counseling with potentially religious clients by professional and student counselors in explicitly Christian or secular settings. *Journal of Psychology and Theology, 11,* 318–328.

Wright, H. N. (1986). *Self-talk, imagery, and prayer in counseling.* Waco, TX: Word.

Wyatt, S. D., & Johnson, R. W. (1990). The influence of counselors' values on clients' perceptions of the counselor. *Journal of Psychology and Theology, 18,* 158–165.

III

PSYCHOTHERAPY WITH RELIGIOUSLY COMMITTED PEOPLE

14

COGNITIVE–BEHAVIORAL THERAPY AND THE RELIGIOUS PERSON

L. REBECCA PROPST

Cognitive therapy is uniquely suited to address the beliefs and assumptions that religious clients bring to psychological treatment. In this chapter, I present an overview of the cognitive–behavioral approach, a discussion of its specific application to religiously committed individuals, a summary of selected research, and a case illustration. To begin, the term *cognitive* refers to any aspect of mentation, including beliefs about self, others, and relationships. It also refers to the patient's inner self-talk or inner dialogue, including both abstractions and mental images.

Lazarus (1991), contended that there is no hard evidence that emotions—including those assumed to be produced by physical causes— occur in the absence of mediating cognitions. For many following this school of thought, however, the traditional distinctions among cognitions, emotions, and behaviors are rapidly breaking down and have been replaced by an information-processing model of human behavior (e.g., see Lang, 1985). Such a model emphasizes that emotional responses provide continuous feedback to a person regarding how prepared he or she is to engage the environment. The person's thoughts, in turn, affect subsequent emotions and influence behavior.

Regardless of the assumed relationship between cognitions and emotions, cognitive–behaviorists have found it clinically useful to assume that emotional and behavioral responses to situations are mediated by perceived meanings or cognitions (Beck, 1976). The basic cognitive model of psychotherapy therefore assumes that changes in cognitive distortions and underlying schemas will produce relief from dysphoric affect and other psychological symptoms. Because of its impact on dysphoric affect, cognitive therapy is often used very successfully with people who have depression or anxiety disorders.

In addition, cognitive therapists have been focusing increasingly on the notion of schema, especially as it relates to personality disorders. According to Segal (1988), schemas are "organized elements of past reactions and experience that form a relatively cohesive and persistent body of knowledge capable of guiding subsequent perception and appraisals" (p. 147). Cognitive therapy primarily works to shift or modify these schemas or core assumptions. The exact approach taken to this process varies with the therapist. However, there are usually three general components to any effective cognitive treatment.

First, the individual must be taught and come to believe that thoughts and assumptions strongly influence emotions and psychological well-being. This process can take many forms, but it is usually most effective if it is experiential. That is, the therapist should use the patient's here-and-now experience to illustrate the model. Second, the patient must be taught to recognize and identify individual thoughts in each specific situation. After the patient can successfully identify individual thoughts, he or she can be trained to identify the themes or underlying assumptions and schemas cutting across many different situations. The third step in cognitive therapy is to challenge and modify the individual thoughts and then address the underlying assumptions and schemas. Most cognitive therapists also include behavioral interventions in the treatment regimen. They may give the patient training in particular social skills, such as assertion or communication skills.

More recently, a greater focus on the individual's assumptions about relationships, or interpersonal schemas, has occurred in cognitive therapy. Muran and Safran (1993) have asserted that the interpersonal schema is abstracted on the basis of interactions with attachment figures and permits individuals to predict interactions in a way that increases the probability of maintaining relatedness to these figures. Many of these ideas are akin to Bowlby's (1980) assertions that humans develop internal working models representing interpersonal interaction relevant to attachment behavior. Thus, a patient might be challenged to examine his or her assumptions about a given relationship and the behavior that would follow naturally from those assumptions. Then, on the basis of the principle of interpersonal complementarity, in which interpersonal responses are contingent on the preceding interpersonal behavior of another person, the therapist encourages the individual to see what types of behavior are pulled from other people's behaviors (Safran & Segal, 1990). Finally, the therapist attempts to modify the client's interpersonal assumptions and behavior.

RELIGIOUS CONTENT IN COGNITIVE–BEHAVIORAL THERAPY

The attitude of cognitive–behavioral therapy toward religion has come full circle, from a disdain and avoidance to an appreciation of religion's influence on cognition, emotion, and, ultimately, behavior. Because of the influence of Albert Ellis (1980)—who contended that all forms of religious belief were pathological and lead to neurosis—cognitive therapy at its inception was quite hostile to the religious beliefs of the patient. Such beliefs were described as leading only to self-defeating behavior and neurosis. Specifically, Ellis viewed such thinking as a regression to magical or unscientific thinking or as a reversion to reliance on religious authority. He believed that any *shoulds*, especially those arising from religious ethics, would only result in excessive guilt and a limiting of one's freedom.

Contemporary cognitive therapy has shifted from the idea that there are certain irrational ideas that cause problems for everyone. An emphasis is placed instead on the notion that there are logical errors in thinking that lead to dysfunction, such as overgeneralization, personalizing (assuming excessive responsibility), mind reading, or catastrophizing (Bedrosian & Bozicas, 1994). The specific content of the belief is thus less important. Therefore, these cognitive errors could be made with either religious or secular beliefs.

The emphasis in cognitive therapy on the importance of personal beliefs may account for its acceptability among many religious persons. In similar fashion, religious beliefs have also become increasingly accepted by cognitive therapists as a focus of treatment outside of religious circles. For example, even authors of nonreligious cognitive therapy books (e.g., Bedrosian & Bozicas, 1994) urge their therapist audiences to consult religious cognitive therapy books (e.g., Propst, 1988), which offer a "number of constructive treatment strategies for use with religiously committed individuals" (Bedrosian & Bozicas, 1994, p. 125).

Elsewhere (Propst, 1988), I have contended that all therapeutic techniques, but especially those based in cognitive therapy, place cognition (i.e., conscious thoughts and beliefs of the individual) at the center of the therapeutic work. Furthermore, this cognitive process of modifying and transforming one's assumptions interestingly bears resemblance to aspects of religious expression. There is, for example, a similarity between cognitive restructuring and the religious idea of "repentance," which comes from Greek, meaning "to change one's mind about how one's self and the world is to be viewed" (Michel, 1967). Consistent with this claim, there appears to be a similarity between the idea of the challenging and transforming of one's assumptions and schema with ideas presented within Christian thinking. For example, cognitive theories of transformation urge individuals to not be influenced by the past and their underlying dysfunctional assumptions but, instead, to understand how the present world dictates their behaviors and to resist that dictation, so that they are not defined by their roles. Likewise, as I have explained elsewhere (Propst, 1988):

> various theologies state that true transformation occurs when we cease gaining our self-definition from those around us, but begin to take our cues from God. Such a process results in a new freedom. We are less dependent upon others' approval. We have less need for all relationships to be perfect. We can be a servant of others, and not a slave. (p. 85)

Thus, both the cognitive therapeutic change models and theological inquiry urge a change of perspective for transformation.

In *Psychotherapy in a Religious Framework: Spirituality in the Emotional Healing Process* (Propst, 1988), I suggested that cognitive restructuring could be defined as a type of spiritual transformation of the mind—a spiritual exercise. Such a characterization of cognitive therapy would make it more acceptable to certain members of the religious community.

Research on the Role of Religious Beliefs in Cognitive–Behavioral Therapy

Cognitive–behavioral therapy is based on the premise that its efficacy can be demonstrated through empirical research. Beck and his colleagues (Beck, Sokol, Clark, Berchick, & Wright, 1992; Hollon & Beck, 1994; Rush, Beck, Kovacs, & Hollon, 1977) have successfully proved therapeutic results. The question of whether or not religious faith can positively contribute to, or even enhance, the clinical therapy process therefore remained to be investigated. I have conducted two studies (Propst, 1980, 1992) that demonstrated the therapeutic effects of the use of religious imagery and interventions within cognitive–behavioral therapy.

In the first study, I found that for religious patients, a cognitive–behavioral therapy-related religious imagery treatment and a religious placebo (a control group consisting of discussion of religious issues) both showed a more positive effect on dependent measures than did a cognitive–behavioral related nonreligious imagery treatment. Both this nonreligious treatment and a self-monitoring only control group were the least effective. For the behaviorally oriented dependent variable (observation of group assertiveness), the religious-imagery treatment was the only treatment that differed significantly from the waiting-list condition. Only nonreligious therapists were used in this study, and all religious treatments and the religion of the patients were Christian.

In a 1992 study, Propst, Ostrom, Watkins, Dean, and Mashburn used more standard cognitive–behavioral treatment, more severely depressed patients, and both religious and nonreligious therapists. This study also assessed the relative efficacy of a religious service delivery program relative to cognitive–behavioral therapy by including a treatment containing nonspecific religious counseling (pastoral counseling), but not the active ingredients of cognitive–behavioral therapy. For this study, patients were solicited through local Christian media as well as the general media. The study was presented as a program for teaching Christians between the ages of 18 and 65 how to cope with depression.

To be accepted into the 1992 study, patients had to score in the depression range on the Hamilton Rating Scale for Depression (HRSD; Hamilton, 1967), not be suicidal, and not meet the criteria for any other clinical diagnosis. The patients who met the criteria were randomly assigned to 1 of 10 therapists (advanced graduate students) or the wait-list control group (WLC). Crossing religiosity of treatment and therapist created four cognitive–behavioral therapy combinations: (a) religious cognitive therapy–nonreligious therapist (RCT-NT); (b) religious cognitive therapy–religious therapist (RCT-RT); (c) nonreligious cognitive therapy–religious therapist (NRCT-RT); and (d) nonreligious cognitive therapy–nonreligious therapist (NRCT-NT). The pastoral counseling (PC) condition involved only religious therapists. The therapists (5 men and 5 women) received extensive training prior to the project. The Christian therapists were graduate students in a religiously oriented clinical psychology program, whereas the nonreligious therapists were from a more traditional counseling psychology training program. Both cognitive treatments focused on cognitive restructuring techniques and behavioral assignments. However, therapists offering religious cognitive therapy gave a Christian religious rationale for the procedures, used religious arguments to counter irrational thoughts, and used religious-imagery procedures (Propst, 1988). Those using standard nonreligious cognitive therapy worked from a compilation of procedures from Beck, Rush, Shaw, and Emery (1979) and from Burns (1980). The PC treatment was developed from a survey assessing currently used counseling procedures of 200 Protestant and Roman Catholic clergy in the local metropolitan area for dealing with depression. This treatment included nondirective listening and discussion of Bible verses or religious themes.

The Beck Depression Inventory (BDI; Beck, Ward, Mendelson, Mock, & Erbaugh, 1961) and a modified version of the HRSD were used to assess depression. The Global Severity Index from the Revised Symptom Checklist (Derogatis, Rickels, & Rock, 1976) was used to assess general psychopathology. General social adjustment was measured with the clinician-rated modified Social Adjustment Rating Scale (Weissman, Paykel, & Prusoff, 1980). Both patient and therapist beliefs were assessed by using a measure of types of religiosity (committed–consensual and extrinsic–intrinsic; Allen & Spilka, 1967; Allport, 1966) and a measure of religious experience and Christian orthodoxy (King & Hunt, 1972).

Results indicated that both the religious cognitive–behavioral treatment patients and the PC patients reported significantly lower posttreatment depression and better adjustment scores than did either the nonreligious cognitive–behavioral treatment or the WLC condition. The difference between cognitive–behavioral treatments was due largely to the superior performance of the nonreligious therapists in religious cognitive–behavioral therapy over the performance of nonreligious therapists in the nonreligious cognitive–behavioral treatments. Religious therapists performed equally well in both conditions.

More specifically, analyses of the therapists' effects using parametric statistics revealed that the difference between the religious and nonreligious cognitive therapy recipients on the BDI, the Social Adjustment Rating Scale, and the Global Severity Index occurred because of differences in performance for the nonreligious therapists. Furthermore, highly significant interactions on the BDI and the Social Adjustment Rating Scale indicated that the nonreligious therapists performed better in the religious cognitive therapy condition than in the nonreligious condition. There were no significant differences between religious and nonreligious cognitive therapy for the religious therapists (see Figure 1). A slightly different pattern emerged on the HRSD. Although the analysis of the HRSD and the Global Severity Index according to standard statistical analyses did not show a significant interaction, it did reveal that the only group performing significantly better than the WLC was the RCT-NT. Analyses of proportions of patients outside the range of dysfunctionality on the HRSD showed the same pattern (see Figures 2 and 3).

A second type of result was obtained on the Social Adjustment Rating Scale and the BDI. Namely, only the RCT-RT group performed significantly better than the WLC on this scale. Finally, an analysis of the proportion of patients outside the range of dysfunctionality on the Global Severity Index showed that the NRCT-RT group was significantly better than the WLC (see Figure 4). To summarize these results, the group that performed the most poorly on all measures was that receiving nonreligious cognitive therapy from nonreligious therapists. The other groups performed somewhat comparably.

Patients in all therapy conditions also remained substantially less depressed at both the 3-month and the 2-year follow-up than at pretest. Also, although a slightly different pattern of results was obtained at the 3-month follow-up, the pattern of results at the long-term (2-year) follow-up again paralleled the posttreatment results. Generally, religious therapists outper-

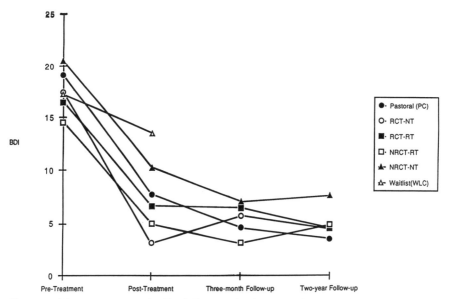

Figure 1. Mean scores on the Beck Depression Inventory by participants from Propst, Ostrom, Watkins, Dean, and Mashburn's (1992) study. RCT = religious cognitive therapy; NRCT = nonreligious cognitive therapy; NT = nonreligious therapist; PC = pastoral counseling; WLC = wait-list control group.

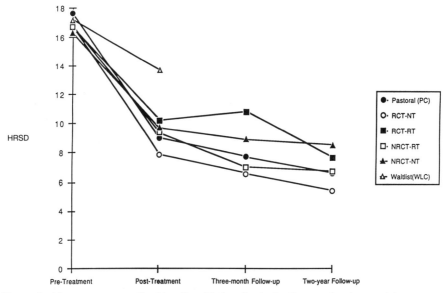

Figure 2. Mean scores on the Hamilton Rating Scale for Depression by participants from Propst, Ostrom, Watkins, Dean, and Mashburn's (1992) study. RCT = religious cognitive therapy; NRCT = nonreligious cognitive therapy; NT = nonreligious therapist; PC = pastoral counseling; WLC = wait-list control group.

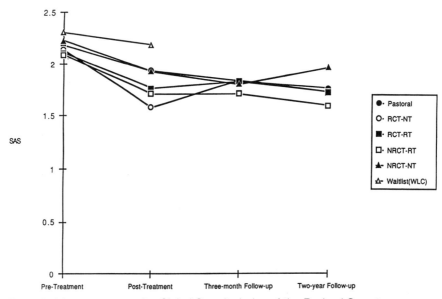

Figure 3. Mean scores on the Global Severity Index of the Revised Symptom Checklist (SCL–90–R) by participants from Propst, Ostrom, Watkins, Dean, and Mashburn's (1992) study. RCT = religious cognitive therapy; NRCT = nonreligious cognitive therapy; NT = nonreligious therapist; PC = pastoral counseling; WLC = wait-list control group.

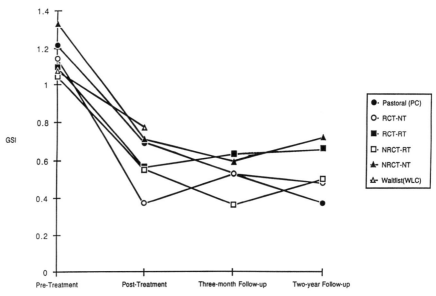

Figure 4. Mean scores on the Social Adjustment Rating Scale by participants from Propst, Ostrom, Watkins, Dean, and Mashburn's (1992) study. RCT = religious cognitive therapy; NRCT = nonreligious cognitive therapy; NT = nonreligious therapist; PC = pastoral counseling; WLC = wait-list control group.

formed nonreligious therapists, but only in the nonreligious cognitive therapy condition. There were no differences between therapists in the religious cognitive therapy condition (Propst et al., 1992).

Overall, these results suggest that the inclusion of religious faith in the therapy process can enhance its therapeutic effects. However, if therapy is given in a religious context by an identified religious therapist, than the inclusion of actual religious content in the therapy sessions themselves may be less necessary. Now that I have reviewed the initial findings about the efficacy of religious cognitive–behavioral therapy, I turn to a presentation of specific interventions. These interventions concern both the content of the cognitions and the operations in thinking.

Religious Cognitive Therapy Interventions

The theoretical perspective of cognitive therapy on religion suggests that cognitive therapy is a highly flexible therapeutic framework for including a patient's religious faith as an active part of the therapeutic process. Although certain general technique requirements are present, the content can probably vary greatly, being limited only by the creativity of the therapist and what research finally shows to be efficacious for the symptoms in question. Using the framework of cognitive therapy, there appears to be at least four categories of religious cognitive therapy interventions: (a) understanding the influence of cognition on emotion and behavior; (b) monitoring cognitions, including thoughts, beliefs, and assumptions; (c) challenging cognitions; and (d) cognitive restructuring and behavior modification.

First, because cognitive therapy emphasizes that patients must understand and believe that their thoughts and assumptions strongly influence their emotions and psychological well-being, religious patients may be given a religious rationale for this framework as well as a religious rationale for assessing their thoughts and assumptions. Thus, theological reflections could actually become some of the tools of cognitive therapy.

I have already provided a few examples of using a Christian rationale for assessing one's thoughts and assumptions (see Propst, 1988). A theological discussion of the value of self-knowledge and self-awareness could be useful for motivating thought monitoring (which is the technique for assessing cognitions). Self-examination is an important theme in both the Hebrew Bible and the New Testament, as well as a strong theme in the works of many Christian writers. Thus, for example, St. Teresa of Avila, a Carmelite nun of the sixteenth century, stated that if we know ourselves better, we will know God better. Similarly, John Calvin (1559/1972), one of the leaders of the Protestant Reformation, stated that the knowledge of God and of ourselves was connected by many ties and it was not easy to determine which of the two precedes and gives birth to the other (p. 37).

The use of such examples may help the religious client adopt a positive view of self-reflection rather than a view that the self-observation required in cognitive treatment means self-absorption.

Religious and theological themes are useful therapeutic tools that provide a motivational language to encourage religious patients to pursue thought monitoring actively and increased awareness of their thoughts and assumptions, as well as to overcome any initial resistance to therapy. With such a motivating language, many of the therapeutic tools originated by Beck—such as the three-column technique (Beck, et al., 1979)—can be made effective for highly religious patients.

After patients accept the value of thought monitoring and can apply this skill, the next process in cognitive therapy is the actual challenging and subsequent changing of thoughts and assumptions. Themes from most religious belief systems can play an important role in this process. Indeed, the religious ideas can actually become cognitive restructuring techniques. For example, some typical challenges to problematic assumptions might be having a patient adopt a problem-solving attitude rather than an attitude of perfectionism. Often, depressed or anxious individuals as well as some individuals with personality disorders have a cognitive schema that says that any type of mistake or a less than perfect solution to a problem can be catastrophic. This attitude may be intensified in some religious individuals because of the assumption that God expects perfection. Such an attitude leads to less risk taking and increased levels of anxiety and depression. Problem solving, on the other hand, means adopting the general orientation toward life that problems are a natural part of life and that coping with those problems is only a natural part of living.

Because many religious individuals' assumptions of perfectionism are rooted in their religious beliefs, challenges to such perfectionistic schemas will be most effective when they also come from those religious beliefs. Thus, for example, most religious thinkers from many belief systems emphasize that life is not perfect and that life has a tragic element. Both the Christian Scriptures and the Hebrew Bible emphasize that people will rarely be problem-free or even find a perfect solution to all their problems. Indeed, faith itself is often a product of difficult situations, according to the New Testament (Heb. 11). For example, even Jesus, the one declared good by God, had many problems. Indeed, the notion that no one is perfect, or even need be, is a common theme in much Christian spirituality. Thus, contemplatives such as St. John of the Cross have actually believed that people's sense of darkness, failure, or abandonment by God is one of the stages of faith (Propst, 1988, pp. 108–109).

Likewise, Karl Barth (1948/1960), a leading twentieth-century theological thinker, noted that the figure of the suffering man—the crucified Jesus—was a threat to Nietzsche's Superman. According to Barth, Nietzsche saw in the suffering Christ the direct opposite of his own ideal. Thus, for example, themes in the New Testament suggest that pain does not imply that one has failed. "But God chose the foolish things of the world to shame the wise. God chose the weak things in the world to shame the strong" (1 Cor. 1:27–29; discussed in Propst, 1988, pp. 41–45). With this theme, Christian patients can begin to challenge their cognitive schemas of perfectionism and high achievement. An explicit integration approach might bring these points of view into the therapeutic discourse (see Tan, chap. 13, this volume). This may lead to a cognitive reframing that may be crucial to treatment outcome.

An additional cognitive restructuring technique that is helpful within a religious context is the use of religious imagery. Lang (1979) viewed images as visual thoughts. These images are not stimuli that individuals respond to; rather, they are individual's responses. Furthermore, images may have a greater capacity than thoughts in a more linguistic mode for intensifying traumatic memories and, thus, may allow patients to focus more fully on emotionally laden ideas, so that patients may more effectively restructure the thoughts and images surrounding a traumatic event.

I have stated (Propst, 1988) that using images of Jesus in calling forth problematic, stressful scenes such as those resulting from posttraumatic stress responses may be useful for many patients. Thus, for example, many Christian female patients who have been sexually or physically abused have been able to allow themselves to experience the image of the abuse, which they have long pushed from awareness, when they imagined Jesus with them in the image. At the point that they are able to visualize Jesus present in that image, the meaning of the image begins to change (Propst, 1988, p. 130–138; see also Tan, chap. 13, this volume). Such an ameliorating of the negative intensty of the image may permit the patient to more fully work through the terrifying aspects of the images and their meanings.[1] Techniques of thought stopping, cognitive rehearsal, and confrontation of dysfunctional forms of thinking (e.g., arbitrary inference and overgeneralization) complement the use of Scripture and theological reflection in the examination of core beliefs and assumptions.

Behavior modification is often also a part of cognitive–behavioral therapy. Here also, religious patients could profit from a religious motivation for behavior changes. For example, some of my own patients—passive, depressed Christian women—would not become more assertive in their abusive marital relationships without a religious rationale for such changed behavior. One depressed woman benefited by seeing herself in the role of

---

[1] For many female patients, the notion of Jesus' maleness may invoke an image or memory of sexual or physical abuse by a male. Therefore, the image of Jesus may be problematic. For some of these women, the notion of Jesus as a victim who had been emotionally and physically abused just as they had may be helpful. Other women have chosen to focus on Jesus as not male, but rather merely human, or in some cases, a woman. Indeed, some contemplative Christian writers have seen Jesus as a mother, so there is support within the Christian tradition for this idea (Juliana of Norwich, 1392/1977).

a Hebrew prophet who is challenging abuse. In that changed self-perspective, she made her concerns clearly known both to her spouse and her boss at work, without the usual guilt that had always accompanied any assertion on her part. After all, she was now God's prophet, speaking out against abuses done to her and others.

CASE ILLUSTRATIONS

Each of the cases described below were ones in which I participated as the primary therapist.

Individual Therapy

A middle-aged female public schoolteacher sought counseling from me because of loneliness and an extended period of crying (Propst, 1993). Her only social outlet was attendance at a local church, in which she took care of the nursery. This patient was chronically depressed, with a secondary diagnosis of an avoidant personality disorder. She was extremely fearful of social contacts, and any type of mild social criticism was devastating to her and extremely embarrassing. When asked to try new, mildly risky social behaviors, she replied, "I could never do that."

Cognitive–behavioral therapy and an explicit integration approach to religious material was selected for this devoutly Christian individual. Because this individual had the cognitive schema that any type of negative emotions, social criticism, or uncomfortable circumstances were unbearable, Jesus was portrayed in therapy as one who chose suffering to accomplish some purpose. Using ideas from the New Testament, I portrayed Jesus not as a passive victim but as someone who laid down his life and experienced uncomfortableness for a purpose. That he actually put himself in difficult situations with possible negative consequences was emphasized. Illustrations from Scripture provided valuable sources of inspiration and aided in the cognitive restructuring for this client. These illustrations were not imposed on the client but, rather, were used to reflect her predominant faith orientation as a devout believer who saw Jesus as the model for human perfection.

When the schoolteacher admitted that she had the assumption that it was always easier to avoid pain, including the pain of possible rejection, I gently asked her whether Jesus had that assumption. She said, "No, he certainly experienced a lot of it." I then emphasized the idea that Jesus had made the choice to go to the cross. Facing that pain resulted in a transformation, namely, the Resurrection. These ideas were new to her, because she had always felt that the Christian ideal was to avoid all pain.

This individual, suffering from avoidant personality traits, firmly believed that negative feelings are bad and that, because she had such feelings, she was unhealthy. Applying Beck's three-column technique (Beck et al., 1979), I asked the patient to rate her belief in the notion that Jesus was vulnerable and in pain, but still a healthy human. She stated that she believed this 100%. I then asked her to rate her belief that, although she was vulnerable and in pain, she was also still a healthy person. Initially she paused and said she only believed this 10%. Then, a look of recognition and a smile came across her face as she stated, "I guess I expect more of myself than I do of Jesus."

Modeling Jesus as the risk taker, this schoolteacher was also able to confront her overbearing, possessive, and highly critical parents and to try new, more risky social relationships. In fact, before therapy was completed, she had even established a romantic relationship. Although she found such a relationship initially threatening, she ventured into the relationship with the thought that "following Jesus means I will risk the pain of a possible rejection."

Group Therapy

Dysfunctional assumptions in overfunctioning women in their marital relationships are also amenable to cognitive restructuring through religious ideas. As Safran has noted (cf. Muran & Safran, 1993), many cognitive schema include the idea of how one should behave interpersonally, including expectations of others' behaviors in response to one's own behaviors in an interpersonal context. Often, depressed women with traditional assumptions about female roles believe that they should care for all activities in the home and do it perfectly, even with, for example, three preschool children. Such behavior is indicative of these individuals' shared belief in what it means to be a "good woman." Some of these assumptions are conscious, but others are not. In cognitive group therapy, a number of depressed women characterized as overfunctioning in their marital relationships realized that they could not assert themselves with their husbands. As each woman described her work burdens—including necessary full-time employment, young children, and the refusal of their spouses to be involved in any home responsibilities—each nodded in agreement. The women initially began to notice in one another that they did not expect their spouses to help. Furthermore, each woman grew to understand how her assumptions and her subsequent behavior influenced her spouse's non-supportive behavior. All of them began to realize that they overfunctioned so that their husbands could underfunction. The notion that overfunctioning behavior was healthy behavior had to be challenged in the course of treatment.

A useful tool for this challenging process was the Christian view of community as a reflection of the Trinity, in which there is equal mutuality and equal give-and-take, with equal responsibility. Also, the point was discussed that there was no hierarchy between the three persons of the Trinity. This notion was presented as a challenging schema to these women's initial views of their marriages. Overfunctioning was redefined as actually being unhealthy. In the actual group context, the notion of mutuality in the Trinity was presented, and individuals were left to apply that notion to their schemas and the schemas of their fellow group members. Group members were quick to make the connections first for other members and then for themselves. It is common that group members are usually more astute at seeing others' dysfunctional assumptions before they can see their own. After the initial idea was presented in the group, members began to challenge each other when they detected overfunctioning in either individuals' actions within group or in their lives outside the group. This process is generally true for introducing theological ideas during cognitive group therapy: It is often most useful to present the ideas and then allow the group members to make the connections for other members after such a cognitive group focus has been established.

CONCLUSIONS

It appears that the effectiveness of cognitive–behavioral therapy can be enhanced if aspects of the patient's religious belief system are used to provide not only a motivation for self-examination, but also a challenge to some of the patient's dysfunctional schemas. It must be acknowledged, however, that this approach to therapy, as with any therapy approach, is not value-free. In most cases, patients are asked to look at their religious beliefs somewhat differently. In other cases, they are asked to pay attention to aspects of their religious beliefs that had heretofore been ignored (e.g., the idea that the Trinity models mutuality of relationships).

Some religious individuals, when confronted with new ideas, may go back to their religious authorities for confirmation. For most patients, the disconfirmation of their dysfunctional beliefs is surprisingly supported by the religious authorities. This is especially the case if the therapist has been careful to stay within the patient's religious tradition. In other cases, patients may find themselves in a conflict between the therapist and their religious community. My clinical experience has shown that, in these cases, many patients find other congregations within the same faith that offer them more support. A few patients will drop out of therapy. However, this is rare if the clinician has been careful to attempt to stay within the bounds of the individual's faith when suggesting reinterpretations.

If the clinician is outside of the individual's faith, it would be important to consult with someone from within the patient's faith to ensure that one's interpretations support the individual's faith. It is also hoped that clinicians from diverse belief systems attempt to define for themselves the healthy aspects of their own religious belief systems, so that these aspects can be used profitably in therapy. I have attempted to do this for my own Christian belief system, and I encourage others to do the same for their belief systems. If such affirmations occur, then religious faith may be a helpful and useful adjunct to cognitive therapy. Indeed, I have found (Propst, 1980, 1992) that it is not necessary for therapists to share patients' actual belief systems to effectively help them use their religious beliefs in the psychotherapy process. What is needed is an understanding on the part of the therapist of how a particular patient's belief system may be effectively and ethically included in the therapeutic process. In summary, cognitive–behavioral therapy offers a treatment approach that is well suited to the examination and modification of all forms of belief, including religious beliefs, as they affect the mental health of the individual.

REFERENCES

Allen, R., & Spilka, B. (1967). Committed and consensual religion: A specification of religion–prejudice relationship. *Journal for the Scientific Study of Religion, 6,* 191–206.

Allport, G. (1966). The religious context of prejudice. *Journal for the Scientific Study of Religion, 5,* 447–457.

Barth, K. (1960). *Church dogmatics: The doctrine of creation* (Vol. 3, Part 2; H. Knight, G. W. Bromily, & R. Fuller, Trans.). Edinburgh: T. & T. Clark. (Original work published 1948)

Beck, A. T. (1976). *Cognitive therapy and the emotional disorders.* New York: International Universities Press.

Beck, A. T., Rush, J., Shaw, B., & Emery, G. (1979). *Cognitive therapy of depression.* New York: Guilford Press.

Beck, A. T., Sokol, L., Clark, D., Berchick, R., & Wright, F. (1992). A crossover study of focused cognitive therapy for panic disorder. *American Journal of Psychiatry, 149,* 778–783.

Beck, A., Ward, C., Mendelson, M., Mock, J., & Erbaugh, J. (1961). An inventory for measuring depression. *Archives of General Psychiatry, 4,* 561–571.

Bedrosian, R. C., & Bozicas, G. D. (1994). *Treating family of origin problems: A cognitive approach.* New York: Guilford Press.

Bowlby, J. (1980). *Attachment and loss* (Vol. 3). New York: Basic Books.

Burns, D. (1980). *Feeling good: The new mood therapy.* New York: Morrow.

Calvin, J. (1972). *Institutes of the Christian religion* (H. Beveridge, Trans.). Grand Rapids, MI: Eerdmans. (Original work published 1559)

Derogatis, L., Rickels, K., & Rock, A. (1976). The SCL–90 and the MMPI: A step in the validation of a new self–report scale. *British Journal of Psychiatry, 128,* 280–289.

Ellis, A. (1980). Psychotherapy and atheistic values: A response to A. E. Bergin's "Psychotherapy and religious values." *Journal of Consulting and Clinical Psychology, 48,* 635–639.

Hamilton, M. (1967). Development of a rating scale for primary depressive illness. *British Journal of Social and Clinical Psychology, 6,* 278–296.

Hollon, S., & Beck, A. (1994). Cognitive and cognitive–behavioral therapies. In A. E. Bergin & S. L. Garfield (Eds.), *Handbook of psychotherapy and behavior change* (4th ed., pp. 428–466). New York: Wiley.

Juliana of Norwich. (1977). *Revelations of divine love.* (M. L. del Mastro, Trans.). New York: Doubleday. (Original written ca. 1392).

King, J., & Hunt, R. (1972). Measuring the religious variables: Replication. *Journal for the Scientific Study of Religion, 11,* 240–251.

Lang, P. (1979). A bio–information theory of emotional arousal. *Psychophysiology, 16,* 495–512.

Lang, P. J. (1985). The cognitive psychophysiology of emotion: Fear and anxiety. In A. H. Tuma & J. D. Maser (Eds.), *Anxiety and the anxiety disorders* (pp. 130–170). Hillsdale, NJ: Erlbaum.

Lazarus, R. S. (1991). Cognition and motivation in emotion. *American Psychologist, 46,* 352–367.

Michel, O. (1967). *Metamelogomai.* In G. Kittel & G. Friedrich (Eds.), *Theological dictionary of the New Testament* (Vol. 4, pp. 626–629; G. Bromiles, Trans.). Grand Rapids, MI: W. B. Eerdmans. (Original work published 1942)

Muran, J. C., & Safran, J. (1993). Emotional and interpersonal considerations in cognitive therapy. In K. Kuehlwein & H. Rosen (Eds.), *Cognitive therapies in action* (pp. 185–212). San Francisco: Jossey–Bass.

Propst, L. R. (1980). The comparative efficacy of religious and nonreligious imagery for the treatment of mild depression in religious individuals. *Cognitive Therapy and Research, 4,* 167–178.

Propst, L. R. (1988). *Psychotherapy in a religious framework: Spirituality in the emotional healing process.* New York: Human Sciences Press.

Propst, L. R. (1992). Spirituality and the avoidant personality. *Theology Today, 49,* 165–172.

Propst, L. R. (1993). Defusing the powers with Jesus as a model of empowerment: Treating the avoidant personality. *Journal of Pastoral Care, 47,* 230–238.

Propst, L. R., Ostrom, R., Watkins, P., Dean, T., & Mashburn, D. (1992). Comparative efficacy of religious and nonreligious cognitive–behavioral therapy for the treatment of clinical depression in religious individuals. *Journal of Consulting and Clinical Psychology, 60,* 94–103.

Rush, A., Beck, A., Kovacs, M., & Hollon, S. (1977). Comparative efficacy of cognitive therapy and pharmacotherapy in the treatment of depressed patients. *Cognitive Therapy Research, 1,* 17–37.

Safran, J. D., & Segal, Z. V. (1990). *Interpersonal process in cognitive therapy.* New York: Basic Books.

Segal, Z. (1988). Appraisal of the self-schema: Construct in cognitive models of depression. *Psychological Bulletin, 103,* 147–162.

Weissman, M., Paykel, E., & Prusoff, B. (1980). *Social Adjustment Scale handbook: Rationale, reliability, validity, scoring, and training guide.* New York: New York State Psychiatric Institute.

15

PSYCHOANALYTIC TREATMENT AND THE RELIGIOUS PERSON

ANA-MARIA RIZZUTO

Freud, the founder of psychoanalysis, considered religion a collective neurosis that provided through its dogmas and rituals an illusory protection against human fragility. According to Freud, the personal religious "neurosis" of an individual was sustained by an infantile attachment to a caring parental figure. A mature adult needed to accept the risks of being alive without having to cling to a protective godhead. For years, analysts followed Freud's dictums without challenging their scientific value. In the past three decades, theoretical changes in psychoanalysis, in particular the introduction of object relations theory, have made it possible to have psychoanalytic theories about religious beliefs that are based on the developmental and dynamic factors that contribute to the formation of the mind and of personal belief. The changes in theory have some impact on the technical approach to the analytic understanding of religious experiences, but the essential analytic technique remains unchanged. Freud himself suggested the probable consequences of using his method:

> If the application of the psycho-analytic method makes it possible to find a new argument against religion, *tant pis* for religion; but defenders of religion will by the same right make use of psycho-analysis in order to give full value to the affective significance of religious doctrines. (1927, p. 37)

Psychoanalysis has proven to be an invaluable tool in understanding the dynamic components of religious beliefs and affects in normal people and neurotics alike. In this chapter, I will first examine the principles of psychoanalytic treatment, followed by a brief discussion of the psychoanalytic understanding of God representations and religious experience, and will conclude with a clinical illustration of the applications of psychodynamic theory and technique.

The psychoanalytic treatment created by Sigmund Freud at the turn of the 20th century has evolved in the course of the years, but its basic technique remains the same. The patient is seen four or five times a week, lying on a couch, while the analyst sits behind, outside the analysand's sight. The patient is invited to say everything and enjoined not to censor thoughts and feelings (free association). The task reveals itself to be a most difficult one. The interplay between the patient's attempts to follow this rule (basic rule) and the obstacles (transference and defenses) that emerge against it give rise to the basic phenomena that constitute the essence of the analytic experience and treatment. Soon the person of the analyst appears to the analysand as an obstacle to his communications (transference). The patient fears physical or psychical harm, from punishment to humiliation, or the rejection of his or her affectionate and sexual wishes. The analysand also discovers that he fears his or her own self, that is, the harsh criticism of the superego demanding that only what it approves can be said. Wishes are put aside, thoughts repressed, images or fantasies denied access to consciousness, and distressful self representations disavowed (defenses). The patient's defensive system, together with the individual's compelling wishes, under the regressive influence of the analytic situation, take control of analytic movement. The analysand, responding to reawakened wishes to obtain what is needed (regression) from the analyst (transferential object), may become demanding, feel entitled, accuse the analyst of withholding a response or experience any other kind of feeling, from intense love to intense hatred. This process is called the transference. It means that the patient experiences the analyst as a figure from the past, most frequently the father, the mother, and, at times, a sibling or another close figure from childhood. These experiences have a powerful psychic reality, conveying a convincing immediacy of feeling. Their sources are unconscious or preconscious experiences, object and self representations, thoughts, wishes, fantasies, and fears from the past that surface to conscious awareness as a result of the progressive lifting of repression (regression) typical of the progression of the analytic process. Through the careful analysis of the patient's convictions, thoughts, feelings, fantasies, wishes, dreams, and verbalizations the analyst helps the analysand trace the origins of such experiences (developmental component) and the processes that have brought the individual to the present conflictive situation (dynamic component). The analyst abstains from any other intervention beyond the questions, clarifications, connections, and interpretations needed to help the patient make sense of what happens in the analysis. The analysis reaches its end when the analysand is capable of recognizing in the experienced present developmental and dynamic processes from the past and is able to recognize them through self-analysis in order to freely achieve conscious goals. At that point, the person is able to recognize the analyst as a different person from the objects of childhood and the transferential bond between them loses its powerful grip (resolution of the transference). In the end, the unconscious wishes modulate their insistence for satisfaction, giving the analysand a broader range of freedom to satisfy present-day desires. The patient is free to go, after mourning the loss of the analyst as the companion of this psychic journey.

Psychoanalytic psychotherapy applies the theoretical tenets of psychoanalysis modified by the lesser frequency of meetings and the face-to-face position of patient and therapist. The issues explored are more limited to conflictive aspects of the patient's personality.

Psychoanalysis and psychoanalytic psychotherapy are not for all patients with psychic problems. The technique is based on understanding and interpretation of unconscious motivations without any other specific gratification for the patient beyond that obtained from the analyst's dedication to help. The technique, therefore, requires the patient's capacity to tolerate frustration, to delay gratification, and to be self-observant. The person's reality testing must be intact to be able to sustain the power of conviction of experienced feelings without confusing them with external reality. These conditions reveal that analysis is the optimal treatment for developmentally and dynamically based intrapsychic conflicts that cause personal suffering without altering basic ego functions or removing the person from being in touch with everyday reality. Analysis, therefore, of necessity, selects its subjects from a high functioning population which is, however, deeply disturbed by conflicts frequently unknown to others. This selection does not mean that the detailed insights and knowledge obtained from such analysands cannot be fruitfully employed, with varied techniques, at the service of any other type of patient.

The psychic religious dimension of human life obtains from psychoanalytic theorizing its most comprehensive developmental and dynamic understanding. Analytic religious insights can be placed at the service of any treatment of psychiatric or medical patients and of the dynamic understanding of religious aspects of any human being.

Before discussing the treatment of the so-called religious person, it is necessary to offer a psychoanalytic theory of how religion and religious objects are constituted as psychic realities and objects.

PSYCHOANALYTIC CONSIDERATIONS ABOUT THE DEVELOPMENTAL AND DYNAMIC COMPONENTS OF RELIGION AND ITS PSYCHIC OBJECTS

Religion, as a cultural manifestation, is a multidimensional phenomenon. It is composed of implicit and explicit beliefs, communal and private rites to express and enact a particular faith about the nature of the ultimate and lasting reality in which a group of human beings assumes they are living their time-limited lives (Glock, 1962). The symbolic and pragmatic systems emerging from the religious life of a community have organizational power to structure moral, legal, and political norms. They encompass precise and subtle modes of interpersonal relatedness as well as modes of judging the members of the group. These modes are implemented in legal codes and in everyday overt and tacit rules to judge the value of an individual and his actions as both a member of the community and a participant in the realm of the ultimate reality. The interplay, at the societal level, of all these factors contributes to the creation of a collective mood, as well as deep lasting and transient emotions. These emotions run through the body of the community with the life-sustaining power the blood has in running through the human body.

The child born in this societal matrix has no option but to be involved in the implicit or explicit religious beliefs, traits, moods, actions, and structures imposed by the power of the dominant religion of his culture. The child's awareness of this participation may become enhanced by direct religious actions and learning demanded of it. The situation may vary according to the prevalence of a single religious group or the communal coexistence, with varied degrees of tolerance or conflict, of diverse religions. In this respect, contemporary America is no longer a religiously unified country. Immigration from Eastern Asiatic countries, a fascination with the religions from the East, the revival of native American and African tribal pride, and many other religious modalities of understanding the world have brought a multitude of religions to live and prosper on American soil. The 1993 Parliament of the World's Religions, held in Chicago in August 1993, demonstrated that religions originating in the four corners of the world have settled and prospered in America's urban and rural landscapes. A child attending public school is exposed to other children practicing religions very different from that of its family and social group.

The individual child, however, must undergo a series of internal processes to integrate into its psychic life the multidimensional complexity of religious life of its group of origin. Religion, in this sense, is a particular case of the processes involved in the formation of a personal psyche. The child must establish meaningful communication with its caretakers and learn to satisfy biological and emotional needs in the modes provided by the culture and the child's parents. The young person must learn to speak the language they speak and, in the process, lose the genetically given potential to pronounce the sounds of other languages. As it happens with language, the internalization of all these patterns of interaction with its parents would provide the child the foundation for its exclusively particular psychic structure, at the price of losing the potential development of others. A similar phenomenon takes place in the internalization of religious beliefs and practices.

Whatever the religion, the child needs to find psychic means to form a representation of the phantom and intangible reality of that which the family religion considers sacred. It may be called God, gods, mana, nirvana, the Great Spirit, or another name. Whatever the religion, the child has to undertake a formidable task. The sacred reality is not directly perceptible. It is alluded to, mentioned, celebrated, feared, appealed to, worshipped, pursued but it is never there to be seen or apprehended by the senses. The child has to create with the psychic tools available to its mind the psychic representation of the sacred and desirable reality offered by the religion of the elders.

The study of the psychic process of the child creating the internal representation of the sacred reality the young person is to find through his religion has just begun. Rizzuto (1979) studied the process of the formation of the representation of the monotheistic God in Jewish and Christian individuals. Other religions have not been studied. Rizzuto's studies show that the process of formation of the God representation follows similar laws to those described by Winnicott in the creating and finding of the mother. Talking about the infant's primary creativity and his need for the illusion that the maternal breast is under the baby's omnipotent and magical control, Winnicott (1953) described the phenomenon: "A subjective phenomenon develops in the baby, which we call the mother's breast. The mother places the actual breast just there where the infant is ready to create, and at the right moment" (p. 11).

The experience provides the infant with what Winnicott calls a transitional object located in a psychic space he called the intermediate area of experience. Winnicott describes this new concept as follows:

> I have introduced the terms "transitional objects" and "transitional phenomena" for designation of the intermediate area of experience, between the thumb and the teddy bear, between the oral eroticism and the true object-relationship, between primary creative activity and projection of what has already been introjected, between primary unawareness of indebtedness and the acknowledgment of indebtedness ("Say: 'ta' "). (p. 2)

The transitional object itself may be any physical object that the baby passionately considers its possession. It "stands for the breast, or the object of the first relationship" and "antedates established reality-testing." In relation to it, "the infant passes from (magical) omnipotent control to control by manipulation (involving muscle erotism and coordination pleasure)" (p. 9). What is so significant about this earliest stage of psychic development is that it "is made possible by the mother's special capacity for making adaptation to the needs of her infant, thus allowing the infant the illusion that what the infant creates really exists" (p. 14).

In the case of the breast and the mother what the infant creates does in fact exist. The experience, however, has dealt with the essential human concern "of the relationship between what is objectively perceived and what is subjectively conceived of" (p. 11). The question, "Did you conceive of this or was it presented to you from without?" (p. 12) must not be asked or even be formulated. Winnicott draws a final and significant conclusion for human development: "In the solution of this problem *there is no health* for the human being who has not been started off well enough by the mother" (p. 11) [my emphasis].

Once the experience has taken place it leaves its indelible mark in the infant's psychic structure as the foundation of all its future interpersonal and cultural life:

> This intermediate area of experience, unchallenged in respect of its belonging to inner or external (shared) reality constitutes the greater part of the infant's experience, and throughout life is retained in the intense experiencing that belongs to the arts and to religion and to imaginative living, and to creative scientific work. (Winnicott, 1953, p. 14)

The Winicottian theory allows for the existence of a transitional space that is capable of encompassing the transformations of early development to the moment of mature adulthood, without losing its potential to find what is created and to create what could be found. This psychoanalytic theorizing is far removed from the original concreteness of the Freudian theory opposing in all psychic instances reality testing to wish fulfillment.

For Winnicott reality testing is as indispensable at all ages as it was for Freud. The difference lies in the fact that together with it there exists the realm of transitional experience where reality testing and subjective creativity enter in a particular mode of experiencing in which subjectivity and objectivity are not to be posed as a question. Does one ask Chagall if his figures are not subject to normal gravity? Does one question the Disney Studios if Donald Duck exists or request a chemist to prove that the geometrical shapes of molecules are factual as depicted? In all these instances the intertwining between creativity and finding is so inseparable that the notion of reality testing proves insufficient.

Religion is a case in point. The sacred reality it addresses can never be photographed or tape-recorded. Without human creativity there could be no religion. Without an enticing existing mysterious reality waiting to be found, the quest for religion would not emerge.

Freud considered God "nothing other than an exalted father"(1913), and religion a regressive fixation and dependence on parental figures needed by those too weak hearted to stand on their own (see Rizzuto, 1979, pp. 13–39). The point in question is whether a person's object of belief results from a fixation to a concrete parent or is a transitional creation that, using parental and self-representations as well as religious teachings, transforms them creatively into that mysterious psychic object called God. The idea proposed in this article is that the child who is developmentally ready creates the sacred reality, God, that its culture has placed there for the young person to find.

Many empirical religious studies (Beit-Hallahmi & Argyle, 1975) find a statistical correlation between the manner in which an individual conceives of God and the character traits of that person's parents. Those studies, however, do not attend to the process of the developmental and dynamic creation of the God representation by the child when the psychic moment arrives (approximately at the age of three) to find the God offered by the culture. Empirical studies that include longitudinal and cross-sectional dynamic documentation of such a process in a particular individual demonstrate that the creation of the God representation is an exquisitely particular process influenced by the nature of the child's relation to the parents and to its own self (Rizzuto, 1979).

What makes God different from other childhood transitional objects is that it is made out of the child's complex representation of the youngster's relationship with its parents. In this respect God, as a psychic representation at the beginning of life, shares the stage with other transitional creations such as monsters, witches, imaginary companions, and other ethereal creatures. These last transitional representations are soon faced by the child's reality testing capacity and lose their "real" existence when their psychic function is no longer needed. God, on the other hand, created as it has been in the transitional space, finds a double reinforcement for its psychic functions. First, at the reality level, God—the invisible and the intangible—is presented to the child who is requested to find the divine being. God, the little believer is told, is there, and has created the child with love, continues to love it, and expects the young one to be good in the presence of a God, who sees people's hearts and may punish them if they are bad. The child is taught to pray and address God with ritual and personal prayers. The transitional reality of God becomes a constant presence in everyday family and communal life. Psychically, the child is very much in need of God at the end of his pregenital years, when the Oedipal experience confronts the wishes to be special to the parent of the opposite sex with impossible conflicts between desire and fear. The resolution of the Oedipal situation requires that the child accepts its place in the family not as an equal to the parents but as their child. It is at this painful moment of necessary humiliation that the child, as Freud demonstrated, transforms earlier formed idiosyncratic God representations into one that includes the consequences of such resolution. This means that the process of *reelaboration* of the God representation follows all the dynamic and defensive laws of satisfaction of wishes and preservation of object ties and of self-esteem. Freud's (1908) theory of sublimation facilitates the understanding of the transformation of oral, anal sadistic, and masochistic as well as phallic suppressed pregenital "perverse elements of sexual excitation" (p. 189) into culturally acceptable practices. God and religion also absorb in their dynamic reworkings the bodily connected instinctual derivatives of resolved and unresolved conflicts with parental figures. Many of them, in their religiously integrated and culturally accepted form become the solid foundations of a personal religion. The case of Louis presented below gives a clinical illustration of some of these concepts.

This God, created and found is a most vital transitional object due to the child's belief that the divine being is always there to love and help, to punish and to reward. God is also available for rejection (see the case of Sybil below) and hatred. The "being always there" is the most frequently mentioned characteristic of God described by the research subjects (Rizzuto, 1979). Psychically, the God representation may be put at the service of maintaining psychic equilibrium, to keep a minimum of relatedness and love in moments of abandonment, to sustain self-respect and hope when the blows of life make it nearly intolerable. It is also available for love and hatred, exaltation and humiliation, as well as for any other feeling that may find difficult integration in human relationships. Furthermore, the divinity becomes a companion for better and for worse. God may offer consolation in lonely moments while remaining an unavoidable witness to secretive actions, sexual explorations, and aggressive wishes. Whatever the situation and the age of the person, from childhood to the moment of death, the transitional God representation is there, consciously or unconsciously, available to be called to psychic duty, whether to be accepted, believed, and loved, or rejected and despised.

The God created and found in the transitional space of religious belief has affective and descriptive characteristics absolutely particular to each person. God traits and disposition are never a matter of indifference. Once created, the God representation affects the sense of self because it establishes a felt dynamic relationship between the believer and his God. Once the psychic representation is believed to be that of an actual existing God, it acquires its full relational reality. Thus, consciously, preconsciously, or unconsciously, the God's representation will, in its reflection of how we have created it and found God through its mediation, affect how we conceive of ourselves. The distress its presence causes at a given moment may bring about a psychic crisis that requires either the reelaboration of the God representation or some changes in the subject's intrapsychic organization. Changes brought about by development would require that such representation be transformed and updated if it is to remain available for conscious belief.

Finally, there is the need to discuss the belief in a factual, transcendent God who is the object of faith and religion. Conscious belief requires that a compatibility be established between the representation of God and the prevailing self-representations. Belief is never free of conflict and of the work of the defenses to maintain such compatibility. If changes occur that overburden the defensive system, an experience of conversion or of rejection of belief may occur. In either case, neither belief nor unbelief are indicators of health or mental illness but pointers to suggest the particular psychodynamic arrangement between the sense of self and the available representation of God.

The psychic changes brought about by each new stage in life, as well as by social shifts and scientific discoveries, require that the representation of God undergo concomitant revision to remain believable. A professor of astrophysics would be hard put to confer belief to a God representation of a creator making mud people, a representation that was convincing to a child in the first grade. An astrophysicist needs a God capable of encompassing the complex evolutionary, mathematical, and spatial realities of the scientific world.

Finally, a word needs to be said about the relationship between the God representation as a transitional creation in the context of a given religion and God, the postulated transcendent being. The representation serves in relation to God the same function it serves with any other reality, material or human. Representations are the *means* the mind has to know existing realities. Without the representation of the breast or of the mother, the child has no means to know the mother. The mother, however, is not the representation. The mother exists on her own right and provides with her timely presentation of the breast the elements that permit the infant to form the found components of the breast representation. Thus, the God sought for by the sincere believer must not be confused with the representation of God. They belong to different layers of reality. The God representation is the psychic means the mind has to seek God. Its developmental and dynamic sources are unconscious and not accessible without psychic exploration. God, on the contrary, appears to the believer as the object of conscious belief in an existing being beyond the limits of the mind.

Spero (1992) proposes a different model to account for the representation of an existing (objective) God:

It is a modified model in that it assumes two distinct lines of development . . . . The first line indicates the trajectory of an objective human object moving toward internalization. . . . The second line indicates the trajectory of an *objective* God object moving on *its* representational pathway toward internalization. . . . Thus while the line of development for the objective *human* object may, indeed, yield anthropocentrically based, internal or endopsychic gods, only the line of development from the objective object known as God can legitimately be said to yield an internalized God representation. For only in [the] latter case has something *really* external and objectively of God been taken inward. (p. 138)

Spero's model creates more problems than it solves. The first problem is that it finds its source in the assumed factual and objective existence of God. Although such affirmation is theologically acceptable, it exceeds the empirical phenomenological field of psychology and psychoanalysis. Neither of them has the epistemological competence to affirm or deny God's existence. The second difficulty is that it postulates the formation of an objective representation of God as the immediate (that is not mediated) result of God's objective existence. This assumption can neither be denied nor affirmed by an empirical discipline that has no way of testing it. Finally, the most difficult problem is that, as presented by Spero, this God-representation is not developmentally connected or integrated with the rest of the formation of the human mind. In Spero's words, the objective God representation only "overlaps" with drives, intrapsychic structures, and human object images. A psychically integrated religious experience based on such distinct and separate God representation does not seem possible.

Spero's theoretical difficulties stem from his manner of conceiving the mind in its epistemological function. He talks about "the belief that mental structures and experience tell us only about the mind and nothing about a distinctive objective reality" (p. 140). That is a misconception. The mind, from the beginning of life is capable of telling the difference between existing realities and mental representations. In the case of God, a non-perceptual being, the issue to be psychologically understood is belief, that is the conviction about God's factual existence and active presence in the believer's life. We need a theory of belief that does justice to a psychodynamic model of the mind.

Other components of religion such as ritual, prayers, celebrations, traditions, scriptures, and the esthetic impressions of ceremonial music are also part of the dialectic processes of attachment and separation from parents. Any one of these elements carries deep emotions and the potential for integration to the community at large or rejection of the family religion and practices. Each result, integration, rejection, or ambivalence reveals, under therapeutic exploration, unconscious motivational and dynamic sources related to libidinal ties and narcissistic balance of self-esteem.

The affective component of the religious experience is its main source of personal meaning. James (1902/1929) recognized that "feeling is the deeper source of religion" (p. 422). The affects that fuel a religious experience are rooted in relational exchanges extending from the beginning of life to the moment when it occurs. In this respect, analytically speaking, all encounters with God, as with any other person, are preceded and conditioned by the psychic structure and by the momentary psychic reality of the person who is having the experience. The joys, conflicts, dramas, and exaltations of the individuals's entire relational life (including past relational moments with God) act as the scaffolding of the personality structure that, in turn, conditions that particular instance of readiness for God's epiphany in the psyche. The final shape of the experience of God is always the result of complex psychic compromises between available representations, accepted and rejected feelings and wishes, superego pressures, and the effort at self-integration aided by defensive maneuvering. All this psychic activity occurs in the context of the reality and affective pressures imposed by circumstances in which the individual finds him or herself. The circumstances include that particular relational moment with God, and God's disposition as assumed to be by the person in that religious instance.

What places all these psychic processes in the transitional space is the profound conviction the believer has that his experience is not only an intrapsychic phenomenon but the actual and internally perceptible relationship with a living God.

CLINICAL APPROACH TO THE TREATMENT OF THE RELIGIOUS PERSON

The theoretical description of the formation of the representation of God in persons of monotheistic faiths and the psychodynamic power of religion, suggests that no child who has grown up in a religious culture may come to treatment without at least a barely conscious representation of God available for belief or unbelief as well as for defensive or compensatory psychic use. Religion may be irrelevant to the person at the moment of coming for treatment, and the therapist must respect the patient's stance. However, the therapist must not forget that in most children the representation of God has played a psychic role during development and that when it emerges it may be fruitfully explored. Attending to God's and religion's appearance in the treatment hours may illuminate childhood's relational vicissitudes as well as the transferential significance of, up to now, repressed beliefs (as in the case of Sybil below). This is the baseline that holds true for all patients.

The analyst is confronted with three types of patients: (a) believers for whom their belief is not a problem, (b) nonbelievers who are at peace with their religious situation and accept the treatment without any religious considerations, and (c) believers who are concerned about their religion and fear that therapy may change their faith or their moral commitments. Some of these patients may request a therapist that shares the same faith.

Confidentiality and Establishing the Therapeutic Relationship

Persons who are members of a religious order, priests, leaders of religious institutions, and lay leaders may fall into any of the three categories mentioned above. From the point of view of psychodynamic understanding they do not require any special handling. Their position in society and the way in which they are referred for treatment may require specific clarifications about confidentiality. If they are referred by their superiors, every effort should be made to clarify the goals of the treatment as those of the patient and not of the superior. Special care is needed when some reporting is necessary for the superior's decisions or for legal implications. The manner of reporting should be discussed with all people involved before the treatment proper begins. It should be agreed that no report is given to the superiors that is not known by the patient. The therapist must not assume responsibility for decisions about the patient. It is the patient who is expected to assume responsibility for her or his relation to the superiors, the community, the religious authorities, and for what he or she wants to do with the situation. These precautions are indispensable to preserving the therapeutic situation as one in which the therapist is exclusively at the service of helping the patient to take charge of his life and psychic needs. This situation is particularly delicate when the patient has made a vow of obedience and may hide his passive gratification or hostility behind it.

Taking a Religious History

Psychoanalysts and psychotherapists who practice psychoanalytically based psychotherapy consider religious issues as normal part of the person's individual psyche and explore them with the same care that they explore any other aspect of psychic life. Up to very recently, many therapists neglected to attend to the religious aspects of their patients' lives. This attitude was due to the absence of a theoretical foundation to understand the great developmental and dynamic significance of all religious issues. The problem was aggravated by the complete absence of education about the psychic significance of religion in psychiatric and psychological training programs as well as in psychoanalytic institutes. Taking a religious history was not considered a normal part of the patient history at the time of evaluation. This omission gave the patients the correct message that exploration of their religious convictions and practices was unrelated and irrelevant to their treatment. This situation is changing currently, but much work remains to be done in the field of psychoanalytic education in relation to the dynamic significance of religion in all persons.

The taking of a religious history must be a matter of course procedure as a family and sexual history are. It can be done with ease once it becomes a routine procedure. It is important to know the religious affiliation of each parent, the family's religious practices and attitudes, as well as its integration or lack of it with the community at large. From the individual concerned, it is important to learn if the person has gone normally through the major landmarks of the faith's rituals (baptism, circumcision, confirmation, etc.) and their private and public significance. Finally, the therapist needs to ask the patient about the present situation in relation to religious institutions, beliefs, and religious practices. Such history will reveal precious data about the patient's religious development and the individual's perceptions of the significant people and self in the process of growing up. A good example is that of a patient who said that her father was a "good" provider for the family to declare a few minutes later that God "never delivers" what she prays for. At that point, the therapist may create a hypothesis (to be explored later) that the patient feels the need to maintain the idealization of her father, whereas God can "tolerate" her angry complaints.

Abstinence and Neutrality

The analyst abstains from revealing religious affiliation, beliefs, or any other personal information. The abstinence is at the service of offering maximal latitude for the development of a transference based on the patient's psychic processes, unrestricted by factual data. On the other hand, the analyst must take with all seriousness whatever beliefs or experiences the patient has. The person's spiritual concerns, faith, doubts, moral quivering and commitments must be explored fully and with the utmost respect. This means that, at times, the therapist may be confronted with personal ignorance. In that case, the therapist may ask the patient factual questions to be instructed about the subject. The therapist must remain aware that the patient describes these facts from a private angle of vision. An example is the case of a religious woman from a contemplative order who complained that she was a "nothing" because her voice in the singing of prayer was "not good." Besides exploring any dynamic issue about the patient's voice and its function, the therapist inquired about the significance of singing in her order.

The abstinence of the therapist in revealing anything private is at the service of preventing misalliances. A Jewish patient may assume that the (assumed) Jewish therapist "thinks exactly like me." This is not a problem as such. It becomes a problem if the therapist, who may happen to be Jewish, omits exploration of an issue because of it. The other side of the problem is the patient avoiding certain subjects based on the assumption that they share religious and social meanings. Example of this is a Jewish patient who took for granted that he was getting "lousy" treatment because he and his analyst (supposedly) were one of those "good for nothing lower Manhattan Orthodox Jews." At first, he said it only in derivative form by being late, not paying, procrastinating, and constantly belittling the analyst. After it was explored, it was clear that it was anathema for him to express the absolute contempt he felt for his parents and his community. The working through of this "religiously forbidden" act allowed him to participate more openly in treatment.

The risk of collusions and avoidances is very high when it is known that the therapist is a religious person, a member of the clergy, or of a religious institution. A feeling of "we", the religious people, may facilitate some trusting disposition but also harbor expectations for special favors, and fantasies of being special. A priest, who is an analyst, discussed in a private presentation how several Catholic patients, after disclosing their darkest secrets, wanted him to absolve them as a priest. The working through of these wishes is a key element in the treatment of such patients. The blurring of roles on the therapist's part closes the possibility of dynamic exploration of wishes and conflicts. The worse consequences are the obliteration of the patient's autonomy, the restriction of his freedom, and the foreclosure of finding a truer religious life.

CASE EXAMPLES

The development of theory and the elaboration of technique find their source in the clinical setting. This section presents four cases that illustrate the interrelation between developmental and dynamic issues and religious thinking, feeling, and beliefs. Each in its own way illustrates the relevance of addressing God representations and religious experiences *in toto* within psychoanalytic treatment.

Emergence of Belief in a Nonbeliever

Laura was the child of a wealthy Jewish family. The family had no religion. Jewish holidays were extended family meals without any reference to their meaning. Laura had never been inside a synagogue, nor had she ever attended Hebrew School. When she was a child a maid brought her once to see Saint Patrick's Cathedral. She had no interest in religion. Her 8 years of analysis disclosed a binding and hateful relation with an obsessive and domineering mother who used food as a way of controlling the child and herself. The mother humiliated the young girl because of her looks and her inability to achieve in school. The father lived in a world of money, romance, and sexualization of every detail of their lives. Glamour, high class, top resorts, flowers, perfumes, love notes between husband and wife, created a life style of unreality and unbearable overexcitement. Laura and her sister felt constantly neglected and left out by the parental couple. The patient developed an eating disorder, and became a flower child of the 60s. When she entered treatment at age 21, her parents tried to control the therapist who informed them that the patient was an adult and that they had to ask their daughter what they wanted to know. The parents hired a person to investigate the therapist but could find nothing to stop the treatment. During her long analysis, Laura was able to separate emotionally from both parents and to free herself from the double bind of hatred and excited overinvolvement with them. To achieve this significant psychic change, the analyst and the patient had to go together through very stormy transference feelings. She feared her analyst would repeat her mother's constant humiliation of her. In turn, she demanded that the analyst behave in the enticing and sexualized ways habitual to her father. The analyst, at first, listened attentively to her fears and complaints, letting her expand freely on her feelings. With progressive clarifications, not unfrequent confrontations of her demands, and carefully timed interpretations of her wishes and fears, the patient became reflective and self-observant. That was the first major change that permitted analytic work. She moved from her pervasive mode of acting out her disowned affects to an analytic effort to understand her feelings and thoughts. During the middle part of the analysis, when this modality became firmly established, the eating disorder became controlled.

During termination she realized that life was limited and that, in the end, she had to die. She began to think about the meaning of life. One day, after an extensive reevaluation of her destructive relation with her mother and father, she felt she was, at last, free from their power. Soon after, she declared that she believed in "a God," *her* God, and she felt she needed a religion. Laura bought a few books on Judaism, and after some reading, felt ready to "create" her own service. She bought a candelabra for her dining room table and invented some very simple sayings, not quite prayers, to say on Friday evening while lighting the candles. Laura declared, "This religion is good enough for me."

Laura's case illustrates the emergence in the transitional space opened by her separation from her mother and father, of God as an existing being, that she found on her own. God's existence as a newly found being could be traced to very early childhood experiences of feeling that the parents were there with her which were revived and reworked during positive transferential moments, particularly during termination.

Refinding the God of Childhood After Working Through a Narcissistic Injury

Sybil came to analysis because of uncontrollable sexual acting out with men. She had no use for religion and frequently laughed at "those ignorant idiots that go to church." She had grown up within an average religious family. The father was a lay assistant who helped in the church and taught religion to the children. Sybil had been a believer and a churchgoer until she was 8 years old. At that point, she went into a religious crisis and rejected God for ever. On the surface, the crisis originated in her praying to God for a special favor. The favor did not come through. She felt enraged and betrayed. She felt that if God was not going to take care of her then she had no use for Him. From that moment on, she never prayed again and only "went through the motions of going to church," full of private mockery and rage. The analysis revealed an intense Oedipal situation, with deep hatred for her mother (a somewhat psychologically limited person) and blind adoration for her father. The analysis followed the normally predicted course. An intense maternal transference cast the analyst in the role of a hateful and "idiotic" maternal figure, that could easily be fooled. The unconscious components of such perceptions betrayed their origin in the maternal figure through slips of the tongue and unexpected associations that surprised the patient and, at times, the analyst. Confrontation was frequently needed to help the patient to listen to the analyst's interpretations, because she was in the habit of discarding the analyst's words as she had done with her mother's. The working through of this situation permitted some new and unexpectedly friendly conversations with her mother and a more balanced view of her father. It was at that point that she recognized the source of her rejection of God. She had felt totally betrayed by her father when he had persistently aligned with the mother in matters of discipline. The final rejection of God took place one day when she felt particularly betrayed by her father. Unable to express her rage to her father, Sybil raged against his God, and made God pay for her father's treason. One day she declared in the analysis that she was going to attend the Holy Week Services and the Easter Vigil. She came back amazed and in tears because she had found "meaning and depth and beautiful words" in the service. From that moment on she attended services most Sundays and continued to be amazed at the "deep things" she heard. It took her some time to see the connections between the narcissistic injury of her Oedipal defeat and her rejection of God.

Transformation of the Representation of God in a Believer

Father Robert was a middle-aged Roman Catholic priest of Polish descent referred by an older priest friend he had consulted as a confessor. He was much liked by his congregation and praised by his pastor because he was hard working and dedicated to his ministry. He could not, however, find any rest or satisfaction in his work nor in the praise he received. Privately, he felt constantly guilty and humiliated by his compelling need to masturbate. The compassionate forgiveness and comments of his confessor did not give him any peace. Robert entered treatment hoping that he would find a way out for his inability to find any rest within himself. His history revealed that he was born too soon after his older sibling, and that his mother, in her inability to handle the two children, sent him to live with his maternal grandmother a few houses down. His father worked many hours and was uninvolved with the family. As soon as he could think, Robert became convinced that he was unacceptable to his mother. Her harsh disposition, her constant criticism, her inability to praise him or any of the children, and her frequent bursts of temper convinced Robert that he was unlovable. This feeling did not become conscious until the middle of the treatment. As a child, he came to believe that he had to be perfect, asexual, and that to be a priest was the only way to gain some respect from his mother. On the other hand, the sisters of his grammar school told him that God loved him as he was. He had enough proof that there was something good about him because he was well liked throughout school by his classmates and teachers alike, and the girls and boys sought his company. He accepted being with them but could not feel involved with them. He went to the seminary, graduated with honors, and went to work in a parish and, although successful as a priest, he could not feel satisfaction and esteem through his ministry.

The analytic psychotherapy helped him deal with the overpowering effect of his relationship with his mother. He could recognize his desperate and useless effort to get her to change and approve of him. He still longed for the affection she never expressed to him and came to see that his masturbation was, in part, a way of soothing himself. His mother, meanwhile, was still treating him as she had done when he was a child. He discovered that his grandmother had loved him but that it had been to no avail. He had identified with his mother and judged himself as sternly as she always did. Furthermore, he discovered that he believed (unconsciously) that the God of his feelings was as harsh as her and impossible to please. The God of his conscious belief was quite different. He did believe in a God who loved him, and it was that belief that had helped him to become a priest. After much work with a female therapist he decided to run an experiment. He took off his Roman collar and attended some social functions in a town where nobody knew him. Soon a woman was attracted to him. They began a friendship. She liked him very much. Finally he disclosed to her that he was a priest. She was surprised but said that she loved him anyway, even if there was no hope of a permanent relationship. In spite of their better intentions, they found themselves making love a few times. She was tender, respectful, sexually involved, and gave with her behavior further evidence that she cared for him. The affair made him guilty, but also pleased. He was amazed that she had loved him without knowing he was a priest. He had convinced himself that people cared only for the priest and not for the man. It was the first time in his life that he discovered that he felt a person cared for him as *himself.* They decided to terminate the affair because he wanted to be celibate as he had promised to be. It was at this point the he began to realize that he had never felt that God loved him and that he was convinced he could not please God. He knew intellectually that he had done all he had to please God; however, he could never feel he had. The therapy helped him to separate his experiences with his mother from the representation of God. He said with amazement, "I didn't know that I believed that God was just like my mother."

Father Robert's case illustrates that his changing the internal compulsion to satisfy an impossible mother (that had provided the prevailing components of the unconscious God representation) and his finding a "proof" that he was lovable, permitted Robert to integrate his dissociated representation of God. The loving God of his Catholic belief (and of his grandmother and the nuns and priests, and classmates who liked him) could now be more of a "felt" God that gave him peace. As a result he became able to accept the praise of others and to enjoy the company of his friends.

In all these cases the therapist must keep in mind that there are significant transferential affective components, spoken and silent, that significantly contribute to the process of transformation of the maternal, paternal, as well as of the God representation. The patient's transferential perceptions, feelings, wishes and expectations prompt the person to anticipate a repetition of the feared original hurts and traumas. The analyst's respectful stance, careful listening, and efforts to understand the patient's experience introduce a major change in the person's expectations. The analyst's careful clarification of feelings and thoughts and the affectively attuned interpretation of unconscious wishes and fears bring about in a progressive and cumulative manner, a modification of the representation of the original objects, of the patient's sense of self, as well as the perception of the person of the analyst, now progressively divested of its transferential features. These major changes modified in a subtle and silent way, and at times overt manner the representation of God that found some of its characteristics in those primary objects.

Illustration of the Dynamic Interaction of Affects, Wishes, Conflicts and Representations During the Analytic Process

Louis, a young man of vivid imagination, resorted to analysis because of his difficulties with women and work. He was very attached to the parental couple, still relating to them as a latency child who appears to be good on the surface, but is secretly devoted to sexual thoughts and victorious vengeful fantasies. During the initial interviews, he wept saying that nobody should take God and his religion away from him. Soon, he wept again out of fear that his father could die. Any therapist could see that he was in the grips of a human drama of father, mother, and son. The drama also had a divine dimension.

At the time of the analyst's first vacation, Louis found the separation very difficult. Upon the analyst's return, he was frantic, clinging, and terrified of his feelings, which were voiced in gruesome, fairy tale metaphors. They seemed to reveal his unconscious guilt. He dreamed about being castrated by his mother. He hinted that if nobody loved him he would kill himself. He went to see his pastor and repeated the sad announcement. The pastor insisted, with scriptures in hand, that God loved him, and that God's love always remains. Louis informed the pastor that he had a woman analyst and asked him to call her. He felt much consoled by the pastor's words and considered their encounter a proof of God's love for him.

The pastor called the analyst who, constrained by confidentiality, listened to his report and thanked him for his concern.

The analysand returned, much improved. He asked if the pastor had called. His question was a formality, he knew that the pastor would keep his promise. A good mood came upon him and, without transition, he had a fantasy of being naked next to his mother and ready and eager to have sex with her. He was surprised that he was describing the fantasy. He felt no guilt and acted as though God had given him permission to have sex with his mother. From that moment on his clingingness diminished, his mood lifted, and he became able, once more, to collaborate in the analytic exploration. What helped him was the analyst's unchallenging acceptance of the first explicit emergence of his wishes. He had expected a devastating punishment for having them, although he could not avoid repeating the manipulation of his parents now enacted with the pastor and the analyst. At this early moment of treatment the analyst did not interpret his unconscious wishes (something to be done later) but helped him to make himself comfortable in the treatment by saying all he had to say. He remained, however, unaware of his sexual wishes toward the analyst and of the interconnections between God, pastor, mother, and analyst.

That was the first of several moments in which God joined the analytic encounter. In other occasions, God returned with punishment and anger; at still others, with consolation and favors. In all these, Louis compared himself to severely tried but favored biblical characters: Job, Daniel, and Jonah. Like them, he felt he had to suffer, while rejoicing in God's interventions, which made them victorious.

It is obvious that God appeared in these hours as another ordinary "person" deeply enmeshed in Louis' family relations as well as in his transferential wishes. Analytic examination of God's representation in these hours indicated that they had their source in an assumed castrating mother as well as in the wished-for, loving and sexual mother of the phallic Oedipal period. There was no conscious trace of the father in the God representation. The father was, however, acted out in the person of the pastor who, as Louis' actions showed, was obligated to tell the analyst that she, the transferential mother, should love him and not leave him.

The cleverness of unconscious processes is shown in its economy of means. In these few hours Louis unconsciously orchestrated a magnificent demonstration of how to keep your God, your mother, your analyst, and your pastor–father, while fulfilling in fantasy the double satisfaction of sex with his mother and narcissistic triumph, without any conscious guilt. All this he could achieve because God was his secret accomplice (as his mother had been) under the Scriptural certification provided by his pastor.

In due time the analysis discovered that the mother, who supplied the representational elements for the God representation of these hours and was the source of Louis' intense despair, had overstimulated him as a small child with her physical games. She too, he believed, had condoned their sexual involvement.

There was more to Louis as a moral and religious person than what these analytic hours reveal. He was a committed and serious believer who honored his personal, moral, and religious obligations with full responsibility. These hours present him at his most regressed state and allowed him to observe the genetic, dynamic, conflictive, and defensive functions that the many aspects of his unconscious God representation had served and could still serve in his psychic life.

This illustration aims specifically at showing that the analyst must not be concerned with the seemingly confusing, at times, unexpected emergence of these aspects of the God representation. It is only through the thorough and unimpeded examination of all these elements that the analysand can work through the fixation to parental figures as well as aspects of God created during childhood at the service of psychic compensation or defense. For these reasons the analyst must follow the patient wherever his associations bring him. The rage of God, his love, neglect, sexuality, favoritism, curses, sadism, or any other belief must be taken with the utmost seriousness. It is only in this complete analytic freedom that the analysand can fully feel the complexities of his relation with his personal God. In so doing he may acquire a new mode of believing purified of its old psychological burdens.

To achieve this desirable goal it is indispensable that the analyst *never* make any pronouncement about God or religion. Technically, such pronouncement disrupts the working through of the personal representation of God and of personal belief. It also conveys to the patient that the analyst knows God for sure, and has the right to demand that the analysand submits to the authority of the analyst. This goes against the aim of the treatment, which is to help the patient find maximal autonomy and internal freedom. It is not the responsibility of the analyst to help the patient find the "true" God and religion. His or her responsibility is to help the patient to find God and religion in the context of her or his past life history and present circumstances.

Similar considerations apply for any other religious issues. The analyst is not a spiritual director. The analytic task is not to guide the patient in the search of God. It is to help the analysands to find their own wish for God and the truth and to enable them to understand the motives that interfere with such wishes.

CONCLUSION

Any patient is potentially a religious person. The psychoanalytic therapist remains always attentive to any appearance of God and religion in treatment, as a normal manifestation of significant developmental and dynamic issue. The appearance of religion and God in the hour are never uncomplicated issues. They bring with them their genetic developmental history, their regressive potential to earlier moments of God's representation formation and transformation in moments of psychic urgency or integration. They carry with them a whole array of dynamic conflicts and the potential to be used as defense. Of these, the most frequent is the resorting to God as a way of avoiding difficult transferential issues. If God is an object with a long conscious history in the life of the individual, it becomes easily available, as it was with Louis, in his regressed transferential moment. At other times, God is unconsciously called upon to reinforce a superego stance insisting that one should not say certain things, making God responsible for avoiding distressing associations.

The other side of the God representation and of religion, as psychic realities, is their equally strong potential to aid in the processes of psychic integration and of relating to the world. These are best illustrated in the cases of Laura, Sybil, and Father Robert. Remembered childhood experiences, therapeutic psychic transformations, and concrete religious participation in a religious practice offer a sense of belonging to a transcendent reality and of relating to a living God.

Religiously committed patients must be treated exactly as any other person. Not to do so would mean to deprive them of the exploration of the sources of their belief and the relation they have with the God to whom they have committed their lives. It must be remembered that a religious act is an act of the total person in a relationship with a living God. Psychoanalysis can only explore the sources and motives of those acts. The religious act *itself* surpasses the scope of psychic exploration.

Finally, there is a need to insist that in all cases, extreme respect and tact are required to deal with religious feelings and beliefs. It may be humiliating for a priest, a nun, or a devout believer to have to admit to themselves that they have a sexualized relationship with God (as Louis did), that they are unwilling to give up a resentment against him (as Sybil), or any other variation of human attachment and conflict. The main task of the therapist is to facilitate all analysands' progressive acceptance of their psychic life as a necessary, even if difficult and painful, process of becoming true to themselves and to their God.

REFERENCES

Beit-Hallahmi, B., & Argyle, M. (1975). God as a father projection: The theory and the evidence. *British Journal of Medical Psychology, 48,* 71–75.

Freud, S. (1908). "Civilized" sexual morality and modern nervous illness. In *The standard edition of the complete psychological works of Sigmund Freud* (Vol. 9, pp. 177–204). London: Hogarth Press.

Freud, S. (1913). Totem and taboo. In *The standard edition of the complete psychological works of Sigmund Freud* (Vol. 13, pp. 1–162). London: Hogarth Press.

Freud, S. (1927). The future of an illusion. In *The standard edition of the complete psychological works of Sigmund Freud* (Vol. 21, pp. 1–57). London: Hogarth Press.

Glock, C. Y. (1962). On the study of religious commitment. *Religious Education Research (Supplement), 57,* 98–110.

James, W. (1929). *The varieties of religious experience.* New York: The Modern Library. (Original work published in 1902)

Rizzuto, A.-M. (1979). *The birth of the living God. A psychoanalytic study.* Chicago: The University of Chicago Press.

Spero, M. H. (1992). *Religious objects as psychological structures: A critical integration of object relations theory, psychotherapy, and Judiasm.* Chicago: University of Chicago Press.

Winnicott, D. W. (1953). Transitional objects and transitional phenomena. In *Playing and reality* (Vol. 1971, pp. 1–25). New York: Basic Books.

APPENDIX
ADDITIONAL READING

McDargh, J. (1983). *Psychoanalytic object relations theory and the study of religion. On faith and the imaging of God.* Lanham, New York, London: University Press of America.

Meissner, W. W. (1984). *Psychoanalysis and religious experience.* New Haven, CT: Yale University Press.

Pruyser, P. W. (1968). *A dynamic psychology of religion.* New York: Harper & Row.

Rizzuto, A.-M. (1991). Religious development: A psychoanalytic point of view. In F. K. Oser & W. G. Scarlett (Eds.), *Religious development in childhood and adolescence* (pp. 47–59). San Francisco, CA: Jossey-Bass.

Rizzuto, A.-M. (1993). Exploring sacred landscapes. In M. L. Randour (Ed.), *Exploring sacred landscapes. Religious and spiritual experiences in psychotherapy* (pp. 16–33). New York: Columbia University Press.

Shafranske, E. P. (1992). Religion and mental health in early life. In J. F. Schumaaker (Ed.), *Religion & Mental Health* (pp. 163–176). New York: Oxford University Press.

Spero, M. H. (1990). Parallel dimensions of experience in psychoanalytic psychotherapy of the religious patient. *Psychotherapy, 27,* 53–71.

16

EXISTENTIAL–HUMANISTIC PSYCHOTHERAPY AND THE RELIGIOUS PERSON

ALVIN R. MAHRER

The purpose of this chapter is to try to answer two questions: (a) How does an existential–humanistic therapist work with a religious person or with religious material, as compared with a person or material that is not especially religious? (b) Do religious–spiritual values, convictions, beliefs, practices, or behaviors have some special role, or little and no role, in the material with which this therapy works; in the theory or model of what human beings are like; in the way in which psychotherapeutic change is understood as coming about; in this therapy's notions of the directions of change; and in the way in which this therapist is with the person throughout the session?

A further question arises in regard to this discussion: Is it more useful to try to tell about the existential–humanistic family in general, or to use an illustrative representive?

One option is to focus on the existential–humanistic family as a whole. That would run into the problem of how to be fair to the impres-

I would like to express my appreciation to Vince Gilpin, CSW, and to Peggy Kleinplatz, PhD, for their help in the preparation of this chapter.

sively different viewpoints and answers of such existential–humanistic family members as Allport, Angel, Angyal, Bakan, Binswanger, Boss, Buber, Bugental, Caruso, Combs, Deikman, Ellenberger, Fischer, Frankl, Fromm, Gendlin, Giorgi, Goldstein, Gurwitsch, Heidegger, Husserl, James, Jaspers, Jourard, Kierkegaard, Laing, Malone, Maslow, May, Merleau-Ponty, Moustakas, Needleman, Perls, Polster, Ouspensky, Rogers, Sartre, Shostrom, Sorokin, Straus, Tillich, van den Berg, Van Dusen, Vespe, Von Eckartsberg, Warkentin, Whitaker, and Wilhelm.

Focusing on the family as a whole would also run into a problem of how to be fair to differing existential–humanistic therapies such as phenomenological therapy, focusing therapy, logotherapy, client-centered therapy, existential therapy, existential analysis, growth therapy, humanistic therapy, Gestalt therapy, Daseinsanalysis, encounter therapy, concentration therapy, feeling–expressive therapy, psycho-imagination therapy, nonrational therapy, intense feeling therapy, experiential therapy, and many others. As one example of how big and tangled this family is, Mahrer and Fairweather (1993) found several dozen substantially different kinds of therapies that were called *experiential psychotherapy*.

The problem is that these therapies do differ a great deal from one another, and the positions of the family members do differ a great deal on the answers to the two central questions. Trying to give answers for the existential–humanistic family as a whole would almost certainly veer toward a diffuse, highly generalized mishmash that represented very little of any particular family members, that told very little of how an existential–humanistic therapist might work with a religious person, and that stayed at a vacuously generalized level of abstraction in telling about the role of religious–spiritual values, convictions, beliefs, practices, and behaviors in this family of psychotherapies. I decline this option.

Another option is to select one of the existential–humanistic therapies, to answer the questions from the perspective of this illustrative representative, and to leave room for the voices of some of the other family members and therapies. This option is, I believe, a better way of trying to answer the two central questions and yet to say something meaningful about the existential–humanistic family and the religious person. I have choosen this option here.

The psychotherapy that will be used as an illustrative representative is one experiential psychotherapy (Mahrer, 1996), and I will try to point out how and where other members of the existential–humanistic family may and may not differ in how to work with the religious person. Yet I know that selecting one experiential psychotherapy, or any member of the family, risks not giving enough voice to other members of this existential–humanistic family, and for that I apologize at the outset.

WHAT IS TO BE USED AS A MEANING OF THE "RELIGIOUS–SPIRITUAL" PERSON?

If we are going to be talking about the religious person, it is probably helpful to have some clear picture of what is meant by religion and spirituality. The word *religion* may be taken as referring to the beliefs, values, and practices of various established religions (Shafranske & Malony, 1990), and the word *spirituality* may be taken as referring to some kind of relationship between the person and a higher force, being, power, or God (Peterson & Nelson, 1987). However, I acknowledge that there are multiple meanings of these two key terms and that how I define *religious* or *spiritual* is far different than many other respectable meanings of the words.

WHAT IS AN EXPERIENTIAL SESSION LIKE, WHETHER OR NOT IT IS WITH A RELIGIOUS PERSON?

In general, what happens in a session of experiential psychotherapy is the same, whether or not the person may be understood as religious.

What Are the Aims and Goals of an Experiential Session?

There are two main aims and goals for each session. One is that the person can become a qualitatively new person. There can be a genuine change in who and what the new person is, in the very inner core and identity of this new person, in how this new person is and acts and interacts. The change is from the inside out, for it starts with the discovery of what is deeper inside the person, then enables what is deeper to be welcomed and appreciated (i.e., integration), and then to become a central part of the new person (i.e., actualization).

The second aim or goal is for the new person to be free of the scenes of bad feelings that were front and center for the old person. There is a letting go of, a freedom from, the scenes and situations that were so bothersome, painful, and troubling for the person who started the session.

What Sequence of Steps Is Followed in an Experiential Session?

Each session proceeds through a sequence of steps or phases. The first step is to discover or access what is called the inner deeper potential for experiencing that is here in this session. The "deeper potential for experiencing" is one version of what the existential–humanistic family holds is deeper in personality, comprises the inner personality structure, and is otherwise pointed toward by related terms such as existential capacities or states, inner felt meanings, or inner possibilities or potentialities. This first step opens by finding a scene of strong feeling, and locating the precise moment of strong feeling in the scene. It is in this moment of strong feeling that the deeper potential for experiencing can be accessed, discovered, sensed, felt, and received.

The second step is to enable the person to welcome, to appreciate, to have integrative good relations with the inner deeper potential for experiencing that was accessed in the first step. Integration means that the person can receive and welcome the inner, alien, deeper potential, regardless of its nature and content. For example, the person now welcomes the deeper potential for experiencing caring for, protecting, nurturing, or a deeper potential for experiencing wickedness, devilishness, mischievousness, or whatever the nature is of this particular deeper potential for experiencing.

The third step is to enable the person to undergo the radical and qualitative shift into literally being this deeper potential for experiencing. The person is given an opportunity to undergo what it is like to be a whole new person who is this deeper potential, and to do so wholly, fully, in an existential leap of faith, and with vigor, wholesomeness, energy, and vibrant aliveness.

The fourth and final step is to enable the person to become a qualitatively new and fuller person, including the integrated and actualized deeper potential that is now a core part of who and what this new person is. By means of rehearsal and in-session sampling, the whole new person faces the possibility of living, existing, being, and behaving as this qualitatively new person in the qualitatively new extratherapy world of the immediate present and prospective future.

The consequence of these four in-session steps is that the person who leaves the session can be a qualitatively new person who is able to be free of the the old person's scenes of bad feelings.

Therapist and Person Are "Aligned" With One Another, Rather Than in a Face-to-Face, Person-to-Person, Interactive Stance

Growing out of existential–humanistic conceptions of how the therapist and person can be with one another (cf. Buber, 1958; Bugental, 1970; Havens, 1974; May, 1989; Rogers, 1975), the therapist and person are continuously "aligned" or fused with one another (Mahrer, in press; Mahrer, Boulet, & Fairweather, 1994). In its practical, concrete meaning, the therapist is "aligned" with the patient when (a) both patient and therapist are attending mainly to what is "out there," to a third entity, to something that draws the attention of the patient, to the cancer or the look on her son's face or to the breathtaking sunrise, and (b) the therapist is so postured and situated that the patient's words seem to be coming from a part of the therapist, or coming in and through the therapist, or as if the therapist and patient are parts of a single person who is voicing the words.

The therapist is aligned with the patient continuously, throughout the session. This aligned stance is in sharp contrast to the common face-to-face stance in which therapist and patient are attending mainly to one another as they engage in a person-to-person interactive conversation about this or that topic, with most of their attention on one another.

By being aligned with the patient, with their attention directed mainly "out there," on some other center, the therapist essentially lets go of the ordinary stream of private thoughts and inferences about the patient, about their relationship, about the way to phrase the interpretation or empathic reflection, about the clinical meaning of the patient's pauses or speech pattern. The therapist essentially lets go of the common therapist identities, roles, and postures, together with the common ways of relating and interacting with the patient if they are face-to-face with each other. The aligned stance is quite different from the ordinary face-to-face stance, and there are some rather bold consequences.

The Aligned Therapist Is Essentially Free of His or Her Own, Personal, Religious–Spiritual Convictions, Attitudes, and Beliefs

The aligned therapist deliberately attends to that third attentional center "out there," and deliberately joins with the person in allowing the person's words to come from a part of the therapist, as if the therapist were saying these words. To this extent, the therapist has essentially left behind the therapist's own personal religious–spiritual convictions, attitudes, and beliefs. This is substantially a disengagement from or minimalization of one's own religious–spiritual history (cf. Shafranske & Gorsuch, 1984), whether or not the therapist reads the Bible, believes in this or that God, or follows any kind of religious practices.

Can therapists accept this proposal? If they can, it means that they are willing to let go of a generally accepted fundamental truth that the therapist's own personal religious–spiritual convictions, attitudes, and beliefs somehow must be potent factors in psychotherapy. This means that "truth" does not hold for the aligned therapist.

The Aligned Therapist Can Work With Just About Any Person, Regardless of the Therapist's or the Patient's Religious–Spiritual Convictions, Attitudes, and Beliefs

If the therapist is well and truly aligned, the session can be a fine one whether or not the therapist or the patient have read the Bible, whether or not one of them is a priest, or whether or not they celebrate the same religious holidays (cf. Bergin, 1980; Malony, 1972; Shafranske & Gorsuch, 1984). The therapist can work with the person whether or not one of them is deeply religious, whether or not both are deeply religious in ways that are flagrantly dissimilar, or whether or not they have similar or dissimilar histories of religious–spiritual experiences.

To the degree that the therapist can accept the notion of being aligned with the person, many religious–spiritual issues can be seen as essentially restricted to face-to-face therapists rather than to aligned therapists.

The Experiential Therapist Shows the Person What to Do, Joins the Person in Doing It, Values and Respects the Person's Immediate Readiness and Willingness to Do It

Throughout the entire session, in going through each step, with therapist and patient attending mainly "out there," the therapist's job is to show the person what to do and how to do it, and to join with the person in doing it. The therapist is the coach-instructor-guide who accompanies the person in undergoing each step.

This means that the therapist is continually asking if doing this particular thing is all right, if the person is ready and willing. Furthermore, the person's immediate state of readiness and willingness is uppermost, required, and essential, and is valued, honored, respected, and followed. There is no pressure by the therapist, no trying to get the person to do it, no "interventions," no applying methods and techniques to get the person to conform or to explain why the person is not being a good patient. If the person is not especially ready and willing to do this immediate thing, that is just fine.

Each Session Is Its Own Complete Mini-Therapy

Each session starts by finding whatever scenes of strong feeling are front and center for this person right now, and each session ends with the qualitatively new person sampling what it is like to be this new person in the present extratherapy world, free of the scenes of bad feelings. Each session goes through the four steps. The specific goals for this session are arrived at in the first step of this session, and the success or failure of this session can be determined at the end of this session and in who and what the person is in the opening of the next session. In so many ways, each session is its own complete mini-therapy, whether therapist and patient decide to have a next session right away or after a bit, whether or not there are many sessions or few sessions, sessions in a bunch or now and again for a long time.

In the balance of this chapter, I will take a closer look at the role of religious–spiritual factors in experiential sessions. In the beginning of a session, what role is played by religious–spiritual factors in determining what the session will focus on, deal with, and target? To what extent do religious–spiritual factors play a role in a picture, or theory, or model of what human beings are like? Do religious–spiritual factors play a substantial role in how psychotherapeutic change is understood as coming about? To what extent and in what ways are experiential psychotherapy's goals and directions of change cordial to those of religion and spirituality? I now want to focus on how the experiential therapist works with a religious person and tries to do this as one illustrative representative of the existential–humanistic family, while shedding light on the rest of the family.

The person we will be following is Samuel, and specifically the initial session with Samuel. He has a responsible position with a very large agency. He and his wife are in their early 40s, and would probably be regarded as moderately religious and observant of their religious principles and practices.

Each Session Opens by Finding a Scene of Strong Feeling, and a Religious–Spiritual Scene Is Just Fine

In the beginning of each session, the important work is to identify the scenes of strong feeling that are front and center for the person right now. If the nature of the scene is religious or spiritual, that is just fine.

The Scenes of Strong Feeling for Samuel

In the beginning of the initial session, Samuel was shown how to find whatever time or incident was front and center on his mind, the focus of whatever strong feelings are here now. He went directly to his recent morbid fascination with reading religious texts on death, occultism, and spells. The scene is sitting in the religious library, pouring over texts before and after work, missing meals, in a state of gripping tension and morbid fascination. "I barely go home! I can't sleep! This is all I do!" Is this when and where the feeling is the strongest, this feeling of being gripped, frozen, in a state of utter frozen tension? No. It was worse about 3 weeks ago. As he was leaving the government building where he works, some crazed, fanatic, dirty, bearded old man accosted him and, with a fierce and hateful look on his face, cackled about how Samuel was doomed to hell. What makes this so terrifying is that he was eerily certain this was the old rabbi of whom Samuel had been frightened as a child, and who had died when Samuel was an adolescent. Here are the two scenes of strong feeling for Samuel.

The Session Starts by Finding Scenes of Strong Feeling; Versus, the Important Target Is the Mental Disorder, the Pathology

There are two main reasons why it is so important for the person to identify the scene of strong feeling:

1. If the scene is accompanied with bad, painful feelings—the heart of what is so hurtful and painful—then the aim is to enable this person to be free of that awful scene. It is no longer to be a part of the person's world.
2. Whether the accompanying feelings are bad or good, the scene can be used as a grand entry or avenue down into the person's own insides, into discovering the inner, deeper potential for experiencing. Scenes of strong feeling are therefore precious in the beginning of each session.

What is not precious, what is not even relevant, is to look for what is commonly called signs and symptoms of mental disorders or pathology. The experiential therapist is not looking for these things, nor are these things helpful in looking for the scenes of strong feeling that are front and center for the person right now.

Religious–Spiritual Scenes Are Welcomed and Used

The helpful guide is that the person is to identify the scene in which feeling is strong. It may be some awful feeling of terror as the brutish man is smashing you again and again. It may be a feeling of ecstasy as you are entranced by the wondrous sunrise. No kind of scene or feeling is declined as long as it is important for the person, is compelling and gripping. Scenes that may be candidly religious or spiritual are precious, welcomed, and useful, whether the person is in a church or synagogue, in a struggle with the devil, hearing an inner voice, staring at the clouds, surrendering to the undertow, or brushing her teeth.

Samuel is sitting in the religious library, magnetized by the texts on death, spells, and the occult. Samuel is accosted by the old man who seems to be the deceased old rabbi. These scenes of strong feeling are welcomed and used whether or not they are considered religious–spiritual.

The person's religious–spiritual concerns, issues, troubles, happinesses, excitements, convictions, beliefs, practices, or behaviors—all of these can be helpful and important avenues into finding this person's own special scenes of strong feeling. The experiential therapist accepts, honors, and welcomes this material (cf. Krippner & Welch, 1992; Lukoff, Lu, & Turner, 1992; Rothbaum, Weisz, & Snyder, 1982; Spilka, 1986; Weisz, Rothbaum, & Blackburn, 1984).

Because the Session Starts With Finding the Scene of Strong Feeling. . . The therapist starts by working with the person to find the scene of strong feeling that is present, central, and of concern now. This is far more important than looking for signs and symptoms of some mental disorder, pathology, maladjustment, or abnormality.

It Is Not Especially Relevant Whether or Not Lots of People Have Religious–Spiritual Convictions and Beliefs. In the beginning of the session, the therapist and person search for when and where there were strong feelings. If the situation is somehow one that is religious or spiritual, that is fine, whether or not surveys show that large proportions of people believe in God, belong to some religion, or have religious–spiritual interests (e.g., Anderson & Young, 1988; Jensen & Bergin, 1988; Spilka, 1986). The therapist would still start with a scene of strong feeling in which the person is caught up in her forbidden thoughts toward the priest even though such concerns may not score high in surveys. A scene of strong feeling is important because it is a scene of strong feeling, and not because a survey confirms that believing in God is checked by a high proportion of respondents.

It Is Not Especially Relevant Whether or Not the Person Is Deeply Religious. The therapist would start by enabling the person to find scenes of strong feeling whether or not the person is deeply religious. If the scene is one in which the person tried to kill herself, or is tortured by recollections of having blown up civilians in the war, or lied about having had a secret abortion, the scenes would be just as precious whether or not the person is deeply religious. The meaning of the scene, and the nature of the strong feeling may vary in deeply religious or nonreligious patients, but it is the scene itself and the nature of the feeling that are important, not whether or not the person is deeply religious.

With Samuel, the work is to find the scenes of strong feeling. The scenes of pouring over the religious texts and being accosted by what seemed to be the deceased rabbi are the working scenes. For this work, it makes little or no difference whether someone regards Samuel as deeply religious or not.

It Is Not Especially Relevant Whether Some Other Therapists Regard Religious–Spiritual Material as "Pathological." It is important to be clear that for the experiential therapist the important opening step is to search for scenes of strong feeling, and that in this therapy, as in many members of the larger family, there is simply no place for notions of pathology, mental disorder, symptoms, or signs of maladjustment or mental illness.

Many religious–spiritual theorists and therapists react against many traditional theorists and therapists who tend to regard some kinds of religious–spiritual convictions, values, beliefs, and practices as pathological or signs and symptoms of mental disorders (Bergin, 1980, 1991; Campbell, 1975; Lukoff, Lu, & Turner, 1992). These religious–spiritual theorists and therapists are bothered that Freud (1949) considered a mystical state of unity and oneness with the world as a serious regression to a primitive narcissistic infantile state, and that this pronouncement was upheld by the Group for the Advancement of Psychiatry (1976). These religious–spiritual theorists and therapists are concerned that so many therapists are so very prone to jump to a pathological meaning when a person says he hears the voice of God or spends many hours studying religious texts, or is compelled by a near-death experience (cf. Moody, 1975; Spero, 1987).

Accordingly, these religious–spiritual theorists and therapists try to argue that (a) there can be simple religious–spiritual, nonpathological dimensions in these supposedly pathological experiences; (b) that these experiences are not necessarily regarded as pathological in many other cultures (Achterberg, 1988; Eisenbruch, 1992; Grof & Grof, 1989; Lukoff, 1991); (c) that religious counselors deal with a host of religious–spiritual concerns that are not pathological (Lukoff, Lu, & Turner, 1992; Young & Griffith, 1989); and (d) that many experiences, such as mystical states, religious conversions, and spiritual visions, far from being pathological, can be seen as indications of a higher plateau, a state of enlightenment, and a sign of actualization (Hood, 1974; James, 1961; Jung, 1973; Maslow, 1968, 1973; Spilka, 1986; Walsh & Roche, 1979).

If a person clings to her religious–spiritual convictions and beliefs, some therapists regard that as pathological. If therapists cling to their convictions and beliefs about pathology, perhaps that too is evidence of pathology. In contrast, the experiential therapist merely searches with the person for scenes of strong feeling, and this replaces a search for what some therapists regard as pathology.

It Is Irrelevant Whether or Not Religious–Spiritual Factors Contribute to "Pathology." Because the experiential therapist and patient look for scenes of strong feeling, it is almost irrelevant whether or not religious–spiritual factors play a part in bringing about what others call pathology. Some may reluctantly admit that religion and spirituality can be used to brainwash a person toward mental disorder, can foster mental disorder by overstressing sin and evil, and can relieve a person of responsibility by placing responsibility in the hands of God (Rothbaum, Weisz, & Snyder, 1982; Weisz, Rothbaum, & Blackburn, 1984). In experiential psychotherapy, it makes little or no difference whether or not religious–spiritual factors contribute to pathology and mental disorders because notions of pathology and mental disorder have essentially nothing to do with the finding of scenes of strong feeling.

The Scene of Strong Feeling Is the Doorway to the Person's Deeper Potentials for Experiencing

Once the therapist and patient identify a scene of strong feeling, they enter into this scene and search for what lies deeper inside the person. In the experiential model of human beings, the insides of the person, the foundations of personality, are comprised of what is called potentials for experiencing. It is the discovery of these deeper potentials for experiencing that is the aim of the first step of an experiential session.

In the Experiential Model of Human Beings, the Basic Foundation Is Composed of Potentials for Experiencing

In the experiential model of human beings, there is something deeper within, something outside the boundaries of the more or less conscious, aware, functioning, behaving, thinking person. Drawing upon some existential–humanistic conceptualizations, what is deeper inside is understood as potential ways of being, possibilities, capacities, capabilities, powers, other personalities, or potentials for experiencing (Alexander & Selesnick, 1967; Burton, 1972; Fadiman, 1980; Fischer, 1985; Kaplan, 1982, 1985; Kapleau, 1967; Kopp, 1971; Mahrer, 1989, 1995; Maslow, 1970; Owens, 1975; Rogers, 1957; Rowan, 1991). Beyond the more or less functioning, thinking, behaving person are deeper potentials for experiencing that relate either well or poorly with one another.

Potentials for experiencing are described as potential ways of being, ways in which this particular person is capable of experiencing. Here are descriptions of some potentials for experiencing: being firm, tough, hard; being in control, on top, in charge; being silly, whimsical, fun-loving; being free, liberated, spontaneous; being close to, bonded with, intimate with; being compassionate, caring, nurturing; being separated, withdrawn, out of; penetrating, entering into, plunging inside; being devilish, mischievous, roguish; being lost, confused, bewildered; being mean, nasty, evil, hurtful.

In this model, if you open up the person and probe down inside, you will arrive at this person's own package of deeper potentials for experiencing. The closer you come to describing this person's own particular deeper potentials for experiencing, the more likely it is that the deeper potentials in this person are different from the deeper potentials for experiencing in many other people.

Deeper Potentials for Experiencing Are Not Generally Religious or Spiritual

If you take a relatively close look at most deeper potentials for experiencing, it seems clear that you are merely describing different kinds of "experiencing," different ways of being with an emphasis on what this person has a capacity to experience. Although you may be inclined to consider some of these religious or spiritual, you may have a hard time showing that just about any deeper potential for experiencing is necessarily and restrictively religious or spiritual. This seems to hold even if the deeper potential for experiencing is described as the experiencing of giving oneself, surrendering, becoming one, or a deeper potential for experiencing a sense of worshipping, adoring, idolizing, and venerating.

In the Experiential Model, There Are No Universal Basic Deeper Potentials for Experiencing, Drives, Motivations, Needs, or Forces

When the therapist and the person discover a deeper potential for experiencing, they know one of this person's deeper potentials for experiencing. In this model, there is no notion that there are universal deeper potentials for experiencing of any kind. Nor are there universal basic drives, motivations, needs, or forces that are to be found in just about every person.

Some existential–humanistic theorists and some religious–spiritual theorists hold that there are inborn, intrinsic, inherent, universal drives, motivations, needs, growth forces, transpersonal yearnings, existential choices, as well as universal, basic religious–spiritual dimensions, connected oneness with the infinite, knowings of basic good and evil, and religious–spiritual values (e.g., Allport, 1950; Angyal, 1965; Bergin, 1985, 1988; Binswanger, 1958, 1967; Frankl, 1959, 1969; Jung, 1973; Maslow, 1968, 1970, 1973; Rogers, 1959, 1970, 1973; Shafranske & Gorsuch, 1984; Yalom, 1980). Here is a relatively important issue on which there is a difference between the experiential model of what lies at the foundation of personality, and what is understood as basic and deeper in some existential–humanistic and religious–spiritual theories.

Discovering Samuel's Deeper Potential for Experiencing

Samuel and I concentrated on the scene in which the feelings were most powerful, the scene in which Samuel is accosted by what seemed to be the deceased rabbi. As we entered into this scene and actually made it alive and real, the precise moment when the feeling is strongest is when the old man's face is only a few inches away, and he is glaring fiercely at Samuel. In this moment, what he accessed was something utterly new. It was an inner deeper sense of being filled with weakness, a frozen helplessness, a soft pliancy, a being utterly docile to the other person. These words were taken as defining a deeper potential for experiencing in Samuel.

In the first step of an experiential session, the therapist and patient open up, access, discover something inside the person, a deeper potential for experiencing. The balance of the session is to enable the person to undergo change.

Change Occurs by Welcoming–Appreciating and Then by Being the Deeper Potential for Experiencing

Once the deeper potential for experiencing is discovered, change means that the person becomes a qualitatively new person, based upon this deeper potential, and it also means that the new person becomes relatively free of the scenes of bad feeling that were so bothersome to the person. How does the therapist help these changes to occur?

The Purpose of Steps 2–4 Is to Help Bring About Change

The purpose of step 1 is to discover or access a deeper potential for experiencing. Once one discovers the deeper potential for experiencing, steps 2–4 are designed to enable change to occur. In step 2, the person is shown how to welcome and to appreciate this deeper potential. Instead of sealing it away, keeping it down, keeping it distant, the person is enabled to love the deeper potential, to cherish and value it, to feel good about it, to bear an integrative, caring relationship toward it, to keep it present, close, and right here.

In the second step of the session, Samuel is able to welcome and appreciate his deeper potential for experiencing softness, pliancy, docility, being weak, and helpless. This is an inner quality in him, not at all a part of the way he is on the surface. Indeed, his actual behavior seems quite alien to this particular way of being. It is apparently rather new and different for Samuel, an inner deeper potential for experiencing.

Once the deeper potential is reasonably welcomed and appreciated, step 3 enables the person to enter into and literally to be this deeper potential for experiencing. Here is a radical and transformative change into being a qualitatively new person who is the deeper potential, and all within scenes and contexts from earlier in the person's life. These scenes may be relatively recent or from long ago.

Step 4 enables the formerly deeper potential to become a part of this qualitatively new person, and for this qualitatively new person to gain a taste, a sample, of what it is like to be this whole new person in the newly available extratherapy world of the present and the prospective future. These three steps constitute the experiential way of helping to enable change to occur.

Steps 2–4 Are Probably Closer to Some Religious–Spiritual Than to Many Traditionally Psychotherapeutic Ways of Helping to Bring About Change

Bergin (1980) talks about a general disillusionment with some of the more traditionally psychotherapeutic ways of trying to help bring about change. Given this state of affairs, Bergin suggests, it may be timely to look elsewhere for ways to help bring about substantive change. For whatever reasons, it seems to me that there is a friendly compatibility between these steps and many of the grand avenues of change that are heralded in both existential–humanistic and religious–spiritual writings.

Step 2 calls for a welcoming–appreciating relationship toward what is within the person, an embracing acceptance and love of that which had been fended off and sealed off as alien and not-me, a wholesale tolerance and caring for what is deeply buried within oneself. This phase of experiential change is hand-in-hand with avenues of change found in much of the existential–humanistic and religious–spiritual literatures.

Steps 3 and 4 involve the radical and transformative change into wholly being the deeper potential, and into being the qualitatively new person based upon the deeper potential. Here is the psychotherapeutic use of surrendering, of submitting, of entrusting oneself. It is the highest sacrificing of who and what one is in the leap of faith to becoming what one can become. It calls for faith, trust, being willing to throw oneself into the abyss of nothingness, existential–humanistic death. This is a cornerstone of existential conceptions of radical change. It is also a cornerstone of many religious–spiritual conceptualizations of radical change.

For Samuel, steps 3 and 4 mean a wholesale letting go of the very person that he is, a leap into being the qualitatively new and different inner deeper person who undergoes and experiences softness, pliancy, docility, being weak and helpless. In step 3, Samuel throws himself into being this whole new person in the context of earlier life scenes and situations. In step 4, Samuel does the same in getting a sample, a foretaste, of what life can be like in the present and prospective future if he were actually being this wholesale new and different person.

However, there are some ways of trying to effect change that are common in many traditional psychotherapies, and in some religious–spiritual change avenues, but are alien to how change is helped to occur in experiential psychotherapy.

The Experiential Steps of Change Do Not Include Trying to Get the Patient to Adopt Your Own Beliefs, Ways of Thinking, and Cognitions. Many traditional therapists try to get the patient to have different thoughts, to adopt the therapist's way of thinking about oneself and the world, to change their cognitions. It is thought that patients will get better if they exchange their wrong way of thinking for the right way of the therapist, if they have different attitudes, philosophies, outlooks, and cognitions. In much the same way, some religious theorists and therapists try to bring about change by trying to get the person to adopt a particular set of religious beliefs, attitudes, outlooks, ways of thinking, and cognitions. Patients are therefore pushed to adopt the belief systems of the cognitive therapist, the feminist therapist, the rational–emotive therapist, the systems therapist, the cognitive–behavioral therapist, or the religious therapist.

Each therapist has sound reasons why his particular set of beliefs and ways of thinking are superior, and should of course be adopted by patients. Whether a psychotherapist or a religionist, it is easy to assert that your own set of beliefs and ways of thinking are the truth: Great conceptualizers have upheld them. Their roots go far back in history. Authorities endorse them. They are confirmed by science. One should not question the basic truth of these beliefs and ways of thinking. The practical proof is that those who accept the right ways of believing and thinking are free of symptoms, turmoil, loneliness, depression, despair, mental disorders, psychopathology, and everything bad (Hole, 1971; Nelson, 1977; Spilka, 1986).

Experiential steps 2–4 do not especially involve trying to get the patient to adopt psychotherapeutic or religious cognitions, ways of thinking, attitudes, thoughts, or beliefs.

The Experiential Steps of Change Do Not Especially Include Trying to Get the Patient to Accept Psychotherapeutic or Religious Kinds of Insights, Understandings, or Explanations of Oneself and the World. Some psychotherapists and some religionists try to get the patient to have a particular way of seeing oneself, understanding oneself, and explaining oneself. The insight, understanding, or explanation is about the kind of person that the patient is, how the person got that way, how and why the person acts and feels and thinks the way the person does, how and why the person is so unhappy or troubled. Some psychotherapists help to bring about insight, understanding, and explanation that is Freudian, Jungian, Sullivanian, Adlerian, Lewinian, behavioral, social learning, systemic, or dozens of other kinds. Likewise, the religionist can also select from dozens of other ways that the person can have insight, understanding, and explanation of himself and his world.

For many psychotherapists and religionists, change is brought by getting the person to have some kind of insight, understanding and explanation; however, these play little or no role in the experiential steps 2–4.

The Experiential Steps of Change Do Not Especially Include Trying to Get the Person to Behave in Ways That Are Considered Normal, Nonpathological, Healthy, Good, or Right. For some psychotherapists, an important way of bringing about change is to try to get the patient to change behaviors. By adopting new behaviors, change is supposed to occur. Typically, the psychotherapist has particular sets of change-producing behaviors for particular mental disorders and problems. The patient who is afraid of being in very tall buildings is to try being in moderately high buildings. The patient who is afraid of intercourse is to engage in simple foreplay without trying to have intercourse. Many psychotherapists have notions of what kinds of behaviors are normal, healthy, nonpathological, and try to get change by doing what they can to get patients to engage in these behaviors.

In much the same way, some religionists believe that change is helped to occur when patients begin carrying out certain kinds of behaviors that are regarded as good, right, pathology-reducing, and change-producing. For example, here are some of behaviors prescribed by Bergin (1980, 1988): The person is to forgive others who caused harm to the person. The person is to regulate and control abusive behavior, addictive behavior, aggressive behavior, as hurtful and pathological. The person is to be committed to her family, responsible to her family, caring for her family. The person is to behave heterosexually rather than homosexually.

Experiential psychotherapy does not count on change occurring through the prescription of a set of behaviors that are regarded as change-producing or generally good for whatever ails the person. Instead, the final part of step 4 includes finding new behaviors that both come from and provide for the new experiencing found in the session, and that enable the qualitatively new person to be this new way in the extratherapy world. These behaviors are typically not part of a general set of behaviors regarded as normal, nonpathological, healthy, good, right, or change-producing.

At the end of the session, Samuel was able to find some new behaviors, in some relatively new scenes and situations, that enabled a newfound sense of experiencing softness, pliancy, docility, letting oneself be weak and pleasantly helpless. Being and behaving in these new ways seemed useful and helpful because they provided for the integrated and actualized potential for experiencing that had been deeper and sealed off in Samuel. They are not part of some list of behaviors considered normal, nonpathological, healthy, good, or right.

The Experiential Steps of Change Do Not Include Placing the Person Into Some Larger Group, System, or Community. Some psychotherapists count on the effects of treating the person by putting the person in a larger group. The group may be the family, a group of patients with the same mental disorder, a setting outside the community, a setting within the community. Change occurs via social factors or systems factors or whatever seems to be helpful by being in the group.

Some religionists share the same kind of notion of how to bring about change. They believe in the change-producing effects of the person being part of a religious group, setting, institution, community. They believe that being in a religious group or setting can help the mentally disordered person function without florid outbreaks of deviance, abnormality, and mental illness (Propst, 1980; Spilka, 1986; Spilka, Hood, & Gorsuch, 1985). Placing a person in some kind of group or setting is not especially a substantive part of steps 2–4 in experiential psychotherapy.

At the end of step 1, the experiential therapist and the person have identified scenes of strong feeling, and have discovered a deeper potential for experiencing. Steps 2–4 show how change is helped to occur. The question of how change is helped to occur is the other side of a further question. What are the directions of change in experiential psychotherapy, and are these simple and straightforward values?

What Are the Preciously Valued Directions of Change in Experiential Psychotherapy?

In just about every experiential session, the person is given an opportunity to undergo steps toward two coupled directions of change.

1. The person is able to become a qualitatively new person. In this new person, relationships between parts of the person are to be more welcoming, accepting, loving (integration), and the discovered deeper potential becomes an integral part of who and what this new person is (actualization).
2. The new person is essentially free of the scenes of bad feeling that were front and center for the old person. These are the directions of change.

Experiential Directions of Change Constitute a Set of Precious Values

The directions of change, in experiential psychotherapy, constitute a simple, frank, straightforward set of preciously held values. The directions of change come from the experiential picture of what human beings can become, what optimal persons can be like, what can be achieved through progressive and successful integration and actualization (Mahrer, 1989, 1996). The directions of change are indeed a value system (cf. Bergin, 1980; London, 1964; Lowe, 1976).

With Samuel, there were two valued directions of change. One is that what had been a deeper potential, sealed off and pushed down, can become an integrated and actualized new part of the new Samuel. He could and did become a qualitatively new person who included being and experiencing a newfound and good-feeling softness, pliancy, docility, a letting oneself be weak and helpless. Second, this qualitatively new person was essentially free of scenes of painfully bad feelings as he is compelled to spend what seemed to him to be inordinate hours pouring into religious texts. Nor were there any further scenes of being terrifiedly accosted by others in incidents that were so shatteringly frightening.

The Experiential Value System Is Not Basic, Fundamental, or Universal. The directions of change are closely tied to the experiential model of human beings and to the experiential theory of how change can be helped to occur. In the experiential model and theory, a person is able to become more integrated and actualized, to become a qualitatively new person who can be free of scenes of bad feelings. But there is no law or developmental power or psychobiological force that determines the person should move in these directions. They are mere possibilities that are available. It is the experiential value system that justifies offering the person the opportunity to move in these directions.

Nor is it presumed that the experiential value system is somehow basic to what human beings are really like, somehow fundamental to the nature of human beings, or universal in any grand sense. It is merely the experiential valued directions of change.

Most Therapists Are Self-Appointed Police of Their Own Lists of What They Approve and Disapprove. The directions of change, in experiential psychotherapy, represent an explicit value system. However, there is no predetermined specific content to the directions of change. There is no list of what is good and bad. It is good to move toward increasing integration and actualization, and it is good to be free of scenes of bad feeling. But the experiential therapist cannot say that here are the deeper potentials that are to be integrated and actualized, or here are the bad-feeling scenes of which patients should be free.

In almost stark contrast, it seems to me that most therapists go about their work with their own detailed predetermined lists of what they approve and what they disapprove, and they are self-appointed police in sniffing out disapproved behaviors and in getting patients to abide by the therapist's own personal list of what is to be approved. In actual functioning, I am struck by how very judgemental, how extremely quick most therapists are to moralize, to find this or that as disapproved. Indeed, it is almost as if most of what most therapists do simply oozes with moralistic judgmental disapproval. They operate out of predetermined working lists of what they approve and disapprove, and impose their lists on patients in most sessions. Most therapists have long lists of what is bad, sick, pathological, symptomatic, unhealthy, abnormal, maladjustive, mentally disordered, deviant, and needing "treatment." This long list is organized under scores and scores of categories labelled narcissism, conduct disorder, sexual abuse, masturbation, homosexuality, overcontrolled, undercontrolled, unemotional, overemotional, obsessively religious, and on and on.

Most therapists have a picture of personality that includes inner, deeper forces, impulses, drives that are to be guarded, controlled, watched over, kept down because they are basically bad, disapproved, grotesque, animal, harmful, uncivilized, savage, immoral, or dangerous. Opening up and letting loose what is inside can lead to killing, sexual abuse, rape, pillage, and hundreds of other disapproved items on the disapproved lists.

Most therapists are bristling with keen vigilance at detecting what this patient presents that can be found on the disapproved list. Once this is found, and it almost always is, then the direction of change is toward what this therapist has on her list of approved values, beliefs, practices, and behaviors. And then most therapists are quite skilled at bringing on the big guns to snuff out what is disapproved and to force the person to conform to the approved list.

I believe that there are some worrisome things about the way in which most therapists' personal lists of what is approved and disapproved virtually dominates most of what occurs in psychotherapy. It is bad enough when a few therapists agree with one another on what is to be approved and disapproved. But something scary seems to happen when many bureaucratic, political, energetically administrative therapists agree with one another. Their shared lists become the professionally approved and mandated goals of therapy, the guiding axioms for psychotherapy, the ways that patients are to be. Patients are to develop particular strategies for coping with stress. Patients are to increase their sensitivity to others. Patients are to become more open, genuine, and honest. It is good to apply self-discipline in the use of alcohol, tobacco, and drugs. Be faithful to your marriage partner. Be committed to family needs and child-rearing (Jensen & Bergin, 1988). Most therapists are self-appointed morality police. It scares me that the list of disapproved and approved values, beliefs, practices, and behaviors determines almost everything that most therapists do.

Therapists apply their lists of approved and disapproved values, practices, behaviors, and beliefs with a dedicated vengeance. They work hard at applying rugged pressure against what they disapprove and toward forcing the patient to conform to what the therapists approve. They are more messianic than a cult of frenetic missionaries. They are by no means passive or mild or nonintrusive. The pressure is applied quickly, with firmness and persistence.

These therapists rarely say, "I have a personal list of the beliefs, values, behaviors, and practices of which I approve and of which I disapprove, and I am going to apply this list to you, and I will be relentless." Instead, most therapists hide and disguise what they do. They depersonalize their personal zeal in applying their personal lists. What they are doing is "providing professional services." They are "treating mental disorders and personal problems." Patients "need" "treatment." They are providing "help." Whatever they are doing is codified as working for the "welfare of the client." They elevate what they are doing to a noble profession, all dressed in the guise of ethical–professional codes. All of this is designed to hide that most therapists are the policing enforcers of their own personal lists of what they approve and what they disapprove in their subjects, who are called clients or patients.

Religious–spiritual proponents are generally more honest in pointing to written lists of what the religion condones and approves, and of what the religion considers bad and disapproved. The list is usually public, stated concretely, and can be studied by just about anyone. Most of the followers of most religions can have a pretty good idea of what is approved and disapproved in their religions. Not so with most therapists. They are much more devious in hiding and disguising their own lists. But their own list of what is approved and disapproved is very powerful, always present, and making its presence felt in what is called the patient's problem, mental disorder, treatment plan, therapeutic goals, and treatment outcome.

Most therapists are seductive and deceptive in what they promise patients. They do not say that I am going to force you to conform to my personal list of what I disapprove and approve. Instead, they indirectly indicate that they will provide understanding, interested listening, someone to talk to, caring and positive regard. They say that I will be your confidante, your friend, and your doctor. The unstated part of the promise is that all of this is in the service of getting you to conform to traits I personally approve and disapprove.

It seems to me that most therapies are saturated with value systems of one kind or another, whether or not these are publicly acknowledged. The directions of change and the picture of what optimal human beings can be, in experiential psychotherapy, are an avowed value system. It is merely one among many, and is not put forth as a value system that is basic, fundamental, or universal.

How Do the Valued Directions of Change in Experiential Psychotherapy Compare With the Various Religious–Spiritual Valued Directions of Change?

Some Striking Similarities. The directions of change in experiential psychotherapy can be seen as quite similar to those of many other psychotherapies in the existential–humanistic family. There are also striking similarities between the valued directions of change in experiential psychotherapy and those of many religious–spiritual directions of change. Indeed, from ancient times to today, some shamans, priests, ministers, healers, mystics, spiritual guides, tzaddiks, teachers, and gurus may likewise be understood as helping the person to achieve a higher level of well-being, a higher plateau of consciousness, enlightenment, awakening, nirvana, satori, growth, fulfillment, or integration and actualization; and to achieve freedom from human misery, inner turmoil, or personal anguish and pain—a cleansing of the soul (e.g., Alexander & Selesnick, 1967; Kaplan, 1982, 1985; Kara, 1979; Kopp, 1971; Spero, 1976, 1987; Watts, 1961; Wheelis, 1958). These two directions of change are valued in some religious–spiritual value systems and are quite close to the directions of change in the value system of experiential psychotherapy.

There is also another way in which the two sets of valued directions of change are similar. In experiential psychotherapy, the pursuit of becoming a qualitatively new person, increasingly integrated and actualized, and the pursuit of becoming free of scenes of painfully bad feelings, is essentially a lifelong enterprise. You may have sessions, on and off, throughout your whole life, with regular or varying periods in between. But the pursuit of these directions of change is a lifelong process. In contrast, most therapies start treatment when there is a treatable problem, and treatment is over when treatment is over. You may return later for further treatment, but the common format is five or ten sessions to treat the problem, and that is that. The religious–spiritual format is much closer to that of experiential psychotherapy than to that of most therapies. That is, for most religions and spiritualities, the practices, pursuits, rituals, and behaviors are generally a lifelong process. It is rare that the religion or spirituality is to be followed for five or ten sessions or prayer, ritual-following, or meditation, and some problem is supposed to be cured. On the issue of a few sessions and that is that, or here is a lifelong process to be carried out, experiential psychotherapy and religious–spiritual pursuits are much closer to each other than either is to most therapies with their limited number of sessions to treat the problem.

But the Directions of Change, in Experiential Psychotherapy, Do Not Generally Include the Carrying out of Particular Religious–Spiritual Practices, Rituals, Behaviors, or Beliefs. In experiential psychotherapy, the person is to move toward becoming optimal, the person is to become a qualitatively new person, the person is to be free of scenes of bad feeling. But here is no list of specific ways of being, specific practices, behaviors, characteristics, or beliefs that go with becoming optimal, or becoming a qualitatively new person, or being free of scenes of bad-feelings. The directions of change are marvelously particularized to this particular person.

In rather sharp contrast, some religions and spiritualities do have a list of relatively specific behaviors, beliefs, rituals, characteristics, and practices that identify the optimal person. Many religions and spiritualities do have specific lists of how the person should be, what the person is to be like, how the person should strive to think, believe, act, and behave. Experiential psychotherapy cannot provide such a list.

Some surveys of therapists indicate that a fair proportion of therapists do share lists of how patients are to be, behave, think, and act (Bergin, 1980, 1985, 1991; Bergin & Jensen, 1990; Jensen & Bergin, 1988). According to these surveys, many therapists' lists include active participation in a religious affiliation, being faithful to one's marriage partner, preference for heterosexual rather than homosexual relationships, making restitution for one's negative influence, and forgiving others who have inflicted harm on you. However, none of these are ways the person is necessarily to be in experiential therapy, nor would experiential psychotherapy have any kind of list of optimal behaviors, practices, beliefs, or actions.

In Experiential Psychotherapy, How Do You Arrive at the Particular Way of Being and Particular Behavior That May Be Good for This Person? Arriving at the particular way of being means finding the deeper potential for experiencing that is to become a central part of how the qualitatively new person is to be. By the end of the first step, the therapist and client have probably discovered what it is, and by the end of the second step the person has probably welcomed and appreciated the deeper potential. The therapist and client know that the person is to become a person who is able to experience whatever the deeper potential is. So the person is to be able to experience gentleness, softness, delicacy, to be independent, autonomous, on one's own, or being dominant, controlling, in charge.

The tougher question is what specific behaviors in what specific situations are fitting, acceptable, useful, and accompanied with good feelings in the actual being of this qualitatively new person. Answering this question is the job of step 4. It relies on the person's own immediate degree of readiness and willingness to be this new way. It relies on a careful set of rehearsals, of tryings-out, of altering and modifying behaviors and situational contexts. It relies on the person's seeing if this way of behaving in this situation context is accompanied with good feelings of tranquility, peacefulness, togetherness, inner harmony, oneness, and good feelings of excitement, aliveness, vibrancy, and joy. It relies on giving each part of the person plenty of opportunity to voice its own reactions to the prospective new way of being and behaving in the likely situation. It relies on the person's own readiness and willingness to be committed to being this way in this situation.

By the end of the initial session, Samuel was able to identify several situations and actual ways to be that seemed to enable this new person to gain a sense of experiencing the newfound softness, pliancy, docility, weakness, helplessness. In the session, he rehearsed and refined ways of allowing himself to be this new way in love-making with his wife, and in spending playtime with both of his children, and also in entrusting more responsibility to particular subordinates in his department. These new ways of being and behaving felt right and good, and he committed himself to perhaps actually undergoing them in his real life after the session.

There Are Some Striking Differences With Religionists and Spiritualists for Whom the Direction of Change Is the Reduction of Mental Disorders and Pathological Problems. Some religionists and spiritualists have essentially accepted traditional psychotherapies' notion that the direction of change is mainly to treat and to reduce the mental disorder and the person's pathological problems. These religionists and spiritualists try to show that religious and spiritual factors can be helpful in treating mental disorders and pathological problems. They try to demonstrate that religious and spiritual backgrounds and beliefs of therapist and patient can make a difference in the treatment of mental disorders and pathological problems. They would like religious and spiritual factors to be more acknowledged in the official nomenclature of mental disorders (Lukoff, Lu, & Turner, 1992). They try to show that the patient's religious and spiritual history, beliefs, and practices can be helpful in understanding the patient's mental disorder and pathological problems.

For experiential therapists, the directions of change include enabling the person to become a qualitatively new person, based upon the person's own deeper potentials, and also to enable the person to be free of the scenes of bad feelings that were so troublesome and painful. For some religionists and spiritualists, the directions of change are mainly to reduce the mental disorder and the pathological problems. The two sets of directions of change seem to be strikingly different.

How Do the Experiential Directions of Change Accommodate or Risk the Person's Own Religious–Spiritual Values, Beliefs, Practices, and Behaviors? In some rather explicit ways, the experiential directions of change accommodate, honor, respect, follow, and take account of the person's own religious–spiritual values, beliefs, practices, and behaviors. All of this occurs mainly in the fourth and final step of the session in which the person is able to taste and sample what it can be like to be the qualitatively new person in the world of the present and prospective future.

Suppose that the deeper potential is the experiencing of defiance, rebellion, opposition, standing up to others. Under what conditions, in what situations, can the new person be this new way? How may the new person behave, what may the new person do, to enable a good-feeling experiencing of being defiant, rebellious, oppositional, standing up to others? It is here that the person's own other potentials for experiencing are explicitly invited to have their say. It is here that the person may decline being and behaving in this new way in particular contexts and in ways that violate or conflict with their person's own religious–spiritual values, beliefs, practices, and behaviors. Whatever the person may finally rehearse and be inclined to carry out, it is to be accompanied with good feelings of integration and actualization. This means that the person's own feelings help to approve or veto the prospective new way of being and behaving. It may feel right to carry out this new-felt experiencing of being defiant, rebellious, and oppositional in standing up to the proposed change in the committee structure at work. It may not feel right, good, solid, exciting, vibrant to be this new way and to behave in new ways with regard to the religious rituals during the religious holiday.

However, there is a way in which the valued experiential directions of change may well risk the person's religious–spiritual values, beliefs, practices, and behaviors. In both existentialism and the experiential model of human beings (Mahrer, 1989), there is a magnificent risk in becoming a qualitatively new person, in the existential leap into the abyss, in letting go of who and what one is, in disengaging from one's own identity and self, in becoming a qualitatively new being based upon the deeper potential. There is a magnificent risk in undergoing truly deep-seated change. The risk is that you may sacrifice, surrender, and no longer be the person whom you were. The risk is that you may enhance, may become more of, or you may no longer be, the person who has the same old religious–spiritual values, beliefs, practices, and behaviors. If the deeper potential is the experiencing of rebelliousness, defiance, and opposition, the risk of integrating and actualizing this deeper potential is that you may no longer be the person you were.

In the existential–experiential model, it is the relatively surface, functioning, operating, behaving, feeling, or thinking person who holds the religious–spiritual values, beliefs, practices, and behaviors. Integration and actualization of what lies deeper, the true becoming of a qualitatively new person usually means risking the surface, functioning, operating person that you are. There may be a change in the person who held those religious–spiritual values, beliefs, and who carried out the religious–spiritual practices and behaviors. The risk of deep-seated existential–humanistic change is that you may also change.

Samuel remained a moderately religious person. But, as indicated in the next session and in subsequent sessions, he seemed to become a qualitatively new person who can undergo and experience a newfound softness, pliancy, docility, being weak and helpless in ways that were accompanied with good feelings. He carried out the changes he had intended to carry out after the session, both at home with his wife and children and also at work. Additionally, there were few if any further instances of being so painfully frozen and terrified as he had been in the scene of being accosted by the old man. The compelling nature of that incident seemed to fade away. He also let go of spending so many hours being engrossed in reading religious texts about death, spells, and the occult, and the frightening intensity of the feelings that gripped him during these periods. He was seemingly free of these scenes of such bad feeling. There were changes, some perhaps dramatic, in Samuel. Yet he remained the moderately religious person he had been before these scenes of bad feeling.

CONCLUSIONS

1. As one illustrative representative of the existential–humanistic family, each session of experiential psychotherapy can enable the person (a) to become a qualitatively new person, based upon the inner deeper potential for experiencing, and (b) to be free of the troubling, bothersome, scenes of strong, bad feeling that were front and center in this session. There is an explicit sequence of steps to help bring about these changes, starting from the person's own scenes of strong feeling.
2. These changes can occur whether or not the person or therapist is religious, and whether or not the scenes of strong feeling are religious–spiritual.
3. In the experiential model of human beings, the basic foundation is composed of deeper potentials for experiencing. These are neither universal nor necessarily religious–spiritual in their nature or content.
4. In experiential psychotherapy, change occurs by welcoming–appreciating (integration) and then by being the deeper po-

tential for experiencing (actualization). This grand avenue of change is also the way in some religions and spiritualities.

5. The experiential directions of change (a) constitute an explicit set of precious values, (b) bear some striking similarities with some religious–spiritual directions of change, (c) are rather different from some other religious–spiritual valued directions of change, and (d) both accommodate and risk the person's own religious–spiritual values, beliefs, practices, and behaviors.

6. Therapists for whom religion and spirituality may be personally meaningful are invited to adopt experiential psychotherapy as one illustrative member of the existential–humanistic family.

REFERENCES

Achterberg, J. (1988). The wounded healer: Transformational journeys in modern medicine. In G. Doore (Ed.), *Shaman's path* (pp. 187–218). Boston: Shambhala.

Alexander, F. G., & Selesnick, S. T. (1967). *The history of psychiatry.* London: George Allen and Unwin.

Allport, G. W. (1950). *The individual and his religion: A psychological interpretation.* New York: Macmillan.

Anderson, R. G., & Young, J. L. (1988). The religious component of acute hospital treatment. *Hospital and Community Psychiatry, 39,* 528–533.

Angyal, A. (1965). *Neurosis and treatment: A holistic theory.* New York: Wiley.

Bergin, A. E. (1980). Psychotherapy and religious values. *Journal of Consulting and Clinical Psychology, 48,* 95–105.

Bergin, A. E. (1985). Proposed values for guiding and evaluating counseling and psychotherapy. *Counseling and Values, 29,* 99–116.

Bergin, A. E. (1988). Three contributions of a spiritual perspective to counseling, psychotherapy, and behavior change. *Counseling and Values, 33,* 21–31.

Bergin, A. E. (1991). Values and religious issues in psychotherapy and mental health. *American Psychologist, 46,* 394–403.

Bergin, A. E., & Jensen, J. (1990). Religiosity of psychotherapists: A national survey. *Psychotherapy, 27,* 3–7.

Binswanger, L. (1958). The existential analysis school of thought. In R. May, E. Angel, & H. F. Ellenberger (Eds.), *Existence: A new dimension in psychiatry and psychology* (pp. 191–213). New York: Basic Books.

Binswanger, L. (1967). *Being-in-the-world.* New York: Harper Torchbooks.

Buber, M. (1958). *I-thou.* New York: Scribner.

Bugental, J. F. T. (1970). *The search for existential identity.* San Francisco: Jossey-Bass.

Burton, A. (1972). *Interpersonal psychotherapy.* Englewood Cliffs, NJ: Prentice Hall.

Campbell, D. T. (1975). On the conflicts between biological and social evolution and between psychology and moral tradition. *American Psychologist, 30,* 1103–1120.

Eisenbruch, M. (1992). Commentary. Toward a culturally sensitive DSM: Cultural bereavement in Cambodian refugees and the traditional healer as taxonomist. *Journal of Nervous and Mental Disease, 180,* 8–10.

Fadiman, J. (1980). The transpersonal stance. In M. J. Mahoney (Ed.), *Psychotherapy process: Current issues and future directions* (pp. 35–44). New York: Plenum Press.

Fischer, C. T. (1985). *Individualizing psychological assessment.* Monterey, CA: Brooks/Cole.

Frankl, V. E. (1959). *From death camp to existentialism.* Boston: Beacon Press.

Frankl, V. E. (1969). *The will to meaning.* Don Mills, Canada: General.

Freud, S. (1949). *Civilization and its discontents.* London: Hogarth. (original work published 1930)

Grof, S., & Grof, C. (Eds.). (1989). *Spiritual emergency: When personal transformation becomes a crisis.* Los Angeles: Tarcher.

Group for the Advancement of Psychiatry (1976). *Mysticism: Spiritual quest or mental disorder.* New York: Author.

Havens, L. L. (1974). The existential use of the self. *The American Journal of Psychiatry, 131,* 1–10.

Hole, G. (1971). Some comparisons among guilt-feelings, religion, and suicidal tendencies in depressed patients. *Suicide and Life-Threatening Behavior, 1,* 138–142.

Hood, R. W. (1974). Psychological strength and the report of intense religious experience. *Journal of the Scientific Study of Religion, 13,* 65–71.

James. W. (1961). *The varieties of religious experience.* New York: Macmillan.

Jensen, J. P., & Bergin, A. E. (1988). Mental health values of professional therapists: A national interdisciplinary survey. *Professional Psychology: Research and Practice, 19,* 290–297.

Jung, C. G. (1973). *Psychology and religion.* Princeton, NJ: Princeton University Press.

Kaplan, A. (1982). *Meditation and kabbalah.* York Beach, ME: Weiser.

Kaplan, A. (1985). *Jewish meditation: A practical guide.* New York: Schoken.

Kapleau, P. (Ed.). (1967). *The three pillars of Zen.* Boston: Beacon.

Kara, A. (1979). The guru and the therapist: Goals and techniques in regard to the question of the chela and patient. *Psychotherapy: Theory, Research and Practice, 16,* 61–71.

Kopp, S. B. (1971). *Guru: Metaphors from a psychotherapist.* Palo Alto, California: Science and Behavior Books.

Krippner, S., & Welch, P. (1992). *Spiritual dimensions of healing.* New York: Irvington.

London, P. (1964). *The modes and morals of psychotherapy.* New York: Holt, Rinehart, & Winston.

Lowe, C. M. (1976). *Value orientations in counseling and psychotherapy: The meanings of mental health* (2nd ed.). Cranston, RI: Carroll.

Lukoff, D. (1991). Divine madness: Shamanistic initiatory crisis and psychosis. *Shaman's Drum, 22,* 24–29.

Lukoff, D., Lu, F., & Turner, R. (1992). Toward a more culturally sensitive DSM-IV. *Journal of Nervous and Mental Disease, 180,* 673–682.

Mahrer, A. R. (1989). *Experiencing: A humanistic theory of psychology and psychiatry.* Ottawa, Canada: University of Ottawa Press. (original work published 1978)

Mahrer, A. R. (1996). *The complete guide to experiential psychotherapy.* New York: Wiley.

Mahrer, A. R. (in press). Empathy as therapist-client alignment. In A. C. Bohart & L. S. Greenberg (Eds.), *Empathy and psychotherapy: New directions to theory, research, and practice.* Washington, D.C.: American Psychological Association.

Mahrer, A. R., Boulet, D. B., & Fairweather, D. R. (1994). Beyond empathy: Advances in the clinical theory and methods of empathy. *Clinical Psychology Review, 14,* 183–198.

Mahrer, A. R., & Fairweather, D. R. (1993). What is "experiencing"? A critical review of meanings and applications in psychotherapy. *The Humanistic Psychologist, 21,* 2–25.

Malony, H. N. (1972). The psychologist-Christian. *Journal of the American Scientific Affiliation, 24,* 129–144.

Maslow, A. H. (1968). *Toward a psychology of being* (2nd ed.). New York: Van Nostrand Reinhold.

Maslow, A. H. (1973). *The farther reaches of human nature.* New York: Viking.

Maslow, A. H. (1970). *Motivation and personality* (2nd ed.). New York: Harper and Row.

May, R. (1989). *The art of counseling.* New York: Gardner Press.

Moody, R. A. (1975). *Life after death.* New York: Bantam Books.

Nelson, F. I. (1977). Religiosity and self-destructive crises in the institutionalized elderly. *Suicide and Life-Threatening Behavior, 7,* 67–74.

Owens, C. M. (1975). Zen Buddhism. In C. Tart (Ed.), *Transpersonal psychologies* (pp. 155–202). New York: Harper & Row.

Peterson, E. A., & Nelson, K. (1987). How to meet your clients' spiritual needs. *Journal of Psychosocial Nursing, 25,* 34–39.

Propst, R. L. (1980). A comparison of the cognitive restructuring psychotherapy paradigm and several spiritual approaches to mental health. *Journal of Psychology and Theology, 8,* 107–114.

Rogers, C. R. (1957). The necessary and sufficient conditions of therapeutic personality change. *Journal of Consulting Psychology, 21*, 95–103.

Rogers, C. R. (1959). A theory of therapy, personality, and interpersonal relationships as developed in the client-centered framework. In S. Koch (Ed.), *Psychology: A study of a science* (pp. 221–231). New York: McGraw-Hill.

Rogers, C. R. (1970). *On becoming a person.* Boston: Houghton Mifflin.

Rogers, C. R. (1973). Some new challenges. *American Psychologist, 28*, 379–387.

Rogers, C. R. (1975). Empathic: An unappreciated way of being. *The Counseling Psychologist, 5*, 2–10.

Rothbaum, F., Weisz, J. R., & Snyder, S. S. (1982). Changing the world and changing the self: A two-process model of perceived control. *Journal of Personality and Social Psychology, 42*, 5–37.

Rowan, J. (1991). *Subpersonalities: The people inside us.* London: Routledge & Kegan Paul.

Shafranske, E. P., & Gorsuch, R. L. (1984). Factors associated with the perception of spirituality in psychotherapy. *Journal of Transpersonal Psychology, 16*, 231–241.

Shafranske, E. P., & Malony, H. N. (1990). Clinical psychologists' religious and spiritual orientations and their practice of psychotherapy. *Psychotherapy, 27*, 72–78.

Spero, M. H. (1976). On the relationship between psychotherapy and Judaism. *Journal of Psychotherapy and Judaism, 1*, 15–33.

Spero, M. H. (1987). Identity and individuality in the nouveau-religious patient: Theoretical and clinical aspects. *Psychiatry, 50*, 55–71.

Spilka, B. (1986). Spiritual issues: Do they belong in psychological practice? Yes—But! *Psychotherapy in Private Practice, 4*, 93–100.

Spilka, B., Hood, R. W. Jr., & Gorsuch, R. L. (1985). *The psychology of religion: An empirical approach.* Englewood Cliffs, NJ: Prentice Hall.

Walsh, R., & Roche, L. (1979). Precipitation of acute psychotic episodes by intensive meditation in individuals with a history of schizophrenia. *American Journal of Psychiatry, 136*, 1085–1086.

Watts, A. W. (1961). *Psychotherapy east and west.* New York: Pantheon Books.

Weisz, J. R., Rothbaum, F. M., & Blackburn, T. C. (1984). Standing out and standing in: The psychology of control in America and Japan. *American Psychologist, 34*, 955–969.

Wheelis, A. (1958). *The quest for identity.* New York: Norton.

Yalom, I. D. (1980). *Existential psychotherapy.* New York: Basic Books.

Young, J. L., & Griffith, E. E. (1989). The development and practice of pastoral counseling. *Hospital and Community Psychiatry, 40*, 271–276.

17

SWITCHING TRACKS: PARALLEL PARADIGMS IN PSYCHOLOGY AND RELIGION

JOHN R. VAN EENWYK

In short, the "sacred" is an element in the structure of consciousness . . .

Mircea Eliade (1971, p. ii)

When religious issues are brought to psychotherapy, how are they to be addressed? Do patients who insist on framing issues solely in religious terms, displaying either ignorance of or hostility to psychological constructs, create an insoluble impasse in psychotherapy? What about therapists who display similar rigidities about religion? When faced with such an impasse, some practitioners confine themselves to the religious perspective of the patient, while others try to convert the patient to one or another of their favorite psychological theories. Neither approach adequately integrates psychology and religion, however, because each demands that one participant defer to the *Weltanschauung* of the other.

Practitioners would do better "to discover the conditions in which systems of truth become mutually convertible and therefore simultaneously acceptable to several different subjects" (as cited in O'Flaherty, 1988, p. 10). In the philosophy of comparative religion, for example, O'Flaherty proposes a theoretical analog to the railroad roundhouse, "that place where all the tracks of a railway meet so that the train may pass from any one track to any other" (p. 10). With regard to psychology and religion, such a roundhouse would be a "place where we can move from the track of one

This chapter was based in part on a previous article, "Switching tracks in psychotherapy: Parallel paradigms in psychology and religion," published in the *Journal of Contemporary Psychotherapy*, 19(4), 1989, Human Sciences Press.

461

person's reality to another's" (p. 10), that is, from religious ideation to psychological constructs and back again.

A good roundhouse should help practitioners to establish dialogues in a language patients understand that respect the orientations of both. Yet the roundhouse is only a switching device, a means of moving from psychology to religion and back again, for

> The roundhouse . . . is a place that we must reach in order to get off our track and onto someone else's track, but it is not a place to settle down into. Like New York, the roundhouse is a place to visit, not a place to live in. (O'Flaherty, 1988, p. 10)

Thus, practitioners who use the roundhouse to enjoin the religious perspectives of those patients who view their lives primarily or exclusively in terms of religious ideation must choose for themselves whatever psychological theory they wish to use in framing interpretations and interventions.

To function as a transition between psychology and religion, such a roundhouse must have a "track" common to both. To see if the roundhouse metaphor is consistent with a psychological theory, in this chapter I compare it with the work of C. G. Jung for two reasons: (a) Jung speaks of agencies within the psyche itself; and (b) he posits a design that informs the intent of those agencies. Seeing how the roundhouse applies to Jung's theories, therefore, should also help to see how it applies to religious issues within the therapeutic context.

THE METAPSYCHOLOGY OF JUNG

Let us assume that the word *agency* refers simply to any functioning capacity that possess some degree of autonomy that, *intent* is the purpose or direction manifested by the activity of the agent, and that *design* is the plan or schema that informs the intent of the agent. How does the psychology of Jung see the relations between these ideas?

Agency

A fundamental principle of Jung's metapsychology is that the ego is only one among many functioning centers in the psyche, all of which participate in the organism's adaptation and growth. They derive from instincts, which motivate the organism, and archetypes, which enable it to recognize the goal of the instinct. For example, the behavior of newborns is hardly the result of rational reflection. One could argue that learning occurs simply as a result of trial and error, but Jung had become intrigued by patients institutionalized at the Burgholzli who seemed to know things that they obviously had never learned. Thus, he reasoned, more than just consciousness must be involved in learning. To the extent that early childhood survival is something more than random trial and error, he reasoned, it must depend less on the ego than on other functioning centers in the psyche. These other agents of psychological development that are involved with psychological growth constitute the basic structure of the psyche.

Instincts generate feelings of need. Archetypes, which are the psychic components of instincts, connect needs with images. Thus, when the instinct of hunger is combined with the archetypal image of the nipple, eating behavior ensues. As instincts and archetypes continue to invest perceptions and experiences with feelings, affectively valenced networks—called *complexes*—are formed. Through their affective valences, or feeling-tones, complexes assimilate similar perceptions and experiences. As time goes on, their influence increases (Jung, 1919/1978).

As potentials for apprehending and organizing experience become activated in a child's interactions with the environment, psychological development progresses. It is by no means a smooth process. For one thing, the child's needs do not always coincide with the environment's. When they don't, frustration leads to an awareness of the disparity between the felt-need and the lack of response from the surround. This awareness stands apart from the feeling-tones of the other complexes and slowly consolidates into an identity of its own. Jung defined this as the experiencing subject of consciousness, which he called the "ego."

The ego is also a complex. Unlike the other complexes, however, whose associations are organized through feelings, the ego's associations cluster around that which is traditionally defined as consciousness: reflection, logic, comparison, differentiation, and definition, for example. Thus, although it shares with the other complexes the capacity to organize perceptions and experiences, such organization is not affectively valenced. By the time the ego develops sufficient power to organize perceptions and experiences through consciousness, the complexes have been doing so through feelings for years. Consequently, the affective power of the complexes competes with the ego's efforts to order things consciously. Sometimes, when the ego chooses to behave rationally, the complexes prove the more powerful, suffusing ego-consciousness with their feeling-tones, leading to emotionally based behavior (Jung, 1934/1978). When behavior is dominated by the complexes, the locus of agency resides in the unconscious.

Jung said that "there is no difference in principle between a fragmentary personality and a complex . . . complexes are splinter personalities" (Jung, 1934/1978, par. 202). Awareness of complexes is an ambiguous enterprise, however, for the ego is generally unaccustomed to acknowledging inner agencies other than its own. Rather, it tends to project their influence onto the surround. If the environment can contain the projections, all proceeds in the classic psychoanalytic fashion: One encounters dimensions of oneself in others. But if it cannot (for example, when the archetypal valence is very high), the ego tends to perceive its projection carriers in the nonmaterial realm. Jung (1928/1978) said,

> [T]he powers which men have always projected into space as gods, and worshiped with sacrifices, are still alive and active in our own unconscious psyche. . . . [This does not mean that the] manifold religious practices and beliefs . . . [can] be traced back, however, to the whimsical fancies and opinions of individuals, . . . [but rather] to the influence of unconscious powers which we cannot neglect without disturbing the psychic balance. (par. 728)

If one's perception of agencies in the cosmos has its counterpart in one's own psyche, then the first attribute of our roundhouse would be the composite nature of the psyche. But Jung's theory also says that the activity of the internal agencies, or complexes, is not simply random. Rather, it is purposive. Thus, Jung's roundhouse can accommodate another element of religion as well, that of intent.

Intent

Jung (1928/1978) was quite adamant about the role that the unconscious plays in psychological development:

> If, therefore, I had to name the most essential thing that Analytical Psychology can add to our *Weltanschauung*, I should say it is the recognition that there exist certain unconscious contents which make demands that cannot be denied, or send forth influences with which the unconscious mind must come to terms, whether it will or no. (par. 713)

The activities of the complexes are not simply random, but compensate one another for the purpose of self-regulation and growth. Grounding his theory on the premise that "there is no balance, no system of self-regulation, without opposition" (Jung, 1917/1978, par. 92), Jung drew the conclusion that "the unconscious processes that compensate the conscious ego contain all those elements that are necessary for the self-regulation of the psyche as a whole" (Jung, 1916/1978, par. 275).

For example, whenever ego functioning fails to consider the multitude of possibilities and dimensions of life, which is an inevitable consequence of the limitations of consciousness, complexes that express opposite perspectives become activated. As the feeling-tones of their associations intensify, images appear that command the ego's attention and elicit its response. These powerful images, called *symbols*, function much like the "fictions" described in theologian David Tracy's writings (1975), which "do not operate to help us escape reality, but to re-describe our human reality in such disclosive terms that we return to the 'everyday' reoriented to life's real—if forgotten or sometimes never even imagined—possibilities" (p. 207). Thus, symbols that are generated by the activity of unconscious agencies reflect their intent to balance the limited perspective of the ego by drawing it into experiences that expand its consciousness.

When the unconscious presents the ego with images that are the opposite of its viewpoint, a tension inevitably develops. Jung (1928/1978) said,

> The development of consciousness and of free will naturally brings with it the possibility of deviating from the archetype and hence from instinct. Once the deviation sets in a dissociation between consciousness and the unconscious ensues, then the activity of the unconscious begins. This is usually felt as very unpleasant, for it takes the form of an inner, unconscious fixation which expresses itself only symptomatically, that is, indirectly. (par. 724)

Sometimes, particularly if the ego is weak or insufficiently developed, it chooses to avoid the task and to suppress the conflict it feels. In this case, it substitutes its own intent (avoidance) for that of the complex (balance and growth). On the other hand, "there exist certain unconscious contents which make demands that cannot be denied, or send forth influences with which the conscious mind must come to terms, whether it will or no" (Jung, 1928/1978, par. 713). These the ego cannot suppress.

Trying to avoid conflict might lead simply to "unpleasant" feelings were that conflict not a manifestation of a design for growth inherent in the psyche. Symbols "pursue definite, unconscious lines of direction which converge upon a definite goal" (Jung, 1916/1978, par. 384). This goal is, according to Jung, the fulfillment of one's potential to meet the challenges of life. The ego that seeks to escape the intent of the unconscious agencies of the psyche risks being in conflict with its own opportunities for psychological development. Like the one who resists the will of God, such an ego finds itself excluded from the "divine" plan.

This is the last, and perhaps most important, aspect of the roundhouse provided by Jung's theories. Practitioners who can discern the underlying intent of the unconscious forces that trouble their patients gain the opportunity to help their patients interpret the design, or meaning, of those forces. At this point it matters little whether such forces are called "unconscious" or "divine," for the result is the same: The ego must expand its consciousness.

Design

If the unconscious plays a part in the development and regulation of the psyche, how does it make its choices? Intent is a fairly automatic process that restores balance through tensions of opposites. On what is the intent of the various agencies within the psyche based? Somewhere there must be a design that considers the end toward which intent is mobilized. Among the more common designs among theories of psychology—including Jung's—are adaptation, survival, and growth. But while most theories are fairly relaxed about how design occurs, most often attributing it to a general urge, drive, or instinct for survival, competence, actualization, or what-have-you, Jung localized it in a supraordinate agency that is the essence of the psyche itself. He called this agency the *self*.

Of course, simply positing an entity such as the self does not guarantee that such an entity exists. Nevertheless to explain how the self stands in relation to the other archetypes, one "post-Jungian" draws an analogy with the endocrine system:

> A bodily parallel would be the glands; they each have their own organizing function, but in health they are regulated or balanced in relation to each other by a dynamic in the whole body. Without that their specific organizing function is useless. In maturation, sometimes one predominates and sometimes another, e.g. sex hormones. So the picture is not one of static "order" but rather a dynamic integration. Similarly, archetypes have their own organizing function but need to be related to the whole. (Samuels, 1985, p. 90)

The self is the dynamic in the psyche that integrates all of its diverse elements, including the ego, into a coherent whole. It demonstrates the same intent as the other archetypes, namely, compensation and balance, but in a more reflective manner. It seeks adaptation, growth, and the fulfillment of each individual's unique potential. By relating the organizing functions of the archetypes to the whole, the self is the agent that integrates the intent of the other agents into its design.

The self runs the show from birth. As the agent that administers the design, it is the archetype of the archetypes, so to speak. As the ultimate source of meaning within the psyche, it produces symbols that "pursue definite, unconscious lines of direction that coverage upon a definite goal" (Jung, 1916/1978, par. 384). For example, when tensions of opposites occur that the ego cannot resolve, the self generates "uniting symbols" that restore the balance. Sometimes called the "transcendent function," this dynamic refers not to some divine or other-worldly character, but to the self's ability to transcend the particulars in which the ego becomes enmeshed (Jung, 1957/1978, pars. 131–193). Consequently,

> The ego stands to the self as the moved to the mover, or as object to subject, because the determining factors which radiate out from the self surround the ego on all sides and are therefore supraordinate to it. The self, like the unconscious, is an *a priori* existent out of which the ego evolves. (Jung, 1954/1977, par. 391)

Given this relationship between ego and self, it is no wonder that Jung believed that uniting symbols are so powerful that they appear in all the major religions of the world: "For psychology the self is an *Imago Dei* and cannot be distinguished from it empirically. The two ideas are therefore of the same nature" (Jung, 1912/1976, par. 612). If the self and God resemble one another phenomenologically, Jung said, the ego will experience them as similar.

Notions of the self as the progenitor of the ego as well as the guardian of design are the basis on which Jung examined data previously considered the domain of religion. Having found Jung's theory to be compatible with the three elements of the roundhouse, I will now examine his technique to see how he applied his theory in the consulting room.

INTRODUCTION TO TECHNIQUE

Essential to Jungian analysis is the sealing off of analyst and patient in a *temenos*, or secured place, where anything can happen. The boundaries of the analytic frame, which include restrictions on contact both within and outside the consulting room, free patient and analyst to experience together the symbols that arise in the patient's psyche, the effect they have on the analyst, and the response of the analyst's unconscious to the material presented by the patient. In effect, patient and analyst mix their psyches together to see what happens (Jung, 1946/1977, pars. 367, 375).

Not surprisingly, this can be quite an intimidating process for the patient. Typically, patients begin their analyses hoping that their analysts will provide them with answers to their questions, solutions to their problems, and ways out of their dilemmas. After all, why else would they pay such high prices to sit with someone for 50 minutes? Yet, how much more difficult is the process of analysis! As Jung said, "the suitably trained analyst mediates the transcendent function of the patient, i.e., helps him to bring conscious and unconscious together and so arrive at a new attitude" (Jung, 1957/1978, par. 146). Thus, the goal of analysis has less to do with understanding symbols, and even less with solving problems, than with forging a working relationship between ego and unconscious.

This principle is especially evident in Jung's views of the transference. He speaks of transference in the classic sense, as having to do with projections of the patient onto the analyst; however, he does not believe that the analyst's counter-transference is necessarily counterproductive, rather,

> a transference is answered by a counter-transference from the analyst when it projects a content of which he is unconscious but which nevertheless exists in him. The counter-transference is then just as useful and meaningful, or as much of a hindrance, as the transference of the

patient, according to whether or not it seeks to establish that better rapport which is essential for the realization of unconscious contents. (Jung, 1920/1978, par. 519)

The projection of the patient that forms the transference reflects the patient's relationship with the unconscious. Consequently, the real focus of the analysis is not so much on the transference to the analyst than to the unconscious.

Of course, much of people's relationships with the unconscious are based on their experiences of their parents. Parents are the ones who first mediate to their children a world that is largely unknown, but in which the children shall have eventually to function. The manner in which parents (biological, adoptive, or surrogate) introduce children to the world around them, as well as to the world within themselves, colors children's relationship with the unknown, the yet-to-be-realized, that which exceeds their powers of rational thought. It is understandable that when analysis begins, patients habitually expect that their analysts will function much as did their parents. Exploring the degree to which that is either accurate or not forms the first level of transference work (Jung, 1946/1977, par. 357, 363).

The second level is that of the patient's transference to the unconscious. Often, the first task of analysis is to make the patient aware that the unconscious exists. Again, giving something a name does not assure insight into, let alone control over, whatever that something is. At its most basic, the word *unconscious* refers simply to that which is not conscious. But given the agency, intent, and design that Jung included in his characterizations of the unconscious, the matter becomes more complex. This unconscious is an "other" that operates alongside the ego within the same psyche. The awareness of dreams, projections, and transferences is all predicated on confusion between what belongs to us and what belongs to others. When patients begin to discern that much of the otherness that they ascribe to the surround is actually themselves, complications ensue.

Much of Jungian analysis is focused on this second level of transference. For example, patients who were taught by their parents that life is simple and "we are only what we perceive ourselves and others to be" have a more difficult time acknowledging the unconscious than do patients who were taught that much of life is virtually unspecifiable. While Jung warned that

> consistent support of the conscious attitude has in itself a high therapeutic value and not infrequently serves to bring about satisfactory results. It would be a dangerous prejudice to imagine that analysis of the unconscious is the one and only panacea which should therefore be employed in every case[,] (Jung, 1946/1977, par. 381)

he also believed that when the agency of the unconscious manifested an unopposable intent, the patient would have to take notice.

It is at this point—when the patient is acutely aware of the activity of the unconscious—that Jungian analysis uses a number of techniques to enrich the relationship between ego and unconscious. The first is the subjective interpretation of unconscious material. With regard to dreams, for example, everything in the dream is taken to be a manifestation of dynamics in the patient's unconscious. If the patient dreams of a goat that nibbles on an olive tree while a snake scampers away, then the the goat, tree, and snake reflect the patient's intrapsychic dynamics.

The significance of the subjective approach is that the patient's input is essential for the interpretation of symbols. What the dream awakens in the patient is as important as the opinion of the analyst. In working with dreams, for example, the patient is placed in the leadership role in the exploration of the unconscious. The analyst is along for the ride, so to speak, lending support, encouragement, and another point of view when the patient gets stuck. Because "in the end it makes very little difference whether the doctor understands or not, but it makes all the difference whether the patient understands. Understanding should therefore be understanding in the sense of an agreement which is the fruit of joint reflection" (Jung, 1943/1977, par. 314). By focusing on their own associations to dream images, patients learn how to explore themselves.

Once an image of the unconscious has been recognized, there are techniques for integrating it with consciousness. It can be represented through a concrete image, as in a drawing or sculpture, or it can be entered into through physical expression, as in dance. Active imagination, whereby patients can ask questions and wait for answers to appear in their imaginations, engages the images from dreams. Such a dialogue stretches the ego into the realm of the unconscious while providing something tangible on which it can focus.

Patients soon discover that their personal unconscious material has a strange resonance with symbols that have influenced humankind throughout its history. In the dream cited above, for example, goats, olive trees, and snakes have had a fairly consistent effect on the human imagination. Consequently, personal symbols open the individual consciousness to the archetypal dynamics on which all human psyches are based. Analysts must be conversant with the diversity and range of images that have been symbolic both to particular groups and to humankind in general. For example, snakes have been seen as symbolic of the devil (the Garden of Eden), healing (the caduceus), resurrection (they shed their skins), the Great Mother (the uroboros), and so on. By amplifying images with their more general counterparts, analysts can demonstrate to patients how that which is personal reflects that which is collective. This helps to relieve the troubling feelings of isolation that everyone feels when besieged by internal chaos. Knowing that humankind has had similar experiences throughout its history makes people feel less crazy when it happens to them.

APPROACHES TO RELIGIOUS MATERIAL

And so, the analytic process aims at relieving distress through the integration of inner psychological dynamics with the ego and with humankind. Ultimately, analysis should be a reconciling experience. Nevertheless, as psychology traces its lineage to science, the other with whom we must perceive a connection—an other that, like God, both transcends and cares about us—resides in ourselves. As William James (1929) said, "Let me then propose, as a hypothesis, that whatever it may be on its *farther* side, the 'more' with which in religious experience we feel ourselves connected is on its *hither* side the subconscious continuation of our conscious life" (p. 502). As is the hither side the domain of science, so is the farther side the domain of religion.

That agency, intent, and design are also metaphors of religion, consider the following statements, one from a historian of religions, the other from a theologian. Mircea Eliade (1985) maintained that "*insofar as he is a spiritual being*, man partakes of a divine condition, and most notably of the function and destiny of the gods of the cosmic structure" (p. 266). Rudolph Otto (1969) wrote that "to become consciously aware of . . . 'the holy' . . . [as] an operant reality, intervening actively in the phenomenal world . . . is a fundamental conviction of all religions, of religions as such" (p. 143). Jung, the son of a clergyman and the grandson of a philosopher, tried to be true to both science and religion, saying,

> It is only through the psyche that we can establish that God acts upon us, but we are unable to distinguish whether these actions emanate from God or from the unconscious. We cannot tell whether God and the unconscious are two different entities. Both are border-line concepts for transcendental work. (Jung, 1952/1977, par. 757)

Both psychology and religion agree fairly well on the existence of agency, from the most concrete to the most abstract: parent, clergy, friends, daily events, unconditioned stimuli, motives, the unconscious, spirits, deities, fate, destiny, and so on.

There is less agreement, perhaps, in their accounts of intent and design. Nevertheless, that diverse agents exist whose actions reveal an intent that is informed by design seems consistent in both psychology and religion. By positing a dimension of the psyche that goes beyond consciousness, Jung proposed a psychological paradigm similar to religious images of transcendence.

Although he believed that "religious questions are primarily psychological questions so far as [practitioners] are concerned" (Jung, 1920/1978, par. 526), Jung also believed that it served little purpose to persuade patients away from their religious beliefs. Over the door to his consulting room was the phrase: "Called or uncalled, God will be present." Jungian analysts do not have as one of the goals of analysis the conversion of patients from religious to psychological perspectives. Usually, the problem is exactly the reverse. Most patients deny that there is any influence on their perspectives and behaviors other than their own egos. Consequently, according to James Hillman (1975), the primary task of Jungian analysis is to bring patients to an awareness of the pantheon of gods that inhabits their souls: "Psychology as religion implies imagining all psychological events as effects of Gods in the soul, and all activities to do with soul, such as therapy, to be operations of ritual in relation to these Gods" (p. 227). Of course, sometimes a considerable amount of time and effort must be expended in the service of disentangling that which patients ascribe to religion from that which is more accurately a function of their own psychology. Like virtually everything else, religion carries its share of projections.

If agency, intent, and design can provide a roundhouse by which to shift back and forth between religion and psychology, how might it work in practice? The following case studies are examples.

CASE STUDIES

The Man Who Lost God

In the Autumn of 1986, a man consulted me for hypnotic age-regression to recover a relationship with God that he had lost when he was in his early teens. He was vague about his age, settling on somewhere around 47, was married and had two children (with whom he felt he had a good relationship), and had a stable job. He felt that his "whole life [was] based on one given point in time" when he experienced a very strong connection to God, a connection that was broken "suddenly and dramatically" around age 13, after which he was left wandering and lost. His only sibling, a brother 3 years older, had recommended hypnosis, preferably with a Jungian analyst. As I am also a practicing clergyman, he consulted me.

He had experienced several traumatic abandonments early in life. He had no memory of his mother and remembered little about his father. Although he was very vague on dates, he knew that he was about 4 to 6 years old when his father was killed in World War II. His mother died 3 years later of tuberculosis, after which he and his brother were sent to stay with an aunt. When she became unable to cope with the emotional and financial burdens of this larger family, she took him and his brother to a church-run orphanage, where they spent the remainder of their childhood years. While there he suddenly developed an intensely close relationship with God. The problem he wished to address derived from a subsequent visit to his aunt's house. Kneeling in the bedroom praying to God, he suddenly thought to himself "Won't you be embarrassed if she sees you praying?" Immediately he felt God's concern for him, which had "helped him out of getting into trouble at the Home," disappear. Distraught, confused, and remorseful, he began to ruminate over the loss. Now, at age 47, he wanted to find God again.

That was all he remembered of his past. Details from the present held little interest. Not particularly talented hypnotically, his age-regression was largely unsuccessful. He decided to terminate. Ten months later he was back, this time, as he said, "for the long haul." In the meantime, his brother had died, his wife was having an affair, and he felt he was losing control of his life. The devastation he felt in his separation from God was his only concern, however, for he felt that current events were simply one more proof that God considered him unworthy. Wishing only to recapture his relationship with God, he resisted any discussion of his wife, children, or career.

The facts as he saw them were these: God had entered his life in a manner that totally transformed his life. He had subsequently betrayed God's trust, whereupon God withdrew from the relationship, leaving him abandoned and depleted. Since that time he had been obsessed with God. It formed the basis for his self-image, marriage, friendships, and social life. In the consulting room, his usually flat affect changed only when speaking of God. As diagnoses and interpretations were nonsense to him, interventions were similarly useless. Consequently, we concentrated on his expressed goal: to recover via hypnosis his connection to God.

After using hypnotic age-regression for a few sessions, he recalled the events that led to his encounter with God: Having been berated at length in front of his friends by the housemother of his living unit, he collapsed into tears, ran upstairs to his room, and paced its length several times. He then knelt down next to his bed and prayed. Suddenly, he felt himself becoming increasingly calm, whereupon brilliant shards of light rained down on him from above. This continued for a while, after which he "blacked out." When he awoke he was very relaxed, at peace with the world, and at one with God. Relationships became easier to establish and maintain. Surrounded by God's love, everything fell into place. As his behavior improved, others in the school noticed and complimented him on it. One year later, just before a visit to his aunt, his housemother warned him against losing this special feeling he had gained. Yet that was exactly what was to happen, for it was during that visit that he lost his relationship with God.

The story of his encounter with God suggested how the roundhouse might interpret his experiences, for he questioned why (the design) God (the agent) had abandoned him (the intent). This made it possible to translate his dilemma into Jung's language and concepts, for example: For what purpose (design) had the self (agent) activated that particular tension of opposites (intent) between separation and merger? Interpretations could then be formulated using his own language, particularly concerning his belief in transcendent forces at work in his life. This helped to alleviate his fears that his beliefs and experiences were peculiar, diminishing thereby his feelings of isolation. As the roundhouse facilitated the interpretation of religious ideation, patterns and dynamics emerged that could be addressed in his current experience.

Perhaps the most illuminating pattern to emerge was that the God whom he sought and the parents he had lost shared a common definition—they had disappeared from his life in radical and unexpected ways. With regard to feelings of loss, however, he was aware only of those associated with his separation from God. That he remembered nothing of his parents' deaths, nor had ever—to his knowledge—actively grieved over their loss, suggested that those feeling were insufficiently integrated into consciousness, leaving him vulnerable to their continuing influence. Later, when his aunt became a parental surrogate, he again experienced the abandonment that was already present in his associations with parental figures. A powerful complex was forming, able to infect any parenting agency with its feeling-tone. As God became a parental figure (loving, guiding, and supporting), it was virtually inevitable that God would abandon him too. Even employers seemed to be associated with the complex, for he had never been able to work successfully under the direction of another. At present, he was self-employed.

He reacted to the complex with intense feelings of guilt. Convinced that his concern about his aunt seeing him praying had led God to abandon him, he sought to become the kind of person with whom God would wish to reconnect. By trying to attract God, he was compensating for his feelings of powerlessness with regard to separation by substituting his own intent for that of the complex. However, he really had been powerless to prevent the losses of those dear to hm. Blaming himself actually inflated him with the presumption of a power he did not have. Even his desire for hypnosis was an attempt to control God through restoring the relationship. According to Jung's view of tensions of opposites, the complex would compensate the inflation by involving him with situations in which he would have to recognize that in some instances he was truly helpless. He was painfully suspended in a paradox: To regain closeness with God he would have to admit his powerlessness.

Particularly problematic was that he had never had the opportunity to work through issues of being loved, supported, guided, and corrected over a long period of time with one set of parents. Consequently, he was inadequately prepared to accept a negative intent serving a positive design. Parents regularly do things for their children's benefit that the children find unpleasant. By the time children leave home, they usually have internalized enough of their relationships with their parents to assist them in discerning their lives' designs. In this manner, says Jung, the powerful agency of the self is mediated by previous encounters with more concrete carriers of its projection. This man, however, had been deprived of parents and surrogates who could carry adequately the projection of the self. At age twelve, there were no concrete containers for the projection, leaving him no insulation from the power of the archetype.

The lack of a substantial projection carrier, combined with the power of the archetype, led quite understandably to his seeing the experience as an encounter with God. The beauty of the roundhouse is that we could discuss it from either the religious or the psychological perspective. If the agency of concern was God, whose perceived intent was to remain separate until he learned what had caused the rift, then the next step in the therapy would be to consider the design that informed the experience. In short, what could he learn about himself from discerning the design? In Jung's words (1950/1977): "The characteristic feature of a pathological recreation is, above all, *identification with the archetype*" (par. 621), that is, by blaming himself and fixating on the relationship he once had, he was identifying with the self. Consistent with his vocabulary, he had to realize that he was usurping God's role.

Using the roundhouse to express this in religious terms, it was possible to observe that this relationship with God had occurred at a time when his helplessness and vulnerability made him particularly receptive. His fixation on regaining this original relationship with God was the antithesis of that original attitude. To try to recapture the earlier receptivity, however, was to open himself to the feelings of that problematic complex associated with abandonment. While other schools of thought have their own ways of dealing with this, Jung's is to see it symbolically. Thus, therapists teach patients to supply for themselves that which was never adequately received from others. In this case, he had to become the parent he had never had.

Here was a unique opportunity to work in present time with problematic dynamics left over the past, for the adult ego contains a number of coping skills that were unavailable when the ego first suffered its trauma. Thus, not only can the ego repattern itself in a way that was impossible originally, but it can also do so in light of the larger puzzle of elements that have evolved into a defensive network. Drawing on his adult knowledge of how good parents behave, he began to learn to quiet his own fears (fixated at 12-year-old level). Imaginal techniques were particularly helpful: Using hypnosis, he saw himself as a young boy, afraid and alone in his bedroom. He did not try to solve the childhood dilemma, but imagined giving comfort and support to his boyhood self, allaying his fear of abandonment.

By seeing his troublesome feelings as symbolic of the dilemmas he faced as a child, he was able slowly and carefully to open himself to them and to reverse his fixation on manipulation and control. As his inflation began to diminish, he reported feeling closer to God. Although he was unable to specify exactly how he felt closer, feeling that he was in the presence of God's love helped him to cope with other feelings that were beginning to emerge in response to the events of his daily life. For example, he was divorcing his wife, changing his residence, and expanding his business. The inevitable powerlessness that attends such experiences reconstituted his fears of abandonment. However, recalling that God's will for him (the design) required that he acknowledge his feelings of powerlessness when they were realistic helped to restore his confidence. Thus, by acknowledging this design, he became more comfortable with the intent of his inner agents. And by acknowledging his feelings, he was living a more authentic existence.

The Woman Who Embraced Death

Cases involving religious issues do not always frame themselves in sectarian terms. There seem to be times in people's spiritual development when they must let go of the religion that teaches them to experience that which teaches their religion. So deeply personal is this experience that it holds a unique place in religion, sometimes referred to as *spirituality*. The following analysis, which consisted of 146 sessions over 3 1/2 years, explored many topics and dynamics. Although the day-to-day interactions were far more complex than one theme can summarize, the motif of death permeated much of the work.

She was 29, a nurse, and dissatisfied with her relationships and vocation. In high school she had not dated much. The one boy with whom she felt particularly close had been killed in an automobile accident while coming to see her. It bothered her that she was still a virgin, was stuck in a dead-end job in a psychiatric ward for children, and was feeling alienated from her religion.

She spent the first few months of the analysis getting to know me and learning how to record and interpret her dreams. After three months she dreamed that a man was threatening to rape her. She didn't want to engage the dream figure through active imagination for fear of "what he might have to say." Six months later she dreamed:

> I was making soup with the meat of a very large snake. I cut the head
> (which was as large as my hand) off the snake, but the snake head still
> had a life of its own—like a chicken with its head cut off, except that

the snake's body had died but the head kept living and it had big fangs and kept biting. I put the snake head on top of the soup water and it floated around the pot, snapping its jaws occasionally. I didn't feel really frightened—it was kinda amusing to watch, but also rather disturbing. I knew the snake head couldn't move without its body, so I was safe. Then my parents' cat got up on the counter and started playing with the snake head. I was afraid she would get bit, and she nearly did, but then she bit the snake head in the brain and it finally died.

This time she wanted to connect with the dream figure. We looked at her personal associations with snakes, soups, her parents' cat, and considered the archetypal amplification of snakes as symbolic of transformation (they shed their skins), the devil (the Garden of Eden), the Great Mother (the uroboros), and healing (the caduceus).

After a little less than a year of analysis, our focus began to change. She was becoming infuriated with her mother's hurt feelings every time she became more independent from her. She felt that her mother was highly manipulative and had kept her too close to her apron strings. About the same time a patient with whom she had been close was transferred to the intensive care unit of the hospital and not expected to live. She said, "I hate all that death stuff." That her feelings toward her mother and toward death had emerged in fairly close proximity to each other intrigued us both.

Shortly thereafter she dreamed that she was in hell bargaining with the devil for the privilege of making love to two other men. In the dream account she wrote, "I figured the devil would probably rape me, but it would be nice to make love with the other two guys." She was very intrigued with what the dream said about the dynamics going on within her psyche. She was curious about death as both a reality of life and an agent within herself. With regard to the latter, what could be its intent? Could it have to do with relationships, vocation, even her mother?

Maybe it had to do with the week before, when she had told her mother of her feelings of entrapment and decided to enforce limits on their relationship by, among other things, confining her mother's telephone calls to one a week. In a few weeks, her anger extended to her father, who had offered little assistance in her efforts to differentiate herself from her mother. She felt that she had been raised by both parents to be a good little suburban housewife, so that her vocational aspirations were either discouraged or unsupported. She decided to consult a faculty advisor about medical school with the goal of becoming a doctor.

Fifteen months into the analysis she summed up "some pretty major strides in personal/spiritual growth" that she felt came from her analytic work: "I have permission to be a separate person from my mother. I believe that it's a good thing for me to be a sexual creature/body person. I am beginning to get some ideas about my academic/vocational gifts." Then, on her way home one night, she passed a store window and saw a ring with a large angel of death on it. Two days later, on Valentine's Day, she ordered it in her size. That night she dreamed that she could feel its weight on her left forefinger as someone asked her "Are you engaged?" Within a week she had the following hypnogogic image while emerging from sleep:

> The angel of death was at the foot of the bed. He came to make love with me, and I was receptive to him, but he was all bones and I said: "I have a space for you and I want to make love with you, but you have nothing to fill me with. You're all bones and no flesh." Then I was looking at his bones—checking them all out. I was feeling very light and euphoric. It felt like my hands were detached from my body and they were floating up.

As she imagined herself in conversation with the angel of death, she suddenly had the strong impression that death was meant to be her teacher. She felt this was confirmed when a young boy in the hospital began speaking of his fears of death one night. Her colleague on duty could not handle this, so she filled in and spoke with him at length. She felt comfortable with the discussion and began to feel more certain that death was not simply an adversary in the practice of medicine.

Soon thereafter she was discussing her images of death with her lover. He became concerned that her dreams and fantasies meant that death was coming for her. She wrote in her daily journal "I believe the Reaper is coming to make friends with me rather than to take me." Nevertheless, her lover seemed to be articulating a fear not only of his own but of hers as well. She was beginning to understand that much of her fear of relationship had to do with the fear of being abandoned. Sources of these fears other than the death of her boyfriend in high school were a mystery. Soon, however, they began to focus on me.

Her progress was suddenly very upsetting. If she got well, she wondered, would I throw her out of analysis? Would it mean the death of our relationship? In our session she felt like sitting and rocking and crying. In her journal she noted that she had adjusted to the presence of death in her work, but was not quite sure what it meant to her personally. After she looked up death in a symbol dictionary, she wrote, "There is more to this Death business than just death. There is new life within this death business. Food for worms." Three months later we were talking about death when she abruptly said, "He wants to give me something." I asked her what she thought that was and she relaxed, concentrated on the image, then looked up at me. "A life," she said. "He wants to give me a life." She began to cry.

After this experience, as she was researching images of death, she happened on the Grimm's fairy-tale of "Godfather Death," which she brought to our session and read. It speaks of a father who looks for a godfather for his son. He rejects God and the devil because both are unfair in their distribution of pain and comfort. He accepts Death because Death makes all people equal. Death then bestows on his godson the power to discern if someone is to live or die, which makes the godson the most famous physician in the world. But when he fails to observe the limits placed on him by Death, he loses his life. This, she felt, resonated strongly with her need to change.

As we began to notice a confluence of death, abandonment, and her mother, cognitive and rational views of death failed to articulate the power of the image. She learned that when she was very young, about 2 years old, her mother had experienced a severe depression that lasted several months. During that time, she was unavailable to her children. We discussed the themes of death and rape in terms of the myth of Persephone's rape by Hades. We wondered if her mother had feared that her daughter had been dragged off to Hades with her but had been left behind when she subsequently reemerged. This might explain her strong identification with her daughter—sewing identical outfits for them both to wear and wanting her daughter to be a housewife like her who would be happily married, have children, and spend time with her mother. Her daughter, for her part, had bought into that role. She was infuriated, for instance, when she discovered a photograph that had been taken in college, which showed her standing with a group of friends holding a sign that read "Hi, Mom!"

She decided to tell her mother how she felt about their relationship. Her mother listened to what she was saying, apologized for not realizing it while it was happening, and offered to help her to get on with her life. When she told about her desire to go to medical school, her mother gave her her blessing. With her mother's acceptance, she became more aware of the inner dynamics of abandonment. For example, after seeing a movie about sexual abuse ("Closetland"), she wrote in her journal:

> Dangerous to have a mind. And always thinking of physiology. Wanting to say "It hurts. It hurts. IT HURTS!" Always wanting to meta-comment on the physiology. And not a moment of trust. . . .
>
> I can see the value of dissociative states. I would be journeying. Meeting the animals. . . . I would journey to meet someone—to try to connect someone with where I am. To call out to the universe. To say Find Me! Someone Find Me. . . . Would someone know I had been abducted? Would someone, anyone, have the courage to speak. To find a voice. To communicate. She is abducted. We must find her. . . .
>
> Dissociative states. Abduction into the blackest parts of my own soul. Madness as Evil. But only when it is not recognized as madness. I think I would know instantly when I had gone mad. But how long could I hold on to the knowledge of madness before I got lost in it? And can't come back? Look inside my own soul for the part I torture.

Look inside my own soul for the part that tortures me. Where did I learn this crazy business that no one can love me for who I am? That I always have to be an anima-woman to be loved? . . .

If I am killed I will need a psychopomp. I will need help crossing over. Think of all the souls in this dark place. Haunting it. Needing a psychopomp. I can journey to psychopomp. To clean up the air of maybe one or 2 lost and confused souls. . . .

I need a real place of safety. I need this place of safety. This place where I can be as much of my Self as I choose to be. Where I can expose my Self as much as I choose. I can conceal as much of me as I choose. From you. And from myself. And when I choose to open myself, a little. The parts that are revealed are accepted. Maybe even loved. A place where I am safe. Where you do not penetrate. Except where you are invited. Where I can feel what I feel when I feel it and if it hurts, it hurts, IT HURTS. I can feel it hurt and I can say NO to my mother trying to soothe it away. NO. I will not have my feelings taken away from me—even if it hurts you to let me feel them. I need this real place. Outside my mind.

Clearly, she believed, she needed to cooperate with death to retrieve the girl who was stuck in Hades without a mother. She wrote:

When I came home from college, I opposed homosexuality in the Church. I also perceived AIDS as one of those judgment diseases. I loved all that judging character crap. Give me structure. Give me rigid rules. To make me feel safe. Sexual repression. Absolutism. Don't think for yourself. Let the Church think for you. A place for everything and everything in its place. Bullshit.

Where once structure had been her salvation, now she needed to go it alone. Like a snake shedding its skin, she had to shed the old identity that was fixated in her relationship with her parents. To do so, she would have to return to that existential place where it had been necessary to construct that identity in the first place, namely, her mother's depression and the abandonment she felt during it. To do that, she would have to experience that darkness herself.

Through her daily journal, her dreams, active imagination, and preparing for medical school, she entered into the death of her old identity. But events were conspiring to bring death into the analytic relationship. A few months later I told her that in 6 months I would close my practice and move to another city. Death was now a very real presence. Even her dreams began to elude her. However, her relationship with the unconscious remained intact. She wrote:

My dreams. They wake me up, then escape me now. All the clear details have faded to broad generalizations within minutes. I let them go. I know I have too much going on right now. John going and [a friend] coming. Then school starting. But I hope they won't always run away like this. I like my dreams, my very clearly detailed images. They are my friends.

Agency, intent, and design gave coherence to the inner and outer, the imminent and transcendent. She had learned to use the roundhouse in her analysis and now was applying it to her daily life. For her, religion, spiritually, and the unconscious had become reflections of one another.

Death was more than a content of thought. It was a category of thought as well. Its image was a reflection of the kind of process that in Jungian terms is called *archetypal*. Death conditioned her perceptions and her experiences. It led her into those dimensions of her psyche where work needed to be done for her to become who she was, rather than who others wanted her to be. Of course, we experienced this together. In her final notes she made it all clear:

> It is like a death. A "planned and wanted" death. Like cancer, with enough time to prepare and to grieve together.
> But in hospice thinking, the soon-to-be deceased has the choice. The corpse chooses his funeral. The music. Perhaps part of the meditation. Some psalm or favorite poetry.
> I did not ask you. I'm sorry I did not ask you. How do you want me to grieve you? How would you like your funeral to go?
> I will make for you a gift. This is something you do not get to choose. But otherwise. Besides. How do you want it to be, this grieving time?
> I feel raw, and I don't want to speak with my parents tonight. I don't want them to know I am ending analysis. Because the growth process will continue, for me.
> Now.
> Perhaps you will say:
> Just be grateful for the time we had together.
> Remember me fondly.
> And get on with your life.
> Generic grieving.
> Any good corpse can say that.
> But what I want to know is:
> How do *you* want me to grieve you?
> What makes you different from the ordinary corpse?
> What makes you *you*?
> Beyond the generic?

Knowing that whatever we face on the outside has its counterpart on the inside gives us the opportunity to transform our circumstances by transforming ourselves. For my part, it is quite reassuring to be able to shift between religious and psychological ideation during analysis. For example, I could have interpreted her images of death as illness unnoticed, depression, or even suicidal ideation. But being able to see death as symbolic of an agent that was carrying out the intent of a design made it possible to be a bit more flexible in my response. I was able to trust that the process had meaning.

CONCLUSION

In this chapter, I have posed the question of how to shift back and forth between religious and psychological metaphors. Looking briefly at religion yielded the possibility that a roundhouse metaphor embracing agency, intent, and design could assist in such work. I then outlined Jung's metapsychology for its consistency with these metaphors. Finally, I applied the roundhouse to two case studies to see how well it opened up religious material to interpretation.

Like computer commands, the role of the roundhouse is restricted to getting the practitioner into the program, so to speak. In this case, the goal is to assist the psychologist in gaining access to the religious language of the patient. Nevertheless, while the roundhouse gets us into the program, it does not tell us what to do when we are there. Once "inside," we can use whatever theories we find most useful to work with our patients' concerns.

REFERENCES

Eliade, M. (1971). *The quest: History and meaning in religion*. Chicago: The University of Chicago Press.

Eliade, M. (1985). *A history of religious ideas* (Vol. 3). Chicago: The University of Chicago Press.

Hillman, J. (1975). *Re-visioning psychology*. San Francisco: Harper & Row.

James, W. (1929). *The varieties of religious experience*. New York: The Modern Library.

Jung, C. G. (1976). Symbols of transformation. In H. Read, M. Fordham, G. Alder, & W. McGuire (Eds.), *The collected works of* C. G. Jung (Vol. 5). Princeton, NJ: Princeton University Press. (Original work published 1912)

Jung, C. G. (1978). The relations between the ego and the unconscious. In H. Read (Ed.), *The collected works of* C. G. Jung (Vol. 7, pars. 202–406). Princeton, NJ: Princeton University Press. (Original work published 1916)

Jung, C. G. (1978). On the psychology of the unconscious. In H. Read, M. Fordham, G. Alder, & W. McGuire (Eds.), *The collected works of* C. G. Jung (Vol. 7, pars. 1–201). Princeton, NJ: Princeton University Press. (Original work published 1917)

Jung, C. G. (1978). Instinct and Unconscious. In H. Read, M. Fordham, G. Adler, & W. McGuire (Eds.) *The collected works of* C. G. Jung

(Vol. 8, pars. 263–282). Princeton, NJ: Princeton University Press. (Original work published 1919)

Jung, C. G. (1978). General aspects of dream psychology. In H. Read, M. Fordham, G. Alder, & W. McGuire (Eds.), *The collected works of C. G. Jung* (Vol. 8, pars. 443–529). Princeton, NJ: Princeton University Press. (Original work published 1920)

Jung, C. G. (1978). Analytical psychology and "Weltanschauung." In H. Read, M. Fordham, G. Alder, & W. McGuire (Eds.), *The collected works of C. G. Jung* (Vol. 8, pars. 689–741). Princeton, NJ: Princeton University Press. (Original work published 1928)

Jung, C. G. (1977). The practical use of dream analysis. In H. Read, M. Fordham, G. Alder, & W. McGuire (Eds.), *The collected works of C. G. Jung* (Vol. 16, pars. 294–352). Princeton, NJ: Princeton University Press. (Original work published 1934)

Jung, C. G. (1978). A review of the complex theory. In H. Read, M. Fordham, G. Alder, & W. McGuire (Eds.), *The collected works of C. G. Jung* (Vol. 8, pars. 194–219). Princeton, NJ: Princeton University Press. (Original work published 1934)

Jung, C. G. (1977). The psychology of the transference. In H. Read, M. Fordham, G. Alder, & W. McGuire (Eds.), *The collected works of C. G. Jung* (Vol. 16, pars. 353–539). Princeton, NJ: Princeton University Press. (Original work published 1946)

Jung, C. G. (1977). A study in the process of individuation. In H. Read, M. Fordham, G. Alder, & W. McGuire (Eds.), *The collected works of C. G. Jung* (Vol. 9, pars. 525–626). Princeton, NJ: Princeton University Press. (Original work published 1950)

Jung, C. G. (1977). Answer to Job. In H. Read, M. Fordham, G. Alder, & W. McGuire (Eds.), *The collected works of C. G. Jung* (Vol. 11, pars. 553–758). Princeton, NJ: Princeton University Press. (Original work published 1952)

Jung, C. G. (1977). Transformation symbolism in the Mass. In H. Read, M. Fordham, G. Alder, & W. McGuire (Eds.), *The collected works of C. G. Jung* (Vol. 11, pars. 296–448). Princeton, NJ: Princeton University Press. (Original work published 1954)

Jung, C. G. (1978). The transcendent function. In H. Read, M. Fordham, G. Alder, & W. McGuire (Eds.), *The collected works of C. G. Jung* (Vol. 8, pars. 131–193). Princeton, NJ: Princeton University Press. (Original work published 1957)

O'Flaherty, W. D. (1988). The philosophical track into the roundhouse of myth. *Criterion, 27*(1), 8–11.

Otto, R. (1969). *The idea of the holy.* Oxford, England: Oxford University Press.

Samuels, A. (1985). *Jung and the post-Jungians.* New York: Routledge, Kegan Paul.

Tracy, D. (1975). *Blessed rage for order.* New York: The Seabury Press.

18

TRANSPERSONAL PSYCHOLOGY AND THE RELIGIOUS PERSON

FRANCES VAUGHAN, BRYAN WITTINE, and ROGER WALSH

Transpersonal psychotherapy is an approach to healing and growth that aims at the integration of physical, emotional, mental, and spiritual aspects of well-being. The goals of transpersonal psychotherapy encompass the classic ones of normal healthy functioning, but go beyond these to include spiritual issues explored from a psychological perspective. Transpersonal psychotherapy differs from other therapeutic approaches in that it reframes the Western psychological tradition in the broader context of the perennial philosophy, the common mystical root of the great world religions (Huxley, 1944; Smith, 1976; Wilber, 1977).

A transpersonal therapist may employ traditional psychotherapeutic techniques, such as free association and analysis of the transference, as well as methods derived from spiritual disciplines, such as meditation and mind training. The client may be encouraged to attend to mind–body processes and explore the inner world of dreams and fantasies, as well as to examine religious beliefs and discuss spiritual experiences. As we will show, some clients may go so far as to have profound spiritual experiences in a psychotherapy setting.

CONTEXT, CONTENT, AND PROCESS IN TRANSPERSONAL PSYCHOTHERAPY

A useful distinction can be made between the *context* of therapy established by the beliefs, values, and state of mind of the therapist; the *content* of therapy, consisting of the client's experience (i.e., what the client talks about); and the *process* of therapy, in which both therapist and client participate and through which healing occurs.

A transpersonal context in psychotherapy is established by the therapist who values the integration of spirituality in the healing process, regardless of whether the client is formally affiliated with an organized religion. The transpersonal therapist should be willing to examine his or her own religious beliefs and attend to his or her own spiritual development. As we will later emphasize, therapy can be considered transpersonal if the therapist is personally committed to a disciplined path leading to spiritual realization.

We therefore recommend that therapists who conduct psychotherapy with religious persons have training in practices that provide them with an experiential basis for their work. A transpersonal therapist is not only sensitive to religious values and beliefs, but has personally explored spiritual and transpersonal levels of consciousness, and is therefore better equipped to assist others who are working with religious and spiritual issues. Just as a 20 year old may not be able to understand the issues of a 50 year old as well as someone closer to that age, a therapist who has not explored his or her own spirituality is less likely to empathize with spiritual issues than one who has. This does not mean that the transpersonal therapist is necessarily religious in the traditional sense; rather he or she is informed about the variety of spiritual issues that may be encountered by religious persons and has had first-hand experience of spiritual dimensions of consciousness.

Similarly, a therapist who has practiced meditation may be better able to assist others who are engaged in similar practices than one who has no meditation experience. Research (Shapiro & Walsh, 1984) indicates that, in addition to better understanding spiritual states of consciousness when they are discussed by clients, meditation training can increase the capacity for empathy in psychotherapists, whereas conventional professional training does not necessarily do so.

The word *transpersonal* means, literally, "beyond the personal." As we will later show, this means that personal work is included in a larger context. Because religion generally provides an individual with a creed, a code of ethics, and a community of like-minded persons who share a particular orientation to life, these cultural and social influences are also taken into account. A transpersonal orientation does not invalidate other approaches, any of which may be relevant to an integrative psychotherapy. It does, however, call for a more expanded context than is usually assumed by other approaches and allows for a vision of the human potential that explicitly includes spiritual experience. In the light of the perennial wisdom of spiritual teachings, it affirms the possibility of living in harmony with others and the environment, reducing fear and greed, and developing compassion and a sense of meaning and purpose in life, regardless of the particular religious beliefs that may be espoused.

The Spectrum of Development

Researchers increasingly divide human development into three major phases: preconventional, conventional, and transconventional; or prepersonal, personal, and transpersonal. Whether it is the development of cognition, morality, faith, motivation, or sense of self, it is clear that one enters the world unsocialized (at a prepersonal or preconventional stage) and is gradually acculturated into a personal or conventional worldview and *modus operandi*, both religious and secular. A few individuals differentiate themselves from their familial past and cultural conditioning to discover who they are as unique individuals, thus developing further into postconventional stages of postformal operational cognition (e.g., the work of Flavell and Arieti), transconventional morality (Kohlberg), universalizing faith (Fowler), self-actualizing and self-transcending motives (Maslow), and a transpersonal self-sense (Wilber).[1]

What is crucial for a contemporary psychological understanding of religion is the recognition that spiritual experience, religious belief, and behavior can occur at any of these stages—preconventional, conventional, or postconventional—and can vary dramatically in form, function, and value according to the stage. Further, it can contribute to psychological health or dysfunction, depending upon how well it can be integrated. In his study of self-actualizing and self-transcending people, psychologist Abraham Maslow (1971) found that all of them had a spiritual orientation to life, but were not necessarily formally religious. Thus, although religion can easily be misused and serve as a defensive maneuver, we believe it is a mistake to equate preconventional magical thinking with all religious thinking, and to overlook religion as a developmental catalyst. The confusion and conflation of preconventional and prepersonal stages of psychological and spiritual development with transconventional and transpersonal stages has been called the *pre/trans fallacy* (Wilber, 1993). Awareness of this distinction is essential for any practitioner of transpersonal psychotherapy who aims at the healthy integration of spiritual impulses and religious practices.

---

[1] For a comprehensive overview of this research and the theory of transpersonal development in general, see the work of Ken Wilber (1980a, 1983, 1995), one of transpersonal psychology's most influential exponents.

Fortunately, relevant research on religion and spirituality is expanding dramatically and includes some useful findings, including the following:

- Growing numbers of contemporary psychoanalytic thinkers are forging new psychoanalytic perspectives and no longer see psychoanalysis and authentic spirituality as incompatible (Coltart, 1992; Kakar, 1991; Shafranske, 1994; Wittine, 1994).
- People who have mystical or peak experiences, far from being necessarily pathological, score above average on multiple measures of well-being (Walsh & Vaughan, 1993).
- Several hundred studies of meditation confirm that it can produce wide-ranging physiological, psychological, and biochemical effects and therapeutic benefits (Shapiro & Walsh, 1984). Intriguing findings include evidence for enhanced creativity, perceptual sensitivity, empathy, marital satisfaction, self-control, and self-actualization. Developmentally, several studies suggest meditation may foster maturation on scales of ego, moral, and cognitive development. Clinical research suggests that it can be therapeutic for several psychological and psychosomatic disorders including anxiety, phobias, posttraumatic stress, insomnia, and mild depression. Regular meditation seems to reduce legal and illegal drug use, blood pressure, cholesterol levels, and the severity of asthma, migraine, and chronic pain (West, 1987; Walsh & Vaughan, 1993).

Unfortunately, most meditation research has been confined to what Maslow (1968) called "means oriented" as opposed to "goal oriented," meaning that researchers have focused on what is easiest to measure rather than on what is most important. In the case of meditation, physiology, biochemistry, and stress have been measured, rather than the subtle subjective shifts in awareness, affect, motivation, and self-sense that are the original goal of meditation practices in the contemplative traditions. There has been more attention to heart rate than to heart opening, even though the cultivation of transpersonal affects and motives such as love, compassion, empathy, and service is a central goal of most meditation practices. Nevertheless, some beginnings have been made. Although much work needs to be done, several studies support classic claims that meditation practice can cultivate a variety of transconventional capacities and transpersonal experiences.

Basic Assumptions of Transpersonal Psychotherapy

Some of the basic assumptions underlying a transpersonal orientation in psychotherapy can be summarized in the following postulates (Wittine, 1990).

Postulate 1

Transpersonal psychotherapy is an approach to healing and growth that addresses multiple levels of the spectrum of identity—prepersonal, personal, and transpersonal.

"Who am I?" and "What am I?" are central questions addressed in both religion and psychology. The quest to find answers to these eternal questions is as ancient as the questions themselves. Wilber (1977, 1980b) suggests that answers depend entirely upon where one is identified in a spectrum of identity. A person's identification is determined by where the person draws the boundary line between what is "I" and "not-I."

Here we will refer back to the three stages of development we cited earlier—prepersonal, personal, and transpersonal. In addition to recognizing these as stages of development, they can also be seen as bands in a spectrum of identity extending from the isolated individual to the wholly inclusive and universal. Each band can be viewed as a mode of consciousness, a way of experiencing ourselves and the world, and a category of unconscious phenomena.

The bands can also be viewed as interpenetrating levels in a "hierarchy of wholes." The higher levels go beyond, yet include, the lower. However, because these levels are interpenetrating, the life concerns of clients can involve all levels *simultaneously*. This point is often underemphasized in hierarchical and developmental models of human functioning, but becomes apparent when one applies these models to clinical work.

Prepersonal Identity. The prepersonal stage of development starts in the womb and extends through the first three or four years of life. In the prepersonal stage we emerge from the surround of mother and begin to consolidate a stable sense of self and world.

Prepersonal consciousness is rudimentary, infantile, innocent, grasping, and dependent, motivated by survival, safety, attachment, and exploratory needs. To a greater or lesser extent, a person in a prepersonal mode of consciousness is entirely fixated on him or herself and has little awareness of others, except as they serve his or her own basic needs. Magical thinking, fantasy, and primary process are this stage's dominant cognitive modes. The prepersonal self-sense fluctuates, sometimes rapidly, as identification moves from one self-representation to another.

Personal Identity. The prepersonal stage of development culminates in the development of personal identity. Our personal identity is a whole constellation of unconscious organizing principles by which we construct ourselves, the world, and ourselves in that world. This constellation has its origins in the patterns of interaction between ourselves as children and our caregivers. Our experiences with siblings, teachers, and peers add to this superstructure. Personal identity is composed of self-images, object representations, memories, beliefs, meanings, and affects with which we are identified. These become the unconscious map to which we refer in order to orient ourselves in our day-to-day lives. The unconscious organizing principles of personal identity may include deeply rooted religious beliefs.

One primary task of transpersonal psychotherapy is identical to that of many other Western approaches to psychotherapy: to facilitate the emergence and development of a stable, cohesive personal identity when this is needed by the client. Psychologist Jack Engler (1986) has pointed out the importance of developing a personal identity before aspiring to self-transcendence. Many clients come to therapy needing a clearer feeling of who and what they are as separate, distinct individuals. They need an experience of self that endures over time rather than a self-sense that fluctuates rapidly between one identification and another. They also need to build the structures of adult life—home, career, family—and achieve a place in the social order. Often this entails *separation–individuation*, the ability to "stand separate from the mother" and becoming autonomous. Thus, when transpersonal psychotherapy supports healing and growth at the personal level, it assists clients in developing an ordered self by replacing nonfunctional concepts of self and other, building boundaries, integrating polarizations, and modifying character structure so clients can interact with others and the world in more fulfilling ways.

Mature development at the personal level involves not only the development of a healthy ego, but unfolding an existential self or authentic individuality. C. G. Jung (1971) calls this further development *individuation*, defined as a process by which one differentiates oneself from one's persona or social image and from the images of one's culture in order to become a unique individual. Jung believed this process was more pronounced in the second half of life because it required a healthy ego and an ability to adapt to the necessary minimum of social norms. It is conceivable that what Maslow (1968) calls self-actualizing needs motivate the process of individuation.

Clients tend to individuate and unfold the unique potentialities of personal identity as they confront what existential therapists term the "basic conditions of being" (Bugental, 1980) or "ultimate concerns" (Yalom, 1980). A human being is embodied, finite, free to make choices and take action, and separate from, yet related to, others. Each person is subject to these givens of existence. Concerns such as aging, the reality of death, existential versus neurotic anxiety and guilt, responsibility, and the relationship of oneself as an individual to others and the collective are often explored by clients in transpersonal psychotherapy in deeply personal ways. The task of transpersonal psychotherapy at this level is to help clients confront these existential givens and thus loosen the hold of the rigidified self-and-world construct so that greater feelings of aliveness and authentic talents and skills may come forth.

Transpersonal Identity. In the course of psychotherapy, some clients begin to recognize that no matter how individuated or self-actualized they become or how much they accomplish, they will never be truly satisfied or fulfilled. The first of the four noble truths of Buddhism—the impermanence, pain, and insubstantiality of embodied existence—may be starkly experienced. They begin to recognize that their personal selves will always feel incomplete. They begin to intuit that they cannot be truly whole until awakened to the wholeness of a deeper, transpersonal level of interconnected identity.

As a result, prompted by an inner imperative, their attention may turn to deeper spiritual questions. The process of individuation described by Jung becomes oriented toward the spiritual goal of realizing the numinous Self—the "pearl of great price," the "jewel in the lotus," the "philosopher's stone." Maslow's self-actualizing needs are superseded by an urge for self-transcendence.

In the Western depth psychological tradition, Jung (1973) was one of the first psychiatrists to recognize the relevance of spiritual experience to psychological health and wellbeing. He said, ". . . the fact is that the approach to the numinous is the real therapy, and inasmuch as you attain to the numinous experience you are released from the curse of pathology" (p. 377). His initial conceptualization of the Self took shape in response to his fascination with Eastern thought. In various writings, Jung compared the Self to *Atman* of Hindu philosophy (1958a), the *Tao* in Chinese philosophy (1967), and *Buddha-mind* in Mahayana Buddhism (1958b). Jung also believed the Self is the "still small voice" of a *spiritus rector* in the psyche, an inner guiding intelligence experienced as outside the conscious ego, which inspires one to develop psychologically and spiritually. According to Jung, the experience of the Self is a defeat for the ego. By this he means that he or she who aspires to hear the still, small voice of the Self must practice humility and cultivate an attitude of submission.

So far so good. Unfortunately, Jung muddied his conception by including all sorts of other religious phenomena as experiences of the Self. At times, Jung uses Self (1968) to mean a God-image, a transcendent symbol that draws together into a meaningful whole the fragments and polarized opposites of one's psyche. For example, Christ, the Buddha, and other religious figures are transcendent symbols, and offer people who connect with them a feeling that they are connected to something greater than their conscious ego, something around which they can integrate their lives. Jung (1969) also believed that synchronicities, in which two events are meaningfully but not causally connected, could be viewed as expressions of the Self. Finally, Jung (1963) uses Self to mean the totality of one's innate potentialities, both personal and transpersonal, conscious and unconscious. The Self is "the hypothetical summation of an indescribable totality. . . . The concept of the Self is essentially intuitive and embraces ego-consciousness, shadow, anima, and collective unconscious in indeterminable extension" (pp. 107–108).

Based upon the perennial philosophy and numerous studies of men and women who practice meditation and other techniques for evoking nonordinary states of consciousness, transpersonal psychology brings clarity and order to Jung's religious vision. Several states and stages of transpersonal experience and development have been identified (Wilber, 1980a, 1995). Here we focus on two of them—the *subtle* and the *causal*—representing levels of increasing subtlety and depth.

The *subtle* is the realm of archetypal images, Platonic forms, subtle sounds and illuminations, and transcendental insights. At this level persons may also experience themselves as imbued with subtle spiritual qualities, such as love, compassion, wisdom, and strength. Jung's Self as *spiritus rector* and God-image belong to this category.

At the subtle level, the inner observer or witness transcends the isolated person and opens onto a vast expanse of awareness that is no longer possessed by the individual bodymind. In Wilber's (1995) words

> *That which* observes or witnesses the self, the person, is precisely to that degree *free* of the self, the person, and *through that opening* comes pouring the light and power of a Self. . . . (p. 281)

A person who is no longer exclusively identified with the individual personality still preserves the personality, but the awareness of a universal Self can be perceived as shining through the personality. This is sometimes described as the power of presence. At this level one may experience directly the Self and a sense of unity with all beings.

The *causal realm* is said to be the unmanifest source or transcendental ground of all the lesser structures—prepersonal, personal, and subtle. Strictly speaking, the realization of the Self as pure being and awareness, as *Atman*, *Tao*, and *Buddha-mind*, belongs to this category. Transpersonal identity at this most profound level is of the Self as one pure continuing presence, one clear, radiant awareness, boundless, unconditioned by mental constructs, yet spontaneously creative, and overflowing with love and compassion. Here the most fundamental subject–object dualism, between the individual self and universal whole, is radically transcended.

From the perspective of transpersonal psychology, then, the Self is the substratum of all modes of consciousness, all types of self-experience, and all categories of unconscious phenomena. It is here, in the formless, causal Self, that the seeker after truth and lover of God (the personal ego) realizes the goal of all striving: the "mystical marriage" with the Beloved, the absolute ground of Being.

As we will show in the case study later in this chapter, transpersonal experiences—whether subtle or causal—sometimes occur in the journey of psychotherapy if a client penetrates beneath a well-entrenched self-identification in a very profound way. These individuals quite naturally begin to consider questions about their relationship to God, ultimate mystery, their place in the evolutionary scheme of things, life after death, and spiritual disciplines. At this point their religious orientation may change or it may take a different form.

The content of transpersonal therapy is the life experience of the client. Because religious clients with spiritual concerns tend to seek out therapists with a transpersonal orientation, the content may be prepersonal, personal, subtle, or causal. If the content is explicitly transpersonal, such as when the client is questioning religious beliefs or trying to make sense out of transpersonal experiences, the therapist may look for the healing potential of such experiences and does not pathologize, discount, or invalidate them, regardless of whether or not they conform to a particular religious expectation. Conventional approaches that tend to devalue such experiences contribute to their repression, abort development, and result in subsequent disturbances (Grof, 1988). On the other hand, skillful examination can explore and interpret the experiences in a way that enhances self-awareness, personal freedom, and social responsibility.

Although transpersonal experiences are potentially healing, their effects are usually temporary unless an effort is made to stabilize the insight gained. Part of the task of psychotherapy with people who have transpersonal experiences is, therefore, the effective integration of subjectively meaningful revelations. If appropriately understood and interpreted, they can contribute significantly to the healing process and to improving the quality of personal relationships as behavior, values, and attitudes begin to change.

Postulate 2

Transpersonal psychotherapy recognizes the therapist's unfolding awareness of the Self and his or her spiritual worldview as central in shaping the nature, process, and outcome of therapy.

Psychotherapy can be considered transpersonal insofar as the therapist seeks to realize the Self as the deepest center of Being. As we mentioned earlier, what differentiates transpersonal therapy from other orientations is its context, not technique or what clients talk about. The difference lies in the centrality of the therapist's spiritual orientation to life. The therapist's spiritual orientation informs his or her therapeutic stance.

Transpersonal therapists are characterized by their dedication to a spiritual path, defined as a disciplined course of action entered into specifically for the purpose of cutting through the ego-mind and opening to the Self. If an individual seeking to become a transpersonal therapist practices meditation or other psychospiritual exercises, the likelihood is that a spiritual perspective will gradually characterize his or her outlook on life, and attributes of the Self will begin to permeate his or her being. Eventually a transpersonal context will inform his or her therapeutic approach. The therapist's spiritual awareness and reliance upon the wisdom and guidance of the Self may or may not be made explicit to the client. If a client is religious or spiritually inclined, therapists may find it useful to openly discuss spiritual issues, even to the extent of using religious terms such as God, Christ Consciousness, Buddha Nature, and Spirit, depending on the religious framework that is meaningful to the client. The therapist may also take a spiritual history to ascertain what religious influences may have contributed to the client's presenting problems. Transpersonal therapists should not, in any event, attempt to impose their own belief system or meditational practice upon a client, maintaining instead an objective stance with respect to the client's beliefs.

Postulate 3

Transpersonal psychotherapy is a process of awakening from a lesser to a greater identity.

As in other perspectives, in transpersonal psychotherapy self-identity and worldview at the prepersonal, personal, and subtle levels are viewed as arising from our thoughts and beliefs. Healing involves the realization of a greater identity that comes to light when unquestioned conceptions of self and world are relinquished.

By gradually relinquishing exclusive identification with a prepersonal identity, one can awaken to personal identity, an embodied individual self-sense that feels authentic; by relinquishing an exclusive identification with personal self, one can eventually awaken to his or her identity as the Self. Former identifications are not necessarily discarded, but are integrated into a more encompassing self-concept. By transcending who we thought we were, we come closer to who we really are, until paradoxically, we come home to the transpersonal Self we never left.

The transpersonal therapist may or may not use specific practices to help clients have transpersonal experiences. Rather, by uncovering various layers of conditioned beliefs, the therapist may persistently help clients identify and let go of self-definitions and patterns that are impeding inner freedom, enhanced self-awareness, and the emergence of a greater identity.

If, in the course of therapy, the resistances and defenses of the lesser identity are gradually relinquished, clients may enter a "dark night" or crisis of awakening. They may become acutely aware that old ways of life have little to offer and that the cost in terms of aliveness and creativity is enormous. This can be compared with what St. John of the Cross (1991) called the dark night of the senses, characterized as a normal stage in spiritual growth when a spiritual seeker, having tired of the "things of the senses," cannot yet depend upon consolation from the "things of God" (p. 361).

In religious patients, such crises may occur if old forms of religious practice are no longer satisfying, or when a person has become disillusioned by dysfunctional aspects of his or her spiritual mentor or community. The client John whom we describe at the end of this chapter, exemplifies someone at this initial stage of the spiritual quest.

It is important that therapists realize that this may be a healing crisis rather than a pathological one. The client appears to be falling apart; however, as we will later show, the crisis may also herald the birth of a new person. One of the functions of the therapist is to act as a midwife to this birth.

Crises that are specifically associated with transpersonal experiences have been described as "mystical experiences with psychotic features," "spiritual emergencies," and "transpersonal crises." They can occur either within or outside a conventional religious setting. What seems clear is that a period of psychological disturbance may often be associated with significant growth and development. Consequently, *some* psychological disturbances, such as those that may occur spontaneously as midlife crises or may be induced by practices such as intensive meditation, if appropriately mediated, can result in a higher level of functioning than before the initial crisis began (Walsh, 1990).

Transpersonal therapists working with religious persons must be prepared to remain psychologically present and supportive with their clients during such experiences of disintegration and reintegration. The most basic preparation they can have is to have undergone their own dark nights and subjective experiences of death and rebirth.

Postulate 4

Transpersonal psychotherapy facilitates the process of awakening by making use of techniques that enhance intuition and deepen awareness of personal and transpersonal realms of the psyche.

According to the perennial philosophy, the truth of ourselves lies within, and healing occurs by expanding our inner awareness. According to Wilber (1995), ". . . the more one *goes within,* the more one *goes beyond,* and the more one can embrace a *deeper identity with a wider perspective*" (p. 257).

To turn attention inward and "Self-ward" and become more fully aware of our deeper identity is a natural human capacity. Learning to live directly from one's internal sense of things and from ever deeper dimensions of being is in itself restorative and healing. However, in most of us, this capacity is blunted (Vaughan, 1979, 1995).

To develop intuition and know the intrinsic wisdom of our deeper Self we must be willing to set aside the dominance of our judging, analyzing mind and shift our attention away from its exclusive focus on the objective world. In this way we can access not only the personal, biographical realms of the unconscious, but transpersonal, collective levels as well (Grof, 1988). Many people can access deeper levels of inner wisdom and intuit within themselves what they need to do to improve the quality of their lives if they are willing to turn attention inward and access these subjective realms. As Perls (1969) noted, "Awareness per se—by and of itself—can be curative."

To achieve the goal of enhancing awareness of the personal and transpersonal realms, transpersonal psychotherapists make use of conventional and nonordinary psychotherapeutic techniques. We believe it is important to be effective therapeutic communicators, to use free association, and to understand the subtle dynamics of the transference relationship; however, transpersonal therapists may also have expertise in using one or more nonordinary techniques that make the unconscious conscious.

Some of the techniques a transpersonal therapist may employ include, but are not limited to, the following:

Bodywork. Transpersonal therapists may employ bodywork, such as hatha yoga, t'ai chi ch'uan, aikido, biofeedback, sensory awareness, and movement therapy. These disciplines train awareness by focusing attention on subtle physical sensations, thereby fostering mind–body integration, self-mastery, and the release of patterns of habitual tension.

Imagery and Dreamwork. These methods include techniques such as dream analysis, active imagination, gestalt dialogue, and the hypnotic induction of altered states. The techniques themselves are neutral and may be used either in service of the ego or for exploring transpersonal dimensions of the psyche. The depth of the work depends not only on the technique, but on how it is used.

For example, if the therapist does not have a transpersonal orientation the spiritual potentials of dreamwork tend to be overlooked. A traditional psychoanalyst, for instance, may interpret dreams as egoic wish fulfilling fantasies while overlooking the fact that dreams have long been an important source of revelation and inspiration to the world's spiritual practitioners. This is not to deny that dreams reflect egoic desires, but to point out that they can also express far deeper aspects of the psyche that will remain unrecognized by therapists and clients as long as the therapist denies their possibility.

Altered States of Consciousness. The use of techniques such as music, fasting, drumming, chanting, dancing, or ingesting drugs to alter consciousness is as old as recorded history. The use of altered states in hypnotherapy and deep relaxation is familiar to most clinicians. The investigation of other nondrug methods for altering consciousness has been pioneered by researchers such as Stanislav and Christina Grof (holotropic breathwork), Elmer and Alyce Green (biofeedback), and Michael Harner (shamanic drumming) (Walsh, 1990; Walsh & Vaughn, 1993). Their work indicates that some altered states can have powerful effects. Hence, some transpersonal therapists have sought to work with such techniques with appropriate clients.

Meditation. Meditation can be a helpful adjunct to therapy by quieting the mind and focusing attention on inner experience. Different types of meditation have different effects, but at the beginning stages most tend to increase self-awareness and sensitivity to how the mind works. A large body of clinical and research literature now attests to the many psychological and psychosomatic benefits of meditation (Shapiro & Walsh, 1984).

Inquiry. Inquiry can be understood as a phenomenological method that involves a search for the truth of one's experience (Wittine, 1990; Vaughan & Wittine, 1994). Phenomenology can be understood as an introspective analysis of the objects of consciousness that studies and describes the intrinsic traits of phenomena as they reveal themselves in awareness. The process of inquiry in psychotherapy may include direct or indirect questioning that can be initiated either by the therapist or the client. The process might well involve general questions such as "Who am I?" or "What is this?," but can broaden to include:

- Where am I now in my life?
- What is trying to emerge from within me at this time? What potential is trying to unfold?
- What is blocking me? Which self-images, object images, and beliefs of the past must I relinquish at this time to support what's emerging from within me?
- What do I need to move through the block?
- What meaning does this period have in the context of my life as a whole?

The client is asked to close his or her eyes, to become relaxed, and to pose one of these or other questions to him or herself. The client should then receive whatever responses seem to arise from within the psyche, and to follow his or her own curiosity by posing further questions and waiting in open receptivity. In this way inquiry becomes an intensive search into the nature of one's physical and emotional experience, into one's beliefs about oneself and one's place in the universe, into the causes of one's psychological distress, and into one's most cherished longings and desires. The purpose of such inquiry is to help clients release themselves from intrapsychic and interpersonal difficulties by deepening self-awareness and insight.

In transpersonal psychotherapy, inquiry is used not only to address personal concerns, but to explore deeper spiritual questions, sometimes leading to direct experience of spiritual realms. Spiritual inquiry in general is an introspective method used in many religious traditions to investigate one's inner experience and to help realize the Self. When practicing spiritual inquiry, one inquires into the very foundation of one's identity, consciousness, and life meaning, attending, with clear and single-minded awareness, to what actually unfolds at successive moments of experience. Such methods of spiritual inquiry, if practiced within a broader context of spiritual development, enable persons to apprehend the truth of who and what they are by direct experience rather than as a concept, idea, or object of reason.

For example, Zen Buddhists who practice the technique of the *koan* in conjunction with sitting meditation practice concentrate on such questions as "Who am I?," "What is my true self?," and "What was the face I had before I was born?" If done with strong faith and determination, concentration in this manner can lead to opening the "Wisdom Eye" and recognizing oneself and the world without distortion (Kapleau, 1968, p. 64).

These questions are not meant to be answered by the discursive mind. They simply orient the inquirer toward the Self. As concentration increases and intensifies, the person may cut through the socially adapted layers of personal identity, including unconscious self-images, and the subtle layers of the psyche to a direct experience of the Self—pure being, awareness, and higher intelligence. Clients who are able to withstand the anxiety of searching beyond the boundaries of their known self will often experience a transpersonal dimension of consciousness, particularly in the later stages of thoroughgoing psychotherapy. Experiences of heightened awareness in which the ego or personal self-sense appears to dissolve into a vaster intelligence, transcendence of dualistic thinking, experiences of light and numinosity, and episodes of unusual peace, joy, love, and compassion are examples.

Disidentification. Meditation and inquiry support the process of disidentification, which is central in transpersonal work. By clearly differentiating the contents of consciousness, such as feelings, thoughts, and fantasies, from consciousness itself, the client may directly experience the transpersonal Self. When the client is ready for it, disidentification exercises (Assagioli, 1965; Wilber, 1980b)—for example, I have thoughts, but I am not my thoughts; I have emotions, but I am not my emotions; I have a body, but I am not my body—affirm identification with pure being and awareness, and the capacity for directing and using psychological processes without becoming exclusively identified with any of them. Disidentification does not imply discarding or repressing self-concepts, but subsuming them in a larger, more encompassing self-sense.

In practice, the transpersonal clinician may use a variety of different methods or techniques, depending upon what is appropriate for a particular client. Because some clients who seek transpersonal therapists are religious or on a spiritual path, practitioners may be called upon to deal with specifically spiritual issues. It is therefore necessary for the therapist to distingush healthy spirituality from pathogenic religious practices.

Transpersonal psychotherapy is often presumed to be most suitable for religious people or for relatively healthy, growth-oriented clients. However, transpersonal techniques can sometimes be helpful in treating some severely disturbed individuals, because accessing the transpersonal dimensions of the psyche can provide a source of inner nourishment. Seymour Boorstein (1996), a psychoanalytically trained transpersonal psychiatrist, cautions that sometimes individuals may come into therapy misusing certain practices such as meditation or altered states of consciousness to avoid relationships or to mask psychopathology. In such cases the therapist may help the client discern the psychodynamic meaning of using these techniques.

A problem for therapists in general is the tendency to impose their own beliefs on their clients, either consciously or unconsciously. Maintaining objectivity and a detached attitude may be particularly challenging for a therapist who has recently discovered a rewarding spiritual practice. An important distinction is made between a pastoral counselor who works within a specific religious tradition that subscribes to certain religious beliefs, and the transpersonal psychotherapist whose commitment is to assist the client to discover his or her own path, rather than recommending a particular system.

For example, a clinician who is familiar with meditation and meditation research (Shapiro & Walsh, 1984) can assess the value of different types of meditative practice for a particular client and make appropriate recommendations, while avoiding some of the pitfalls of a dogmatic or narrow approach.

Spiritual Issues in Psychotherapy

Spirituality is inextricably interwoven with psychological health. Psychologist Abraham H. Maslow (1970), one of the founders of transpersonal psychology, believed that every individual is born with spiritual needs and a longing for transcendent experiences. He found that the healthiest individuals are those with a well integrated, deep sense of spirituality in life.

In contrast to organized religion, which provides a community of social support, spirituality is a subjective experience that exists both within and outside of traditional religious systems. Spirituality may be theistic, as in Christianity, Judaism, and Islam, nontheistic as in Buddhism, or polytheistic as in Hindu and shamanic traditions. Whatever the form of religious observances, specific problems tend to be associated with certain stages of spiritual development.

Stages of Spiritual Development

Each stage of the spiritual quest presents specific challenges. Challenges for beginning spiritual seekers include self-deception, self-doubt, fear of self-knowledge, guilt, and feelings of unworthiness. Lack of discernment and self-betrayal are not uncommon when a person first becomes aware of a desire for learning about spirituality. Often a seeker may look for a teacher without being able to evaluate the authenticity and integrity of the individual who claims to have special knowledge about spiritual development. Beginners may also be prone to inflation when they think they have found the one true way.

For the intermediate seeker who has made a commitment to the pursuit of spiritual development, ego-inflation can be fueled by spiritual insights. Feelings of elation associated with ego-inflation are often followed by deflation or depression. At this stage a person may also experience a conflict between the desire for inner development and the demands of the outer world. In some cases, suffering may be perceived as more desirable than happiness, particularly if suffering is believed to achieve spiritual merit.

In the more advanced stages of spiritual development, a spiritual practitioner who has begun to disidentify from egoic self-concepts may encounter a dark night of the soul in which life is perceived as meaningless suffering and desire is supplanted by aversion to life.

The advanced seeker must also be aware of the subtle pseudorealizations that can be extremely pleasurable and seductive. At every stage, attractive illusions may promise escape from the pain of existential realities. At any stage, the failure to temper spiritual ambition with the ordinary tasks of everyday life is potentially pathogenic.

A clinician working with religious persons and spiritual issues in psychotherapy should be able to differentiate pathological patterns from healthy spirituality at any stage. In contrast to pathogenic illusions of spirituality, authentic, healthy spirituality can be an asset in treating psychological dysfunction by providing a person with a felt sense of meaning and purpose in life. Healthy religious and spiritual attitudes can also contribute to reducing anxiety and alleviating depression by providing a sense of orientation and belonging in relation to the cosmos, nature, and the human community.

Denial of the Shadow

Ego defenses of projection and denial can easily be reinforced by some forms of religiosity. Religious groups that regard themselves as unique in their dedication to the one true way tend to divide the world into believers and nonbelievers, those who are awake and those who are asleep, those who are on a path and those who are not. Any dichotomy that reinforces the position that what *we* believe is right and what *others* believe is wrong leads to denigration of the outsider and unquestioning obedience. These hallmarks of cult behavior can be found not only in religious groups, but also in contemporary secular society and institutions (Diekman, 1990).

Ego inflation and projection of the negative shadow are evident in the devaluing of outsiders. Healthy spirituality does not presume that there is only one way to find the truth. Respect for other people's traditions and beliefs is an essential ingredient of healthy spirituality.

Because the psychological mechanisms of projection and denial operate unconsciously, those who see themselves as good whereas others are regarded as evil are generally not aware of projecting their unacknowledged impulses onto their enemies. It takes a certain degree of psychological maturity to acknowledge that the shadow, symbolizing what we most fear and dislike, must be uncovered in ourselves.

Spiritual Experiences

The first glimpse of states of consciousness that transcend ordinary reality can be both fascinating and seductive. A taste of bliss or a sense of being at home in the universe can be more compelling than other desires. Although such experiences can help people wean themselves from chemical addictions and have become a valuable tool for recovery (Grof, 1993; Grof & Grof, 1989, 1990), problems may develop if a person does not have a solid psychological foundation that enables him or her to recognize the value of the experience without idolizing the person or the method that induced it.

Transpersonal experiences often stimulate psychological growth and development. A clinician may be called upon to distinguish those experiences that contribute to psychological health from those that are regressive and potentially damaging. In the context of therapy, any experience, regressive or visionary, can be potentially rewarding, provided that the therapist can make appropriate interpretations and does not confuse genuine experiences of self-transcendence with regressive pathology, as in the pre/trans fallacy mentioned above. Both reductionistic interpretations of genuine mystical experiences and glorification of poorly differentiated prepersonal experiences can be detrimental to psychological health. For example, in working with a Catholic nun who had joined a convent after a profound mystical experience as a young adult and subsequently became disillusioned with religious life, it was useful to differentiate her subjective experience from her subsequent interpretations and assumptions about what it implied for her life.

If the longing for spiritual renewal is no longer satisfied by conventional religion, many forms of false mysticism tend to emerge. Substitute gratifications take many forms, including drugs and alcohol. Whenever critical intelligence is discarded in favor of blind devotion to a particular experience, person, or cause, addiction becomes a risk. Furthermore, sharing these experiences with a group can lead to a feeling of belonging that is a welcome alternative to a sense of social isolation and alienation.

A person who is searching for an authentic spiritual path can benefit from being able to raise questions and explore alternatives with a therapist who understands that spirituality, unlike religion, does not require obedience to a particular set of beliefs or prescribed dogma. If healthy spirituality is to flourish, it needs to be validated and supported by those who have gained some wisdom in their own search.

The capacity for healthy spirituality is innate. It exists in every human being and is not limited to any set of doctrines or practices. From a psychological perspective, spirituality is a universal experience, not a universal theology. Spirituality can be religious or nonreligious. It can be found at the heart of the great religions and in no religion. Spirituality can be found anywhere, not only in temples, churches, synagogues, and monasteries, but also in music and dance, in the beauty of nature, or the intimacy of a love relationship, and in any moment of ordinary life.

THE CASE OF JOHN

In the pages that follow, we illustrate some of our themes by describing in detail the process of transpersonal psychotherapy with John, a 44-year-old attorney who comes from a prosperous, devoutly religious Roman Catholic family.

In his first therapy session, John slumped down into the couch in his therapist's consulting room. "I'm in a really bad place," he exhales. His anxiety fills the room. "I've got it all. Good wife, two great kids, wonderful job, no money problems. What the hell have I got to complain about?" He pauses, as if looking at himself in an unwelcome mirror. "What happened to the golden boy with all the promise? How come I have to have a drink every night to get home and two more once I get there?"

John's background is not unusual. He was an imaginative child whose sensitivity and social skills were nurtured by a well-educated, yet deeply depressed mother. John made his mother proud by regularly serving as an altar boy at Mass and excelling at a major Catholic university in theology, psychology, and philosophy. He described his father as an ambitious businessman who had established an international reputation by being hard-nosed and shrewd. John wanted to follow in his father's footsteps. His ambitions were fueled by a secret longing to receive his father's love. He patterned himself on the popular image of the successful man—dynamic, extroverted, athletic, intellectually sophisticated, knowledgeable of the arts, dynamic and forceful in business—all the while remaining deeply religious. He married Ellen, a woman who matched his own social status, and together they had two children.

John began therapy because he felt empty and apathetic, anxious and depressed. Two years before his first session his closest male friend died of a heart attack. Six months prior to the first session a colleague in his firm was killed unexpectedly in a boating accident. Clearly John was confronting impermanence, but it was also dawning upon him that he was psychologically dying, suffocating under unquestioned ways of living and worn out habits of thought and feeling. John was struggling between psychic aliveness and psychic death. John said he was creatively stagnant, no longer growing. He said he felt spiritually dead!

John's confrontation with finitude became one of two major themes that unfolded during his therapy. The other concerned his identity. During the second therapy hour he reported the following event. Four years before, when he had just turned 40, John trekked with two other men to Machu Picchu high in the Andean mountains. One evening as they gazed into the campfire in the lonely mountain air, John talked openly to his friends about his troubles—how he was disappointed by his wife's lack of attentiveness, the heavy responsibilities of raising his children, the layers of falseness he felt at home and at work.

Later that night after his buddies went to sleep, John stayed awake gazing into the dying campfire. As he recalled this experience he said thoughtfully to his therapist,

> Everything became very quiet. For a few moments I felt strangely uplifted and alive. I felt totally unburdened, completely free. For the first time in my life I felt at one with myself. I was just myself—whole and complete, perfectly myself, not like my father or my mother, or anybody else. I also felt that I was a part of it all, like one star in the constellation of life.

Then, with his voice breaking with emotion, he said, "I want nothing more than to live like that—to be fully myself, at one with the world, and completely free."

What is the therapist to do for a client such as John who is in the throes of a midlife crisis? Like most depth psychotherapists, a transpersonal therapist listens, gathering information about his childhood, his parents and siblings, his life style, and so forth. The therapist might ask John what he thinks is the matter, how he handles his anxiety, what other goals he has. He or she would also inquire as to what sources of hope and support the client has, for these could be crucial if he commits himself to the kind of thoroughgoing psychotherapy he needs.

In John's case, as his story unfolds, the therapist listens to *what* he says and, even more significantly, to *how* he says it, noticing which aspects of his inner life he attends to and which ones he neglects. As John examines his experience, does he primarily use rational thinking? Does he focus on facts and details? Does he objectify and evaluate his experience? Does he look for quick solutions to deep-rooted concerns? Does he emphasize objective modes of inquiry, or does he express a deeper connection to his subjective world by bringing forth memories? Feelings and emotions? Deeper thoughts? Fears and apprehensions? Wants and longings? Dreams, fantasies, and imaginings? Intuitions? One of the therapist's tasks is to help John learn to inquire in as many ways as possible, and to become aware of aspects of his subjectivity that have been more or less neglected. Eventually he may freely associate to his concerns, readily accessing his deeper thoughts, feelings, memories, imaginings, intuitions, and anything else that goes on in his awareness.

The therapist's task is to help John become accustomed to experiencing a realm of his psyche that is deeper, more subjective, and less accessible than the discursive intellect, yet remains on this side of the Self as pure, unconditioned being and awareness. In Jungian analysis this is the realm of soul, where conscious and unconscious come together. The movement in Jungian analysis is away from the ego or personal self with its strictly outerworld focus toward a widening of consciousness into the realms of the unconscious. This realm is the source of artistic inspirations and creativity, of nighttime dreams and waking fantasy states. By bringing together conscious and unconscious, one accesses not only prepersonal and personal unconscious phenomena, but transpersonal states as well.

To enter this subjective realm, John will be encouraged to inquire into his actual felt experience as it unfolds within him during the course of each therapy hour. He will be asked to (a) focus his awareness on an issue he genuinely cares about, (b) be curious and concerned about himself and this issue, (c) open his awareness as fully as possible to whatever he inwardly experiences, and (d) describe whatever he experiences as freely and openly as possible. When John is fully immersed in his stream of immediate inner experiencing and unselfconsciously absorbed in the telling and retelling of his concerns he is likely to make new discoveries in energetically charged flashes of direct knowing. We emphasize the phrase "energetically charged" because these flashes are far more than simply mental insights. They are keenly experienced with one's whole being.

As John accesses his own subjective world, the therapist must also access his or her own, attempting to enter John's world and imagining being in his shoes. He or she may listen and reflect about how it feels to be with John, perhaps imagine what it might be like to be John, or to be the people with whom he interacts in his life. The therapist may also imagine how John feels being here, and how what the therapist says and does affects him.

This process gradually brings awareness to the unconscious organizing principles out of which John constructs his personal identity—the structure of his experiencing, the characteristic ways in which John experiences himself and his world—from a perspective within, rather than outside, his unique frame of reference.

In this way John will learn that he experiences himself and his world through the filter of these unconscious organizing principles, and therefore tend to perceive the present in terms of the past. John will gradually discover that he is identified with these structures and in many ways believes that he is in fact nothing but these structures. These identifications compel him to think, feel, perceive, and act in ways that match those structures, and often result in personal and interpersonal difficulties.

During the course of therapy, the therapist will repeatedly bring John's awareness to these structures as they are enacted both in John's life outside therapy and in his relationship to the therapist (the transference relationship). As the therapist does this, the hold of these structures on his psyche is likely to be reduced. At some point following considerable investigation and disidentification from the structures, John may experience himself as the Self, as pure being, awareness, and higher intelligence. In John's case, this actually occurred; John came to experience himself as pure spirit, distinct from the structures of personal identity.

As John entered his subjective realm and described his concerns, he gradually began to learn he was unconsciously enacting at least three basic personal structures.

First, John had the persona of a charming go-getter—outgoing, compulsively performing and entertaining. These personality traits brought him the attention he wanted, but others' responses no longer satisfied him. As John began his inquiry in therapy, the therapist commented that he seemed to be entertaining and performing even in the therapy itself. This helped John discern the deeper dimensions of the structure. Hidden behind his charming facade was a compulsion to take care of others. John had learned to be exceptionally adept at sensing the wishes of others and automatically giving them what they expected. He responded so well that he rarely noticed his own thoughts, feelings, and desires. He became especially sensitive to hints of depression in others, and concluded it was his duty to cheer them up. He began to learn this way of being in order to entertain his depressed mother and thereby gain her love. As John inquired further, he discovered that this structure was related to a second one.

John's second identity structure was composed of a frustrated, oppressed self in relation to a critical father who had grandiose expectations that his son would be socially successful in ways like him. In John's daily life, this structure was triggered whenever he felt his wife and children were particularly demanding, and whenever he was confronted by the exacting standards of professional life. When functioning in this structure, John wanted freedom from limited, overly rigid paternal rules and expectations, while at the same time he felt the threat of punishment for authentic self-strivings. John thwarted and frustrated himself by conforming to his internalized system of social codes. As this came to the surface in therapy, John gradually became aware of how he felt hurt by and angry toward his perfectionistic father, and how he felt a conflict between the resultant aggressive impulses and his fear of condemnation.

This recognition brought John to an even deeper, more central part of his prepersonal and personal identity. John's anger and authentic self-strivings conflicted with his very deep longing to feel loved, admired, and affirmed. John uncovered feelings of fear and dependency. He recognized that in a deep, prepersonal place he was full of insecurities, terrified of being alone, and longed to feel affirmed—not for his charm, athletic and intellectual prowess, and capacity to make others happy, but for other more fundamental creative and spiritual drives. He felt ashamed of his need for affirmation that seemed unacceptable and made him feel unworthy of love.

During the course of therapy, John became aware of each of these structures. He discovered how each of them affected him and how each influenced his thoughts and feelings toward himself and toward his world. When the therapy brought him awareness of his underlying despair and neediness, he felt that he was "at the end of his rope." He sensed that there was nothing else in him, that he was a helpless creature who desperately needed his mother and father to save him from his loneliness and look after him in a world of people whose standards he could not meet. Some of these feelings emerged in his relationship to the therapist, whom he began to see as the withholding mother and perfectionistic father who required that he meet certain standards before being loved.

Spiritual Realization in Psychotherapy

As this process of illuminating the structures of personal identity goes on, a client may gradually disidentify from limiting configurations of self and world and uncover other aspects of experience that feel more authentic and creative. Some clients inquire so deeply that they may temporarily become disidentified from their personal identity. At this point the structures of the ego-personality are discovered to be only objects in consciousness that need not control behavior or experience. It is important to note that premature disidentification can be problematic if a person has avoided working with the structures of personal identity. In John's case, experiencing fully the memories, fantasies, beliefs, and states of mind and emotion associated with personal identity preceded disidentification, which led to a sense of freedom and autonomy. Those who do the work of claiming their ego-personality may then discover that they are more than personal identity, that in fact their true identity is the Self. This is what happened to John.

As John probed ever more deeply into his psyche and worked to understand and reexperience his dependency and fear, his experience of desperately needing to be affirmed began to dissolve. Despite the fact that his helplessness had felt so real, John's identification of himself as frightened and needy proved in the end to be another cognitive–affective structure. In one session John experienced himself as exploding. The structure itself seemed to break apart, but because John was identified with his dependency, he felt himself break into a thousand pieces, like atoms shooting off at random.

At this point John became very anxious. He said he felt pried loose from his moorings, that he could hold on to nothing. He thought that he was dying, at the very least falling into a terrible, lonely nothingness. Wilson van Dusen (1972), the existential phenomenologist, calls this experience the "horrible satori":

> Satori is an uncommon but normal experience. Awareness of one's self as an individual temporarily disappears and there follows a spontaneous blossoming of awareness of the real nature of creation. The gate to satori is through the death of self. The individual who stumbles into this realm may feel himself terrified. He may feel like he is dying or completely losing his mind. The result is a horrible, half-born satori. (p. 160)

In such cases the presence of a skilled therapist may be crucial for a positive resolution. The therapist suggested to John that he simply let go, let the experience unfold, and see where it took him. He was quiet for nearly 10 minutes. Then he gently began to weep. He said that while he was silent he had "slipped into another plane of awareness" where he felt "deeply at peace" and "boundlessly free." He explained that he had lost all sense of individuality, that the hard lines differentiating him from everything else dissolved, and that he began to feel he was a vast "no-thingness," composed of empty space permeated by a fiery "scintillating and intelligent" substance. What's more, he felt total acceptance of everything! He felt radiantly alive and aware, and pregnant with possibility. For those few moments he felt totally liberated from his "reactive self," meaning his usual system of beliefs and emotions.

Later, he said that he had to "come down" from this state in order to know "where" he was and describe it, for he felt that this dimension was beyond the mind. Even as he spoke his thought processes seemed distinct from him, as though he were a sea of light in which thoughts arose like bubbles only to burst and disappear as quickly as they appeared.

John later referred to this state as an experience of "God." He came away from it believing that it was always there, but that in developing an identity based upon what the world seemed to require, he had lost touch with the depth dimension of his own being and awareness. In this moment John regained that depth and discovered that his identity as the Self, as pure contentless being and awareness was "pregnant with possibility," and no longer bound by the limiting constructions of personal identity. John differentiated his true nature from John-as-compliant self, John-as-frustrated rebel, and John-as-despairing and dependent. The result was a profound experience of inner freedom.

An experience such as John's does not end psychotherapy. In fact it can be a precondition for a deeper personal and spiritual exploration. After his spiritual experience, John began to use his therapy to inquire even more concentratedly into these fundamental questions:

- What does this experience of emptiness and spaciousness mean for my life?
- Given this experience, who am I really and fundamentally, and who or what is really in charge?
- What do the deaths of my friends mean for me, in view of this experience of the spirit and the larger purpose of my life? What are these deaths saying? And what are they asking of me as a response? What does the greater intelligence within me say about the meaning and purpose of these events?

Clients who are not already involved in meditation or some other authentic practice may at this point become deeply immersed in it, and if the therapist is able, psychotherapy may take on the characteristics of spiritual direction (Durckheim, 1989; May, 1982), focusing more on discerning spiritual guidance than uncovering personal history.

John's continuing inquiry led him to question many of his values, such as his personal desire for recognition, and he began to think about how he could serve and contribute to his family and his community. When John completed therapy he had already become committed to a meditation practice and was actively involved in community affairs.

It is beyond the scope of this chapter to discuss the subtleties and nuances that occur when psychotherapy becomes a process of spiritual inquiry. However, it seems evident that the therapeutic relationship can only support an open ended exploration of spirituality to the extent that the therapist is committed to his or her own spiritual growth. Although any good therapist can offer emotional support, those who have first-hand experience of transpersonal realms can be instrumental in helping clients experience those realms within themselves, thereby providing a new frame of reference for evaluating religious beliefs.

CONCLUSION

Psychotherapy with religious persons and spiritual seekers can be a meaningful process when both therapist and client are open to exploring this vital area of human experience and when the therapist is familiar with methods that help clients distinguish between the Self on the one hand and personal identity on the other. The therapist's understanding of religious experience is crucial. Although many forms of psychotherapy do not address spiritual issues, the possibility of meaningful spiritual inquiry is present in any therapeutic relationship that recognizes the value at a certain point of exploring and disidentifying from unquestioned identity constructs. If the awareness of the Self that lies beneath the superstructure of conditioned identity and religious dogma is overlooked, both therapist and client may be deprived of a powerful source of inspiration, healing, and renewal.

In summary, transpersonal psychotherapy offers the religious or spiritually inclined client an opportunity to explore, in a safe and supportive setting, the interior realms of the psyche and to discover his or her unique, authentic spirituality in a way that contributes to psychological health and maturity.

REFERENCES

Assagioli, R. (1965). *Psychosynthesis*. New York: Hobbs, Dorman.

Boorstein, S. (Ed.). (1996). *Transpersonal psychotherapy* (2nd ed.). Cupertino, CA: Science & Behavior Books.

Bugental, J. (1980). *The search for authenticity: The fundamentals of an existential-analytic approach*. New York: Irvington.

Coltart, N. (1992). The practice of psychoanalysis and Buddhism. In *Slouching towards Bethlehem: Collected writings*. New York: Guilford Press.

Deikman, A. (1990). *The wrong way home*. Boston: Beacon Press.

Durckheim, K. G. (1989). *The call for the master: The meaning of spiritual guidance on the way to the Self*. New York: Dutton.

Engler, J. (1986). Therapeutic aims in psychotherapy and meditation: Developmental stages in the representation of self. In K. Wilber, J. Engler, & D. Brown (Eds.), *Transformations of consciousness*. Boston: Shambhala.

Grof, C. (1993). *The thirst for wholeness*. San Francisco: Harper.

Grof, C., & Grof, S. (1990), *The stormy search for the self*. Los Angeles: Tarcher.

Grof, S. (1988). *The adventure of self-discovery*. Albany: State University of New York Press.

Grof, S., & Grof, C. (Eds.). (1989). *Spiritual emergency*. Los Angeles: Tarcher.

Huxley, A. (1944). *The perennial philosophy*. New York: Harper.

John of the Cross. (1991). *The dark night*. In K. Kavanaugh & O. Rodriquez (Trans.), *The collected works of St. John of the Cross* (Rev. Ed., pp. 353–457). Washington, D.C.: Institute for Carmelite Studies.

Jung, C. G. (1958a). Foreword to Suzuki's "Introduction to Zen Buddhism." In R. F. C. Hull (Trans.), *The collected works of C. G. Jung* (Vol. 11, pp. 538–557). Princeton, NJ: Princeton University Press. (Original work published 1939)

Jung, C. G. (1958b). The holy men of India. In R. F. C. Hull (Trans.), *The collected works of C. G. Jung* (Vol. 11, pp. 576–586). Princeton NJ: Princeton University Press. (Original work published 1944).

Jung, C. G. (1963). *Mysterium coniunctionis*. In R. F. C. Hull (Trans.), *The Collected works of C. G. Jung* (Vol. 14, 2nd ed.). Princeton, NJ: Princeton University Press.

Jung, C. G. (1967). Commentary on *"The secret of the golden flower."* In R. F. C. Hull (Trans.), *The collected works of C. G. Jung* (Vol. 13, pp. 1–56). Princeton, NJ: Princeton University Press. (Original work published 1957)

Jung, C. G. (1968). *Aion: Researches into the phenomenology of the Self*. In R. F. C. Hull (Trans.), *The Collected works of C. G. Jung* (Vol. 9, ii). 2nd edition. Princeton, NJ: Princeton University Press. (Original work published 1959)

Jung, C. G. (1969). Synchronicity: An acausal principle. In R. F. C. Hull (Trans.), *The collected works of C. G. Jung* (Vol. 8, pp. 417–531). Princeton, NJ: Princeton University Press. (Original work published 1952)

Jung, C. G. (1971). *Psychological types*. In R. F. C. Hull (Trans.), *The collected works of C. G. Jung* (Vol. 6). Princeton, NJ: Princeton University Press.

Jung, C.G. (1973). *Letters* (Vol. I: 1906–1950) (R. F. C. Hull, Trans.). Princeton, NJ: Princeton University Press.

Kakar, S. (1991). *The analyst and the mystic: Psychoanalytic reflections on religion and mysticism*. Chicago: University of Chicago Press.

Kapleau, P. (1968). *The three pillars of Zen*. New York: Harper & Row.

Maslow, A. H. (1968). *Toward a psychology of being*. New York: Van Nostrand.

Maslow, A. H. (1971). *The farther reaches of human nature*. New York: Viking.

May, G. (1982). *Care of mind, care of spirit: Psychiatric dimensions of spiritual direction*. New York: Harper & Row.

Perls, F. (1969). *Gestalt therapy verbatim*. Lafayette, CA: Real People Press.

Shafranske, E. (1994). Psychoanalytic praxis and religious experience. *Psychology of religion newsletter of the American Psychological Association, Division 36, 19(3)*.

Shapiro, D., & Walsh, R. (Eds.). (1984). *Meditation: Classic and contemporary perspectives*. New York: Aldine.

Smith, H. (1976). *Forgotten truth: The primordial tradition*. New York: Harper & Row.

Van Dusen, W. (1972). *The natural depth in man*. New York: Harper & Row.

Vaughan, F. (1979). *Awakening intuition*. New York: Doubleday.

Vaughan, F. (1995). *The inward arc* (2nd ed.). Nevada City, CA: Blue Dolphin Press.

Vaughan, F., & Wittine, B. (1994). Psychotherapy as spiritual inquiry. *Revision, 17*, 2, 42–48.

Walsh, R. (1990). *The spirit of shamanism*. Los Angeles: Tarcher.

Walsh, R., & Vaughan, F. (Eds.). (1993). *Paths beyond ego: The transpersonal vision*. Los Angeles: Tarcher.

West, M. (Ed.). (1987). *The psychology of meditation*. Oxford: Clarenden Press.

Wilber, K. (1977). *The spectrum of consciousness*. Wheaton, IL: Quest.

Wilber, K. (1980a). *The Atman project*. Wheaton, IL: Quest.

Wilber, K. (1980b). *No boundary*. Boston: Shambhala.

Wilber, K. (1983). *A sociable god*. New York: McGraw-Hill.

Wilber, K. (1993). The pre-trans fallacy. In R. Walsh & F. Vaughan (Eds.), *Paths beyond ego: The transpersonal vision* (pp. 256–266). Los Angeles: Tarcher.

Wilber, K. (1995). *Sex, ecology, spirituality*. Boston: Shambhala.

Wittine, B. (1990). Basic postulates for a transpersonal psychotherapy. In R. Valle & S. Halling (Eds.), *Existential-phenomenological perspectives in psychology*. New York: Wiley.

Wittine, B. (1994, November). Journey on the razor-edged path: Critical stages, dangers, and distortions on the way to the Self. In *Psychotherapy in a spiritual context*, Annual Symposium of the Berkeley Psychotherapy Institute, Berkeley, California.

Yalom, I. D. (1980). *Existential psychotherapy*. New York: Basic Books.

19

MARITAL AND FAMILY THERAPY WITH RELIGIOUS PERSONS

LEN SPERRY and PAUL GIBLIN

When religiously committed families or couples seek the services of a psychotherapist, they come with a system of religious beliefs and values that affect their attitudes, thoughts, and behaviors. Their religious orientation and religiosity influence various aspects of family life, from ideals about marriage and family purpose, to family size, power, sexuality and intimacy, gender roles, and methods of raising and disciplining children. As such, religion can serve as either an important resource or a significant source of resistance in therapy. Accordingly, it is incumbent on psychotherapists to understand the role and meaning of religious beliefs and practices of religiously committed couples and families. In this chapter, we briefly overview a number of relevant clinical theories, assessment methods, and interventions useful in working with such families and couples. We follow with a review of religious beliefs and practices that can facilitate or impede therapeutic work with this client population. Finally, we present case materials illustrating the clinical application of these concepts and discuss how these relate to some common presentations of religiously committed couples and families. Our discussion and case illustrations are drawn from an explicitly Christian orientation that reflects our personal faith and concerns the majority of cases in which we have sought to integrate religion and clinical practice. It is our view that the clinical issues involved in such an integration are found in any attempt to understand a couple's or family's religious faith commitment, no matter what is the specific nature of their beliefs, traditions, and practices.

RELEVANT THEORY AND CONCEPTS FROM MARITAL AND FAMILY THERAPY APPROACHES

Marital and family therapy differs from individual therapy in a number of respects. Rather than focusing on a single individual with a problem or concern, the therapist focuses on the individual within his or her marriage or family and defines problems as relational issues. The therapist typically relates to the couple or the entire family rather than to a single person and observes the interactions of the couple or family members rather than relying on the report of one member. Furthermore, therapy tends to be directed toward changing the structure and process of the relationship rather than toward merely achieving insight. Subsequently, such changes in structure and process lead to changes in the behavior and experience of all individuals in the relationship.

The current literature reflects an ever-increasing number of schools of thought and approaches to marital and family therapy. It is beyond the scope of this chapter to review all or many of these schools and approaches. We refer readers to the *Handbook of Family Therapy*, Volumes 1 (Gurman & Kniskern, 1981) and 2 (Gurman & Kniskern, 1991), for an extensive description of the major approaches. Here, we describe some overarching themes or constructs inclusive of these major approaches.

All couple and family relationships can be characterized in terms of three metaconstructs that essentially combine and integrate concepts and principles of most marital and family therapy schools and approaches. These three constructs are (a) boundaries, or inclusion; (b) power, or control; and (c) intimacy (Doherty & Colangelo, 1984; Doherty, Colangelo, Green, & Hoffman, 1985; Fish & Fish, 1986).

Boundary issues in families are those that center around membership and structure: membership in the sense of who is involved in the marital or family system and to what degree, and structure in terms of the extent to which family members are part of, but at the same time apart from, the couple subsystem or family unit. Boundary issues also refer to interpersonal boundaries, specifically, the degree of intrusiveness that will be accepted in the relationship. For a married couple, commitment to their relationship is a core boundary issue, as are partners' relative commitments to jobs, extended family, friends, and other outside interests. For children, boundaries usually center around the sense of belonging to the family, while having a sense of being recognized as an individual.

In terms of family therapy approaches, the structural approach (developed by Minuchin, 1984) and the contextual approach (advocated by

Boszormenyi-Nagy, 1987) emphasize the inclusion or boundary dimension of family functioning. Such therapeutic efforts are primarily directed at assessing and intervening in the boundary and role patterns to modulate the extent of enmeshment and distancing within the nuclear family—particularly the boundaries involving the marital–parental subsystem and sibling subsystems—as well as intergenerational boundaries (Doherty & Colangelo, 1984).

Power issues include responsibility, control, discipline, decision making, and role negotiation. Family interactions continually involve overt as well as covert attempts to influence decisions and behavior. Control or power issues are typically tied to issues of money, reward, and privileges. They also manifest themselves in more subtle ways, such as escalation of conflict or one-upmanship in efforts to regulate other family members' behavior. Couple interaction also involves struggle for control of the relationship in various ways. Essentially, the basic dynamic in marital conflict revolves around who tells whom what to do under certain circumstances. Both couple and family interactions range emotionally from positive to negative and politically from laissez-faire, to democratic, to autocratic. Thus, power becomes a metarule for all decisions about boundaries as well as intimacy. It determines which member or partner will pursue and which will distance, as well as how this is accomplished.

In terms of family therapy schools, the strategic approach (advocated by Haley, 1976), the interactional approach (developed by the Mental Research Institute Group; Watzlawick, 1984), and the behavioral system (such as described by Jacobson, 1981) emphasize this power and control dimension of family functioning. These therapeutic approaches focus on changing the family's rule system for mutual regulation. This can be accomplished directly, by returning the parent's authority with regard to a troubled adolescent or by teaching a feuding couple communication and problem-solving skills, or indirectly, such as with a paradoxical prescription to neutralize a specific power struggle between siblings (Doherty & Colangelo, 1984).

Intimacy issues in families are evident in areas like self-disclosure, friendship, caring, and appreciation of individual uniqueness. Intimacy involves negotiating emotional as well as physical distance between partners or among family members. In either instance, the goal is to balance a sense of autonomy with feelings of belonging. When issues of affection in a family become a source of difficulty, they can be manifested in various ways that result in such complaints as "You don't understand my feelings," "I'm being taken for granted," or "The romance has gone out of the relationship."

The psychoanalytic and object relations approach (such as the approaches of Ackerman and Framo), family systems theory (developed by Bowen), the symbolic–experiential approach (described by Whittaker), and the humanistic–communications approach (advocated by Satir) emphasize the intimacy dimension in couples and families. These approaches place a premium on optimal family functioning and self-differentiation. Resolving issues of boundaries and control is viewed as a prerequisite to helping partners or family members relate in a healthy, intimate fashion (Doherty & Colangelo, 1984).

Because these metaconstructs of boundaries, power, and intimacy are broad and inclusive, they can be quite useful in assessing and formulating treatment issues with all couples and families, irrespective of their religious affiliations or belief systems. The therapist may find it useful or necessary to translate these constructs with certain religiously committed clients. Salinger (1987) has attempted an initial translation of some of these notions for the conservative Protestant who may be concerned about the concordance of such constructs with biblical concepts of family functioning. Salinger noted that the Bible provides rather clear guidelines for family structure, boundaries, power, and conflict resolution as well as intimacy and personal development. He indicated that there are scriptural guidelines for resolution of interpersonal conflict coupled with respect and valuing of all family members, and these provide strong forces against triangulation and scapegoating processes.

RELIGIOUS BELIEFS AND PRACTICES THAT INFLUENCE THERAPY

Couples and families experiencing problems can derive significant benefits from religion. They may use their religious beliefs, values, and practices as well as their association with religious groups as resources and for support. Such religious concepts and support mechanisms may prove beneficial in therapy. Therapists can assist religiously committed couples and families in using religion as a tool for growth. For instance, therapists can encourage the development of religious practices that support family cohesion, such as family rituals and customs associated with religious holidays. Furthermore, they can encourage the replacement of religious practices that negatively affect growth and functioning with more positive religious behaviors. For example, parents can be counseled to substitute limit setting and forgiveness for threats and guilt when talking to adolescents about attendance at religious services.

Of course, this requires that therapists understand and are sensitive to couples' and families' religious beliefs and practices. But which religious beliefs and practices are helpful to families and facilitate the therapeutic process, and which do not? A survey of family life professionals' perceptions of religious beliefs and practices helpful to families (Brigman, 1984) identified love, faith, hope, forgiveness, grace, reconciliation, parenthood of

God, and divine worth of people as helpful. Similarly, they identified loving, caring, sharing, giving to others, taking responsibility, and shared religious observances as lifestyles or behaviors that helped strengthen families. Furthermore, these professionals perceived that the social support and networking that religious groups and organizations provide can greatly strengthen families. Brigman (1992) believed that such affiliations not only reduce loneliness and isolation by fostering a feeling of belonging and acceptance but also ease the burden of guilt and contribute to a sense of hope.

Several studies have demonstrated a positive relationship between marital satisfaction and spiritual well-being or religious maturity (Anthony, 1993; Dudley & Kosinski, 1990; Hunt & King, 1978; Roth, 1988). Empirical studies of healthy family functioning and family strengths have repeatedly identified religion as a significant variable. How religion and spirituality interact with dimensions of marital and family life has been addressed in recent theory building (Giblin, 1993; Robinson & Blanton, 1993; Schumm, 1985) or theory testing (Hatch, James, & Schumm, 1986) research.

Giblin (1993) proposed that, in a therapeutic context, the affective, cognitive, and behavioral shifts from marital conflict to marital satisfaction are potentially mediated by a couple's spiritual resources and that there is a sense in which the dynamics accompanying marital conflict are the direct inverse of those present with marital spirituality. Robinson and Blanton (1993) proposed a model of marital strengths with intimacy as the central characteristic and religious orientation as a major influence on intimacy, commitment, and communication. Schumm (1985) reviewed the family strengths research and proposed a path model whereby religious orientation was the driving force among five other family strengths. Although all three of these models were derived independently and showed considerable overlap, there are as yet no empirical data to support them.

On the other hand, some religious attitudes can be detrimental to families (Pruyser, 1977). Religious beliefs and practices that could be harmful to families were also identified by family life professionals in Brigman's (1984) study. These included rigid doctrine that is insensitive to human need; negativity regarding such issues as family planning, sexuality, divorce, and remarriage; and an overemphasis on such concepts as sin—a judgment leading to guilt feelings and low self-esteem. Other harmful beliefs and practices identified were the promotion of traditional, patriarchal gender roles as bias toward the indissolubility of marriage on any grounds and an emphasis on the individual to the exclusion of emphasis on the family, particularly with regard to activities that separate family members (Brigman, 1984).

Just as it is important for the therapist working with religiously committed couples and families to evaluate whether religious beliefs and practices contribute to integration and growth or to disintegration, so too must the therapist ascertain clients' expectations and perceptions of therapy. Generally speaking, the more orthodox or conservative their religious beliefs, the more sensitized and concerned clients are about therapists attacking their beliefs or encouraging them to go against their religious beliefs or the standards of the religious group to which they belong (Brigman, 1992; Koltko, 1990). Such perceptions and expectations are less likely to be present among those with less conservative beliefs, irrespective of creed. For instance, although Sanuas's (1989) review of several epidemiological studies showed that, in comparison with other religious groups, a high percentage of contemporary Jews undergo psychotherapy, Wikler (1986) found that Orthodox Jews entered therapy very reluctantly, and only after they had tried to solve their problems on their own or by talking with friends and rabbis. Sensitive to the stigma attached to psychotherapy, these individuals relied on their own resources in finding a therapist. In addition, for Orthodox Jews, the religious beliefs of the therapists were a major issue in choosing a counselor. Denton and Denton (1992) indicated that family therapists are somewhat reluctant to work with conservative Christians, stating that "one of the more perplexing subcultural groups for most family therapists is Protestant fundamentalists" (p. 182). In a study comparing therapists' ratings of fundamentalist families or nonfundamentalist families in therapy, these researchers found that therapists rated fundamentalist families to be significantly less healthy than nonfundamentalist families on three of four factors. Although fundamentalist families were rated as holding clearer expectations of how family members were to behave in relation to one another, nonfundamentalist families were rated healthier on such factors as intimacy, caring without smothering, and encouraging personal development and individualization while maintaining generational boundaries. Furthermore, involvement with a particular church and specific religious beliefs and practices had a significant impact on family organization and functioning of fundamentalist families. Nonfundamentalist families were found to encourage age-appropriate responsibilities and individuation by allowing members to exercise their own judgment in appropriate ways, did not perceive change to be a threat, and maintained appropriate boundaries between nuclear family affairs and extended family members. On the other hand, fundamentalist families were much more enmeshed, discouraged members from exercising personal judgment, perceived change as a threat, and had problems with boundaries between nuclear family and extended family members.

In his classic family therapy text *Generation to Generation: Family Process in Church and Synagogue*, Friedman (1985) emphasized working with nonfundamentalist, nonorthodox families. He reported that despite sociological differences, there are essentially no differences among Jewish families and Christian families (both White and Black), when it comes to symptom location, triangles, homeostasis, and the like.

Assessment of Spirituality and Religion in Marital and Family Work

Clinicians need to be able to accurately assess the influence of spirituality and religion in clients' lives. Is the valence negative, with the spiritual contributing to withheld emotions (e.g., because anger is not to be felt or expressed), distorted thoughts (e.g., crises are punishments from God), or dysfunctional behavior (e.g., the married man who is about to "give it all up"—including wife and children—to "follow the Lord")? On the other hand, is the valence of the religious positive but underused? That is, might the religious be better used in the service of therapeutic change and growth? In assessment the therapist must typically examine the following factors: (a) awareness (on the therapist's part) of the place that spirituality and religion has in his or her life; (b) an understanding of the differences between religion and spirituality; and (c) a means of assessing client spirituality and religion.

Self-Awareness

Family therapy training emphasizes self-awareness in the service of the therapeutic use of the self. Coursework and supervision typically include construction of one's family genogram and analysis of response patterns to the "facts" of one's history. Experiential exploration of one's feelings and beliefs related to gender, culture, and stage of life are necessarily addressed. Along with Aponte (1985), we urge therapists to conduct a thorough examination of clients' religious journeys, values, and beliefs. Ideally, this reflective process should occur in a supportive supervisory–peer context that challenges blind spots and expands perspectives.

Spirituality Versus Religion

Is there a difference between spirituality and religion, and, if so, what difference does the difference make? A student of ours made this distinction: "Spirituality is about going fishing and thinking about God and life, while religion is about going to church and thinking about fishing!" Religion is born of awareness of the transcendent together with expression of that awareness in conceptual, cultural, and social form (Ellswood, 1990). Religion is about a shared belief system (dogma) and communal ritual practice (liturgy). However, for many people today religion carries a negative connotation:

> Spirituality, as opposed to religion connotes a direct, personal experience of the sacred unmediated by particular belief systems prescribed

by dogma or by hierarchical structures of priests, ministers, rabbis, or gurus. (Berenson, 1990b, p. 59)

Spirituality is about people's search for meaning and belonging and the core values that influence behavior. It has been variously defined as "harmonious interconnectedness—across time and relationships" (Hungelmann, 1985, p. 149), "the human capacity to experience and relate to a dimension of power and meaning transcendent to the world of sensory reality" (Anderson, 1985, p. 21), and "the experience of consciously striving to integrate one's life in terms not of isolation and self-absorption but of self-transcendence toward the ultimate value one perceives" (Schneiders, 1986, p. 255).

Benner (1989) made this helpful distinction between religion and spirituality: "Not all spirituality is religious, and not all religious spirituality is Christian" (p. 20). All people are created spiritual beings as they experience a yearning for self-transcendence and surrender. This quest becomes religious in relation to some higher power and the individual responds to this relationship with prayer and worship. Clinicians should be aware that this quest takes many forms and requires a respectful acceptance of others' faith commitments and an appreciation of the nuances of individual religious experience. For example, Christian spirituality, in our experience, is one subset of religious spirituality in response to Father, Jesus, and Spirit. Such a response reflects an unique aspect that is central to Christianity: belief in the tripartite nature of God. An appreciation of spirituality, therefore, involves a consideration of the quest for meaning in its most universal form and in its most specific religious expression.

In the context of marital and family therapy, we find it most helpful to focus on the spiritual and religious as the search for meaning; the experience of the meaningful in relationships (love, acceptance, and forgiveness); the value dimension of people's lives together; and the manner in which people communicate, manage conflicts, maintain commitment, and make decisions in relationship to their ultimate values, including the transcendent. We find it less helpful to focus on religious beliefs, theology, or religious practice and have learned that clients are generally pleasantly surprised to think about, explore, and play with the "spirituality of the ordinary" in their lives.

Assessment Strategies

Clinicians need a flexible means for assessing clients' spirituality or religion. It is helpful to think of a continuum ranging from informal questioning and conceptualizing, on the one hand, to use of formal assessment tools on the other. In terms of less formal inquiry, the clinician might ask about the place of God, religion, church and community, prayer, and time in clients' lives. He or she might ask about the felt or thought place of

God, religion, and spirituality in dealing with the issues that bring clients to therapy and to the eventual resolution of these problems. The therapist wants to understand the degree to which religion and spirituality influences feelings, thoughts, and behaviors in the system, ranging from no influence, to some influence but basically outside the system, to some influence on behavior or thoughts, to an encompassing influence on all three dimensions of feelings, thoughts, and behaviors (DiBlasio, 1988; Giblin, 1993). Posing questions about time (e.g., alone vs. couple or family time and quality of time [free–meaningful vs. meaningless–compulsive]) and space (alone–private space vs. enmeshment) helps to reveal the value and practice of centering, reflection, and contemplation among clients. This, of course, assumes that individuals need a regular amount of quiet time and space in order to nurture the spiritual.

In the beginning phase of treatment, we may use Pruyser's (1976) seven categories for "pastoral diagnosis" and inquire about the following:

1. Awareness of the holy: What does one hold sacred? What does one revere?
2. Providence: Where is trust or hope in the client's life?
3. Faith: To what does the client commit himself or herself?
4. Grace or gratefulness: For what is the client thankful? What has he or she been given? And has one been forgiven for or been forgiving?
5. Repentance or sin: How has a client dealt with mistakes? Where does he or she place responsibility?
6. Communion: With whom does the client reach out, care for, and feel cared for?
7. Sense of vocation: What sense of satisfaction and purpose does the client find in life and work?

A number of formal assessment tools have been developed from Pruyser's (1976, 1977) work.

At the more formal end of the continuum, the clinician may use one of several easily administered, psychometrically valid and reliable assessment instruments. Analysis of responses to individual questions will reveal family member attitudes and practices, often with greater depth and detail than might surface in interviews. Two such instruments are the Spiritual Well-Being Scale (SWB; Ellison, 1983) and the Spiritual Experience Index (SEI; Genia, 1990, 1991). These consist of 20 and 38 questions, respectively, and are answered on 6-point Likert scales. The SWB comprises two subscales: Existential Well-Being (measuring a person's sense of life purpose and satisfaction) and Religious Well-Being (measuring the nature of a person's relationship with God). These two subscales are summed for an overall spiritual well-being score. The SEI was developed to assess spiritual maturity from an object relations, developmental perspective. The SEI is intended to correlate with a five-stage model of spiritual maturity or faith. These stages are as follows:

1. Egocentric faith, dominated by splitting;
2. Dogmatic faith, characterized by rules of fairness and clearly defined obligations, defensiveness, and utilitarian use of doctrine;
3. Transitional faith: religious searching and doubting;
4. Reconstructed internalized faith, characterized as a more internal, differentiated, and personally integrating religious system; and
5. Transcendent faith, for which Genia (1990) listed 10 criteria.

Both the SWB and the SEI can help therapists begin to conceptualize the functional, interactive nature of the God–family relationship. (For a comprehensive description and evaluation of several dozen different spiritual assessment tools, refer to Fitchett, 1993.)

Regardless of whether the clinician uses a more or less formal assessment method, the goal is to discriminate between healthy or dysfunctional religion and spirituality in the marital or family system. This means being able to determine, for example, whether family members form coalitions with God in an effort to gain extra power, control, or authority; if religious conflict serves as a "stalking horse" to present underlying family conflict; or if marital or family conflict arises out of fundamentally different religious commitments (Pattison, 1982). It also means being able to determine how spirituality and religion contribute to affect (from defensiveness to openness), thinking (from certainty and absoluteness to tentativeness), and behavior (from revenge to forgiveness; Giblin, 1993).

Finally, the clinician needs to attend to patterns of intimacy and distance in both marital and family and God relationships. This assumes that there is a high concordance between closeness and distance among intimates and closeness and distance in relationship with God. For example, Worthington (1990) has couples graph these cycles for themselves and for their relationship to God. Couples generally find strong parallels between the two plots, which helps demonstrate the imminent, incarnational nature of God. Likewise, change in family relationships can result in change in the perceived relationship with God, and vice versa. For instance, differentiation from an idealized, distant parent could result in the loss of both the idealized parent and God concepts and relationship (Ranges, 1980). Clinicians need to be aware of religious transference and alterations in faith experiences that occur during therapy.

Intervention With Religiously Committed Couples and Families

Respect for and incorporation of the spiritual and religious into marriage and family therapy does not necessitate using a body of specific techniques. Quite the opposite: More harm is likely to be done to clients by clinicians equipped with ready scriptural reference for each presenting problem, by untimely or overused prayer, and by the simplistic rendering of the mysterious and paradoxical sides of life. Clinicians need a range of flexible approaches, including (a) therapeutic use of self; (b) a sense of how explicitly–directly or implicitly–indirectly the religious dimension can be used; and (c) consideration of the appropriateness and timing of interventions, such as prayer with or for clients, scriptural correlations, bibliotherapy, forgiveness or thanksgiving work, gestalt or empty chair techniques, dreams, and networking with church or spiritual resources.

We have spoken thus far about a range of assessment strategies for dealing directly or indirectly with a couple or family's relationship with the transcendent or God (i.e., spiritual assessment). It is our belief that all human beings are spiritual; open to a sense of life greater than themselves; draw meaning and purpose in relation to that greater sense; and are at heart relational, inclusive of self, others, creation, and the transcendent, God, or higher power. When clients are both aware of and able to articulate their relationships with the transcendent, we speak of a more direct–explicit involvement of this dimension in therapy. For example, Where do you think God is in your decision making? What do you think God wants for you each and for your marriage? What is your memory of Jesus dealing with his anger? However, when clients lack such awareness or articulation, we involve the spiritual in a more indirect–implicit fashion, never speaking directly about God but always keeping an ear open for understanding their value, belief, and meaning systems. The categories and questions generated by psychologist Paul Pruyser (1976) are especially helpful for the more implicit–indirect assessment and intervention strategies. (For a related discussion see Tan, chap. 13, this volume.)

Therapeutic Use of Self

More important than any other single factor is the therapist's own spiritual journey and his or her awareness of and ability to articulate that process. At best, the couple or family needs to know that they have found a "spiritual friend."

A spiritual friend is familiar with the religious resources, scriptures, rituals, traditions, and spiritual reading materials that the client mentions. And if not directly familiar with these resources, he or she does homework to become more so. Perhaps more importantly, he or she has first-hand experience of the client's struggles with finding meaning, with experiences of loss, psychological–emotional–spiritual death, and knows about hope and resurrection—new life. At worst, they need to know that their values and beliefs will be respected and that they will not be shamed, ridiculed, or evangelized. Below are some key themes that we believe each clinician needs to make meaning of for himself or herself. We have found these themes to be particularly salient for Christian psychotherapists, and they illustrate the kind of inquiry that is useful for clinicians to undertake in assessing the spirituality that they bring to the therapeutic relationship.

God's presence. Where is God to be found?: Above, outside, in the world? Is God dead? Is He in you or me or in "the between" (Berenson, 1990a)? Our belief is in a God imminently present in the everyday familial, work, marital, and home lives of each person. As Hart (1989) has pointed out, "where the action is in a person's life, God is most present and active" (p. 117). God is present not simply in the Sabbath or Sunday churchgoing, in scripture reading, or in personal prayer. God's presence is enfleshed in the love, care, sacrifice, intimacy, and forgiveness of people's lives together. That presence is often evident after the fact and is usually accessed upon reflection.

Decision making and change. How do the values humans hold and the decisions we make embody the spiritual and religious? What we most deeply want, God also wants for us. The trick is to know what we want and to be able to go after it singlemindedly. The pulls of denial and addiction (May, 1988), materialism, careerism, and egoism (Watchell, 1983) are strongly opposed to our recognition of deep desires. The more open people are to evaluating their decisions in trusted relationships, the more likely it is that they will overcome blind spots and make good decisions.

What are the dynamics of change and growth? Is it a cognitive, affective, or behavioral shift that initiates and maintains lasting change? From a spiritual perspective, growth or change takes time and typically involves waiting and letting go. Hendrix (1988) has noted that what one partner needs the most is what the other partner is the least able to give, as well as being the precise area where that partner needs to grow.

Change and growth involves differentiation in relation to God as well. It is painful but all too easy to go along with the cultural and religious narrative for marital and family life: that is, being "with the program" while failing to listen to the deeper feelings and stirrings of self, partner, and family members. An example of this would be when, in the name of "healthy religious practice," one represses anger while extending care and self-sacrifice at the expense of self-awareness and one's own needs.

Sin and suffering. How are we to make meaning of tragedy and suffering in our lives? Do these things come from God as punishment for sins or are they needed for character development? Who is to blame for pain, evil, and suffering? Why does God not answer prayers? From a spiritual perspective, as therapists we distinguish between curing and healing. The former refers to finding some way around or through a problem or ailment. *Healing,* on the other hand, refers to bringing back to wholeness, to being at peace with and in the correct relationship with self, other, and God. As therapists, we recognize that we participate in the healing process, but that we do not bring about the healing. Although we do not understand why suffering and evil are present, we believe that they are not from God and that God works with everyone in suffering and evil for good. In our view, God represents life, freedom, healing, and growth, and efforts to interpret God's ways most often distance us from a couple's or a family's pain.

This question arises: Is sin an act omitted or committed? From a spiritual perspective, humans are made up of freedom and creative possibility mixed with finite limitation. Individuals are sinful to the degree that they deny either or both polarities of their existence (i.e., "denial of death" or the divine). Typically, sin is thought of primarily in terms of limitation. All humans are sinners: We act out of our conditionedness, we have "sore points," we have "shadow sides," and we make mistakes. We are most likely sinful when we fail to own our limitations or to accept responsibility for our contribution to marital and family conflicts. However, as Becker (1973) noted in *The Denial of Death*, we are equally susceptible to failure at owning our heroic, creative (i.e., spiritual) side.

Images of and experiences of God. How are the voice, face, and person of God imagined? At best, people's God concepts are an admixture of the parental (God as father figure [Freud], God as preferred parent [Adler], God as same sex [social learning theory], and God as extension of self [self-esteem theory]; Spilka, 1975), religious institutions (Coles, 1990), and the developmental and imaginative, along with familial and religious influences (Rizzutto, 1979). How we as therapists imagine God—whether as distant, demanding, and critical or warm and nurturing—will likely influence the process and outcome of therapy with clients who are religiously committed. For example, in the first case study that follows, we discuss a client, Betty, whose image of God was entirely punitive, demanding, and unforgiving. For the client to begin to forgive herself and accept her behaviors when she experienced this same judgment and nonacceptance from her spouse and parents presented an almost unsurmountable obstacle to therapy.

Paradoxical and symbolic. What is the clinician's experience of the mysterious, paradoxical, and symbolic sides of life? Religious experience is often described as indescribable, as ineffable. To have life one needs to be willing to lose one's life. In letting go, dying to self, and trusting to God, one finds new life. Yet one needs to love others as one loves oneself. One needs to be willing to risk all for the sole treasure deep in one's heart. *Negative capability* is a psychoanalytic style of listening described as the capacity to be in uncertainty and doubt without any irritable reaching after fact and reason (Scharff & Scharff, 1987). The clinician sensitive to the spiritual may use this technique not only in search of therapeutic effectiveness but also out of a belief and experience of being open to the mysterious ways of the spiritual. These are some of the areas that we attend to as we work with the religious dimensions of therapy with couples and families.

Direct–Explicit Versus Indirect–Implicit Use of the Religious

The clinician needs to be able to determine how directly or indirectly the spiritual and religious dimension is to be used. In our practice, we tend to be cautious, moving slowly and only after a relationship has developed with the couple or family. We like to deal with the spiritual by way of play, posing such questions as "I wonder how God accepts you when you find it so hard to accept yourself?" and "I wonder what God thinks about this decision?" Alternatively, we might hint or suggest, "I was thinking about you two when I heard the scripture readings on Sunday." The goal is to plant seeds, to suggest alternative ways of looking at and experiencing relationships, and to create an openness to experiment (i.e, to cooperate with the spiritual).

CASE MATERIAL

In the two case descriptions that follow, we illustrate various interventions that we have used with religiously committed clients.

Jack

Jack was a 38-year-old, highly verbal, minimally insightful, married man. He had two children and a third was born in the time that he was in therapy. He was Roman Catholic, a graduate of parochial high school and college, a weekly participant in a men's prayer and scripture study group, and a daily churchgoer. Jack was dissatisfied with his professional work and envisioned that his true calling was to be an evangelizer, a minister, or, perhaps, a missionary. He was about to "give it all up" to follow his "call," and he had declared bankruptcy to pay off debts. He reported marital satisfaction but appeared minimally committed to either marriage or parenting.

In terms of spiritual assessment, Jack's was a "spirituality of the ideal": fueled by perfectionist images and characterized by a litany of *shoulds* and a focus on his own self (i.e., "How am I doing?" "How do I match up to the ideal?"). This is in contrast to a "spirituality of the real," which begins with one's personal reality and asks "What is God doing in my life?" In other words, the latter is a God-centered rather than a self-centered spirituality (Broccolo, 1990).

In Jack's case, the issue was one of an explicit sense of spirituality. Jack was quite aware and articulate about his Christian belief system, to the degree of feeling called to professional ministry. However, his faith system appeared to function in a largely defensive fashion, for several reasons:

1. It called him away from responsible partnering, parenting, and economic providing.
2. It bolstered an otherwise weak sense of self and provided a sense of uniqueness.
3. It had little to do with any altruistic sense of service.

In terms of Pruyser's (1976) categories of pastoral diagnosis, Jack presented as follows:

1. Awareness of the holy: Jack strongly identified with the church and it rituals. He was an active church participant on the daily level. He spoke of a strong sense of God, a God who was primarily otherworldly.
2. Providence: Jack had little sense of trust in himself and placed entire trust in God and God's representatives, the clergy.
3. Faith: Jack struggled with an appropriate locus for his commitments. It was surprising how little impact his wife's pregnancy and child's birth had on him during therapy.
4. Grace and gratefulness: Jack had little sense of thanksgiving for his life and relationships; instead, he had a strong sense of existential guilt for not being more successful with his life.
5. Repentance: Jack had a legal, rule-governed sense of morality and would not take work that would apparently compromise his values.
6. Communion: Jack had little sense of connectedness.
7. Vocation: This was a primary area of therapy: What was he called to do with his life? What would provide him with a sense of meaning? There was a strong sense that Jack was operating less out of his heart's desires than on the basis of an external sense of what he should be doing.

Overall, Jack presented with what seemed to be a fairly rigid belief system, a strong sense of connectedness to the institutional church, and with much less of a sense of personal spirituality.

Betty

Betty entered therapy with Brad, her ex-husband. She was 47 years old, a bright and hard-working divorced woman who came to therapy for relationship counseling in dealing with her ex-husband. She was a mother of six grown children, one of whom had been diagnosed with cancer only months after Betty separated from her husband. Betty had not intended to divorce but simply to find emotional space outside of an oppressive marriage. However, her husband served her with divorce papers before the year was out. Her son died 2 years after the divorce, but not without an infinite number of prayers and heroic medical efforts by Betty. Betty was nonetheless blamed for her son's death by her ex-husband and her elderly parents, all of whom pointed to her marital separation as the catalyst for the son's illness. Betty's grief and rage were palpable, and her search for faith was passionate but filled with doubt and questioning. Her upbringing allowed for little anger or vulnerability, much independence, and dogmatic religious practice.

Next, we describe some of the interventions that we used in therapy with Jack and with Betty.

Prayer

Therapists can pray with or for clients. Many spiritually sensitive therapists prepare for their work with a form of centering prayer, a desire to be open to the spiritual in both self and clients. In our experience, far fewer clinicians actually incorporate in-session prayer and most do so only after assessing client comfort levels with this intervention. We ask clients or clients may report about prayer (i.e., what their "friend" thinks or feels about their situation). We may variously include relevant religious figures, saints, or deceased ancestors in prayers. Detailed examples of in-session prayer in separate cases with an individual, couple, and family can be reviewed in Wimberly's (1990) book.

Returning to our case studies, Betty had a distant, sickly mother from whom she had received no nurturing. She had long ago learned to be independent, a caretaker, and to "keep a stiff upper lip." She had had no positive female role models. In one session, Betty and one of us prayed to Mary, the mother of Jesus, that she might become the mother Betty never had. Mary was a strong, competent woman who, like Betty, also let go of her son at a very young age, and Mary had wept. This positive identification allowed Betty to begin to trust and express her deep grief and to begin to befriend her spiritual self.

Dreams

Dreams have been referred to as the "royal road to the unconscious" and as "God's language." Religious communication is frequently conveyed in dreams in the Scriptures. In marital and family work, dreams provide access into both the unconscious and the religious. For example, Betty had an extraordinary dream within the first few days of her son's death. The dream took place in heaven, and her completely healed son bounded across an open, sunny field to greet her. He wanted to tell her that he "was doing fine, that God was OK," and that he was with two, elderly loved neighbors.

The dream was amazingly confirmed by a neighbor who had also lost a son and reported having Betty's dream the same week. This dream sequence was returned to during therapy as a means to explore and challenge Betty's otherwise negative and judgmental image of God.

Scriptural Correlation

The clinician who is familiar with the Scriptures may share associations depending on the degree to which this may enhance the therapeutic process. If done correctly, this intervention allows the couple or family an expanded perception, may help to normalize their conflicts, and might assist in overcoming their sense of isolation. For instance, Jack narcissistically identified himself with many scriptural references of self-sacrifice and "following the Lord." The therapeutic task with him was to begin to temper his religious enthusiasm with "rules of discernment" drawn from his familiar background in Ignatian spirituality and to increase dialogue of "vocation" with his spouse and other community members. He was offered the frequent observation that, in the therapist's experience and reading of scriptures and spiritual works, conversion or change of heart, behavior, and the fundamental way of living one's life was most frequently fashioned out of repeated small steps rather than through major leaps. Jack's "leaps of faith" would cut him off from as yet barely nurtured marital and family commitments. He had received no external affirmation of his gifts and talents for ministry from his religious community. The therapist's task was to balance a mirroring of Jack's enthusiasm with wondering aloud about how and why he did not receive affirmation or recognition for his gifts from the faith community, as do most ministers during their ministerial training.

Forgiveness and Acceptance

At the heart of the spiritual perspective is the sense of interconnectedness, unity, and equality. Whereas conflict highlights differences and punctuates interactions with clear villain and victim perceptions, the spiritual focuses on similarities and shares equal responsibility for initiating change. We have found the spiritual to provide strong support for cognitive and behavioral interventions aimed at interrupting reactive cycles in a marriage or family. Time-out strategies and self-talk might include reflection on what one is saying "down deep" or what God's will is for the client in this interaction. Alternatively, it might involve saying something like this: "When you are so angry with each other and only aware of each other's negatives, try to imagine how God sees and accepts you and him or her." Looking at clients' family of origin models for acceptance, forgiveness, caring, and thanksgiving may expose poor modeling of these spiritual activities and allow partners to begin to be more accepting of one another. Needless to say, therapeutic work focused on forgiveness is enhanced by the addition of the spiritual perspective.

Bibliotherapy

It is important to assess the impact of literature, movies, and videos on clients and the therapeutic process as well. In cases where readings chosen by clients may serve to maintain their rigid defensiveness, readings prescribed by therapists may economically expand perspectives, correct misinformation, challenge misperceptions, and contribute to a sense of belonging and understanding. Clinicians need to have read whatever they assign, must follow up on their assignments, and must process client understanding or interpretation of the material.

Gestalt, Empty Chair, and Letter-Writing Techniques

Gestalt therapy, empty chair scenarios, and letter writing are all techniques that can be used to include God and God concepts in therapy for both assessment and intervention. Betty, for instance, had a strong, positive, idealizing transference with one of us in therapy. She found him to be accepting, nonjudgmental and a person of faith. Her longing for a warm and accepting God was counterbalanced by a rage and sense of abandonment by God. We brought Betty's otherwise well-censored feelings and images into the room by inviting God into the empty chair, listening to an imagined dialogue between Betty and God, and taking turns sitting in and speaking from God's chair. We also took turns writing "letters from heaven," again imagining a dialogue between Betty and God. The comparison of different perspectives was broadening for her.

CONCLUSION

It has been our experience that many clients increasingly seek a clinician who not only deals with their conflicts but also recognizes their spiritual journey, their search for values, and their need for "care of the soul." For the religiously committed couple or family, finding God in the midst of conflict as they seek to resolve differences and broaden their horizons is tremendously empowering and freeing. We believe the challenges and the rewards in doing therapy with clients who are religiously committed are abundant. To tap into the spiritual is to tap a wellspring (or wildfire) of energy. Berenson (1990b) noted this transformation in his attention to the spiritual:

Recently, having done four therapy sessions back to back without a break, I was struck by how alive and exhilarated I felt. Fifteen years ago, the same four sessions would have left me drained and exhausted. The difference comes from allowing expression to the power of the "between," the vital current that connects my clients and me. (p. 67)

Similar to work with any clients who differ from therapists by way of gender, ethnicity or culture, or age and life stage, work with clients who are religiously committed challenges therapists to go back to their own understandings, values, and beliefs. If the spiritual and religious has not been an area of attention and nurture in the therapist's life, then engaging such areas in clients' lives will be threatening or painful. On the other hand, when this is an area of growth for therapists, then engaging clients around spiritual issues and resources will be exciting and produce further growth for both client and therapist.

In terms of research possibilities in this area, the sky's the limit. Many questions about the relationship between spirituality and therapy await exploration. To name but a few examples: How could spiritual resources (prayer individually or as a couple) enhance marital therapy with couples who are religiously committed? How would asking a faith community to regularly pray for an (anonymous) couple or a family enhance the outcome of therapy for that couple or family? How does prayer by the therapist influence therapeutic outcome, and in what ways? These and many more issues are in need of examination.

REFERENCES

Anderson, D. (1985). Spirituality and systems therapy. *Journal of Pastoral Psychotherapy, 1,* 19–32.

Anthony, M. (1993). The relationship between marital satisfaction and religious maturity. *Religious Education, 88,* 97–108.

Aponte, H. (1985). The negotiation of values in therapy. *Family Process, 24,* 223–238.

Becker, E. (1973). *The denial of death.* New York: Free Press.

Benner, D. (1989). Toward a psychology of spirituality: Implications for personality and psychotherapy. *Journal of Psychology and Theology, 8,* 19–30.

Berenson, D. (1990a, September–October). Between I and thou. *Family Therapy Networker,* p. 32.

Berenson, D. (1990b). A systemic view of spirituality: God and twelve step programs as resources in family therapy. *Journal of Strategic and Systemic Therapies, 9,* 59–70.

Boszormenyi-Nagy, I. (1987). *Foundations of contextual therapy: Collected papers of Ivan Boszormenyi-Nagy.* New York: Brunner/Mazel.

Brigman, K. (1984). Churches helping families: A study of the effects of religion on families and how churches can help strengthen families. *Family Perspectives, 18*, 77–84.

Brigman, K. (1992). Religion and family strengths: Implications for mental health professionals. *Topics in Family Psychology and Counseling, 1*(1), 39–52.

Broccolo, G. (1990). *Vital spiritualities: Naming the holy in your life*. Notre Dame, IN: Ave Maria Press.

Coles, R. (1990). *Spiritual life of children*. Boston: Houghton Mifflin.

Denton, R. T., & Denton, M. J. (1992). Therapists' ratings of fundamentalists and non-fundamentalist families in therapy: An empirical comparison. *Family Process, 31*, 175–185.

DiBlasio, F. (1988). Integrative strategies for family therapy with evangelical Christians. *Journal of Psychology and Theology, 16*, 127–134.

Doherty, W. J., & Colangelo, N. (1984). The family FIRO model: A modest proposal for organizing family treatment. *Journal of Marital and Family Therapy, 10*, 19–29.

Doherty, W. J., Colangelo, N., Green, A. M., & Hoffman, G. (1985). Emphases of the major family therapy models: A family FIRO analysis. *Journal of Marital and Family Therapy, 11*, 299–303.

Dudley, M., & Kosinski, F. (1990). Religiosity and marital satisfaction: A research note. *Review of Religious Research, 32*, 78–86.

Ellison, C. (1983). Spiritual well-being: Conceptualization and measurement. *Journal of Psychology and Theology, 11*, 330–340.

Ellswood, R. (1990). Religion. In R. Hunter (Ed.), *Dictionary of pastoral care and counseling* (pp. 683–687). Nashville, TN: Abingdon Press.

Fish, R., & Fish, L. S. (1986). Quid pro quo revisited: The basics of marital therapy. *American Journal of Orthopsychiatry, 56*, 371–384.

Fitchett, G. (1993). *Spiritual assessment in pastoral care: A guide to selected resources*. Decatur, GA: Journal of Pastoral Care Publications.

Friedman, E. H. (1985). *Generation to generation: Family process in church and synagogue*. New York: Guilford Press.

Genia, V. (1990). Religious development: A synthesis and reformulation. *Journal of Religion and Health, 29*, 85–99.

Genia, V. (1991). The Spiritual Experience Index: A measure of spiritual maturity. *Journal of Religion and Health, 30*, 337–347.

Giblin, P. (1993). Marital conflict and marital spirituality. In R. Wicks & R. Parsons (Eds.), *Clinical handbook of pastoral counseling: Vol. 2* (pp. 237–241). New York: Paulist Press.

Gurman, A. J., & Kniskern, D. P. (Eds.). (1981). *Handbook of family therapy*. New York: Brunner/Mazel.

Gurman, A. J., & Kniskern, D. P. (Eds.). (1991). *Handbook of family therapy* (Vol. 2). New York: Brunner/Mazel.

Haley, J. (1976). *Problem-solving therapy*. San Francisco: Jossey-Bass.

Hart, T. (1989). Counseling's spiritual dimension: Nine guiding principles. *Journal of Pastoral Care, 43*, 111–118.

Hatch, R., James, D., & Schumm, W. (1986). Spiritual intimacy and marital satisfaction. *Family Relations, 35*, 539–545.

Hendrix, H. (1988). *Getting the love you want: A guide for couples*. New York: Harper & Row.

Hungelmann, J. (1985). Spiritual well-being in older adults: Harmonious interconnectedness. *Journal of Religion and Health, 24*, 147–153.

Hunt, R., & King, M. (1978). Religiosity and marriage. *Journal for the Scientific Study of Religion, 17*, 399–406.

Jacobson, N. (1981). Behavioral marital therapy. In A. S. Gurman & D. P. Kniskern (Eds.), *Handbook of family therapy* (pp. 556–591). New York: Brunner/Mazel.

Koltko, M. E. (1990). How religious beliefs affect psychotherapy: The example of Mormonism. *Psychotherapy, 27*, 132–141.

May, G. (1988). *Addiction and grace*. San Francisco: Harper & Row.

Minuchin, S. (1984). *Family kaleidoscope*. Cambridge, MA: Harvard University Press.

Pattison, E. (1982). Management of religious issues in family therapy. *International Journal of Family Therapy, 4*, 140–163.

Pruyser, P. (1976). *The minister as diagnostician*. Philadelphia: Westminster Press.

Pruyser, P. (1977). The seamy side of current religious beliefs. *Bulletin of the Messenger Clinic, 41*, 329–340.

Ranges, C. (1980). Finding religious roots in the family tree. *The Family, 8*, 71–74.

Rizzutto, A. (1979). *The birth of the living God: A psychoanalytic study*. Chicago: University of Chicago Press.

Robinson, L., & Blanton, P. (1993). Marital strengths in enduring marriages. *Family Relations, 42*, 38–45.

Roth, P. (1988). Spiritual well-being and marital adjustment. *Journal of Psychology and Theology, 16*, 153–158.

Salinger, R. J. (1987). Family therapy: Overview. In D. G. Benner (Ed.), *Psychotherapy in Christian perspective* (pp. 298–304). Grand Rapids, MI: Baker Book House.

Sanua, V. D. (1989). Studies in mental illness and other psychiatric deviances among contemporary Jewry: A review of the literature. *Israel Journal of Psychiatry and Related Sciences, 26*, 187–211.

Scharff, D., & Scharff, J. (1987). *Object relations family therapy*. Northvale, NJ: Jason Aronson.

Schneiders, S. (1986). Theology and spirituality: Strangers, rivals, or partners? *Horizons, 13*, 253–274.

Schumm, W. (1985). Beyond relationship characteristics of strong families: Constructing a model of family strengths. *Family Perspective, 19*, 1–9.

Spilka, B. (1975). Parents, self and God: A test of competing theories of individual religion relationships. *Review of Religious Research, 16,* 154–165.

Watchell, P. (1983). *The poverty of affluence.* New York: Free Press.

Watzlawick, P. (1984). *The invented reality.* New York: Norton.

Wikler, M. (1986). Pathways to treatment: How Orthodox Jews enter therapy. *Social Casework: The Journal of Contemporary Social Work, 67,* 113–118.

Wimberly, E. (1990). *Prayer in pastoral counseling.* Louisville, KY: Westminster/ John Knox Press.

Worthington, E. (1990). Marriage counseling: A Christian approach to counseling couples. *Counseling and Values, 35,* 3–15.

20

THE 12-STEP PROGRAM

RONALD E. HOPSON

The 12-step program of Alcoholics Anonymous (AA) has provided the model for the plethora of "anonymous" group movements that exists today. L. P. Kurtz (1990) reported the existence of over eighty 12-step-related fellowships and 125,000 separate chapters. Such fellowships of common suffering as Narcotics Anonymous, Cocaine Anonymous, Adult Children of Alcoholics Anonymous, Emotions Anonymous, Gamblers Anonymous, Sex and Love Addictions Anonymous, and Overeaters Anonymous all subscribe to the 12-step model of recovery. There are also such groups as Nar-Anon, Al-Anon, and Al-Ateen to support family and friends of people who are struggling with alcohol and narcotic addictions. AA has now spawned over a half-million different "anonymous"-type groups in America alone, with more than 16 million persons involved in these groups (Buxton, Smith, & Seymour, 1987).

Rather than attempt to discuss each of the many 12-step fellowships, in this chapter I focus on AA as the exemplary and oldest 12-step fellowship. The terms *AA* and *12-step program* are used interchangeably throughout the discussion. I begin by outlining a brief history of AA to provide a context for understanding the structure and spiritual focus of 12-step programs. I discuss alternatives to the 12 steps of AA as they reflect objections to certain aspects of AA and differing opinions on the nature of addiction. I then offer an analysis of the therapeutic efficacy of 12-step programs.

Finally, I discuss 12-step programs in light of their role in the culture, their relationship to traditional religious organizations, and their place in the practice of psychotherapy.

A BRIEF HISTORY OF AA

The origins of AA lie in a rare statement made by a therapist to his patient: "I cannot help you." With these words, Carl Jung unknowingly launched the search for sobriety that was to develop into AA and the 12-step movement. Rowland H. had been a patient of Carl Jung and had been unable to cease excessive use and abuse of alcohol despite the disturbance it was causing in his life. After extensive analytic work, to no avail, Jung declared that what Rowland H. required to rescue himself was a spiritual or religious experience. Shortly after leaving treatment with Jung, Rowland H. found his way into an evangelical religious movement called the *Oxford Group* (not associated with the 19th century movement within the Church of England).

The Oxford Group movement was founded by the evangelist Frank N. D. Buchman. Buchman came on the scene in America during a period of tremendous religious growth in the United States during the first part of the twentieth century. At one time it was thought that Buchman's movement had spread worldwide, to over 60 countries. Buchman's movement, later renamed *Moral Rearmament*, "sought to win individuals, especially among students, intellectuals, the wealthy, and those influential in political life and labour . . . 'to remake men and nations' . . . [and] . . . to effect 'personal, social, racial, national, and supranational change' " (Latourette, 1953, p. 1419).

Rowland H. was able to achieve sobriety through his experiences with the Oxford Group movement, after which he left England and returned to the United States to work with other alcoholics through the Oxford Group in New York. One of the people who Rowland H. assisted in becoming sober was Edwin T., who was a friend of Bill W., the eventual founder of AA.

Edwin T. convinced Bill W. that "release from alcohol" was possible through the religious discipline of the Oxford Group. Bill W. managed to achieve sobriety through the assistance of his physician, Dr. William Silkworth; however, he then experienced profound depression. The depression precipitated a conversion experience that was to provide the impetus for his vision of a society of alcoholics: "If each sufferer were to carry the news of the scientific hopelessness of alcoholism to each new prospect, he might be able to lay every newcomer wide open to a transforming spiritual experience" (W., 1961/1987, p. 20). Bill W. was given a copy of William James's *Varieties of Religious Experience* (1961). James's work provided the conceptual basis for the necessity of ego collapse and the acknowledgment of powerlessness, which became known as the first step of AA.

The understanding of alcoholism on which AA is based was offered by Carl Jung (1961) in his reply to a letter from Bill W.:

> [the] craving for alcohol [is] the equivalent on a low level, of the spiritual thirst of our being for wholeness, expressed in medieval language [as] the union with God ... You see, "alcohol" in Latin is *spiritus*, and you use the same word for the highest religious experience as well as for the most depraving poison. The helpful formula therefore is: *spiritus contra spiritum.* (p. 21)

The perspective of the AA movement on alcoholism, as explicated in the "Big Book" of AA, expands on Jung's conceptualization. AA declares that the alcoholic is unable to exercise choice with regard to drinking and that the power to live without drinking must come from a source other than (and greater than) the self:

> Lack of power, that was our dilemma. We had to find a power by which we could live and it had to be a Power greater than ourselves. The abuse of alcohol is a sign of an underlying spiritual disorder which can only be addressed through surrender to a higher (spiritual) power: Our liquor was but a symptom. So we had to get down to causes and conditions. (AA, 1976, p. 64)

According to AA, the remedy for the spiritual problem of alcoholism involves the restoration of power and order to a disempowered and disordered life. This restoration is effected by following certain steps that are suggested by AA as the route back to sanity. Exhibit 1 shows the 12 steps to recovery through AA.

PERSPECTIVES ON 12-STEP PROGRAMS

Much controversy has been generated over the spiritual aspect of AA. Although some claim that the spiritual aspect of 12-step programs is nothing more than religion and is a major impediment to AA's broader success (e.g., Ellis & Schoenfeld, 1990), others (Buxton et al., 1987) claim that the spiritual aspect of AA is not necessarily religious and is one of the most important aspects of the program.

Advocates of the spiritual dimension of AA insist that AA is not a religion, maintaining that AA allows for a range of religious conviction, from sectarian to atheistic (Twerski, 1990). Chappel (1990) has cited the fact that AA counts Muslims, Catholics, and Hindus among its membership. Membership in religious organizations is, by definition, mutually exclusive; therefore, AA could not be a religion. AA was, in fact, investigated by the Catholic Church because of its Protestant roots, and approval was

EXHIBIT 1
The 12 Steps of Recovery Through Alcoholics Anonymous

1. We admitted we were powerless over alcohol—that our lives had become unmanageable.
2. Came to believe that a power greater than ourselves could restore us to sanity.
3. Made a decision to turn our will and our lives over to the care of God as we understood him.
4. Made a searching and fearless moral inventory of ourselves.
5. Admitted to God, to ourselves, and to another human being, the exact nature of our wrongs.
6. Were entirely ready to have God remove all these defects of character.
7. Humbly asked Him to remove our shortcomings.
8. Made a list of all persons we had harmed and became willing to make amends to them all.
9. Made direct amends to such people wherever possible, except when to do so would injure them or others.
10. Continued to take personal inventory, and when we were wrong promptly admitted it.
11. Sought through prayer and meditation to improve our conscious contact with God as we understood Him, praying only for knowledge of His will for us and the power to carry that out.
12. Having had a spiritual awakening as the result of these steps, we tried to carry this message to alcoholics, and to practice these principles in all our affairs.

Note. Excerpted from *Alcoholics Anonymous* (1952).

granted for Catholics to join AA.[1] Obviously, no religion would grant permission for its adherents to be members of another religion. The religious dimensions of the Oxford movement were removed by the founders of AA to avoid the pitfalls of involvement in specific religious traditions (E. Kurtz, 1979). Buxton et al. (1987) has insisted that 12-step programs are not religious in nature because members are not required to accept any particular concept of deity, nor are there particular rituals and beliefs to which members must adhere.

The 12-step programs view spirituality in recovery from addiction as the basis of a lifestyle change. Rather than denying the reality of his or her condition, the addict must begin to see the addiction as destructive to the self. Spirituality involves an assertion of the will to bring one's behavior in line with the reality of one's condition. Acknowledgment of one's helplessness leads to the recognition that one must turn to something outside the self to begin the process of recovery (Buxton et al., 1987, p. 280). That something outside the self that will support recovery is the higher power.

---

[1] This involved an informal perusal of the 1939 edition of *Alcoholics Anonymous* by an anonymous official of the New York Archdiocesan chancery (See Kurtz, 1979). This was carried out to assess whether any tenets of the new group would conflict with Catholic doctrine.

Recovery is made possible at the junction between the surrendered self and the higher power. The quest that has compelled someone to use a substance is redirected toward the beneficent higher power. Valliant and Milofsky (1982) as well as Ludwig (1985) have found spiritual elements (increased hope and faith) to be salient in the initiation and maintenance of recovery.

Those who object to the spiritual dimension of AA, however, reject supporters' claims that AA is not a religious program (Ellis & Schoenfeld, 1990). Ellis and Schoenfeld also deplore the dependency implicit in the 12-step model. They criticized the view that the chemically dependent person is prone to dependence and that the goal of treatment is to transfer this dependency to a more benign object. As an alternative to the spiritual–religious perspective of AA, Ellis and Schoenfeld have offered Skinner's humanist alternative 12 steps (see Ellis & Schoenfeld, 1990). According to Ellis and Schoenfeld, Skinner's 12 steps offer a nontheistic alternative to the 12 steps of AA. However, although these steps may eliminate conceptions of God, it is not clear how they avoid the fostering of dependency that Ellis and Schoenfeld also criticized. The humanistic 12 steps simply shift the dependency from God (as God is understood by each individual), to "fellow men and women." Essentially, Skinner's steps modify the rhetoric with little modification of the fundamental components of the 12-step model: surrender, willingness, fellowship, and relationship. Although eschewing the word God, ironically, the humanist 12 steps preserve the essential spirit of the 12-step model.

Such programs as Rational Recovery and the Secular Organization for Sobriety have arisen to offer secular alternatives to the spiritual dimension of 12-step programs. Rational Recovery criticizes the apparent reliance in AA on nonrational processes (e.g., Step 2) for recovery. The work of Albert Ellis has heavily influenced the Rational Recovery movement, whose adherents maintain that impulsive behavior is a consequence of distorted thinking. They believe that the focus for remediation should be on rational thinking.

Despite the objections regarding the spiritual elements of AA and other 12-step programs, Tournier (1979) observed, AA is the preeminent method of alcoholism treatment in American society and the cornerstone of virtually all contemporary rehabilitation efforts. Yet, even with the ubiquity of 12-step programs, skepticism and objections about such programs continues, and their effectiveness is a continuing source of debate (Brandsma, Maultsby, & Welsh, 1980).

Skepticism about the effectiveness of 12-step programs has generally fallen into one of the following four categories, described here in relation to AA (L. P. Kurtz, 1990): (a) AA has never been proven effective by scientific standards; (b) AA is culturally inappropriate for any group other than middle-class White men; (c) AA is antiscientific and antiprofessional; or (d) AA simply substitutes dependence on the program for dependence on substances and does not address the intrapsychic pathology giving rise to addictions. I address each of these categories in turn below.

It has been exceedingly difficult to assess the effectiveness of AA or other 12-step programs rigorously (Bebbington, 1979). The evaluation of AA's effectiveness is fraught with methodological quagmires, such that researchers lament over the "elusiveness of hard data" (Bebbington, 1979). McCrady and Irvine (1989) reviewed studies of the effectiveness of AA and found only two methodologically rigorous (e.g., randomized clinical trial) studies, neither of which demonstrated that AA was more effective than alternative treatments.

Findings regarding the effectiveness of AA and other 12-step programs have been inconclusive. Emrick (1987) concluded that AA had not been proven to be uniformly and uniquely effective in the treatment of alcoholism and questioned the prevailing practice of treatment professionals universally referring recovering persons to AA. However, Zinberg and Bean (1981) maintained that AA is the most successful treatment modality and should be recommended in conjunction with psychotherapy.

Osborne and Glaser (1981) found AA members to be more socially stable and affiliative and more often members of the middle class than their non-AA counterparts. This finding supports the objection that 12-step programs are culturally inappropriate for minority members of the society. Other groups have risen as sociocultural alternatives to traditional 12-step groups. Men in Recovery, for example, is aimed at African American men. Members of this group maintain that the experience of African Americans in the United States has been such that the mandate to surrender and admit powerlessness is detrimental to the psychological well-being of African American men. Zitter (1987) has stressed the importance of empowerment in working with chemical dependency within African American families and communities. Likewise, Williams (1992) critiqued what he saw as the individualistic focus of 12-step programs and the emphasis on anonymity as anathema to the experience of many recovering African American people. He maintained that the African American heritage is essentially communal, and so the fate of each person in the community is crucial to the well-being of the entire community. An emphasis on anonymity is thus inappropriate for a group of people who have been rendered invisible in the larger culture. Both Williams and Zitter maintained that recovery is best facilitated by group cohesion and community support.

Similarly, the organization Women for Sobriety decries the ethic of dependency that they argue is promoted in AA. In its place, Women for Sobriety stresses healthy self-esteem, autonomy, and individual responsibility through the application of 13 steps to sobriety.

Each of the groups described above offers a different conceptualization of the addictive problem than does AA. The relative success of these groups in garnering members (the Secular Organization for Sobriety reports an international membership of over 20,000) raises the question of the nature of addictive problems, which I address in the following section.

The concern that 12-step programs are antiscientific and antiprofessional may relate to the proliferation of certification programs in the treatment of addictions. Those seeking to work with addicted persons may obtain certification through various certification bodies which may not be affiliated with academic institutions or health care licensing boards. These programs do not require specific training in an applied discipline, such as social work or clinical psychology, and reflect the conviction among many 12-step members that having suffered the same malady is the best qualification for helping another. Also, concerns about intolerance among 12-step members may lead to opposition between professionals and the self-help communities (L. P. Kurtz, 1990).

Finally, the objection that 12-step programs simply substitute dependence on the program for other forms of dependence and thus, do not address the intrapsychic pathology responsible for addiction comes back to the long-standing question of the nature of addiction.

The Nature of Addiction

H. Shaffer (1985) has argued that the understanding of addiction is in a preparadigmatic stage. The description of most forms of addiction as *disease* is best understood as a metaphor. According to Shaffer, there is no uniform agreement about the nature of addictive disease. Is its etiology primarily psychological, sociological, biological, genetic, or biochemical?

Several models of addiction have been offered over the past century. Emil Kraepelin's 1907 textbook of clinical psychiatry included a category for alcohol abuse. Alternatively, William James, writing in 1902, maintained that alcohol abuse was a symptom of a spiritual problem. As cited above, this view was to be crucial in the founding of AA. Sigmund Freud's observations and speculations on the roots of mental illness led his primary apologist, Otto Fenichel (1945), to locate alcohol and other addictions as intrapsychic problems rooted in the vicissitudes of emotional development in the earliest stages of life. This view has been expanded in the work of various contemporary psychodynamic theoreticians and is discussed further below. (See Morgenstern & Leeds, 1993, for a summary of psychodynamic views of addiction.)

During the early part of the twentieth century, addiction (prototypically, alcohol abuse) was considered to be evidence of moral turpitude. The experiment with prohibition in the United States and the religious rhetoric that surrounded the consumption of alcohol demonstrates the view that alcohol abuse was a consequence of a disordered will resulting from moral weakness and sin (Baron, 1962).

The work of Jellinek (1960) was a turning point in the understanding of alcoholism in America. Jellinek argued that alcoholism met all of the criteria for a disease entity. Although the nature of alcoholism and other addictions has not been found in subsequent research to fit the criterion of physical disease, Jellinek's work completed the alteration of the understanding of alcoholism begun by Kraeplin, and alcoholism came to be understood as a physical disease entity. More recently, as reflected in an Institute of Medicine (1990) report from the National Institutes of Health, alcoholism has been understood to be a biopsychosocial phenomena, integrating the various etiological perspectives.

Objections to the Disease Concept

As a consequence of the success of the medical-disease view of alcoholism, the disease concept has become the predominant contemporary understanding of addiction. Peele (1989) has argued strongly against the classification of alcoholism and other addiction–impulse problems as diseases. He has maintained that the construal of addictive behaviors as diseases renders human beings passive victims rather than active agents in the construction of their lives. Furthermore, the proliferation of such diseases contributes to increasing insularity in U.S. society. Therefore, people retreat to a stance of diseased individualism, which results in the diminution of community spirit, and this process, for Peele, is the essence of the problem of addictions.

Kaminer (1992) has also criticized the proliferation of categories of dependency and addictions. She concurred with Peele that the popularization of addictions is leading to a culture of victims who refuse to take responsibility for their actions. Furthermore, Kaminer saw the implicit standard in the self-help movement as the elimination of all problems. And she saw the emphasis on God as a defensive illusion that belies the contingent nature of life and offers "platitudes billed as revelations" (Kaminer, 1992, p. 127).

The 12-step programs have accommodated the disease model primarily in the service of eliminating the stigma attached to behaviors that have been considered historically to result from moral failings. Psychodynamic therapists have achieved an uneasy alliance with 12-step advocates as they argue that self-help methods may be useful adjuncts in the treatment of addictive problems (Bean-Bayong, 1985; Dodes, 1988).

Psychological Analysis of Addiction and the 12-Step Program

I have examined the nature of addiction with attention to the therapeutic elements of AA (Hopson, 1994). My findings have suggested that the addictive phenomena reveal perceptual and experiential anomalies to which the addicted person is susceptible. As has been suggested theoretically (Krystal & Raskin, 1970), addicted people report experiencing intense feelings for which language is inadequate. The intense feelings are experienced as potentially overwhelming and result in a "short circuit," wherein feelings become an impulse to action (Wurmser, 1978) as a way of managing these feelings. The addicted person is unable to recognize these feelings or put them into words. Wurmser described the addicted person as unable to use the "verbal band out of the spectrum of symbolic processes" (1978, p. 234), which may function to ameliorate intense feelings. Along with these intense feelings comes a disruption in the sense of the movement of time. There is a sense of being caught or frozen in time, and time ceases to move. The addicted person also reports lacking a sense of agency or efficacy and lacking the capacity to self-regulate feelings and behaviors. Finally, the addicted person reports experiencing a lack of connection to oneself and others as well as an intense sense of alienation from self and others.

The experiential and perceptual anomalies of the addictive experience are addressed by the 12-step program. The fundamental tool of 12-step programs is language. Members of AA begin speaking with the phrase "My name is _____ and I'm an alcoholic." This sentence serves to reinforce a member's sense of selfhood and links him or her to the community of alcoholics. The cornerstone of 12-step programs is the custom of telling one's story in AA meetings. Schafer (1992) has argued that telling one's story plays a critical role in the establishment of an "emotionally coherent account of one's life" (p. 34). The construal of one's life as a story provides a sense of continuity in time for the self. It also makes change possible, because a narrative perspective views the person as efficacious in constructing the narrative and, thus, the narrative may be reconstructed (Sarbin, 1986). Telling one's story also provides a series of lessons in using language to represent the self. As people hear their story through the stories of others, opportunities for consolidation of a sense of self and identification with others are provided. These opportunities directly address both the sense of alienation from the self and alienation from others.

In addition to enabling one to tell one's story, the AA program provides certain verbal strategies to intervene with the sense of intense feelings and the impulse to acquire the substance of abuse. Phrases such as "easy does it" and "take it easy" provide cognitive strategies to intervene with potentially overwhelming emotional experiences.

Wallace and Rabin (1960) cited Freud's view that one's sense of time is developed through periodic interruptions in the experience of gratification. If these interruptions are too frequent or intense for the child, then a disturbance in temporal perspective may develop (Ingram, 1979). The intensity of feelings reported by addicted persons may precipitate a temporal disturbance as "time ceases to move." The result of this process is the often frantic search for relief that characterizes the addict in search of his or her substance of choice. No obstacle is too formidable as the addicted person seeks to reestablish the sense of being in time that has been threatened. McInerney's (1991) elucidation of Heidegger illustrates this problem:

> Time is an essential parameter of that action-oriented system of meaning through which we encounter . . . others, and ourselves. . . . every moment of world-time is understood with respect to some actual or potential action. Every "now" is experienced as the appropriate or inappropriate time to do something. (p. 123)

For the addict, with the collapse of time, "now" is experienced as the appropriate time to act. Several sayings have developed within AA that address the problem of the experience of time. "This too shall pass," "First things first," and—perhaps, the most famous saying—"One day at a time" provide cognitive strategies to restore temporality and order and to mitigate intense feeling states. "This too shall pass" reminds the person of the movement of time and orients him or her toward the future. "One day at a time" addresses the experience of the collapse of past and future and the corresponding sense of overwhelming that accompanies the loss of future time perspective. "First things first" offers the possibility for prioritizing and establishing order and limits in one's life.

Other dimensions of the AA program also address the issue of temporality. Members of AA are encouraged to select a particular meeting that they consistently attend (this is referred to as a "home meeting"). Members also develop the expectation that others of their group be in attendance, thus offering to the addicted person the opportunity to practice a lifestyle of regularity and predictability.

The addictive experience is also characterized by a sense of alienation from self and others. One of the primary consequences (and perhaps, antecedents) of addiction is shame (E. Kurtz, 1982; Ramsey, 1988). Kaufman (1985) understood shame to be an essentially interpersonal phenomena in which the "interpersonal bridge" between oneself and others is broken. Shame leaves a person feeling visible, defective, alone, and alienated from others. In the case of the addicted person, shame may be intensified because of the moral sanctions that attend certain forms of addictions (e.g., addiction to drugs or sex).

The sharing of stories addresses the interpersonal dimension of shame. AA lore maintains that the addicted person suffers from "terminal uniqueness." The 12-step program offers a context of reciprocal self-revelation (Flores, 1988) in which the addicted person may hear stories of others who have done things of which they too are ashamed; in this way, each person may feel less unique and less alienated.

The historical emphasis on fellowship in AA and other 12-step movements also addresses the experience of interpersonal alienation. The 12-step programs provide an interpersonal network that is "available at once to provide unconditional acceptance and support to the newcomer and, together with a sponsor, bring about an end to the member's isolation" (Spiegel & Mulder, 1986, p. 38). The structure of AA maintains the necessity of relationships to sustain and regulate the self. Mack (1981) has argued that the success of AA may be attributed to this insight regarding the necessity of emotionally relevant participation with others. Similar to Bateson's (1972) views regarding alcoholism, Mack suggested that the person never functions as a solitary entity. The ethos of the fellowship of AA provides the feedback that is necessary for the individual to adequately guide his or her life. This view accords with the theoretical views of Kohut (1977) and others, who maintain that self structures are built up as a consequence of interactions with others and, so, may be modified in therapeutic ways by appropriately nurturing and supportive contact with others.

The failure in self-governance (Mack, 1981) is understood to be rooted in inadequate ego development and the unavailability of appropriately supportive others in early development. That is, the containing and mirroring functions of early caregivers was not good enough to support the development in the child of sufficient self-care and regulatory functions (Khantzian, Halliday, & McAuliffe, 1990). The addictive behavior is understood as an attempt to compensate for these deficits. The structure and steps of 12-step programs provide a framework for the restoration of order, coherence, and relationship.

Psychological Analysis of the 12 Steps

The 12 steps are summarized in AA programs in the following manner:

Steps 1–3: Give up.
Steps 4–7: Own up.
Steps 8–9: Make up.
Steps 10–12: Grow up.

Step 1 defines the problem initially as alcohol (or whatever issue around which the particular 12-step program is constructed). However, paradoxically, after defining the problem specifically, there is no further mention of the manifest problem (e.g., alcohol) until the last step, which reminds the member to carry the message to others struggling with the same manifest problem. Thus, although acknowledging the focus of the problem, the 12 steps offer a total lifestyle solution. The fragmentation characteristic of traditional views of human functioning (Becker, 1962) is avoided. Rather,

12-step programs insist on the unity, complexity, and interrelatedness of human experience.

The often-cited denial of the addicted person is addressed through the first step with the acknowledgment of powerlessness. An effective television commercial illustrating the nature of denial depicts an elephant in the living room while a family sits together watching television. The mother serves beverages, and the family behaves as though the elephant is not in the room, sometimes straining to see around the elephant. This illustrates the idea that the nature of denial necessitates that individuals remain vigilant with regard to that which is being denied if the denial is to be effective. Therefore, the person in denial is divided within the self. The admission of powerlessness (surrender) begins the process of unification of the self. Step 1 also involves admitting a loss of control, which is crucial for establishing motivation for the change necessary for recovery to begin (Prochaska, DiClemente, & Norcross, 1992).

The act of surrender called for in Step 3 ("made a decision to turn will and life over to God"), is a consequence of hitting bottom, or "deflation at depth" (E. Kurtz, 1979, p. 23). This element is considered a necessary aspect of the conversion experience in 12-step programs. Tiebout (1961) observed that this was a controversial element early in the life of AA. Traditionally, the therapist's task has been to minimize clients' suffering and intervene to prevent harm; however, it was the insight of AA that this process of "hitting bottom" was necessary to provide the intrinsic motivation to change.

The first three steps place the addicted person in the midst of a paradox. There is acknowledgment of the addicted person's inability to control the self and, paradoxically, a call for the alcoholic to exercise the will to surrender control of the self to a beneficent higher power. The steps embrace this paradox by acknowledging the reality of volition in the midst of the loss of volition. Despite the lack of a sense of efficacy, the possibility of agency is assumed as the addicted person is charged to act. However, this action is not in keeping with the sense of alienation from self and others and the corresponding loss of control. Rather, the action proposed assumes relationship with a beneficent power greater than the self. This element of submission and surrender may be highly important in working with religiously committed persons. Steps 2 and 3 address the transpersonal dimension of alienation by offering an other to which the addicted person may turn, unashamedly.

Steps 4–7 ("made moral inventory," "admitted wrongs," "were ready for defects to be removed," and "asked that shortcomings be removed") continue to intervene with the individual's sense of shame and alienation. Psychoanalytic insights regarding the costs of repression (e.g., the return of the repressed) are confirmed in the charge to uncover, acknowledge, and let go of one's shortcomings. The initial movement in the process of letting go involves uncovering and acknowledging. This is in accordance with Kaufman's (1985) view that the links between shame and life events must be made conscious and reworked. The addicted life may be described as a life of pretensions in the quest for perfection (Kurtz, 1979). As these pretensions are acknowledged, the addicted person need no longer hide behind them, and, therefore, the true self may be met and affirmed. The true self is not a static self that never changes. Rather, precisely because the power to change is offered from outside the self, change is possible. Step 7 offers possibility in the face of the dread that comes with hitting bottom.

The importance of a source beyond the self for assistance may be understood dynamically. Addictive behavior, although initially experienced as ameliorative to the individual, becomes admittedly self-destructive. Although the addictive behavior expresses the immediate hope of relief from some intolerable internal state (Wurmser, 1978), the negative consequences of the behavior reveal an ambivalent attitude of the addicted person toward the self. There is at once the desire for relief, as expressed in the addictive behavior, and the desire for punishment, as expressed in the addictive behavior despite the knowledge that the consequences will be harmful. The behavior in relation to the self may be seen as a fusion between self-love (the desire for relief) and self-contempt (the desire for punishment).

Implied in the invitation to surrender to the higher power is the beneficence of the higher power. AA literature understands this moment of surrender as the movement of faith (AA, 1976). Steps 2 and 3 maintain that despite the "insane" behavior of the addicted person, assistance is available. This assistance is not conditional on sane behavior but, rather, is offered without necessity of merit. The attitude of the higher power toward the self may be described as entirely accepting and nonambivalent. Thus, as one relies on the higher power for assistance in ceasing destructive behaviors, the accepting attitude of the higher power counterbalances the negative side of the ambivalence toward the self and provides the impetus for making nondestructive decisions in relation to the self. The acceptance by the higher power is a priori: The addicted person need only exercise the courage to accept acceptance, which, for the theologian Paul Tillich (1952), is an act of faith.

The role of the higher power as a counterbalance to self-contempt may explain why the higher power may be anything so designated by the person. Anything construed by the individual as offering acceptance and help without conditions may play the role of the higher power (e.g., many 12-step members claim the group itself as their higher power). The higher power mobilizes the addicted individuals' will on behalf of their well-being rather than punishment. The will of the individual is brought into line with a different perspective on the self: self-love rather than self-contempt. The spiritual dimension of 12-step programs effects this transformation from self-contempt to self-love through the higher power.

Steps 8 and 9 ("willingness to make amends" and "made amends where possible," respectively) address the necessity of reparation. Psychoanalytic insight maintains that reparation is a crucial element in the development of the capacity to hope and feel concern for oneself and others (Klein, 1975). The feelings of guilt and shame that attend acknowledging one's shortcomings can result in a sense of perennial badness unless effective reparation is possible (Segal, 1974). Steps 8 and 9 offer a procedure for bringing about such reparations so that further injury cannot occur. The powerlessness and lack of agency or efficacy characteristic of the addictive experience is also addressed by offering the possibility of reparation. Contrary to the addict's view of the self as lacking efficacy and agency, the 12-step member comes to see himself or herself as an effective agent in the world, capable of making an impact on others for good or ill. Intrapersonal and interpersonal alienation is addressed in the making of amends.

Twelve-step programs offer a view of the human being as in process, as continually becoming human. The goal of life is not to become holy or perfect, as may be the quest in some religious traditions, but, rather, to achieve "a way of life that accepts imperfection as imperfection" (E. Kurtz & Ketcham, 1992, p. 111). Human existence is seen as relating oneself to oneself, others, and transcendence (God). Maturity is achieved through the recognition of full subjectivity of the self and others. Self and others are not viewed as means to an end (I–it), instead, self and others are viewed as ends in themselves (I–thou; Buber, 1958). The objectification of the self and others that is a consequence of alienation is avoided through conscious contact with oneself and others. The final three steps of the 12-step program ("continue to take personal inventory," "sought to improve conscious contact with God," and "carry message to other addicted persons and practice these principles in all affairs") are offered to increase the member's conscious contact with his or her self and other people. The 12-step program assumes that acknowledging one's shortcomings and limitations is a continuing challenge, thus a higher power is again invoked to aid in this process. The 12-step member is invited to a lifestyle conversion through the message to "practice these principles in all [their] affairs."

Twelve-Step Programs and Culture, Religion, and Therapeutic Psychology

The fellowship and spirituality of AA, as well as the emphasis on the therapeutic, place it and other 12-step programs at the intersection of religion and therapeutic psychology. Twelve-step programs may provide fertile ground for continuing dialogue between religion and therapeutic psychology. An understanding of the relationship between 12-step programs, religion, and therapeutic psychology may enhance the efficacy of each. Also, the presence and proliferation of such programs in America suggest that neither religion nor therapeutic psychology have adequately addressed some of the cultural issues that are raised in 12-step programs.

Religion

The religious scene in America after World War I was characterized by two theological systems: fundamentalism–piety and humanist–idealist liberalism (Ahlstrom, 1972). E. Kurtz (1979) maintained that elements of the pietistic and humanist–liberal tradition could be clearly seen in the structure of AA. The pietistic influence can be seen in the 12-step emphasis on surrender and conversion as facilitated by a higher power, whereas the humanist–liberal tradition is reflected in the pragmatic and pluralist ethos of AA. The founders of AA cited William James as the source of their emphasis on the importance of spiritual experience to instigate change. The founders also embraced James's understanding of the variety of modes of spirituality that are possible, providing the basis for AA's tradition of tolerance for diversity.

Smith (1963) understood religion as the amalgam of two different phenomena: cumulative tradition and faith. To him, cumulative tradition is the institutional dimension of religion. In keeping with Protestant tradition then, faith can be understood as the personal dimension of religious experience:

> Faith is personal. It is not a fixed something, but the throbbing actuality of a myriad of someone's ... theologies, rites, [and] moralities, and congregations are not faith, they are expressions of faith and form the ground of faith. (Smith, 1963, p. 189)

This view of faith accords with the understanding of spirituality within 12-step groups (Buxton et al., 1987). The thwarted quest for a deeper spiritual dimension of living is the fundamental problem of addiction (Woodman, 1987). Twelve-step programs emphasize personal spirituality and provide the tools needed to avoid the pitfalls of traditional institutionalized religion.

Bellah, Madsen, Sullivan, Swidler, and Tipton (1985) have suggested that the emphasis on spirituality in American culture arises from disenchantment with the institutionalized church in its function as facilitator of personal growth. They saw the pitfalls of institutional religion to be "a temptation to authoritarianism, on the one hand, and too-easy compromise with, and even coaptation by, the power of this world on the other" (p. 244).

Reiff (1966) argued that institutionalized religion's success within U.S. culture may have rendered the church obsolete in its spiritual function for the individual:

> The failure of Christianity resembles that of Communism: both have been wrecked by success; neither could resist incorporation into social orders that were partly their own creation. . . . Historically, the Christian spiritual perception, which had attacked the established moral demands of its time, took on an institutional form, and moreover, had a revolutionary effect on some aspects of the social system—for example, on the status of women. At the same time, the Church was incorporated into the social system and survived, powerful and yet defeated in its ideal intention by that very incorporation. (Reiff, 1966, pp. 250, 259)

Reiff's comments correspond with Carl Jung's (1958) view that religious institutions may prevent access to a fuller range of experience by which people critique societal mores and customs. Reiff maintained that the religious institution is only vital inasmuch as it stands apart from the established social order and maintains a critical stance toward the popular morality of the culture. Twelve-step programs are structured to avoid authoritarianism, institutionalization, and coaptation. The 12 traditions (AA, 1952) provide the underpinnings for the structure of 12-step programs (see Exhibit 2).

Traditions 2 and 8 ensure against the development of autocratic leadership and exclusivism within the 12-step movement. E. Kurtz (1979) and Mack (1981) suggested that the lack of hierarchy in AA is an important counterbalance to the tendency toward narcissism, which may be expressed as grandiosity or self-denigration. Traditions 4, 6, 7, 9, 10, and 12 attempt to keep AA from institutionalization. These traditions provide the rationale for what has been described as "organizational anarchy" because they emphasize autonomy for each group, minimal organizational structure, neutrality with regard to outside issues, and anonymity.

In contrast to creeds, confessions, and dogma, the 12 steps are offered as a guide available for the taking, rather than a mandate that individuals must accept. The 11th tradition maintains that the AA program is based on attraction, not promotion, and, indeed, the founders of AA soon came to understand that proselytizing interfered with the effectiveness of their message (E. Kurtz, 1979). The structure offered to the 12-step member maintains the advantage of providing a systematic view of life, while not crushing individuality and spontaneity under the weight of a constricting system of inviolable rules.

I have suggested above that the addicted person experiences a failure of self-regulation and is relatively lacking in the capacity to use symbolic processes (e.g., language). Language as symbol may contain paradox and

EXHIBIT 2
The 12 Traditions of Alcoholics Anonymous

1. Our common welfare should come first; personal recovery depends upon AA unity.
2. For our group purpose there is but one ultimate authority—a loving God as He may express Himself in our group conscience. Our leaders are but trusted servants; they do not govern.
3. The only requirement for AA membership is a desire to stop drinking.
4. Each group should be autonomous except in matters affecting other groups or AA as a whole.
5. Each group has but one primary purpose—to carry its message to the alcoholic who still suffers.
6. An AA group ought never endorse, finance, or lend the AA name to any related facility or outside enterprise, lest problems of money, property, and prestige divert us from our primary purpose.
7. Every AA group ought to be fully self-supporting, declining outside contributions.
8. Alcoholics Anonymous should remain forever nonprofessional, but our service centers may employ special workers.
9. AA as such, ought never be organized; but we may create service boards or committees directly responsible to those they serve.
10. Alcoholics Anonymous has no opinion on outside issues; hence, the AA name ought never be drawn into public controversy.
11. Our public relations policy is based on attraction rather than promotion; we need always maintain personal anonymity at the level of press, radio, and films.
12. Anonymity is the spiritual foundation of all our traditions, ever reminding us to place principles before personalities.

Note. Excerpted from *Alcoholics Anonymous* (1952).

transmit the reality of something beyond that to which it immediately refers:

> In this function language casts off, as it were, the sensuous covering in which it has hitherto appeared ... [and] ... gives way to purely symbolic expression which, precisely in and by virtue of its otherness, becomes the vehicle of a new and deeper spiritual content. (Cassirer, 1953)

Bloom (1992) suggested that religious traditions that emphasize the literal meaning of sacred texts suffer from an inability to sustain metaphor. These traditions may, ironically, close off the very depths of spiritual experience that they claim to seek. The range of interpretive possibilities invited in the 12-step tradition and the paradoxical function of the 12 steps in providing both boundary and possibility reveal the spiritual nature of the 12-step program.

The 12-step tradition calls for people to speak in meetings about how they were, what happened to them, and how they are now. Twelve-step members are encouraged to share their wounds with others in the fellowship. This practice echoes Marion Woodman's (1987) view that "the God comes in through the wound" (p. 64). The practice of revealing one's wounds (telling the story of one's wrongs and shortcomings) serves a confessional function that is substantially different from confession in traditional Judeo–Christian religion. The goal of confession in religion is renunciation and overcoming of sin. However, the very act of renunciation contains a denial of the intractable nature of one's sinfulness (limitations). Thus, although denied, sin in its full ramifications is ever present through the return of the repressed. The goal of confession in the 12-step tradition is identification. One does not confess for the sake of achieving perfection, but to remind oneself and others of the reality of human finitude and imperfection (Kurtz & Ketcham, 1992) and to bring one's self-perception in line with this reality. Thus, the fact of one's sinfulness (limitations) is not an occasion for shame but, rather, is simply a given of human existence. Hearing one's own story spoken by others makes possible identification and the affirmation of the reality of human finitude.

Culture

Bateson (1972) understood alcoholism as an attempt to correct the errant epistemology that, he suggested, characterizes our current age. The compulsive behavior is a tireless yet fruitless effort to effect the relatedness to self, others, and transcendence for which the addict longs. Schaef (1987) has characterized contemporary American society as an addictive system. According to her, cultural values promote an illusion of control, self-sufficiency, denial, and acquisitiveness. These illusions have taken the place of reality, and reality (finitude, relative dependency, and the spiritual dimension) has been sacrificed in the service of participation in the addictive system.

Alcoholism and the proliferation of other addictions may be symptomatic of the failures of the prevailing cultural values (Schaef, 1987). AA and other 12-step programs offer a prescription for the age of anomie and alienation that appears to be upon us (see "Growing up scared," 1994). The structure of AA may be understood as a commentary on the grandiosity, rugged individualism, and consequent cultural narcissism that has been said to characterize modern Western life (Lasch, 1979). The proliferation of 12-step programs attests to the costs that such values as individualism and acquisitiveness have exacted on the persona. In addition, the growth of such programs points to the relative inadequacy of society's current therapeutic structures to meet these needs.

Although it has been suggested that the essence of religious experience is discontent and its resolution (James, 1961; Spilka, Hood, & Gorsuch, 1985), current trends suggest that mainline religious institutions are not offering adequate resolution and people are looking to spiritual–individualistic or fundamentalist–authoritarian movements to find resolution. Reiff (1966) suggested that when a culture has exhausted its particular "symbolic capital," it must be infused with new capital from the unconscious or from the collective unconscious. The 12-step movement may be seen as evidence of this new capital in light of the decline of traditional religious structures.

Therapeutic Psychology

Therapeutic psychology has its roots in the applied psychology movement, which burgeoned during and after the Second World War (Hilgard, 1987). As demand for psychological services grew after the Second World War, psychologists began rendering psychotherapy, initially under the supervision of psychiatrists and later as an autonomous part of professional practice. Training programs in clinical psychology grew as a consequence of an infusion of money through the Veterans Administration. These programs were located in university departments of psychology, where they had to compete with academic psychology for respectability. Thus, the natural science methods that had been appropriated by academic psychologists became the principal tools for knowledge acquisition among clinicians. As Koch (1959–1963) noted, "from the earliest days of the experimental pioneers, man's stipulation that psychology be adequate to science outweighed his commitment that it be adequate to man" (p. 783).

The consequence of the history of therapeutic psychology is that psychotherapy has often been indifferent to, if not directly opposed to, religious–spiritual considerations (Bergin, 1980). Clinical psychologists have reported a low degree of institutional religious involvement, although some have acknowledged the personal importance of spirituality (Bergin & Jensen, 1990). Two thirds of Americans in 1985 reported religious commitment to be very important or the most important aspect of their lives (Gallup, 1985). Together with the proliferation of 12-step programs, this suggests the need for spiritually sensitive therapeutic elements in American culture. The lack of attention paid by psychology training programs to the spiritual–religious dimension of living has resulted in a call for the profession to reconsider its attitude toward religious–spiritual attitudes (Shafranske & Malony, 1990). The negative relationship between alcohol and drug usage and religiosity (Cochran, Beeghley, & Bock, 1988) also suggests that religion and spirituality may play a significant role in avoiding addiction.

The recommendation that Carl Jung made to Rowland H. acknowledged the importance of the religious and spiritual dimension for change with regard to alcoholism. Although the spiritual dimension of change is seldom an explicit aspect of theorizing in the psychotherapy literature, aspects commonly thought to be in the spiritual domain may be important for effecting change in psychotherapy. Frank (1973) has argued that psychotherapy is in continuity with many other forms of healing and shares essential characteristics: lessening of the state of demoralization, instilling trust and hope, and mobilizing the person's active participation in the healing endeavor. Similarly, Applebaum (1988) suggested that feeling rather than cognition, needfulness, and the expectation of external help are major aspects of healing in psychotherapy. Strupp (1972) also stated that trust is an essential element in the psychotherapeutic process. Nino (1990) has offered Augustine's *Confessions* as an analogue for psychotherapy that embraces the importance of the role of transcendence in healing. Contrary to the view that religion is only marginally relevant or even anathema to the psychotherapeutic endeavor, the religious commitment of people may be an important asset in psychotherapy.

It has been suggested that all healing endeavors involve faith as an essential element in the healing process (Kiev, 1964). Hopson (1992) has argued that faith may be expanded beyond the religious domain and appropriately applied to the psychotherapeutic context: Change in psychotherapy involves confrontation with the unknown, which can arouse fear that has been likened to the fear of death (Bugental & Bugental, 1984). As I have explained elsewhere (Hopson, 1992),

> Resistance to change in psychotherapy is overcome through faith. As the patient embraces the anxiety that attends change, a new more trustworthy ground of being (higher power) is experienced, thus facilitating change. The creation of a new self out of dissociated, repressed, or denied aspects of the self is made possible by an act of faith. This new creation is embarked upon by an act of the total personality, an act of faith. Resistance to the creation of a new self is seen as fundamentally a crisis of faith—the maintenance of an old life-constricting faith, or the embracing of new life-expanding faith . . . psychotherapeutic "cure" is ontological, not intellectual. (p. 102)

The wisdom of 12-step programs is to acknowledge the ontological nature of recovery from addiction. Overcoming addiction involves a realignment of one's faith. Concepts familiar to religiously committed people—such as God, faith, and conversion—are embraced in the 12-step tradition to facilitate a sense of self-efficacy and relatedness to others. The tradition of 12-step programs attempts to avoid the pitfalls of institutional religion while embracing the spiritual dimension of religious insight.

The goal of psychotherapy began as the elimination of neurosis in order to return patients to the "normal misery" of living. As therapeutic psychology developed, interest grew in adjustment, amelioration, curing, and even facilitating peak experiences (Napoli, 1981). With the exception of certain forms of existential psychotherapy and pastoral psychotherapy, the spiritual dimension of change has been largely ignored. Faith and spirituality have been largely considered the domain of religion.

The failure of traditional psychotherapeutic endeavors to adequately address the problem of addiction may in part be related to the willingness of those with traditional psychotherapeutic perspectives to ignore the role of spirituality in any attempts to make significant life changes. However, because "divine interventions intervene" (Keller, 1990), the spiritual dimension of 12-step programs may serve to inform more traditional therapeutic endeavors of the advantages of including spirituality in any understanding of change.

CONCLUSION

Twelve-step programs have exploded onto the cultural landscape in America since the 1960s and have found similar success in other parts of the world. Despite the relative dearth of scientific evidence for the effectiveness of 12-step programs, they continue to be supported by most people in the professional treatment community, and variations of such programs have been spawned to address issues ranging from excessive eating to gambling. Since the founding of the Society for Alcoholics Anonymous, 12-step programs have insisted that the spiritual dimension must be addressed in any attempts to remediate lifestyle problems. An analysis of the 12 steps suggests that, beneath such specific problems as addiction, lies the more general and persistent problem of human living: the negotiation of our finitude. Twelve-step programs offer a structured approach to dealing with such concerns. In doing so, these programs bridge the gulf between religion and therapeutic psychology.

Through their spiritual focus and organizational anarchy, it has been suggested, 12-step programs avoid some of the pitfalls of organized religion and therapeutic psychology. Such programs provide prescription without dogma, structure without institutionalization, and spirituality without exclusion, while addressing the inherent uneasiness of life at the close of the twentieth century. In contrast to the prevailing ethos of Western culture, 12-step programs celebrate the reality of human limitation and the necessity of relationship in community. The structure of 12-step programs accords with Hillman and Ventura's (1992) insistence that personal healing must take place in a community infused with a sense of connection with oneself, others, the other, and the world.

REFERENCES

Ahlstrom, S. (1972). *Religious history of the American people*. New Haven: Yale University Press.

Alcoholics Anonymous. (1939). Alcoholics Anonymous; The story of how many thousands of men and women have recovered from alcoholism. New York: Author.

Alcoholics Anonymous. (1952). *Twelve steps and twelve traditions*. New York: Author.

Alcoholics Anonymous. (1976). *Alcoholics Anonymous*. New York: Alcoholics Anonymous World Services.

Applebaum, S. (1988). Psychotherapy, a subset of healing. *Psychotherapy: Theory, Research, and Practice, 25*, 201–208.

Baron, S. (1962). *Brewed in America: A history of beer and ale in the United States*. Boston: Little, Brown.

Bateson, G. (1972). *Steps to an ecology of mind*. San Francisco: Chandler Publishing.

Bean-Bayong, M. (1985) Alcoholism treatment as an alternative to psychiatric hospitalization. *Psychiatric Clinics of North America, 8*, 501–516.

Bebbington, P. (1979). The efficacy of Alcoholics Anonymous: The elusiveness of hard data. *British Journal of Psychiatry, 128*, 572–580.

Becker, E. (1962). *The birth and death of meaning*. New York: Free Press of Glencoe.

Bellah, R., Madsen, R., Sullivan, W., Swidler, A., & Tipton, S. (1985). *Habits of the heart*. New York: Harper & Row.

Bergin, A. E. (1980). Psychotherapy and religious values. *American Psychologist, 48*, 95–105.

Bergin, A. E., & Jenson, J. P. (1990, Spring). Religiosity of psychotherapists: A national survey. *Psychotherapy, 27*, 3–7.

Bloom, H. (1992). *The American religion*. New York: Simon & Schuster.

Bradley, A. (1988). The case for a valuation of Alcoholics Anonymous. *Alcohol, Health, and Research World, 12*, 1192–1199.

Brandsma, J., Maultsby, M., & Welsh, R. (1980). *Outpatient treatment of alcoholism: A review and comparative study*. Baltimore: University Park Press.

Buber, M. (1958). *I and thou* (2nd rev. ed.) (R. G. Smith, Trans.). New York: Charles Scribner's Sons.

Bugental, J., & Bugental, E. (1984). A fate worse than death: The fear of changing. *Psychotherapy: Theory, Research, and Practice, 21*, 543–549.

Buxton, M. E., Smith, D. E., & Seymour, R. B. (1987). Spirituality and other points of resistance to the 12-step recovery process. *Journal of Psychoactive Drugs, 19*, 275–286.

Cassirer, E. (1953). *The philosophy of symbolic forms, Vol. 1. Language*. New Haven, CT: Yale University Press.

Chappel, J. N. (1990). Spirituality is not necessarily religion: A commentary on "Divine intervention and the treatment of clinical dependency." *Journal of Substance Abuse, 2*, 481–483.

Cochran, J. K., Beeghley, L., & Bock, E. W. (1988). Religiosity and alcohol behavior: An exploration of reference group theory. *Sociological Forum*, 3, 256–276.

Dodes, L. (1988). The psychology of combining dynamic psychotherapy and Alcoholics Anonymous. *Bulletin of the Menninger Clinic*, 52, 283–293.

Ellis, A., & Schoenfeld, E. (1990). Divine intervention and the treatment of chemical dependency. *Journal of Substance Abuse*, 2, 459–468.

Emrick, C. D. (1987). Alcoholics Anonymous: Affiliation processes and effectiveness as treatment. *Alcoholism: Clinical and Experimental Research*, 11, 416–423.

Fenichel, O. (1945). *The psychoanalytic theory of neurosis*. New York: W. W. Norton & Co., Inc.

Flores, P. (1988). Alcoholics Anonymous: A phenomenological and existential perspective. *Alcoholism Treatment Quarterly*, 5, 73–94.

Frank, J. (1973). *Persuasion and healing*. Baltimore: Johns Hopkins University Press.

Gallup, G. (1985). *Religion in America* (Gallup Rep. No. 236). Princeton, NJ: Princeton Religion Research Center.

Growing up scared. (1994, January 10). *Newsweek*, 123, 42–49.

Hilgard, E. R. (1987). *Psychology in America: A historical survey*. Orlando, FL: Harcourt Brace Jovanovich.

Hillman, J., & Ventura, M. (1992). *We've had a hundred years of psychotherapy—And the world's getting worse*. San Francisco: HarperCollins.

Hopson, R. (1992). The role of faith in the psychotherapeutic context. *Journal of Religion and Health*, 31(2), 95–105.

Hopson, R. E. (1994). Why AA Works: A psychological analysis of the addictive experience and the efficacy of Alcoholics Anonymous. *Alcoholism Treatment Quarterly*, 12, 1–18.

Ingram, D. H. (1979). Time and timekeeping in psychoanalysis and psychotherapy. *American Journal of Psychoanalysis*, 39, 319–328.

Institute of Medicine. (1990). *Broadening the base of treatment for alcohol problems*. Washington, DC: National Academy Press.

James, W. (1961). *The varieties of religious experience: A study in human nature*. New York: Collier-MacMillan.

Jellinek, E. M. (1960). *The disease concept of alcoholism*. Harlan Park, NY: Hillhouse Press.

Jung, C. (1958). *Psychology and religion: West and east* (R. F. C. Hull, Trans.). New York: Pantheon Books.

Jung, C. (1987). The Bill W.–Carl Jung letters. *Revision*, 10(2), 19–21.

Kaminer, W. (1992). *I'm dysfunctional, you're dysfunctional*. Reading, MA: Addison-Wesley.

Kaufman, G. (1985). *Shame: the power of caring*. Cambridge, MA: Schenkman Books.

Keller, M. (1990). But "devine interventions" intervene. *Journal of Substance Abuse, 2*, 473–475.

Khantzian, E. J., Halliday, K. S., & McAuliffe, W. E. (1990). *Addiction and the vulnerable self*. New York: Guilford Press.

Kiev, A. (1964). *Magic, faith and healing*. New York: Free Press of Glencoe.

Klein, M. (1975). *Love, guilt and reparation and other works: 1921–1945*. New York: Dell Publishing.

Koch, S. (Ed.). (1959–1963). *Psychology: A study of science* (Vols. 1–6). New York: McGraw-Hill.

Kohut, H. (1977). *The restoration of the self*. New York: International Universities Press.

Kraepelin, E. (1907). *Clinical Psychiatry; A Textbook for students and physicians*. New York: The Macmillan Co.

Krystal, H., & Raskin, H. A. (1970). *Drug dependence: Aspects of ego function*. Detroit, MI: Wayne State University Press.

Kurtz, E. (1979). Not God: A history of Alcoholics Anonymous. Center City, MN: Hazelden.

Kurtz, E. (1982). Why AA? The intellectual significance of Alcoholics Anonymous. *Journal of Studies on Alcohol, 43*, 38–80.

Kurtz, E., & Ketcham, K. (1992). *The spirituality of imperfection*. New York: Bantam Books.

Kurtz, L. P. (1990). 12-step programs. In Thomas J. Powell (Ed.), *Working with self-helps* (pp. 93–119). Washington, DC: National Association of Social Work Press.

Lasch, C. (1979). *The culture of narcissism*. New York: Norton.

Latourette, K. S. (1953). *A history of Christianity*. New York: Harper and Brothers.

Ludwig, A. M. (1985). Cognitive processes associated with "spontaneous" recovery from alcoholism. *Journal of Alcohol Studies, 46*, 53–58.

Mack, J. (1981). Alcoholism, A.A., and the governance of the self. In M. Bean & N. Zinbery (Eds.), *Dynamic approaches to the understanding and treatment of alcoholism* (pp. 128–162). New York: Free Press.

McCrady, B. S., & Irvine, S. (1989). Self-help groups. In R. K. Hester & W. R. Miller (Eds.), *Handbook of alcoholism treatment approaches: effective alternatives* (pp. 447–480). Elmsford, NY: Pergamon Press.

McInerney, P. (1991). *Time and experience*. Philadelphia: Temple University Press.

Morgenstern, J., & Leeds, J. (1993). Contemporary psychoanalytic theories of substance abuse: A disorder in search of a paradigm. *Psychotherapy: Theory, Research, Practice, Training, 30*, 194–206.

Napoli, D. (1981). *Architects of adjustment*. Port Washington, NY: Kennikat Press.

Nino, A. (1990). Restoration of the self: A therapeutic paradigm from Augustine's confessions. *Psychotherapy: Theory, Research, Practice, Training, 27*, 8–18.

Osborne, A. C., & Glaser, F. B. (1981). Characteristics of affiliates of Alcoholics Anonymous: A review of the literature. *Journal of Studies on Alcohol, 42,* 661–675.

Peele, S. (1989). *The diseasing of America.* Lexington, MA: Lexington Books.

Prochaska, J. O., DiClemente, C. C., & Norcross, J. C. (1992). In search of how people change: Applications to addictive behavior. *American Psychologist, 47,* 1102–1114.

Ramsey, E. (1988). From guilt through shame to AA: A self-reconciliation process. *Alcoholism Treatment Quarterly, 7,* 87–107.

Reiff, P. (1966). *The triumph of the therapeutic: Uses of faith after Freud.* New York: Harper & Row.

Sarbin, T. (1986). *Narrative psychology: The storied nature of human conduct.* New York: Praeger.

Schaef, A. W. (1987). *When society becomes an addict.* New York: Harper & Row.

Schafer, R. (1992). *Retelling a life.* New York: Basic Books.

Segal, H. (1974). *Introduction to the work of Melanie Klein.* New York: Basic Books.

Shaffer, H. (1985). The disease controversy: Of metaphors, maps and menus. *Journal of Psychoactive Drugs, 2,* 65–76.

Shafranske, E., & Malony, H. N. (1990). Clinical psychologists' religious and spiritual orientations and their practice of psychotherapy. *Psychotherapy, 27*(1), 72–78.

Smith, H. (1963). *The meaning and end of religion.* New York: MacMillan.

Spiegel, E., & Mulder, E. (1986). The anonymous program and ego functioning. *Issues in Ego Psychology, 9,* 34–42.

Spilka, B., Hood, R. W., & Gorsuch, R. L. (1985). *The psychology of religion: An empirical approach.* Englewood Cliffs, NJ: Prentice Hall.

Strupp, H. (1972). On the technology of psychotherapy. *Archives of General Psychiatry, 26,* 270–278.

Tiebout, H. M. (1961). Alcoholics Anonymous: An experiment of Nature. *Issues in Ego Psychology, 9,* 34–42.

Tillich, P. (1952). *The courage to be.* New Haven: Yale University Press.

Tillich, P. (1957). *The Protestant era.* Chicago: University of Chicago Press.

Tournier, R. (1979). Alcoholics Anonymous as treatment and ideology. *Journal of Studies on Alcohol, 40,* 230–239.

Twerski, A. J. (1990). Is divine intervention really a drawback? *Journal of Substance Abuse, 2,* 485–487.

Valliant, G. E., & Milofsky, E. S. (1982). Natural history of male alcoholism, IV. Paths to recovery. *Archives of General Psychiatry, 39,* 127–133.

W., B. (1987). The Bill W.—Carl Jung letters. *Revision, 10*(2), 19–21. (Original work published 1961)

Wallace, M., & Rabin, A. I. (1960). Temporal experience. *Psychological Bulletin*, *57*, 213–233.

Williams, C. (1992). *No hiding place*. San Francisco: HarperCollins.

Woodman, M. (1987). Worshipping illusions: An interview with Marion Woodman. *Parabola: The Magazine of Myth and Tradition*, *12*(2), 56–67.

Wurmser, L. (1978). *The hidden dimension: The psychodynamics of compulsive drug use*. Northvale, NJ: Jason Aronson.

Zinberg, N., & Bean, M. (1981). Alcohol use, alcoholism, and the problems of treatment. In M. Bean & N. Zinberg (Eds.), *Dynamic approaches to the understanding and treatment of alcoholism* (pp. 1–35). New York: Free Press.

Zitter, M. L. (1987, March–April). Culturally sensitive treatment of black alcoholic families. *Social Work*, 130–135.

IV

AFTERWORD

21

RELIGION AND THE CLINICAL PRACTICE OF PSYCHOLOGY: A CASE FOR INCLUSION

EDWARD P. SHAFRANSKE and H. NEWTON MALONY

We return in this closing chapter to the central question posed in the introduction: What is the influence of religion as a variable in mental health and psychological treatment? Broadly stated, the issue concerns the inclusion of religious issues in the clinical practice of psychology. Consideration of "inclusion" is crucial to this discussion because it defines the relationship between the science and profession of psychology and the domain of human experience referred to as religion. Furthermore, such a determination regarding inclusion establishes the parameters of treatment and standards of care, delimits the scope of legitimate psychological research and scholarship, and dictates the course of education and clinical training. It is our view that religious issues should be included within the clinical practice of psychology. We believe that this inclusion is justified in light of four interrelated factors: the professional ideal of cultural inclusion; the substantial evidence of religion as a cultural fact; the developing body of theoretical, clinical, and empirical research literature concerning religion as a variable in mental health; and the appreciation of psychological treatment as a value-based form of intervention. We conclude our discussion with an appraisal of current education and training respective of religious issues and suggest a model for training and future research.

In positing that religion be included as a variable in psychological treatment, we are not issuing a universal statement regarding the positive

561

or negative valence of the effects of religion on individuals. Rather, we are calling for an appreciation of the significance of religion in mental health and treatment. We find ourselves to be in agreement with certain critics of religious belief, such as Ellis (1970, 1980, 1983), in the respect that we mutually appreciate the significance of religion. We agree, as well, that some religion can be toxic and can impede healthy adjustment. However, we are more inclined to perceive that religion can have a positive as well as a negative effect on mental health. Our charge to the profession is to address both sides of the religious question and to engage in an "on the one hand . . . on the other hand" dialogue until, like Tevye of "Fiddler on the Roof" fame, we "run out of hands." Religion is too important to be automatically excluded from the psychotherapeutic task. In fact, we conclude that religion ought to be one of those issues that *invariably is included* in all psychological treatment.

Failing to include religious concerns in psychotherapy would be similar to not exploring problems associated with drinking alcoholic beverages—a far-too-common occurrence in physical examinations. If psychotherapists fall into the habit of not addressing religion in their work, they, like some physicians, may miss an extremely formative aspect of personal adjustment.

THE PROFESSIONAL IDEAL OF BEING CULTURALLY INCLUSIVE

The APA *Monitor* is replete with job announcements that include the statement that a given institution is an "equal opportunity employer." Sometimes, such phrases are followed by explanatory statements that no discrimination in hiring will be made on the basis of gender, ethnicity, or culture, to name only a few of the qualifiers that are often seen. Such announcements reflect an ideal of not making professional decisions on the basis of nonessential characteristics over which people have little or no control.

Even though, in our culture, religion is seen as self-chosen aspect of life rather than something with which one is born, it is almost always included in the list of individual traits to be ignored. Most important, we psychologists commit ourselves, as do members of other mental health professions, to bracket our preconceptions and to make our professional decisions as bias-free as possible. Principle D of "The Ethical Principles of Psychologists and Code of Conduct" of APA (1992) directs psychologists to be aware of cultural, individual, and role differences, including those that are due to religion and to try to eliminate the effect on their work of these biases (cf. p. 1599).

Interestingly enough, while the goal of being bias-free is still a worthy professional ideal, we have come to feel that attending to such issues as gender, race, or culture in the psychotherapeutic task is crucial. In the same document on ethics and code of behavior, (cf. 1992, p. 1601, Standard 1.08 Human Differences) mandates that special training, experience, consultation, or supervision in dimensions of human differences or diversity, including religion, may be required to ensure the competence of the services they render, or else they should make appropriate referral. It appears that what is *proscribed* in job selection is *prescribed* in psychotherapy (Jackson, 1990). In fact, training in cultural diversity is now required for licensure in several states. Furthermore, the publication of this volume by APA may provide additional evidence for the appreciation that is placed on cultural differences and features of diversity. Moreover, the literature is full of articles comparing treatment outcomes for therapist–client backgrounds that are similar or different in a number of the variables considered nonessential in job announcements such as those in the APA *Monitor*.

As Bergin and Jensen stated, "every therapeutic relationship is cross-cultural experience" (1990, p. 3). Indeed, even among those pairings that counselors have considered most ideal, there are inherent cross-cultural differences that should not be ignored even among those who claim they exude total empathy, congruence, and warmth. Psychotherapists who remain unaware of gender, ethnic, and cultural differences do so at their own risk, according to current professional literature (Stricker et al., 1990). Although the data regarding whether same or different pairings on these issues is the preferable condition are inconclusive, what is certain is that the differences should be considered (Nagayama-Hall & Malony, 1983).

What is surprising is how often religion has been left out of those lists of differences that should be intentionally reflected on in psychotherapy. Illustrative of this tendency is the list given by Jackson (1990, p. 209) that suggested we should attend to "related variables such as sex, socioeconomic status, generational issues, and education levels" in addition to racial and ethnic differences. Her list included no mention of religion. Pope, Sonne, and Holyrod (1993) are among the few authors who have included religious differences between clients and therapists among important issues to consider.

Although external racial differences have been the dominant theme in writing about differences that should be considered in psychotherapy (cf. Stricker et al., 1990), a broader understanding of cultural differences includes "*internalized* values and beliefs (as well as . . . emotional and mental qualities" (VandeCreek & Merrill, 1990, p. 196). These authors continue their description of cultural diversity by stating, "Culturally different individuals do not necessarily have overt physical characteristics or identifiable ethnic heritages that distinguish them from the dominant cultural group (p. 196). Such beneath-the-skin "values and beliefs . . . emotional and mental qualities" might well include religious concerns. The bonds of affiliation, as Durkheim contended, may be established through the ideological commitments that people hold. Belief in a common vision of reality, or rather a shared, social construction of reality (Berger, 1963), may be a far more potent social glue than the color of one's skin, cultural heritage, or gender.

There is some evidence that religion may play an equal, and at times dominant, force in group affiliation and identification. Indeed, Kosmin and Lachman (1993), the authors of a major study of religion in contemporary American society, concluded, "religious identification and belief tend to crosscut racial and ethnic divisions among Americans and to provide a largely unappreciated level of social cohesion and consensus on core values" (p. 116). Religious identification for some may be the thread that unites individuals into a social unit. Features of diversity are not isolated. The question should not be posed as to which factor alone provides the agency of influence. Gender, ethnicity, religion, and a host of other factors conjoin to contribute to one's cultural identity, affiliations, and values. As Lovinger (Chapter 12, this volume) suggests, cultural differences are complex phenomena; one needs to look beyond the general identification of religious denomination to the diverse interactions between ethnicity, religious denomination, and locality. The point is that religion must be taken account of as a factor in any appreciation of individual difference and cultural diversity.

Suffice it to say, as the next section will show, we are convinced that religion is, indeed, one of those critical aspects of culture that is focal for a significant number of those who seek psychological treatment. Quite apart from religion's frequent exclusion from the lists of important differences to which therapists should attend, a recent survey revealed that religious issues often arise in therapy (Shafranske & Malony, 1990). As we will show in a later section, this does not mean that the religious concerns that clients bring with them are always realistic, healthy, or treatment-enhancing. However, neither can it be asserted that these religious concerns are entirely destructive or tangential to adjustment and cure. Psychotherapists should keep an open mind and be willing to explore religious concerns as an important component of cultural diversity.

RELIGION AS A CULTURAL FACT

In the previous section, we argued for inclusion of religion in psychological treatment on the basis of professional ideals and principles. Our justification in this section now turns to the basis of facts and statistical probability. The question to be asked is "What is the likelihood that a given client will be religious?" Our pragmatic, clinical presumption underneath that question is "If it can be demonstrated that a majority of persons who seek psychotherapy are religious, would it not be appropriate always to explore that aspect of their life in treatment?" The review of the survey data as presented by Hoge (Chapter 1, this volume) provides a compelling answer to the question. In his words, "Religion in America is as alive as ever, but it is diversifying" (p. 38). The answer to our question, therefore, is not a simple one. Both facets of his conclusion will need to be taken into account by clinicians: first, that it is likely that a majority of clients are religious and, second, that the form of religious commitment, experience, and affiliation cannot be taken for granted but must be carefully examined in light of religious diversification.

The first point deserves further amplification. The findings of the National Survey of Religious Identification indicated that approximately 90% of Americans identify with a religion (cf. Kosmin & Lachman, 1993, p. 2). Barna (1992) reported the results of a national survey that found that 86% of Americans believe in God, 70% believe that there is a God who answers prayers, 64% consider themselves to be religious, 49% attended a religious service in the past week, and 47% consider faith to be relevant to the way they live their lives. Of interest is the historical finding of the continuing rise in religious affiliation: "At the time of the American Revolution, only 17 percent of Americans belonged to a church. By the Civil War that had risen to 37 percent. After a postwar dip, the number of adherents rose to 50 percent and in 1980 was up to 62 percent. A 1994 Gallup Poll found that 68% of American's belong to a particular church or temple." (Clark, 1994, pp. 1041–1042). Furthermore, a *U.S. News & World Report* ("Spiritual America," 1994, p. 48) found that 62% say religion is increasing in influence on their lives. Our review of the data leads us to agree with the conclusions of Kosmin and Lachman (1993, p. 279) that, "An outstanding feature of America today is that the vast majority of people identify with a religion" (See also Gallup, 1985). In light of these data it is probable that the majority of clients seeking professional consultation are in some fashion religious.

We turn briefly to Hoge's second point concerning religious diversification. As he points out, the religious landscape of the United States is becoming increasingly diverse. Through the cultural influence of assimilating immigrants, increased tolerance of religious differences, and trends that point to rising conservatism while simultaneously a weakening in church authority, assumptions about the nature of an individual's religious faith and commitment will be at best speculative. The question will demand to be put, not as "Are you religious?" but rather, "How are you religious?" As was found in the research on intrinsic and extrinsic motivation in religion, the emphasis needs to be placed on the internal structure and functions of an individual's religiousness. As the United States becomes increasingly individualistic and multicultural, clinicians will need to consider the multiverse of features that contribute to the psychosocial aspects of their clients' lives and present psychological status.

If these data and our conclusions are correct, there is a strong likelihood that clients will bring with them a significant religious component when they come for psychotherapy. At the very least, the therapist should ask Socratic questions designed to assess the degree to which the client is relating religious convictions and attitudes to the problems that he or she is facing. These relationships may be conscious states of mind and beliefs of which the clients are well-aware. They could also be unconscious or subconscious God representations, beliefs, and traits of behavior that function as organizing schemata outside of conscious awareness. Nevertheless, if the surveys are correct, a significant proportion of clients who come to therapy have incorporated religion into their personal, cultural experience.

Because of the pervasiveness of organized religion in the United States, it can be predicted that clients will express this dimension of their experience within the terms of one of the major religious traditions. This will likely be true in spite of Barna's (1992) observation that Americans are tending toward more private, less institutional spiritual expression and Roof's (1993) conclusion that much contemporary religious experience is occurring outside of traditional religious institutions. Nevertheless, we believe that, in light of the sociological data, it is incumbent that clinicians develop at least a rudimentary understanding of religion in its institutional expressions. As illustrated by Lovinger (Chapter 12, this volume), the nuances of institutional beliefs and practices are exceedingly varied and play a decisive role in an individual's psychology. The familiarity of religious traditions that can be gleaned through a study of comparative religion will need to be complemented by a clinically sophisticated inquiry of the client's unique religiousness. This will necessarily include an understanding of religious commitments within the family of origin; religious education; formative faith experiences; present challenges within the context of faith development (Fowler, Chapter 6, this volume; 1981); and current involvement in a religious congregation, faith community, or spiritual tradition.

RELIGION AS A VARIABLE IN MENTAL HEALTH

The professional ideal of cultural inclusion and the body of sociological data establishing religion as a cultural fact are sufficient and convincing justifications for attending to religiosity in the clinical practice of psychology. There is a third domain of knowledge to which we now turn that bolsters that claim: religion as a variable in mental health. Throughout this volume, numerous studies have been cited and case illustrations presented that suggest that religion as a variable is significant in psychological health. Our aim in this section is not to recite this body of literature in its specifics but rather to elucidate a number of considerations and conclusions that are relevant to clinical practice.

Evaluating and comparing results in the empirical literature are difficult in light of the varied procedures that have been used to operationalize the variables of religion and mental health. Religious commitment and involvement, for example, can be measured through a number of indexes including religious motivation, belief, affiliation, and practice. The diversity of factors is ever more the case in assessing mental health. Psychological functioning can be inspected from a number of perspectives involving numerous variables. For example, mental health can be assessed by self-report of phenomenological states of mind, such as anxiety, or by actuarial tests and scales such as the Minnesota Multiphasic Personality Inventory; by structured diagnostic interviews as those used in catchment studies, or through objective measures of psychophysiological correlates of psychological states. Religion and mental health appear to be complex domains that contain a number of diffuse, interrelated, and, at times, confounding factors. A number of reviews of the empirical literature have investigated the relationship between religion and mental health (Batson & Ventis, 1922; Becker, 1971; Bergin, 1983; Bergin, Stinchfield, Gaskin, Masters & Sullivan, 1988; Gartner, Larson, & Allen, 1991; Masters & Bergin, 1992; Sanva, 1969; Schumaker, 1992). Each in their own way has contributed to the demonstration of a relationship between variables associated with religion and mental health.

Gartner (Chapter 7, this volume) found a way through this complexity and identified a number of mental health variables that correlated with religion. His comprehensive review found that religious involvement correlated with positive or beneficial mental health variables in respect to physical health, mortality, suicide, drug use, alcohol abuse, delinquency and criminal behavior, divorce and marital satisfaction, well-being, health outcome, and depression. Furthermore, he reported that religious involvement has been found to be associated with the following features of psychopathology: authoritarianism, dogmatism, suggestibility, and dependence. This survey of the literature, taken with the earlier cited reviews, demonstrates that a significant relationship exists between religious involvement and measures of mental health. Religious involvement appears to be a significant variable among the numerous factors that influence psychological functioning. It is not an insignificant finding that this is also the case in physical health. Levin (1995; Levin & Vanderpool, 1991) found that religiousness correlated with positive physical health correlates in 83% of the studies that investigated that relationship.

That religiousness is a factor in mental health and psychological treatment was formally acknowledged by its inclusion in the *Diagnostic and*

Statistical Manual of Mental Disorders (DSM-IV). The 1994 edition of the DSM-IV (American Psychiatric Association) included the following:

> V. 62.89 Religious or Spiritual Problem. This category can be used when the focus of clinical attention is a religious or spiritual problem. Examples include distressing experiences that involve loss or questioning of faith, problems associated with conversion to a new faith, or questioning of spiritual values that may not necessarily be related to an organized church or religious institution. (p. 685)

This inclusion reflects the awareness that religious and spiritual concerns play a role in the mental health of individuals.

We conclude that religion plays a significant role in psychological health and therefore requires to be considered within the clinical practice of psychology. In light of this conclusion, a further question results: "In what ways might clinicians include the variable of religion within their practice of psychology?"

RELIGION AND CLINICAL PRACTICE

A sensitive appraisal of religion contributes to two interrelated aspects of psychological consultation: assessment and treatment. Assessment involves the development of a comprehensive understanding of the client with particular emphasis placed on areas of psychological difficulty, psychiatric symptoms, and maladjustment. Treatment concerns the application of psychological knowledge and procedures to the amelioration of psychological conflict, maladaptive behavioral responses, and psychiatric complaints leading to improved mental health and psychosocial functioning. Religion as a cultural fact and as a clinically significant variable should be taken into account within the assessment process.

Clinical Assessment

Elements of religious involvement, including beliefs, practices, and affiliations, should be assessed in terms of their dynamic role in supporting or impeding mental health. The development of a treatment plan should include consideration of aspects of a client's religious involvement that may serve as resources or present obstacles to the therapeutic work. Assessment of an individual's religious orientation, beliefs, practices, and affiliations provides a unique aperture in which to inspect the client's mode of understanding and relating to themselves and to others (Malony, 1988, 1992a, 1993).

Our review of the literature leads us to suggest that the empirical findings concerning religion as operationalized in terms of intrinsic and extrinsic orientation are of particular note to clinical practice and a starting point for our discussion. As introduced earlier, what is of clinical significance may rest not so much on whether particular clients are religious or not nor in what congregation they affiliate, but rather, "How are they religious?" and furthermore, "What role does religious involvement play in the client's psychology?" Such an approach focuses on the functions, purposes, and dynamics that religious involvement plays in the client's mental health. The literature on intrinsic and extrinsic religiousness points in this direction toward a functional appraisal of religious motivation. Although we do not believe that the model of intrinsic and extrinsic orientation fully captures the entire spectrum of religious experience, we nonetheless value its conceptual and methodological facility to tease out an essential difference found between separate individuals' ways of being religious.

On the basis of the model put forward by Allport and Ross (1967) and refined by a number of empirical researchers (see Donahue, 1985, for comprehensive review), intrinsic religious orientation involves religion as an end in itself: It provides answers to essential existential questions; extrinsic religiousness derives its impetus from utilitarian aims; and it is a means to obtain security, status, and self-justification. Allport and Ross succinctly puts the distinction as follows: "the extrinsically motivated individual *uses* his religion, whereas the intrinsically motivated *lives* his" (p. 434). Masters and Bergin (1992) have concluded that intrinsic religious orientation is positively related to mental health, and Bergin, Payne, and Richards (Chapter 11, this volume) suggest that "the base of this effect is a sense of purpose and meaning in life." The function that religious involvement serves in the life of the client will provide a central focus in a clinical interviewing and treatment. To the extent that religiousness is based on an intrinsic orientation, religious involvement may serve as a potential resource toward the aim of mental health. The discovery of an extrinsic orientation may alert the therapist to psychological tendencies in the client that may pose vulnerabilities respective of mental health and portend liabilities to the treatment process (e.g., a disposition to prejudice, authoritarianism, and cognitive inflexibility).

The point is not to definitely assign the descriptive nomenclature of intrinsic or extrinsic to a client's religiousness for the sake of categorization or pejorative judgment. Such a use would be akin to the misunderstanding and misapplication of diagnostic taxonomies as simply procedures of labeling or stigmatizing. Rather, we view the inquiry of religious orientation as a contribution to a comprehensive understanding of how an individual experiences, makes sense of and lives in the world. Furthermore, our discussion of intrinsic and extrinsic religiousness does not imply that the clinical assessment of the nature and function of religion be limited to such an inquiry. Allport's model may serve as an initial focus of exploration in light of its heuristic value and the research evidence of its relationship to mental health variables.

Meissner (Chapter 9, this volume) contributes to the qualitative and functional assessment of religious belief systems. His analysis provides criteria for determining those aspects of belief systems that are in service of psychological health and adaptation and those that are destructive and, in summary, pathological. Meissner's sophisticated reading and expansion of Rokeach allows for an assessment of the content and functions of religious, or for that matter, any belief, be it derived from popular, artistic, or scientific domains. Clinicians may develop through the course of assessment and treatment an understanding of the structure and function of a belief in terms of degrees of openness versus closedness and rigidity versus flexibility. Such an appraisal establishes whether religious beliefs are on the side of health or illness.

Religious beliefs and practices need also to be assessed in terms of their location within the cultural background and milieu of the client. Lovinger (Chapter 12, this volume) convincingly points out that a given belief or practice must be understood within the normative experience of a given cultural, denominational, and local religious community. Practices and beliefs that lie outside of the milieu may suggest deviance and prompt the clinician to assess the psychological function of the religious involvement further.

In keeping with their belief and value commitments, religions provide prescriptions for living. An important index to assess is the relationship between salience, which concerns the importance that an individual places on faith commitments, and lifestyle, which involves the application of beliefs and values to specific ways of behaving. It logically follows that for those for whom religion has a high salience, the living out of such beliefs and values will be of importance. Psychological distress and conflict may ensue when there exists an incongruence between the salience of faith commitments and lifestyle. It has been our clinical experience that clients experience anxiety and, at times, depression in circumstances in which such an incongruence exists. The clinician, therefore, should be mindful of assessing, in addition to the functions, and cultural location of religious involvement, the relationship between holding religious beliefs and values and living them.

In our view the client's religious involvement and beliefs should initially be assessed through four criteria: religious orientation, degree of openness or closedness in structure and function, relationship to normative religious and cultural experience, and congruence between salience and the degree to which the religious tradition's prescripts are followed. Through such an approach religiousness can be understood and assessed without relying solely on the subjective opinion of the clinician or correspondence to the clinician's personal belief system. Such an appraisal may provide important diagnostic and clinical information regarding the antecedents and dynamics of psychological distress and psychopathology. Beliefs that are highly idiosyncratic and are at odds with the client's present religious tradition indicate potentially disturbed thinking that may contribute to or be a symptom of mental illness. The ability to commit to beliefs and values and yet remain open to others of different faith orientations results in an openness to relationship rather than to a closed insularity that may lead to suspicion and alienation. Religious involvement that provides a sense of personal meaning and coherence to life experience and supports affiliation in a faith community presents a potential resource for mental health.

It is important, as well, to assess religious involvement from a developmental perspective. Fowler (Chapter 6, this volume; 1981) presents an important vantage on which to understand the trajectory of faith development. This perspective emphasizes that religious faith is not a static entity but rather a dynamic process. In our clinical experience we have found that crises of faith often parallel or prompt changes in psychological status. For example, the understanding of a patient's depression is enhanced through an appreciation of the particular faith challenge of a given developmental stage. Such an understanding can be a significant asset to clinical assessment.

Finally, an appreciation of religion as a potential resource for mental health is required. We agree with Pargament (Chapter 8, this volume; Pargament and Maton, in press) that "psychologists have much to gain by learning about, learning from, and working with the religious world in an effort to promote mental health" (p. 215). Pargament and his collaborators (see this volume for a review) have demonstrated empirically that religion can be a potent source of support and coping, particularly in the adjustment to crisis. As a culturally sanctioned institution, religion provides beliefs, rituals, and social affiliations that assist the individual in constructing a personal philosophy of significance. The clinician needs to be sensitive to the functions that religious involvement serves in this regard. An assessment needs to take into account the influence of religion as a potential source of support for, as well as a potential impediment to, mental health.

We assert that a comprehensive assessment of an individual should include an appreciation of religious background and current involvement, including beliefs, practices, and affiliations (Malony, 1992a; Lovinger, Chapter 12, this volume). This assessment necessitates a qualitative inquiry into the structure and function of religious involvement and its location in the cultural milieu and developmental status of the individual.

Psychological Treatment as a Value-Based Intervention

It is our view that psychological treatment involves the whole person—that it is an impossibility to simply treat symptoms or aspects of psychological functioning in isolation. With this premise in mind we assert that treatment will inevitably come in contact with the client's values and religious and spiritual life. Furthermore, we assert that treatment involves not only the values of the client but also those of the therapist.

We agree with Bergin (cf. 1991; Chapter 11, this volume) that the major premise that psychotherapy is value-free or value-neutral has become untenable. Psychological procedures, in themselves, are not value-neutral but rather emanate from particular world views and faith commitments. The prescription of a psychotropic medication or behavior therapy or psychoanalysis or existential psychotherapy to a patient presenting with depression involves a clinical decision that is rife with the values and particular world view of the clinician. Mental health professionals make such decisions on a daily, and perhaps, constant, minute-to-minute basis, in providing consultation and treatment. We do not intend to minimize the influence of clinical training; rather, we are asserting that embedded within clinical decision-making and practice procedures are beliefs and values concerning the nature and meaning of human life. London (1964) suggested that there are three signal elements explicit or implied in all systems of psychotherapy: (a) a theory of personality, which addresses itself to the nature of the person and behavior; (b) a superordinate moral code; and (c) a body of therapeutic techniques, which are deliberate means of influencing behavior (cf. London, 1964, p. 25). We concur with this view that psychotherapy inevitably involves the expression of beliefs and values.

Clinicians bring their own personal values to the clinical setting; the idea that one could park one's faith commitments and ways of organizing experience at the office door seems to us to be a naive notion. Worthington (1988) helpfully suggests that the therapist brings two sets of values: those idiosyncratic to the clinician as a person and those values specific to the mode of treatment that is offered. We agree, however, with Beutler, Machado, and Neufeldt (1994, p. 240) "that in practice, one's professional and personal values become so intertwined that it is virtually impossible to differentiate among them."

Recent writing within the field of psychoanalysis also contributes to this discussion. The term *intersubjectivity* has been introduced to emphasize the dyadic nature of the analytic relationship and to stress the mutual influence of each participant on the process of psychotherapy (Natterson, 1991; Stolorow, Atwood, & Brandchaft, 1994). This literature suggests that the therapist actively participates and co-constructs rather than merely observes reality. The psychotherapist's "irreducible subjectivity" plays a significant role in the treatment process (cf. Renik, 1993). No longer can the psychoanalytic therapist, or therapist of any stripe, be considered a blank screen or detached, objective, scientific observer. The values of the clinician enter into the treatment process at each turn. This particularly important in light of the fact that psychotherapy at its core involves elaborating and ascribing meanings to human experience. In this regard, psychological treatments that involve the interpretation of experience function in ways that are remarkably similar to those of religion. Both religion and science provide models that are used to make sense of the world. Each provides a hermeneutic for the interpretation of experience. Furthermore, the faith commitments inherent in the therapeutic system provide sources of inspiration and promises of a better life. Each intends through its praxis to initiate and extol behaviors toward a valued aim. The differences between them are in matters of degree rather than absolute contrast (cf. Barbour, 1974, p. 171). It is in the territory of ontological beliefs and personal lifestyle that religion and psychology most clearly enjoin or conflict.

Through religion "spheres of relevancy are created that orient human values and ultimately determine behavior" (Shafranske, Chapter 5, this volume). Psychology as a profession participates, as well, in the polity as an agent of social influence. In their own ways both seek to influence the direction of individuals' lives and of the culture. Both religion and psychology contribute to an individual's construction of meaning and values. We agree with Frank (1973) that psychotherapy involves interpersonal persuasion and the inculcation of a set of meanings and values that combat demoralization and encourage behavioral change.

The goal of eliciting behavior change through the interpretation of experience marks the entry into the most fundamental aspect of being human. A not-uncommon presumption about human beings is that their behavior is characterized by two basic motives—sense making and meaning seeking (Malony, 1986, pp. 37–39). Certainly most existential and many humanistic psychologists would agree with this depiction of human nature (Yalom, 1980). Religion, defined broadly as including traditional, institutional, newer religious movements, and individual spiritual practices, has always been one of the prime ways in which the search for meaning was assuaged (cf., Allport, 1950/1961). Batson and Ventis (1982) concluded that religiousness included not only external-means and internal-ends features, related to Allport's extrinsic and intrinsic religious orientation, but also included a dimension of "quest" that emphasizes an incompleteness and tentativeness that "involves honestly facing existential questions in all their complexity, while resisting clear-cut, pat answers" (pp. 149–150).

The twofold motivational model of sense making and meaning seeking implies that along with the pragmatic impulse to make sense of one's environment and function successfully within it (cf. Kelly, 1955), individuals seek overarching understandings of meaning for their lives and try to affirm values and purposes on which to base their existences. Viktor Frankl (1959) has labeled this impulse the "will to meaning."

Although it is not necessary to extend this presumption as far as Frankl (1975) goes in calling this impulse "religious," it does seem evident, from numerous sources, that there may be a universal "need to experience oneself as a part of a meaningful universe" (Van der Lans, 1991, p. 317). At the very least, this need could be labeled *quasireligious* in the sense that Yinger (1970) meant when he defined religion as "a system of beliefs and practices by means of which a group of people struggle with the ultimate problems of life" (p. 7).

Our argument is this: Quite apart from the statistical evidence of modal religion noted earlier, there is warrant for encouraging psychotherapists to explore how their clients are meeting the basic search for meaning in their lives. We are drawing attention to this feature of psychology—that in its intent to ameliorate psychiatric symptoms a confrontation of beliefs and values necessarily occurs. The relevance of the answers to this exploration may be only minimal for the pragmatic, corollary need to make sense of life; however, it is presumed that overall life adjustment would be deeply influenced. Meaning and purpose will serve as an umbrella over or a circle around all else and, even, may often become the core issue of concern in psychotherapy (cf. Tillich, 1957).

To ignore or exclude attention to religious issues in psychotherapy may be profoundly short-sighted, from this point of view. As Jones (1993) so decisively asserted, "As a species we need to know that our life is meaningful and purposeful" (p. 2). Although Allport (1950/1961) concluded that there were many ways this could be accomplished, he correctly stated that religion was the primary way human beings met these basic needs. In this modern, or perhaps postmodern, age, we may speculate that psychology as well as religion presents a paradigm through which meaning may be constructed.

Having argued that meaning making becomes one nexus where psychology and religion intersect, the matter before us now is "How should religion be included in psychological treatment?" To reaffirm our position, the question is not stated "Should religion be included in psychological treatment?" for we believe that religious issues are necessarily involved. We concur with Tan (Chapter 13, this volume) that there are two major models concerning the actual use of religion in clinical practice.

> *Implicit integration* of religion in clinical practice refers to a more covert approach that does not initiate the discussion of religious or spiritual issues and does not openly, directly, or systematically use spiritual resources like prayer and Scripture or other sacred texts, in therapy. . . . *Explicit integration* of religion in clinical practice or psychotherapy refers to a more overt approach that directly and systematically deals with spiritual or religious issues in therapy, and uses spiritual resources like prayer, Scripture or sacred texts, referrals to church or other religious groups or lay counselors, and other religious practices. (this volume, p. 368)

As demonstrated in the section in this volume on clinical treatment, there are a number of approaches that may be used. Psychoanalytic therapists may explore God representations and religious experience in terms of the dynamic conflicts and transference implications that are expressed within analysis (Rizzuto, Chapter 15, this volume; Jones, 1993; Meissner, 1984; Shafranske, 1995). Cognitive–behavioral therapists may use cognitive restructuring and desensitization procedures to embolden clients toward positive behavioral adjustment (Propst, Chapter 14, this volume). Family therapists may analyze the dynamic and structural functions of religious involvement in the equilibrium of the system (Sperry & Giblin, Chapter 19, this volume). Existential–humanistic therapists may view religious experience as offering the deeper potential for experiencing and for the elucidation of meaning (Mahrer, Chapter 16, this volume; Frankl, 1975). Transpersonal therapists may use a variety of techniques, drawing from religious and spiritual experiences of the client, to an appreciation of transpersonal view of the self (Vaughn, Walsh, & Wittine, Chapter 18, this volume). Analytical psychotherapy views religious symbolism and dreams as important inroads to the understanding and resolution of psychological complexes leading to individuation. Twelve-step programs explicitly integrate spirituality within the course of treatment (Hopson, Chapter 20, this volume). Although the therapeutic techniques and philosophies vary, each share an appreciation of the relevance of religious experience in the psychotherapeutic work.

The heart of the issue remains concerning the degree of implicit and explicit integration. Our recommendations concerning dealing with religious issues in psychological treatment are threefold. First, therapists should take into consideration the influence of religion, in both its institutional form and private, more idiosyncratic expression, in the life of the client. Such a consideration takes into account the potential of such involvement to enhance or impede psychosocial functioning. Such assessments are rendered with utmost respect for the autonomy of the client and with an understanding that includes of diversity and cultural identity.

Second, therapists should be mindful that psychological treatment involves the interplay of the values of the client and therapist alike and acknowledge that clinical interventions are value-laden communications. Although this may mar the patina of objectivity that we as scientists like to assume exists in our treatments, such an acknowledgment actually assists in keeping our personal biases in check. Bergin et al. (Chapter 11, this volume) put the issue well: "A sensitive line exists between exploring and even critiquing values, faith, beliefs, and spiritual constructs while pursuing psychological integrity, versus examining these highly individualized perspectives with pre-emptive judgements" (p. 314). It is incumbent that therapists consider the role of values, beliefs, and faith commitments as they affect the psychological health of the client. However, such an assessment should be based on clinical criteria rather than on personal bias.

Third, explicit integration should be conducted within the parameters of the training of the therapist and with the expressed consent of the client. Furthermore, such an understanding calls for the respect for the autonomy of the client and clear demarcation of professional boundaries.

Younggren (1993) recently voiced the concern that "if one chooses to practice psychology from a spiritual or religious framework, then that practitioner has a professional responsibility to be in touch with those effects and to make sure that they do not become destructive" (p. 8). We fully concur with this position. However, we are firmly convinced that those who choose to practice psychology from a nonreligious framework need to do the same. The issue, again, is not whether faith commitments and values affect mental health and treatment but, rather, how the therapist addresses that reality. Through the considerations that we have put forth and the recommendations that follow, religiousness as a cultural fact and as a feature of an individual's psychology may be addressed within treatment.

EDUCATION, CLINICAL TRAINING, AND RESEARCH

One of the hallmarks of professional standards is that clinicians should practice within the scope of their competence. This standard appears to be in some jeopardy in light of survey research that indicates that psychologists and other mental health professionals rarely receive education and clinical training respective of religious issues (Shafranske, Chapter 5, this volume; Shafranske & Gorsuch, 1985; Shafranske & Malony, 1990; Bergin & Jensen, 1990). In this section we propose a number of measures to redress and remedy the current status of training. Note that we advocate a three-pronged approach that includes education, clinical training, and research. It is our view that each requires the other. Pedagogy demands a research base of knowledge on which clinical applications can be recommended, supervised, and investigated. Furthermore, we assert that clinical psychology hold firm to its tradition as an applied science (Fowler, 1990). We begin our discussion with education.

We acknowledge that these suggestions are ambitious, but we believe it is important to state what an ideal curriculum would look like to assess the degree to which specific training models are approximations. The ideal plan would include four components: a "values in psychological treatment" component, a "psychology of religion" component, a "comparative-religion" component, and a "working with religious issues" component.

Values in Psychological Treatment

This component addresses what we feel to be the core problem in including religion in the psychotherapeutic task. It is the problem that psychologists have on two fronts: one a scientific front and the other a personal front. Our training as social–behavioral scientists has been dominated by a "methodological atheism" at best and a "materialistic bias" at worst. Both are understandable. They reflect our scholarly heritage and current understanding of behavioral causation.

Psychology, anchored to the positivistic agenda of modern science, eschewed understandings of human events that could not be operationalized within an empirical framework. Furthermore, the belief was inculcated that through certain scientific procedures a factual, objective reading of reality could be obtained. Religious thinking was seen to be anathema to the scientific mind (Albee, 1991; Ellis, 1980). The relative isolation of religiousness from clinical studies, or its reduction to a nomothetic variable such as church identification, created a climate in which religiousness was assumed to be an irrelevant or blatantly pathological feature. We can recall that in our own clinical training religion was mentioned only in respect to the frequency of religious ideation in the psychoses. This is not to suggest that such an observation be omitted, but rather, that the whole story was not presented. By the whole story we mean the faith commitments within religion and within science.

A critical assessment is required of the status of the epistemological foundations of science. Through such an inspection models of religion and science can be appreciated in respect to the values that undergird their respective authority (Barbour, 1974). The objectivity that science purports emanates from a perspective of beliefs and values in as much as religion declares its authentic grasp of teleology on the basis of faith. Jones (Chapter 4, this volume) demonstrates the necessity of a thorough understanding of epistemology and an appreciation of "the variety of extraempirical factors that shape the scientific process." We share in his concern that other forms of human knowing complement those of science. Furthermore, we find an affinity with O'Donohue's (1989) conceptualization of the clinical psychologist as "metaphysician-scientist-practitioner." We suggest that the postmodern critique of science rattles the boundaries between models of knowing and calls for developing more comprehensive understandings of phenomena from a variety of disciplines and perspectives (Rosenau, 1992). Although this may shake the solidarity that is offered by the promise of objectivity, the gain may be found in a fuller grasp of the nature of things (cf. Rorty, 1991).

In essence, we are calling for and envision a curriculum that addresses the underlying value commitments that establish the canon of science and influence its application within clinical practice. Such an investigation will include a philosophical inquiry into the nature of facts, scientific practices, models of validation and falsification, and the assumptions on which clinical theories and treatments are based. We believe this is critical for the profession of psychology and essential if "a constructive relationship for religion with the science and profession of psychology" (Jones, Chapter 4, this volume) is to be achieved.

This component of the curriculum would also include an investigation of the role of personal values of the clinician as they are expressed in clinical thinking and practice. This involves an introspection and clarification of personal beliefs and religious experiences. Such an exercise is in keeping with discussions particularly within the psychoanalytic and analytical orientations concerning countertransference, within the humanistic–existential tradition concerning authenticity and the use of the self, and the role of therapist values and attributes in the comprehensive field of psychotherapy and counseling. We concur fully with Bergin's (1983) recommendation:

> Because religious cognitions, emotions, and behaviors, as documented here, are so pervasive, potential clinicians should understand the cultural content of their clients' religious world views rather than deny the importance of these views and coerce clients into alien liguistic and conceptual usages. To achieve this goal, the clinical students and practioners should be aware of their own religious impulses. Spiritual tendencies are common among us, but they are symbolized and expressed under many aliases. (p. 180)

An investigation of the religious beliefs, values, and faith commitments of the clinician-in-training complements the goal of training in cultural diversity. Furthermore, it amplifies the intersection of clinical technique, training, and clinician subjectivity that influence the treatment process. This is relevant, particularly in light of the survey research that shows that psychologists and other mental health professionals as a group are less likely to affiliate with organized religion as compared with the general population (Shafranske, Chapter 5, this volume). We might ask what are the factors that explain this "religiosity gap" (Lukoff, Lu, & Turner, 1992) and what impact might this have on clinical practice?

There is a further point of intersection that contains both the scientific and the personal. This area concerns the training process itself, in which an apprentice is brought into the scientific and professional paradigm, is schooled in its values, and procedures, and is supported in the development of new a identity and afforded a social affiliation within the community of the discipline and guild. As Kuhn (1970) and others (Pickering, 1992; Turner, 1994) have noted, the work of science is a profoundly social enterprise. The practices and habits that define the field contain silently within their structure a core of principles, values, and assumptions. It behooves the profession, particularly its subspecialty of social psychology, to understand the social influences that influence the developing scholar and clinician and to make explicit the value dimensions of its claims and practices. Could it be that the paradigm disallows religiousness in its confines (see Gartner, 1986)? Should that be the case, the profession's spirit of inclusiveness would be violated and certain sources of knowledge would be summarily isolated from contribution and investigation. Furthermore, how does the paradigm accommodate different modes of knowledge and values commitment? (Eckhardt, Kassinove, & Edwards, 1992). This component in the curriculum would provide an ongoing assessment of the process of acculturation into the profession and emphasize to the novice clinician the importance of recognizing personal and scientific beliefs and values within the clinical practice of psychology.

The question of values in psychotherapy should be addressed within the context of a critical appraisal of values as related to indexes of mental health. We posit that empirical research will contribute to an understanding of essential human values that by definition correlate with psychological health. The pedagogical component concerning values will be enhanced to the extent that research can demonstrate their virtues. Such a demonstration establishes therapy recommendations and their implicit moral values on empirical as well as theoretical grounds.

Psychology of Religion

The second component in our ideal training model for clinicians would include study of the psychology of religion. Although there is a need to understand the psychopathology of religion, there is an even greater need to appreciate the role of religion in the normal developmental process. Although many graduate sociology programs include such courses, such study has been rare for psychology. It is probably not too far fetched to say that many clinicians have not gone much deeper than a cursory reading of Freud and, perhaps, William James and are mostly unaware of the rich tradition of psychological interest in religion. There are number of fine surveys of this field that could be used to introduce psychotherapists to the understandings of religion from a psychological point of view (Batson, Schoenrade, & Ventis, 1993; Malony, 1992b; Spilka, Hood, & Gorsuch, 1985; Wulff, 1991). An exposure to the psychology of religion provides a fascinating history of American psychology in addition to its examination of essential issues concerning religion in individual and cultural experience.

Wulff's overview (Chapter 2, this volume) demonstrates that many of the most sophisticated contributors to American psychology have addressed the subject of religion. A survey of their thinking not only illuminates our understanding of religious experience but also provides a unique context to discern how their theories addressed difficult epistemological problems concerning consciousness, human motivation, and depth psychology. Vande Kemp's "Historical Perspective: Religion and Clinical Psychology in America," (Chapter 3, this volume) provides a sophisticated, comprehensive, and convincing statement of the long-standing integration of psychology and theology and religion. These chapters taken together suggest that graduate training in psychology would be lacking without attention to the psychology of religion.

Comparative Religions

Some study of general psychology of religion would lead naturally to a survey of comparative religions as well as various forms of spirituality. The diversity is enormous. There is a need for clinicians to have some appreciation of the variety. If nothing else, such a study would keep therapists from premature claims that they knew what was or was not orthodoxy for other traditions. In addition, an understanding of religious diversity would assist the clinician in making determinations regarding particular beliefs and practices in respect to normative religious practice in a given faith community. As Lovinger pointed out, such knowledge is required for a clinical assessment to be proffered (Chapter 12, this volume). Moreover, such a study might provoke a greater appreciation for the ways in which various religious traditions provide guidelines for well-being and fulfilling life adjustment.

In light of our review of religion as a cultural fact and the profession's call for increased sensitivity and attention to cultural diversity, such a survey seems warranted. Furthermore, in the United States, and perhaps, throughout the industrialized world, there is increasing cultural diversity within national borders. A study of comparative religion would contribute to the broadly defined goal of multicultural awareness.

Clinical Training

The last component of such an ideal training model would include instruction and supervision in dealing with religious issues in psychotherapy. Fortunately, a number of excellent resources are available. These include foundational essays such as that of Bergin (1983, 1985) as well as volumes such as Lovinger (1985, 1990), Randour (1993), Spero (1985), and Stern (1985). All of these materials include discussions of the inevitable presence of values in counseling; the religious convictions of the therapist; the means for assessing underlying world views; procedures for handling complicating and enhancing mentation; and the importance of addressing, rather than ignoring, religious and spiritual matters in the course of treatment.

Furthermore, we believe that graduate programs and internship facilities should provide direct training and supervision that includes assessment of religiousness as a variable in mental health and exposure to implicit and explicit models of addressing religious issues in psychological treatment. Support for such a recommendation appears to be developing in a number of professional associations. It is of note that in accordance to the APA principles that were previously cited the Office of Accreditation includes religion as one aspect of multicultural sensitivity that site visitors take into consideration in evaluating a program's education in cultural diversity. The American Psychiatric Association recommends, as well, that religion be considered in the evaluation and treatment of patients within residency training (Post, 1995). Furthermore, a recent conference sponsored by the National Council of Schools of Professional Psychology included a presentation on religious issues (Tan, 1993).

We believe that this proposed curriculum is a logical extension of the call for diversity training proposed by such authors as Vaughn (1988) and Wyatt and Parham (1985) and is consistent with the ethical standards for practice. The establishment of such a curriculum can only be maintained through an empirical demonstration of the importance of factors of religion in mental health.

Research

Our understanding of the influence of religion in the life of the individual and as a force within the culture is established through rigorous intellectual scholarship that includes empirical research. The relationship among religious beliefs, religious orientation, spiritual practices, and lifestyles based on specific moral and religious values and mental health require correlational and prospective research. We need to develop research methods and instruments that capture the constituent aspects of religious faith and practice that go beyond global assessments of affiliation and belief. Methods that investigate the dynamic functions of religious involvement will help to establish both the uniqueness of the faith dimension and those aspects of religious experience that might be applied to nonreligious populations.

Within clinical psychology further empirical work is required in the area of therapist–client value matching and its effects on treatment. Rigorous controlled studies are required to establish the efficacy of treatment regimens that explicitly integrate religious resources. Furthermore, more complete understanding of the faith dimension as the agent of change in 12-step programs is required and its implications for the treatment of other mental disorders. Fortunately, there are a number of ongoing research programs that are contributing to this field. Bergin and his colleagues' studies on values, lifestyle, and mental health and Pargament's ongoing work on religion as a resource are two examples that come to mind (Bergin et al., Chapter 11, this volume; Pargament, Chapter 8, this volume). The support of research in this area will be founded on the appreciation of religion as an elemental force in determining values which lead to behaviors which impact the mental health status of persons. Last, such research will contribute to an appreciation of religion as a coconstituent of cultural identity.

The curriculum that we propose will be based on a foundation of clinical research and collaborative intellectual efforts including, but not limited to, the disciplines of clinical and counseling psychology, social psychology, psychiatry, anthropology, sociology, philosophy, and religious studies. The inclusion of religion as a variable within mental health within graduate applied psychology curricula attunes scholars and clinicians to the breadth of human experience and values that inspire individuals to actions that ultimately affect individual and corporate well-being.

We conclude that the beliefs, practices, values, and affiliations, expressed within the structure of a formal religious body or held privately, hold the potential to be significant variables in mental health. In our society whose members almost universally identify themselves as religious and as a culture of diverse peoples and faiths, clinicians need to be mindful of the role that religion may serve in promoting or impeding mental health. We conclude that religion in all of its varied expressions and nuances be included in the clinical practice of psychology. This requires a commitment within the profession to mount a sustained effort to better understand the influence of religious involvement on psychological functioning, mental health, and psychological treatment.

REFERENCES

Albee, G. W. (1991). Opposition to prevention and a new creedal oath. *The Scientist Practitioner, 1*(4), 30–31.

Allport, G. (1961). *The individual and his religion.* New York: Macmillan. (Original work published 1950)

Allport, G. W., & Ross, J. M. (1967). Personal religious orientation and prejudice. *Journal of Personality and Social Psychology, 5*, 432–443.

American Psychiatric Association (1994). *Diagnostic and statistical manual of mental disorders (4th ed.).* Washington, DC: Author.

American Psychological Association. (1992). Ethical principles of psychologists and code of conduct. *American Psychologist, 47*, 1597–1611.

Barbour, I. (1974). *Myths, models, and paradigms.* New York: Harper & Row.

Barna, G. (1992). *What Americans believe: An annual survey of values and religious views in the United States.* Ventura, CA: Regal Books.

Batson, C. D., Schoenrade, P., & Ventis, W. L. (1993). *Religion and the individual.* Oxford, England: Oxford University Press.

Batson, C. D., & Ventis, W. L. (1982). *The religious experience.* Oxford, England: Oxford University Press.

Becker, R. (1971). In M. Strommen (Ed.), *Research on religious development: A comprehensive handbook*. New York: Hawthorn.

Berger, P. L. (1963). *An invitation to sociology: A humanistic perspective*. New York: Doubleday.

Bergin, A. E. (1983). Religiosity and mental health: A critical reevaluation and meta-analysis. *Professional Psychology: Research and Practice, 14*, 170–184.

Bergin, A. E. (1985). Proposed values for guiding and evaluating counseling and psychotherapy. *Counseling and Values, 29*, 99–116.

Bergin, A. E. (1991). Values and religious issues in psychotherapy and mental health. *American Psychologist, 46*, 394–403.

Bergin, A. E., & Jensen, J. P. (1990). Religiosity of psychotherapists: A national survey. *Psychotherapy, 27*, 3–7.

Bergin, A. E., Stinchfield, R. D., Gaskin, T. A., Masters, K. S., & Sullivan, C. E. (1988). Religious life-styles and mental health: An exploratory study. *Journal of Counseling Psychology, 35*, 91–98.

Beutler, L., Machado, P., & Neufeldt, S. (1994). Therapist variables. In A. E. Bergin & S. L. Garfield (Eds.), *Handbook of psychotherapy and behavior change* (pp. 229–269). New York: Wiley.

Clark, C. S. (1994, November). Religion in America. *CQ Researcher* (Vol. 4, No. 44). Washington, DC: Congressional Quarterly.

Donahue, M. J. (1985). Intrinsic and extrinsic religiousness: Review and meta-analysis. *Journal of Personality and Social Psychology, 48*, 400–419.

Eckhardt, C., Kassinove, H., & Edwards, L. (1992). Religious beliefs and scientific ideology in psychologists: Conflicting or coexisting systems? *Psychological Reports, 71*, 131–145.

Ellis, A. (1970). The case against religion. *Mensa Journal, 138*.

Ellis, A. (1980). Psychotherapy and atheistic values: A response to A. E. Bergin's "Psychotherapy and religious values." *Journal of Consulting and Clinical Psychology, 48*, 635–639.

Ellis, A. (1983). *The case against religiosity*. New York: Institute for Rational Emotive Psychotherapy.

Fowler, J. W. (1981). *Stages of faith: The psychology of human development and the quest for meaning*. San Fransico: Harper & Row.

Fowler, R. D. (1990). Psychology: The core discipline. *American Psychologist, 45*, 1–6.

Frank, J. D. (1973). *Persuasion and healing: A comparative study of psychotherapy* (Rev. ed.). Baltimore: The Johns Hopkins University Press.

Frankl, V. (1959). *Man's search for meaning: An introduction to logotherapy*. New York: Pocket Books.

Frankl, V. (1975). *The unconscious god*. New York: Simon & Schuster.

Gallup, G. (1985). Fifty years of Gallup surveys on religion. *The Gallup Report, 36*.

Gartner, J. D. (1986). Antireligious prejudice in admissions to doctoral programs in clinical psychology. *Professional Psychology: Research and Practice, 17,* 473–475.

Gartner, J., Larson, D., & Allen, G. (1991). Religious commitment and mental health: A review of the empirical literature. *Journal of Psychology and Theology, 19,* 6–25.

Jackson, J. S. (1990). The therapeutic equation and cross-cultural psychology. In G. Stricker, E. Davis-Russell, E. Bourg, E. Duran, W. R. Hammond, J. McHolland, K. Polite, & B. E. Vaughn (Eds.), *Toward ethnic diversification in psychology education and training* (pp. 206–210). Washington, DC: American Psychological Association.

Jones, J. W. (1993). Living on the boundary between psychology and religion. *Psychology of Religion Newsletter: American Psychological Association Division 36, 18*(4), 1–7.

Kelly, G. A. (1955). *The psychology of personal constructs* (Vol. 1). New York: Norton.

Kosmin, B. A., & Lachman, S. P. (1993). *One nation under God. Religion in contemporary American society.* New York: Crown Trade Paperbacks.

Kuhn, T. S. (1970). *The structure of scientific revolutions* (2nd ed.). Chicago: The University of Chicago Press.

Levin, F. (1995, April). *Epidemiology of religion.* Paper presented at the Spiritual Dimensions in Clinical Research Conference, National Institute for Healthcare Research. Washington, DC.

Levin, F. S., & Vanderpool, H. Y. (1991). Religious factors in physical health and the prevention of illness. *Prevention in the Human Services, 9*(2), 41–64.

London, P. (1964). *The modes and morals of psychotherapy.* New York: Holt, Rinehart & Winston.

Lukoff, D., Lu, F., & Turner, R. (1992). Toward a more culturally sensitive *DSM-IV*: Psychoreligious and psychospiritual problems. *The Journal of Nervous and Mental Disease, 180,* 673–682.

Malony, H. N. (1986). *Integration musings: Thoughts on being a Christian professional.* Pasadena, CA: Integration Press.

Malony, H. N. (1988). The assessment of optimal religious functioning. *Review of Religious Research, 30,* 3–5.

Malony, H. N. (1992a). Religious diagnosis in evaluating mental health. In J. F. Schumaker (Ed.), *Religion and mental health* (pp. 245–256). Oxford, England: Oxford University Press.

Malony, H. N. (1992b). *Psychology of religion: Personalities, problems, possibilities.* Grand Rapids, MI: Baker Book House.

Malony, H. N. (1993). The uses of religious assessment in counseling. In L. B. Brown (Ed.), *Religion, personality, and mental health* (pp. 16–28). New York: Plenum.

Masters, K. S., & Bergin, A. E. (1992). Religious orientation and mental health. In J. F. Schumaker (Ed.), *Religion and mental health* (pp. 221–232). Oxford, England: Oxford University Press.

Nagayama-Hall, G. C., & Malony, H. N. (1983). Cultural control in psychotherapy with minority clients. *Psychotherapy: Theory, Research and Practice, 20,* 131–142.

Natterson, J. (1991). *Beyond countertransference.* Northvale, NJ: Jason Aronson.

O'Donohue, W. (1989). The (even) bolder model: The clinical psychologist as metaphysician-scientist-practioner. *American Psychologist, 44,* 1460–1468.

Pargament, K., & Maton, K. (in press). *The psychology of religion and coping.* New York: Guilford Press.

Pickering, A. (1992). *Science as practice and culture.* Chicago: University of Chicago Press.

Pope, K. S., Sonne, J. L., & Holyrod, J. (1993). *Sexual feelings in psychotherapy: Explorations for therapists and therapists-in-training.* Washington, DC: American Psychological Association.

Post, S. (1995, April). *Religious studies and scientific freedom.* Paper presented at the Spiritual Dimensions in Clinical Research Conference, National Institute for Healthcare Research. Washington, DC.

Randour, M. L. (Ed.). (1993). *Exploring sacred landscapes.* New York: Columbia University Press.

Renik, O. (1993). Analytic interaction: Conceptualizing technique in light of the analyst's irreducible subjectivity. *Psychoanalytic Quarterly, 62,* 553–571.

Roof, W. C. (1993). *A generation of seekers.* San Fransico: HarperCollins.

Rorty, R. (1991). *Objectivity, relativism, and truth. Philosophical papers* (Vol. 1). Cambridge, England: Cambridge University Press.

Rosenau, P. M. (1992). *Post-modernism and the social sciences.* Princeton, NJ: Princeton University Press.

Sanua, V. (1969). Religion, mental health, and personality: A review of the empirical studies. *American Journal of Psychiatry, 125,* 1203–1213.

Schumaker, J. F. (Ed.). (1992). *Religion and mental health.* Oxford, England: Oxford University Press.

Shafranske, E. (1995). *The analysis of religious beliefs and God representations: Technical considerations.* Paper presented at the meeting of the International Psychoanalytic Studies Organization, San Francisco.

Shafranske, E., & Gorsuch, R. (1985). Factor associated with the perception of spirituality in psychotherapy. *Journal of Transpersonal Psychology, 16,* 231–241.

Shafranske, E., & Malony, H. N. (1990). Clinical psychologists' religious and spiritual orientations and their practice of psychotherapy. *Psychotherapy: Theory, Research, Practice, Training, 27,* 72–78.

Spero, M. H. (1985). *Psychotherapy of the religious patient.* Springfield, IL: Charles C Thomas.

Spilka, B., Hood, R. W., Jr., & Gorsuch, R. L. (1985). *The psychology of religion: An empirical approach*. Englewood Cliffs, NJ: Prentice-Hall.

Spiritual America. (1994, April 4). *U.S. News and World Report*, pp. 48–59.

Stern, E. M. (1985). Psychotherapy of the religiously committed patient. New York: Haworth.

Stolorow, R., Atwood, G., & Branchaft, B. (1994). *The intersubjective perspective*. Northvale, NJ: Jason Aronson.

Stricker, G., Davis-Russell, E., Bourg, E., Duran, E., Hammond, W. R., McHolland, J., Polite, K., & Vaughn, B. E. (1990). *Toward ethnic diversification in psychology education and training*. Washington, DC: American Psychological Association.

Tan, S.-Y. (1993). Training in professional psychology: Diversity includes religion. In American Psychological Association (Ed.), *Clinical training in professional psychology: National Council of Schools of Professional Psychology mid-winter conference, January 19 to January 23, 1993* (pp. 183–196). Washington, DC: American Psychological Association.

Tillich, P. (1957). *The dynamics of faith*. New York: Harper & Row.

Turner, S. (1994). *The social theory of practices. Tradition, tacit knowledge, and presuppositions*. Chicago: University of Chicago Press.

VandeCreek, L., & Merrill, W. (1990). Mental health services for the culturally different. In G. Stricker, E. Davis-Russell, E. Bourg, E. Duran, W. R. Hammond, J. McHolland, K. Polite, & B. E. Vaughn (Eds.), *Toward ethnic diversification in psychology education and training* (pp. 195–201). Washington, DC: American Psychological Association.

Van der Lans, J. (1991). What is the psychology of religion about? Some considerations concerning its subject matter. In H. N. Malony (Ed.), *Psychology of religion: Personalities, problems, possibilities* (pp. 313–322). Grand Rapids, MI: Baker Book House.

Vaughn, B. E. (1988, spring). Incorporating multicultural issues in professional training. *National Council of Schools of Professional Psychology Newsletter, 2*(3), 3–8.

Worthington, E. L., Jr. (1988). Understanding the values of religious clients: A model and its application to counseling. *Journal of Counseling Psychology, 35*, 166–174.

Wulff, D. M. (1991). Psychology of religion: Classic and contemporary views. New York: John Wiley & Sons.

Wyatt, G. E., & Parham, W. D. (1985). The inclusion of culturally sensitive course materials in graduate school and training programs. *Psychotherapy, 22*, 461–468.

Yalom, I. D. (1980). *Existential psychotherapy*. New York: Basic Books.

Yinger, J. M. (1970). *The scientific study of religion*. New York: Macmillan.

Younggren, J. N. (1993). Ethical issues in religious psychotherapy. *Register Report, 19*(4), 1, 7–8.

AUTHOR INDEX

Numbers in italics refer to listings in the reference sections.

Genia, V., 519–520, *530*
George, L. K., 218, *236*
Gergen, K., 118, 120, *143*
Gholson, B., 118, 121, *143*
Gibb, L. L., 200, *207*
Gibbs, H. W., 220, *235*
Giblin, P., 515, 519–520, *530*
Gifford, S., 87, *98*
Gill, D. S., 91, *97*
Gill, J. J., *321*
Gillette, V., 233, *235*
Ginsburg, M., 194, *208*
Glaser, F. B., 538, *557*
Glass, D., *320*
Glasser, W., 85, *98*
Glen, N. D., 193, *207*
Globetti, G., 191, *207*
Glock, C. Y., 273, *293*, 412, *430*
Goldbrunner, J., 79, 90, *98*
Goldfried, M. R., 312, *323*
Goldsmith, W. M., 84, *108*, 302, *321*
Goleman, D., 136, *143*
Goli, V., *236*
Goodyear, R. K., 379, *381*
Gordon, D., 273, *293*
Gorsuch, R. L., 8, *16*, 45, *68*, 69, 83, *98*,
      114, 117, *143*, *146*, *162* 191, 198,
      207, 220, *238*, 437, 444, 448, *460*,
      550, *557*, 576, 579, 585–586
Gottlieb, N. H., 189, 191, *207*
Graff, R. W., 200, *207*
Graham, J. M., 200, *212*
Graham, T. W., 189, *207*
Gravey, F. J., 200, *208*
Greaves, D. W., 312, *321*
Greaves, M., 86, *111*
Greeley, A. W., 31–33, 37, *40*
Green, A. M., 512, *530*
Green, L. W., 189, 191, *207*
Greenberg, D., 230, *239*
Greenberg, J. R., 65, *68*
Greenberg, R. F., *209*
Greenwold, M. A., *144*, *322*, *383*
Greer, B. A., 329–330, *361*
Greer, J., 347, *363*
Gregory, M., 90, *98*
Grevengoed, N., 223–224, *235*, *238*
Griffin, G. E. E., 91, *98*
Griffith, E. E., 194, *207*, 442, *460*
Grof, C., 442, *458*, 499, *507*
Grof, S., 80, 82–83, *98*, 442, *458*, 491,
      494, 499, *507*

Grollman, E. A., 82, *98*
Group for the Advancement of Psychiatry,
      441, *458*
Grünbaum, A., 244–245, 247–248, *266*
Guerney, B. J. R., 271, *294*
Guinn, R., 191, *207*
Guntrip, H., 57, *68*
Guntrip, H. H. J. S., 78, 87, 91, *98*
Gupta, A., 194–195, *207*
Gurman, A. J., 512, *530*
Gurnee, H., 85, *98*
Guy, R. F., 193, *207*
Gyaltshan, Y., 83, *98*

Hadaway, C. K., 26–27, *40–41*
Haddad, Y. Y., 342–343, *361*
Hagan, R. A., 230, *236*
Haley, J., 513, *530*
Halifax, J., 83, *98*
Hall, J. R., 197, *213*, 224, *239*
Halliday, K. S., 543, *556*
Hamilton, M., 395, *406*
Hammond, W. R., *586*
Handelman, S. A., 310, *324*, 370, *385*
Hansen, B. K., 302, *321*
Harari, C., 302, *321*
Harder, M. W., 273, 279, *293*, *295*
Hardyck, J. A., 277, *293*
Hart, H., 227, *236*
Hart, T., 522, *531*
Hartshorne, H., 91, *99*
Harvey, P. D., 196, *205*
Hasin, D., 191, 192, *207*
Hassan, M. K., 195, 198–199, *207*
Hastings, E., 149, *161*
Hastings, H., 149, *161*
Hatch, J. W., 233, *235*
Hatch, R., 515, *531*
Hathaway, W., *238*
Hathaway, W. L., 220, *235*
Havenarr, J. M., 302, *321*
Havens, J., 79, 86, *99*
Havens, L. L., 436, *458*
Hays, R. D., 191, *208*
Hebl, J. H., 233, *235*
Heckler, V. J., 200, *209*
Heckmann, R. C., 232, *239*
Heie, H., 86, *99*
Heintzelman, M. E., 195, *208*
Heller, P. L., *235*
Helsing, J. K., 190, *208*

Hendrix, H., 522, *531*
Henry, W., 155, 157, *161*
Herb, L., 218, *238*
Herek, G. M., 198, *208*
Hertsgaard, D., 194–195, *208*
Hess, R. E., 219, *238*
Hesse, M., 119, *143*
Hicks, R. C., 200, *212*
Higgins, L. M., 341, *361*
Higgins, P. C., 192, *208*
Hilgard, E. R., 551, *555*
Hillman, J., 90, 99, 471, *481*, 553, *555*
Hiltner, S., 87, *99*
Hinkle, J. E., 83, *100*
Hinsie, L. E., 247, *266*
Hirsch, W., 82, *99*
Hixon, L., 87, *99*
Hjelle, L. A., 200, *208*
Hoch, Z., 197, *208*
Hoekema, A. A., 337, *361*
Hoelter, J., 190, 196, *208*
Hoffding, H., 218, *236*
Hoffman, E., 82, *99*
Hoffman, G., 512, *530*
Hoffman, T. J., 331, 333, *363*
Hogan, R., 198, *208*
Hoge, D. R., 27, 31–32, 37–38, *40*
Hohmann, A., 191, *207*
Hole, G., 447, *458*
Holifield, E. B., 87, 99, 114, *143*
Hollon, S., 394, *406–407*
Holyrod, J., 563, *585*
Homans, P., 81, *99*
Hood, R., 114, *146*
Hood, R. W., 45, 69, 197, 200, *213*, 224,
    239, 442, 448, *458*, 460, 550, *557*,
    579, *586*
Hope, D., 311, *321*
Hopkinson, G., 273, 290, *295*
Hopping, M., 200, *208*
Hopson, R., 552, *555*
Hopson, R. E., 540, *555*
Horton, A. L., 220, *236*
Horton, W. M., 91, *99*
Hostie, R, 90, *99*
Houde, K. A., 78, 84, *99*
Houghston, M. J., 193, *212*
House, J. S., 190, *208*
Houselander, F. C., 79, *99*
Houser, B. B., 193, *204*
Houskamp, B., 78, *110*
Houts, A., 117, *144*

Howard, G., 75, *100*, 118, 120, *143*
Howard, G. S., 298, *321*
Hoyle, R. H., 135, *143*
Hundleby, J. D., 191, *208*
Hungelmann, J., 518, *531*
Hunsberger, B., 379, *387*
Hunt, R., 396, 406, 515, *531*
Hunt, R. A., 83, *100*, 193, *208*
Hunter, J. D., 331, 339–340, *361*
Hutch, R., 136, *143*
Huxley, A., 483, *508*
Hyman, H., 198, *208*

Iannaccone, L. R., 24, *41*
Imber, S., *320*
Imber-Black, E., 233, *236*
Ingalls, W., 77, *100*
Ingram, D. H., 541, *555*
Inman, D. J., 190, *204*
Institute of Medicine, 540, *555*
Irvine, S., 538, *556*
Ishler, K., 237, *362*

Jackson, D. A., 226, *238*
Jackson, J. J., 193, *208*
Jackson, J. S., 563, *584*
Jacobi, Y., 90, *100*
Jacobs, D., *236*
Jacobsen, E., 273, *293*
Jacobson, N., 513, *531*
Jacquet, Jr., C., 220, *236*
Jaekle, C. R., 87, *96*
Jahn, E., 90, *100*
Jahoda, M., 82, *92*
James, D., 515, *531*
James, W., 13, 16, 46, 52–53, 68, 83, *100*,
    161, 166–167, 178–180, 186, 272,
    290, *293*, 419, *430*, 442, *458*, 470,
    481, 534, 539, 550, *555*
Jamnia, M. A., 75, *93*
Jansen, D. G., 200, *208*
Jaspers, K., 66, *68*
Jeeves, M., 75, *100*, 116, *144*
Jeeves, M. A., 86, *104*, 116, *145*
Jellinek, E. M., 540, *555*
Jenkins, C. D., 189, *208*
Jenkins, P. H., 219, *238*, 303, *323*, 367,
    384
Jenkins, R., 219, 223, *236*
Jensen, J., 113, 139, *142*

Merrill, W., 563, 586
Meseguér, P., 90, 103
Metzner, H. L., 190, 208
Meyers, I. B., 55, 69
Michaelsen, R. R., 81, 103
Michel, O., 394, 406
Mickleburgh, W. E., 304, 323
Miller, A., 171, 186
Miller, E. J., 282, 284, 294
Miller, H. L., 195, 213
Miller, W. R., 86, 104, 138, 145, 309–310, 323, 365, 384
Mills, L. L., 195, 206
Milofsky, E. S., 537, 557
Minear, J. D., 190, 210
Minirth, F. B., 89, 103
Minuchin, S., 75, 104, 271, 294, 512, 531
Misiak, H., 79, 104
Mitchell, S. A., 65, 68
Mittlemann, B., 84, 103
Moberg, D. O., 193, 210
Mock, J., 395, 405
Modias, R., 363
Montalvo, B., 271, 294
Moody, R. A., 442, 459
Mookherjee, H. N., 191, 210
Moon, G. W., 379–380, 384
Moore, R. L., 79, 104
Moore, R. V., 81, 104
Morgan, C. L., 91, 104
Morgan, J., 79, 104
Morgenstern, J., 539, 556
Morris, P. A., 194–195, 210
Morris, R. J., 197, 200, 213, 224, 239
Mounier, E., 78, 104
Mowbray, C. T., 233, 235
Mowrer, O. H., 75, 85, 104, 376, 384
Muchnik, B., 195, 210–211
Mulder, E., 543, 557
Müller, F. M., 76, 104
Muller-Freienfels, R., 73, 104
Muran, J. C., 392, 403, 406
Murphy, H. B. M., 196, 210
Murray, J. A. C., 90, 104
Myers, D. G., 86, 104, 116, 145
Myers, J. K., 190, 194, 209–210, 218, 236

Naeem, S., 196, 203
Nagayama-Hall, G. C., 563, 585
Nagy, I. B., 277, 294
Napoli, D., 552, 556

Naranjo, C., 83, 104
Narramore, B., 86, 95, 116, 143
Natan, T., 195, 206
Nathanson, D. L., 171, 186
National Academy of Sciences, 117, 122, 145
Natterson, J., 571, 585
Needham, R., 44, 69
Needleman, J., 278, 294
Nehemkis, A. M., 195, 212
Neill, S. C., 90, 104
Nelson, A. A., 369, 384
Nelson, F. I., 447, 459
Nelson, F. L., 190, 211
Nelson, K., 435, 459
Neufeldt, S. A., 313, 320, 572, 583
Neusner, J., 29, 40
Nevo, B., 196, 198, 204
Newcomb, M. D., 191, 210
Newman, J., 238
Nicholi, A. M., 191, 210, 271–272, 274, 294
Niebuhr, H. R., 176, 186
Niederland, W. G., 257–259, 267
Niehardt, J. G., 82–83, 104
Nietzsche, F., 260, 267
Nino, A., 552, 556
Norcross, J. C., 312, 323, 544, 557
Novek, S., 82, 104
Novelly, R. A., 200, 213
Nuttin, J., 79, 105
Nye, F. I., 192, 210

O'Brien, M. E., 221, 237
O'Connor, T., 192, 204, 213
Oden, T. C., 114, 145
Odenwald, R. P., 79, 110
O'Donnell, J. M., 72, 105
O'Donohue, W., 115, 118, 120–121, 124, 129, 138, 145, 309, 317, 323, 577, 585
O'Flaherty, W. D., 461–462, 482
Ofshe, R., 275, 278, 295
Ogden, D., 131, 142
Olsen, H., 237, 238
Olthuis, J., 121, 145, 317, 323
Omran, A. R., 287–288, 294
Ornstein, R. E., 83, 104–105
Ortberg, Jr., J., 372, 375, 386
Osborne, A. C., 538, 557
Ostfeld, A. M., 190, 214

Ostow, M., *105*
Ostrom, R., 140, *146*, 311, *323*, 369, *385*, 395, 397–398, *406*
Otto, R., 470, *482*
Owen, G., 316, *323*
Owens, C. M., 443, *459*

Paden, W. E., 221, *237*
Page, S. H. T., 374, *384*
Paine, M., 76, *105*
Paisey, T., 193, *211*
Paloma, M., 311, *323*
Paloutzian, R. F., 45, 69, 114, *145*, 193, *210*, 230, *237*, 328, *362*
Pande, N., 224, *235*
Pargament, K., 223–224, *235–236*, 571, *585*
Pargament, K. I., 199, *210*, 215–216, 218–224, 229, 231–233, 235, 237–239, 303, *323*, 350–351, *362*, 367, *384*
Parham, W. D., 581, *586*
Park, C. L., 218, 222–223, 232, *238*
Parloff, M., *320*
Parsons, T., 1, *17*
Partridge, K. B., 189–190, *205*
Patai, R., *363*
Patterson, C. H., 298, *323*
Pattison, E., 520, *531*
Pattison, E. M., 271, 287–288, 294–295
Pattison, M., 274, *295*
Paykel, E., 396, *407*
Paykel, E. S., 190, *210*
Payne, I. R., 219, *238*, 300, 303–304, 310, *319*, *323*, 365, 367, 370–371, 378–380, *381*, *384*
Pearson, P. R., 196, *206*
Peaston, M., 78, *105*
Pecheur, E., 369, *385*
Peck, M. S., 33, *40*, 92, *105*, *161*, 374, 376, *385*
Peele, S., 540, *557*
Pellegrin, V. B. H., 200, *211*
Pendleton, B., 311, *323*
Pendleton, B. F., 340, *362*
Pennebaker, J. W., 222, *238*
Pepper, M. P., 194, *209*, 218, *236*
Peres, Y., 197, *208*
Perls, F., 494, *508*
Persinger, M. A., 200, *209*, *211*
Peters, R., 133, *145*

Peterson, E. A., 435, *459*
Peterson, J. D., 380, *382*
Pfister, O., 90, 98, *105*
Philipchalk, R. P., 86, *105*
Piaget, J., 181, *186*, 217, *238*
Pickering, A., 578, *585*
Pieper, C., *236*
Piercy, F. P., 200, *209*
Pierpont, J., 77, *105*
Pilkonis, P., *320*
Piwowarski, M., 195, *211*
Plantinga, A., 134, 136, *145*
Polanyi, M., 65, 69, 74, *105*
Polite, K., *586*
Poloma, M. M., 340, *362*
Pope, K. S., 563, *585*
Porter, N., 76, *105*
Possage, J., *362*
Post, S., 581, *585*
Potts, R., 300, *324*
Powell, L. H., *321*
Pratt, C., 223, *239*
Pratt, J. B., 91, *105*
Price, V. A., *321*
Princeton Religious Research Center, 25–26, 30, 33, *40*, 149, *161*, 197, *211*
Privette, G., 365, *385*
Prochaska, J. O., 544, *557*
Progoff, I., 76, 91, *105*
Propst, L. R., 86, *105*, 138, 140, *146*, 309, 311, *323*, 369, 372, 375, *385*, 393–395, 397–402, 405, *406*, 448, *459*
Proudfoot, W., 277–278, *295*
Prusoff, B., 396, *407*
Pruyser, P., *161*, 349, *362–363*, 515, 519, 521, 525, *531*
Pruyser, P. W., 56, 69, 79, 86, *105*, 248, 267, *363*, *431*
Psychological Studies Institite, 80, *105*
Puryear, H. B., 194, *209*
Pyle, C. M., *232*
Pym, T. W., 86, *106*

Quackenbos, S., 365, *385*
Query, J. N., 191, *211*

Rabin, A. I., 541, *558*
Rabin, D. D., *321*

Salinger, R. J., 514, *531*
Salter, N. E., 230, *236*, 271, 273–274, *294*
Salzman, L., 271, *295*
Samuels, A., 466, *482*
Sandler, H. M., 194, *206*
Sanford, J. A., 90, *107*
Sanford, R. N., *203*
Sanua, V. D., 192, 195, 198, *211*, 567, *585*
Sarason, S., 120, *146*
Sarbin, T., 541, *557*
Savary, L. M., 90, *107*
Scanzoni, J. H., 193, *211*
Scarborough, E., 74, *107*
Schacter, S., 277, *292*
Schaef, A. W., 550, *557*
Schaefer, C. A., 220, *238*
Schaer, H., 90, *107*
Schafer, R., 541, *557*
Scharff, D., 523, *531*
Scharff, J., 523, *531*
Schatzman, M., 258, *267*
Schillebeeckx, E., 244, *267*
Schmall, V., 223, *239*
Schmieding, A., 116, *145*
Schmitt, A., 90, *107*
Schneiders, S., 518, *531*
Schoenfeld, E., 535, 537, *555*
Schoenrade, P., 45, *67*, 579, *582*
Schreber, D. P., 256–257, 262, *267*
Schroeder, B. L., 200, *212*
Schroeder-Slomann, S., 116, *145*
Schuller, D. S., 83, *107*
Schulte, J., *363*
Schultz, R., 193, *205*
Schumaker, J. F., 202, *212*, 567, *585*
Schumm, W., 515, *531*
Schumm, W. R., 193, *212*
Schwartz, L. L., 227, 230, *239*, 271, *295*
Scott, E. M., 187, *212*
Scott, G. G., 369, *387*
Scroggs, R., 353, *363*
Seamands, D., 372, 374, *385*
Secord, P., 118, *145*
Sedman, G., 273, 290, *295*
Segal, H., 546, *557*
Segal, Z., 392, *407*
Segal, Z. V., 393, *407*
Segall, M., 218, 220, *239*
Segaller, S., 90, *107*
Selesnick, S. T., 443, 452, *457*
Seligman, L., 299, *324*, 367, *385*
Seligman, M. E. P., 339, *363*

Sethi, S., 334, *363*
Seymour, R. B., 533, *554*
Shaffer, H., 539, *557*
Shafii, M., 343, *363*
Shafranske, E. P., 84, *107*, 138, *146*,
    153–159, *161–162*, 309–310, 314,
    324, 348, *363*, 366, *385*, 431, 435,
    437, 444, 460, 486, 508, 551, *557*,
    564, 575–576, *585*
Shamblin, J. B., 190, *213*
Shapiro, D., 484, 486, 495, 497, *508*
Shapiro, E., 290, *295*, 307, *324*
Sharman, H. B., 75, *107*
Shaver, P., 230, *239*, 277–278, *295*
Shaw, B., 395, *405*
Shea, T., *320*
Sheatsley, P., 198, *208*
Sheehan, W., 288, *294*, 304, *322*
Sheikh, A. A., 83, *107*
Sheikh, K. S., 83, *107*
Sheldon, W. H., 73, 91, *107*
Shelp, F., *236*
Shepher, J., 197, *208*
Sherill, K. A., *144*
Sherkat, D. E., 340, *361*
Sherrill, K. A., 322, *383*
Shrimali, S., 220, *239*
Shriver, Jr., D. W., 157, *161*
Shrum, W., 193, *212*
Shuttleworth, F. K., 91, *99*
Siegel, J. M., 232, *239*
Siegler, I. C., 218, *236*
Silver, R. C., 218, *237*
Silverman, M., *237*
Silverman, W. H., 199, *210*
Silverstone, H., 82, *107*
Simmonds, R., 279, *293*
Simmonds, R. B., 229, *239*, 273, 276, *295*
Simmons, T., 336, *363*
Simon, H., 126–127, 136, *146*
Simon, J., 278, *295*
Simpkinson, C. H., 82, 88, 92, 96, *107*,
    366, *382*, *385*
Sims, J., 155, *161*
Sinclair, U., 83, *107*
Singer, M., 271, 275, 277, 283, 287, *295*
Skinner, B. F., 48, *69*
Sklo, M., 190, *208*
Smart, R. G., 191, *203*
Smedes, L., 374, *385*
Smiley, H., 302, *324*
Smith, D. E., 533, *554*

600   AUTHOR INDEX

Smith, D. R., 195, *212*
Smith, H., 483, *508*, 547, *557*
Smith, J. H., 310, *324*, 370, *385*
Smith, S. A., 300, *324*
Smith, T., 149, *162*
Smith, W. C., 46, 69
Sneck, W., 347, *363*
Snow, D. A., 227, *239*
Snyder, S. S., 440, 442, *460*
Snyder, W. U., 199, *213*
Sokol, L., 394, *405*
Sollod, R. N., 314, *324*, 367, *385*
Sonne, J. L., 563, *585*
Sorensen, A. E., 200, *212*
Sotsky, S., *320*
Spark, G., 277, *294*
Spellman, C. M., 195, *212*
Spendlove, D. C., 195, *212*
Spero, M. H., 82, *108*, 241, 267, 309, *320,*
   324, 365, *385*, 417–418, *430–431,*
   442, 452, *460*, 580, *585*
Sperry, R. W., 115, *146*
Spiegel, E., 543, *557*
Spiegelman, J. M., 82, *108*
Spilka, B., 45, 69, 83–84, 98, *101–102,*
   108, 114, *144*, *146*, 157, *161*, 187,
   212, 220, *237*, 365, *385*, 396, *405,*
   440–442, 447–448, *460*, 523, *532,*
   550, *557*, 579, *586*
Spilka, B. P., 196, *204*
Sponte, H., 517, *529*
Sporawski, M. J., 193, *212*
Spray, S., 155, *161*
Sripat, K., 195, *205*
Staats, A., 123, *146*
Stacey, D., *363*
Stack, S., *212*
Stacy, A. W., 191, *208*
Stagner, R., 78, 84, *108*
Stanik, P., *237*, *362*
Stanish, W. M., 195, *212*
Starbuck, E. D., 228, *239*
Stark, R., 24, *40–41*, 190, 192–194, 198,
   212, 273, *293–294*
Stark-Adamec, C., 200, *212*
Staudt, V., 79, *104*
Steele, R. E., 303, *323*
Stein, M. S., 218, *236*
Sterba, R., 273, *295*
Stern, D., 169, *186*
Stern, E. M., 309, *324*, 365, *386*, 580, *586*
Stern, K., 90, *108*

Stern, M. E., 138, *146*
Stern, M. S., 194, *209*
Stewart, M., 276, *295*
Stewart, R. A. C., 200, *213*
Stifler, K., 347, *363*
Stillion, J. M., 190, *213*
Stinchfield, R. D., 304, *319*, 567, *583*
Stolorow, R., 572, *586*
Stone, C. L., 29, *41*
Stout, G. F., 91, *108*
Strachan, R. H., 86, *108*
Stricker, G., 563, *586*
Strommen, M., 83, *107*
Strommen, M. P., 45, 69, 83, *107*, 299, *324*
Strupp, H. H., 129, 140, *144*, 298, *321,*
   369, *383*, 552, *557*
Stuart, G. C., 78, 86, *108*
Sturkie, J., 376, *386*
Sullivan, C. E., 304, *319*, 322, 567, *583*
Sullivan, M., 223, *238*
Sullivan, W., 547, *554*
Sullivan, W. M., 330, *360*
Sundberg, N. D., 230, *236*
Sunua, V. D., 516, *531*
Suttie, I. D., 56, 69
Swidler, A., 330, *360*, 547, *554*
Syme, S. L., 190, *204*
Szasz, T. S., 309, *324*

Tamir, A., 195, *206*
Tan, S. Y., *108*, 138–139, *147*, 306–309,
   324, 365, 367–369, 371–372,
   375–377, 379–380, *382*, *386*, 581,
   586
Tanner, J., 190, *210*
Tart, C. T., 82, *108*
Tennison, J. C., 199, *213*
Terruwe, A. A. A., 79, *108*
Thielman, S. B., *144*, 322, *383*
Thompson, E., 233, *235*
Thompson, L., *321*
Thomsen, R., 289, *295*
Thoresen, C., 310, *325*
Thoresen, C. E., *321*
Thorsen, P. L., 199, *210*
Thurman, C., 375, *386*
Tiebout, H. M., 544, *557*
Tillich, P., 91, *108*, 176, *186*, 545, *557,*
   574, *586*
Tipton, S. M., 330, *360*, 547, *554*
Tiryakian, E. A., 23, *41*

Weisz, J. R., 440, 442, *460*
Welch, M. R., 232, *239*
Welch, P., 440, *459*
Wellisch, D. K., 191, *205*, 276, 283, *296*
Welsh, R., 537, *554*
Welter, P. R., 377, *387*
Weltha, D. A., 196, *213*
Wenegrat, B., 280, *296*
Werme, P. H., 187, *212*
Werner, H., 71, *111*
West, D. W., 195, *212*
West, M., 486, *509*
Westman, A. S., 195, *213*
Westphal, M., 257, 259, *267*
Wheelis, A., 452, *460*
White, F. J., 376–377, *387*
White, M., 191–192, *205*
White, V. F., 76, 79, 90, *111*
Whitehead, A. N., 52, *70*
Whiting, R., 233, *236*
Whitt, H. P., 327, *360*
Wichem, F. B., 89, *103*
Wickstrom, D. L., 197, 199, *213*
Widaman, K. F., 191, *208*
Wikler, M., 516, *532*
Wilber, K., 87, *111*, 483, 485, 490, 493, 496, *509*
Wilcox, C., 340, *363*
Wilcox, D. A., 309, *321*
Wilkins, M. M., 220, *236*
Willard, D., 378, *387*
Williams, C., 75, *111*, 538, *558*
Williams, D. R., 232, *239*
Williams, P. W., 331, *362*
Williams, R. L., 195, *213*
Williams, S. K., 90, *107*
Willis, D. E., 379, *384*
Wilson, R. W., 199, *213*
Wilson, W., 195, *213*
Wilson, W. P., 274, *296*, 369, 384, *387*
Wimberly, E., 526, *532*
Windham, G., 191, *207*
Winger, D., 379, *387*
Winnicott, D. W., 56, *70*, 171, *186*, 253, *267*, 413–414, *430*
Witcutt, W. P., 79, *111*
Wittine, B. W., 80, *111*, 486–487, 495, *509*
Witztum, E., 230, *239*

Wolfe, D. L., 86, *99*
Wolfram, T., 379, *383*
Wolman, B., 87, *111*
Wolterstorff, N., 120–121, 134–136, *145*, *147*, 317, *325*
Woodman, M., 547, 550, *558*
Woodward, W. R., 72, *111*
Woolcott, P., 79, *111*
Woolfolk, R., 130, *147*
Wootton, R. J., 230, *239*
Worthington, E., 520, *532*
Worthington, E. L., 138, *147*, 369, *382*
Worthington, Jr., E. L., 309, 311, 315, *325*, 365–366, 369, 379–380, *387*, 572, *586*
Wortman, C. B., 218, 223, 234, *237*
Wright, F., 394, *405*
Wright, G. L., 84, *108*
Wright, H. N., 375, *387*
Wright, K., *213*
Wright, S., 223, *239*
Wright, W., 220, *236*
Wulff, D. M., 45–46, 49–50, 55, 61–62, 65, *70*, 83, *112*, 114, *147*, 151, 156–157, *162*, 186, 579, *586*
Wurmser, L., 541, 545, *558*
Wuthnow, R., 65, *70*
Wyatt, G. E., 581, *586*
Wyatt, S. D., 369, *387*
Wykle, M., 218, 220, *239*

Yalom, I. D., 444, *460*, 488, *509*, 573, *586*
Yancey, P., 224, *239*
Yinger, J. M., 574, *586*
Young, J. L., 194, *207*, 441, 442, 457, *460*
Young, M., 192, *213*
Younggren, J. N., 576, *586*

Zander, A., 275, *292*
Zegans, L. S., 290, *294*
Zilboorg, G., 79, *112*
Zilli, A. S., 195, *204*
Zimmerman, V., 194, *208*
Zinberg, N., 538, *558*
Zinnbauer, B., 229, *239*
Zitter, M. L., 538, *558*
Zuckerman, D. M., 190, *214*

SUBJECT INDEX

Diagnostic and Statistical Manual of Mental Disorders, inclusion of religious or spiritual problems, 568

Dichotomists, 73

Disease, alcoholism as, 539–540
objections to, 540

Disidentification, 496–497

Diversity
dealing with value dilemmas, 315–316
issue with respect to rights and dignity, 307–308

Divorce, relationship with religion, 193

Dogmatism, correlation with religiosity, 199

Dreams, in marital and family therapy, 526–527

Dreamwork, 494

Drug use, relationship with religion, 191–192

Eastern Orthodox Church, 332, 334

Education
association with religion, 197
comparative religions, 580
to deal with religious issues, 158–159
effect on importance placed on religion, 150–152

Ego, 463–464
relationship to self, 466–467
relationship with unconscious, 467–468

Emotions, relationship with cognitions, 391–392

Empty chair scenarios, marital and family therapy, 528

Episcopal church, divisions, 329

Erikson, Erik, views on religion, 58–59

Evangelicals, 28, 339–340

Existential–humanistic psychotherapy, 433–457
aligned therapist
can work with just about any person, 437–438
essentially free of personal, religious–spiritual convictions, 437
change occurs by welcoming–appreciating and by being

the deeper potential for experiencing, 444–448
closer to religious–spiritual than to traditional psychotherapy, 445–448
experiential directions of change, 448–456
accommodating or risking person's religious–spiritual values, 454–456
arriving at a particular way of being, 453–454
compared with religious–spiritual valued directions, 452–456
no predetermined specific content, 449–450
as set of precious values, 449–452
experiential session
aims and goals, 435
as complete mini-therapy, 438–439
open by finding scene of strong feeling, 439–442
sequence of steps, 435–436
use of religious–spiritual scenes, 440–442
scene of strong feeling, as doorway to deeper potentials for experiencing, 442–444
steps of change do not include trying to change behaviors, 447–448
therapist and person are "aligned" with one another, 436–438
therapist as coach-instructor-guide, 438

Experience
accountability to, commonalities and distinctions between religion and science, 123–124
shared, charismatic group, 278–279

Experiential approach, 13

Experiential model of human beings, 443

Faith, 47
characterization, 168
conjunctive, 170, 174–175
distinguished from religion, 168
in healing process, 552
individuative–reflexive, 170, 173–174

Integration (*continued*)
    professional society organization, 78–80
Integrity, 75–76
Intelligence, association with religion, 197
Intersubjectivity, 572–573
Intimacy issues, marital and family therapy, 513–514
Intrapersonal integration, 377–378
Islam, 342–343

James, William, 165–185
    differences with faith-development theory, 180–184
        development and conversion, 182
        feeling Self and construing self, 181
        grounding convictions and overbeliefs, 182–184
        pluralism in faith and religious experience, 180–181
    overbeliefs, 167, 182–184
    pluralistic universe, 178, 183
    similarities with faith-development theory, 176–180
        empirical approach, 177–178
        generic unity underlying manifestations of religion and faith, 178–179
        nonreductionistic and indirectly apologetic, 176–177
        pragmatist and functional approach combined with normative evaluative criteria, 179–180
    "twice-born" orientation, 182
    Varieties of Religious Experience, 166–167
    views on religion, 52–53
Jehovah's Witnesses, 337–338
Jews, liberal attitudes on moral questions, 37
Journals, integrative, 82–83
Judaism, 331–332
Jung, Carl
    in Alcoholic Anonymous's history, 534–535
    concept of self, 489–490
    metapsychology, 462–467
        agency, 462–464
        design, 465–467

intent, 464–465
    on transference, 467–468
    views on religion, 53–55
Jungian analysis
    approaches to religious material, 470–471
    case studies, 471–480
        man who lost God, 471–475
        woman who embraced death, 475–480
    goal, 467
    relationship between ego and unconscious, 467–468
    subjective interpretation of unconscious material, 469
    transference, to unconscious, 468–469

Kohut, Self psychology, 57–58
Künkel, Fritz, integration, 77–78

Laboratories, integrative, 83
Letter writing, marital and family therapy, 528
Leuba, James, views on religion, 48
Literature, theoretical, 89–91
Longevity, religious commitment and, 190

Manipulation, forcible conversion of vulnerable people, 229
Marital and family therapy, 14–15, 311–312, 511–529
    boundary issues, 512–513
    case material
        Betty, 525–526
        interventions, 526–528
        Jack, 524–525
    constructs, 512
    intimacy issues, 513–514
    power issues, 513
    religious beliefs and practices that influence therapy, 514–524
        assessment of spirituality and religion, 517–520
        assessment strategies, 518–520
        clients' expectations and perceptions, 516

direct–explicit versus indirect–implicit use of the religious, 524

intervention, 520–524

positive and detrimental attitudes, 515

self-awareness, 517

spirituality versus religion, 517–518

therapeutic use of Self, 521–523

theory and concepts, 512–514

Marital satisfaction, relationship with religion, 193

spiritual well-being or religious maturity, 515

Maslow, Abraham, views on religion, 63–64

Mass delusion, 247–248

belief systems as, 248–249

Mature adjustment, religious, indices, 349–350

Mean making, 573–574

Meditation, 495

Eastern forms, 135–136

Men in Recovery, 536

Mental health

behavior concepts and personal orientation and lifestyle, 306

outcome, religious commitment and, 194

relationship with religion, 187–189, 201–202, 303–304

Mental health professionals, consensus on values, 297–298

Mental philosophy, 74

Metapsychology, Jung, 462–467

Millennial Churches, 337–338

Moral attitudes, 35–36

Moral philosophy, 74

Motivational model, sense making and meaning seeking, 573

Nation of Islam, 341–342

Naturalism, 136

New Age movement, 33–34

New Scripture Churches, 335–337

Object-relations theory, 56–58

Organizations, devoted to religious therapy, 88–89

Oxford Group movement, 534

Papal authority, acceptance of, 32

Paradoxical side of life, 523

Passionate devotion, commonality and distinction between religion and science, 126

Pastoral care, psychologizing, 114

Pathology

of beliefs, see Beliefs

markers, 347–349

Peak experiences, 65

Pentecostal churches, 330, 340

Perfectionism, religious individuals' assumptions of, 400

Personal behavior, religious concern with, 34

Personal identity, 487–488

Personality theory, religious presuppositions, 129–130

Personality therapy, Christian, literature, 90–91

Personal religious behavior, 33–34

definition, 23

Physical health, association with religion, 188–190

Political attitudes, correlation with religious commitment, 34

Postpositivistic philosophy, science, 118–122

Power issues, marital and family therapy, 513

Prayer

in clinical practice, 371–375

for deliverance, 374

differential forms and uses, 311

inner healing, 371–374

in marital and family therapy, 526

potential misuses, 374–375

Preferencing process, 317

Prejudice, relationship with religious commitment, 197–198

Prepersonal identity, 487

Privatism scale, 330

Professional societies, for integration, organization, 78–80

Protestant churches

mainline, 334–335

membership trends, 26–29

Protestants, conservative attitudes on moral questions, 37

Psychiatric hospitals, Christian, 89
Psychiatric intervention, charismatic group, 289–291
Psychoanalysis, 13, 409, 430
    abstinence and neutrality, 421–422
    case examples
        dynamic interaction of affects, wishes, conflicts and representations, 427–429
        emergence of belief in nonbeliever, 422–424
        God representation transformation, 425–426
        refinding the God of childhood after narcissistic injury, 424
    changes in theory, 409
    confidentiality and establishing therapeutic relationship, 420
    evolution, 410–411
    requirements of patient, 411
    taking a religious, 420–421
    transference, 410
Psychological distress, as antecedent to joining charismatic group, 271
Psychological intervention
    charismatic group, 289–291
    value-laden nature, 10–11
Psychological literature, attention to religious and psychotherapy, 365–366
Psychological science, intractable difficulties intrinsic to, 133
Psychological theories, values as integral part, 309–310
Psychologists
    abstaining from revealing personal information, 421–422
    affiliation and practice of religion, 154–156
    broad and deep acquaintances with religious faith and tradition, 66
    educational and training to deal with religious issues, 158–159
    engaging values, 301–303
    honesty about value-ladenness of mental health enterprise, 139–140
    ideological orientations, 154
    as "metaphysician-scientist-practitioner", 309

narrowing influences of our own religious views, 66
    neutrality, 421–422
    peer accountability in moral–religious dimensions, 140–141
    religious and spiritual beliefs, affiliations, and practices, 7, 151, 153–154
    role of religion in lives, 113–114
    sectarian programs, 139
    training, 138–139
    use of interventions of religious nature, 157–158
    variance between attitudes and behaviors and clinical addressing of religion, 157–158
    view of religion as valuable, 153–154
Psychologists Interested in Religious Issues, 79
Psychology
    bias against theistic and spiritual perspectives, 298–299
    constructive relationship with religion, 132–141
        constructive mode, 135–136
        critical–evaluative mode, 134–135
        dialectical relationship, 137
        foundations, 132–134
        implications, 138–141
        major forms of interaction, 134–138
    formal interaction with religion, 114–115
    history of term, 72
    incorporation of values and worldviews into scientific process, 133–134
    philosophical, ethical, and religious dimensions, 138
    of religion, 43–67, 579–580
        Erikson's views, 58–59
        Freud's views, 50–52
        Fromm's views, 62–63
        historical factors, 44–45
        humanistic psychology, 59–67
        James' views, 52–53
        Jung's views, 53–55
        Kohut's Self psychology, 57–58
        Leuba's views, 48
        Maslow's views, 63–64

neglect in introductory textbooks and departmental curricula, 44

object-relations theory, 56–58

on finding a viable point of view, 64–67

Skinner's views, 48–49

trends, 45–46

Vetter's views, 49–50

religious resources and, 233–234

Psychosis, relationship with religion, 196

Psychotherapeutic theory, religious presuppositions, 129–130

Psychotherapists

religiously zealous, 314

values among, 305–306

Psychotherapy, 352–354

associated with religion, 198–200

client's religious issues, 353–354

guidelines for providing services to religious people, 308

initial obstacles, 352–353

integrating spiritual and secular techniques, 310–313

as moral enterprise, 128–131

overlap with moral–religious domain, 131–132

secular approaches, alien values framework, 305

spirituality, 497

spiritual realization, 504–506

12-step programs and, 551–553

values, *see* Values

Quasireligious, 574

Quest scale, 61–62

Rational Recovery, 537

Referral, to religious group, in clinical practice, 375–376

Religion

anxiety and, 195–196

in assessment and treatment, 11

as asset, 52–59

association with intelligence and education, 197

as bipolar potential, 59–67

clinical practice, *see* Clinical practice

commonalities and distinctions with science, 122–126

accountability to experience, 123–124

analogical models, 125

goals, 124–125

human enterprises, 125–126

passionate devotion, 126

subject matter, 122–123

concept of, 46–47

concern with both ends and means of significance, 216–217

constructive relationship with psychology, 132–141

constructive mode, 135–136

critical–evaluative mode, 134–135

dialectical relationship, 137

foundations, 132–134

implications, 138–141

major forms of interaction, 134–138

cumulative tradition, 168

definition, 435

differentiation from spirituality, 517–518

distinguished from faith, 168

distortions in, 66–67

as force for health or psychopathology, 9–10

as hope and wisdom, 58–59

implicit and explicit integration, *see* Clinical practice

inclusion in clinical practice, *see* Clinical psychology

as infantile wish fulfillment, 50–52

integration into child's psychic life, 412–413

interaction with

profession of clinical psychology, 128–132

science of psychology, 126–128

as irrationality and pathology, 48

Jung's definition, 54

as liability, 47–52

longevity and, 190

mental health and, 303–304

as moral net, 203

no relationship with pathology, 327

physical health and, 188–190

prejudice and, 197–198

psychoanalytic considerations, 412–419

psychology of, 5, 579–580

Religion (*continued*)
    see Psychology, of religion
    psychosis and, 196
    as reinforced behavior, 48–49
    relationship with
        delinquency and criminal behavior, 192
        divorce and marital satisfaction, 193
        drug use, 191–192
        mental health, 187–189, 201–202
    relationship with suicide, 190
    relevance
        in clinical practice, 157
        effect of education, 150–152
        general population, 149–150
    repositioning in intermediate "illusionistic" realm, 56
    resources, psychology and, 233–234
    as response to unpredictable situations, 49–50
    role in lives of psychologists, 113–114
    as search for significance, 216–217
    self-esteem and, 196–197
    sexual disorders and, 197
    supposed separateness and exclusivity with science, 116–118
    as therapeutic relation, 56–58
    as transformed narcissism, 57–58
    12-step programs and, 547–550
    as variable in mental health, 8, 566–568
    variance of commitment and expression, 2
    as way to human excellence, 52–53
    as way to wholeness, 53–55
    as web of significance, 2
Religiosity, correlation with
    authoritarianism, 198–199
    rigidity and dogmatism, 199
    suggestibility and dependence, 199
    tolerance of ambiguity, 199
Religious, direct–explicit versus indirect–implicit use, 524
Religious adjustment, empirical measures, 350–352
Religious affiliation, rise in, 565
Religious belief, 31–32
    definition, 22
Religious clients

preference for use of prayer and Scripture in therapy, 369
    response to therapy adapted to religious values, 140
Religious commitment
    depression and, 194–195
    measures, 188, 202
    mental health outcome and, 194
    prevalence, 304–305
    relationship with
        self-actualization, 199–200
        well-being, 193–194
Religious conversion, 227–231
Religious coping styles, 346
Religious denominations, 328–343
    African American churches, 341–342
    Catholicism, 332–334
    Fundamentalist, Evangelical, Holiness, and Pentecostal, 338–340
    Islam, 342–343
    Judaism, 331–332
    Millennial churches, 337–338
    New Scripture churches, 335–337
    Protestantism, 334–335
Religious experience, 165–185
    affective component, 419
    feelings, 166
    pluralistic universe, 166
    resistance to verbal expression, 43
Religious factors, assessment in psychotherapy, 346–352
    empirical measures of religious adjustment, 350–352
    mature adjustment indices, 349–350
    pathology markers, 347–349
Religious identity, interrelationship with cultural identity, 5
Religious imagery, 356, 394–395, 400
Religious issues, in therapy, informed consent and open agreement, 313
Religious leaders, confidence in, 32
Religious life, diversity and flexibility, 231–232
Religious maturity, relationship with marital satisfaction, 515
Religious objects, psychoanalytic considerations, 412–419
Religious orientation, assessment, 60–62

Religious preference, 24–25
    definition, 22
    of psychologists, 154–156
Religious prevention, conservation of significance, 219
Religious reframing, conservation of significance, 222–225
Religious rituals, conservation of significance, 221–222
Religious sentiment, as cultural force, 1
Religious support, conservation of significance, 219–221
Religious therapy, organizations devoted to, 88–89
Religious traditions
    differences within, 11
    psychological findings or theories and, 114–115
Religious values, patient–therapist similarity, 140
Research, 581–582
Resistance, 356–358
Rigidity, correlation with religiosity, 199
Rites of passage, religious, 225–227
Ritual purification, conservation of significance, 221–222
Roman Catholic Church, 332–333

Sacred
    making search for significance distinctive and powerful, 232
    reappraisal, 224–225
Sacred texts, use in clinical practice, 375
Satori, 505
Schemas, 392
Schreber, Daniel Paul, theocosmological system, 256–263
    belief that God was changing him into a woman, 256–257
    comparison with Zoroastrianism, 257, 260–262
    delusions as beliefs, 259–263
    division of God into upper and lower Gods, 257
    identification with castrated figure of mother–victim, 259
    inability to demonstrate falseness of belief, 262
    projective system, 258–259
Science
    commonalities and distinctions with religion, 122–126
        accountability to experience, 123–124
        analogical models, 125
        goals, 124–125
        human enterprises, 125–126
        passionate devotion, 126
        subject matter, 122–123
    as cultural and human phenomenon, 120–121
    postpositivistic philosophy, 118–122
    of psychology, interaction with religion, 126–128
    supposed separateness and exclusivity with religion, 116–118
Scientists, studies of religious beliefs, 151
Scripture, use in clinical practice, 375, 527
Sect, definition, 334
Secularization model, 23–24
Secular Organization for Sobriety, 539
Secular psychotherapy, integration with spiritual, 310–313
Segregation, opposition to integration, 73–75
Self, 489–490
    relationship to ego, 466–467
    therapeutic use, marital and family therapy, 521–523
    in universalizing faith, 175–176
Self-actualization, 65
    relationship with religious commitment, 199–200
Self-awareness, 517
Self-esteem, relationship with religion, 196–197
Selfhood, unconscious aspects, 174
Seventh-day Adventists, 337
Sexual disorders, association with religion, 197
Shame, feeling in addicted people, 542
Significance
    coping methods, 217
    search for, 216–231
Sin, 522–523
Situation, reframing, 222–223
Skinner, B. F., views on religion, 48–49
Social attitudes, correlation with religious commitment, 34
Social control, charismatic group, 280–282

Social issues, with important religious elements, 34–38
Social reality, delusions and, 247
Spiritual, definition, 21
Spiritual commitment, prevalence, 304–305
Spiritual issues, dealing with in psychotherapy, 376–377
Spirituality, 33, 47
    definition, 435
    development, in therapist and client, 377–378
    differentiation from religion, 517–518
    in recovery from addiction, 536–537
    transpersonal psychology, 497
Spiritual psychotherapy, integration with secular, 310–313
Spiritual well-being, relationship with marital satisfaction, 515
Subject matter, commonality and distinction between religion and science, 122–123
Suffering, 522–523
Suggestibility, correlation with religiosity, 199
Suicide, relationship with religion, 190
Symbolic side of life, 523
Symbols, 464–465
Systems theory, as charismatic group model, 282–285

Temporal lobe epilepsy, hyperreligiosity and, 200
Tests, bias of authors, 201
Textbooks
    focused on religion, 85–87
    treatment of religion, 84–85
Theology, individual, 356
Theories, appraising of, 119–120
Therapeutic alliance, triadic, 184–185
Therapeutic relationship, establishing, 420
Therapists
    increased religious or spiritual orientation, 366
    personal background, 354
    predetermined lists of what is approved or disapproved, 450–451
    role of personal values, 578

sets of values brought into clinical setting, 572
treatment of clients with religious issues, 354–358
    countertransference, 358
    problems tied to specific Biblical texts, 355–356
    religious imagery and individual theology, 356
    resistance and transference, 356–358
    values clashes and worldviews, 359–360
Therapy relationship, transmissions of values, 317
Therapy units, Christian, 89
Thought control, charismatic group, 276–278
Thought monitoring, 399–400
Training
    to deal with religious issues, 158–159
    psychology of religion, 579–580
Transference, 410
    Jung's views, 467–468
    to unconscious, 468–469
Transitional object, 413–415
Transpersonal identity, 489–491
Transpersonal psychology, 14, 483–507
    addressing multiple levels of spectrum of identity, 487–491
    altered states of consciousness, 494–495
    assumptions, 486–497
    bodywork, 494
    case of John, 500–506
    causal realm, 490
    context, content, and process, 484–485
    denial of the shadow, 498–499
    development spectrum, 485–486
    disidentification, 496–497
    entering subjective realm, 502–503
    facilitating awakening process, 493–497
    goals, 483
    imagery and dreamwork, 494
    inquiry, 495–496
    institutions offering training, 81–82
    meditation, 495
    personal identity, 487–488

process of awakening from a lesser to a greater identity, 492–493
prepersonal identity, 487
spiritual developmental stages, 498–500
spiritual experiences, 499–500
spirituality, 497
subtle realm, 490
therapist's unfolding awareness of Self and spiritual worldview as central in therapy, 491–492
transpersonal identity, 489–491
Transpersonal Psychology Interest Group, 79–80
Trichotomists, 73
Truth value
belief system, 243–246
lack of grounds to determine, 249
Twelve-step programs, *see* Alcoholics Anonymous

Unconscious
relationship with ego, 467–468
role in psychological development, 464–465
transference to, 468–469
Unification church, 285–287

Values
among psychotherapists, 305–306
clashes in therapy, 359–360
diversity and professional training, 307–310
in psychological theories, 309–310

psychotherapy, 297–319, 576–579
attending to client's and engaging therapist's values, 301–303
background, history, and issues, 298–301
concerns, cautions, and caveats, 313–315
consensus, 305–306
ethically relativistic therapist stance, 300
future directions, 315–317
impact of, 317
informed consent and open agreement, 313
intermediate range of values similarity between client and therapist, 302
making implicit values explicit in therapy, 306
separation between personal and professional, 313
trends, 318
Varieties of Religious Experience, 166–167
Vetter, George, views on religion, 49–50

Well-being, relationship with religious commitment, 193–194
Winicottian theory, 413–414
Women, religious role, 38
Women for Sobriety, 538
Worldview assumptions, 121, 359–360
influences of sciences, 133

Zoroastrianism, 257, 260–262

ABOUT THE EDITOR

Edward P. Shafranske is Professor of Psychology at the Graduate School of Education and Psychology at Pepperdine University and is a member of the faculty of the Southern California Psychoanalytic Institute. Dr. Shafranske has presented and published extensively in the psychology of religion. His primary emphasis has been in the psychoanalytic study of religious experience in which he has addressed both Freudian and contemporary object relations and self psychology contributions to the field. In addition, he has conducted a number of surveys of psychologists focusing on the relationship between religious affiliation and belief and the clinical practice of psychology. He is a past president of APA Division 36: Psychology of Religion, serves on a number of editorial boards, and has conducted continuing education programs in the psychology of religion for the American Psychological Association.

Dr. Shafranske received a PhD in clinical psychology from United States International University and a PhD in psychoanalysis from the Southern California Psychoanalytic Institute. He completed full psychoanalytic training at the Southern California Psychoanalytic Institute and co-directs its Center for the Psychoanalytic Study of Religious Experience. His research and clinical interests concern the function of religious belief and affiliation in mental health and psychotherapy and the interface of psychoanalytic treatment and cognitive science. He is currently examining the process of psychodynamic psychotherapy and issues concerning the clinical training of psychologists. In addition to academic and research activities, Dr. Shafranske maintains a private practice in clinical psychology and psychoanalysis in Irvine, California.